CARBON CAPTURE AND STORAGE

Carbon Capture and Storage (CCS) is increasingly viewed as one of the most significant ways of dealing with greenhouse gas emissions. Critical to realising its potential will be the design of effective legal regimes at national and international level that can handle the challenges raised but without stifling a new technology of potential great public benefit. These include: long-term liability for storage; regulation of transport; the treatment of stored carbon under emissions trading regimes; issues of property ownership; and, increasingly, the sensitivities of handling the public engagement and perception.

Following its publication in 2011, *Carbon Capture and Storage* quickly became required reading for all those interested in, or engaged by, the need to implement regulatory approaches to CCS. The intervening years have seen significant developments globally. Earlier legislative models are now in force, providing important lessons for future legal design. Despite these developments, the growth of the technology has been slower in some jurisdictions than others. This timely new edition will update and critically assess these updates and provide context for the development of CCS in 2018 and beyond.

Carbon Capture and Storage

Emerging Legal and Regulatory Issues

Second Edition

Edited by
Ian Havercroft, Richard Macrory
and Richard Stewart

·HART·
PUBLISHING
OXFORD AND PORTLAND, OREGON
2018

Hart Publishing
An imprint of Bloomsbury Publishing Plc

Hart Publishing Ltd	Bloomsbury Publishing Plc
Kemp House	50 Bedford Square
Chawley Park	London
Cumnor Hill	WC1B 3DP
Oxford OX2 9PH	UK
UK	

www.hartpub.co.uk
www.bloomsbury.com

Published in North America (US and Canada) by
Hart Publishing
c/o International Specialized Book Services
920 NE 58th Avenue, Suite 300
Portland, OR 97213-3786
USA

www.isbs.com

HART PUBLISHING, the Hart/Stag logo, BLOOMSBURY and the
Diana logo are trademarks of Bloomsbury Publishing Plc

First published 2018

First edition published 2011

© The editors and contributors severally 2018

The editors and contributors have asserted their right under the Copyright, Designs and Patents
Act 1988 to be identified as Authors of this work.

All rights reserved. No part of this publication may be reproduced or transmitted in any form or by any means,
electronic or mechanical, including photocopying, recording, or any information storage or retrieval
system, without prior permission in writing from the publishers.

While every care has been taken to ensure the accuracy of this work, no responsibility for loss or damage
occasioned to any person acting or refraining from action as a result of any statement in it can be
accepted by the authors, editors or publishers.

All UK Government legislation and other public sector information used in the work is Crown Copyright ©.
All House of Lords and House of Commons information used in the work is Parliamentary Copyright ©.
This information is reused under the terms of the Open Government Licence v3.0 (http://www.
nationalarchives.gov.uk/doc/open-government-licence/version/3) except where otherwise stated.

All Eur-lex material used in the work is © European Union, http://eur-lex.europa.eu/, 1998–2018.

British Library Cataloguing-in-Publication Data
A catalogue record for this book is available from the British Library.

ISBN: HB: 978-1-50990-958-2
ePDF: 978-1-50990-961-2
ePub: 978-1-50990-960-5

Library of Congress Cataloging-in-Publication Data

Names: Havercroft, Ian, editor, author. | Macrory, Richard, editor, author. | Stewart, Richard B., editor.

Title: Carbon capture and storage : emerging legal and regulatory issues / edited by Ian Havercroft,
Richard Macrory and Richard Stewart.

Description: Second edition. | Portland, Oregon : Hart Publishing, 2018. | Includes bibliographical
references and index.

Identifiers: LCCN 2017050497 (print) | LCCN 2017052192 (ebook) | ISBN 9781509909605 (Epub) |
ISBN 9781509909582 (hardback) | ISBN 9781509909612 (ePDF)

Subjects: LCSH: Carbon sequestration—Law and legislation.

Classification: LCC K3593.5.C37 (ebook) | LCC K3593.5.C37 C375 2018 (print) | DDC 344.04/633—dc23

LC record available at https://lccn.loc.gov/2017050497

Typeset by Compuscript Ltd, Shannon
Printed and bound in Great Britain by CPI Group (UK) Ltd, Croydon CR0 4YY

To find out more about our authors and books visit www.hartpublishing.co.uk. Here you will find extracts,
author information, details of forthcoming events and the option to sign up for our newsletters.

Contents

Contributors' Biographies xiii
List of Abbreviations xix
Table of Cases xxi
Table of Legislation xxiii

Introduction 1
Richard Macrory, Ian Havercroft and Richard B Stewart

1. Geological Factors for Legislation to Enable and Regulate Storage
   of Carbon Dioxide in the Deep Subsurface 5
   Stuart Haszeldine and Navraj Singh Ghaleigh
   I. Introduction 5
   II. Outline of CCS, Similarities to and Differences from Established
       Subsurface Industries 7
       A. Hydrocarbon Exploration and Production 7
       B. Geothermal Exploration and Production 8
       C. Shale Gas Production 8
       D. Carbon Dioxide Storage 9
   III. Concepts of Subsurface Zoning 9
   IV. Concepts of Injection and Storage 11
   V. Guidance on Storage Sites and Monitoring Zones 12
       A. Accommodating Imperfect Sites 13
       B. How much CO_2 can Leak? 13
           i. Natural Processes of Trapping 13
           ii. Tracking and Fingerprinting CO_2 14
       C. Pressure Processes and Extent Around the Injection Site 14
   VI. CO_2 Injection 15
       A. Types of Trapping 15
       B. Geometries of CO_2 Trap 16
       C. Effects of CO_2 Injection 16
       D. Consequences of CO_2 Injection 17
       E. Incomplete Containment 17
       F. Role of Demonstrations and Evolving Regulation 18
       G. Operational Interventions 18
           i. In Salah, Algeria, Onshore 18
           ii. Snøhvit, Norway, Offshore 20
       H. Accidents 21
   VII. Enhanced Oil Recovery 23
   VIII. Storage Liability 25

		A. Member State as Insurer for Validation Projects 25
		B. Site Specific Monitoring is Required but Total Leakage is Small 26
		C. How to Progress? 27
	IX.	Progress and Outlook for CCS and Paris 2015 28
	X.	Summary 30

2. Implementation of the Directive on the Geological Storage of Carbon Dioxide 33
Maria Velkova

    I. Introduction 33
    II. Details of the EU Legislation 34
        A. Allowing Storage or Not 34
        B. Assessing Storage Capacity 35
        C. Permitting of CO_2 Storage Sites 37
        D. Preparing for CCS Retrofitting for New Large-scale Combustions Plants 38
    III. Beyond the Legislation 39
    IV. Conclusions 41

3. The CCS Directive: Did it Stifle the Technology in Europe? 43
Leonie Reins

    I. Introduction 43
    II. The Legislative History, The Public Debate and Collingridge— What a Dilemma 44
        A. The Legislative History of the CCS Directive 45
        B. The Public Debate 47
        C. The Dilemma 49
    III. Risk Management and the CCS Directive 50
        A. The Underlying Principles: Prevention? Precaution? 50
        B. The Underlying Principles: Conservatism! 52
    IV. Conclusion 57

4. Germany: A Country without CCS 59
Ludwig Krämer

    I. Obligation to Allow CO_2 Storage? 59
    II. Limitation to Pilot Projects 61
    III. The Elaboration of the CO_2 Storage Act of 2012 62
    IV. The German Act and the Land Legislation 64
    V. The Actual Situation and Discussion of CCS in Germany 67
    VI. Reasons for the German Rejection of CCS Technology 68
        A. Public Acceptance 68
        B. Environmental Reasons 69
        C. Economic Reasons 71
        D. Policy Considerations 72
    VII. Concluding Remarks 73

Contents   vii

5. **Public Participation in UK CCS Planning and Consent Procedures**.................75
   Meyric Lewis and Ned Westaway
   I.   Introduction 75
   II. CCS in the UK Planning Regime..77
        A. Power Plants 77
           i.   The Former Regime 77
           ii. The Planning Act 2008 77
           iii. The Carbon Capture Readiness Regulations 2013..................78
        B. Pipelines 79
        C. CO$_2$ Storage 79
        D. The Carrington Decision 80
        E. Yorkshire-Humber Pipeline and White Rose CCS Project.............81
   III. Public Participation and National Policy Statements 83
        A. The Energy NPSs..83
        B. Consultation on NPSs 84
        C. The Aarhus Convention 86
        D. Strategic Environmental Assessment...87
        E. A Dedicated NPS on CCS? 88
        F. Limitations of, and Modifications to, NPSs....................................89
   IV. Public Participation at the Application and Project Stages 90
        A. Pre-Application Consultation 90
        B. Examination of NSIPs 92
        C. Environmental Assessment of NSIPs 95
        D. The Decision on the NSIP Application 97
        E. Offshore Pipelines and Storage...98
   V.   Conclusion 99

6. **CCS in the US Climate Change Policy Context**..101
   Michael B Gerrard and Justin Gundlach
   I.   Introduction 101
   II. CCS/U Technologies 102
   III. The Current Climate Policy Context and CCS/U 104
        A. US Climate Policy...105
        B. Laws Addressing CCS/U Activities and Facilities.........................106
           i.   Regulations and Carbon Capture 106
           ii. Carbon Transport Regulations...108
           iii. Carbon Sequestration Regulations...109
           iv. CCS/U RD&D 110
        C. Siting Sequestration Reservoirs: Politics atop Legal
           Requirements 112
        D. CCS/U Will Not Become Commercially Viable until
           Climate Policy Becomes Coherent and Stable 113
   IV. The Future Climate Policy Context and CCS/U 115
   V.   Conclusion 117

viii   Contents

7. **Confronting the Bleak Economics of CCS in the United States** 119
   David E Adelman
   I.   The Economics of Low-Carbon Electricity 120
   II. Current and Future US Policies for Promoting CCS 125
   III. Conclusion 130

8. **Gaining Economic Credit for CCS in the United States** 133
   Robert F Van Voorhees
   I.   Introduction 133
   II. National Level Credit 133
        A. Credit for Carbon Dioxide Sequestration under Section 45Q 133
            i.   Secure Geologic Storage—IPCC Guidelines 134
            ii. Secure Geologic Storage—Subpart RR 135
            iii. Questions about Subpart RR 136
            iv. Subpart RR Reporting 138
        B. Investment Tax Credits under Sections 48A and 48B 139
        C. Advanced Fossil Energy Project Loan Guarantees 140
   III. State and Regional Credits 141
        A. California Cap-and-Trade Program 141
        B. Regional Greenhouse Gas Initiative 142
        C. State Severance Tax Reductions 143
            i.   Certification of Sequestration 144
            ii. Monitoring and Verification 144
            iii. Railroad Commission Certification Rule 145
            iv. Other States 145
   IV. Voluntary Carbon Credit Market 146
   V.   Conclusion 146

9. **The Legal Framework for Carbon Capture and Storage in Canada** 149
   Henry J Krupa
   I.   Authority—Canada's Constitutional Structure 149
   II.   The Regulation of GHG Emissions 152
         A. Canada and International: Climate Change Law 152
         B. General Regulation of Air Emissions 164
         C. Specific Regulation of GHGs 165
         D. Market-based Approaches to Reduce GHG Emissions 167
         E. Direct Support and Regulation of CCS 173
   III. Geophysical Survey and GHG Emissions Sources 180
   IV.   Subsurface Property Rights 183
   V.   The Regulatory Framework 186
   VI.   The Liability Framework 191
   VII. Conclusions 200

10. **Pore Space Ownership in Western Canada** 203
    Nigel Bankes
    I.   The Common Law Rules 204
    II. Alberta 205

	III. British Columbia 207
	IV. Saskatchewan 209
	V. Conclusions 210

11. The Regulation of Underground Storage of Greenhouse Gases in Australia 213
Meredith Gibbs
    I. Introduction 213
    II. Overview of Australia's GHG Storage Legislation 214
        A. Approaches to Regulation 214
        B. GHG Storage Tenure 216
        C. Environmental, Health and Safety 218
        D. Managing Competing Interests 219
            i. Federal and Victorian Offshore Acts 220
            ii. Victorian and Queensland Onshore Acts 220
        E. Enforcement 222
    III. Long-term Liability 223
        A. What is Long-term Liability? 223
        B. How do the Acts Deal with Long-term Liability? 224
            i. Federal Offshore Act 224
            ii. Victorian Onshore, Victorian Offshore and Queensland Onshore Acts 225
        C. Why the Difference in Liability Regimes? 227
        D. 'De-risking' Early Mover Projects 229
    IV. Conclusion 230

12. Tenure, Title and Property in Geological Storage of Greenhouse Gas in Australia 231
Michael Crommelin
    I. Introduction 231
    II. Land Tenure 231
    III. Title 234
        A. Offshore Areas 234
        B. Coastal Waters 235
        C. Onshore 236
    IV. Property 238
        A. Dealings and Registration 239
        B. Security of Title 239
    V. Conclusion 242

13. Transportation of Carbon Dioxide in the European Union: Some Legal Issues 245
Martha M Roggenkamp
    I. Introduction 245
    II. Transporting CO_2 Via Pipelines 246
        A. Qualifying CO_2 Pipelines 246
        B. Health, Safety and the Environment 248

            i.   Health and Safety Regulation 248
            ii.   Protecting the Environment 249
            iii. Leakages and Impact on Climate Change 251
       C. The Use of CO_2 Pipelines 252
            i.   Pipeline Owners and Users 252
            ii.   Third-party Access Regime 253
            iii. National Developments 254
       D. Other CO_2 Pipelines 255
  III. Transport of CO_2 by Ship 257
       A. Qualifying CO_2 Transport by Ship 257
       B. Offshore Safety and the Environment 257
            i.   Safety Regulation 257
            ii.   Leakages and Climate Protection Offshore 259
            iii. Liability Offshore 259
       C. Transport 261
  IV. Cross-border Transportation of CO_2 Offshore 261
  V. Trans-European Networks 262
       A. EU Legal Framework 262
       B. Carbon Dioxide Networks 263
  VI. Conclusion 265

14. **Regulation of Carbon Dioxide Pipelines: The US Experience and a View to the Future** 267
Philip M Marston
  I. Introduction: A Word of Context 267
  II. CO_2-based Enhanced Oil Recovery and the Role of CO_2 Pipelines 269
       A. The CO_2-EOR Process 269
       B. CO_2 Supply and Demand 274
            i. CO_2 Supply: Large, 'Bulky' Increments of Both 'N-CO_2' and 'A-CO_2' 274
            ii. CO_2 Markets: Large, Long-lived 'Bulky' Demand Increments 276
       C. CO_2 Pipelines: the 'Few-to-Few' Midstream Component of an Integrated Industry 278
  III. The Current Regulatory Framework for CO_2 Pipelines in the United States 281
       A. Federal Regulation of Construction and Operation 281
            i.   Jurisdictional Status under the Natural Gas Act 282
            ii.   Jurisdictional Status under the Interstate Commerce Act 283
            iii. Jurisdictional Status under the Mineral Leasing Act of 1920 Administered by the Bureau of Land Management 285
            iv. Conclusion as to Federal Regulatory Jurisdiction over CO_2 Pipelines 286
       B. State Regulation of Construction and Operation 286
       C. Safety Regulation 288

		i.	The Federal Statutory Framework for Pipeline Safety Regulation..288
		ii.	Regulatory Implementation for CO_2 Pipelines in 1991.......291
		iii.	State Safety Regulation..292
		iv.	Safety Record of CO_2 Pipelines 293
	IV.	Related Issues: Pipeline Standards; Control of Product Specifications; and Capacity Allocation 293	
		A.	CO_2 Pipeline Standards...293
			i. ASME B31.4 293
			ii. Other Standards and Recommended Practices for CO_2 Pipelines..294
		B.	Managing CO_2 Stream Quality Specifications 295
			i. A Word of Caution: 'One Size' CO_2 Stream Quality Specifications will not Fit All Projects..................................295
			ii. Illustrative Pipeline Quality Specifications for CO_2 Pipeline Stream..299
		C.	Capacity Planning and Allocation: Ensuring Service While Avoiding Excessive Costs 300
	V.	Conclusion 306	

15. Long-Term Liability and CCS..307
    Ian Havercroft
    I. The Challenge 307
    II. Emergence of the CCS-Specific Regime..308
        A. The Nature of Liability 309
        B. Similarity in Approach 309
        C. Reliance upon Existing Liability Mechanisms 311
        D. Transfer and Long-Term Stewardship 311
    III. Constraints and Challenges 312
        A. The Scope and Practicality of Transfer Provisions 313
        B. Technical Cooperation 315
        C. Liability Post-Transfer...316
        D. Climate Change Liabilities 317
    IV. Conclusions and the Way Forward...318
        A. Assessing Different Forms of Liability..318
        B. Positive Models of Law and Regulation 319
        C. Project-Specific Experience...320

16. Carbon Capture and Storage: Commercial Arrangements for Managing Liability Risks 323
    Daniel Lawrence
    I. Introduction: The Complexities of CCS and the Many Links in the CCS Chain...323
    II. Key Roles and Risks in a CCS Project 326
    III. Categories of Risks/Liabilities Associated with a CCS Project, and How Legal Liability Risks May Arise in Practice 327

	IV.	Mechanisms for Apportioning Liability Risks	329
	V.	Incentivising CCS—Liability Considerations	334

17. No Visible Means of Legal Support: China's CCS Regime 337
Navraj Singh Ghaleigh

	I.	Introduction: Whither Law?	337
	II.	Environmental Law in China	339
		A. Basics of the Chinese Legal System	339
		B. Environmental Law Making and Enforcement	342
		C. The Turn to the Climate	344
	III.	Carbon Capture and Storage and China	347
		A. Policy and Pilots	347
		B. The Adequacy of Amending Extant Regimes	347
		C. State-Owned Enterprises	350
	IV.	The Problem of Law and the Environment in China	352
		A. Hostility to Legal Codes	352
		B. Administrative Measures and the Rule of Law	353
		C. Enforcement	354
		D. Corruption	356
	V.	Conclusion	357

Pulling the Threads Together 359
Ian Havercroft and Richard Macrory

I.	The Context of Legal Development	359
II.	Emergence of CCS-Specific Legislation	361
III.	Future Perspectives for Regulation	363

Index 367

Contributors' Biographies

David E Adelman holds the Harry Reasoner Regents Chair in Law at the University of Texas School of Law. Professor Adelman's research focuses on the many interfaces between law, science and innovation. His articles have addressed such topics as the tensions between legal and scientific evidentiary standards in regulatory decision making, development of effective policies for promoting innovation relevant to addressing climate change, and more recently empirical studies of clean air regulations and environmental litigation. Professor Adelman received a BA from Reed College, a PhD in chemistry from Stanford University, and a JD from Stanford Law School. Following law school, he clerked for the Honorable Samuel Conti of the United States District Court for the Northern District of California. Prior to entering academia, Professor Adelman was a Senior Attorney with the Natural Resources Defense Council and an associate with the law firm Covington & Burling in Washington, DC.

Nigel Bankes is professor of law and holder of the chair of natural resources law at the University of Calgary, Alberta, Canada. He is vice-chair, Board of Directors, for the Canadian Institute of Resources Law, and an adjunct professor with the KG Jebsen Centre for the Law of the Sea at UiT, the Arctic University of Norway. Dr Bankes's research work covers a number of areas, including carbon capture and storage, indigenous property rights in settler states in the circumpolar arctic, unitisation and joint development agreements in marine areas, and the Columbia River Treaty.

Michael Crommelin is Zelman Cowen Professor of Law in the University of Melbourne. He holds the degrees of BA and LLB (Hons) from the University of Queensland, and LLM and PhD from the University of British Columbia. He was Dean of the Melbourne Law School from 1989 until 2007, and in 2010. He has held visiting academic appointments at the University of British Columbia, Georgetown University, the University of Virginia, and l'Université Panthéon-Assas Paris II. His teaching and research interests are in constitutional law, comparative law, and resources and energy law. He was President of AMPLA-The Resources and Energy Law Association in 1986, and is currently a member of the American Law Institute and a fellow of the Australian Academy of Law.

Michael B Gerrard is the Andrew Sabin Professor of Professional Practice at Columbia Law School, where he teaches courses on environmental law, climate change law and energy regulation, and is Director of the Sabin Center for Climate Change Law. He also chairs the faculty of Columbia University's Earth Institute and is Senior Counsel at the law firm Arnold & Porter Kaye Scholer. A prolific writer in environmental law and climate change, Professor Gerrard twice received the Association of American Publishers' Best Law Book award for works on environmental law and brownfields.

He has written or edited 11 books, including *Global Climate Change and US Law*, the leading work in its field, and the 12-volume *Environmental Law Practice Guide*.

Navraj Singh Ghaleigh is Senior Lecturer in Climate Law at the University of Edinburgh, where he is the Head of the Public Law Subject Area and Director of two LLM programmes: LLM in Global Environment and Climate Change, and LLM in Law and Chinese. He has published widely on the nature of climate law and its inter- and infra-disciplinary nature. His current research interests relate to climate law in East Asia, and the operation of climate constitutionalism in the light of the Paris Agreement.

Dr Meredith Gibbs is a Partner at the law firm HWL Ebsworth, specialising in environmental, water and climate law, representing private and government clients in the energy, resources, agriculture, property and telecommunications sectors. She is listed in Australia's 'Best Lawyers' for her expertise in climate change law, natural resources law, energy law and government practice. Dr Gibbs holds a PhD (Law and Politics) from the University of Otago, New Zealand, and an LLB (Honours) and BA from the Australian National University. In 2016 she was appointed the inaugural Legal Fellow of the Global CCS Institute and delivered a research program focused on effective enforcement of underground storage of carbon dioxide. She publishes in the areas of climate change law, environmental law, indigenous rights and reparative justice, and has a number of publications on Australia's regulatory framework for underground storage of carbon dioxide.

Justin M Gundlach is an Associate Research Scholar at Columbia Law School and a Fellow at the Sabin Center for Climate Change Law. His academic publications and work as a litigator have focused on issues relating to energy, climate change and environmental protection.

Ian Havercroft is the Global Lead—Legal and Regulatory at the Global CCS Institute, and is based in Melbourne, Australia. He was previously an academic at University College London's Faculty of Laws, where he taught on the environmental law programme and undertook contracted research for a range of organisations, including governments and industry. He co-founded and managed the UCL Carbon Capture Legal Programme between 2007 and 2010. He had acted as an expert reviewer or an adviser to a number of organisations on carbon capture and storage law and regulation; these include the International Energy Agency and the IEA Greenhouse Gas R&D Programme. He holds undergraduate and postgraduate degrees in law, and in 2012 was appointed as an Honorary Visiting Senior Research Fellow at University College London's Faculty of Laws.

R Stuart Haszeldine is Professor of Carbon Capture and Storage at the University of Edinburgh, Director of Scottish Carbon Capture and Storage, and Director of Storage at the UK CCS Research Centre academic network. He trained as a geologist, and since 1981 has worked on gas, oil and coal extraction, fracking and nuclear waste disposal. From 2004 he has focused on CO_2 storage, biochar, and climate engineering to re-capture emitted fossil and bio-carbon. Professor Haszeldine has advised governments in Scotland and the UK, including serving on the influential

2016 Oxburgh review of carbon capture and storage. North Sea geology is now recognised as a European-sized CO_2 storage asset. He was elected FRSE in 2002, awarded the Geological Society William Smith Medal for applied geology in 2011, and in 2012 was appointed OBE for services to climate change technologies.

Dr Ludwig Krämer is Director of the environmental law consultancy 'Derecho y Medio Ambiente' in Madrid. He studied law and history in Kiel, Munich and Paris (ENA), and gained an LLD from the University of Hamburg. Dr Krämer was a judge at the Landgericht Kiel, and between 1972 and 2004 an Official of the Commission of the European Community, Environmental Department, successively responsible for legal and enforcement issues, waste management and environmental sustainability. He is a Visiting Professor at University College London. Dr Krämer has lectured on EU environmental law in more than 60 European and North American universities, having written 20 books and more than 260 published articles on the subject.

Henry Krupa is a senior counsel in the Environmental and the Energy & Emissions Trading Groups in the Toronto office of McMillan LLP. He is Co-Chair of the firm's Environmental Law Group. He provides legal and strategic advice to the environmental, energy, natural resources and government-relations sectors on all aspects of international, national and sub-national environmental law, including legislative and regulatory analysis and counselling, transactions and due diligence, environmental compliance and permitting, enforcement and litigation, and development and brownfields' redevelopment. He has extensive experience representing clients in numerous complicated transactions involving regulatory matters. Typical matters include assisting clients in complex mergers, acquisitions and regulatory processes involving industrial, oil, gas, forestry and mining resources; defending clients in prosecutions and civil actions resulting from violations of federal or provincial environmental laws; and assessing and handling all aspects of complicated brownfield transactions. He has a LLM in Environmental Law and Policy.

Daniel Lawrence is a senior environmental and regulatory lawyer in Freshfields Bruckhaus Deringer's Environment, Planning and Regulatory Group. He advises on a broad range of environmental, regulatory and permitting issues, and on proceedings affecting a wide variety of industry sectors, with particular experience of the energy sector. He has extensive experience of negotiating and documenting the allocation of environment-related risks and liabilities in projects and other transactions, and also of advising on regulatory enforcement actions and other disputes. His experience includes advising on consenting and other regulatory issues relating to onshore and offshore pipelines and installations, and he was involved in advising on the UK Government's competition for the UK's first end-to-end carbon capture and storage project. He has a LLM in Environment, Planning and Regulatory law, and is a former chairman of the UK Environmental Law Association.

Meyric Lewis is a barrister practising in Environmental and Planning Law at the Chambers of Andrew Tait QC, Francis Taylor Building, Temple, London. His work involves close examination of the environmental implications of major infrastructure and development projects for promoters, public authorities and objectors. He appears in public inquiry and court proceedings at all levels. He formerly served as counsel for the Secretary of State defending challenges to planning decisions in the High Court and Court of Appeal. Notable cases include *Bolton Metropolitan Council v Secretary of State* (House of Lords, impact of the Trafford Centre on Greater Manchester); *Goodman v LB Lewisham, Bateman v S Cambs DC, Evans v Secretary of State* (all Court of Appeal, environmental impact assessment); Surrey Waste Plan Public Examination (objection to impact of waste incineration on Thames Basin Heaths Special Protection Area); and the HS2 Parliamentary Petition Hearings (impacts of long-term construction).

Richard Macrory is a barrister and Professor of Environmental Law at University College London. He was first chair of the UK Environmental Law Association and founding editor of the *Journal of Environmental Law*. Richard Macrory has been a member of the UK Royal Commission on Environmental Pollution and a board member of the Environment Agency in England and Wales. He led the Cabinet Office Review on Regulatory Sanctions in 2006. Professor Macrory directed the UCL Carbon Capture Legal Programme between 2007 and 2012.

Philip M Marston has specialised in energy law since entering law practice in 1976 with Morgan, Lewis & Bockius. He has focused on legal, regulatory, business and policy aspects of the energy industries in private practice as well at the Federal Energy Regulatory Commission (FERC) in various senior roles. At FERC, during the 1980s, he was one of the architects of a competitive, open access regulatory framework for natural gas markets. Since founding MARSTON LAW (www.marstonlaw.com) in 1998, his clients have included energy suppliers and customers, as well as natural gas, oil and CO_2 pipelines and or shippers. In recent years, he has advised extensively on the regulation of CO_2-based enhanced oil recovery. He has served on various advisory bodies. These include the International Energy Agency's task force on a CCS Model Regulatory Framework and its CCS Regulatory Network forums; the CO_2 Pipeline Task Force of the Interstate Oil and Gas Compact Commission (including as a principal author of the final report); the US Chamber of Commerce Energy Committee; and the natural gas advisory committee of the New York Mercantile Exchange. In 2013, Philip Marston authored a book-length report for the Global CCS Institute in Australia on the legal and regulatory framework for CO_2-EOR and CCS. His JD degree is from the University of Virginia School of Law. He has co-authored a book, and has published and spoken widely on energy regulatory issues in French as well as English.

Leonie Reins is Assistant Professor at Tilburg Institute for Law, Technology and Society, Tilburg University, The Netherlands. She previously was a Post-Doc at KU Leuven in Belgium where she also wrote her PhD thesis on the coherent regulation of energy and the environment in the EU. In addition, she worked for a Brussels-based environmental law consultancy providing legal and policy services for primarily public sector clients.

Martha M Roggenkamp is Professor of Energy Law at the University of Groningen, Director of the Groningen Centre of Energy Law and Academic Director of the LLM Energy & Climate Law. She also the Academic Coordinator of the executive LLM

'North Sea Energy Law Programme' and the faculty's research programme, 'Energy & Sustainability. Martha Roggenkamp has published widely on energy law issues since the early 1990s and has edited several energy law monographs, such as *Energy Law in Europe*, 3rd edn (Oxford, Oxford University Press, 2016). She is also editor-in-chief of the series *Energy & Law* published by Intersentia (Antwerp), and a member of the editorial board of the Dutch *Journal of Energy Law* and of the editorial committees of the *Journal of Energy and Natural Resources Law*, the *International Energy Law Review* and the *Renewable Energy Law and Policy Review*. She also holds the chair of the Dutch Association of Energy Lawyers and is a board member of the Groningen Energy and Sustainability Platform.

Richard B Stewart is University Professor and John Edward Sexton Professor of Law at New York University (NYU) School of Law, and recognised as one of the world's leading scholars in environmental and administrative law. Prior to joining the NYU School of Law faculty, Stewart had served as a Byrne Professor of Administrative Law at Harvard Law School and a member of the faculty of the Kennedy School of Government at Harvard; Assistant Attorney General in charge of the Environment and Natural Resource Division of the US Department of Justice, and Chairman of the Environmental Defense Fund.

Maria Velkova is a policy officer who has been working for the European Commission since 2008. In her current position she is responsible for the implementation of the EU Directive on the geological storage of carbon dioxide and for the 2020 greenhouse gas reduction target for road transport fuels of the EU Fuel Quality Directive. Before joining the European Commission, Maria Velkova worked in the areas of enterprise policy, renewable energy and energy efficiency in the Bulgarian public administration. She has Masters degrees in Environmental Change and Management from Oxford University and in European Economic Studies from the College of Europe in Bruges. Her Bachelors degree is in European Business Administration from the University of National and World Economy, Sofia.

Robert F Van Voorhees is Executive Director of the Carbon Sequestration Council (a US association of petroleum companies and electric utilities), Executive Director of the Underground Injection Technology Council, and Of Counsel at the law firm Bryan Cave LLP in Washington, DC. He has practised law in environmental and energy regulation since the 1970s, with a focus on regulation of subsurface and related operations since 1985. He was instrumental in facilitating the development of multi-stakeholder recommendations for a US regulatory framework for carbon capture and storage; contributed to the development of regulatory framework recommendations by the International Energy Agency and the World Resources Institute; and is active in the ISO Technical Committee 265 development of international standards for carbon dioxide capture, transportation and storage.

Ned Westaway is a barrister specialising in planning and environmental law, based at Francis Taylor Building in London. He has appeared in the Supreme Court and Court of Appeal, and is consistently rated as a leading junior by Chambers and Partners under Planning, Environment and Agricultural & Rural Affairs, which comments, among other things, that he is 'not afraid to go to court with a case that is out of the ordinary—he is very environmentally minded and has a good sense of the principles'. Ned Westaway is a Trustee of the United Kingdom Environmental Law Association and is standing counsel for the Campaign for National Parks. He regularly speaks and write on legal issues, and is a visiting researcher at University College London.

List of Abbreviations

AGD	Acid Gas Disposal
API	American Petroleum Institute
ASME	American Society of Mechanical Engineers
BAT	Best Available Techniques
BLM	Bureau of Land Management
BREF	Best Available Techniques Reference Document
CCR	Carbon Capture Readiness
CCS	Carbon Capture and Storage (in the US, also Carbon Capture and Sequestration)
CCS/U	Carbon Capture, Sequestration and Utilisation
CCUS	Carbon Capture Utilisation and Storage
CO_2e	Carbon dioxide equivalent
CO_2-EOR	CO_2-based Enhanced Oil Recovery
DCO	Development Consent Order
EIA	Environmental Impact Assessment
ELD	Environmental Liability Directive
ETS	Emissions Trading System
EU	European Union
EOR	Enhanced Oil Recovery
EGR	Enhanced Gas Recovery
EPA	Environmental Protection Agency
FERC	Federal Energy Regulator Commission
GCCSI	Global Carbon Capture Storage Institute
GHG	Greenhouse gas
HRA	Habitats Regulations Assessment
ICC	Interstate Commerce Commission
IEA	International Energy Agency
IGCC	Integrated Gasification Combined Cycle
ISO	International Organization for Standardization
IPC	Infrastructure Planning Commission
IPCC	Intergovernmental Panel on Climate Change
IPPC	Integrated Pollution Prevention and Control
IRM	Internal Revenue Manual
IRS	Internal Revenue Service
KSpG	Gesetz zur Demonstration der dauerhaften Speicherung von Kohlendioxid (Act on demonstrating the permanent storage of CO_2)
LCOE	Levelised Cost of Electricity
LNG	Liquid Natural Gas
MRV	Monitoring, Reporting and Verification

MVA	Monitoring, Verification and Accounting
MST	Monitoring Sampling and Testing
NDC	Nationally Determined Contribution
NCP	National Carbon Policy
NETL	National Energy Technology Laboratory
NGCC	Natural Gas Combined-cycle
NPC	National People's Congress
NPS	National Policy Statement
NRDC	National Development and Reform Commission
NSIP	Nationally Significant Infrastructure Projects
NSPS	New Source Performance Standard
OGA	Oil and Gas Authority
OPS	Office of Pipeline Safety
PHSMA	Pipeline and Hazardous Materials Safety Administration
R&D	Research and Development
RD & D	Research, Development and Demonstration
RGGI	Regional Greenhouse Gas Initiative
RRC	Texas Railroad Commission
SASAC	Stated-owned Asset Supervision and Administration Commission
SEA	Strategic Environmental Assessment
SOE	State-Owned Enterprise
SPV	Special Purpose Vehicle
TEC	Treaty establishing the European Community
TENs	Trans-European Networks
TFEU	Treaty on the Functioning of the European Union
TPA	Third Party Access
UIC	Underground Injection Control
UNFCCC	United Nations Framework Convention on Climate Change

Table of Cases

Abraham v Wallonia Case C-2/07 [2008] ECR I-1197 96
ANR Pipeline Co v Iowa State Commerce Comm'n, 828 F 2d 465 (1987) 290
Associated Gas Distributors v FERC, 824 F 2d 981 (DC Cir 1987) 302
Bank of NSW v The Commonwealth (1948) 76 CLR 1 240
Berkeley v Secretary of State for the Environment [2001] 2 AC 603 95
Bisson v Brunette Holdings Ltd, [1993] OJ No 3378 193
Bowen-West v Secretary of State for Communities and Local Government [2012] EWCA Civ 321 96
California v Lo-Vaca Gathering Company, 379 US 366 (1965) 277
Cadia Holdings Pty Ltd v New South Wales (2010) 242 CLR 195 232
Canada Steam Ship Lines Ltd v The King [1952] UKPC 1 332
Cardoza-Fonseca 480 US 421 (1987) 284
Chance v BP Chemicals Inc 670 NE 2d 985 (Ohio 1996) 226
Commission v Ireland Case C-392/96 [1999] ECR I-5901 96
Commission v Spain Case C-227/01 [2004] ECR I-8253 96
Cunningham v Commonwealth of Australia [2016] HCA 39 240–41
Cortez Pipeline Company, 7 FERC ¶ 61,024 (1979) 109, 282
Cudgen Rutile (No 2) Pty Ltd v Chalk [1975] AC 520 232
Denbury Green Pipeline-Texas, LLC v Texas Rice Land Partners, Ltd 363 SW3d 192 (Tex. 2017) 287
Durham Holdings Pty Limited v New South Wales (2001) 205 CLR 399 .... 233, 242
E E Caledonia Ltd v Orbit Valve Company Europe [1993] 4 All ER 165 332
Exxon Corp v Lujan, 970 F.2d 757 (10th Cir 1992) 275, 285
FPC v Florida Power & Light Co, 404 US 453 (1972) 277
HS2 Action Alliance Limited v Secretary of State for Transport [2013] EWCA Civ 920 87
ICM Agriculture Pty Ltd v The Commonwealth (2009) 240 CLR 140 240
Inter-Environnement Bruxelles ASBL v Région de Bruxelles- Capitale (C-567/10) [2012] 2 CMLR 909 87
Interprovincial Coop Ltd v Manitoba, [1976] 1SCR 477 193
Just v British Columbia, [1989] 2 SCR 1228 194
Mabo v Queensland [No 2] (1992) 175 CLR 1 231–32
Mann v Saulnier, [1959] NBJ No 12 193
Mongrue v Monsanto Co 249 F 3d 422 226
Morgan v Hinton Organics (Wessex) Ltd [2009] EWCA 86
Motor Vehicle Mfrs Ass'n v State Farm Mutual Auto Ins Co, 463 US 29 284
Massachusetts v EPA 549 US 497 (2007) 101
Multiple Access Ltd v McCutcheon, [1982] 2 SCR 161 150
Newcrest Mining (WA) Ltd v The Commonwealth (1997) 190 CLR 513 240
Nomarchiaki Aftodioikisi Aitoloakarnanias v Ipourgos Perivallontos, Khorotaxias kai Dimosion Ergon Case C-43/10 [2013] Env LR 453 87
North Dakota v EPA Case No 15–1381 (DC Circuit, 13 October 2016) 106, 111
North Dakota v Heydinger 2016 WL 3343639 106
Nuclear Energy Institute v EPA 373 F3d 1251 113

Olympic Pipe Line Co v City of Seattle, 437 F 3d 872 290
R v Latouche [2010] AJ No 631 150
R (HS2 Action Alliance Limited) v Secretary of State for Transport [2014] UKSC 3 87
R (Beebee) v Poole BC [1991] 2 PLR 27 95
R (Gate) v Secretary of State for Transport [2013] EWHC 2937 92
R (Greenpeace Ltd) v Secretary of State for Trade and Industry [2007] EWHC 311 85
R (London Borough of Hillingdon) v Secretary of State for Transport [2010]
   EWHC 626 .... 87, 89
R (Little) v Secretary of State for Trade and Industry [2002] EWHC 3001 77
R (Hardy) v Pembrokeshire CC [2005] EWHC 1872 96
R (Medway Council) v Secretary of State for Transport, Local Government
   and the Regions [2002] EWHC 2516 85
R (Rankin) v Rotherham MBC [1990] 1 PLR 93 95
R (Redcar and Cleveland BC) v Secretary of State for Business Enterprise
   and Regulatory Reform [2008] EWHC 1847 99
R (Thames Blue Green Economy Ltd) v Secretary of State for Communities
   and Local Government [2015] EWCA Civ 876 89
Re Seaport Investments Ltd [2007] NIQB 62 87
Ricoh Europe Holdings BV & Ors v Spratt & Anor [2013] EWCA Civ 92 332
Rylands v Fletcher (1868) LR 3 HL 330 193
Safeway Stores Ltd & Ors v Twigger & Ors [2011] 2 All ER 841 332
Shell Oil Co v City of Santa Monica, 830 F 2d 1052 (9th Cir 1987) 290
Sierra Club v Mississippi Pub Serv Comm'n 82 So 3d 618 (Miss 2012) 107
Smith v UMB Chrysler (Scotland) Ltd [1978] 1 WLR 165 332
TEC Desert Pty ltd v Commissioner of State Revenue (Western Australia) (2010)
   241 CLR 576 239
Terre wallonne ASBL and Inter-Environnement Wallonie ASBL v Région wallonne
   (Cases C-105/09 and C-110/09) [2010] ECR I-5611 87
The Commonwealth v Hazeldell Ltd (1918) 25 CLR 552 242
The Commonwealth v WMC Resources Ltd (1998) 194 CLR 1 241
The Corporation of the City of Kawartha Lakes v Director, Ministry
   of the Environment, 2012 ONSC 2708 189
Thomas Jefferson Univ v Shalala, 512 US 504 (1994) 284
Tock v St John's Metropolitan Area Board, [1989] 2 SCR 1181 193
Walters v Whessoe (1960) [1968] 2 All ER 332
Western Australia v Ward (2002) 213 CLR 1 231–32
Wik Peoples v Queensland (1996) 187 CLR 1 233
Wychavon DC v Secretary of State for the Environment [1994] Env LR 239 95

Table of Legislation

INTERNATIONAL

Convention on the Prevention of Marine Pollution by Dumping of Wastes
and Other Matter (London Convention) 1972 .... 261, 265
Convention for the Protection of the Marine Environment of the North-East
Atlantic (OSPAR Convention) 1998 .... 261, 362
International Convention for the Safety of Life at Sea 1974 257–58
International Convention on Liability and Compensation for Damage in Connection
with the Carriage of Hazardous and Noxious Substances by Sea 1996 259–60
Paris Agreement 2015 .... xiv, 1, 4, 7, 29, 147, 152–57, 160,
168, 337–38, 346, 359–61, 365
UN Framework Convention on Climate Change 1992 .... 85, 115, 147, 152–53,
157, 344–46

AUSTRALIA

Aboriginal Heritage Act 2006 (Vic) 218
Australian Courts Act 1828 (UK) 232
Barrow Island Act 2003 (WA) 213, 215, 229, 238, 362
Coal Acquisition Act 1981 (NSW) 233
Coastal Management Act 1995 (Vic) 218
Coastal Waters (State Powers) Act 1980 (Cth) 234
Coastal Waters (State Title) Act 1980 (Cth) 234
Coastal Waters (Northern Territory) Powers Act 1980 (Cth) 233–35, 242
Dangerous Goods Act 1985 (Vic) 218
Environment and Protection Act 1970 (Vic) 218
Environment Protection and Biodiversity Conservation Act 1999 (Cth) 218
Environment Protection (Sea Dumping) Act 1981(Cth) 218
Flora and Fauna Guarantee Act 1998 (Vic) 218
Geological Storage Act 2008 (Vic) 215
Geothermal Energy Act (NT) 2009 233
Geothermal Energy Act 2010 (Qld) 233
Geothermal Energy Resources Act 2005 (Vic) 233
Greenhouse Gas Geological Sequestration Act 2008 (Vic) 236–39, 314, 362
Greenhouse Gas Storage Act 2009 (Qld) 215, 237–39, 362
Land Act 1958 (Vic) 226
Mineral (Acquisition) Ordinance 1953 (Cth) 233
Mineral and Energy Resources (Common Provisions) Act 2014 (Qld) 239
Mines (Amendment) Act 1983 (Vic) 233
Mining Act 1971 (SA) 233
Native Title Act 1993(Cth) 231–32
National Parks Act 1975 (Vic) 218

New South Wales Constitution Act 1855 (UK) 232
Offshore Petroleum and Greenhouse Gas Storage Act 2006 (Cth) 214–15, 233–35,
                                                            238–39, 241–42, 310, 313, 363
Offshore Petroleum and Greenhouse Gas Storage Act 2010 (Vic) 236, 239
Offshore Petroleum and Greenhouse Gas Storage (Environment) Regulations
    2009 (Cth) 90, 95, 218
Offshore Petroleum and Greenhouse Gas Storage (Greenhouse Gas Injection
    and Storage) Regulations 2011 (Cth) 219–20
Offshore Petroleum and Greenhouse Gas Storage Regulations 2011(Vic) 220
Offshore Petroleum (Safety) Regulations 2009 (Cth) 218
Personal Property Securities Act 2009 (Cth) 238
Petroleum Act 1990 (Vic) 233
Petroleum Act 2000 (SA) 215
Petroleum and Geothermal Energy Resources Act 1967 (WA) 233
Petroleum and Geothermal Energy Act 2000 (SA) 233, 236, 238–39, 363
Petroleum (Submerged Lands) Act 1967 (Cth) 234, 241–42
Seas and Submerged Lands Act 1973 234
Water Act 1989 (Vic) 218

CANADA

Canada Health Act 151
Canada Oil and Gas Operations Act 196, 198
Canadian Environmental Assessment Act 151, 188, 190
Canadian Environmental Protection Act 156, 163, 166
Carbon Capture and Storage Funding Act (Alberta) 176
Carbon Capture and Storage Funding Act (Extension of Expiry Date) Amendment
    Regulation (Alberta) 176
Carbon Capture and Storage Statutes Amendment Act (Alberta) 110, 174–75,
                                                                                     185, 196, 200
Carbon Sequestration Tenure Regulation (Alberta) 110, 175
Carbon Tax Act (British Columbia) 172–73
Climate Change and Emissions Management Act (Alberta) 165, 171, 318
Climate Change and Emissions Reductions Act (Manitoba) 165, 171
Climate Change Mitigation and Low-carbon Economy Act (Ontario) 170
Climate Leadership Act (Alberta) 172, 175
Climate Leadership Regulation (Alberta) 172
Crown Minerals Act (Saskatchewan) 184, 209
Drilling and Production Regulation (Manitoba) 180
Emissions Tax on Coal and Petroleum Coke Act (Manitoba) 171
Ending Coal for Cleaner Air Act (Ontario) 161
Energy Resources Conservation Act (Alberta) 175
Environmental Assessment Act (Saskatchewan) 178, 188–89, 191
Environmental Management and Protection Act (Saskatchewan) 197
Environmental Protection Act (Ontario) 164, 188
Environmental Protection and Enhancement Act (Alberta) 197
Environmental Quality Act (Quebec) 179
Exploration Licences, Production and Storage Leases for Oil and Gas in Ontario
    Regulation (Ontario) 184

Table of Legislation xxv

Greenhouse Gas Emission Control Regulation (British Columbia) 173–74
Greenhouse Gas Emissions Regulations (Nova Scotia) 165
Greenhouse Gas Emission Reporting Regulation (British Columbia) 165
Greenhouse Gas Industrial Reporting and Control Act (British Columbia) 173–74
Greenhouse Gas Reduction Targets Act (British Columbia) 172
Kyoto Protocol Implementation Act 152–53
Land Act (British Columbia) 185
Management and Reduction of Greenhouse Gases Act (Saskatchewan) 171, 178
Management of Greenhouse Gas Act (Newfoundland and Labrador) 165
Metallic and Industrial Minerals Tenure Regulation (Alberta) 176
Mineral Resources Act (Nova Scotia) 184
Mines and Minerals Act (Alberta) 175, 185, 205–07, 310, 314–15, 318, 363
Mines and Minerals Administration Regulation (Alberta) 176
Mining Act (Ontario) 184
Mining Act (Quebec) 179, 184
Negligence Act (Ontario) 194
Oil and Gas Act (Manitoba) 180, 184
Oil and Gas Activities Act (British Columbia) 174, 186, 190–91, 196–98, 208
Oil and Gas Conservation Act (Alberta) 110, 196–97, 206, 363
Oil and Gas Conservation Act (Saskatchewan) 177, 196
Oil and Gas Conservation Regulations (Saskatchewan) 196
Oil Sands Emissions Limit Act (Alberta) 158, 165
Ontario Energy Board Act (Ontario) 185
Ontario Regulation 496/07 Cessation of Coal Use—Atikkoan, Lambton, Nanticoke
    and Thunder Bay Generating Stations 161
Petroleum and Natural Gas Act (British Columbia) 174, 185, 197, 207
Petroleum Resources Act (Nova Scotia) 184
Pipeline Act (Alberta) 196
Pipeline Act (British Columbia) 196
Pipelines Act (Saskatchewan) 77, 196
Quantification, Reporting and Verification of Greenhouse Gas Emissions Regulation
    (Ontario) 165
Reduction of Carbon Dioxide Emissions from Coal-fired Generation of Electricity
    Regulations 161, 163, 166–67
Regulations Designating Physical Activities 190
Regulation Respecting a Cap-and-Trade System for Greenhouse Gas Emission
    Allowances (Quebec) 169
Regulation Respecting Mandatory Reporting of Certain Emissions of Contaminants
    into the Atmosphere (Quebec) 165
Regulation respecting petroleum, natural gas and underground reservoirs (Quebec) 179
Regulations Respecting Reductions in the Release of Methane and Certain
    Volatile Organic Compounds (Upstream Oil and Gas) 166
Specified Gas Emitters Regulation (Alberta) 165, 175
Specified Gas Reporting Regulation (Alberta) 171
The Constitution Act 1867 .... 149, 151, 205
Underground Hydrocarbons Storage Act (Nova Scotia) 184
Underground Storage Act (New Brunswick) 184
Water Act (Alberta) 185, 218

CHINA

Environmental Protection Law 1979 ....342–43, 349, 354
Energy Conservation Law 2007 343
Renewable Energy Law 2005 343–44
Law on Prevention and Control of Air Pollution 1987 348
Tort Liability Law 2010 356

GERMANY

Gesetz zur Demonstration der dauerhaften Speicherung von Kohlendioxid
  (Kohlendioxid-Speicherungsgesetz - KSpG) 2012 .... 61, 362

EU

Directive 2011/92/EU on the assessment of the effects of certain public and private
  projects on the environment 33, 95, 246
Directive 2003/87/EC establishing a scheme for greenhouse gas emission allowance
  trading within the Community 39, 259, 310–11, 333
Directive 2009/73/EC of 13 July 2009 concerning common rules for the internal
  market in natural gas 253
Directive 2009/20/EC on insurance of ship owners for maritime claims 260
Directive 2009/71/Euratom establishing a Community framework for the nuclear
  safety of nuclear installations 60
Directive 2009/31/EC on the geological storage of carbon dioxide 33–34, 37, 43, 49,
                                                                  59, 72, 75, 245, 310–11, 313, 315, 333
Directive 2010/75/EU on industrial emissions (integrated pollution
  prevention and control) 33, 51–52
Directive 2004/35/EC on environmental liability with regard to the prevention
  and remedying of environmental damage 250, 259, 310–11, 329
Regulation 347/2013 on guidelines for trans-European energy infrastructure 263

UK

Carbon Capture Readiness (Electricity Generating Stations) Regulations 2013 78
Electricity Act 1989 ....38, 77–78, 80
Energy Act 2008 ....75–76, 79, 80–81, 98
Energy Act 2013 90
Energy Act 2008 (Consequential Modifications) (Offshore Environmental Protection)
  Order 2010 98
Infrastructure Planning (Applications: Prescribed Forms and Procedure)
  Regulations 2009 90
Localism Act 2011 78
Marine and Coastal Access Act 2009 80
Offshore Petroleum Production and Pipe-lines (Assessment of Environmental Effects)
  Regulations 1999 98–99

Table of Legislation xxvii

Offshore Petroleum Activities (Conservation of Habitats) Regulations 2001 98
Planning Act 2008 .... 75–78, 83–84, 87–91, 93, 95, 97–98
Pipelines Act 1962 77
Storage of Carbon Dioxide (Amendment of the Energy Act 2008 etc)
  Regulations 2011 80
Storage of Carbon Dioxide (Inspections etc.) Regulations 2012/461 80
Storage of Carbon Dioxide (Licensing etc.) Regulations 2010 .... 80, 98
Storage of Carbon Dioxide (Termination of Licence) Regulations 2011
  SI 2011/1483 317
Town and Country Planning Act 1990 .... 77, 97

US

Accountable Pipeline Safety and Partnership Act 1996 289
American Reinvestment and Recovery Act 2009 110
California Global Warming Solutions Act 2006 141
California Code of Regulations (CCR) 79, 142
Carbon Pollution Emission Guidelines for Existing Stationary Sources: Electric Utility
  Generating Units, 80 Fed Reg 205 .... 105, 136, 160
Clean Air Act 1970 .... 101, 105–09, 111, 114–15
Clean Coal FutureGen for Illinois Act of 2011 110
Consolidated Appropriations Act, 2008 105
Emergency Economic Stabilization Act 2008 111
Energy Improvement and Extension Act 2008 134
Energy Policy Act 2005 .... 110–11, 140
Energy Independence and Security Act 2007 .... 103, 110
Energy Tax Incentives Act 2005 140
Federal Requirements Under the Underground Injection Control (UIC) Program
  for Carbon Dioxide (CO2) Geologic Sequestration (GS) Wells, 75 Fed
  Reg 77229 .... 109, 126, 274
Final Carbon Pollution Standards for New, Modified and Reconstructed Power Plants,
  80 Fed Reg 64510 106
Global Warming Solutions Act 2006 Cal Stat c 488 .... 106, 141
Hazardous Liquid Pipeline Act 1979 .... 108, 288–89
Hazardous Materials Transportation Act 1975 108
Hazardous Waste Management System: Conditional Exclusion for Carbon Dioxide
  (CO2) 79 Fed Reg 350 109
Hepburn Act 1905 .... 283, 285
ICC Termination Act 1995 .... 109, 283–84
Interstate Commerce Act 1887 .... 282–84, 286
Land Policy and Management Act 1988 285
Light-Duty Vehicle Greenhouse Gas Emission Standards and Corporate Average
  Fuel Economy Standards 75 Fed Reg 25324 105
Mandatory Reporting of Greenhouse Gases, 74 Fed Reg 56260 105
Mandatory Reporting of Greenhouse Gases: Injection and Geologic Sequestration
  of Carbon Dioxide 75 Fed Reg 75,060 135–36
Mineral Leasing Act 1920 .... 275, 285–86

xxviii Table of Legislation

Natural Gas Act of 1938 ....109, 174, 185, 197, 207, 275, 282–83, 286
Natural Gas Pipeline Safety Act of 1968 288
Oil and Natural Gas Sector: Emission Standards for New, Reconstructed,
    and Modified Sources, 81 Fed Reg 35823 105
Pipeline Safety Act 1992 289–90
Pipeline Safety Reauthorization Act 1988 ....108, 288–89, 291
Pipeline Safety, Regulatory Certainty, and Job Creation Act 2011 ....289–90, 292
Prevention of Significant Deterioration and Title V Greenhouse Gas Tailoring Rule,
    75 Fed Reg 31514 105
Reconsideration of Standards of Performance for Greenhouse Gas Emissions From New,
    Modified, and Reconstructed Stationary Sources: Electric Utility Generating Units,
    81 Fed Reg 27442 106
Safe Drinking Water Act 1974 .... 109, 126, 363
Standards of Performance for Greenhouse Gas Emissions From New, Modified,
    and Reconstructed Stationary Sources: Electric Utility Generating Unit 80
    Fed Reg 64509 .... 105, 115
Texas Administrative Code 16 145
Transportation of Carbon Dioxide by Pipeline; Final Rule, 56 Fed
    Reg 26922 (1991) 108, 291
WIPP Land Withdrawal Act 1992 113

Introduction

RICHARD MACRORY, IAN HAVERCROFT AND RICHARD B STEWART

WHEN THE FIRST edition of this book was published in 2011, legislation concerning carbon capture and storage (CCS) was emerging in a number of jurisdictions. Since then legislative developments have grown apace, and as the chapters in this book illustrate, there is now a far greater understanding by lawyers of the critical legal challenges and complexities involved. Some would argue that CCS is not a new technology as such, since many of the core elements of the CCS process have been seen in practice for many years. What is new, however, is its potential role as a technology for climate change mitigation, and the scale and integration of the key elements—capture, transportation and long-term storage—that will needed if it is to make a significant contribution in the coming decades. The 2015 Paris Agreement on Climate Change has provided a new urgency and powerful framework for the greater deployment of CCS.

Law by itself cannot resolve all the challenges needed to secure the development of CCS. Economics, short-term government policies and adverse public perception in a number of countries have inhibited the commercial deployment of CCS in recent years. A robust legal framework, while vital for securing industrial and public confidence, must also offer a degree of flexibility to adapt to new understandings and knowledge, particularly given the long timescales involved. Legislation must also avoid stifling innovation by over-prescriptive requirements. It is not an easy balance to secure.

The effective design of regulation requires a good understanding of the science and technology involved. There will always be some uncertainties, especially when dealing with a field such a geology, but the critical question is the nature and extent of these uncertainties, and the risks they may imply. In Chapter 1, Stuart Haszeldine, one of the world's leading geologists specialising in CCS, and international lawyer Navraj Singh Ghaleigh provide a comprehensive and robust analysis of the technology, emphasising what we can already learn from experience to date, and indicating what this implies for the future design of CCS law and regulation. They note the similarities with long-established activities such as mining and oil production, but highlight significant differences that need to be addressed. As they note, 'CCS stretches existing expertise of the subsurface, but does not require entirely new innovation'.

The next four chapters of this volume (Chapters 2–5) focus on CCS in Europe. The European Union's (EU's) CCS Directive was an early example of legislation dealing with all aspects of the technology and in the context of climate change. Maria Velkova of the European Commission considers the core elements of the Directive and its role in the EU's wider energy and climate change policies. Leonie Reins takes a more critical view of the Directive, and argues that it was adopted too early in the developmental stage of the technology. Early legislative intervention, far from encouraging CCS, may have inhibited its commercial development. The Directive does not require EU Member States to provide storage sites within their territories, and Ludwig Krämer's case example of Germany provides a salutary example of the consequences of the failure by industry and government to secure public support for CCS. Furthermore, the decision to explore land-based storage facilities exacerbated tensions between the Federal Government and *Länder*, heightening internal political tensions. German legislation is now confined to pilot plants. The United Kingdom (UK) avoided some of these issues by focusing its policy on developing offshore CCS storage facilities. Yet the technology is at a stage where government economic support for demonstration plants remains essential, and the decision of the Treasury in 2015 to suddenly withdraw funding support for the first demonstration plant has halted further development for the time being. Meyric Lewis and Ned Westaway consider how the UK has implemented the CCS Directive into national law, but also how it is set against national planning procedures for developing large infrastructure projects. Here we see another tension in the construction of law—the streamlining of procedures for giving the green light to developments considered to be in the national interest against the need to accommodate public consultation and local interests. Over 30 years ago, Lord Flowers, a distinguished nuclear scientist and former chairman of the UK Royal Commission on Environmental Pollution, noted that 'there comes a time in the development of any new technological enterprise when its acceptability by the public at large may be its dominating feature'. This was written in the context of the development of civil nuclear power,[1] but could equally apply here to the deployment of CCS.

The United States (US) has had a long experience in the capture of carbon dioxide (CO_2), its transportation, and its use and disposal in the context of enhanced oil recovery. But it is only recently that its significance in contributing to climate change mitigation has risen higher on the policy and legal agendas. In Chapter 6, Michael B Gerrard and Justin Gundlach analyse current developments and note the inchoate nature of legal underpinning, with 'almost no purpose-built Federal legislation, a growing raft of federal regulations and Executive Orders, and a diverse list of state laws and local ordinances'. In their view, without a coherent and stable climate change policy, including the imposition of a robust carbon price, CCS as a technology for climate change mitigation is unlikely to become commercially viable. Achieving this will be all the more challenging at federal level, given the highly politicised nature of the climate change debate and the election of President Trump and a Republican-controlled Congress. In Chapter 7, David E Adelman focuses on the need to understand and re-evaluate the potential of CCS in the US in the context of dramatic changes in electricity markets and the increasing uncompetitiveness of coal plants compared to the low price of natural gas, as well as the declining cost of renewables and electricity storage. He is sanguine about the potential contribution of enhanced oil recovery and tax incentives to substantially changing the economics of CCS, and urges greater investment by government in fundamental CCS research,

---

[1] R Macrory (ed), *Commercial Nuclear Power—Legal and Constitutional Issues* (London, Imperial College Centre for Environmental Technology, 1982).

with a more systematic focus on industrial sources where CCS remains the only option for mitigating CO_2 emissions. Robert F Van Voorhees accepts in Chapter 8 that political efforts to impose a national price on carbon in the US have effectively stalled, and focuses on the range of tax and fiscal incentives that have been introduced at both federal and State level.

Canada and Australia are two jurisdictions that have seen impressive developments in CCS legislation in recent years, and perhaps both have benefitted from a less highly-charged politicisation of the climate change debate than that seen in the US. The provinces of Western Canada in particular are currently global leaders in the development of CCS projects on a commercial scale. In Chapter 9, Henry Krupa provides an extensive overview of the legal and regulatory developments in Canada, at both federal and provincial levels. He concludes that the regulatory frameworks in all the provinces are now adequate to meet the needs of CCS, but that those provinces which already had extensive experience of the oil and gas industry have had the advantage in developing their legislation. Nigel Bankes focuses in Chapter 10 on how three of Canada's provinces have dealt with the challenging legal issues of the ownership of pore space, involving both common law principles and legislative intervention. In Chapter 11, Meredith Gibbs considers the developments in Australian legislation over the last decade, at both Federal level and State level. The country now has one of the world's most developed and comprehensive legal frameworks for CCS. Yet she notes there are some worryingly differences in the various laws, particularly in relation to the treatment of long-term liability. These can be explained by the political background to the legislative developments, but can create unnecessary uncertainty and risk for investment. Michael Crommelin's focus on Australian CCS law in Chapter 12 largely covers important and complex questions of tenure and ownership. In his view, the Australian approach to the question of underground storage of CO_2 has derived from principles and practices evolving since the nineteenth century in the treatment of public land and natural resources such as minerals and petroleum, but is one that 'rests precariously on the uncharted divide between public and private law'.

A key element of CCS is the transportation of 'supercritical' CO_2 from its source to the final storage site, generally through pipelines, and this is an area that brings its own set of legal issues. In Chapter 13, Martha M Roggenkamp conducts a detailed legal analysis of transportation issues, both by pipeline and by ship, and against the context of the framework afforded by the EU CCS Directive. Third-party access to pipelines is a key issue of importance, which the Directive addresses. But the author notes that the Directive itself does little in the way of encouraging the significant transportation networks that will likely be needed if CCS is to realise its potential in the context of climate change mitigation. Here the concept of Trans-European Networks, introduced in 1992 and applying to CO_2 transportation since 2013, may prove of immense importance. In Chapter 14, Phillip M Marston addresses legal issues in the US, where the regulatory framework has been developed almost exclusively for the needs of CO_2 transportation in the context of enhanced oil operations and where over 8,000 miles of CO_2 pipelines are in operation. The lengthy regulatory experience—the first CO_2 pipeline was built in the 1930s—is impressive, and often overlooked by other jurisdictions. However, as policy makers consider how CCS can be employed in the context of climate change mitigation, the author warns of the dangers of failing to respect the legal, commercial and operational realities under which CO_2 transportation and disposal in the context of enhanced oil recovery are conducted.

Carbon capture and storage for climate change mitigation requires the secure storage of CO_2 for hundreds of years, well beyond the likely lifetime of the initial storage operator. Liability issues have, as a consequence, been a distinctive challenge in developing CCS legislation. Channelling liability towards the storage operator, with provisions for the eventual transfer of responsibility to the state, has been a common model in many jurisdictions. In Chapter 15, Ian Havercroft considers, in a comparative analysis across a number of countries, how subtle but significant differences have developed in the treatment of liability—both as to the conditions of transfer and as to the types of liability that are encompassed. The commercial development of CCS, as with other major infrastructure projects, is likely to involve a number of different entities. Whatever the provisions of the legislation, in practice liability risks may be spread by commercial arrangements among the different parties involved, and Daniel Lawrence addresses the challenges involved in Chapter 16. As he notes, 'the willingness of commercial entities to participate in a CCS project will be influenced by the extent to which potential liabilities can be allocated/shared effectively amongst the various CCS project participants (and/or their insurers), including the extent to which liabilities can be shared with/allocated to the state'.

China is now the world's largest emitter of CO_2, and houses nearly half of the world's existing coal-fired generating stations. Yet China's endorsement of the Paris Climate Change Agreement suggests that CCS will play an increasingly significant role in the country. Navraj Singh Ghaleigh's consideration of the law in China in Chapter 17 is therefore of special importance. He notes that despite policies promoting CCS, China lacks a dedicated CCS legal regime and relies upon amendments and additions to existing environmental laws. But he warns against analysing the Chinese system against Western conceptions of law: 'the Chinese approach bears only a slight resemblance to a system of generally applicable rules applied impartially, and enforceable via independent courts'. The role of state-owned enterprises, their relationship to government, and the use of bureaucratic agreements and plans are likely to be as important to achieving the securing the implementation of CCS as any formal legislation.

We are immensely grateful to all the authors for their contributions. We would particularly like to thank Kathryn St John and Alec Bombell, students at the UCL Faculty of Laws, for their assistance. They have learnt much about CCS law—whether the technology will prove a critical technology for their generation remains to be seen.

Lastly, we would like to give special thanks to our copy-editor from Hart Publishing, Catherine Minahan, who has showed immense professionalism and patience in her work on this book.

Richard Macrory
Ian Havercroft
Richard B Stewart
July 2017

1

Geological Factors for Legislation to Enable and Regulate Storage of Carbon Dioxide in the Deep Subsurface

STUART HASZELDINE AND NAVRAJ SINGH GHALEIGH

I. INTRODUCTION

COMBUSTION AND CONVERSION of carbon have been basic energy and feedstock sources during the evolution and rise of industrialised society. Since the 1750s, fossil fuels—coal, then oil, then methane gas—have succeeded one another in providing dense energy storage in portable, easily extractable and cheap forms. However efficiently these fossil fuels, or indeed biomass, are used in combustion, or are transferred to different energy vectors such as hydrogen, or used in petrochemical products, the fossil or biological carbon ultimately emitted into the atmosphere is still carbon dioxide (CO_2). It is clear, first, that this increased rate of CO_2 emission instigated by industrialisation has produced increased atmospheric CO_2 content, leading to global warming and climate change. Secondly, the dissolution of increased CO_2 from the atmosphere into the upper ocean is producing a measurable increase in the acidity of ocean water. One solution to this dilemma of cheap energy, combined with undesirable CO_2 emissions, is to invent, perfect and deploy the suite of technologies collectively known as carbon capture and storage (CCS). The aim of such an exercise is to apply technological solutions that can either capture the carbon before combustion, with the fossil fuel, or recapture the carbon after combustion of fossil fuel. Once captured, purified and compressed into a liquid state, this CO_2 can be transported for tens, hundreds or even thousands of kilometres by a truck, train, pipeline or pressurised ocean tanker. Sites of underground geology can be identified using known geological principles, and the liquid CO_2 can be injected deep below ground into microscopic pore space. This can occur in a variety of subsurface geological contexts, ranging from enhancement of oil recovery, to pressurised refilling of depleted oil- or gas-fields, to displacing ambient pore water in deep saline formations. Once in place, the environmental requirement is that CO_2 should remain stored deep below ground for tens of thousands of years into the future.[1] This will reduce the excess rate, and total mass, of fossil carbon emission,

---

[1] PU Clark et al, 'Consequences of twenty-first-century policy for multi-millennial climate and sea-level change' (2016) 6 *Nature Climate Change* 306.

and enable the Earth's self-regulating system to return to its equilibrium of the past 10,000 years.

Carbon capture and storage has received a great deal of publicity, and is politically well favoured. Among the reasons for that favour are the important factors that CCS enables fossil fuel consumption and electricity supply to continue towards 2050 with very similar industrial and infrastructure and institution systems to the past 150 years. Clean-up of the undesirable CO_2 emissions can be effected at a few large, centralised installations, with little impact on the majority of consumers. Carbon capture and storage can be developed rapidly, but, where fitted onto electricity, must also deliver at a cost comparable to competing sources of electricity from renewables, and can, in many cases, enable the continued use of domestically accessible, secure supplies of fossil fuels. As the price of renewable electricity generation continues to tumble rapidly,[2] all of utility-scale solar photovoltaic (PV), onshore wind and (especially) offshore wind are becoming cheaper in price than new-build coal plants without CCS. Therefore it is very difficult to foresee a demand to make progress into commercial coal-fuelled electricity markets, with CCS as an added expense and infrastructure, unless local or cheap coal/lignite is available. The main selling point of CCS fitted to gas-fuelled power plants would be that output is controllable, and deliverable when the sun does not shine, the wind does not blow or the tide does not flow. It remains moot as to the utility of expensive CCS fitting on power plant that may run for only tens of days per year. However, as with many apparently simple new propositions, the detailed development, engineering, commercialisation and regulation of such a new industry requires that new alliances are made profitably, that new ways of planning or developing surface industry and land use are considered, and that new ways of understanding licensing and regulating the use of the subsurface are discovered (the focus of this chapter).

An additional pressure is that commercialisation of CCS on electricity is intended to occur over a timescale of one or two decades. This is an entirely unprecedented rapid rate of change for multiple items of very large equipment within the global and industrialised energy system. Although there is often a singular focus on CCS fitted to electricity, it is very important to recognise that the economic benefits of CCS extend laterally across whole economies. Thus CCS can be fitted onto industries where emissions occur due to intensive fuel use (such as aluminium smelting), or where emissions are inherent in the chemical processes: cement manufacture, ammonia making and multiple types of petrochemicals, iron ore conversion to steel. These can be sites with very low capture costs, but yet still commercially difficult to put CCS into effect because global competition means that suppliers are not (yet) able to charge premium prices for introducing products into low-carbon supply chains. Additionally, in temperate climate industrial cities, the decarbonisation of heat supply is being evaluated through the substitution of methane by hydrogen. If made from methane, this hydrogen will require massive industrial CCS.

---

[2] McKinsey, 'Winds of change? Why offshore wind might be the next big thing' *McKinsey Quarterly* (18 May 2017), at www.globaladvisors.biz/inc-feed/20170518/winds-of-change-why-offshore-wind-might-be-the-next-big-thing/.

Additionally, widespread availability of hydrogen can enable fuel-cell utilisation in transport. Carbon dioxide derived from industrial, hydrogen or transport supplies can have very different business models from that for electricity, and may prove possible to fund by its addition into the adaptation of existing distribution networks. The deep geological storage of CO_2 would be similar in all cases.

The progress of CCS research, and that of commercial project development, is reviewed at the end of this chapter, as is the looming shortfall of new projects and the chasm which could be partly filled by CCS, between predicted warming, pledges pursuant to the Paris Agreement 2015 with Nationally Determined Contributions commitments to reduce emissions, and the much greater reductions necessary to achieve and maintain a 2°C warming limit.

II. OUTLINE OF CCS, SIMILARITIES TO AND DIFFERENCES FROM ESTABLISHED SUBSURFACE INDUSTRIES

A. Hydrocarbon Exploration and Production

Investigation and exploitation of legal subsoil—here focusing on deep geology—has been occurring for many decades. The most extensive industries are: oil and gas (hydrocarbon) exploration and production; groundwater production and use; coal and mineral mining; and the more recent engineering to extract geothermal heat. Of these, the hydrocarbon industries have a uniquely comprehensive suite of experience and high-technology expertise in the visualisation, investigation and modelling that allows exploitation of deep sedimentary basins.[3] Exploitation typically occurs to depths of 4 km, and less frequently to depths of 8 km, in both onshore and offshore settings. Liquid oil or gas is extracted from the deep subsurface by means of boreholes, resulting in reduced subsurface pressures. In many cases this extraction is augmented and increased by the injection of additional water from the surface or surrounding sea. In about 180 cases worldwide, there has been, and is, experience of injecting natural CO_2 to enhance oil recovery, as this can repressurise the deep hydrocarbon reservoir, driving the oil upwards, and CO_2 can also chemically dissolve into the oil, forming a less viscous fluid that flows more easily to the surface. The volumes of fluid handled by the hydrocarbon industry on a daily basis are indeed massive: for the US alone, the figures are 16 million barrels/day (2.54 Mm^3) hydrocarbon-produced fluids and 38 million barrels/day water injection. Carbon dioxide injection for full-scale CCS would be similar in scale. It is clear that substantial expertise exists in the hydrocarbon industry to enable the understanding of 3D geometry of porous rock bodies in the deep subsurface, the understanding of the impermeable seal that seals such a reservoir, and the mechanical and fluid engineering necessary to circulate such large amounts of fluid on a routine daily basis.

---

[3] B Lovell, *Challenged by Carbon: The Oil Industry and Climate Change*, 1st edn (Cambridge, Cambridge University Press, 2009).

However, the CCS proposition[4] contains substantial differences from these established hydrocarbon industries. First is the philosophical difference of polarity, in that oil and gas are produced, whereas CO_2 will be injected for disposal. Secondly, the production of oil and gas leaves a lesser fluid volume in the deep subsurface (there is no empty space in the subsurface), whereas the injection of CO_2 will place a greater volume of fluid into the subsurface. Thirdly, the production of hydrocarbon is a high-value product, produced during a timescale of years to decades, where production can be halted or increased at will with only commercial penalties. By contrast, CO_2 storage requires projection and accurate prediction not just during the 30-year life span of a CO_2 storage operation, but also into the geological longer term to provide assurance of 10,000 years of retention. Fourthly, the ineffective production of hydrocarbon simply carries a penalty of lost potential income, whereas failure of CO_2 storage carries a penalty or a fine outweighing the value of the price paid for CO_2, and additionally carries a hard-to-quantify-and-limit risk of damage to climate or to local life around a leakage point in the future.

B. Geothermal Exploration and Production

Although extraction of heat from the shallow earth crust is nowhere near the industrial scale, or the commercial value, of the hydrocarbon industry, there are similarities in geological circumstance. Low temperature geothermal production and CO_2 storage both require the use of porous and permeable bodies of reservoir rock, of regional extent (ie tens of kilometres). Geothermal borehole development has extensive experience in injecting circulation waters to acquire the associated heat. In many cases, this is a demonstrably successful system. However, in some well-known instances (Soultz, Basel), a series of small earth tremors (magnitude 2.0–3.5 on the Richter scale) have been created, leading to public disquiet and the halting of a project. These provide important indications that the stress field in sedimentary rocks of the 1–3 km subsurface is in close balance and can easily be perturbed by small increases of fluid pressure. Earth tremors can be expected during CO_2 injection.

C. Shale Gas Production

Since the mid-1990s, it has become apparent in the US that large volumes of methane gas can be extracted from mudrocks in the intermediate depth subsurface, which were previously regarded as having zero resource potential. The mechanism of production is to drill boreholes spaced at 1–3 km intervals, and to enhance the flow of gas from the mudrock by means of creating new fracture networks. This is done by injection of pressurised water, deliberately creating small earth tremors as a consequence of the new fracture networks. In these cases, public disquiet appears to be

---

[4] RS Haszeldine, 'Carbon Capture and Storage: How Green Can Black Be?' (2009) 325 *Science* 1647.

much less of an issue, even though the subsurface operation is of a very similar type and a very similar effect to that of geothermal heat mining. The difference may be that many of these shale explorations have been in sparsely populated areas of the US, and also that the above-ground population is much more accustomed to, and content with, the consequences of subsurface drilling and exploitation.

D. Carbon Dioxide Storage

Several settings are envisaged for storage of CO_2 in the deep subsurface. These are likely to incur different effects around the immediate injection site, and these effects are discussed at greater length in section III. Compared to the established industries described here, CO_2 storage requires much better predictions into the future than the oil industry has been accustomed to making. The predictions must also include a better understanding of the three-dimensional geometry of connected rock bodies below ground, which is a question never previously considered in detail. For enhanced oil recovery, challenges and technologies are similar to those already known, so that the regulation and legal difficulties may be much better defined. For injection and storage into passive depleted methane gas-fields or oilfields, the CO_2 injection is likely to be well constrained, with a detailed suite of information derived during production of the hydrocarbons and a good understanding of the local rock-body geometry, its connections and its yield points. Carbon dioxide injection into saline formations is significantly more challenging. If individual structures can be identified, similar to hydrocarbon trapping structures, these may be the easiest to map their limits, monitor and demonstrate CO_2 retention. If, however, CO_2 is injected into the much larger storage spaces available in dipping saline formations without discrete structural traps, then the monitoring, demonstration of CO_2 location and retention will be potentially much more difficult, with a clear choice to trade off adequate precision against excessive expense. In all saline formation settings, the long-term prediction of CO_2 migration, combined with pressure increases, will require detailed and site-specific assessment.

III. CONCEPTS OF SUBSURFACE ZONING

Injection of CO_2 into the deep subsurface may produce several geological effects. These can be considered as (i) direct physical effects and (ii) indirect communication effects. It is useful to consider the subsurface as a series of three zones, each of which possesses certain attributes to contain injected CO_2 (see Figure 1.1). First, the basic requirement is a primary reservoir, combined with a primary seal, together with a side seal and under seal. The primary seal may not directly overlie the reservoir, resulting in a 'waste zone' above the primary reservoir, which may become occupied by CO_2. Secondly, above the primary seal is a thick sequence, normally of sedimentary rocks, which comprises the overburden. This may contain secondary and tertiary reservoirs, with secondary and tertiary seals. However, this may also contain steeply dipping, or vertical, pathways of preferential gas or fluid leakage from the present day, or in the recent geological past. These can act as opportune leakage routes for rapid CO_2 migration, and require careful baseline evaluation, followed by monitoring. Thirdly, above the overburden lies the 'surface environment' where groundwater may be extracted or exploited, and the shallow subsurface may contain living organisms even before the seabed is reached. Fourthly, above the shallow subsurface is the marine water column, or soil and atmosphere, where CO_2 may become diluted and dispersed.

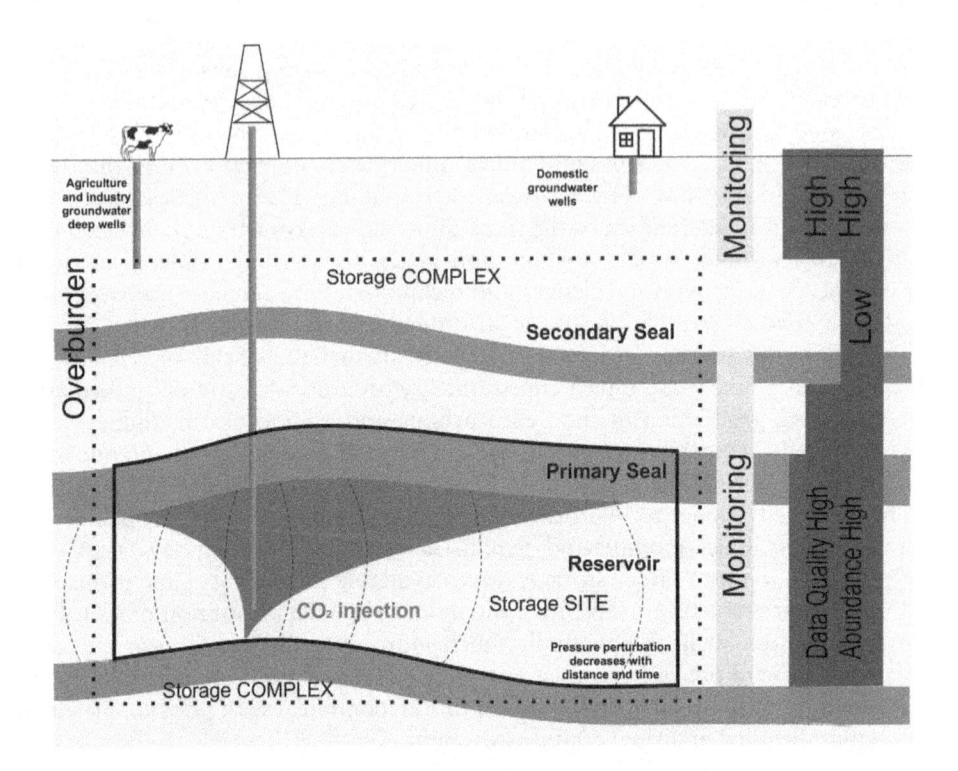

Figure 1.1: Cartoon section through two-dimensional cut of Earth's layering
Note: Vertically exaggerated and not to scale, approximately 2–4 km vertically, and 20–40 km laterally. Shows a borehole injecting CO_2, which forms a plume though time, trapped beneath the primary seal. Outlines of Site under EU-ETS legislation, and Complex under CCS Directive legislation are shown.

In terms of planning for resource use, these different subsurface zones may well have, or be planned to have, different uses. For example, the shallow zones may require to be preserved for groundwater extraction, such that any input of more saline water would be highly undesirable. At deeper levels the use of secondary or tertiary saline formations may be planned for geothermal heat extraction, or for water extraction, or even for methane gas or hydrogen storage. An additional factor may be interference with hydrocarbon production beneath a CO_2 storage reservoir, or more directly threatening effects if the same reservoir is shared both as a CO_2 storage site and 20 km laterally as a hydrocarbon production zone, which may often be operated by a different commercial entity under a different hydrocarbon licensing regime. In the nascent CO_2 licensing regimes of the UK, EU, US and Canada, it seems that hydrocarbon production has 'priority'. What that means in practice remains to be negotiated case by case, because over-prioritisation of hydrocarbons would sterilise most regions identified as CO_2 storage resources.

IV. CONCEPTS OF INJECTION AND STORAGE

These different zones (see Figure 1.1) also have a conceptual use, in that together they can be considered as an injection zone and its adjacent surroundings (the storage Site), where CO_2 is then placed into the reservoir. There is a zone of routine low-level monitoring in the waste zone and primary seal above the reservoir. Above the monitoring zone can be considered a potential zone of remediation, where reservoir engineering interventions can be made to secure leaks and enhanced monitoring can be deployed if leaks are detected. Above the remediation zone is the majority of the storage complex, which extends up to the base of the shallow subsurface. The introduction of the storage complex concept is very helpful to physically and legally contain secondary migration of CO_2 in the subsurface.

Defining subsurface zones in three-dimensional space enables monitoring to be focused onto the boundaries, for determination of the success of CO_2 retention. However, there needs to be clarity on what is intended. Is the intention to inject captured greenhouse gas and prevent stored CO_2 from reaching the shallow depth biosphere, land surface and atmosphere to drive global warming? Or is the intention to make a detailed assessment of all subsurface effects of that injection, which could include changes of deep water chemistry in the storage reservoir site, the displacement of ambient pre-injection water (or other fluids), the detection of fluid pressure pulses and the attribution of induced seismicity. Clearly the first is more aligned with the objective of CO_2 storage; and although the second approach may feel more comforting to a regulator, it is immensely onerous for a storage operator, for little practical benefit.

In principle, the lateral extent of a 'storage complex' could be many tens of kilometres; however, it is probable that for practical purposes the licensing authority will wish to restrict the area to a few kilometres diameter. Migration of small amounts of CO_2 from the primary reservoir and along bounding faults is not necessarily a problem under this conceptualisation. Although such migration would be unplanned and unexpected, it will trigger enhanced and detailed monitoring once detected by the low-level background monitoring. Carbon dioxide could migrate through the overburden, to be dispersed or retained by a secondary, or even a tertiary, seal.

The concept of permanent storage is elusive in geological timescales. Depending on the context, it could mean hundreds or thousands of years from a human societal perception; or it could mean tens of millions of years in the context of a sedimentary basin receiving stored CO_2; or it could mean many hundreds of millions of years during the lifetime of the Earth. For the purpose of climate mitigation, a pragmatic timescale for storage is linked to the duration needed for the Earth's climate system to dispose of excess (post-industrial) CO_2. That can be taken as a minimum 1,000–10,000 years, so that any leakage in that timescale can be viewed as 'failure'.

Natural CO_2 accumulations clearly demonstrate that it is possible to retain high concentrations of pure CO_2 in single subsurface locations for timescales of tens of thousands, or even tens of millions, of years. However, technical factors in extrapolating results of reservoir engineering models mean that small uncertainties in the measurement of a storage site at the present day, propagate into larger uncertainties further into the future. Consequently, it is very difficult to make precise predictions even for timescales of thousands or tens of thousands of years. Predictions for timescales of millions of years into the future are often made using techniques to statistically combine an assemblage of risks assessed at the present day, and multiply by what is envisaged as a full suite of possible future circumstances. In such situations, it is extremely difficult to state that there will be zero leakage in all cases, even though the overwhelming majority of simple future scenarios demonstrate zero, or minimal, leakage. There is a clear danger that over-regulation may attempt to provide 'guarantees' of secure storage into the far future. A more pragmatic approach will take a nuanced and risk-based approach, on the understanding that the natural world is neither black nor white but composed of many shades of grey. The state may ultimately take over liability for stored CO_2, but in doing so is entitled to ask the storage operator for predictability.

A wrong conception has arisen resulting from a misreading of section 1.6.3 of the Special Report of the Intergovernmental Panel on Climate Change (IPCC) on CCS.[5] This states that a leakage rate of 0.001 (0.1 per cent) or more in 5,000 years has to be unacceptable. This has frequently been misinterpreted to imply that a leakage rate of 0.1 per cent *is expected*. That is untrue. A combination of good site choice together with a competent subsurface operator should mean that leakage rates will be much less than 0.1 per cent in 5,000 years. It is also incorrect to assume that *all* storage sites will leak in a similar manner at a similar rate. Information from natural oil accumulations and methane gas-fields clearly shows that such assumptions are unjustified, and retention at sites that are performing well is much better than this, for millions of years. Evidence from over 30 years of engineering experience with methane gas storage in porous subsurface reservoirs also demonstrates that significant leakage is improbable. Each subsurface storage site will be individual, and will need individual assessment and individual treatment, even though common approaches, rules and processes are expected to be available.[6]

V. GUIDANCE ON STORAGE SITES AND MONITORING ZONES

Here the concept of a subsurface 'storage complex' is examined (see Figure 1.1). This involves a much larger volume, to be defined by the licence applicant, and could

---

[5] B Metz et al, *Carbon Dioxide Capture and Storage: Special Report of the Intergovernmental Panel on Climate Change* (Cambridge, Cambridge University Press, 2005), at www.ipcc.ch/pdf/special-reports/srccs/srccs_wholereport.pdf.

[6] T Lairer and H Obro, 'Environmental and Safety Monitoring of the Natural Gas Underground Storage at Stenille, Denmark' in DJ Evans and RA Chadwick (eds), *Underground Gas Storage*, Special Publication 313 (London, Geological Society, 2009) 81.

extend from beneath the reservoir for several kilometres vertically up to the shallow subsurface, without reaching the shallow subsurface.

A. Accommodating Imperfect Sites

Expecting, and legislating for, total security of storage is unreasonable, although desirable. There are several ways around this problem. A realistic approach may be to legislate for the possibility of small-scale unintended leakage. Several modelling studies show that the small 'tongue' at the leading edge of a CO_2 plume immediately beneath the primary seal is extremely difficult to contain within a Site (eg Figure 1.1, extreme ends of CO_2 plume). If 1 per cent of CO_2 is predicted to leak from a Site into the complex within 1,000 years by this well-understood process, and does not leave the storage complex into the biosphere or atmosphere, is that a terminal problem? This could simply result in the site operator's paying a penalty to reimburse the regulator for the expense of monitoring leakage outside the primary reservoir. Alternatively, an operator may choose to under-fill a site, to avoid the possibility of leakage—that could become a problem for governments if pre-owned storage resources are handed back; can a second operator be licensed, and who would be responsible if any CO_2 were to leak at a later date? It is again important to realise that a correctly undertaken site evaluation and site-choosing process is essential before any CO_2 injection occurs. If this has been undertaken correctly, the risk of unplanned leakage is minimal, and it would be entirely unreasonable to expect and legislate for insurance of all of the injected CO_2 to be released.

B. How much CO_2 can Leak?

i. Natural Processes of Trapping

It is impossible for all injected CO_2 to leak from the storage site reservoir, and very improbable that any significant quantity of CO_2 will leave the storage complex to reach the biosphere or surface. The only CO_2 mobile for catastrophic leakage in the short term (days to years) is the dense phase (fluid and gas) CO_2 in the wellbore and pipeline. As explained in the 2005 IPCC Special Report on CCS,[7] there are several processes operating that act to retain CO_2 in porous rock in the deep subsurface. During injection, the risk of unplanned leakage increases progressively, as pressure within the reservoir increases and could reactivate boundary faults or— very rarely—break the top seal. The quantity of free phase CO_2 also increases. This is also the time at which maximum industrial intervention is occurring, with greatest on-site capability for continual monitoring, intervention and remediation. During injection, and continuing rapidly (weeks, years) after injection ceases, fluid CO_2 is dissolving in residual pore water, CO_2 movement leaves behind isolated bubbles of

---

[7] Metz et al, n 5 above.

fluid CO_2 (residual saturation trapping) and reactions occur, which are usually geologically slow (multiple millennia), to form new minerals by consuming the CO_2 as a reactant. All these processes reduce the quantity of mobile CO_2. Residual saturation and dissolution are most important in retaining CO_2 in sandstone reservoirs, and between 20 and 80 per cent of CO_2 can be immobilised by this process.[8] That means a mode of only 60 per cent CO_2 can physically leak, and that leakage will move into overlying aquifers, where additional residual saturation trapping can occur, leaving very little CO_2 capable of reaching the land surface.

The point of maximum risk of catastrophic leakage, then, is in the closing stages of injection. After that point, the processes of CO_2 dissolution into pore water, physical dissipation of excess pressure and migration-assisted trapping irrevocably decrease the risk of CO_2 leakage. Individual simulation and calculation will be needed for each storage site, but the quantity of CO_2 able to leak as discrete fluid or gaseous CO_2 quickly reduces to just a very few tens of per cent.

ii. Tracking and Fingerprinting CO_2

The quantity of dissolved CO_2 will be useful to determine, for actuarial purposes of calculating the possible leakage. This can be achieved remotely by seismic reflection survey geophysics, as CO_2 brine has a sonic velocity different from that of brine with fluid CO_2 bubbles, and from brine with no CO_2. Calibration and verification can be achieved by resampling the reservoir brine plus CO_2, and using oxygen and carbon stable isotopes to geochemically determine the amount of pore water-to-CO_2 interaction.[9]

To identify and fingerprint CO_2 that has migrated as a gas phase, or which has dissolved into pore water and migrated, it is possible to use the tiny mixture of noble gases dissolved into the CO_2 as a fingerprint. Sophisticated understanding of the abundances and ratios of different noble gas isotopes can produce quantitative insights to the sources of CO_2, the quantity of subsurface water contacted and the differences from CO_2 derived from other capture owners. Noble gases and stable isotope signatures of CO_2 have been trialled in a quasi-litigation setting at Weyburn, to successfully rebut accusations of CO_2 leakage.[10]

C. Pressure Processes and Extent Around the Injection Site

Excess pressure will extend for many kilometres beyond the physical CO_2 plume, and excess pressure will usually be a limiting physical condition on injection rates, close

---

[8] NM Burnside and M Naylor, 'Review and implications of relative permeability of CO_2/brine systems and residual trapping of CO_2,' (2014) 23 *International Journal of Greenhouse Gas Control* 1.

[9] S Serno et al, 'Using oxygen isotopes to quantitatively assess residual CO_2 saturation during the CO_2CRC Otway Stage 2B Extension residual saturation test' (2016) 52 *International Journal of Greenhouse Gas Control* 73.

[10] SMV Gilfillan et al, 'Using noble gas fingerprints at the Kerr Farm to assess CO_2 leakage allegations linked to the Weyburn-Midale CO_2 monitoring and storage project' (2017) 63 *International Journal of Greenhouse Gas Control* 215.

to the boreholes. Because of the density difference between CO_2 and brine in the reservoir, the vertical column thickness of CO_2 produces a pressure disequilibrium at the base of the top seal, which augments the excess pressure due to the increased volume of fluid during injection. This can cause new fractures in the overlying cap rock. Or, more likely, a reactivation of slippage along faults within the rock volume of this transient pressure bubble. Modelling of the subsurface shows that measurable pressure increases are expected at 30–50kms distance from the injection sites.[11] These are likely to cause small-scale seismicity, barely detectable at the land surface, and with minimal or no damage to the built environment. The pressure pulse decays away during a few decades, by slow movement of water or CO_2 pore fluid into the waste zone above the reservoir and beneath the seal, laterally away from the injection site, and also down into sediments beneath the injection site.[12]

Pressure could interact with other users of the subsurface, within several tens of kilometres. If two injection sites overlap, the excess pressures will be additive, so that cooperation is needed to avoid inadvertent fracture of adjacent top seal to storage—so damaging the viability of that property. Equally possible is that CO_2 injection could overlap with hydrocarbon extraction—in which case the effects may be broadly neutral, but detailed planning of pressure management at the hydrocarbon site could be affected. In hydrocarbon exploitation by extraction, there is not normally any concept of pressure trespass or damage to adjacent assets or users. Although there is no known engineering problem, it remains to be seen if pressure trespass will be established as a legally serious problem for CCS.

VI. CO_2 INJECTION

A. Types of Trapping

It is conceptually well understood that several types of trapping are possible. During the injection and site operation phase, physical retention of fluid CO_2 is required. When this CO_2 moves through the whole space of the reservoir, residual saturation trapping becomes important, forming small bubbles of CO_2 isolated in different pores. This can be an important effect in timescales of only years to decades, and may retain up to 30 per cent of the injected CO_2. During timescales of several decades to a few thousand years, dissolution of injected CO_2 into the subsurface brine or hydrocarbon becomes important; this will usually result in a fluid more dense than the original brine, so that dissolved CO_2 will sink within the sedimentary basin to produce secure storage, rather than rise to form a potential leak. Natural accumulations and engineering simulations both show that this type of secure storage can be promoted by designing CO_2 injection to encounter the maximum volume of

---

[11] Q Zhou et al, 'Modeling Basin- and Plume-Scale Processes of CO_2 Storage for Full-Scale Deployment' (2010) 48 *Groundwater* 494.
[12] C McDermott et al, 'Screening the geomechanical stability (thermal and mechanical) of shared multi-user CO_2 storage assets' (2016) 45 *International Journal of Greenhouse Gas Control* 43.

pore water. Reaction of dissolved CO_2 with surrounding rock can sometimes produce new minerals; such reactions can occur rapidly in new or fractured minerals, or in high-flux situations close to boreholes. However, in the majority of the rock and CO_2 volume, these reactions in natural situations are extremely slow (tens of thousands to millions of years) and absorb only a few percentage points of injected CO_2. It seems probable that the greatest risks of CO_2 escape from the primary reservoir occur during the physical retention period, ie including the period of site operation. This is at a time when monitoring can be most intense.

B. Geometries of CO_2 Trap

Although the consideration of each storage site will be different in detail, there are fundamentally only two types. The first, structure traps, provide a geometric shape that retains buoyant CO_2. The easiest of these concepts is that of a dome, which can be described as an anticline, or fold, with down-dips in all four compass directions. The above-ground analogy would be an isolated smooth sloped hill. Here, CO_2 will be retained within the dome topography, provided that the primary seal is not fractured. Similar containment can be achieved with a range of geological structures including fault blocks, unconformities or 2-D anticline folds. Such geographically confined storage sites enable monitoring to be clearly focused, and there is no direct interaction between injected CO_2 and other subsurface users. The second type is a layer of reservoir rock, which lies at an angle (dip) to the horizontal. In these cases, retention of CO_2 requires an overlying primary seal, together with a combination of residual saturation trapping, dissolution, or very large pore volume.

C. Effects of CO_2 Injection

Injection of CO_2 will produce several effects in saline formations. Three such effects are highlighted here. First, injected CO_2 is a fluid of extremely low viscosity and so can migrate rapidly through porous reservoirs. Experience at the Utsira injection site, combined with numerous computational reservoir models, clearly shows that a thin 5–10m zone of fluid CO_2 can migrate at 1m/day laterally along the top of a saline formation, beneath the seal. Thus the small amount of CO_2 in that leading edge of the plume may be important for concepts of trespass, even though it is volumetrically insignificant. The second effect is that a great volume of CO_2 remains in the injected plume. This type of trapping is likely to be more difficult to monitor and fully quantify, if there is a requirement that all the CO_2 must be closely tracked. A third effect of storage in aquifers also provides situations where pressure waves or CO_2 from one operator may move in the subsurface to become mingled with pressure waves or CO_2 from a second operator. If the CO_2 from different operators needs to be distinguished into the future, it will be necessary to fingerprint individual operators' CO_2 using parts per billion of suitable labelling gases or compounds.

D. Consequences of CO_2 Injection

Several aspects of CO_2 injection may produce unhelpful effects. The most debated of these is the far-field pressure wave, or transient 'pulse'. When CO_2 is rapidly injected as additional fluid into a sealed, or more normally only partially sealed, saline formation, an increase of pressure can be anticipated. To avoid artificially induced fracturing of the geological seal overlying the primary reservoir, the limits of additional pressure increase can be calculated and closely audited during the injection time period. The pressure pulse will affect an area many times that of the liquid CO_2. This can affect multiple operators within one saline formation; the pressure pulses will interact such that injection into neighbouring structures A and B can increase the background pressure of a new storage site development, structure C, before any CO_2 has been injected, and so reduce the storage capacity of structure C. Licensing may have to treat sites as connected groups. Reservoir engineering simulations show that a pressure pulse decreases to background within a few decades of injection ceasing. In confined formations, or geo-pressured deep settings, this pressure increase will define the limits of possible CO_2 injection. In the more normal circumstance of partially open and partially connected saline formations, CO_2 injection will depend on the rate of pressure dissipation. If safe pressure limits were exceeded during injection, and fracturing of the overlying seals became a problem, it would be possible simply to stop injecting, or to extract a few per cent of the injected CO_2 to decrease pressure.

A second consequence of CO_2 injection is the potential in the far-field to induce movement of brine from the deep saline formation. If such fluids, containing very salty and metal-rich water, do reach extraction zones for drinking water for agricultural wells, problems of water pollution could, in theory, occur. However, calculations using the volume of injected CO_2 for a 25-year storage lease, compared to the whole porosity volume available within the rock, show that groundwater tables will shift, on average, only a few tens of millimetres vertically.

E. Incomplete Containment

It is well understood that CO_2 could escape from the site of its injection, by several methods. These are all capable of being predicted during the site choice and evaluation stages. As discussed in section IV, because of the variation in, and precise nature of, natural subsurface systems, it is impossible to guarantee 100 per cent containment into the indefinite future. There are multiple possibilities for small-scale leakage through the primary seal. This is why monitoring of the storage site needs to be undertaken, and why the highest quality of baseline survey is essential, because all future work will be referenced onto that baseline. The method of monitoring will depend on the exact site. Conventional oil industry methods have been, and will be, adapted. Regulations need to accommodate these possibilities. It is not yet possible to place established probability values on all of these features, because engineered CO_2 storage has never been undertaken in these diverse settings for any period of time. It will be necessary to gain learning about the quantification of unplanned migration by means of experimentation at a number of validation storage sites. Defined structures offer the greatest certainty of CO_2 location. Regionally extensive saline formations are likely to involve laterally extensive CO_2 migration and could result in the movement of CO_2 outside a geographically constrained licence area, even though that is unlikely to constitute a leak returning to the surface. Where pore space is not owned by the federal state (such as in the US) then this could produce situations of trespass into different property. Any of these idealised situations could result in CO_2's occurring in hard-to-predict or unexpected locations above the primary seal, or in slow diffuse leakage if the primary seal has not been adequately assessed or is damaged during injection.

F. Role of Demonstrations and Evolving Regulation

Projects to demonstrate CCS are usually discussed in the context of their capture and power-plant technology. However, an equally important point is that demonstrations of subsurface storage capability still need to be undertaken. A diverse suite of subsurface environments exists within any individual sedimentary basin, and also worldwide. Commercial-sized demonstrations (greater than 1 Mt CO_2 per year) have the opportunity to test the validity of different types. Only after such demonstrations have been undertaken are problems discovered and solved; once this occurs, more precise and prescriptive legislative guidance can be given. Legislators should beware of over-prescription before enough validation projects are undertaken globally. These injection projects, at industrial scale, will provide effective in situ average measures of real-world migration speeds of the CO_2 plume, of dissolution, and pressure pulse increase and decay, to compare with and refine the theoretical predictions made beforehand. There is potential to gain strong benefit from sharing of results because, with the learnings being gained at the controlling microscopic scale, petrophysical properties of rocks are considered portable from one setting to another. A sandstone in Texas can behave identically to a sandstone beneath the UK North Sea.

G. Operational Interventions

Great efforts are made by many regulators to install monitoring equipment and secure operational standards at CO_2 injection sites. However equally, or more, important are the abilities to use the knowledge and undertake actions to ensure secure storage if operations do not perform as planned. Two examples of commercial-scale CO_2 storage can demonstrate this.

i. In Salah, Algeria, Onshore

In Salah is the location of the Krechba gasfield, in a deep subsurface closed anticline fold in Carboniferous sandstones as part of the gasfield complex of the central

Algeria desert. The natural gas methane produced is high in CO_2 (10 per cent mole volume), and so needs to be separated before sale and pipeline transport northwards to the coast. A consortium of Sonatrach, Statoil and BP decided to use this separated pure CO_2 for re-injection, to test the ability to create local storage globally at CO_2 gas production sites. The legal and regulatory institutional oversight of CO_2 storage in Algeria is believed to be effective but minimal. The injection reservoir was pragmatically chosen to be the deeper, down-dip, extension of the gasfield reservoir. That is water-filled at about 1,800m. This would be geologically well understood, and shared the same thick and impermeable mudrock seal that had clearly retained methane plus CO_2 in the main reservoir. A potable aquifer is regionally widespread within 400m of the surface, and needs protecting. It was always clearly known that this reservoir falls far outside the factors recommended for 'best practice' CO_2 storage, with a low permeability of 10mDarcy, being thin (just 20m), and the entire site having a geological history showing many kilometres of uplift from deep burial to its present depth. Subsurface geological mapping shows many NW–SE fault trends (some of which are reversed in movement due to uplift), apparently linking up from the deep non-reservoir basement into the shallower reservoir. However, if this type of poor site adjacent to gas production could be developed and operated with secure performance, that would open the possibility of similar developments with minimal infrastructure at numerous gas fields with high CO_2 content. The site was used as a test bed for extensive and detailed monitoring with all plausible science techniques and technology instruments. Injection of 0.74 Mt CO_2/yr commenced in early 2004, with the intention to store 17–20Mt CO_2 through a 30-year production project. Several comprehensive assessments of risks were undertaken[13] before development, and a design limit was set for the upper limit of injection pressure to be 24–29 MPa (3,500 to 4,200 psi). Risk of CO_2 leakage upwards through re-activated and re-opened fractures was considered improbable but of high impact. Consequently, the boundary of the subsurface CO_2 licence was set shallow and above the most likely seal. Pre-existing boreholes, fractures and faults were recognised as the most likely CO_2 leakage routes.

After three years of injection, surface surveying detected a minor leak of CO_2 gas from the wellhead of KB-5, a disused borehole. The CO_2 was unexpected, due to faster than anticipated migration along faults and factures. This well had been recognised as poorly cemented after abandonment, by pre-emptive surveys before CO_2 injection had started. This was managed by re-sealing the well to a better standard.

By October 2008 a surface uplift of a 5–10mm/yr became detectable above some parts of the injection site around well KB-502. This used low-cost satellite surveys from InSAR—radar frequency interferometry, now available at low cost for several surveys per year. At the same time, modelling calculations indicated that injection pressures had exceeded those intended. Thus a possibility emerged that CO_2 had migrated vertically up though re-opened fractures associated with geologically old

---

[13] CM Oldenburg, 'Leakage risk assessment of the In Salah CO_2 storage project' (2011) 4 *Energy Procedia* 4154.

and geologically ancient basement fault zones. Carbon dioxide injection rates were reduced, to reduce the pressure effects. Further simulation of injection and of rock mechanics[14] demonstrated that the clusters of fractures re-opened by the excess pressures could be 3,500m long, 50m wide and extend 350m upwards from the reservoir. Surface displacement was due to pressurised CO_2 migrating from the reservoir into clusters of fractures within the caprock but not breaking through the caprock.

The continued growth of the opened fracture created a risk. Leakage of CO_2 up to the potable aquifer and land surface could have been possible. That risk had already been identified by intensive multi-technique monitoring. That had been managed by a reduced rate of CO_2 injection, and eventually to cessation of injection in 2008. In Salah is a good example of the stringently self-regulated operation of a CO_2 storage site. A full risk appraisal had been undertaken before borehole drilling, and intensive monitoring was deployed using remote sensing at low cost. That was able to detect unpredicted behaviour and link to pre-arranged programmes of action—and to provide support where necessary. Tough regulation is good, but must also be adequately enforced—by an informed regulator and /or by self-imposed fear of practical and reputational damage.

ii. Snøhvit, Norway, Offshore

Snøhvit is the northernmost gasfield in Europe, exporting LNG from the Barents Sea continental shelf of Norway. The field is operated by Statoil, who have decided to clean the natural CO_2 mix 5–8 per cent from the commercial hydrocarbon gases and to store geologically store CO_2 in the deep subsurface to prevent climate change emissions. The commercial logic is driven by the same offshore tax penalty of 500 NOK/ton that encouraged gas clean-up and CCS at Sleipner, and CCS was a condition imposed by the Norwegian Parliament when consenting the project. Carbon dioxide is produced offshore, brought onshore to separate from LNG, and the CO_2 is returned offshore through a dedicated pipe and 0.7Mt/yr CO_2 are reinjected to the deep subsurface. The onshore LNG plant emits about 900,000t CO_2/yr—about 2 per cent of Norwegian GHG—but is covered under different legislation for onshore emissions with no tax penalty. This produces 4.3 Mtonnes LNG/yr, equivalent to 38 million barrels of oil. Injection of 99 per cent pure CO_2 started in April 2008, initially using the 2,560m subsealevel Tubåen Formation, deeper than the gas reservoir. The detailed formal legal definition of the storage site is not publicly available. But Statoil, as operator, certainly made several suites of different assessments and predictions for several subsurface localities. Detailed monitoring of downhole fluid pressure and seismic reflection surveys showed that the site was not performing as well as anticipated, so that CO_2 was not spreading evenly through the storage reservoir but was instead restricted to one small reservoir compartment. That CO_2 was imaged on seismic reflection, and the excess pressure was continually

---

[14] AP Rinaldi and J Rutqvist, 'Modeling of deep fracture zone opening and transient ground surface uplift at KB-502 CO_2 injection well in Salah, Algeria' (2013) 12 *International Journal of Greenhouse Gas Control* 155.

monitored, so that when pressure increase approached close to rock fracture pressure, all injection was stopped before any adverse blowout. During initial evaluation of the site by Statoil, a Plan B was already defined. A new borehole was drilled during 2011 into the shallower Stø Formation, which is not geologically segmented by faults and is a down-dip extension of the producing reservoir. This has performed well, in line with predictions of CO_2 injection. During autumn 2016, a second injection borehole was planned and drilled into a different part of the Stø Formation, which now enables options to be chosen for the rate of injection into each hole.

The lessons from Snøhvit are as follows:

(1) Carbon dioxide storage development can occur without being supervised by specific EU legislation on CCS.
(2) A competent operator is vital during these initial learnings on how to choose and develop storage sites. An operator who is experienced in the deep subsurface problems that can arise adds greatly to the resilience of operation and the remedial choices rapidly available in controlling and modifying the injection at the storage site.
(3) An experienced and competent operator of hydrocarbon fields will inevitably make several plans. In case of events becoming unexpected, a substitute (and well-costed and already evaluated) borehole plan exists, which can be enacted very rapidly.

H. Accidents

An understandable fear with any industrial technology, particularly a newly developing large-scale technology, is that of catastrophic accident. Several false analogies are often made to illustrate CO_2 storage in the subsurface. One of the most common of these is the Lake Nyos incident in Cameroon. Here, a volcanic lake trapped free gaseous CO_2 beneath a deep column of water. When this was disturbed by submarine rockfall, the gas bubble erupted rapidly through the water column to spread onto the surrounding land, and killed 1,600 people. This analogy is incorrectly applied to subsurface CO_2 storage. In the subsurface case, CO_2 cannot rise through intact porous rock, or even through fracture networks, at such a rapid rate. There are many studies of natural CO_2 seeps worldwide, and none has shown this extreme rate of CO_2 leakage. Where historical records exist, it appears that the risk of death to the affected population from natural CO_2 seeps is about 10,000 times less than the probability of death in a car accident.[15]

A different type of fear is that of a borehole failure. Blowouts, due to excess subsurface pressure, are not known frequently in CO_2 boreholes. One such incident at Sheep Mountain, a natural CO_2 accumulation, was closed down using standard oil and gas remediation techniques, within weeks. Unanticipated incidents do, of

---

[15] JJ Roberts, RA Wood and RS Haszeldine, 'Assessing the health risks of natural CO_2 seeps in Italy' (2010) 108 *Proceedings of the National Academy of Sciences* 16545.

course, occur in the offshore. A spectacular example was the BP-operated failure in the Gulf of Mexico in 2010. Although this demonstrably leaked large amounts of oil into the ocean, it is also remarkable how rapidly new and untested technology was built, experimented with, and eventually successfully deployed—within a timescale of only weeks. Although this leak was a poorly-handled public relations disaster, a case can be made that it was a commendable technical recovery. This gives confidence that even unexpected and new incidents can be mitigated rapidly, without the entire oilfield (or CO_2 storage site) becoming emptied. As alluded to in section V.B.i, there are now several pieces of work to show that leakage of CO_2 injected under planned and designed pressure constraints cannot be as extreme as hydrocarbon blow-outs; and the total CO_2 in a catastrophic leak can be only a very few per cent of the CO_2 injected.

An example of onshore leakage of CO_2 by spectacular blowout from an onshore borehole occurred in Serbia. This is worthy of note because it shows that mitigation and control can be achieved at low cost with basic equipment.[16] The overpressured Becej CO_2 field experienced a blowout at the end of 1968, killing several people. Uncontrolled gas flow lasted for six months, until the deep borehole collapsed to reduce the flow for an additional month, which created a crater at the surface that also collapsed to block the remaining flow, except for a few bubbles that rose continually to the surface. A total loss of 17 Bm3 is calculated. In mid-2007 an artificial borehole seal was applied using a mix of silica gel and urea, emplaced through a specially drilled diagonal relief well intersecting the blowout. That forms a solid cross-linked polymer capable of retaining geopressure. Leakage is reported to have been reduced to a tiny yearly quantity.

Borehole problems of a different kind were remediated in Mississippi during CO_2 injection for CO_2-Enhanced Oil Recovery (CO_2-EOR—see section VII). An abandoned borehole had not been adequately sealed, and although not used for CO_2 injection, was excessively pressured during CO_2 injection and flowed CO_2 plus oil and drilling mud from 650m to the land surface for 37 days from 9 August 2011. Surface effects included deaths of several animals due to the settling of dense CO_2 in hollows, but there is no recorded harm to humans. The borehole crossed two exploited aquifers in the subsurface, but no contamination was recorded in either. As to this author's speculation on the cause: the depth of leakage is around the transition from CO_2 fluid to CO_2 gas, so it is possible that a phase transition and very large-volume expansion created the pressure drive for leak-off. The operating company was fined $650,000, and halted the leak by drilling a new well to cement the inadequately abandoned well. Reports state that serious local surface effects required removal of 32,000 bbl of liquids from the site, plus 27,000 tons of contaminated soil plus drilling mud. Subsequently, 28 abandoned legacy wells in the oilfield, dating from the 1940s and 1950s, were pre-emptively remediated to modern standards. Two additional blowouts through Mississippi legacy wells occurred in 2007,

---

[16] L Lakatos et al, 'Prevention of Vertical Gas Flow in a Collapsed Well Using Silicate/Polymer/Urea Method' (2009), SPE International Symposium on Oil Field Chemistry, Society of Petroleum Engineers.

and CO_2 bubbled slowly to the surface in a Louisiana incident in 2013, which was remediated by injecting chemical treatment downhole.

The two examples above indicate the difficulties of pressure management, and the difficulties of guaranteeing the security of 100 per cent of tens of thousands of legacy boreholes during onshore operations. Arguably the local damage caused, although significant, is still less than the dispersed damage caused to global climate by not injecting CO_2. And it should also be noted that all these occurrences were in onshore CO_2-EOR operations, where standards are much lower than operations offshore, and where standards of design are much lower than for boreholes or sites specifically planned for CO_2 injection and retention. Are these few incidents a 'price worth paying' for the wider environmental benefits of accelerating and enabling CO_2 injection? That has not been legally tested. The issue, though, is of permissive local state legislation, focused on enabling oil production rather than enforcing CO_2 retention.

VII. ENHANCED OIL RECOVERY

In addition to the 'aquifer injection' style of CO_2 injection analysed in section VI, there is the possibility to engage in very large-tonnage utilisation of CO_2. This is by injecting fluid-phase CO_2 into operating, or partly depleted, oilfields, which, in the correctly chosen geological circumstances, has the effect of producing additional oil that would otherwise be left permanently in the ground. This is known as CO_2-EOR, and has been an established and profitable business practice in the USA since 1972. Careful distinction should be made from other technological types of EOR—such as polymers, solvents, steam, brightwater—which do not use or store CO_2. A closely similar technique is the injection of methane CH_4, to reduce oil viscosity. More than 100 such projects are operating CO_2 injection at any one time[17] in USA, Canada, Brazil, Trinidad and Turkey. These projects are motivated not by storage of CO_2 for climate mitigation, but by the commercial magnet of producing an additional 5–20 per cent of the original oil in place from established fields.

Typically in the USA, a CO_2-EOR project will purchase CO_2 from a natural source, or increasingly a CCS-engineered project, transport the CO_2 by pipe, inject it into many tens of boreholes on an onshore field, produce additional oil, and separate and re-inject the CO_2 to produce yet more oil (to save costs of purchasing additional CO_2). The CO_2 used remains below ground and is not vented to air—although some of the CO_2 could be recovered and used for EOR in a different oilfield.

In the US, rules provide tax incentives to develop CO_2-EOR, from the perspective of enabling extra domestic oil production to aid national security of fuel supply. Thus CO_2-EOR is an excellent way of making CCS projects much more commercially profitable, typically reducing the wholesale price of electrical power from a CCS plant by \$20–40/MWhr, about 30 per cent. Thus CO_2-EOR can be seen as a proven method of commercialising CCS.

---

[17] *Oil and Gas Journal*, '2014 Worldwide EOR Survey', at www.ogj.com/articles/print/volume-112/issue-4/special-report-eor-heavy-oil-survey/2014-worldwide-eor-survey.html.

A weakness in that argument is the carbon accounting balance of CO_2 injected and stored, versus the extra carbon costs of engineering operations plus the extraction refining and combustion of additional produced oil. In the US, carbon from extra produced oil is often not considered as an emission, as equivalent amounts of oil would be conventionally produced, eventually, from some other State and used in combustion. However, in terms of carbon accounting for the environmental benefit, it is important to add the carbon emission from extra oil, as the CO_2 supplied for EOR has already been derived by capture from combusting hydrocarbon. There cannot be a double benefit from the same CO_2, but there can be a benefit if CO_2 is derived from CCS fitted onto a first combustion site, that CO_2 is stored for CO_2-EOR and remains stored within the reservoir, and the oil is combusted *and* CCS is fitted to that. That requires knowledge and regulation along the whole CCS chain. Alternatively, we suggest that a more portable accounting method can be hypothesised, which is locally based. First, CO_2 is injected and oil produced, but because stored CO_2 has a value for climate purposes, there is an incentive to store more, rather than economise on purchase of the amount stored. Thus the maximum tonnage of CO_2 is incentivised to be used in a project, not the minimum. Secondly, after the production of additional oil has ceased, the licence or permit stipulates that injection of CO_2 must continue for a specified tonnage, for example for another 10 or 20 years of operation. This stores CO_2 in an established site, with good monitoring, and cumulatively tips the carbon accounting balance to net negative.[18] The pipelines delivering CO_2 are paid for by oil profits and are built to last 60 years; the ancillary engineering equipment, boreholes and CO_2 capture technologies are all established more frequently than in a non-profit state-funded case of CCS development. So more CCS equipment is built, learnings and cost reduction are gained, and more CO_2 is stored sooner.[19]

In legal attribution, it may be necessary to determine how securely stored the CO_2 is. That can be monitored by measurement of the geochemistry of pore waters in the oilfield.[20] This shows that CO_2 in EOR dissolves rapidly with the pore water it is forced to contact, and so CO_2 is dissolved, or is in residual saturation, and is about 40 times more securely stored than in aquifer injection. And ownership of CO_2 can be fingerprinted by minute traces of noble gases that are intimately mixed in with CO_2 from different origins, but in different ratios which allow diagnostic fingerprinting. There could of course be problems of ownership, CO_2 attribution and liability during the lifetime of one asset. During the initial oil production, company A owns the oil but produces only part, and leaves residual saturation of unproduceable oil in much of the field pore space. The field is sold to company B, who injects

---

[18] J Stewart and RS Haszeldine, 'Can producing oil store more carbon?' (2015) 49(9) *Environmental Science and Technology* 5788.

[19] Scottish Carbon Capture and Storage (SCCS), *CO_2 storage and enhanced oil recovery in the North Sea* (SCCS, 2015), at www.sccs.org.uk/images/expertise/reports/co₂-eor-jip/SCCS-CO₂-EOR-JIP-Report-SUMMARY.pdf.

[20] S Serno et al, 'Oxygen isotopes as a tool to quantify reservoir-scale CO_2 pore-space saturation' (2017) 63 *International Journal of Greenhouse Gas Control* 370.

CO_2 and produces more oil: is tax payable differently on the continued production of oil contrasted with tax payable on additional oil produced? And who owns the residual oil abandoned by Company A? After oil production ceases, the field is sold to company C, who operates this as a storage site by injecting CO_2 through established infrastructure. Does Company C have liability for CO_2 injected by Company B? And if a borehole not used for CO_2 operations leaks CO_2, is company A liable for its incorrect sealing?

VIII. STORAGE LIABILITY

Who retains the future liability for stored CO_2, and especially for CO_2 that may migrate in directions originally unpredicted? This is a scary question for producers, project developers who may import CO_2, storage operators, regulators and governments. Different jurisdictions are assembling different approaches—from the very conservative actuarial approaches of the EU, to the pragmatic experience-based cooperative of Alberta, to the mutually negotiated licences of Western Australia and the not publicly stated experience of Norway. These all have very different impact on the valuation of risk and the financing of a project to cover the 'what if'.

A. Member State as Insurer for Validation Projects

A cautious regulatory and licensing approach can easily become too negative, and act as a blockage to projects being developed, by placing too high a liability burden on initial project proposers. Two approaches can help to mitigate this problem.

First the financial method, by which risk can be shared. This can be a method adapted from the 1957 Price-Anderson Act approach to US nuclear power, where the site operator is liable for the first parts of a problem, but ultimately a Member State government can also provide enabling support by becoming the formal underwriter of last resort, which is inevitably its position in any case. It should be possible to construct a 'staged liability' to cover CO_2 storage, by means of defined partnership between operators, insurance companies and governments. For example, an operator could hold the first £100 million of liability (which could remediate 50 boreholes onshore, or three remedial boreholes offshore), with an insurance company holding the next £500 million of liability (which would cover installation of a large new offshore platform or pipeline) and the Member State government holding liability beyond that; the exception being negligence or deliberate malpractice, in which case full liability would remain with the operating company.

Second is to improve scientific understanding of the potential problem. In effect to ask 'How much CO_2 could leak?' This requires a greater knowledge of the national sub-surface—an activity that may well be based on compilation of previously existing industry information, but which has to be led and funded by the state. This knowledge is important in the context of uncertainty concerning long duration slow leakage. Does indefinite liability remain held by the site developer—very difficult to hold in conventional year-end actuarial compilations—or does the state take over liability at some point after CO_2 injection has ceased and routine monitoring shows the CO_2 plume to be behaving within the range of predictions for adequate site performance? The state (and indeed the developer) can be greatly aided by some additional confidence in how much (or indeed how little) CO_2 could leak. As described in section V, the leakable amount is small, and is greatest at the point in time where injection ceases, but that is also the point in time when maximum resources are available to reduce or fix any problems.

B. Site Specific Monitoring is Required but Total Leakage is Small

The most extreme CO_2 example may be the Becej blowout in Serbia.[21] Here, a total loss of control of the well resulted in unrestricted flow to the surface from the highly overpressured CO_2 accumulation over 209 days, followed by slower seepage for a further 39 years until the leak was sealed.[22] Comparing this natural system at extreme overpressure, to intended excess injection pressure engineered during CO_2 storage of just 5–10 bars, shows that engineered storage has minimal risk of blowout or leakage—a risk of leakage of maybe 1 Mt CO_2/yr, about the same as the injection rate of CO_2 into one borehole.

Chronic, slow leakage or migration outside the licensed storage complex has also been discussed in the preceding sections. How important is this? As an analogy, consider oil trapping and migration in the North Sea hydrocarbon basins. In the North Sea there are about 300 commercial-sized oilfields, charged with oil and gas from about 90 million years ago. Mass balance calculations suggest that about 90 per cent of all the oil ever generated in the North Sea is unaccounted for. Even at the worst case, assuming that all this oil leaked from oilfields (rather than still being distributed today by residual trapping in sub-economic accumulations), it would still produce a maximum leakage of 1 per cent per million years from all oilfields. That is about one million times more optimistic than the leakage rates implied and expected to be insured for under the EU CCS Directive legislation.[23] Directly considering CO_2 in the deep subsurface, it is difficult to measure directly, but it is clearly possible to measure leakage incidents in the deep subsurface. As with the examples of Snøvhit or In Salah,[24] existing monitoring technology derived from hydrocarbon geoscience can be modified so that the incident can be adequately detected and remedial action taken, a long time before there is any material or climate impact. Some 20–60 per cent of injected CO_2 will be retained in the reservoir by residual saturation, at least a further 40 per cent will dissolve in groundwater contacted by

---

[21] Lakatos et al, n 16 above. See also section VI.H.
[22] A total loss of 17 billion M^3 is stated, and converting that at surface density equates to 33 M tonnes—around 1 Mt/yr. During the first months of unrestricted blowout, the loss of CO_2 is estimated to have been 0.5 billion M^3, ie just 0.9 Mt CO_2. This blowout and CO_2 loss was driven by the extreme natural overpressure of the CO_2 accumulation, stated to be an original 151 bar pressure at 900m depth, ie an excess pressure of 91 bars, during blowout over three years this lost 34 bars of pressure drive.
[23] See further on the CCS Directive ch 2 by Velkova in this volume.
[24] See sections VI.G.i and ii.

migrating CO_2—longer migration means more dissolution—and additional residual saturation (dynamic or migration-assisted trapping) will also occur along the migration path. And even if CO_2 reaches the soil horizons or seabed sediments, at least 60 per cent of that small amount can be trapped within tens of metres of the ground or seabed surface. Migration to the surface is only feasible at large scale along fault zones[25] or broken boreholes (see above), and is sealed where the overburden sediments are overpressured.

It seems very probable that, for legal or actuarial assessment of liability, even for storage sites of many tens or hundreds of million tonnes of CO_2, the total liability from catastrophic or chronic leakage is very low. Consequently it is immense over-regulation to require that the full financial value of all CO_2 injected has to be insured, or held as a bond, in case of leakage. Rigorous site choice and appropriate operations and monitoring should greatly reduce these risks.

C. How to Progress?

An industry, or state activity, to store CO_2 securely does not develop automatically. There are hurdles comprising geological knowledge, regulation, licensing and control institutions, and either state mandates and funding or creation of a viable business model. An individual capture to storage project could be proposed, agreed and built to operate within three to five years. But to establish a durable and formal framework is a lot more complex, and global experience shows that this process can easily take 10 years. The fundamental basis is geological knowledge, which is particular to the individual country. Unless that is compiled and convincingly demonstrated, there can be no serious political leadership or commercial interest. Evaluation of storage is the essential first step.

Although the engineering principles and processes of CO_2 storage are well understood globally, it is understandably the case that policy advisers in individual countries may prefer to start domestic CO_2 storage with a short-duration or smaller-size project to 'validate' the activity. The purpose of validation projects is to explore designs, concepts and operations that are well-enough studied to provide confidence in experts and informed decision makers. At this stage of a project, onerous or cooperative legality and regulation can help or hinder. Although applying the fullest secure legal fixtures onto CO_2 storage may appear administratively desirable, it is important to recognise that too much regulation at the start can discourage investors and developers. In the Norwegian example, existing hydrocarbon knowledge and legislation was adapted within two years of 1994 to enable the first CO_2 injection for storage and transfer decades of knowledge and experience from that sector. In the EU CCS Directive example, a legislative approach has been viewed as rigorous to harsh, and as remotely designed by adminstrators. No commercial CO_2 storage

---

[25] JJ Roberts et al, *Natural CO_2 sites in Italy show importance of overburden geopressure, fractures and faults for CO_2 storage performance and risk management* (London, Geological Society of London Special Publications, 2017) 458, at www.research.ed.ac.uk/portal/files/38216786/SP458.14.full.pdf.

projects have developed. In the Alberta example, hydrocarbon and acid gas disposal legislation has been adapted, together with risk mitigation by a pooling of long-timescale leakage risk (operated by the Government). Storage projects are now operating. In the Western Australia example, co-design between the developer and the provincial state has created mutually acceptable and operational solutions. Treating the first validation projects in a flexible way, with some method to share risk and act as guarantor, should allow the first projects to proceed. Results from first projects will rapidly improve certainty, and will enable price structures and risk allocation systems to evolve, which enables subsequent routine projects to become insurable and more appropriately legislated and controlled.

IX. PROGRESS AND OUTLOOK FOR CCS AND PARIS 2015

Has the theoretical concept and practical engineering of CO_2 storage proceeded rapidly? The concept of CCS on an industrial scale, as a way of reducing CO_2 emissions, can be traced to 1977 and Cesare Marchetti,[26] who suggested CO_2 storage in depleted gas- or oilfields, or deep ocean currents. The UK potential to store large tonnages of CO_2 in geological pore space was proposed in 1991 by BGS[27] followed by the first storage appraisal.[28] No commercial projects have resulted. By contrast in Norway, the 1994 Bruntland Report, *Limits to Growth*, had particular resonance, as Norway had become an affluent nation based on oil production, coupled with environmental concern. A concern to reduce emissions of CO_2 from offshore industrial hydrocarbon activities in 1994 resulted in the Norwegian Parliament placing a tax on offshore emissions at around \$50/tonne CO_2. That had an immediate effect, prompting Statoil to develop offshore of Norway the world's first application of CCS for climate protection. That has operated successfully from 1996. Carbon dioxide from produced hydrocarbons at the Sleipner field has to be separated for commercial sale purity. The extra tax incentivises CO_2 to be injected into the nearest available geological aquifer sandstone, 1 km beneath the seabed, and has continued without incident for 20 years. No environmental rules or regulations or permits specific for CO_2 were applied. Norway has the only two offshore CO_2 storage projects operating today (2017) in a commercial environment. A clear inference from these two histories, similar in geology on opposite sides of the North Sea, is that multi-decade government commitment with clear and closely focused taxation, linked to more substantial environmental regulation for carbon emissions reduction, results in much more effective policy instruments than expecting markets to innovate, or nudging with ephemeral individual politicians heading up environmental or climate departments of government.

---

[26] C Marchetti, 'On Geoengineering and the CO_2 Problem' (1977) 1 *Climatic Change* 59.
[27] D Holliday et al, 'A Preliminary Study of the Feasibility of Underground Storage of Carbon Dioxide', BGS Technical Report No WE/91/20 (1991) Nottingham, British Geological Survey.
[28] S Holloway and R van der Straaten, 'Joule II project' (1995) 36 *Energy Conversion and Management* 519.

During the years since Sleipner commenced operations in 1966, CCS projects have nudged into existence around the globe, and stored 22.1 Mt CO_2 in 2012, increasing to 40.3 Mt CO_2/yr in 2017—compared to 32.1 Gt CO_2 in global emissions registered in 2016. New CCS projects have added diversity, with increased capacity at the Decatur biofuel plant in Illinois, opening CCS retrofit on the Petra Nova coal power plant, and new-build new process iron and steel plant in Abu Dhabi. A further five projects are expected to open in the years to 2020, including the first in China at Yanchang coal-to-chemicals plants, with captured CO_2 to be used for EOR in the Xinjiang region, and the gas-sweetening project around Gorgon offshore NW Australia. But there are failures too—after 10 years of discussion the Netherlands ROAD project was cancelled in 2017 because of lack of political support for coal power. The Kemper County gasification coal project was also cancelled in 2017 after immense cost over-runs and failure to make the gasification operate commercially. After 2020, the future for CCS is very unclear. The reduction in political leadership by the US (2017) is likely to slow technology improvement, and CCS remains without a profitable business model—other than selling CO_2 to EOR, or environmentally-predicated price support. Due to this lack of momentum, the large-scale routine installation of CCS is impossible before 2025, and it seems increasingly inevitable that the rate of construction will be around 100 to 1,000 times too small to meet 2°C warming limits in 2050. A political step-change is needed, such as the introduction of targeted carbon taxes at $40-80/tonne CO_2, mandatory storage, or an unprecedented move to 'leave fossil fuels in the ground'.

The UN Paris Climate Agreement of December 2015, which came into effect in November 2016, committed nations to the limiting of global warming, two-thirds of which is caused by energy transport and feedstock combustion of fossil fuels, and the remedy for which requires unprecedented reduction of greenhouse gas emissions. Can this be achieved without CCS? The slow and dispersed installation of CCS in many different forms worldwide means that learning rates for cost-reduction are, and will be, slow. And it also means that a track record of success to reduce the perception of risk by investors or insurers will build experience only slowly. These factors have profoundly negative implications for the ability to use CCS as a practical means of mitigation in limiting climate warming to less than 1.5°C, or in keeping emissions below the cumulative tonnage required to stay 'well below 2°C' indefinitely into the future. Technologically, forms of CCS are operating and have been proven in many diverse settings worldwide. Carbon dioxide storage can be legislated, regulated and closely monitored to ensure high-quality performance. The shortfall is not in expertise but in political will to make CCS inevitable and routine, and in the consequent inability to innovate a financially profitable step-change in the way that business-as-usual fossil fuel combustion or conversion is tacitly permitted to release its emissions into the common global atmosphere and oceans.

A negative spiral could result from lack of established CCS. In simple terms, if CCS cannot become credible, lower-cost and de-risked, energy emissions will not be captured. If CCS does not exist then Bio-Energy CCS (BECCS), using biomass to re-capture and store already emitted CO_2, will not exist. If BECCS does not exist then it is harder to develop CCS for process industries. It is still harder to develop Carbon Dioxide Reduction (CDR) to engineer the removal of emitted CO_2

from atmosphere. In the International Energy Agency/International Renewable Energy Agency scenario (2017), for a 66 per cent chance of keeping below 2°C, the use of CCS increases to 3Gt/yr CO_2 by 2050. In the most recent IPCC Report on climate and impacts, 2014,[29] in Figure SPM7, from the 147 scenarios examined, only three to six scenarios without CCS have a probability greater than 66 per cent of maintaining CO_2e at or below the 450 ppm required for 2°C or less warming by 2100. Keeping below 2°C implies reducing emissions by 40–70 per cent from 2010 values by mid-century. Put simply: No CCS = No 2°C.

To achieve 2°C without the use of CCS requires about 2.5 times greater global expenditure[30] than if CCS is widely used throughout the economy. Avoiding CCS requires: (i) that land use becomes profoundly carbon negative; and/or (ii) that enhanced weathering chemical sequestration is massively deployed; and/or (iii) that the oceans become used as chemical storage facility for dissolved carbonate.[31] Or, at a lesser cost but as a much more interventionist action of questionable legality, deliberate planetary engineering might be commenced to manipulate the thermal reflectivity of the atmosphere.[32] Logic, financial and economic modelling all point to CCS as the best and least expensive solution economy-wide. In 2017, it seems that logic is not enough.

X. SUMMARY

It is suggested that carbon capture and storage should become a significant part of global efforts to reduce emissions of fossil CO_2, which will remove the drivers for climate change and ocean acidification. It stretches existing expertise of the subsurface, but does not require entirely new innovation. The fundamental end-point of CCS is to place CO_2 underground, where storage will be secure for thousands of years into the future. Experience in industrial capture, transport and injection of CO_2 may be gained from decades of commercial activity in established industries, such as hydrocarbons, geothermal heat, shale gas and methane storage. A legal framework for CO_2 storage is needed for any state undertaking CO_2 storage activity. It is easy for this newly-drafted regulatory and licensing system to become too onerous and risk-averse. A typical legal approach recognises different sizes of subsurface containment, in the 'primary reservoir' and in the 'storage complex', to which different definitions of leakage and different penalties apply. Injection of CO_2 into deep subsurface reservoirs will produce several effects, both in the near-field and in the far-field. That includes increased pressure in connected subsurface fluids, which may extend for tens of kilometres away from an injection site. And it also includes the potential to displace existing deep saline fluids into shallower depths and the potential for CO_2

---

[29] IPCC 2014 AR5 Report WG3 Summary for policymakers, at www.ipcc.ch/report/ar5/wg3/.
[30] ibid Figure 6.24.
[31] ibid Figure TS 17.
[32] JA Dykema et al, 'Stratospheric controlled perturbation experiment: a small-scale experiment to improve understanding of the risks of solar geoengineering', *Philosophical Transactions of the Royal Society A* **372**: 20140059, at dx.doi.org/10.1098/rsta.2014.0059.

migration out of a storage site to follow a narrow path, along which rapid migration occurs. All of these effects are more extensive than direct contact with physical CO_2. However, all of them are known, understood and can be adequately monitored from the surface using existing technology. Storage sites are individual, and injection of CO_2 into subsurface trapping structures will be easier to license, monitor and regulate than injection of CO_2 into very large regionally extensive saline formations. The problems of insurance and of long-term liability for stored CO_2 are important for many legislators. Well understood scientific knowledge about how CO_2 dissolves in deep pore fluids, how CO_2 leaves small droplets of isolated residual saturation and the small excess pressures needed to inject CO_2—all show that storage will be secure for many tens of thousands of years. Leakage points of highest risk are if CO_2 intersects natural geological fault zones of fractures along which CO_2 can flow; or if CO_2 encounters poorly sealed legacy boreholes. Study of accidents and blowouts at CO_2 boreholes, or practical operations of fully commercial engineered storage sites, shows that there is no reason to predict that a storage site will leak all its CO_2. Experience shows that a storage site will leak less than 1 million tonnes of CO_2 per year from a catastrophic accident. There is no evidence to show inevitable chronic low-rate leakage from all storage sites. Consequently, the financial insurance needed against leakage need be only tiny in comparison to the amount of CO_2 stored. Insurance for repair and remediation of a detected poor performance or leak is more useful and quantifiable. It is credible for a developer to guarantee more than 90 per cent, and likely up to 99 per cent, retention of CO_2 during the next 1,000 years. Consequently, requiring 100 per cent security of storage rather than 99 per cent is unreasonable, and at present is technically undetectable. A realistic approach may be to legislate to accommodate the possibility of small-scale intended leakage. This may result in the operator paying a fine to repair future leakage outside the primary reservoir. Ultimately, it is the Member State government that is the insurer of last resort, and which will bear ultimate liability. Making this explicit for early validation projects is a helpful change, which removes a major commercial barrier to commercial CCS operations. The discussion should really be around how rapid is the timescale for liability transfer from developer to state, rather than whether liability should be transferred.

Remember: No CCS = No 2°C.

2

Implementation of the Directive on the Geological Storage of Carbon Dioxide

MARIA VELKOVA

I. INTRODUCTION

COUNCIL DIRECTIVE 2009/31/EC of the European Parliament and of the Council on the geological storage of carbon dioxide (the CCS Directive) was adopted as part of the 2009 climate and energy package. It provides a legal framework for the environmentally safe geological storage of carbon dioxide (CO_2). It aims to ensure that there is no significant risk of leakage of CO_2 or damage to public health or the environment, and to prevent any adverse effects on the security of the transport network or storage sites, thereby addressing public concerns. The Directive also contains provisions on the capture and transport components of CCS, though these activities are covered mainly by existing European Union (EU) environmental legislation, such as the Environmental Impact Assessment Directive[1] and the Industrial Emissions Directive.[2]

The European Commission has published two reports on implementation of the CCS Directive. The first implementation report covered the period until April 2013 and presented an overview of how different Member States transposed the Directive.[3] The second implementation report covered the period May 2013–April 2016 and focused only on the articles, which have had practical application in Member States of the EU.[4] The European Commission also carried out a thorough

---

[1] Council Directive 2011/92/EU of 13 December 2011 on the assessment of the effects of certain public and private projects on the environment [2011] OJ L26/1.
[2] Council Directive 2010/75/EU of 24 November 2010 on industrial emissions (integrated pollution prevention and control) [2010] OJ L 334/17.
[3] European Commission, 'Report from the Commission to the European Parliament and the Council on the Implementation of Directive 2009/31/EC on the geological storage of carbon dioxide' COM (2014) 99.
[4] European Commission, 'Report from the Commission to the European Parliament and the Council on the Implementation of Directive 2009/31/EC on the geological storage of carbon dioxide' COM (2017) 37.

review of the CCS Directive, as required by Article 38, and evaluated the Directive for its effectiveness, efficiency, coherence, relevance and EU added value in 2015.[5] The Commission's review report was based on an extensive evaluation study.[6] The Commission concluded that the Directive is fit for purpose: it provides the regulatory framework needed to ensure safe CO_2 capture, transport and storage, while allowing the Member States sufficient flexibility to adjust regulation to their national or project-specific circumstances.

This chapter draws on the above reports in order to derive conclusions, which may be of use to jurisdictions, which have not yet developed thorough legislation to regulate the capture, transport and storage of CO_2.

II. DETAILS OF THE EU LEGISLATION

Unlike EU Regulations, which have immediate effect within Member States, EU directives require Member States to bring into force laws, regulations and administrative provisions necessary to comply with their provisions. This had to be done for the CCS Directive by 25 June 2011.

A. Allowing Storage or Not

The CCS Directive has the particularity that Member States can choose whether and where they allow storage of CO_2 on their territory: in Article 4(1), the CCS Directive confers the right to Member States to determine the areas from which storage sites may be selected. This also includes the right not to allow storage in any part of a Member State's territory. In principle, all provisions of a Directive must be transposed into the national legal systems, even if national policy means they are unlikely to be invoked (for example, environmental impact assessment requirements for proposed nuclear power stations). The CCS Directive, however, gives very explicit discretionary powers to Member States in respect of storage, which has allowed a more flexible approach to be adopted in respect of transposition.

This flexibility was used by the Member States to adjust to their national circumstances. Whereas most Member States allow geological storage of CO_2, some have chosen to restrict partially or entirely storage on their territory. For example, The Netherlands, the UK and Sweden are allowing storage only offshore. Even if storage offshore is more expensive, it generally avoids public concerns. The Netherlands and the UK can also use their depleted hydrocarbon reservoirs, and profit from their knowledge of the geology and managing of offshore operations.

---

[5] European Commission, 'Report on review of Directive 2009/31/EC on the geological storage of carbon dioxide', COM (2015) 576, Annex accompanying the document Report from the Commission to the European Parliament and the Council Climate action progress report.

[6] 'Study to support the review of Directive 2009/31/EC on the geological storage of carbon dioxide (CCS Directive)' (Luxembourg, Publications Office of the European Union, 2015).

The Czech Republic, Germany and Poland have decided to take a more cautious approach and have imposed various temporal and quantitative limits. Storage of CO_2 in natural rock formations will not be authorised in the Czech Republic before 1 January 2020. Germany has imposed restrictions on the annual quantity of CO_2 that can be stored: 4 Mt CO_2 is the national total, and 1.3 Mt of CO_2 is permitted per storage site. In addition, five German federal states[7] are preparing decisions or have passed laws limiting or banning underground storage of CO_2, including for research purposes. The underpinning reasons for the bans in Germany are prioritising uses of the underground, such as for geothermal energy, energy storage or mining, or safeguarding against environmental and tourism concerns. Lastly, storage is allowed in Poland only for demonstration purposes.

A few Member States do not allow geological storage of CO_2, such as Austria, Croatia, Estonia, Ireland, Latvia and Slovenia. Member States are not required to justify the decision to ban storage. Other Member States do not allow CO_2 storage on part of or the whole territory due to the unsuitability of their geology for such storage: Finland, Luxembourg and the Brussels Capital Region of Belgium.

It is important to note that even when banning geological storage, Member States are required to transpose all provisions of the Directive that govern the capture and transport of carbon dioxide. In this way, the CCS Directive allows every Member State to adapt the provisions to its national circumstances with regard to geology, national energy policy and public perception. At the same time, it creates the necessary legal certainty for investors to construct large-scale installations for CO_2 capture and pipelines for transport, even in countries that have banned storage.

B. Assessing Storage Capacity

The CCS Directive requires those Member States that intend to allow geological storage of CO_2 on their territory to undertake an assessment of the available storage capacity (Article 4(2)). The Directive does not prescribe the methodology or detail of these assessments. Most Member States have carried out at least some assessment of their storage capacity. For example, an overview of CO_2 storage capacity across the EU was provided by the EU GeoCapacity project,[8] which estimated for the 21 participating Member States theoretical storage potential of 87 Gt CO_2 (69 Gt in deep saline aquifers, 17 Gt in depleted hydrocarbon fields and 1 Gt in unmineable coal beds). The level of detail, extent and accuracy of the assessments varies, and it is related in most cases to the interest of Member States to develop favourable conditions for development of the technology and/or to knowledge of the underground linked to oil and gas exploration. The Joint Resources Council (JRC) is currently developing the first European CO_2 atlas in close cooperation with the European Geological Surveys, based on a harmonised CO_2 storage assessment methodology.

---

[7] Lower Saxony, Schleswig-Holstein, Mecklenburg-Western Pomerania, Saxony-Anhalt and Bremen.
[8] T Vangkilde-Pedersen et al, 'EU Geocapacity: Assessing European Capacity for Geological Storage of Carbon Dioxide' (D16 WP2 Report, 2009), at www.geology.cz/geocapacity/publications, 166.

The Directive gives the criteria for characterisation and assessment of geological formations, and thus their suitability to serve as storage sites. This is done in three steps: data collection, building 3-D static geological earth models and characterisation of storage dynamic behaviour. Such detailed characterisations and assessments have been done only in a few Member States in preparation for pilot and demonstration projects. Most of this work has been supported through research or demonstration programmes at national and/or EU level.

For example, in the UK, as part of the Front End Engineering and Design study work under the UK CCS Commercialisation Competition, appraisal work was carried out on the Goldeneye and Endurance stores.[9] The UK also undertook a CO_2 Storage Appraisal Project on five further stores.[10] The project confirms that there are no major technical hurdles to storing industrial-scale CO_2 offshore in the UK, with sites able to service mainland Europe as well as the UK. This project identified 20 specific CO_2 storage sites (from 579 potential sites), which together represent the tip of a very large national CO_2 storage resource potential, estimated to be around 78 $GtCO_2$. The top 15 per cent of this potential storage capacity would last the UK around 100 years.

The Netherlands is planning to update its national CO_2 transport and storage plan in 2017. The update will examine which storage sites will become available in the future, whether those sites might be technically and geologically suitable, when they will become available and what their storage capacity is.

Some regions have started working together to develop common, transboundary solutions for the transport and geological storage of CO_2 where there is a shared resource like the North Sea or the Baltic Sea. The CCS network under the Baltic Sea Region Energy Cooperation with Estonia, Germany, Finland, Norway and Sweden aims to move from theoretical assessment of the potential though better characterisation and modelling of reservoirs, cap rock and fault zones to pilot studies, and tests characterisation of commercial storage sites. In the most optimistic scenario, this will take around 15 years.[11] The Nordic CO_2 storage atlas was produced by the Nordic CCS Competence Centre. It provides a comprehensive overview of storage sites in the Nordic countries—Denmark, Norway, Sweden and Iceland. These networks may facilitate the transparent and non-discriminatory access to CO_2 transport networks and CO_2 storage sites for operators in Member States where there is no possibility of underground storage. Belgium, The Netherlands, the UK and France are also exploring possibilities of developing hubs for industrial and power CO_2 emissions in the areas of the ports of Amsterdam and Rotterdam, Grangemouth, Tees Valley and Fos-sur-Mer.

The majority of current storage assessments made in the Member States are static and do not include aspects such as flow calculations, migration pathways and

---

[9] Department of Energy and Climate Change, 'Peterhead and White Rose Key Knowledge Deliverables' (June 2015), at www.gov.uk/government/publications/peterhead-and-white-rose-key-knowledge-deliverables.

[10] Energy and Technologies Institute, 'Strategic UK CCS Storage Appraisal' (2017) www.eti.co.uk/project/strategic-uk-ccs-storage-appraisal/.

[11] N Nordbäck, 'CCS Network Task Force—Geological CO_2 Storage' (April 2015), at basrec.net/wp-content/uploads/2015/04/D1-Nicklas-Lindbäck.pdf.

dissolution effects. Studying these parameters would be necessary for choosing the most appropriate monitoring techniques and for the optimisation of potential CO_2 storage projects. These detailed and reliable assessments, along with planning of transport networks through their realisation, have very long lead times. Given the state of these preparations, only very few projects can be expected to see ground up to 2030. While the EU can reach its climate goals in 2030 without CCS, deep decarbonisation for some industrial processes becomes more difficult without CCS. Therefore, it is in the interests of Member States with carbon-intensive industries and power generation and/or appropriate geology to facilitate the planning of transport and storage networks and the detailed assessment of storage sites.

C. Permitting of CO_2 Storage Sites

The core of the EU CCS Directive is introducing common rules for managing geological storage sites, including permitting, monitoring, measures to prevent significant irregularities, corrective measures, managing liability, closure, post-closure and transfer of responsibility.

No storage sites in the EU have started operating yet. There have already been two draft permits, however, on which the European Commission has given an overall positive Opinion as required by Article 10: for the P18-4 reservoir of the ROAD project in The Netherlands in 2012,[12] and for the Goldeneye reservoir of the Peterhead project in the UK in 2016.[13] The Dutch Competent Authority issued the permit for the P18-4 reservoir in 2013.[14] Due to delays and changes in the ROAD project, a new storage site, the Q16 Maas, is being explored for which an application for a permit is planned to be submitted in 2017. Even if no injection of CO_2 has been carried out in these sites yet, the extensive requirements for permitting, including detailed site characterisation and assessment and financial security, have been satisfied. This shows that the Directive gives ample flexibility to account for the particularities of the projects. Solutions have been found even for liabilities, which can be potentially difficult to estimate. For example, one uncertainty, raised by stakeholders during the review of the Directive, is linked to the price of CO_2 and the potential need to surrender allowances at an unknown date in the future. The ROAD project had reached an agreement with the Competent Authority to cap this liability for the P18-4 reservoir to the worst case blow-out in a well, which can be repaired in three months according to the corrective measures plan.

---

[12] European Commission, 'Commission Opinion relating to the draft permit for the permanent storage of carbon dioxide in block section P18-4 of block section P18a of the Dutch continental shelf, in accordance with Article 10(1) of Directive 2009/31/EC of 23 April 2009 on the geological storage of carbon dioxide' COM (2012) 1236.

[13] European Commission, 'Commission Opinion on a draft permit for the permanent storage of carbon dioxide in the depleted Goldeneye gas condensate field located in blocks 14/28b, 14/29a, 14/29e, 20/3b, 20/4b and 20/4c on the United Kingdom Continental Shelf' COM (2016) 152.

[14] 'Permit for the storage of carbon dioxide in the P18-4 reservoir' (Dutch Ministry of Economic Affairs, 2013).

Another concern raised by stakeholders is the long period before transfer of responsibility, which, according to the Directive, is a minimum of 20 years, unless the competent authority is convinced that all available evidence indicates that the stored CO_2 will be completely and permanently contained. Due to the novel nature of geological storage of CO_2, the Dutch authority requires a 20-year period before transfer of responsibility in the permit for the P18-4 reservoir. The UK authority, however, was planning to agree provisionally to a shorter period. The prospective operator of the Peterhead project was planning to request transfer of responsibility six years after closure: five years monitoring and one year for processing of data. Then the UK competent authority would have had to consider the request to transfer the responsibility if the surveys previewed in the plan demonstrated containment of the stored CO_2 and no irregularities were detected, which could have been as early as six years.[15]

D. Preparing for CCS Retrofitting for New Large-scale Combustions Plants

The CCS Directive requires in Article 33 that when applying for operating licence, operators have to assess the technical and economic feasibility of carbon capture, transport and storage. If the assessment is positive, space on the installation site must be set aside for the equipment necessary to capture and compress CO_2.

Assessments were carried out in Belgium (1), the Czech Republic (1), Germany (5), Romania (6), Poland (10), Slovenia (1) and Spain (5). All assessments found that CCS is not economically feasible. Some further difficulties were found for some of the plants—no suitable storage sites in Belgium and Estonia, or technical incompatibility with the flexible operation of a plant.

Despite the lack of positive assessment for the economic feasibility for CCS retrofitting, many of the permitted power plants are setting aside land for the equipment to remove and compress CO_2, and are designed in such a way that CCS can be connected later on without major layout modifications, eg in the Czech Republic, Estonia, Germany and Poland. It can be concluded that even if the conditions for triggering obligations under this article have not been met, the obligation to carry out assessment for CCS readiness may have had the effect of prompting operators to take precautionary measures and prepare for a future CCS retrofit.

The legislation in the UK goes beyond the requirements of the CCS Directive and grants permissions to power plants only if they can prove that they will meet the technical and economic feasibility conditions during the life-time of the power station. Permits for 14 power plants have been approved based on guidance provided by the authorities.[16] The economic assessments show that it is economically

---

[15] The Peterhead project is currently suspended after the UK discontinued its CCS commercialisation competition at the end of 2015.

[16] See Department of Energy and Climate Change, 'Carbon Capture Readiness (CCR)' (November 2009), at www.gov.uk/government/uploads/system/uploads/attachment_data/file/43609/Carbon_capture_readiness_-_guidance.pdf. See also the Scottish Government, 'Thermal Power Stations in Scotland: Guidance and Information on Section 36 of the Electricity Act 1989 under Which Scottish Ministers Determine Consents Relating to Thermal Power Stations', at www.gov.scot/resource/doc/917/0095764.doc.

feasible that CCS could be retrofitted to the proposed power plants given an appropriate carbon price.

III. BEYOND THE LEGISLATION

The CCS Directive was adopted in expectation of a number of projects going online before 2015.[17] The Directive aims at ensuring environmentally safe capture, transport and geological storage of CO_2, to set a level playing field for all operators and to reduce administrative burden through streamlining regulation. Carbon capture and strorage itself is incentivised through the EU Emissions Trading Scheme (ETS) Directive.[18] The Commission's position on CCS has been confirmed in a number of policy communications.[19] To reach the decarbonisation targets, CCS will need to be deployed from around 2030 onwards in the fossil fuel power sector.[20] In the longer term, CCS may be the only option available to reduce direct emissions from large-scale industrial processes.[21]

In addition to the common legal framework and the incentive through the EU ETS, the EU is providing financial support through the European Energy Programme for Recovery (EEPR),[22] the NER300 programme,[23] and the EU Research and Innovation programme Horizon 2020,[24] and in the future will be doing so through the Connecting Europe Facility[25] and the Innovation Fund.[26]

---

[17] In June 2008, the European Council asked the Commission to propose as soon as possible an incentive mechanism for Member States and the private sector to ensure the construction and operation of up to 12 CCS demonstration plants by 2015 to contribute to mitigation of climate change.

[18] Directive 2003/87/EC of the European Parliament and of the Council of 13 October 2003 establishing a scheme for greenhouse gas emission allowance trading within the Community [2003] OJ L275/32.

[19] Eg, in the Commission's Communications, 'The Future of Carbon Capture and Storage in Europe' COM (2013) 180 and 'A Roadmap for moving to a competitive low carbon economy in 2050' COM (2011) 112.

[20] European Commission, 'Energy Roadmap 2050' COM (2011) 885.

[21] European Commission, 'A policy framework for climate and energy in the period from 2020 to 2030' COM (2014) 15.

[22] Regulation (EU) No 1233/2010 of 15 December 2010 establishing a programme to aid economic recovery by granting Community financial assistance to projects in the field of energy [2010] OJ L 346/5.

[23] The NER300 programme is one of the world's largest funding programmes for innovative low-carbon demonstration projects and has awarded a total of €2.1 billion to 38 renewable energy projects and one CCS project. See European Commission, 'NER 300 Programme' (January 2017), at ec.europa.eu/clima/policies/lowcarbon/ner300/.

[24] Regulation (EU) No 1291/2013 of 11 December establishing Horizon 2020—the Framework Programme for Research and Innovation (2014–2020) and repealing Decision 1982/2006/EC [2013] OJ L347/104.

[25] Innovation and Networks Agency, 'Connecting Europe Facility' (January 2017), at ec.europa.eu/inea/en/connecting-europe-facility.

[26] In its proposal for amending the EU ETS Directive 2003/87/EC establishing a scheme for greenhouse gas emission allowance trading within the Community (COM (2015) 337), the European Commission proposes to set up an Innovation Fund to be endowed with €450 million allowances under the EU ETS to support CCS as well as innovative renewable energy and energy-intensive industry, in order to enhance cost-effective emission reductions and low-carbon investments.

These actions at EU level are not enough, though, as CCS is still at demonstration stage and projects cost much more as they are first-of-a-kind. In addition, the current carbon price cannot ensure a business case without further public support. Sufficient national support is still lacking. Even the UK, which had set aside £1 billion to support two large-scale demonstration projects, cancelled the funding at the end of 2015.[27] As a result, as of January 2017, there is only one ongoing project in the EU, the ROAD project in The Netherlands, which may start injecting CO_2 before 2020. This rate of progress with large-scale CCS in Europe is much slower than expected.[28]

It is important to maintain support for commercial-scale demonstration projects in both the power and the industry sectors, as this is essential to gain experience, public confidence and to bring costs down. With a view to future CCS deployment, it is essential to advance knowledge on potential CO_2 storage sites and to plan shared CO_2 transport and storage infrastructure around key industrial hubs. Power-generation and other industrial projects, as well as the transport infrastructure and storage sites, have long lead times, so it is important that Member States consider CCS as part of their long-term energy and climate planning, ideally up to 2050. Energy policy is a national prerogative, however the EU has agreed a number of energy and climate targets and objectives for 2030 and 2050.[29] This is why the EU Member States have agreed to exchange information and monitor their progress towards achieving these targets through the Governance of the Energy Union. According to the proposal for the Governance, the European Commission will facilitate this process, can issue recommendations and may propose EU measures if there is a risk that targets will not be reached.[30] This process is very important as it will encourage the Member States to plan long term. Carbon capture and storage may not be needed in 2030, but for reaching the greenhouse gas emission targets in a cost-efficient way, CCS may be required in the power and industry sectors of some Member States. However, due to the high current cost and complexity of the technology, investments are delayed, which may mean higher costs in the long run. Through the Governance of the Energy Union, Member States will be able to plan cost-effective national policies for reducing the greenhouse gas emissions and to identify when and what low-carbon investments are best to be made, including investments in CO_2 transport and storage infrastructure.

---

[27] For more on the UK CCS commercialisation competition, see Department for Business, Energy and Industrial Strategy, 'UK carbon capture and storage: government funding and support' (November 2015), at www.gov.uk/uk-carbon-capture-and-storage-government-funding-and-support.

[28] Preliminary estimates, carried out with a view to assessing the impact of the Directive and referred to in the impact assessment of the Commission, indicated that 7 million tonnes of CO_2 could be stored by 2020, and up to 160 million tonnes by 2030; and that the CO_2 emissions avoided in 2030 could account for some 15% of the reductions required in the Union.

[29] EU renewable energy target, energy efficiency target, electricity interconnection target and greenhouse gas reduction targets for 2030; overall objective to reduce greenhouse gas emissions for 2050.

[30] European Commission, 'Proposal for a Regulation of the European Parliament and of the Council on the Governance of the Energy Union' COM (2016) 759.

IV. CONCLUSIONS

The EU CCS Directive so far has had limited application due to the lack of business case for developing large-scale CCS projects. The available evidence and the consultation of stakeholders during the review of the Directive suggest, however, that the Directive strikes the right balance between introducing common rules for managing CCS projects across the EU and allowing Member States to account for national particularities. The Directive streamlines and creates certainty for the process and requirements of permitting and management of geological storage sites for CO_2 in the EU. It is likely that it will ensure high levels of protection of the environment and human health by minimising the risk of leakage of CO_2 from geological storage sites.

Due to the long lead times for preparing, permitting and the building of transport and storage infrastructure, Member States that plan to use CCS for reducing emissions need to identify their needs for storing CO_2 underground. The proposed Governance of the Energy Union foresees that Member States will plan forward, to exchange information and comment on one anothers' energy and climate policies with a view to reaching the common EU targets. The Governance will be a useful tool for the Member States to plan the necessary low-carbon investments. This could be especially beneficial for infrastructure projects, including CO_2 transport and storage infrastructure, because of the long preparation times needed.

3

The CCS Directive: Did it Stifle the Technology in Europe?*

LEONIE REINS

I. INTRODUCTION

THE CARBON CAPTURE and Storage (CCS) Directive, a legal regime on the geological storage of carbon dioxide (CO_2),[1] establishes a legal framework for the environmentally safe geological storage of CO_2 to contribute to the battle against climate change.[2] The purpose of environmentally safe geological storage is the permanent containment of CO_2 to prevent and eliminate negative effects, as well as any risks to the environment and human health.[3] The CCS Directive amends the Water Framework Directive,[4] the Waste Directive[5] and several other Directives.[6] Due to its technological and financial challenges, the technology involves high risks, including regulatory ones.[7] The European Commission states that 'although the components of CCS are all known and deployed at commercial scale, integrated

---

* This contribution is based on Leonie Reins, *Regulating Shale Gas: The Challenge of Coherent Environmental and Energy Regulation* (Cheltenham, Edward Elgar, 2017).
[1] Council Directive 2009/31/EC of 23 April 2009 on the geological storage of carbon dioxide and amending Council Directive 85/337/EEC, European Parliament and Council Directives 2000/60/EC, 2001/80/EC, 2004/35/EC, 2006/12/EC, 2008/1/EC and Regulation (EC) No 1013/2006 [2009] OJ L140/114 (CCS Directive).
[2] For an analysis of the structure and content of the Directive and the individual provisions, refer to M Doppelhammer, 'The CCS Directive, its Implementation and the Co-financing of CCS and RES Demonstration Projects under the Emissions Trading System (NER 300 Process)' in I Havercroft, R Macrory and RB Stewart (eds), *Carbon Capture and Storage: Emerging Legal and Regulatory Issues* (London, Hart Publishing, 2011), 94–100.
[3] CCS Directive, Art 1.
[4] Council Directive 2000/60/EC of 23 October 2000 establishing a framework for Community action in the field of water policy [2000] OJ L327/1.
[5] Council Directive 2006/12/EC of 5 April 2006 on waste [2006] OJ L 114/9.
[6] See also KJ De Graaf and JH Jans, 'Environmental Law and CCS in the EU and the Impact on the Netherlands' in MM Roggenkamp and E Woerdman (eds), *Legal design of carbon capture and storage: developments in the Netherlands from an international and EU perspective* (Antwerp, Intersentia, 2009) 158f.
[7] A McHarg and M Poustie, 'Risk, Regulation, and Carbon Capture and Storage: The United Kingdom Experience' in DN Zillman et al (eds), *The Law of Energy Underground: Understanding New Developments in Subsurface Production, Transmission, and Storage* (Oxford, Oxford University Press, 2014) 249.

systems are new. A clear regulatory framework is thus required, and the EU's CCS Directive provides this.'[8]

In the EU it was estimated that by 2030 the CCS technology could foster 15 per cent of the carbon emission reductions required.[9] However, in practice, the technology has not taken off yet within the EU. Consequently the aim of this chapter is not to review and assess the regulatory framework applicable to CCS in an exhaustive manner,[10] but to ask whether this framework has actually stifled the development of the technology.

The chapter argues that the CCS Directive was adopted too early in the developmental stage of the technology. Even though it has been promoted as an instrument to foster its development, it has in fact had the opposite result—namely the restriction of its development by being too burdensome and by fuelling public concerns.

The reasoning underlying this argument is twofold. First, it is based on the Collingridge dilemma relating to the control of new technologies, which will be explained in more detail in section II and will subsequently be applied to CCS, more precisely on the legal history and reasoning behind the Directive, as well as the underlying public debate. Secondly, it will be argued the risk management approach taken by the Commission in developing the legislation diverted from the typical approach of precaution and prevention, which is normally used when dealing with new or emerging technologies.

II. THE LEGISLATIVE HISTORY, THE PUBLIC DEBATE AND COLLINGRIDGE—WHAT A DILEMMA

In terms of the regulation of new or emerging technologies, the variable of 'time' is decisive in determining the point for regulatory intervention.[11] In social science theory this is referred to as the Collingridge dilemma relating to the control of new technologies. Accordingly,

> [a]ttempting to control a technology is difficult, and not rarely impossible, because during its early stages, when it can be controlled, not enough can be known about its harmful social consequences to warrant controlling its development. By the time these consequences are apparent, control has become costly and slow.[12]

The Collingridge dilemma originated in social science, but in applying it to a legal context, the question posed to lawyers is essentially about the right point of

---

[8] See European Commission, *Carbon Capture and Geological Storage* (January 2017), at ec.europa.eu/clima/policies/lowcarbon/ccs/index_en.htm, 'Ensuring safe and environmentally sound CCS'.
[9] See CCS Directive, n 1 above, Recital 5.
[10] This is done, eg, in the contributions in Roggenkamp and Woerdman (eds), n 6 above.
[11] See also LB Moses, 'Why have a theory of law and technological change?' (2007) 8 *Minnesota Journal of Law, Science & Technology* 589, 597; and LB Moses, 'Agents of change: how the law "copes" with technological change' (2011) 20 *Griffith Law Review* 763. As well as G Majone, 'Political Institutions and the Principle of Precaution' in JB Wiener et al (eds), *The Reality of Precaution: Comparing Approaches to Risk Regulation in the United States and Europe* (Washington, DC, RFF Press, 2010) 420.
[12] D Collingridge, *The Social Control of Technology* (New York, St Martin's Press, 1980) 19.

regulatory intervention in any technological development. Regulatory intervention at a premature stage is difficult because of possibly 'insufficient, conflicting or confusing data about the nature and impact of the new technology'.[13] The adverse impact on a society or the environment is not clear, or rather is subject to uncertainty. An efficient regulatory regime thus may not be possible to establish at this point. If, however, the regulatory intervention comes too late in the technology development chain, the technology will have become entrenched in society and 'influence and change become correspondingly more difficult [slow and expensive[14]] to effect'.[15] From a legal perspective, the precautionary principle may be raised where intervention takes place at an early stage. It provides a general framework for law and policymakers to intervene, even if there are still uncertainties associated with a technology, but without implying 'when in doubt opt out'.[16] In applying this framework of analysis to CCS, and in illustrating its relevance regarding the CCS technology, the legal history of the CCS Directive and the public debate surrounding the technology first needs to be analysed.

A. The Legislative History of the CCS Directive

The legislative history and context of the CCS technology evolved against the backdrop of CCS being perceived as an option to mitigate the impacts of climate change and to meet the 2°C global warming target.[17] Competitiveness of the EU economy and industry, especially vis-à-vis the United States[18] and Australia, is recognised as a key reason for the development of CCS. The CCS Directive stipulates that '[i]t would allow European industries to become leading players in a potentially burgeoning global market for CCS technology'.[19] Despite the potential impact of the technology, the legislative history and context did not generate much public reaction. Several working groups were set up by the second and third European Climate

---

[13] G Laurie, SH Harmon and F Arzuaga, 'Foresighting Futures: Law, New Technologies, and the Challenges of Regulating for Uncertainty' (2012) 4 *Law, Innovation and Technology* 1, 5f.
[14] LB Moses, 'How to Think about Law, Regulation and Technology: Problems with "Technology" as a Regulatory Target' (2013) 5 *Law, Innovation and Technology* 1, 8.
[15] Laurie et al, n 13 above.
[16] G Van Calster, D Bowman and J D'Silva, '"Trust me, I'm a Regulator": the (In)adequacy of EU Legislative Instruments for Three Nanotechnologies Categories' in M Goodwin, BJ Koops and R Leenes (eds), *Dimensions of Technology Regulation* (AH Oisterwijk, Wolf Legal Publishers, 2010) 230. Sunstein, however, is of another opinion. He argues that the precautionary principle paralyses, because risks are everywhere and the principle in itself forbids action. The application of the principle hence results only in prioritising and shifting risks. See also CR Sunstein, *Laws of Fear: Beyond the precautionary principle* (Cambridge, Cambridge University Press, 2005) 26f.
[17] European Commission, 'Staff Working Document, Accompanying document to the Proposal for a Directive on the geological storage of carbon dioxide: Impact Assessment' COM (2008) 2 (CCS Impact Assessment).
[18] See, for a comparison of law and policy approach to CCS in the US and Europe, EJ Wilson and AJ Gibbons, 'Deploying Carbon Capture and Storage in Europe and the United States: A Comparative Analysis' (2007) 4 *Journal for European Environmental & Planning Law* 343.
[19] CCS Impact Assessment, n 17 above, 15.

Change Programmes (ECCP II and III), which stressed the need for a European CCS policy and legislative framework.

Separate legislation for CCS was considered necessary as the applicability of existing Directives, such as the Waste Framework Directive,[20] the Landfill Directive[21] and the Water Framework Directive,[22] created some regulatory problems.[23]

As with many EU policy proposals, the process was accompanied by various stakeholder meetings and a public consultation.[24] The consultation generated 787 replies and generally signalled support for the planned European policy proposal to create an enabling legal framework for the activity.[25] Concerns were mostly related to the fact that investments in CCS could delay or halt efforts in the areas of renewable energy and energy efficiency policy.[26] The legislative progression of the Directive was therefore a fairly smooth process. There was still a lack of general awareness of the technology, and CCS had not really yet touched a public chord, as was to happened later.[27]

Further, in terms of the regulation, law and policymakers in the EU had a dual objective from the very beginning for CCS: managing the environmental risks of the technology, as well as addressing commercial barriers to its development. There was a need for the creation of incentives for development.[28] Investors look not only for legal certainty and stable legal framework for their investments, but also for economic incentives.[29] Policymakers therefore departed from the presumption that it is sufficient to leave it to the market to invest in the technology,[30] and felt that incentivisation of CCS was crucial for its development.[31] With the inclusion of

---

[20] Council Directive 2008/98/EC on waste [1998] OJ L312/3. The Directive would potentially include captured CO_2 under the broad definition of waste, thus making it subject to specific waste permit requirements of Arts 9 and 10 of the Directive.

[21] Council Directive 1999/31/EC of 26 April 1999 on the landfill of waste [1999] OJ L 182/1. The Directive bans all liquified waste at landfills.

[22] The issue whether the technique would fall under underground injection as included in Art 11(3)(j).

[23] See also MJ Mace, C Hendriks and R Coenraads, 'Regulatory challenges to the implementation of carbon capture and geological storage within the European Union under EU and international law' (2007) 1 *International Journal of Greenhouse Gas Control* 253, 259.

[24] European Commission, 'Capturing and storing CO_2 underground: should we be concerned?' (Public consultation, European Commission, 2007) and CCS Impact Assessment, n 17 above, 18. See, for an initial overview of the consultation results, 'Consultation on the Impact Assessment of the Enabling Legal Framework for CCS' (May 2007), at ec.europa.eu/clima/events/articles/0004_en.

[25] CCS Impact Assessment, n 17 above, 10.

[26] ibid 15.

[27] See also P Ashworth and C Cormick, 'Enabling the Social Shaping of CCS Technology' in Havercroft et al (eds), n 2 above, 254f.

[28] European Commission, 'Communication on Sustainable power generation from fossil fuels: aiming for near-zero emissions from coal after 2020' COM (2006) 843, 8. The Commission Communication even included three objectives of a EU regulatory framework: 'ensure the environmentally sound, safe and reliable operation of CCS activities; remove unwarranted barriers to CCS activities in current legislation; provide appropriate incentives proportionate to the CO_2 reduction benefits'. CCS Impact Assessment, n 17 above, 2, 4.

[29] MM Roggenkamp and E Woerdman, 'Looking Beyond the Legal Uncertainties of CCS' in Roggenkamp and Woerdman (eds), n 6 above, 349. See also E Woerdman and O Couwenberg, 'CCS in the European Emissions Trading Scheme' in Roggenkamp and Woerdman (eds), n 6 above.

[30] CCS Impact Assessment, n 17 above, 19. See also W Grevers and L Luten, 'Introduction to the CCS chain: Technological aspects and safety risks' in Roggenkamp and Woerdman (eds), n 6 above, 11.

[31] R Purdy and I Havercroft, 'Carbon Capture and Storage: Developments under European Union and International Law' (2007) 4 *Journal for European Environmental & Planning Law* 353, 364.

CCS into the EU Emissions Trading System (ETS), the Commission believed it had established such an incentive,[32] alongside Commission funding programmes[33] and Member States' own initiatives.[34] The Commission stated that '[t]he EU is committed to supporting CCS both financially and with regulatory steps'.[35] Indeed the focus was not so much on 'if' but rather on 'how', and under which enabling framework and conditions.[36] This can already be derived from the four possible options identified in the legislative Impact Assessment regarding CCS action at EU level. It was concluded that that 'Option 0—no enabling policy at EU level' would have negative impacts on employment and competitiveness.[37] The other options considered encompassed including CCS within the emissions trading regime, making CCS mandatory after a certain time, and providing investment subsidies in addition to inclusion within the ETS.[38] Additionally, the impact assessment already includes suggestions for CO_2 storage site selection (Annex III) and a methodology for the carrying out of an environmental impact assessment (EIA) (Annex V).

B. The Public Debate

The initial problem regarding CCS was one of public awareness[39,40] rather than public acceptance. According to a Special Eurobarometer study from 2011 on public awareness and acceptance of CCS, just over 10 per cent of 13,000 participants said 'they had heard of CCS and knew what it was', whilst 18 per cent 'had heard of it but did not really know what it was'.[41] Awareness was especially low in Spain, Poland, the Czech Republic and France, where more than 75 per cent of the respondents claimed that they had not heard of CCS.[42] One possible explanation for these statistics is that CCS is not as obviously visible as other energy technologies or fracking, essentially adding a few components to existing facilities, and consequently failing to generate much public reaction.

---

[32] For a detailed discussion see Woerdman and Couwenberg, n 29 above, 97.

[33] See, eg, the NER300 Programme.

[34] For a case study on CCS development framework in the UK, see E Peters, 'What can be done to help the development of a UK CCS industry?' (2007) 4 *Journal for European Environmental & Planning Law* 393.

[35] European Commission, 'Communication on the Future of Carbon Capture and Storage in Europe' COM (2013) 180, 3.

[36] For an overview and discussion of economic considerations associated with CCS, see Woerdman and Couwenberg, n 29 above, 99ff.

[37] CCS Impact Assessment, n 17 above, 85.

[38] ibid. This was rejected, however, as it would have been feasible only at substantial additional cost. See De Graaf and Jans, n 6 above, 180.

[39] This is not the case anymore. In Europe, two demonstration projects have been delayed or abandoned due to public opposition. See I Havercroft, R Macrory and RB Stewart, 'Introduction' in Havercroft et al, n 2 above, 4, as well as Ashworth and Cormick, n 27 above, 251.

[40] C Fouillac, 'CO_2 Capture Transport and Storage, a Promising Technology for Limiting Climate Change' in JB Saulnier and MD Varella (eds), *Global Change, Energy Issues and Regulation Policies* (Haarlem, Springer Netherlands, 2013), 139.

[41] European Commission, 'Special Eurobarometer 364: Public Awareness and Acceptance of CO_2 Capture and Storage' (2011) 10.

[42] ibid 75.

Linked to the lack of awareness among the population is the public's perception of relatively few risks relating to CCS.[43] Most concerns related not to environmental and human health issues directly but to the fact that 'the technology was insufficiently mature to be mandated, and that the implications of doing so were unclear'.[44]

That risk perception is lower can also be derived from the fact that 60 per cent of respondents from the Eurobarometer study agreed that 'capturing and storing CO_2 should be compulsory when building a new coal-fuelled power plant'.[45] Generally, the awareness is rather low even in countries with major EU co-financed CCS projects.[46] The Eurobarometer study revealed that 61 per cent would be 'worried' and 24 per cent even 'very worried' if an underground storage site for CO_2 were to be located within 5 km of their home.[47] Indeed, the general acceptance of CCS can differ greatly from acceptance of a project in one's immediate neighbourhood.[48] Offshore storage projects in the UK,[49] The Netherlands and Italy have gained the acceptance of the public.[50] In Spain, initial public opposition to a site was overcome by a 'dedicated information and engagement campaign'.[51] An exception to the general perception of low risk regarding CCS is the public debate that took place in Germany.[52] There, public opposition was mentioned as one of the key reasons for the delay in the transposition of the CCS Directive, eventually leading to the halt of the German pilot projects.[53]

Nevertheless, the Commission correctly stressed 'that public acceptance should not be assumed without prior assessment'.[54] Indeed, the review of the CCS Directive indicated that the design and content of the Directive as such is a problem for the few existing cases involving public opposition. More concretely, industry stakeholders consider that the CCS Directive 'sends too many signals about "uncertainties

---

[43] See also H de Coninck et al, 'Is CO_2 capture and storage ready to roll?' (2007) 4 *Journal for European Environmental & Planning Law* 406. Not even non-governmental organisations, while being sceptical, are completely against the technology: ibid 407.

[44] European Commission, Proposal for a Directive on the geological storage of carbon dioxide and amending Council Directives 85/337/EEC, 96/61/EC, Directives 2000/60/EC, 2001/80/EC, 2004/35/EC, 2006/12/EC and Regulation (EC) No 1013/2006 COM (2008) 18 (CCS Proposal), 2; as well as CCS Impact Assessment, n 17 above, 10.

[45] European Commission, 'Special Eurobarometer 364: Public Awareness and Acceptance of CO_2 capture and storage', n 41 above, 13.

[46] ibid 77.

[47] ibid 92.

[48] M Haenchen, P Cocco and U Kastrup, *Use of the Underground—Background Document for EEA Scientific Committee Seminar* (EEA, 2015) 405.

[49] For a case study on public participation in CCS planning in the UK, refer to L Meyric and N Westaway, 'Public Participation in UK CCS Planning and Consent' in Havercroft et al (eds), n 2 above, 277–96. The authors conclude that the adequacy and effectiveness of the public involvement in the UK largely remains uncertain. For an analysis of the general approach taken towards the regulation of CCS in the UK, refer to McHarg and Poustie, n 7 above.

[50] European Commission, 'Communication on the Future of Carbon Capture and Storage in Europe', n 35 above, 18.

[51] ibid.

[52] For a discussion of the situation of CCS in Germany, see L Kramer, 'Germany: A Country without CCS' in this volume.

[53] ibid.

[54] ibid.

and lack of safety" of CCS, and thus that the Directive is indirectly hampering public acceptance';[55] and that public opposition and concern are best addressed at local and individual project levels. The CCS experience shows that binding regulation in the form of a Directive, that is, a minimum form of legal certainty and harmonisation,[56] does not necessarily have a positive influence on public acceptance of a project. On the contrary, according to the draft Recommendations for the review of the CCS Directive, 'both industry and one NGO ... feel that the over-prescriptive requirements of the Directive and Guidance Documents are a factor in the slow progress of CCS, both directly and indirectly by *fuelling public concerns*'.[57] The stakeholders call for more 'flexibility at the MS [Member State] level [which] is key to further development of CCS'.[58]

C. The Dilemma

Turning back to the Collingridge dilemma discussed at the start of section II, this might help to explain why the technology did not really take off. Intervention might have come too early in the development of the technology and procedure, thereby failing to provide enough leeway for industry to further engage in the activity.[59] For example, the closure and post-closure obligations, as established in the Directive, are perceived to be 'too heavy a burden' on the CCS industry, in addition to not being 'flexible enough given the often very different conditions ... [hence] they are considered to be hampering CCS deployment'.[60] While the public at first had little awareness or concern about the risks of the technology, this changed after adoption of the Directive. The 'over-prescriptive requirements of the Directive'[61] did not match the stage of the technology, and thus not only stifled its development but also helped increase public concerns. The stakeholder consultation concludes that

> the overall approach of the Directive has been to treat CCS as a hazardous activity, which has led the public to approach the topic with more caution than necessary. Some industry stakeholders (especially Oil & Gas related) mentioned that the knowledge of and experience with all elements of CCS is not well reflected in the Directive, which treats CCS as something entirely new.[62]

---

[55] Ricardo-AEA et al, 'Support to the review of Directive 2009/31/EC on the geological storage of carbon dioxide—Task 2: Assessment of the CCS Directive on the basis of evaluation and prospective questions—progress report' (October 2016), at www.qualenergia.it/sites/default/files/articolo-doc/CCS-Directive-evaluation-Final-Report%281%29.pdf, 8.

[56] See also De Graaf and Jans, n 6 above, 157.

[57] Ricardo-AEA et al, 'Support to the review of Directive 2009/31/EC on the geological storage of carbon dioxide—Task 3: First Draft Recommendations' (October 2016), at 9 (emphasis added). See also S Haszeldine, 'Geological Factors in Framing Legislation to Enable and Regulate Storage of Carbon Dioxide Deep in the Ground' in Havercroft et al (eds), n 2 above, 18.

[58] Ricardo-AEA et al, n 57 above, 8.

[59] Another important reason that CCS did not evolve as intended is the fact that the carbon price per t/ CO_2 dropped from €40 at the initial planning stage in 2008 to less than €5 in 2011 due to the (European) financial crisis, and thus no investment incentives—and consequently no business case—existed.

[60] Ricardo-AEA et al, n 57 above, 8f.

[61] ibid 9.

[62] ibid 10.

As such, one can conclude that the 'new in technology' is not really the critical factor—what matters is whether the underlying science is new, and this was not the case here.

III. RISK MANAGEMENT AND THE CCS DIRECTIVE

The argument so far has been that one reason for the slow development of CCS in Europe was that the legislator intervened at too early a stage of the development of the technology with a measure that was inappropriately strict. The second justification for arguing that the CCS Directive stifled the development of the technology will now be considered. This concerns the underlying risk management approach used when drafting the Directive. Whereas the Directive and the general regulatory approach applied some aspects of precautionary and prevention risk management, such as, for example, the issuance of BATs (Best Available Techniques, see further in section III.A), the Commission itself argues that the risk management principle of conservatism is the overarching risk management principle used for CCS.

One could indeed have expected that, due to the fact that the risks are known, the use of a 'conservatism' approach in drafting the Directive (further explained in section III.B) would have promoted the technology instead of stifling it. However, just because the risks are known, regulation would not have been necessary to the extent that the Directive provides for this. As will be explained, the application of a conservatism approach has led to overregulation of the technology.

A. The Underlying Principles: Prevention? Precaution?

The role of law within science, as Laurie et al suggest, is the assessment 'from a theoretical perspective, whether the law is an enabler or a prohibitor of technologies'.[63] At best, law should promote the development of a technology without compromising the protection of the society and the environment from uncertainties and risks associated with the technology.[64] As such, law and risk management at best 'neutralise the threat' or 'turn it to our advantage'.[65] The principles of precaution and prevention are the tools in European law to help strike this balance and implement this approach in practice.[66] This section starts from the perspective that

---

[63] Laurie et al, n 13 above, 10. See also Moses, 'Agents of change: how the law "copes" with technological change', n 11 above, 767.

[64] Laurie et al, n 13 above, 12 and 14f. See also A Stirling, 'Science, Precaution, and the Politics of Technological Risk' (2008) 1128 *Annals of the New York Academy of Sciences* 95, 96.

[65] JC Pitt, 'Anticipating the Unknown: The Ethics of Nanotechnology' in F Jotterand (ed), *Emerging Conceptual, Ethical and Policy Issues in Bionanotechnology* (Dordrecht, Springer, 2008) 113.

[66] Prevention and precaution are not free-standing legal principles of EU law as such, but under Art 191 of the Treaty on the Functioning of the European Union (TFEU), policy on the environment at EU level 'shall be based' on these and other environmental principles (rectification at source and polluters pay) expressed in the article.

law in general, and more specifically at the EU level, imposes control on the management of 'known' risks through the invocation of the prevention principle; whereas regarding 'uncertainties' or 'unknowns', the law is more process- rather than outcome-based and guided by the precautionary principle. As Van Asselt concludes:

> The [European] institutions use the fact that the experts are unable to provide this demand for certainty to label the problem as 'uncertain'. Subsequently, this labelling forms the basis for conducting a certain policy strategy, namely invoking the precautionary principle in a risk-aversive manner.[67]

Looking at the regulatory approaches taken in respect of the CCS technology, it becomes apparent that the European institutions intervened at a very early stage in the CCS development process, and did so with a strict and binding measure. In order to explain this, one could have recourse to the precaution and prevention principles, serving as the underlying risk management principles in the EU. Indeed, it would seem logical and convenient to argue that the regulatory approach taken for the CCS technology is based on the precautionary principle.[68] On this basis, CCS would be treated as a genuinely new technology, which had yet to be developed within Europe and had no real precedent in other jurisdictions. Consequently, the impacts associated with the technology are uncertainties rather than risks, as it is not only a question of likelihood but of the possibility of 'unknown unknowns'.

Alternatively, one could argue that the regulation of CCS is based on the prevention principle, and hence that it is a technology with known unknowns (risks) where it is a question of the likelihood of these risks occurring in practice. It would thus be treated as a modification of existing technologies that have been used before, and as such not as a new technology per se. This would indeed be an easy way out of the discussion on underlying risk management principles, but this argument does not really reflect the actual situation.

Hence, in accordance with the prevention principle, the Commission, rather than choosing 'opt-out', introduced a regime of foresight that is living up to the best techniques available. Indeed, BAT (Best Available Techniques) Reference Documents are one tool for risk management and implementing the prevention principle in practice.[69] The concept of BAT was first introduced by the IPPC Directive 2008/1/EC, and it is now contained in the Industrial Emissions Directive 2010/75/EU.[70] According to Article 3(10) of the Directive:

> 'best available techniques' means the most effective and advanced stage in the development of activities and their methods of operation which indicates the practical suitability

---

[67] M van Asselt, E Vos and T Fox, 'Regulating Technologies and the Uncertainty Paradox' in M Goodwin, BJ Koops and R Leenes (eds), *Dimensions of Technology Regulation* (AH Oisterwijk, Wolf Legal Publishers, 2010) 277.

[68] As, eg, argued on the international level in M Brus, 'Challenging complexities of CCS in Public International Law' in Roggenkamp and Woerdman (eds), n 6 above, 26ff.

[69] On the role of BAT and BREFs in the European (risk) regulatory process, refer to M Lee, *EU Environmental Law, Governance and Decision-Making*, 2nd edn (Oxford and Portland, ME, Hart Publishing, 2014) 119ff.

[70] Council Directive 2010/75/EU of 24 November 2010 on industrial emissions (integrated pollution prevention and control) [2010] OJ L334/17.

of particular techniques for providing the basis for emission limit values and other permit conditions designed to prevent and, where that is not practicable, to reduce emissions and the impact on the environment as a whole ...[71]

BAT or EU Best Available Techniques Reference Documents (BREFs) are documents applicable to industrial activities providing, for example, operating conditions and emission rates.

For CCS, no horizontal BREF (reference document containing information on the BAT) exists.[72] So far, BAT and BREF include only provisions in respect of capture and transport, not storage, though the activity is included in the updated BREF on Large Combustion Plants.[73] Furthermore, CCS activity is subject to inclusion in the update on the BREFs on Cement and Lime Manufacturing and Mineral Oil and Gas Refineries.[74] In terms of risk management, the issuance of BAT bypasses the step of risk analysis and jumps directly to the phase of risk reduction.[75] This is certainly appealing when confronted with 'new' technologies associated with a vast number of risks. The problem with applying BAT to technologies that are surrounded by risks, is that these technologies might well become over- or indeed under-regulated, as it is not possible to determine the exact impacts beforehand.[76]

B. The Underlying Principles: Conservatism!

The problem that technologies surrounded by risks might be over- or under-regulated is why the Commission put forward that it had employed the regulatory principle of 'conservatism' concerning the regulatory regime of CCS. The Commission itself explains this principle as follows:

> [I]f the risk profile of a new activity (A) is comparable to that of an existing activity (B) already covered by a risk management framework, then that risk management framework

---

[71] The definition in Art 3(10) continues: '(a) "techniques" includes both the technology used and the way in which the installation is designed, built, maintained, operated and decommissioned; (b) "available techniques" means those developed on a scale which allows implementation in the relevant industrial sector, under economically and technically viable conditions, taking into consideration the costs and advantages, whether or not the techniques are used or produced inside the Member State in question, as long as they are reasonably accessible to the operator; (c) "best" means most effective in achieving a high general level of protection of the environment as a whole'.

[72] Despite its having been asked for by several institutions, such as the European Parliament Committee on the Environment, Public Health and Food Safety in its draft opinion on Supporting Early Demonstration of Sustainable Power Generation from Fossil Fuels (2008/2140(INI)).

[73] European Commission, 'Reference Document on Best Available Techniques for Large Combustion Plants' (2006). This is currently under review: 'Best Available Techniques (BAT) Reference Document for the Large Combustion Plants, Industrial Emissions Directive 2010/75/EU' (2016) draft. See also De Graaf and Jans, n 6 above, 180.

[74] See, eg, P Zakkour, 'Task 2: Choices for regulating CO_2 capture and storage in the EU' (European Commission Discussion Paper, 2007) 22.

[75] GE Marchant, DJ Sylvester and KW Abbott, 'Risk Management Principles for Nanotechnology' (2008) 2 *NanoEthics* 43, 45. Also a general problem with the practical application of the precautionary principle. See SF Hansen and JA Tickner, 'The precautionary principle and false alarms—lessons learned' in European Environmental Agency, *Late lessons from early warnings: science, precaution, innovation* (European Environment Agency, 2013) 18.

[76] See also Moses, 'Why have a theory of law and technological change?', above n 11, 601f.

is also adequate, effective and proportionate for managing the risks of activity A, and no consideration of further options is necessary. The risk profiles of two activities A and B are comparable if activity A does not present new risks that activity B does not, and it does not present significantly greater or lesser risks than does activity B.[77]

Regulation of the technology therefore resulted in a conservative regulatory approach. So far, the principle of 'conservatism' is unique in European law-making. With the exception of the Impact Assessment for CCS, the principle of conservatism has not been included in any other policy documents of the Institutions, nor is it part of any better regulation or better law-making initiatives of the Commission.[78] It is also not included in the updated Better Regulation Package of May 2015,[79] which is made up of the Better Regulation Guidelines,[80] the Regulatory Fitness and Performance Programme (REFIT) plan and other policy documents.[81]

The explanation for the principle adopted by the Commission is far from clear, as it raises the questions of who is able to judge this and against which criteria? If science were to play a role in decision making, that decision making would be trapped in a vicious circle. Proper risk management as interpreted from the perspective of the principle of conservatism requires sound science. However, as already established, proper risk management is an option to deal with a degree of uncertainty regarding a technology in situations where sound science is absent. This leads to another question, namely, how this principle interacts with and relates to the precautionary and prevention principles?

The reference to the principle of conservatism as a regulatory approach for CCS was already included in the first proposal of the Directive as presented by the Commission.[82] It was absent, however, from the preparatory documents submitted by the working groups.[83] It has not been taken up or commented on by the other European Institutions (neither in the Council and Parliament, nor in the Economic and Social Committee) in the legislative procedure. The wording of 'conservative measures' (not phrased as a 'principle', however) was mentioned for the first time in a study conducted on 'risk analysis of the geological sequestration of carbon dioxide' for the UK Department of Trade and Industry (DTI) in 2003.[84] It has been taken up in a study by FIELD and ECOFYS,[85] which refers to 'conservative'

---

[77] CCS Impact Assessment, n 17 above, 23.
[78] European Commission, 'European Governance: Better lawmaking' COM (2002) 275.
[79] European Commission, 'Better regulation for better results: An EU agenda' COM(2015) 215.
[80] European Commission, 'Commission Staff Working Document: Better Regulation Guidelines' SWD (2015) 111.
[81] ibid 110.
[82] European Commission, n 44 above, 5.
[83] Such as, eg, in Second European Climate Change Programme, 'Report of Working Group 3: Carbon Capture and Geological Storage (CCS)' (2006). See also Zakkour, n 74 above; and ERM, 'Task 3: Incentivising CO_2 capture and storage in the European Union' (European Commission Discussion Paper, 2007).
[84] M Vendrig et al, 'Risk analysis of the geological sequestration of carbon dioxide' (DNV, DTI Report No R246, 2003). However, the study is not accessible anymore. The author of this chapter contacted both DNV Consulting and the authors to request a copy, without success.
[85] C Hendriks, MJ Mace and R Coenraads, 'Impacts of EU and International Law on the Implementation of Carbon Capture and Geological Storage in the European Union' (FIELD, ECOFYS, June 2005), at pdf.wri.org/ccs_impact_of_eu_law_on.pdf.

measures mostly in relation to the precautionary principle,[86] but without explicitly defining the meaning of 'conservative'.

The Commission in turn seems to have taken up the concept of 'conservatism' in the CCS Impact Assessment and developed it further as the 'regulatory principle of conservatism'. It seems indeed that the principle has been 'invented' by the Commission and used in the context of CCS for the first and so far only time, at least so consciously and explicitly. This statement is supported by the fact that reference to the principle in scholarship in the European regulatory context is largely missing.[87] Only one published article has been identified regarding the use of this principle, and this in a US regulatory context and with a different definitional approach.[88] In the European context, one reference to the application of conservative measures in the context of CCS has been identified.[89] However, it was written by the leading authors of the FIELD and ECOFYS study, and hence the conclusion that 'the precautionary principle requires that conservative measures be taken where scientific knowledge is not complete'[90] is not surprising.

Based on the principle of conservatism, the Commission, in its Impact Assessment, reviewed the existing legislation on the individual elements of the CCS technology (capture, transportation and storage) separately. The Impact Assessment clarifies the underlying premises: 'A conservative approach was taken, in the sense that the default option for regulating a CCS component was taken to be the existing legal framework that regulates activities of a similar risk (if one exists).'[91] The Commission came to the conclusion that while for some elements, for example regarding EIA and environmental liability, the existing legal framework can be used,[92] for other elements, especially relating to storage, a new legal framework was needed.[93] The former part (use of existing framework) is an articulation of the traditional risk management approach, meaning that the legislator usually tries 'to apply the current

---

[86] ibid. They state that 'the precautionary principle requires that conservative measures be taken where scientific knowledge is not complete': ibid at 40 and 55. General reference to conservative measures is further included ibid at 14 and 50.

[87] It has, eg, not been included in the overview of regulatory innovation in the EU: G Van Calster, 'An Overview of Regulatory Innovation in the European Union' (2009) 11 *Cambridge Yearbook of European Legal Studies* 289.

[88] JR Young and WP Dey, 'Uncertainty and Conservatism in Assessing Environmental Impact under §316(b): Lessons from the Hudson River Case' (2002) 2 *The Scientific World* 30. This relates to a US case study and has to be read in the context of US regulatory law. Young and Dey employ a rather different definition of the principle than does the European Commission. The Commission uses the principle in the context of proportionate assessment and risk regulation regarding two activities associated which comparable risks, while Young and Dey argue that the principle is used regarding 'highly uncertain' activities and more in the sense of the European interpretation of the precautionary principle. They put forward, eg, that 'The precautionary approach explicitly recognizes the uncertainty of biological information and the imperfect ability of management policies to assure that biological targets are met. In recognition of this uncertainty, targets are set in a conservative manner.' Further, they put forward that the more certainty is gained, the more the conservative approach of regulation is reduced; which in 'European speak' would mean a shift from precaution to prevention: see ibid at 31, 34 and 35. Hence, the article was not considered to be helpful when analysing the European interpretation and meaning of the principle.

[89] Mace et al, n 23 above, 259.

[90] ibid.

[91] CCS Impact Assessment, n 17 above, 2, 32.

[92] European Commission, n 44 above, 2.

[93] CCS Impact Assessment, n 17 above, 2.

regulation to new technologies'.[94] This entails making recourse to 'default rules' on ownership, liability and environmental legislation.[95] The conservative regulatory principle might as well be nothing more than the application of traditional risk management concepts in a new wrapping.

The Commission decided not to amend the existing legislation relevant to the storage stage, such as the ETS Directive, the IPPC Directive, now Industrial Emissions Directive (IED), or existing waste legislation, as it was not considered appropriate to deal with storage.[96] Rather, and to a certain extent, contradictorily, as the CCS Directive in the end amends certain existing legislation, the Commission came to the conclusion that 'one single framework will be sufficient',[97] and that the CCS Directive managed to create a climate change 'mitigation option, and that it is done safely and responsibly'.[98]

It is striking that the Impact Assessment on CCS does not include a reference to the prevention principle at all, and includes few references to precaution in contexts other than risk regulation.[99] The Directive itself does not include any reference to these principles. However, the conservative approach principle is discussed and used as reasoning for regulatory design decisions in multiple instances.[100] One would be right to wonder why the traditional risk governance and environmental principles of precaution and prevention were not deemed appropriate and/or applicable in establishing a governance approach for CCS.

The lack of references can be explained by the fact that CCS, as already established, is not a real 'new technology', hence neither of these principles is at the forefront of reasoning and the drafting of regulatory intervention. Indeed, CCS is rather a modification of an existing technology, namely, conventional oil and gas drilling. As such, 'enough technical experience on CCS is available around the globe (and also with European industry)',[101] although the 'existence of potentially serious risks [of CCS] with irreversible consequences has been mentioned. [However, t]here is no consensus on the existence of such risks.'[102] The 'storage' part of the technology is still at the centre of risk discussions,[103] especially regarding carbon leakage and related liability. This is more about regulatory uncertainty, meaning how to close this regulatory gap, rather than scientific uncertainty. More precisely, it is about *how*, meaning through which regulatory mechanism or tool the technology can best be addressed, rather than about *what* the impacts of the technology

---

[94] Haenchen et al, n 48 above, 20. Even if the current legal framework has not been drafted with CCS in mind. See also Purdy and Havercroft, n 31 above, 353. See also Coninck et al, n 43 above, 407f, for an overview of existing Directives and concerns regarding their applicability.
[95] Haenchen et al, n 48 above, 20.
[96] CCS Proposal, n 44 above, 5.
[97] ibid 7.
[98] ibid 2. This is upheld by Roggenkamp and Woerdman, who conclude that 'the CCS Directive provides ample opportunities for CCS. We have found no outspoken inconsistencies or blunt mistakes in the CCS Directive. In principle, it provides a solid legal basis': Roggenkamp and Woerdman, n 29 above, 350.
[99] Once in relation to costs and failure to invest (CCS Impact Assessment, n 17 above, 47) and once regarding the risk of leakage (ibid 67).
[100] See ibid 2, 25, 32, 41 and 54.
[101] Ricardo-AEA et al, n 57 above, 6.
[102] CCS Proposal, n 44 above, 4.
[103] S Bode and L Dietrich, 'Regulating Carbon Capture and Storage in the European Union: An Economic and Legal Analysis' (2008) 2 *Carbon Climate Law Review* 196, 200.

are as such. In short, while the use and combination of the technology might be new, the underlying science is not, hence CCS is subject to prevention rather than precaution.[104] This goes hand in hand with the Eurobarometer findings on the acceptance of CCS, which showed that '[t]here was a lower level of caution about CCS technology among those who had greater knowledge about it'.[105]

Derived from the definition of the conservatism principle as established by the Commission and the way in which it is used to justify the legislative framework for CCS, the conservatism principle links the 'traditional' precautionary and preventive principles at the proportionality stage.[106] The Commission itself refers to the 'interests of proportionate assessment' in the definition of the conservatism principle, and establishes the criteria of adequateness, effectiveness and proportionality as the reference point of a risk management framework.[107] That implies that the principle of conservatism can in fact be considered a 'correction to the precaution and prevention principles', in the sense that the traditional principles are associated with either 'new' technologies and scientific uncertainties in the former case (precaution), and/or known risks and likelihoods in the latter case (prevention). Table 3.1 illustrates these approaches.

Table 3.1: Relationship between the principles of precaution, prevention and conservatism

Circumstance	Regulatory principle
Uncertainty: unknowns and unquantifiable	Precaution
Risk: known unknowns and likelihood	Prevention
Risk: known and quantifiable	Conservatism

The conservatism principle arguably comes into play for technologies where there is already a certain legislative framework available; the technology is only a modification of an already existing technology, and hence not all aspects need go through regulatory scrutiny on the grounds of proportionality considerations. This is further supported by a finding of the FIELD and ECOFYS study: with reference to the 2003 DTI study, they conclude that 'the generic risk assessment included a relatively

---

[104] Interestingly, Mace et al list the polluter pays and the precautionary principles (as well as the principle of intergenerational equity) as the key principles of international law applicable to CCS. This is especially striking, as the prevention principle has a more established role in international law. However, it seems likely that the authors are confusing precaution and prevention, as in the following section they speak about 'risks' relating to CCS and precaution, whereas it should in that case have been rather 'uncertainties' and precaution, or 'risks' and prevention. Mace et al, n 23 above, 254.

[105] European Commission, 'Special Eurobarometer 364: Public Awareness and Acceptance of CO_2 Capture and Storage in Europe', n 41 above, 113.

[106] In addition, Lierman puts forward that 'The principle of proportionality is a principle that helps to balance conflicting principles and interests.' S Lierman, 'Law as a complex adaptive system: the importance of convergence in a multi-layered legal order' (2014) 21 *Maastricht Journal of European and Comparative Law* 611, 629.

[107] CCS Impact Assessment, n 17 above, 23.

high degree of conservatism and that there is significant scope for the individual risks associated with actual applications to fall within acceptable limits'.[108] The regulatory 'principle of conservatism' is arguably the traditional risk management approach in a new package, and as such a regulatory practice or a 'risk assessment tool'[109] rather than a defined concept or principle.[110]

IV. CONCLUSION

The discussion on the regulatory framework for CCS started from the general positive presumption of making the technology work. Law should thus have been an enabler of the technology: The Directive's intention was to create (financial) incentives to promote a fast introduction of CCS.[111] The idea was that without financial support, as well as regulatory clarity, CCS would not take off.[112] However, in retrospect, one is bound to conclude that the CCS Directive, as it was drafted, did not implement this approach in practice. Due to low carbon prices and other complications,[113] CCS did not prove a viable technology, as it failed to provide sufficient incentives for its investors.[114] Large-scale public investment for the financing of demonstration projects and a detailed regulatory framework have been used in an attempt to make the technology work in practice.[115] As has been concluded, however, a 'simpler and more committed regulatory framework would [arguably] prove both cheaper and more effective in the long run'.[116] Ex-ante regulation is certainly important, but what can be learned from the experience with CCS is that technological development and the development of the regulatory framework should go hand in hand.

---

[108] Hendriks et al, n 85 above, 55.
[109] The 'risk management tool versus principle discussion' is not a new one and has been debated regarding the ALARA (As Low As Reasonably Achievable) approach in nuclear power, for example. See also S Lierman and L Veuchelen, 'The optimisation approach of ALARA in nuclear practice: an early application of the precautionary principle? Scientific uncertainty versus legal uncertainty and its role in tort law' (2006) 15 *European Environmental Law Review* 98, 99.
[110] As has been also argued for the 'command and control' approach: Van Calster, n 87 above, 294.
[111] See also Woerdman and Couwenberg, n 29 above, 97f.
[112] This is also stressed by Mace et al, n 23 above, 260, who state that '*In a context of rising greenhouse gas emissions, where CCS is very costly and geological storage shown to be safe, a variety of economic incentives may be needed to encourage the uptake of CCS technology and to increase its cost-efficiency through large-scale application.*' A discussion of several forms of incentives, especially regarding tax law, can be found in JN Bouwman and IJJ Burgers, 'The Law as a barrier or tool for promoting CCS' in Roggenkamp and Woerdman (eds), n 6 above, 321–44.
[113] See also European Commission, 'Communication on the Future of Carbon Capture and Storage in Europe', n 35 above, 16.
[114] See also D Langlet, 'Transboundary Dimensions of CCS: EU Law Problems and Prospects' (2014) 8 *Carbon and Climate Law Review* 198, 198; as well as A Boute, 'CCS Under the Project-Based Kyoto Mechanism' in Roggenkamp and Woerdman (eds), n 6 above, 74. For a discussion of different instruments providing efficient incentives, such as a carbon tax, double credits, a closure of the cost gap and mandatory CCS, see Woerdman and Couwenberg, n 29 above, at 106–23.
[115] See also I Havercroft and R Macrory, 'Pulling the Threads Together' in Havercroft and et al (eds), n 2 above, 301.
[116] McHarg and Poustie, n 7 above, 274.

Further, the regulatory framework applicable to CCS was adopted under the environmental competence of the Treaty prior to Lisbon, and thus prior to the introduction of the Energy Title. Even though the Directive was adopted with the procedure laid down in Article 251 of the Treaty establishing the European Community (TEC) (now Article 294 TFEU), and hence with the ordinary legislative procedure, it could be argued that, at least in theory, due to the changes introduced in the Lisbon Treaty, adoption would now be more difficult. Whereas for the environmental legal basis the threshold of unanimity in decision making was that a measure had to '*significantly* affect[t] a Member State's choice between different energy sources and the general structure of its energy supply' (emphasis added), Article 194(1)(b) TFEU states that '[Union] measures *shall not affect* a Member State's right to determine the conditions for exploiting its energy resources, its choice between different energy sources and the general structure of its energy supply'. In this sense, the threshold under Article 194 TFEU is lower and measures are more difficult to pass as they just have to 'affect' (as opposed to 'significantly' affect). Hence Article 194 TFEU lays down the competences under which the EU can adopt legal measures, but also sets its boundaries, through the second paragraph in particular. Hence one could conclude that a measure on CCS in the form we have today would not be so easy to adopt under the new set-up of energy and environmental competences. Carbon capture and storage is a cross-cutting energy and environmental issue, which might also affect European energy policy. One could further argue that mandatory CCS might affect the Member States' right to determine their own energy resources, as CCS does not function in conjunction with all energy sources. It does, however, function in combination with coal-fuelled power plants (and certain industry facilities). Admittedly, this argumentation is not very strong, but it cannot be disregarded completely. What can be concluded, however, is that, from today's perspective, a CCS measure against the background of the horizontal division of competences post-Lisbon is rendered more difficult, if not impossible, to establish.

4

Germany: A Country without CCS

LUDWIG KRÄMER

COUNCIL DIRECTIVE 2009/31/EC on the geological storage of carbon dioxide (the CCS Directive)[1] was adopted on 23 April 2009. It was based on Article 175 TEC, the present Article 192 TFEU, which provides the legal basis for environmental action, and required the EU Member States to adopt the necessary legislative and regulatory provisions to transpose the requirements of the CCS Directive into national law by 25 June 2011.

I. OBLIGATION TO ALLOW CO_2 STORAGE?

The precise obligations for Member States that flow out of the provisions of the CCS Directive might not be altogether clear. This refers in particular to the question whether Member States have to allow the geological storage of carbon dioxide (CO_2) in their territory and set the corresponding legislative framework for that.

Article 2 of the CCS Directive indicated that the Directive applies to the geological storage of CO_2 in the territory of Member States, their exclusive economic zones and their continental shelves. Article 4(1) provided:

> Member States shall retain the right to determine the areas from which storage sites may be selected pursuant to the requirements of this Directive. This includes the right of Member States not to allow for any storage in parts or in the whole of their territory.

And Article 4(2) continued:

> Member States which intend to allow geological storage of CO_2 in their territory shall undertake an assessment of the storage capacity available in parts or in the whole of their territory ...

The doubts as to the meaning of these provisions stem from the fact that Article 4(1) provided for the right, but possibly also of the obligation, of Member States to determine those areas within their territory suitable for the geological

---

[1] Council Directive 2009/31/EC of 23 April 2009 on the geological storage of carbon dioxide and amending Council Directive 85/337/EEC, European Parliament and Council Directives 2000/60/EC, 2001/80/EC, 2006/12/EC, 2008/1/EC and Regulation (EC) No 1013/2006 [2009] OJ L140/114 (the Directive).

storage of CO_2. The second sentence of Article 4(1) could then be understood to refer to the right of Member States to prohibit the storage of CO_2 within these suitable areas, but not in the whole of their territory.

However, such an interpretation of the CCS Directive appears impossible. Indeed, the provision in the second sentence of Article 4(1), that Member States have the right not to allow for any storage of CO_2 in their territory, is clear and unambiguous. It is not limited in any way to those parts of their territory that are suitable for the geological storage of CO_2. This understanding of Article 4(1) is supported by Article 4(2), which only requires Member States to make an assessment of the storage capacity in their territory when they 'intend to allow' such storage. Thus, where a Member State does not intend to allow the geological storage, it is not obliged to identify suitable storage areas.

This interpretation is confirmed by considerations of general EU law. There is no provision in the EU Treaties that obliges Member States to provide for the construction of specific industrial installations or infrastructure: whether a Member State elects to build nuclear power plants, waste incinerators, nuclear waste deposits, sky-scrapers or motorways, that is its own, sovereign decision. It is for this reason that the provisions relating to trans-European networks for transport, energy and communication, which provide for the construction of the necessary transnational projects for these networks (Articles 170–172 TFEU), motorways, railway lines, electricity lines, etc, explicitly require, in Article 172(2) TFEU, the approval of the Member State concerned, when a project relates to its territory.

The EU practice follows these considerations: about half of the 28 EU Member States do not have nuclear power plants in their territory. They thus did not translate Directive 2009/71/Euratom establishing a Community framework for the nuclear safety of nuclear installations into national law.[2] And the Commission did not ask these Member States to transpose the Directive into their national legal order.

This means in concrete terms that the EU may not oblige any Member State to provide for the construction of CO_2 storage facilities in its territory.

The same conclusion follows from Articles 192 and 193 TFEU. Article 193 TFEU provides that when the EU has adopted an environmental measure under Article 192 TFEU—as is the case with the CCS Directive—Member States are entitled to maintain or introduce more stringent environmental protection measures. As the Directive was rightly based on the present Article 192 TFEU—a storage facility for CO_2 is an environmental measure that might raise some environmental problems such as land use, possible leakages, impact on groundwater, etc—Member States are allowed to adopt measures that further reduce or eliminate such risks altogether, and may thus, on the basis of Article 193 TFEU, completely prohibit the construction of CO_2 storage facilities in their territory.

This means in the present case that the CCS Directive may not oblige any Member State to provide for the construction of CO_2 facilities in its territories. It does not require Member States to provide for installations concerning the geological storage

---

[2] Council Directive 2009/71/Euratom of 25 June 2009 establishing a Community framework for the nuclear safety of nuclear installations [2009] OJ L172/18.

of CO_2. Rather, Member States are free to decide whether they want to establish this technology in their territory.

Neither can it be argued that a Member State has to adopt the necessary legislative framework in order to transpose the CCS Directive into the national legal order because the Member State's political decision not to allow the geological storage of CO_2 might be changed at a later time. The clear wording of Article 4(1) and (2) of the Directive does not allow such an interpretation. It follows from these provisions that as long as the intention of a Member State not to allow the storage exists, that Member State is not obliged to make an assessment of suitable storage sites and—as a logical consequence—transpose the other provisions of the Directive into its national legal order. Any other interpretation of Article 4 would have had to lay down the obligation of Member States in clear, unambiguous terms.

II. LIMITATION TO PILOT PROJECTS

On 27 August 2012, Germany adopted legislation to transpose the CCS Directive into national law, but limited the possibility for the storage of CO_2 to pilot, research and demonstration projects, and also limited the annual storage capacity for each installation (1.3 million tonnes of CO_2) and for the whole German territory (4 million tonnes of CO_2).[3] The KSpG provided that it may be amended after 2018, if the necessity for further legislative measures becomes obvious, The question is whether such a limitation of the transposing legislation is compatible with EU law.

It was argued in section I that a Member State is not obliged to allow the storage of CO_2 in its territory, and that the Member State is not obliged to transpose the provisions of the CCS Directive on storage into its national legal order. If this reasoning is correct, no objection can be made against national legislation that only allows the storage of CO_2 for pilot, research or demonstration purposes (argument *a maiore ad minus*); indeed, when a total prohibition of CO_2 storage is compatible with EU law, a limitation of CO_2 storage to pilot and demonstration projects is all the more permitted, as the desired result of the CCS Directive is complied with in part. This might be different for the transport of CO_2, as such transport may occur from a Member State other than Germany through Germany to a third—EU or non-EU—state. However, the quantitative restrictions in the KSpG refer only to the storage of CO_2, not to its transport. The transport of CO_2 in German territory is neither quantitatively nor as to research or demonstration purposes limited by the German Act.

It follows from this that the KSpG of 2012 is compatible with EU law. There is no question of non-implementation of the CCS Directive by Germany. This is apparently also the opinion of the European Commission, which had started a procedure against Germany, under Article 258 TFEU, for not having transposed the provisions

---

[3] Gesetz zur Demonstration der dauerhaften Speicherung von Kohlendioxid ('Act on demonstrating the permanent storage of CO_2'—hereinafter KSpG)), BGBl 2012, Pt I, 1726.

of the CCS Directive in time—by 25 June 2011—but which terminated this procedure with the adoption of the KSpG of 17 August 2012. The Commission did not start new procedures for partial implementation of the Directive.

The German approach to the storage of CO_2 differs from that of several other countries, in particular from that of the United States (US), the United Kingdom (UK), Australia and Canada. For this reason, it appears appropriate to examine how the Act of August 2012 came into being, what the reactions of the German public were, why there does not appear to be any prospect of authorising the storage of CO_2 in Germany and what Germany considers to be an alternative to the storage of CO_2.

III. THE ELABORATION OF THE CO_2 STORAGE ACT OF 2012

Large-scale public discussion on CCS technology started with the Commission proposal for a directive of 2008,[4] which later became the CCS Directive. In that year, Vattenfall, one of the four big energy producers in Germany, put into operation a pilot project (30 MW) for the CO_2 capture of its lignite-fired power plant (1600 MW) at the Schwarze Pumpe site in Brandenburg. The CO_2 was captured by oxy-fuel combustion, but was then emitted into the air, as the intended underground storage in Ketzin (Brandenburg), some 400 km away, only became available in 2011.

In the same year, 2008, another of the big four energy producing companies, RWE, announced the construction, by 2014,of a lignite-fired power plant at Goldenberg (Hürth) in the *Land* of Nordrhein-Westfalen. The plant was to have a capacity of 450 MW. The company informed the public that the CO_2 would be captured and transported, via a 600-km pipeline, to the *Land* Schleswig-Holstein, where it would be stored in the underground. It had already explored the underground in Schleswig-Holstein for general research purposes, without publicly revealing its CO_2 storage plans. Not even the regional government in Schleswig-Holstein and other public authorities had been made aware of RWE's plans.

While Nordrhein-Westfalen is a highly industrialised region, Schleswig-Holstein is much less industrial. The land is predominantly agricultural, and agriculture and tourism are the largest contributors to economic output for the region. However, strong winds across the land area hint at the economic potential of wind energy. When the RWE plans to store CO_2 in Schleswig-Holstein became known, there was an almost immediate strong negative public reaction. Citizens' initiatives sprang up, mayors, local councils and other public authorities expressed their opposition to the storage plans, farmers and their associations, local church representatives and local political parties (conservatives, liberals, social democrats and, in particular, the Green Party) almost unanimously opposed the storage of CO_2 in the *Land*.

---

[4] European Commission, 'Proposal for a Directive of the European Parliament and of the Council on the geological storage of carbon dioxide and amending Council Directives 85/337/EEC, 96/61/EC, Directives 2000/60/EC, 2001/80/EC, 2004/35/EC, 2006/12/EC and Regulation (EC) No 1013/2006 COM (2008) 18.

Confronted with this massive movement, which found an echo with all parties in the *Land* Parliament, the *Land* government, which initially favoured the storage plans, changed its position. This was a decisive step, as in Germany, permits for industrial installations are granted by the *Land* governments, not by the Federal Government.[5]

The same public opposition arose in Niedersachsen, the Land adjoining Schleswig-Holstein, where geologically appropriate sites were also thought to exist. The citizens' protests were similarly supported by all political parties and by the Christian-Democrat Government.

The third *Land* involved was Brandenburg, a lignite-producing *Land* of the former German Democratic Republic, which is characterised by low levels of industrial development and a high unemployment rate. In 2008, in Ketzin (Brandenburg), the German Centre for Geological Research started to store CO_2 underground in a site with a capacity of some 60,000 metric tonnes. No technical problems or leakages appeared and no opposition from local people or groups was noted, until the events in Schleswig-Holstein and Niedersachsen also gave rise to some—limited—local citizens' initiatives in opposition to CCS technology. Brandenburg was more receptive to CCS technology, as it considered that this might allow the further exploitation of the lignite resources in the Land.

In April 2009, the Federal Government, which was by then composed of a coalition of the Christian-Democrat and Social-Democrat parties, submitted a bill to the German Parliament, in order to transpose the CCS Directive into German law. The Bill largely followed the provisions of the Directive. In conformity with the German Constitution, the Bill was first to be discussed by the Second Legislative Chamber (Bundesrat), where the *Länder* were represented. During the discussions in this Chamber, Schleswig-Holstein and Niedersachsen asked for the right of the *Länder* to oppose the CCS technology in their territory, referring to Article 4 of the CCS Directive. Brandenburg viewed the Bill favourably, but clarified that it was not ready to be the only Land that would allow the storage of CCS. Several other *Länder* asked for (minor) amendments of the Bill, as they were afraid that the CCS technology would facilitate the construction and further use of coal(lignite)-fired power plants. Finally, the Second Chamber adopted a Resolution approving the Bill, but suggesting a number of amendments.[6]

In the First Chamber (Bundestag), the controversies continued, as the deputies from Niedersachsen and Schleswig-Holstein persisted in having a provision inserted into the Bill to allow the prohibition of CCS technology at *Land* level. This created some difficulties for the Federal Government, as the Land governments were of the same political party. In view of the upcoming general elections, scheduled for September 2009, it was not considered opportune to give the impression that the political parties were split over the question of CCS—all the more so as public opposition against the technology in Germany continued to manifest itself. In the end, the Bill was not discussed in the First Chamber and became obsolete with the dissolution of the Parliament and new elections in September 2009.

---

[5] An exception are permits for nuclear installations, which are granted by the Federal Government.
[6] Bundesrat, Beschluss, of 15 May 2009, Drucksache 282/2009.

The general elections led to a Christian-Democrat-Liberal Federal Government. In April 2011, this Government submitted a new bill to the German Parliament. The 2011 Bill differed from the Bill of 2009 in two significant ways: first, it emphasised that it was limited to introducing a pilot phase for CCS, during which only pilot, research and demonstration projects would be authorised; secondly, it gave considerable discretion to the *Länder* to allow or disallow CO_2 storage in their territories.

The Bill was discussed in the Second Chamber in 2011. As the nuclear accident at Fukushima (Japan) had happened in March 2011, and the German Federal Government had decided, in June 2011, to progressively close all nuclear power plants, the discussions on the CCS Bill in the Second Chamber were very politicised. There was a general fear that the Bill would favour the construction of new coal(lignite)-fired power plants and slow down the support of renewable sources of energy. On this and other grounds, Niedersachsen and Schleswig-Holstein altogether opposed the Bill and found support in other *Länder*. In September 2011, the Second Chamber rejected the Bill completely.[7] It did not even ask for the Mediation Committee, a Constitution-based body, composed of representatives from the First and the Second legislative chambers, to be convened, to find compromises between the two Parliamentary Chambers on legislative texts. However, the Federal Government asked the Mediation Committee to convene and find a compromise. The Mediation Committee finally did find such a compromise solution, which allowed the adoption of the Bill by the First Chamber on 27 August 2012.

IV. THE GERMAN ACT AND THE LAND LEGISLATION

The German Act (KSpG)[8] limited the application of the CCS Directive in Germany to the piloting and demonstration of technologies for the permanent storage of CO_2 in underground geological formations.[9] Carbon dioxide storage facilities capable of being authorised under the KSpG (Article 2) included those:

(1) for which a complete application had been introduced before 31 December 2016;
(2) that were not capable of storing more than 1.3 million metric tonnes of CO_2 per year; and
(3) that did not exceed an overall storage in Germany of 4 million metric tons of CO_2 per year.

The permits were to be granted by the competent *Land* authority where the site was located. They might be granted for an indefinite time in the future. And nothing was

---

[7] Bundesrat, Beschluss, of 23 September 2011, Drucksache 487/11.
[8] KSpG, n 3 above.
[9] See ibid, Art 1: 'Dieses Gesetz … regelt zunächst die Erforschung, Erprobung und Demonstration von Technologien zur dauerhaften Speicherung von Kohlendioxid in unterirdischen Gesteinsschichten.' ('This Act shall deal … in a first step with the research, tentative use and demonstration of technologies to permanently store carbon dioxide underground.').

foreseen as to the repeal of a permit—though the specific *Land* permit might, of course, contain provisions in this regard.

While the storage of CO_2 was thus limited, the capture and the transport of CO_2 in Germany was not. Permits for capture or transport follow the general administrative rules on permitting economic activities. With regard to the transport of CO_2, the approach chosen by the KSpG opened the way for storing CO_2 in the German Exclusive Economic Zone, where permits are granted by the Federal Government, not by the *Länder*. Similarly, the Act did not limit the export of CO_2 from Germany to other countries.

The Act gave the *Länder* the right to decide whether they would allow the storage of CO_2 in their territory (see Article 2(5) KSpG):[10]

> The Länder may decide that the tentative use and demonstration of permanent storage is only admissible in certain areas or is inadmissible in certain areas. When a decision in accordance with sentence 1 is taken, other options to use a potential storage site, the geological specificities of the area and other general interests shall be weighed.

This provision was strongly discussed during the legislative process. The *Länder*, led by Schleswig-Holstein and Niedersachsen, insisted on obtaining the possibility of prohibiting CCS storage in their territories altogether. The other *Länder*, in particular Brandenburg and Nordrhein-Westfalen—both *Länder* with considerable coal and lignite resources—were much less determined. However, faced with strong public opposition to CCS, they did not wish to openly oppose what became Article 2(5) KSpG, in order not to suffer losses in federal or regional elections. Indeed, it is remarkable that the opposition to the CCS technology was not oriented along political party lines but was more a question whether coal (lignite) would and should have a place in the German energy-climate change strategy. And the opposition to the CCS technology was not limited to citizen initiatives or local groups; reputable researchers, public bodies and academics also supported the opposition to CCS.

Decisive for the inclusion of Article 2(5) KSpG was probably that the CCS Directive had allowed Member States to refuse to authorise CO_2 storage in their territories. As Germany is a federal state, where the *Länder* have extensive competences to decide on the kind of installations or infrastructures they want to establish,[11] it would have been anomalous to imposean obligation on them, via federal legislation, to accept CO_2 storage.

---

[10] ibid, Art 2(5): 'Die Länder können bestimmen, dass eine Erprobung und Demonstration der dauerhaften Speicherung nur in bestimmten Gebieten zulässig ist oder in bestimmten Gebieten unzulässig ist. Bei der Festlegung nach Satz1 sind sonstige Optionen zur Nutzung einer potenziellen Speicherstätte, die geologischen Besonderheiten der Gebiete und andere öffentliche Interessen abzuwägen.' ('The Länder may decide that testing and demonstration of permanent storage is only allowed in certain areas or not allowed in certain areas. When decisions according to sentence 1 are taken, other options for using a potential storage site, the geological specificities and the area and other public interest issues shall be weighed.')

[11] The permits for nuclear installations, which are governed by federal legislation, constitute the only exception. The corresponding legislation was adopted in Germany in the 1950s, when environmental concerns were not an issue and the euphoria as to the benefits of nuclear technology was general in economic circles.

Article 2(5) KSpG is drafted in ambiguous terms: the Ministry for Economic Affairs within the Federal Government, which was responsible for leading on the proposals, probably was, overall, more open to the general authorisation of CCS, and did not want to give complete freedom to the *Länder* to prohibit the storage of CO_2. The reference to certain areas where such storage could be allowed or prohibited was an attempt to limit the *Länder* discretion—though a rather clumsy one—which in the end was unsuccessful.

Be that as it may, if there was such an intention by the Federal Government, it was counteracted by the *Länder*: both Schleswig-Holstein and Niedersachsen introduced regional legislation that prohibited the storage of CO_2 in their territories.[12] Both *Länder* proceeded in the same way in order to reach that objective: a regional government Bill established five geological areas in Schleswig-Holstein and five in Niedersachsen, examined the suitability of these areas for CO_2 storage and concluded that none of the areas was apt for such storage, although the underlying data on the geological suitability of the areas were not made public. Both governments also invoked geothermal and other uses of the ground, but the two Acts themselves simply declared CO_2 storage in the five different areas—which covered the whole of the Niedersachsen and the Schleswig-Holstein territories—to be prohibited. The Schleswig-Holstein government also invoked the negative impact on tourism as a reason for not allowing CO_2 storage.

The *Land* Mecklenburg-Vorpommern did not even try to argue that its territory was not apt to receive CO_2 storage installations. It adopted an Act consisting of three short articles, which prohibited CO_2 storage in Mecklenburg-Vorpommern.[13]

In the three *Länder*, all political parties in the regional parliament favoured the prohibition, so that the Bills were adopted without any parliamentary discussion. And nobody—not even at the federal level—asked the question whether the regional declarations that the areas were not apt for CO_2 storage were compatible with the KSpG. Article 5 KSpG provided that the Federal Agency for Geological Science and Raw Materials (Bundesanstalt für Geowissenschaften und Rohstoffe) should establish the areas in Germany where CO_2 storage was possible. The Federal Ministry for Economic Affairs should then publish 'the assessment of the potential for permanent storage'.[14] This assessment had not yet been published, so that any possible contradictions between the *Land* decisions regarding the unsuitability of an area and the federal assessment of its suitability remained unresolved; de facto, the *Land* legislation prevailed.[15]

Until mid-2016, no other German *Land* legislated on CO_2 storage.

---

[12] Schleswig-Holstein Gesetz zur Regelung der CO_2-Speicherung im Untergrund, of 27 March 2014, GVBl; Schleswig-Holstein 2014, no 4, 65; Niedersächsisches Kohlendioxid-Speicherungsgesetz, of 14 July 2015, GVBl; Niedersachsen, no 10, of 21 July 2015, 130.

[13] Mecklenburg-Vorpommern, Kohlendioxid-Speicherungsausschlussgesetz, of 30 May 2012, GVBl. Mecklenburg-Vorpommern, 2012, 142.

[14] See KSpG, Art 5(5): 'Das Bundesministerium für Wirtschaft und Energie veröffentlicht die Bewertung der Potenziale für die dauerhafte Speicherung.' ('The Federal Ministry for Economic Affairs and Energy shall publish the assessment of the potential for permanent storage.').

[15] It should be noted that the *Länder* were allowed, according to Art 2(5) KSpG, to take into consideration 'other general interests', while the federal list of the Ministry of Economic Affairs and Energy was to be based on geological considerations only.

For the rest, the German KSpG largely followed the provisions of the CCS Directive; the different provisions are therefore not set out here in detail. At some points the KSpG more precisely specified the rights and obligations under the Directive. In places, the protection of health and safety, as well as of the environment, was strengthened; for example, the operator of a site may only transfer its responsibility to the public authorities after 40 years,[16] while the CCS Directive allows such a transfer after 20 years or an even shorter period.[17]

V. THE ACTUAL SITUATION AND DISCUSSION OF CCS IN GERMANY

The energy producer RWE, which had planned, in 2008, the construction of a power plant with CCS technology in Hürth (Nordrhein Westfalen), abandoned its plans in 2009, when it became aware of the strong opposition of the local population in Schleswig-Holstein, where it had planned to store the captured CO_2.

Actually, RWE is planning a new lignite-fired power plant in Niederaussem (Nordrhein-Westfalen), with a pilot project for the capture of CO_2. The energy producer EON has a pilot project on CO_2 capture running at its power plant in Staudinger (Grosskrotzenburg-Hessen). Also, in 2011, EON installed a pilot project for the capture of CO_2 in its coal-fired power plant in Wilhelmshaven (Niedersachsen); transport and storage issues were not part of the project, which was apparently ongoing in 2016.

Another large German energy producer, Vattenfall, had planned, since 2008, a commercial, lignite-fired power plant with CCS technology in Jänschwalde (Brandenburg). However, in 2011 it abandoned this plan, arguing that the legislative uncertainty in Germany did not give it sufficient planning and investment security. In 2014, Vattenfall announced that it would sell all its lignite-fired power-plants in Germany and re-orientate the company's strategy towards more environmentally friendly technologies.

In 2008, the Geoforschungszentrum Potsdam (Centre for Geological Research Potsdam, GFZ) established a pilot project for the storage of CO_2 in Ketzin (Brandenburg).[18] Over the years, about 67,000 tons of CO_2 were stored underground, at a depth of some 630 to 650 metres. The energy producer Vattenfall brought about 15,000 tonnes of CO_2 from its pilot project at the Schwarze Pumpe power plant (Brandenburg) to Ketzin, which were also stored underground. What is remarkable is that there were no demonstrations, nor was there public opposition to the Ketzin project. No accident or incident (leakage) was reported at the storage site.

The Ketzin project was brought to an end in 2013, for reasons which were not altogether clear. There is an ongoing Ketzin research project (2014 to 2017) concerning the post-injection monitoring and post-closure phases in general. Final results have not yet been made public.

---

[16] Art 30 KSpG.
[17] CCS Directive, n 1 above, Art 18(1)(b).
[18] The permit for that project had been granted under the German Bundesbergbaugesetz ('Federal Mountain Act'), of 13 August 1980, BGBl Pt I, 1310.

For the rest, discussion of CCS technology in Germany has come to an almost complete standstill since 2012. There are no public or scientific discussions on the pros and cons of the use of this technology in Germany. Probably the main reason for this is that the *Länder* Schleswig-Holstein and Niedersachsen publicly announced that, from 2012, CO_2 storage in their territories was completely prohibited, and adopted legislation to this effect. The other *Länder* were not willing to appear to be supporting such storage sites, being afraid of the public reaction to such an announcement.

VI. REASONS FOR THE GERMAN REJECTION OF CCS TECHNOLOGY

A. Public Acceptance

The public reaction in the *Länder* Schleswig-Holstein, Niedersachsen and—to a lesser extent—Brandenburg with regard to CCS technology is one link in the long post-war history of Germans protesting against industrial installations or infrastructure measures. The public reaction started with the attempt by NATO and the German Federal Government, in the late 1950s, to equip the German army with nuclear weapons, which met with considerable opposition in post-war Germany. This— initially mainly pacifistic reaction—grew to general opposition to nuclear power plants, which were planned and constructed in the 1960s and later. Protesters succeeded in preventing the construction of a nuclear power plant in Whyl (*Land* Baden-Württemberg, mid-1970s), a nuclear waste treatment plant in Wackersdorf (*Land* Bayern, 1980s), a final storage plant for nuclear waste in Gorleben (*Land* Niedersachsen, 1980–2015) and North-South German overland electricity lines to bring electricity from German offshore and onshore windfarms (Schleswig-Holstein!) to the more industrialised German South (*Land* Bayern, 2011–2015). Any construction of nuclear plants was accompanied by heavy demonstrations, which also extended to the construction of motorways, airports (Munich, Frankfurt, Berlin) or railway stations (Stuttgart 21). These protesters were mainly motivated by environmental concerns, but the churches (Catholic and Protestant), farmers' associations, academics and other groups of civil society sympathised with or even supported the protests, so that the opposition could not be declared to be anarchic, anti-capitalist or socialist.

This attitude of protest persists in present-day Germany. The Green Party, which is today the third biggest political party in Germany, is a direct emanation of these protest movements, and the German media easily side with the protesters.

It is in light of this background that the opposition against CO_2 storage plants must be interpreted.[19] The protests in Schleswig-Holstein played a leading role

---

[19] See also K Karohs, 'A sustainable technology? How citizens movements in Germany frame CCS and how this relates to sustainability' (Master's thesis, Uppsala University, 2013); K Pietzner, 'Media coverage for carbon capture and storage (CCS) projects in Germany: analysis of 1115 regional newspaper articles' (2014) 63 *Energy Procedia* 7141.

in this movement. The strategic error of RWE, to start exploring underground in Schleswig-Holstein for appropriate storage sites without informing the public or the Land government, raised considerable concerns. The slogan, 'Why should we be the waste-bin (toilet) of industrial activities which take place in Nordrhein-Westfalen, some 600 km away?' quickly found support from the Schleswig-Holstein public[20] and strengthened their general NIMBY ('Not In My Backyard') attitude. To this were added the economic and ecological arguments against CO_2 storage, which will be discussed in sections VI.B and C.

The opposition in Niedersachsen followed similar lines, though Niedersachsen had more industry, including more underground activities (geothermic development, gas extraction, etc). Both *Länder* had, according to preliminary findings by federal bodies, the largest number of sites for storing CO_2 underground. Following this orientation by Schleswig-Holstein and Niedersachsen, the *Land* Brandenburg declared that it was not ready to be the only *Land* where CO_2 was to be stored, and consequently it would also vote against the use of CCS technology in Germany. The other *Länder* kept silent, but when voting in the Second Chamber (Bundesrat), they also rejected approval of the technology. Their main reason was that they wanted to retain the power to decide on the use of CCS technology in their territories and not hand it over to the Federal Government.

The problems involved in convincing the German public to accept CCS technology are also reflected in opinion polls. In 2010, about 8 per cent of the German population favoured the further extension of renewable energy installations, while 74 per cent opposed the construction of new coal/lignite-fired power plants.

B. Environmental Reasons

The environmental arguments raised by the opponents to CO_2 were not at all limited to those that had been raised by environmental organisations or the Green Party. Reputable environmental agencies also raised doubts as regards the usefulness of CO_2 storage in Germany. The main argument was that CO_2 storage was not necessary to fight climate change. Commercially viable storage plants, it was argued, would not be available before 2025. By then, predicted increases in demand for renewable sources of energy made it more reasonable to invest in renewable energies than in coal/lignite-fired power plants. This argument is supported by scientific data: while renewable energy sources contributed 6.2 per cent to the German electricity supply in 2000, they contributed 10.2 per cent in 2005 and 17.0 per cent in 2010. By 2015, their contribution had increased to 32.6 per cent. Optimists argued that by 2050, 100 per cent of Germany's energy needs could be met with electricity sourced from renewable energies, although this included a 10–20 per cent share of imported electricity.

Furthermore, a strong argument from the environmental side in Germany related to the external costs that could be avoided by the use of renewable energies: external

---

[20] It is significant that the Schleswig-Holstein government indicated, during the CCS discussions, that its opposition to CO_2 storage might cease when the economic benefit of the whole project was realised in Schleswig-Holstein (ie, when the construction of the power plant took place in this *Land*).

costs are costs for climate change, environment and health matters, which are not included in the energy price paid by users but are paid by the taxpayer. The German Umweltbundesamt (Federal Environment Agency) estimated the following external costs in 2012 for the different energy sources:[21]

Lignite	10.7% kWh
Coal	8.9% kWh
Nuclear	(11.5–34.0% kWh)
Gas	4.9% kWh
Photovoltaic	1.2% kWh
Water	0.2% kWh
Wind	0.3% kWh

In view of this, it was argued that federal assistance should be given to renewable energy projects rather than to CCS technology projects, as CCS was already an outdated technology.

To these general climate change arguments, more basic environmental arguments were added. For example, the Federal Agency for the Environment examined the impact of CO_2 storage on groundwater, the soil, human health and safety, flora and fauna, biodiversity and the landscape in general.[22] It identified uncertainties and problems in all of these sectors. It held in particular that the long-term effects of such storage—600 or 1,000 years—were unclear, and concluded, '[t]he storage of CO_2 underground does not constitute a sustainable measure of climate protection'.

The Federal Expert Council on Environmental Issues (Sachverständigenrat für Umweltfragen) critisised the CCS Bill—which later became the KSpG—and stated:[23]

> At present, many technical, ecological and financial questions concerning CCS technology are unanswered, and it is open whether its application in Germany makes sense. The ecological risks of CO_2 storage are largely not researched. Already today there are signs of competition on using underground spaces; potential future conflicts of use, for example

---

[21] Dessau, 'Umweltbundesamt: Schätzungen der Umweltkosten in den Bereichen Energie und Verkehr' ('estimations of the environmental costs of the energy and transport sectors') (2012).

[22] Federal Agency for the Environment, 'Umweltbundesamt: Stellungnahme des UBA: Landesgesetz zum Kohlendioxid-Speicherungsgesetz erarbeiten' ('Statement on Carbon Dioxide Storage') (2013) 9.

[23] Sachverständigenrat für Umweltfragen: Abscheidung, Transport und Speicherung von Kohlendioxid. Der Gesetzentwurf der Bundesregierung im Kontext der Energiedebatte (Berlin, 2009): 'Sind derzeit noch viele technisch, ökologische und finanzielle Fragen im Zusammenhang mit der CCS-Technologie ungeklärt und es ist offen, ob ihre Anwendung in Deutschland sinnvoll ist. Die ökologischen Risiken der Lagerung von CO_2 sind weitgehend unerforscht. Konkurrenzen um die Nutzung der unterirdischen Räume zeichnen sich bereits heute ab, potenzielle zukünftige Nutzungskonflikte, etwa mit der tiefen Geothermie, können jedoch nach dem heutigen Wissensstand noch nicht hinreichend bewertet werden. Durch die Verpressung von CO_2 in unterirdische Strukturen würden aber flächenmässig grosse Bereiche für andere Nutzungen blockiert.'

with deep geothermal energy, are not able to be appropriately assessed according to the present state of science. The storage of CO_2 in underground structures would block large areas for other uses.

It also underlined that: multinational energy producers obtained underground property rights free of charge following examination of the underground area; details such as leakages had not been comprehensively dealt with; and the responsibility for damage was transferred to the state after some 30 years, which meant that the taxpayer bore the risk of any later damage.

The overall message sent to the German public—which is today, more or less the general consensus (with the exception of vested interests)—is that CO_2 storage is a technology with considerable risks and uncertainties for humans and the environment, that it is not necessary for climate change reasons and that any money spent would better be invested in renewable sources of energy. In particular, the growing conviction in Germany that electricity needs in Germany—and in Europe—by 2050 can largely, or even completely, be covered on the basis of renewable energies,[24] has reduced the interest in CCS.

C. Economic Reasons

Economically, the four big German energy producers—EON, RWE, EnBW and Vattenfall—abandoned projects for CCS between 2009 and 2011. The official arguments concerned the legislative uncertainty and the lack of acceptance of CO_2 storage by the German public. However, it is not certain that these arguments tell the full story. It became progressively clear that the investments in carbon capture would be considerable, and that up to 40 per cent more energy would be needed for the production of electricity by a plant with a CO_2 capture system. At the same time, the efficiency rate of the power plant would decrease by up to 30 per cent. Overall, electricity from coal (lignite) produced with the help of CCS might make the electricity 60–80 per cent more expensive, which made it uncompetitive with electricity produced from renewable energy sources.

Furthermore, industrial emitters for which CO_2 storage might be relevant—especially those in the steel, cement and chemical industries—did not publicly show any interest in storage projects. This is all the more remarkable as operators have the legal right—except in the three *Länder* which prohibited CO_2 storage—to obtain a permit, as long as they comply with the KSpG. The *Land* authorities do not have any discretion to refuse such an application.

In view of this, it appeared doubtful that a power plant capable of capturing, transporting and storing CO_2 would be economically viable. No official statements were ever made by any of the four big energy producers in this regard. However, it is worth noting that plants with CCS technology have not been constructed in

---

[24] See, eg, Umweltgutachten, Sachverständigenrat für Umweltfragen (Umweltgutachten, 2012) ch 1, paras 71 and 87.

Western Europe,[25] and the only plant to have received financial support from the EU[26]—the White Rose Project (UK), which received €300 million in 2014— may not proceed following the UK Government's decision in 2015 to withdraw financial support of £1 billion for its CCS competition. All this international European discussion seems to indicate that the technology for capturing CO_2 in competitive conditions is not yet available in Europe.

Irrespective of this, the public discussion in Germany indicates that CCS is profitable when generous public funding is made available. Since 2012, when the KSpG was adopted, no company has announced steps to invest in CCS technology in Germany. Even the European Commission's invitation to German energy producers to submit CCS projects in order to obtain generous EU financial support—up to €300 million per project—did not cause them to prepare and submit CCS proposals. This appears to indicate that private business does not envisage the possibility of installing profitable new coal power plants with CCS technology in Germany. This conclusion might be supported by the fact that coal-fired power plants have a lifetime of some 25 years. During periods of such length, the share of renewable energies in overall German energy consumption is likely to increase considerably, making a power plant a doubtful profitable investment.

Public opposition to CO_2 storage may thus be one reason for the decision not to invest in new CCS-equipped coal-fired power plants in Germany; another is most certainly the lack of the prospect of gaining money through such investments.

D. Policy Considerations

The political situation in Germany must be taken into consideration. In 2011, the nuclear accident in Fukushima (Japan) and the strong reaction to it in Germany caused the German Government, some five months before general German elections, to decide to stop all nuclear energy production in Germany. The *Land* government in Baden-Württemberg, where several nuclear plants were located, was less decisive and voiced its support for nuclear energy. This led to the result that in Baden-Württemberg, the governing Conservative Party, which had governed the *Land* for some 40 years, lost its majority; a prime minister from the Green Party was installed instead. In Schleswig-Holstein, the almost unanimous opposition of local political parties, including local Conservative Party groups, to CO_2 storage made the Conservative *Land* government change its initial cautious readiness to accept CO_2 storage to complete opposition, which the government then also defended during the discussions at Federal level.

---

[25] See European Commission, 'Climate action progress report, including the report on the functioning of the European carbon market and the report on the review of Directive 2009/31/EC on the geological storage of carbon dioxide' COM (2015) 576, Annex 2: 'Report on review of Directive 2009/31/EC on the geological storage of carbon dioxide'.

[26] See European Commission, 'Award Decision under the second call for proposals of the NER 300 funding programme' COM (2014) 4493.

The political assessment of the possibility to have CO_2 storage facilities installed in Germany was best expressed by the then Secretary of State for the Environment, Mr Altmeier, who publicly declared in July 2012, before the final adoption of the KSpG:[27]

> We must be realistic: against the will of the population CO_2 storage in the soil cannot be imposed. Germany is densely populated. Possibly, the technology will, in the medium term, be attractive for industrial installations. At present, I do not see political acceptance for coal or lignite-fired power plants in any Land.

There is no sign whatsoever that the political climate in Germany with regard to CO_2 storage has changed since 2012: any political party that would come out in public in favour of such storage will be most likely lose out in *Land* or federal elections. The absence of public discussions on CO_2 storage between 2012 and 2016 has also favoured the strict opposition to this technology. And the strength of the German Green Party and general 'green' positions in German policy are elements that are likely to remain stable during the coming years and decades.

The argument that coal is, worldwide, an important energy source, and will maintain that function for decades, is of no relevance in Germany. Of course, the four big German energy producers are not prevented from participating in CCS pilot, demonstration or even commercial projects in other European countries, in China, India or elsewhere. However, nobody in Germany argues that CO_2 storage in Germany should be permitted in order to increase the possibility of exporting German know-how to other countries at a later stage. There is not the slightest indication that German public authorities would consider such a strategy.

VII. CONCLUDING REMARKS

The KSpG indicated in Article 44(1) that the German Government would report, by the end of 2018, on the experience with the CCS legislation and on the experience with the implementation and application of the CCS Directive within the EU. As there is no discussion on CCS in Germany at present, it cannot be predicted what the Government will report and decide. One option might be to authorise one or more CO_2 storage projects in the German Exclusive Economic Zone. In this Zone, the competence for granting permits lies with the Federal Government, not with the *Länder*. However, up till now, no company has indicated an interest in developing CO_2 storage in the North Sea or submitted an application for a permit. Opposition against any such project in the North Sea is guaranteed. Opponents argue that there might be negative impacts on the Waddenzee, a well-protected natural habitat on the coasts of Germany, The Netherlands and Denmark. At present, no detailed exploration of appropriate storage sites in the North Sea has taken place.

---

[27] Altmeier in Saarbrücker Zeitung, of 23 July 2012: 'Wir müssen realistisch sein: Gegen den Willen der Bevölkerung ist eine Einlagerung von CO_2 im Boden nicht durchzusetzen. Deutschland ist dicht besiedelt. Die Technik ist möglicherweise mittelfristig für Industrieanlagen attraktiv. Für Steinkohle- und Braunkohlekraftwerke mit CCS-Technologie sehe ich derzeit in keinem Bundesland eine politische Akzeptanz.'

In 2010, the Federal Government published an energy strategy up to the year 2050.[28] This strategy announced:[29]

> As a first step, demonstration projects for the use of CCS and the safety of storage sites shall allow the collection of experience ... Until 2020, two of the twelve demonstration projects which are to be financially supported by the EU and which provide for a permanent storage of CO_2 shall be established in Germany. Furthermore, a storage project for industrial CO_2-emissions (for example a common project for industry-biomass-CO_2) shall be realised. The demonstration phase will the basis of an assessment for a decision on a possible commercial use of the CCS-technology.

This energy strategy of 2010 was significantly amended by the German decision in 2011 to progressively switch off all nuclear power plants. However, it was not formally amended.[30] As regards CCS, there was no follow-up whatsoever of the announcement in the 2010 strategy. Since 2011, the German Government has undertaken no initiative to have CO_2 storage plants established in Germany.

New developments might lead Germans to change their negative stance as regards CCS technology, though there is, at present, on environmental, economic and political grounds, no obvious reason why the German Government should suddenly authorise such projects. It would not find support for such an initiative from the German public, German industry and German scientific circles, which view CCS as an expensive technology that is not necessary to achieve a low-carbon economy by 2050. The likelihood is thus great that Germany will remain a country without CO_2 storage.

---

[28] Bundesregierung, 'Energiekonzept für eine umweltschonende, zuverlässige und bezahlbare Energieversorgung' ('Energy strategy for the environmentally friendly, reliable and affordable availability of energy') (September 2010).

[29] 'Zunächst sollen in Demonstrationsvorhaben Erfahrungen mit dem Einsatz von CCS und der Sicherheit von Speichern gesammelt warden ... Bis 2020 sollen auf der Basis des CCS-Gesetzes zwei der zwölf EU-weit förderfähigen Demonstrationsvorhaben mit dauerhafter Speicherung von CO_2 in Deutschland gebaut werden. Darüber hinaus soll ein Speicherprojekt für industrielle CO_2-Emissionen (z.B. ein Gemeinschaftsprojekt für Industrie-Biomasse-CO_2) errichtet werden. Die Demonstrationsphase wird als Entscheidungsgrundlage für einen möglichen kommerziellen Einsatz der CCS-Technologie evaluiert.'

[30] See, however, *Bundesministerium für Wirtschaft: Ein Strommarkt für die Energiewende* (Berlin, 2014); *die Energie der Zukunft* (Berlin, 2014); *Bundesministerium für Umwelt: Aktionsprogramm Klimaschutz 2020* (Berlin, 2014).

5
Public Participation in UK CCS Planning and Consent Procedures

MEYRIC LEWIS AND NED WESTAWAY*

I. INTRODUCTION

IN MANY RESPECTS the United Kingdom (UK) is ideally placed to promote carbon capture and storage (CCS). It has an ageing stock of coal and gas-fired power stations and, in the North Sea, a range of possible storage locations. The UK has a legally binding objective to reduce carbon emissions for the year 2050 by 80 per cent of 1990 levels.[1] The Committee on Climate Change said in October 2015 that 'CCS is very important for reducing emissions across the economy and could almost halve the cost of meeting the 2050 target'.[2]

The UK Government consulted early on CCS[3] and, at least in regulatory terms, has shown considerable foresight. The Energy Act 2008, for example, pre-empted the European Directive on geological CO_2 storage (CCS Directive).[4] Permission for new carbon capture facilities and onshore CO_2 pipelines falls within the streamlined consent procedure for nationally significant infrastructure projects under the Planning Act 2008 (Planning Act).

The Overarching National Policy Statement for Energy (EN-1), published under the Planning Act, states that 'at least 22 GW of existing electricity generating capacity will need to be replaced in the coming years, particularly to 2020'—around a quarter of the UK's current electricity generating capacity.[5] It sets out the

---

* The authors are grateful to Horatio Waller and Merrow Golden for their assistance in updating this chapter.
[1] Climate Change Act 2008, s 1.
[2] Committee on Climate Change, *Power sector scenarios for the fifth carbon budget* (Committee on Climate Change, October 2015), at www.theccc.org.uk/wp-content/uploads/2015/10/Power-sector-scenarios-for-the-fifth-carbon-budget.pdf, 6–24.
[3] Department of Energy and Climate Change (DECC), 'Towards Carbon Capture and Storage: Government Response to the Consultation' (DECC, April 2009).
[4] European Parliament and Council Directive 2009/31/EC of 23 April 2009 on geological storage of carbon dioxide and amending Council Directive 85/337/EEC, European Parliament and Council Directives 2000/60/EC, 2001/80/EC, 2004/35/EC, 2006/12/EC, 2008/1/EC and Regulation (EC) No 1013/2006 [2009] OJ L140/114 (CCS Directive).
[5] DECC, *Overarching National Policy Statement for Energy (EN-1)* (DECC, July 2011) para 3.3.7.

Government's policy to achieve this by ensuring that power stations are 'carbon capture ready' and bringing forward demonstration projects. Paragraph 3.6.5 of EN-1 notes:

> The Government is leading international efforts to develop CCS. This includes supporting the cost of four commercial scale demonstration projects at UK power stations. The intention is that each of the projects will demonstrate the full chain of CCS involving the capture, transport and storage of carbon dioxide in the UK. These demonstration projects are therefore a priority for UK energy policy.

The first consent for a 'carbon capture ready' plant was granted in the Spring of 2010. Further, development consent applications under the Planning Act for a cross-country CO_2 pipeline and a coal-fired power station fitted with CCS technology were recommended for approval in August 2015 and January 2016 respectively.

However, the future of CCS in the UK was put in considerable doubt following the surprise decision of the UK Treasury on 25 November 2015 to cancel funding for the demonstration projects. It appears that the UK no longer intends to be a pioneer of CCS technology, although the legal and planning framework is in place for the relatively early implementation of CCS if financial support can be found.

This chapter sets out the scope for public participation in the decisions on CCS under the Planning Act and Energy Act 2008 and provides a preliminary assessment of its adequacy. The chapter focuses on the position in England and Wales.[6]

At the outset it is appropriate to note that there is an inevitable tension between the urgency to implement CCS and the need to guarantee a fair, legally compliant participative role for the public in the planning process. Two past examples from within the UK are instructive. First, the promotion of waste incinerators has met powerful public opposition in the planning process. The fact that the policy was in response to pressing environmental targets—under the Landfill Directive[7]—increased rather than mitigated the difficulties experienced by local authorities in discharging their waste disposal duties. Secondly, the Government's 1994 approval of the deep-sea disposal of Shell's Brent Spar end-of-life oil storage buoy caused massive public controversy. In the face of adverse public opinion and a vigorous campaign by Greenpeace, Shell withdrew the plans and disposed of the facility onshore by recycling. Shell had undertaken a technically compliant environmental assessment of the impacts of the facility. Greenpeace was more generally concerned with the principles to be applied to the disposal of all abandoned energy facilities in the North Sea; given that Brent Spar was the first such facility to have come to the end of its operational life, it was seen to set a precedent. As the Royal Commission on Environmental Pollution later noted, good practice means not just engaging with the public on an environmental assessment, but opening up to public involvement the questions that should be addressed in any subsequent study,[8] and this had not happened in this case.

---

[6] That is the territorial extent of the Planning Act 2008 (see s 240); the provisions of the Energy Act 2008 apply to England, Wales, Scotland and Northern Ireland (see s 112).

[7] Council Directive 1999/31/EC of 26 April 1999 on the landfill of waste [1999] OJ L182/1.

[8] Royal Commission on Environmental Pollution, *Setting Environmental Standards* (Twenty First Report, Cm 4053, 1998) 8.33.

II. CCS IN THE UK PLANNING REGIME

A. Power Plants

i. The Former Regime

Until March 2010, the UK procedure for authorising power stations of over 50 MW generating capacity was by way of a consent granted by the Secretary of State under section 36 of the Electricity Act 1989, usually accompanied by a direction of deemed planning permission.[9] This process was designed to overcome some of the problems with using the ordinary, localised planning system for decisions on substantial energy infrastructure, where it was important that wider, national energy policy was fully taken into account.

The Electricity Act 1989 gave the Secretary of State a broad discretion over whether to hold a public inquiry.[10] Essentially, the Secretary of State had to ask whether the issues could only be properly assessed by holding a public inquiry. The fact that an application was highly controversial from the point of view of the general public, or that the issues involved were of great value and importance, did not of itself justify holding one.[11] The only exception was where the objection came from the relevant local planning authority. In that situation, the Secretary of State was obliged to cause a public inquiry to be held,[12] an example of a legal obligation, rather than statutory discretion, to do so.

ii. The Planning Act 2008

The Planning Act brought about a significant change. It introduced an entirely new form of statutory development consent for 'nationally significant infrastructure projects' (NSIPs). This is a single procedure, which replaces the need to obtain, amongst other things, planning permission,[13] pipeline construction authorisation[14] and consent under section 36 of the Electricity Act 1989.[15] Significantly, development consent may include consent for the compulsory acquisition of third-party land necessary for an NSIP.[16]

The construction or extension of an onshore electricity generating station with capacity of more than 50 MW is recognised as a NSIP,[17] so development consent under the Planning Act will be required for most CCS capture facilities.

The aim of the Planning Act is to avoid lengthy planning inquiries by setting out policy at a national level, in the form of a National Policy Statement (NPS), and

---

[9] Town and Country Planning Act 1990, s 90(2).
[10] Electricity Act 1989, sch 8, para 3(2).
[11] *R (Little) v Secretary of State for Trade and Industry* [2002] EWHC 3001 (Admin) [25]–[26] (Stanley Burnton J).
[12] Electricity Act 1989, sch 8, para 2(2)(a).
[13] Town and Country Planning Act 1990, s 70.
[14] Pipelines Act 1962, s 1(1).
[15] Planning Act 2008, s 33(1).
[16] ibid ss 122–134.
[17] ibid ss 14(1)(a) and 15(2).

imposing a time frame of 12 months for decision making on applications for new projects. This prevents discussion of high-level policy being an issue for debate in the decision-making process. The problem the Planning Act seeks to address in this regard is exemplified in the field of energy infrastructure by the inquiry over Sizewell B, the nuclear power station in Suffolk, which took place in the early 1980s. That inquiry lasted two years and 340 sitting days, only 30 of which addressed local issues.[18]

As enacted, the Planning Act provided for the establishment of an independent Infrastructure Planning Commission (IPC), which was to decide upon development consent for nationally NSIPs. However, the IPC was abolished by the Localism Act 2011 and the decision-making function was transferred to the Secretary of State.[19] The new procedure is that, following receipt of an application for development consent, the Secretary of State will appoint an inspector, or a panel of three to five inspectors, to examine an application. That examining authority will then make a recommendation to the Secretary of State as to the decision to be made on the application.[20]

Under the Planning Act, there are three opportunities for public participation:

(a) public consultation on draft NPSs;[21]
(b) consultation by the developer during preparation of the application to the Secretary of State; and
(c) the making of relevant representations and the subsequent submission of evidence to, or appearance at, hearings before an examining authority appointed by the Secretary of State to consider the NSIP.

The previous Coalition Government prepared draft NPSs on energy and fossil fuel-fired power stations, which include reference to carbon capture requirements. These went out to consultation between November 2009 and February 2010, and the final versions of the NPSs were published in June 2011.

iii. The Carbon Capture Readiness Regulations 2013

The Secretary of State has further control over maximising the CCS potential of power plants through the Carbon Capture Readiness (Electricity Generating Stations) Regulations 2013,[22] which regulate how orders for development consent under the Planning Act, or for consent under section 36 of the Electricity Act 1989, for the construction of combustion plants with a rated electrical output of 300 MW or more (including extensions to combustion plants that will result in, or add to, this

---

[18] House of Commons Energy and Climate Change Committee, *The proposals for national policy statements on energy, Third Report of Session 2009–10* (House of Commons Energy and Climate Change Committee, 23 March 2010) vol 1, para 1.
[19] Localism Act 2011, s 128 and sch 13.
[20] Planning Act 2008, s 61, as amended by the Localism Act 2011.
[21] ibid s 5.
[22] Carbon Capture Readiness (Electricity Generating Stations) Regulations 2013 (SI 2013/2696) (CCR Regulations).

level of output) need to be assessed. In short, the Secretary of State has no power to make a development consent order (DCO) for these projects unless he has determined whether particular conditions[23] have been satisfied in respect to the feasibility of CCS.[24] The same requirement applies to the appropriate authority with regard to a relevant section 36 consent (for a project of this scale).[25] Furthermore, if those conditions are met, and the DCO/consent is granted, it must include a requirement that suitable space be set aside for equipment to capture the CO_2 produced.

B. Pipelines

Carbon dioxide pipelines come within the Planning Act by virtue of section 14(1)(g). At present, there is no NPS to cover CO_2 pipelines. National Policy Statement EN-4[26] covers gas and oil pipelines; however, the Secretary of State's view is that 'natural gas' does not cover CO_2 but the sort of natural gas supplied to customers for energy.[27] Paragraph 1.8.2 of EN-4 sets out that the NPS 'may be useful in identifying impacts to be considered in applications for pipelines intended to transport other substances', but that is as far as it goes.

C. CO_2 Storage

There is no NPS specifically covering CO_2 storage. Since the UK is essentially contemplating long-term sequestration in the sea-bed beyond the limits of the territorial sea, which ends at 12 nautical miles from the coast,[28] CO_2 storage would fall outside the scope of both the Planning Act and normal domestic planning restrictions. The Planning Act applies to Renewable Energy Zones, but does not otherwise apply to or make provision in section 14 for future application to NSIPs outside territorial waters.

The Energy Act 2008 provides a framework for the licensing of offshore areas for CO_2 storage. The geographical scope of the regulatory framework was extended in 2011 so that it now covers onshore in England and Wales, Northern Ireland and

---

[23] Referred to as the 'CCR conditions' in the CCR Regulations and defined in reg 2(2). These conditions require suitable storage sites to be available for all expected emissions of CO_2, and that it is technically and economically feasible to both (i) retrofit the plant with the equipment necessary to capture that CO_2 and (ii) transport such captured CO_2 to the storage sites (reg 2(2)(a)–(c)).
[24] CCR Regulations, regs 3(1) and 4(1).
[25] ibid regs 5(1) and 6(1).
[26] DECC, *National Policy Statement for Gas Supply Infrastructure and Gas and Oil Pipelines (EN-4)* (DECC, July 2011).
[27] G Scott, Head of Energy Infrastructure Planning and Coal Liabilities, on behalf of the Secretary of State for Business, Energy and Industrial Strategy, 'Application for Development Consent for the Yorkshire and Humber CCS Cross Country Pipeline' (Department of Business, Energy and Industrial Strategy, Decision Letter, 11 January 2017), at infrastructure.planninginspectorate.gov.uk/wp-content/ipc/uploads/projects/EN070001/EN070001-003920-Secretary%20of%20State%20Decision%20Letter%20including%20the%20Statement%20of%20Reasons.pdf, para 4.4.
[28] Territorial Sea Act 1987, s 1.

Scotland, and in the adjacent internal waters, in addition to the territorial sea and waters in a Gas Importation and Storage Zone.[29]

The appropriate licensing authority is determined by the location of the activity in accordance with devolutionary arrangements. Following the Energy Act 2016, regulatory functions with respect to offshore oil and gas rests with the newly established Oil and Gas Authority (OGA) for the territorial sea adjacent to England, Wales and Northern Ireland. The OGA also gained the Secretary of State's regulatory powers in respect of onshore oil and gas licensing in England. Regulatory functions in respect of onshore oil and gas in Scotland, Wales and Northern Ireland, and offshore oil and gas in Scotland, reflect the devolutionary arrangements.[30]

The licensing authority may grant a licence for the storage of CO_2. The Energy Act 2008 leaves much of the detail to secondary legislation, although it anticipates that a licence will cover both financial security and provisions about closure of a storage facility.[31] The Storage of Carbon Dioxide (Licensing etc) Regulations 2010 (as amended) cover the conditions for the granting of licences and exploration permits, the operator's storage obligations, closure of the storage site, the post-closure period and financial security requirements.[32] The licence and its conditions must be made available in a public register.[33]

In addition to a licence, operators must obtain a lease from the Crown Estate in respect of the area they wish to use for offshore storage. Also, offshore CCS activities will very likely require a marine licence from the Marine Management Organisation.[34] We do not discuss these aspects further in this chapter.

D. The Carrington Decision

In April 2010, the Government granted consent under section 36 of the Electricity Act 1989 to the 1,520 MW Carrington gas power plant in Greater Manchester.[35] This was the first such consent decision to take account of CCS in light of the November 2009 guidance on 'carbon capture readiness' (CCR). The Secretary of State considered that the proposal met the CCR criteria, in particular:

— the allocation of 12.1 hectares of land was seen as sufficient space for the carbon capture plant and equipment;

---

[29] Storage of Carbon Dioxide (Amendment of the Energy Act 2008 etc) Regulations 2011 (SI 2011/2454) and Energy Act 2008 (Storage of Carbon Dioxide) (Scotland) Regulations 2011 (SSI 2011/224). As enacted, the Energy Act 2008 applied to the UK territorial sea and the Gas Importation and Storage Zones (s 1).

[30] The detailed arrangements are provided for in s 18 of the Energy Act 2008.

[31] Energy Act 2008, ss 20(3) and 21.

[32] The Storage of Carbon Dioxide (Inspections etc) Regulations 2012 (SI 2012/461) amend the Storage of Carbon Dioxide (Licensing etc) Regulations 2010 (SI 2010/2221), most notably by providing for the inspections of CO_2 storage complexes and amending a number of definitions in the 2010 Regulations.

[33] Storage of Carbon Dioxide (Licensing etc) Regulations 2010 (SI 2010/2221), reg 9.

[34] Marine and Coastal Access Act 2009, s 65.

[35] G Scott, Head of Development Consents and Planning Reform Team, DECC, on behalf of the Secretary of State for Energy and Climate Change, 'Application for consent to construct and operate a 1520MW combined cycle gas turbine generating station at Carrington, Greater Manchester' (DECC, Decision Letter, 1 April 2010), at itportal.decc.gov.uk/EIP/pages/projects/CarringtonSection36.pdf.

— the mooted post-combustion technology was adequately described, such that no significant technical barriers to retrofitting could be foreseen;
— the Morecombe South Field in the East Irish Sea was identified as a suitable storage area for the captured CO_2;
— the pipeline could be installed within the broad corridor identified without significant problems likely to preclude the route; and
— the retrofitting of carbon capture plant and operation of CCS would be potentially viable during the lifetime of the proposed development.

The opinions of the Environment Agency and departmental specialists were sought in coming to these conclusions, but no public inquiry was held. The developer of the Carrington proposal had entered into early discussions with Trafford Metropolitan Borough Council, which did not maintain an objection to the application, nor were any other objections received that would have been a consideration in deciding whether or not to hold an inquiry.

However, it is unlikely that Carrington is a useful indication of the public appetite for participation or ease of planning process for CCS projects. First, gas as a fuel for energy is far less controversial than coal, which is likely to incite more public opposition[36]—in this context, it is noteworthy that of 44 combined cycle gas turbine installations that received consent in the 1990s, only a few, if any, went to public inquiry. Secondly, the proposal did not actually involve implementing a CCS proposal. Thirdly, subsequent decisions on power stations involving CCS will be made under the streamlined procedure under the Planning Act.

E. Yorkshire-Humber Pipeline and White Rose CCS Project

The first CCS application to be considered under the Planning Act was National Grid's application for development consent for the Yorkshire and Humber Carbon Capture Transportation and Storage Cross Country Pipeline. The proposal was for approximately 72 km of onshore pipeline routed from the proposed White Rose CCS Project at Drax in North Yorkshire via a proposed multi-junction at Cambleforth to a land-fall point near Barmston in the East Riding of Yorkshire. The multi-junction was intended to facilitate the connection of multiple pipelines from other regional CO_2 emitters. The offshore elements of the scheme would be subject to a separate consenting regime under the Petroleum Act 1998 and Energy Act 2008.

A single inspector, sitting as examining authority, held a number of hearings in January and February 2015, and produced a report on 19 August 2015 recommending that consent be granted, as well as the compulsory acquisition of land.[37]

---

[36] See, eg, E Rochon et al, *False Hope: Why Carbon Capture and Storage Won't Save the Climate* (Greenpeace International, May 2008).
[37] A Mead, Examining Authority, 'Yorkshire and Humber Carbon Capture and Storage (CCS) Pipeline, Examining Authority's Report of Findings and Conclusions' (The Planning Inspectorate, 19 August 2005), at infrastructure.planninginspectorate.gov.uk/wp-content/ipc/uploads/projects/EN070001/EN070001-003913-Examining%20Authority%20Recommendation%20Report.pdf.

The examining authority noted the Government's support for CCS and considered that the Yorkshire and Humber region provided 'an excellent opportunity for a demonstration project to form the basis for a regional network, capturing large volumes of substantial emitters'.[38]

A second DCO application for a new coal-fired power plant and carbon capture facilities, called White Rose, adjacent to the existing Drax power station in Yorkshire, was considered by another single-inspector examining authority at hearings in July 2015. Again, the examining authority recommended that consent be granted. Her report of 14 January 2016 concluded that the proposed development complied with national policy.[39] It was very significant that White Rose was one of the demonstration projects supported by the NPSs:

> The innovative nature of the proposed CCS element of the generating station is supported by EN-1 ... which would accord with national energy policy to meet emission targets, whilst enabling the UK to continue to use fossil fuels as part of its generating capacity. As part of the demonstration project, there is a clear need for the project to be delivered and there are no viable alternatives to it.[40]

Paragraph 4.7.6 of EN-1 states that '[a]ny decision on a planning application for a new coal-fired generating station should be made independently of any decision on allocation of funding for CCS'. However, following the examination of the White Rose CCS Project, the Government announced that it was withdrawing *all* funding for CCS demonstration projects in the UK. This led to the refusal of consent to the White Rose NSIP on 13 April 2016. While the Secretary of State noted that there was a need for the development, consent was withheld as the applicant had insufficient funds and it was clear that no other funding was available.[41] That also fatally undermined the case for compulsory acquisition of land.

After some delay, on 11 January 2017 the Secretary of State also refused consent for the Yorkshire-Humber Pipeline, noting that EN-1 does not provide support for CCS infrastructure in isolation and that '[t]he withdrawal of the Government's £1bn funding for the CCS competition has had significant impacts on the background against which the application has been considered'.[42] In other words, without White Rose, the need case for the pipeline was significantly diminished and the applicant had not demonstrated that other CO_2 emitters would come forward to justify

---

[38] ibid para 4.0.7.
[39] E Hill, Examining Authority, 'White Rose Carbon Capture and Storage Project, Examining Authority's Report of Findings and Conclusions and Recommendation to the Secretary of State for Energy and Climate Change' (The Planning Inspectorate, 14 January 2016), at infrastructure.planninginspectorate.gov.uk/wp-content/ipc/uploads/projects/EN010048/EN010048-000817-Examining%20Authority's%20Recommendation%20Report%20and%20Recommended%20Development%20Consent%20Order.pdf.
[40] ibid para 6.2.20.
[41] G Scott, Head of National Infrastructure Consents and Coal Liabilities, on behalf of the Secretary of State for Energy and Climate Change, 'Application for Development Consent for the White Rose Carbon Capture and Storage Project' (DECC, Decision Letter, 13 April 2016), at infrastructure.planninginspectorate.gov.uk/wp-content/ipc/uploads/projects/EN010048/EN010048-000820-Secretary%20of%20State%20for%20Energy%20and%20Climate%20Change%20decision%20letter%20and%20statement%20of%20reason.pdf.
[42] Scott, Yorkshire-Humber Decision Letter, n 35 above, para 5.3.

the pipeline.[43] The applicant had sought to argue that the pipeline would provide the 'back-bone' for a future CCS network, but the Secretary of State concluded that there would be no network without the requisite funding.[44]

These decisions demonstrate on the one hand the speedy and effective examination of CCS applications and on the other the vulnerability of CCS to the vicissitudes of politics and economics. Certain further points of relevance from the decisions are discussed in the remaining sections of this chapter.

III. PUBLIC PARTICIPATION AND NATIONAL POLICY STATEMENTS

National Policy Statements are fundamental to the Planning Act. They set the basic criteria for specified types of development. Where policy is set out in an NPS, the examining authority and Secretary of State are entitled to disregard representations that relate to the merits of that policy.[45] Indeed, the Secretary of State must generally make his determination 'in accordance' with a relevant NPS.[46] The NPSs therefore represent the most significant statements of high-level national policy for some time. Their implications for guiding decisions on the scale, nature and location of NSIPs—and the consequential effects on those affected by them—are far-reaching.

A. The Energy NPSs

In November 2009, the Government drew up an initial suite of six NPSs, which underwent public consultation until 22 February 2010. Two of the NPSs are directly relevant to CCS: the Overarching National Policy Statement for Energy (EN-1)[47] and National Policy Statement for Fossil Electricity Generating Infrastructure (EN-2).[48] The NPSs give surprisingly little policy priority to particular types of energy. They conclude that 'there are benefits of having a diverse mix of all types of power generation. It means we are not dependent on any one type of generation or one source of fuel or power and so helps to ensure security of supply.'[49]

Given that the Planning Act contemplates NPSs identifying, among other things 'the amount, type or size of development ... appropriate nationally or for a specified area' and 'one or more locations ... suitable (or potentially suitable) or unsuitable for a specified description of development', the lack of specificity in EN-1 and EN-2 is perhaps surprising. It may be noted that the most controversial of the NPSs, EN-6, concerned the nuclear sector where locations for new reactors were specifically proposed.

---

[43] ibid paras 5.3, 5.9 and 5.10.
[44] ibid paras 5.8–5.10.
[45] Planning Act 2008, ss 87(3)(b), 94(8)(b) and 106(1)(b).
[46] ibid, s 104(3); but subject to exceptions specified in s 104(3)–(8) (see section IV.D).
[47] DECC, EN-1, n 5 above.
[48] DECC, *National Policy Statement for Fossil Fuel Electricity Generating Infrastructure (EN-2)* (DECC, July 2011).
[49] DECC, EN-1, n 5 above, para 3.3.4.

On CCS, EN-1 restates the policy that all new combustion plants of greater than 300 MW capacity and of a type covered by the EU's Large Combustion Plant Directive[50] must be 'carbon capture ready' (CCR).[51] Whether a proposed development is CCR is to be assessed under guidance issued in 2009 by the Department of Energy and Climate Change (DECC).[52] This guidance requires that the proposal is able to demonstrate sufficient space for carbon capture equipment, technical feasibility of retrofitting, a suitable area for storage, a feasible CO_2 transport corridor and (perhaps most problematic of all) economic feasibility of the full CCS chain covering retrofitting, transport and storage.[53] Guidance is offered by EN-1 on the form of the supporting documents for such a proposal.[54] The licensing authority should consult the Environment Agency on the technical and economic feasibility assessments.[55] Further information is provided in EN-2 on the matters that the licensing authority should take into account.

The NPSs set as a priority for CCR coal-fired generating stations, as they have the highest CO_2 emissions.[56] Thus, in addition to satisfying the CCR criteria already noted, new coal-fired stations must have CCS on at least 300 MW net (or, if smaller, all) of their proposed generating capacity from the outset.[57] Operators of fossil fuel generating stations are also under a general obligation to comply with any applicable Emission Performance Standards, outside the consents process.[58]

B. Consultation on NPSs

Before an NPS can be 'designated' by the Secretary of State, there must be public consultation in accordance with the procedure under sections 7 and 8 of the Planning Act.[59] The nature of the obligation to consult is loosely expressed: the Secretary of State must undertake 'such consultation, and arrange for such publicity, as [he] thinks appropriate'.[60] There is no obligation to consult the public generally.

This is not obviously consistent with the White Paper, *Planning for a Sustainable Future*, of May 2007, which commented on the far-reaching and authoritative nature of NPSs, then noted at paragraph 3.22 that 'the Government is committed to

---

[50] European Parliament and Council Directive 2001/80/EC of 23 October 2001 on the limitation of emissions of certain pollutants into the air from large combustion plants [2001] OJ L309/1.
[51] DECC, EN-1, n 5 above, para 4.7.10.
[52] ibid.
[53] ibid.
[54] ibid para 4.7.11–4.7.15.
[55] ibid para 4.7.16.
[56] DECC, 'The Government Response to the Consultation on the Revised Draft National Policy Statements for Energy Infrastructure' (DECC, June 2011), at www.gov.uk/government/uploads/system/uploads/attachment_data/file/47861/1945-govt-resp-consultation-on-nps.pdf, para 3.23.
[57] DECC, EN-1, n 5 above, para 4.7.5; and DECC, EN-2, n 48 above, para 2.3.6.
[58] DECC, EN-2, n 48 above.
[59] Planning Act 2008, s 5(4) and s 8(1).
[60] ibid, s 7(2).

ensuring thorough and effective consultation before policy statements are finalised and adopted'. At paragraph 3.25 the White Paper said:

> [O]nce published in draft, consultation on national policy statements should be thorough, effective, and provide opportunities for public scrutiny of and debate on government proposals. Consultation will need in particular to follow best practice, including setting out clearly the proposals on which views are sought, allowing sufficient time for responses, ensuring wide accessibility, encouraging effective stakeholder participation and ensuring that views are taken into account before final policy proposals are developed ... The aim should be to enable effective and appropriate debate on national infrastructure needs and policy.[61]

The consultation undertaken for the six initial NPSs was the subject of criticism. Some key concerns expressed were:

— that the consultation period was hurried[62] and that this was aggravated by two factors: the need to complete representations six weeks earlier in order to present them as evidence to the Parliamentary Select Committee; and the fact that many energy and climate change experts were deeply involved in the Copenhagen UNFCCC negotiations during the consultation period;
— that there was a limited number of consultation responses, far fewer than, for example, the draft South West Regional Spatial Strategy, which received around 35,000 responses;[63]
— that just six national events were held, with one hour of 'question and answer' at each;[64]
— that there was a level of predetermination and a lack of genuine consideration of reasonable alternatives in the draft NPSs.

It is vitally important—especially from the point of view of concerned members of the public—that consultation should be meaningful and effective. The national courts have shown a willingness to quash policies where consultation is unfair.[65] Consultees must be made aware of the consultation and given an opportunity to comment on the substantive material before the decision-maker at an early stage.

However, there is no such thing as a perfect consultation, and the consultation over the energy NPSs is not obviously an instance, to use the language in the *Greenpeace* case, where 'something has gone clearly and radically wrong' such as to support a challenge in the courts.[66]

---

[61] HM Government, *Planning for a Sustainable Future: White Paper* (Cm 7120, 2007) para 3.25.
[62] See House of Commons Energy and Climate Change Committee, *The proposals for national policy statements on energy*, n 18 above, oral evidence of Hugh Ellis, vol 2, ev 2.
[63] ibid, oral evidence of Fiona Howie, vol 2, ev 34.
[64] ibid, written evidence of Friends of the Earth, vol 2, ev 342, para 69(c).
[65] *R (Greenpeace Ltd) v Secretary of State for Trade and Industry* [2007] EWHC 311, [2007] Env LR 29; and *R (Medway Council) v Secretary of State for Transport, Local Government and the Regions* [2002] EWHC 2516, [2003] JPL 583.
[66] *Greenpeace* [2007] EWHC 311 [116].

In June 2011, the Government issued written responses to the consultation,[67] Parliamentary scrutiny of the drafts,[68] an impact assessment[69] and a document appraising the sustainability of the NPSs.[70] This was swiftly followed by the publication of the final NPSs in July 2011.

Interestingly, most of the consultation responses to EN-2 concerned CCS.[71] Some of the consultation responses suggested that because CCS is as yet unproven, it should not be required on fossil fuel generating stations.[72] A few respondents also suggested that it should be applied equally to gas-fired generating stations.[73] The Government's response was that the NPSs made clear that CCS is not yet proven, and on that basis the Government decided to fund four demonstration projects.[74] The only change made to the draft NPSs of direct relevance to CCS was to open the CCS demonstration funding to gas-fired stations as well as coal-fired stations.[75]

C. The Aarhus Convention

It could be argued that the nature of the consultation on the energy NPSs was not consistent with the 1998 Convention on Access to Information, Public Participation in Decision-making and Access to Justice in Environmental Matters (the Aarhus Convention).[76] The UK ratified the Convention in 2005 and it is at least highly persuasive, if not directly effective, in national law.[77] Most notably, the Convention provides that where plans or programmes are likely to have an impact on the environment, 'reasonable time-frames' should be set out for public participation[78] and there should be 'early public participation, when all options are open and effective public participation can take place'.[79] But, again, it may well be that the UK courts would have regarded the time-frames discussed in section II.B as reasonable, and the opportunity for public participation to have come early enough in the process, to have allowed interested parties to participate effectively.

---

[67] DECC, Government Response to Consultation on Revised Draft NPSs, n 56 above.

[68] DECC, 'Government's Response to Parliamentary Scrutiny of the Revised Draft National Policy Statements for Energy Infrastructure' (DECC, June 2011), at www.gov.uk/government/uploads/system/uploads/attachment_data/file/37054/2007-govt-resp-to-parl-scrutiny-draft-nsps.pdf.

[69] DECC, 'Energy National Policy Statements Impact Assessment' (DECC, 15 June 2011), at www.gov.uk/government/uploads/system/uploads/attachment_data/file/47863/1944-energy-nps-final-impact-assessment.pdf.

[70] DECC, 'Appraisals of Sustainability of energy National Policy Statements: Monitoring Strategy' (DECC, June 2011), at www.gov.uk/government/uploads/system/uploads/attachment_data/file/47865/1936-aos-monitoring-strategy-nps.pdf.

[71] DECC, Government Response to Consultation on Revised Draft NPSs, n 56 above, para 3.21.

[72] ibid para 3.22.

[73] ibid.

[74] ibid paras 3.23–3.25.

[75] ibid p 152.

[76] Convention on Access to Information, Public Participation in Decision-Making and Access to Justice in Environmental Matters (Aarhus, Denmark, 25 June 1998) 2161 UNTS 447 (Aarhus Convention).

[77] See the observations of the Court of Appeal in *Morgan v Hinton Organics (Wessex) Ltd* [2009] EWCA Civ 107, [2009] Env LR 30, [22]; contrast with R McCracken QC, 'The IPC—Challenge or Opportunity' [2009] 37 *JPL Occasional Papers* 7, note 2.

[78] Aarhus Convention, Art 6(3).

[79] ibid, Art 6(4).

D. Strategic Environmental Assessment

Strategic environmental assessment (SEA) is mandatory for 'plans and programmes' that are likely to have significant environmental effects. It now appears to be accepted that an NPS is a 'plan' within this definition, since it sets the framework for future development consent of environmental impact assessment (EIA) projects.[80] The Court of Appeal referred to the 'paradigm cases of plans and programmes which set the framework for a development consent' as including 'a national policy statement under section 5 of the Planning Act 2008',[81] and this appears to have been affirmed on appeal to the Supreme Court.[82] This approach seems compatible with the position that an NPS 'has effect ... on the decisions by the Infrastructure Planning Commission (IPC) [now the Secretary of State] on applications ... that fall within the scope of the NPSs'.[83]

Consequently, NPSs must be subject to SEA, which includes a measure of public participation.[84] Further (and in any event) under section 5(3) of the Planning Act, the Secretary of State must carry out 'an appraisal of the sustainability of the policy' before designating a statement as an NPS. The Appraisal of Sustainability for the energy NPSs purports to have been undertaken in a manner that incorporates the requirements of the SEA Directive.[85]

Strategic environmental assessment is an onerous requirement that at least for the time being continues to have the force of law in the UK. The assessment must be set out in a separate environmental report, yet operate in parallel with, and influence, the development of the plan.[86] Also, the assessment must identify and evaluate 'reasonable alternatives taking into account the objectives and the geographical scope of the plan or programme'.[87] The Appraisal of Sustainability for the energy NPSs deals

---

[80] *HS2 Action Alliance Limited v Secretary of State for Transport* [2013] EWCA Civ 920, [2013] WLR(D) 308 (*HS2 Action Alliance Limited* (CA)). See also *Encyclopedia of Planning Law and Practice* (2017), vol 4, para 2-5643.1. Interestingly, the Government had argued that an NPS should not be regarded as a 'plan or programme' under the Directive in *R (London Borough of Hillingdon) v Secretary of State for Transport* [2010] EWHC 626 (Admin), and the issue had been left unresolved by the High Court (*HS2 Action Alliance Limited* (CA) [43]).

[81] *HS2 Action Alliance* (CA) [53] (Lord Dyson MR and Richards LJ).

[82] *R (HS2 Action Alliance Limited) v Secretary of State for Transport* [2014] UKSC 3 [36]–[42], specifically [29], where reference is made to the Court of Appeal's finding on the 'paradigm case' of a statutory development plan but no mention is made of NPSs. The Supreme Court affirmed the approach in Cases C-105/09 and C-110/09 *Terre wallonne ASBL and Inter-Environnement Wallonie ASBL v Région wallonne* [2010] ECR I-5611; Case C-567/10 *Inter-Environnement Bruxelles ASBL v Région de Bruxelles- Capitale* [2012] 2 CMLR 909 and Case C-43/10 *Nomarchiaki Aftodioikisi Aitoloakarnanias v Ipourgos Perivallontos, Khorotaxias kai Dimosion Ergon* [2013] Env LR 453.

[83] DECC, EN-1, n 5 above, para 1.1.1. See also Planning Act 2008, s 104.

[84] In some circumstances an NPS might also need an appropriate assessment of the implications on a European protected site in view of that site's conservation objectives. See Conservation of Habitats and Species Regulations 2010 (SI 2010/490), reg 61 and *Encyclopedia of Planning Law and Practice* (2017), vol 4, para 2-5643.1.

[85] European Parliament and Council Directive 2001/42/EC of 27 June 2001 on the assessment of the effects of certain plans and programmes on the environment [2001] OJ L197/30 (SEA Directive); DECC, Monitoring Strategy, n 70 above, 1.1.

[86] SEA Directive, Arts 4(2) and 6(2); *Re Seaport Investments Ltd* [2007] NIQB 62, [2008] Env LR 23.

[87] SEA Directive, Art 5(1).

with this aspect bluntly by dismissing all eight alternatives as not being 'reasonable alternatives' requiring evaluation; this suggests a somewhat blinkered outlook. As WWF noted in their written representations to the Parliamentary Select Committee, '[o]nly if real alternatives had been considered, such as different technology mixes, might the process have been able to influence the direction of the NPSs'.[88] In relation to CCS, no alternatives were offered either to the CCR requirement, or to the decision to fix the obligatory carbon capture at large-scale coal-fired power stations at 300 MW.

There are clear time-limits for bringing a legal challenge to a NPS, set out in section 13 of the Planning Act. The adoption of an NPS, and the legality of the process which led to it, can only be challenged through judicial review,[89] and only once the NPS has been designated or published.[90] The claim form must be filed before the end of the period of six weeks beginning with the day after the NPS was designated or, if later, published.[91] No legal challenge was brought against the energy NPSs on grounds either that the SEA was deficient, or that there was insufficient public consultation.

E. A Dedicated NPS on CCS?

Carbon capture and storage is only a minor part of the NPSs, and it is dealt with in a generalised way. The NPS does not give a strong policy steer to the technology, and in particular it does not attempt to specify locations, technology choices or operators. This is perhaps surprising, given the need for geographical 'clustering' of capture projects, recognised, for example, in the Government's 2010 CCS strategy.[92] Public participation requirements are more pressing where a policy may predetermine a locality.[93] Also, if matters such as the appropriateness of the proposed technology, or even the desirability of CCS at all, are not debated as part of this exercise, objectors may find themselves unable to raise such questions at subsequent stages in the progression and consideration of NSIP applications.

An NPS on CCS could also explicitly set out policy for (i) pipelines, (ii) storage sites and (iii) other CO_2-emitting industries, such as cement kilns, steel works and

---

[88] See House of Commons Energy and Climate Change Committee, *The proposals for national policy statements on energy*, n 18 above, written evidence of WWF, vol 2, ev 759, para 3.15; vol 2, ev 578, para 3.13.

[89] Planning Act 2008, s 13(1)(a).

[90] *Hillingdon London Borough Council v Secretary of State for Transport* [2017] EWHC 121 (Admin), [2017] WLR(D) 54 [57].

[91] Planning Act 2008, s 13(1)(b). This provision has been strictly interpreted. See recently *Hillingdon*, n 90 above.

[92] HM Government, *Clean coal: an industrial strategy for the development of carbon capture and storage across the UK* (March 2010), at ukccsrc.ac.uk/system/files/publications/ccs-reports/DECC_Coal_154.pdf, para 2.21.

[93] See, eg, the Secretary of State's additional consultation requirements where a proposed NPS identifies one or more locations as suitable, or potentially suitable, for a specified description of development (Planning Act 2008, s 7(5) and s 8(1)).

chemical plants—all of which are not incorporated in the current NPSs. This would provide an integrated policy basis at the highest level.

Politically, it is highly unlikely that any such new NPS will be brought forward. In any event, the advice of the Parliamentary Committee should be borne in mind for any new energy NPS. That report concluded that '[i]t is clear that the Government's consultation has not gone far enough in engaging the public' and that 'for future NPSs [the Government should consider] more innovative ways, particularly with regard to Greenfield sites, in which it can engage the public in these important documents'.[94]

F. Limitations of, and Modifications to, NPSs

There is nevertheless a limitation to reliance on policy, even policy of the highest level. As it was put in *R (London Borough of Hillingdon) v Secretary of State for Transport*: 'It is a trite proposition in administrative law that no policy can be set in stone. It must be open to reconsideration in the light of changing circumstances.'[95] In *Hillingdon*, the High Court was of the view that the position on climate change, and the need to reduce aviation emissions, had changed so significantly that a policy position favouring a third runway at Heathrow Airport that did not take account of those issues was rendered challengeable.[96]

More recently, in *Thames Blue Green Economy*,[97] the Court of Appeal did not rule out a role for the public in seeking modifications to NPSs. Sales LJ held that the underlying strategic merits of a project cannot be reconsidered when the project comes for determination under section 104 of the Planning Act, because those arguments would have already been decided on through the governing NPS when it was designated. But, he continued, 'in a genuine case where new circumstances arise it would be open to a person to approach the Secretary of State to invite him to revisit the National Policy Statement'.[98] Sales LJ argued that this was the proper approach on the basis that the same procedural protections would apply to this type of reconsideration under the Planning Act.[99] A decision by the Secretary of State not to carry out a review of an NPS is challengeable.[100]

It is noteworthy in this regard that if consent is granted for a new combustion generating station, operators must submit reports on the technical aspects of its CCR to the Secretary of State. The reports must be submitted within three months of the commercial operation of the power station and every two years thereafter.[101]

---

[94] House of Commons Energy and Climate Change Committee, *The proposals for national policy statements on energy*, n 18 above, vol 1, para 120.
[95] *R (London Borough of Hillingdon) v Secretary of State for Transport* [2010] EWHC 626 (Admin), [2010] JPL 976 [51] (Carnwath LJ).
[96] ibid [94]–[97].
[97] *R (Thames Blue Green Economy Ltd) v Secretary of State for Communities and Local Government* [2015] EWCA Civ 876.
[98] ibid [14].
[99] Planning Act 2008, s 6(6)–(7), but see also s 6(8).
[100] ibid, s 13(2).
[101] DECC, EN-1, n 5 above, para 4.7.17.

Further, this links with the duty of the Secretary of State under the Energy Act 2013 to provide Parliament with yearly statements of the carbon intensity of electricity generation in the UK in relation to that year following the making of a decarbonisation order.[102] As demonstration projects develop, circumstances are likely to change again. National Policy Statement EN-2 states that it 'will be subject to review by the Secretary of State in order to ensure that it remains appropriate [for decision-making purposes]'.[103] The door is left open to future arguments—on either side—that CCS is less or more viable than the NPS may suggest, and that, as a result, for example, the 300 MW CCS requirement for coal plants should be respectively softer or stricter.

The Planning Act provides an ongoing duty on the Secretary of State to review each NPS when he considers it appropriate,[104] and the ability to suspend the jurisdiction of the examining authority to consider a relevant application until the NPS is replaced.[105] Any replacement NPS is subject to further public consultation and potential challenge as if it were a new NPS, discussed in section II.B.

IV. PUBLIC PARTICIPATION AT THE APPLICATION AND PROJECT STAGES

A. Pre-Application Consultation

The Planning Act places a considerable burden on the promoter of an NSIP to consult as part of the pre-application process. This is considered to be 'crucial to the effectiveness of the major infrastructure consenting regime',[106] which will lead to fully evolved applications that are better understood by the public and ensure that 'the important issues have been articulated and considered as far as possible in advance of submission of the application to the Secretary of State'.[107] The Government hopes that this 'allows for shorter and more efficient examinations'.[108] The Secretary of State may refuse to accept an application that does not comply with the pre-application consultation requirements.[109] The provisions in the Planning Act are bolstered by separate regulations[110] and statutory guidance produced by the Secretary of State.

---

[102] Energy Act 2013, ss 1 and 3. The Energy Act as enacted placed the Secretary of State under a duty to provide a triennial assessment of CCS technology (s 5), but this was replaced by the new reporting requirement under the Energy Act 2013 (s 1(8)).

[103] DECC, EN-2, n 48 above, para 1.6.1. See also Department for Communities and Local Government (DCLG), 'National Policy Statements' (Letter to Chief Planning Officers, DCLG, 9 November 2009) Annex, para 10.

[104] Planning Act 2008, s 6(1).

[105] ibid s 108.

[106] DCLG, *Planning Act 2008: Guidance on the pre-application process* (DCLG, March 2015) para 15.

[107] ibid.

[108] ibid.

[109] Planning Act 2008, s 55(3)(e).

[110] Infrastructure Planning (Applications: Prescribed Forms and Procedure) Regulations 2009 (SI 2009/2264) as amended (Infrastructure Planning Applications Regulations).

There are three components to pre-application public participation. First, under section 42, the applicant has a duty to consult those with an interest in the land,[111] relevant local authorities and certain official bodies prescribed by the regulations.[112] Secondly, under section 47, the applicant must prepare and publish a statement setting out how it proposes to consult 'people living in the vicinity of the land'[113]— a 'Statement of Community Consultation'—and carry out consultation in accordance with that statement.[114] Local authorities must be involved in this, and regard must be given to their responses prior to publication.[115] Thirdly, the applicant must publicise the proposed application under section 48 in local and national newspapers. The manner of this publicity is prescribed by regulations.[116] Responding to such publicity is the only direct means by which the wider and general public will be involved in the pre-application process.

The applicant must have regard to any responses generated by the processes outlined above 'when deciding whether the application that the applicant is actually to make should be in the same terms as the proposed application'.[117] This is manifested in the need for the applicant to produce a consultation report to accompany the application,[118] which sets out the responses and what account is taken of them together with a summary. An application will be accepted for examination only if the pre-application consultation requirements have been met.

Ultimately, however, the developer has control over this consultation process. Statutory guidance produced by the Department for Communities and Local Government (DCLG) provides some expectations, for example that 'an inclusive approach is needed to ensure that different groups' are involved.[119] It also advises against a 'one-size-fits-all' approach[120] and states that

> whilst consultation should be thorough and effective, there will be a variety of possible approaches to discharging the requirements, and that consultation will need to be proportionate. We understand that promoters will have their own approaches to consultation, and already have a wealth of good practice on which to draw.[121]

In practice, the Secretary of State has been reluctant to refuse to accept applications that purport to comply with pre-application consultation requirements. Further, the opportunity to challenge the adequacy of pre-application consultation is restricted— it can only be brought within six weeks of the final decision on development consent,[122] that is, after the examination process during which interested parties will have had an opportunity to restate their arguments before an examining authority. By that stage, any pre-application issues are likely to be water under the bridge,

---

[111] Planning Act 2008, s 44(1).
[112] ibid s 42(1); Infrastructure Planning Applications Regulations, reg 3 and sch 1.
[113] Planning Act 2008, s 47(1).
[114] ibid s 47(7).
[115] ibid ss 47(2) and (5).
[116] Infrastructure Planning Applications Regulations, reg 4.
[117] Planning Act 2008, s 49(2).
[118] ibid s 37(3)(c).
[119] DCLG, *Guidance on pre-application process*, n 106 above, para 54.
[120] ibid para 11.
[121] ibid para 13.
[122] Planning Act 2008, s 118(7).

either superseded by the examination process or difficult to rectify. Therefore, while pre-application consultation provides a valuable opportunity for public participation, its scope and effect largely depend upon the resources and attitude of the project promoter, and to a lesser extent local authorities.

In relation to *who* is consulted, neither the Planning Act nor the DCLG guidance gives a definition of 'the vicinity of the land', but it would appear to mean a relatively tightly drawn area. The guidance encourages applicants to consider consultation beyond 'those living in the vicinity of the land',[123] and notes that 'applicants may also wish to strengthen their case by seeking the views of other people who are not statutory consultees, but who may be significantly affected by the project'.[124] However, even if applicants are so encouraged, they are under no legal duty to extend the scope of consultation. For a CO_2 capture facility, this implies that it may not be necessary to consult those affected by the route of a related transportation pipeline or concerned about geological storage. Overall, there is an inevitable tension between the requirement for effective consultation and the promoters' interests in developing their own plans.

An interesting example of litigation on the scope of pre-application consultation under the Planning Act is *R (Gate) v Secretary of State for Transport*.[125] There, pre-application consultation for a motorway link stated that the route and road type 'will not be open for consultation or change'. In the High Court, Turner J said that 'it may seem very strange indeed that the consultation should be presented in such limited terms'.[126] However, the context in that case was that a very similar proposed development had gone through an extensive consultation process six years previously, which dealt with the proposed route and road,[127] and there was no evidence to suggest there had been any significant change in circumstances in the interim period, likely to justify a reversal of the arguments.[128] Furthermore, the Court noted the examining authority's conclusion that people had not been precluded from making arguments on the proposed route. The judge held that although in one respect the consultation process fell short of ideal, 'it is not the function of this court retrospectively to micromanage for perfection. Taken as a whole, the consultation process was a fair one and not susceptible to review.'[129] While *Gate* was a case on its own facts, it does reinforce the view that there are difficulties for those seeking to use the courts to hold applicants to account over pre-application consultation.

B. Examination of NSIPs

Once accepted, applications are examined in front of a single inspector, or a panel of three to five, in each case known as 'the examining authority'. The examining

---

[123] DCLG, *Guidance on pre-application process*, n 106 above, para 56, and see also paras 26 and 27.
[124] ibid para 26. See also para 27 encouraging applicants to consult 'widely', as 'there will be a range of national and other interest groups who could make an important contribution during consultation'.
[125] *R (Gate) v Secretary of State for Transport* [2013] EWHC 2937 (Admin).
[126] ibid [39].
[127] ibid [40]–[47].
[128] ibid [49(iv)].
[129] ibid [50].

authority has a great deal of discretion in deciding how to conduct the examination of an application.[130] However, the examining authority must hold a preliminary meeting in order to consider representations about how the application should be examined.[131] Interested parties entitled to participate in this meeting include any 'person who has made a relevant representation'.[132] This initial meeting is important, as it may be the only opportunity the parties have to meet face-to-face with the decision-maker.[133]

Following the preliminary meeting, the examination begins and may be disposed of entirely by written representations. However, that is unusual. In practice, there are two main opportunities for hearings: those in relation to 'specific issues' under section 91 of the Planning Act, and 'open-floor hearings' under section 93. A third opportunity exists under section 92, where the application involves compulsory acquisition of land.

Hearings about specific issues must be held where the examining authority considers it necessary to ensure that:

(a) there is adequate examination of the issue; or
(b) an interested party has a fair chance to put its case.[134]

Open-floor hearings are an alternative, which must be arranged if the examining authority receives notification from at least one interested party before a deadline that they wish to take part in such a hearing.[135]

Two points can be observed at this stage. First, it is essential in order to guarantee participation at hearings that members of the public—if not directly affected by a proposed NSIP—have made relevant representations at the preliminary stages of examination in order to participate. Secondly, no party has a right that particular specific issues will be examined at hearings.

Where issue-specific hearings are held, they must be held in public.[136] However, questioning is controlled, and there is strictly limited scope for cross-examination of witnesses by other parties, which is an essential part of a traditional public inquiry process. The examining authority will decide whether to allow cross-examination, and will also determine the scope of and time permitted for any such questioning.[137] There is a 'principle' that questioning should be undertaken only by the examining authority, except where it is necessary to ensure adequate testing of representations, or that a person has a fair chance to put his or her case.[138] The scope and nature of questions is very much determined by the examining authority. In practice, the examining authority has developed a practice whereby it issues written questions to the parties ahead of hearings and expects written responses. Hearings are an adjunct

---

[130] Planning Act 2008, s 87(1).
[131] ibid s 88(2); see generally s 102.
[132] ibid s 102(1)(e).
[133] McCracken QC, n 77 above, 17.
[134] Planning Act 2008, s 91(1).
[135] ibid, s 93.
[136] ibid, s 94(2).
[137] ibid, ss 94(4) and 94(7).
[138] ibid.

to the written process. Even for complex issues, they rarely last more than one or two days.

While challenging, it is fair to say that the examination process has proved to be fairly effective. The main challenge is dealing with the volume of written documentation that is produced and adequately testing other parties' cases in the limited time available. The Yorkshire-Humber Pipeline examination was heard over five days, with four issue-specific hearings spread over three separate days. The White Rose CCS Project only had a single issue-specific hearing to consider all environmental impacts. However, for both of the CCS NSIPs, reserve days for additional hearings were not used. It appears that the written materials and limited hearings sufficed, at least as far as the examining authority was concerned, to cover all material issues.

There is a clear tension between the rights of interested parties to make oral representations at hearings and the wide discretionary powers of the examining authority to control the process. This tension is policed by section 94(6) of the Planning Act, which provides that the examining authority's powers 'may not be exercised so as to deprive the person entitled of all benefit of the entitlement'. The wording is perhaps unfortunate, as it implies that the examining authority will be able to deny the parties a certain amount of the benefit.

Another tension is the need for speedy decision-making. The Planning Act requires that examinations must be completed within six months, and the examining authority must report to the Secretary of State within a further three months.[139] This is potentially problematic if unforeseen or complex technical issues arise during examination, which may be envisaged for CCS technology. The deadlines can be extended by the Secretary of State, but extensions are seldom used and are politically and administratively sensitive, as the Secretary of State must make a statement to Parliament. A further issue arises if modifications to a project are sought after the initial application or during the examination process. The expectation is that this will not be necessary, as applications should have been fully prepared in advance of submission. However, where changes are made, especially where they are or may be considered 'material', applicants are encouraged to explain the change clearly at the earliest possible opportunity, and to carry out non-statutory consultation. This may have implications for timing and timetabling. In practice, examining authorities tend to accommodate such non-statutory consultation within the examination period; the White Rose CCS Project is an example of where this was achieved. Post-DCO changes are governed by a separate process.[140]

To date there have been 118 applications made for DCOs under the Planning Act, and of those that have been determined, consent has been given to the vast majority.[141] The focus on written information and strict controls on the inquisitorial process tend to favour the granting of consent, especially for well-resourced applicants able to comply with all of the procedural requirements and provide (often voluminous) written material containing the required data and necessary responses.

---

[139] ibid, s 98.
[140] ibid, s 153 and sch 6.
[141] To date only four NSIPs have been refused consent, two of which were CCS projects, recommended for approval but refused on account of the withdrawal of funding.

C. Environmental Assessment of NSIPs

The planning arrangements for CCS cannot be divorced from the need for EIA and Habitats Regulations assessment (HRA), both stemming from obligations under European law. Initially, the UK was slow to appreciate the full impact of environmental assessment as a procedural instrument bolstering public participation.[142] It is now firmly, and memorably, settled in the UK domestic context that EIA is 'an inclusive and democratic procedure prescribed by the Directive in which the public, however misguided or wrongheaded its views may be, is given an opportunity to express its opinion on the environmental issues'.[143] At present the Government's intention on the UK's leaving the European Union appears to be to leave the basic infrastructure of environmental assessment in place, although it may be subject to modification in due course.

Carbon dioxide capture facilities of an annual capacity of 1.5 Mt or more and CO_2 pipelines with a diameter of more than 800 mm and a length of more than 40 km are subject to automatic EIA.[144] Both the Yorkshire-Humber Pipelines and the White Rose CCS Project were EIA development. Smaller facilities require EIA only where they are likely to have significant effects by virtue of their size, nature or location.[145]

The Infrastructure Planning (Environmental Impact Assessment) Regulations 2009[146] set out the procedural requirements for decisions on NSIPs. For EIA development, the decision-maker on an NSIP application must take environmental information into account in his or her decision.[147] Before starting consultation, under section 42 of the Planning Act 2008 the applicant must notify the Secretary of State that the proposal is EIA development;[148] this triggers a duty on the Secretary of State to notify consultation bodies,[149] but this does not expressly include concerned residents or other members of the public.

In fact, the EIA process under the Infrastructure Planning EIA Regulations seems oddly out of kilter with the public element of NSIP consultation. Under regulation 10, the section 47 consultation statement must state that the application is for EIA development, and set out how it is intended to consult on 'preliminary environmental information'. There is no requirement to provide copies of the full environmental statement to the public, and the statement does not have to be prepared until the time of the application to the Secretary of State. This sits uneasily with the emphasis

---

[142] See, eg, *R (Beebee) v Poole Borough Council* [1991] 2 PLR 27; *R (Rankin) v Rotherham MBC* [1990] 1 PLR 93; and *Wychavon DC v Secretary of State for the Environment* [1994] Env LR 239.
[143] *Berkeley v Secretary of State for the Environment* [2000] UKHL 36, [2001] 2 AC 603, 615 (Lord Hoffmann).
[144] European Parliament and Council Directive 2011/92/EU of 13 December 2011 on the assessment of the effects of certain public and private projects on the environment [2011] OJ L26/1 (EIA Directive), Annex I, points 16, 23 and 24.
[145] ibid, art 2(1).
[146] Infrastructure Planning (Environmental Impact Assessment) Regulations 2009 (SI 2009/2263) (Infrastructure Planning EIA Regulations).
[147] ibid reg 3.
[148] ibid reg 6.
[149] ibid reg 9. Consultation bodies are defined at reg 2.

in the Planning Act on pre-application consultation. It also raises questions as to whether the role afforded to the concerned public comes in early enough in the application process and is adequate from the point of view of effective participation in environmental decision-making, as envisaged under Article 6(4) of the EIA Directive.

A more fundamental issue is that CCS is necessarily a chain of three components: capture, transportation and storage. Particularly for the first full-scale plants, there may be questions as to the adequacy and acceptability of the transportation route and the ultimate storage facility, even if it is many miles away.

This was the complaint in relation to two liquefied natural gas terminals, in *R (Hardy) v Pembrokeshire CC*.[150] The claimants pleaded that there had not been a comprehensive EIA, as associated dredging in the harbour, construction of jetties, construction of a power station and construction of a distribution pipeline had not been considered. The claim was dismissed on procedural grounds, but it highlights the possibility of such challenges. The first question is whether the 'project' itself is properly a 'stand-alone proposal'.[151] It is well-established that a developer should not be able to avoid EIA by 'salami-slicing' what is, in reality, a single scheme into smaller components.[152] For example, in *Commission v Spain*[153] the European Court of Justice (ECJ) held that it was improper to consider a 13 km section of railway separately, given that it was part of a larger 251 km project. Even where a project is distinct, EIA requires an assessment of 'direct *and indirect* effects'.[154] In a case involving modifications to an airport's infrastructure, for example, the ECJ held that the effects of increased use were relevant to the EIA, and said:

> [I]t would be simplistic and contrary to that approach to take account, when assessing the environmental impact of a project or of its modification, only of the direct effects of the works envisaged themselves, and not of the environmental impact liable to result from the use and exploitation of the end product of those works.[155]

Any environmental impacts of storing CO_2 should at least be considered as an indirect impact of sequestration.

Carbon capture and storage therefore poses a dilemma in EIA terms. The approach in the CCS Directive and UK law, to grant development consent separately for the three elements of the CCS 'chain' of capture, transportation and storage, does not sit easily with established EIA practice. The requirement to demonstrate 'carbon capture readiness', which involves identifying a pipeline route and storage area,

---

[150] *R (Hardy) v Pembrokeshire County Council* [2005] EWHC 1872 (Admin), [2006] Env LR 16.
[151] The language used in *Bowen-West v Secretary of State for Communities and Local Government* [2012] EWCA Civ 321, [2012] Env LR 22.
[152] Case C-392/96 *Commission v Ireland* [1999] ECR I-5901; Case C-227/01 *Commission v Spain* [2004] ECR I-8253, [2005] Env LR 20.
[153] Case C-227/01 *Commission v Spain*, n 152 above.
[154] Council Directive 85/337/EEC of 27 June 1985 on the assessment of the effects of certain private and public projects on the environment [1985] OJ L175/40, Art 3 (emphasis added); and Town and Country Planning (Environmental Impact Assessment) (England and Wales) Regulations 1999 (SI 1999/293), sch 4, para 4.
[155] Case C-2/07 *Abraham v Wallonia* [2008] ECR I-1197, [2008] Env LR 32 [43].

strengthens the argument that at least some consideration should be given to potential environmental impacts from those parts when consenting to the capture facility. 'Salami slicing' the EIA into three independent assessments potentially undermines the ability to take a global or cumulative overview of environmental effects.

The approach in EN-2 envisages separate consents but states that a condition should be added to any consent that before construction can commence, the applicant should provide evidence that all necessary consents, licences and permits are in place for construction of the full CCS chain, including storage.[156] Such a requirement was recommended to be added to the White Rose CCS Project. The CCR Regulations, discussed in section II.A.iii, preclude consent unless the availability and feasibility of transportation and storage are assured. These provisions provide some reassurance. In particular, the environmental impacts of the whole chain should have been considered before work begins on any component of CCS. However, this is not a comprehensive assessment prior to a single development consent decision having regard to all impacts.

There was no attempt, as part of the White Rose CCS Project, to consider the environmental impacts of transportation and storage.[157] Nor was there any attempt as part of the Yorkshire-Humber Pipeline to consider the impacts of sequestration and storage. The exception to this was in relation to impact on habitats. The Government's nature conservation adviser, Natural England, expressed concern in the Yorkshire-Humber Pipeline examination about the division of consents. This led to the production of a 'Shadow Appropriate Assessment Report' covering the offshore elements of the scheme. Overall, the examining authority concluded that 'at this time all reasonable effort has been made in order to provide the necessary information to inform the assessment of in-combination effects of the onshore and offshore elements of the overall scheme', but that 'more detail' could be considered by the Secretary of State separately.[158] Subject to that, the UK approach to the Yorkshire applications would have involved at least four piecemeal consents: capture, onshore transportation, offshore transportation and storage.

D. The Decision on the NSIP Application

The final decision on an NSIP application must take into account, amongst other things, 'any other matters which the Secretary of State thinks are both important and relevant'.[159] The Planning Act deliberately avoids the language of 'material considerations', which have to be taken into account in the Town and Country Planning Act 1990 decision-making system.[160] Arguably, this gives the decision-maker greater

---

[156] DECC, EN-2, n 48 above, para 2.3.10.
[157] Except to the extent that a 'Greenhouse Gas Assessment' was produced, examining in broad terms the proposal's potential CO_2 emissions against Emission Performance Standards—understandably that took into account the operation of the transport and storage elements.
[158] Mead, Examining Authority's Report, n 37 above, para 5.5.5.
[159] Planning Act 2008, s 104(2)(d).
[160] Town and Country Planning Act 1990, s 70(2).

freedom to exclude otherwise material factors from the purview of its decisions, but this is yet to be tested. It would be surprising, however, if the autonomy of the decision-maker on an NSIP application could exclude what should properly be viewed as a material matter in the context of a decision, simply on the basis of his or her own subjective judgement that the matter in question was not 'important and relevant'.

As noted in section II.A, the decision on the application must be made in accordance with a relevant NPS. But there are important exceptions.[161] First, the NPS need not be followed where it would breach international or domestic obligations or duties—this would include obligations under the CCS Directive. Secondly, policies in the NPS can be ignored where the decision-maker 'is satisfied that the adverse impact of the proposed development would outweigh its benefits'.[162] This is a striking departure from the general thrust of the Act, and opens the door to successful arguments from members of the public that there may be wider disbenefits to a scheme.[163] In practice, examining authorities are unlikely to allow arguments to be made that relate to the merits of an NPS. In any event, it is clear that this balancing exercise enables the Secretary of State to weigh the NPS statement of national need against the 'particular detriments' of a specific development consent order in specific circumstances.[164]

E. Offshore Pipelines and Storage

Conspicuous by its absence is reference to public consultation or other forms of public participation in the Energy Act 2008. On the other hand, major offshore pipelines and storage sites within the scope of the CCS Directive must undergo EIA. For offshore pipelines, EIA obligations are set out in discrete regulations.[165] For CO_2 storage, regulation 6(3)(h) of the Storage of Carbon Dioxide (Licensing etc) Regulations 2010 provides that an application for a storage permit must include the information specified in the EIA Directive.

In either case, the approach appears to envisage only a minimal level of public participation. This would follow the established model for offshore oil and gas development, with relatively passive adverts in the specialised press inviting comments within a set period.

However, the offshore stage of the CCS process is likely to be controversial. The potential for CO_2 leakage, and the ethics of long-term disposal, are both complicated

---

[161] Planning Act 2008, s 104(4)–(9).
[162] ibid, s 104(7)
[163] Although an argument that s 104(7) afforded an opportunity to consider new arguments for strategic alternatives to a scheme, where that scheme was governed by a NPS which had dealt with the question of alternatives, was unsuccessful in *Thames Blue Green Economy Ltd*, n 97 above, [14] and [16].
[164] ibid [16].
[165] Offshore Petroleum Production and Pipe-lines (Assessment of Environmental Effects) Regulations 1999 (SI 1999/360) and the Offshore Petroleum Activities (Conservation of Habitats) Regulations 2001 (SI 2001/1754) as amended by the Energy Act 2008 (Consequential Modifications) (Offshore Environmental Protection) Order 2010 (SI 2010/1513).

issues on which the public may feel entitled to be properly heard. From this point of view, it is disappointing that fuller public participation—at least allowing for the examination of specific concerns, if not a broader debate[166]—is not currently accommodated.

A question will likely arise as to who is the 'public concerned' in relation to offshore seabed sites owned by the Crown. For example, the regulations for offshore pipelines set out that a notice must be published in newspapers, etc, on such occasions 'as to be likely to come to the attention of those likely to be interested in, or affected by, the relevant project'.[167] It is unclear what the scope of this obligation is for projects far from land. If tested, the courts may take a restrictive approach to the standing of interested persons in relation to offshore development.[168]

V. CONCLUSION

Clearly, including CCS technology in NPSs, highest-level policy documents with legal force, can greatly facilitate its subsequent favourable progression through the planning system. The principle of four demonstration projects was established and not open to question during the examination of the White Rose CCS Project and Yorkshire-Humber Pipeline applications. Those applications also demonstrate how a streamlined planning system can permit a measure of public participation within a tightly controlled timetable. In both cases the projects were recommended for approval with apparently few dissenting voices. It was the Government's lack of financial commitment, rather than public concerns, that undid those schemes. That said, the White Rose CCS Project and Yorkshire-Humber Pipeline applications are valuable examples of the consenting process for CO_2 capture and onshore transportation.

The abandonment of funding for CCS in the UK also means that no applications for offshore transportation and storage have been forthcoming. This means that the consenting process for the whole CCS chain in the UK remains untested. However, it appears that while the public would be consulted on the offshore elements of CCS, and a basic form of mandatory EIA would apply, there would be limited scope for public participation.

As this chapter highlights, environmental assessment is an area of difficulty. Carbon capture and storage is a novel and complex technology, with likely environmental impacts occurring at different places in the chain. To assess these impacts adequately when authorising one part of that chain poses a challenge. The UK's

---

[166] Along the lines of the national debate over genetically modified organisms of the 1990s; see discussion in C Abbot and M Lee, 'The usual suspects? Public participation under the Aarhus Convention' (2003) 66 MLR 80, 94–101.
[167] Offshore Petroleum Production and Pipe-lines (Assessment of Environmental Effects) Regulations 1999, reg 9(2A).
[168] See, eg, *R (Redcar and Cleveland BC) v Secretary of State for Business Enterprise and Regulatory Reform* [2008] EWHC 1847 (Admin). In that case, a local authority was not able to insist on the holding of an inquiry because the offshore location of a wind farm requiring s 36 consent was outside its jurisdiction.

approach, to assess the impacts separately but require all consents to be in place before works can commence, is pragmatic but somewhat artificial. Also, it only applies to capture facilities at power stations. There remains the possibility for gaps in assessment and for works on CCS projects to proceed prior to the assessment of each part of the chain. Prudent operators will seek to incorporate into EIAs and appropriate assessments at least an outline of the potential in-combination effects of the other elements of CCS.

In that regard, the more limited public participation over the offshore elements of CCS may be an issue. While the procedures are not yet tested, unless the expression of wider public opinion is appropriately accommodated in the process, there is a risk that these will give rise to similar difficulties, and could lead to the same sort of public controversy that surrounded Brent Spar.

Whether or not further experience of public participation in CCS projects is forthcoming in the UK, as this chapter shows, there are some valuable lessons that can be learned from the regulatory architecture and experience to date.

6

CCS *in the US Climate Change Policy Context*

MICHAEL B GERRARD AND JUSTIN GUNDLACH

I. INTRODUCTION

LIKE A LARGE ship, climate and energy policy in the US is turning slowly. Since the Supreme Court's 2007 *Massachusetts v EPA* decision,[1] that turn has included the direct regulation of greenhouse gases (GHGs) as pollutants, using tools provided by the Clean Air Act, as interpreted by the Environmental Protection Agency (EPA) and federal courts. But the death of the Waxman-Markey cap-and-trade bill in the Senate in 2010 signalled that climate and energy policy was about to become one of the most heavily contested partisan battlefields of the Obama Presidency. All efforts since to regulate GHG emissions and encourage a decarbonisation of the US energy and transportation sectors have been piecemeal, almost wholly unsupported by new legislation, and subject to aggressive litigation.

Nascent carbon capture, sequestration and utilisation (CCS/U) technologies have garnered support from both sides of this politicised fight. Proponents of action to address climate change view CCS/U as a potentially important means of preventing catastrophic climate disruptions during a transition away from fossil fuels. Proponents of maintaining rather than shuttering fossil-fuelled (and especially coal-fired) electricity generation capacity view CCS/U as a way to make that capacity compatible with looming GHG emissions controls. As the technologies' operational and financial profiles come into focus, these opposing parties' current agreement that CCS/U should be developed and deployed will almost certainly be accompanied by disagreement over how regulations should guide that deployment.

Following a short summary of CCS/U technologies, this chapter discusses the current state of US climate policy and of regulations that pertain to CCS/U. It then also considers CCS/U technologies in the context of climate policy circa 2030, with an eye to achieving substantial decarbonisation of the US economy by 2050.

---

[1] *Massachusetts v EPA*, 549 US 497 (2007).

II. CCS/U TECHNOLOGIES

Documents describing climate and energy policy often refer to CCS/U as an integrated suite of tools, but it would be more accurate to describe it as a set of discrete technologies and techniques that *could* be integrated, and that relate to carbon dioxide (CO_2) capture, transport, storage and utilisation. Each of these categories is at a different stage of development and deployment.

Capture technologies can usefully be subdivided into three categories: pre-combustion, post-combustion, and post-combustion with oxyfuel. All three of these consume energy, resulting in an 'energy penalty' that varies with fuel stock and plant design but generally amounts to at least 10–30 per cent of the power generated.[2] They also require significantly more water than facilities without carbon capture capability.[3] Pre-combustion capture extracts hydrogen from a fuel stock like coal or natural gas, then derives energy from the combustion of the hydrogen and compresses rather than combusting the other component gases for transport, storage or utilisation. Only custom-built (rather than retro-fitted) facilities could perform this process, which is still being developed and refined.[4] Post-combustion capture, which entails the extraction of CO_2 from the gases exhausted by a fossil-fuelled boiler before they enter a flue, is performed already for various purposes, notably including injection into deep wells for enhanced oil and gas recovery (EOR/EGR),[5] and can be performed by equipment added to retrofitted power plants or industrial facilities.[6] Adding an oxyfuel element to post-combustion capture entails the extraction of nitrogen from air fed *into* the boiler, which facilitates extraction of CO_2—as well as other pollutants—from gas exhausted by the boiler during combustion. Like standard post-combustion capture, the equipment required for an oxyfuel process can be added to existing facilities through retrofit.[7]

---

[2] US Congressional Budget Office, 'Federal Efforts to Reduce the Cost of Capturing and Storing Carbon Dioxide' (Washington, DC, Congressional Budget Office, 2012) 2 (reporting energy penalty range of 15–30%); S Vasudevan et al, 'Energy penalty estimates for CO_2 capture: Comparison between fuel types and capture-combustion modes' (2016) 103 *Energy* 709, 712–14.

[3] K Gerdes and C Nichols, 'Water requirements for existing and emerging thermoelectric plant technologies' (Morgantown, WV, US Department of Energy National Energy Technology Laboratory, 2009) (estimating 41–96% more water use follows from addition of carbon capture process to various facility and fuel types); H Zhai, ES Rubin and PL Versteeg, 'Water Use at Pulverized Coal Power Plants with Post-combustion Carbon Capture and Storage' (2011) 45 *Environmental Science & Technology* 2479, 2481 (estimating that supercritical pulverized coal power plant would withdraw 80% more water and consume 86% more water with an amine-based post-combustion carbon capture system installed). The increase in water usage varies by technology: ibid 2482 (noting that addition of carbon capture to dry cooling plant makes for more extreme jump in relative water withdrawals and consumption).

[4] P Folger, *Carbon Capture: A Technology Assessment* (Washington, DC, Congressional Research Service, 2014) 13–14.

[5] See Carbon Capture & Sequestration Technologies @ MIT, 'Commercial EOR Projects using Anthropogenic Carbon Dioxide' (September 2016), at sequestration.mit.edu/tools/projects/index_eor.html (listing commercial EOR projects). See also generally US National Energy Technology Laboratory, 'Carbon Dioxide Enhanced Oil Recovery' (US National Energy Technology Laboratory, March 2010).

[6] C Fu and T Gundersen, 'Carbon Capture and Storage in the Power Industry: Challenges and Opportunities' (2012) 16 *Energy Procedia* 1806, 1807–08.

[7] ibid 1808.

Transport of extracted, purified and compressed CO_2 is a fully mature technology that would be more widely deployed if more commercial applications required it.[8] In 2005, the Intergovernmental Panel on Climate Change's Special Report on CCS stated that '[t]he transport of CO_2 by pipeline has been practiced for over 25 years'.[9] Because CO_2, whether in gas or compressed, liquefied form, behaves like other substances routinely transported via pipeline, truck, train and tanker ship, few—if any—research and development (R&D) or demonstration projects are necessary to prove that CO_2 transport is technically and commercially viable.[10]

Several approaches to sequestration of CO_2 have been demonstrated, but none has been deployed on a large scale. One, called 'mineral carbonation' or 'mineralisation', turns carbon injected into basalt formations into a solid.[11] Others entail injection of CO_2 in a 'supercritical' or pressurised, semi-fluid state into one of three types of stable geologic formation: depleted oil or gas formations, unmineable coal seams or saline aquifers.[12] These approaches can be employed in onshore and offshore sequestration reservoirs,[13] though offshore locations present additional technical challenges, such as deep-water site characterisation and the development of infrastructure to connect onshore sources to offshore injection sites.[14] For all of these, successful CO_2 sequestration requires thorough site characterisation and injection, as well as monitoring, verification and accounting (MVA) of the reservoir's integrity and continued capacity to contain the sequestered CO_2.[15] Current

---

[8] N Jain, A Srivastava and TN Singh, 'Carbon Capture, Transport and Geologic Storage: A Brief Introduction' in V Vishal and TN Singh (eds), *Geologic Carbon Sequestration* (Cham, Springer International, 2016) 3, 10.

[9] R Doctor and others, 'Transport of CO_2' in B Metz et al (eds), *IPCC Special Report on Carbon Dioxide Capture and Storage* (Cambridge, Cambridge University Press, 2005) 189.

[10] ibid 181.

[11] JM Matter et al, 'Rapid carbon mineralization for permanent disposal of anthropogenic carbon dioxide emissions' (2016) 352 *Science* 1312, 1312–14.

[12] See National Energy Technology Laboratory and US Department of Energy, Carbon Storage Atlas 5th edn (US Department of Energy, 2015) (collecting characterisations of different types of potential sequestration sites). See also Energy Independence and Security Act of 2007, § 702(a) (instructing Department of Energy to coordinate conduct of 'geologic sequestration tests ... in a variety of candidate geologic settings', including 'operating oil and gas fields, depleted oil and gas fields, unmineable coal seams, deep saline formations, deep geologic systems that may be used as engineered reservoirs to extract economical quantities of heat from geothermal resources of low permeability or porosity, and deep geologic systems containing basalt formations').

[13] The Sleipner CO_2 Storage Project, eg, located in the middle of the North Sea between Norway and Scotland, is the world's first commercial sequestration project. It injects some of the CO_2 separated from an adjacent natural gas extraction operation in a deep saline aquifer situated in a large sandstone formation, and thereby enables Norway's Statoil to avoid paying a carbon tax on that operation. Seismic monitoring has not detected leakage. Carbon Capture & Sequestration Technologies @ MIT, 'Sleipner Fact Sheet: Carbon Dioxide Capture and Storage Project' (September 2016), at sequestration.mit.edu/tools/projects/sleipner.html.

[14] Offshore Storage Technologies Task Force, 'Technical Barriers and R&D Opportunities for Offshore, Sub-Seabed Geologic Storage of Carbon Dioxide' (Final Report, Offshore Storage Technologies Task Force, 2015) ii.

[15] The use of MVA instead of the conventional MMV—for monitoring, measurement and verification—is indicative of the critical importance of tools that keep an account of stored CO_2, because the regulatory regime generally expected to give rise to a robust deployment of CCS/U technologies will result chiefly from the assignment of a price to units of CO_2. US National Energy Technology Laboratory, 'Best Practices for Monitoring, Verification, and Accounting of CO_2 Stored in Deep Geologic Formations—2012 Update' (US Department of Energy, 2012) 13–14.

sequestration research focuses less on injection, which can be accomplished with technologies used for EOR by the oil and gas sector, than on site characterisation and MVA technologies and techniques.[16]

Utilisation is both newer and more wide-ranging than the other categories of technologies and techniques discussed here. Candidates being explored for commercial CO_2 utilisation include: CO_2-intensive cement curing; infusion into polycarbonate plastics; mineralisation for use as construction materials; use as a chemical feedstock, including for fertilisers; and use in cultivation of algae for biofuels.[17]

III. THE CURRENT CLIMATE POLICY CONTEXT AND CCS/U

Climate policy in the US is currently inchoate. It comprises almost no purpose-built federal legislation, a growing raft of federal regulations and executive orders, and a diverse list of state laws and local ordinances. It does not assign a nationwide price to CO_2 emissions, and the prices currently set by auctions for such emissions at the regional and State levels ($4.54 per ton in the northeast[18] and $12.73 per ton in California[19]) are far below the $36 amount prescribed by US Government's estimate for the Social Cost of Carbon—the amount of climate-related damage attributable to each unit of anthropogenic GHGs emitted into the atmosphere.[20] This section reviews these climate-related authorities, laws and regulations that touch CCS/U, and the legal and political processes involved in siting sequestration reservoirs onshore or offshore. It then discusses implications of the current climate policy context for CCS/U's development and deployment.

---

[16] Site characterization: J Litynski et al, 'US DOE's R&D Program to Develop Infrastructure for Carbon Storage: Overview of the Regional Carbon Sequestration Partnerships and other R&D Field Projects' (2013) 37 *Energy Procedia* 6527. See also, eg, HK Hvidevold, 'Layout of CCS monitoring infrastructure with highest probability of detecting a footprint of a CO_2 leak in a varying marine environment' (2015) 37 *International Journal of Greenhouse Gas Control* 274. MVA: National Energy Technology Laboratory, 'Best Practices for Monitoring, Verification, and Accounting of CO_2 Stored in Deep Geologic Formations 2012 Update' (DOE/NETL-2012/1568) (National Energy Technology Laboratory, 2012). See also, eg, R Esser et al, 'MVA Activities: SWP Farnsworth Unit Project' (National Energy Technology Laboratory, 2015), at www.netl.doe.gov/File%20Library/Events/2015/carbon%20storage/proceedings/Esser-poster.pdf.

[17] See RM Cuéllar-Franca and A Azapagic, 'Carbon capture, storage and utilisation technologies: A critical analysis and comparison of their life cycle environmental impacts' (2015) 9 *Journal of CO_2 Utilization* 82, 87; X Lim, 'How to Make the Most of Carbon Dioxide' (2015) 526 *Nature* 628; TE Müller et al, 'Opportunities for Utilizing and Recycling CO_2,' in W Kuckshinrichs and J-F Hake (eds), *Carbon Capture, Storage and Use* (Cham, Springer International, 2015) 67.

[18] Regional Greenhouse Gas Initiative (RGGI), 'CO_2 Auctions, Tracking and Offsets', at rggi.org/market/co_2_auctions/results (listing results of 7 September 2016 auction for allowances for qualifying facilities located in participating States: Connecticut, Delaware, Maine, Maryland, Massachusetts, New Hampshire, New York, Rhode Island and Vermont).

[19] California Air Resources Board, 'California Cap-and-Trade Program, Summary of Joint Auction Settlement Prices and Results' (August 2016), at www.arb.ca.gov/cc/capandtrade/auction/results_summary.pdf.

[20] US Interagency Working Group on Social Cost of Carbon, 'Technical Support Document: Technical Update of the Social Cost of Carbon for Regulatory Impact Analysis Under Executive Order 12866' (US Interagency Working Group on Social Cost of Carbon, May 2013, revised 2015). The $36 estimate is the average result of three climate models for 2015, assuming a 3% discount rate: ibid 3.

A. US Climate Policy

Federal statutes generally omit any mention of climate change, much less prescribe measures to address it. One exception to that rule, the FY2008 Consolidated Appropriations Act, illustrates how modest such exceptions are: it appropriates funds to the EPA to gather data for inclusion in a US GHG emissions inventory.[21] At present, no federal statute calls expressly and directly for restrictions on GHG emissions from mobile or stationary sources. All federal authority to impose such restrictions rests on the Clean Air Act, which was passed in 1970 and amended in 1977 and 1990.[22] Regulations implementing Clean Air Act requirements with respect to GHGs have been politically contentious and subjected to aggressive litigation,[23] and their incremental accumulation has yielded a patchwork of source- and sector-specific rules rather than an integrated, economy-wide approach.[24]

Other federal components of US climate policy all address it indirectly or via the activities of federal agencies and their contractors. Those components include: renewable energy facility tax preferences scheduled to terminate in 2020 or 2022;[25] funding for research, development and demonstration (RD&D) projects relating to renewables, the electric grid and energy efficiency, amongst others;[26] and a stack of executive orders directing, for instance, that sea level rise and other climate change-related factors be incorporated into the flood insurance rate maps that define for legal purposes what is and is not a flood plain.[27]

---

[21] Consolidated Appropriations Act, 2008, Pub L No 110–161, tit II, 121 Stat 1844, 2128 (27 December 2007).

[22] Clean Air Act, 42 USC §§ 7401–7515.

[23] See, eg, AM Wyatt, 'Clean Power Plan: Legal Background and Pending Litigation in West Virginia v EPA' (Washington, DC, Congressional Research Service, 2016) 1 ('The CPP has been one of the more singularly controversial environmental regulations ever promulgated,' and the controversy surrounding the Rule is reflected in the enormous multi-party litigation over the Rule in the [DC Circuit]').

[24] Listed in chronological order: EPA, Mandatory Reporting of Greenhouse Gases, 74 Fed Reg 56260 (30 October 2009) (citing Clean Air Act § 307(d)), codified at 40 CFR pt 98; EPA & National Transportation Highway Safety Administration, Light-Duty Vehicle Greenhouse Gas Emission Standards and Corporate Average Fuel Economy Standards; Final Rule, 75 Fed Reg 25324 (7 May 2010); EPA, Prevention of Significant Deterioration and Title V Greenhouse Gas Tailoring Rule, 75 Fed Reg 31514 (3 June 2010); EPA, Standards of Performance for Greenhouse Gas Emissions From New, Modified, and Reconstructed Stationary Sources: Electric Utility Generating Units, 80 Fed Reg 64509 (23 October 2015); EPA, Carbon Pollution Emission Guidelines for Existing Stationary Sources: Electric Utility Generating Units, 80 Fed Reg 205 (23 October 2015); EPA, Oil and Natural Gas Sector: Emission Standards for New, Reconstructed, and Modified Sources, 81 Fed Reg 35823 (3 June 2016); EPA, Finding That Greenhouse Gas Emissions From Aircraft Cause or Contribute to Air Pollution That May Reasonably Be Anticipated To Endanger Public Health and Welfare, 81 Fed Reg 54422 (15 August 2016).

[25] IRC §§ 45 (production tax credit), 48(a) (investment tax credit).

[26] See generally F Sissine, 'Renewable Energy R&D Funding History: A Comparison with Funding for Nuclear Energy, Fossil Energy, and Energy Efficiency R&D' (Washington DC, Congressional Research Service, 2014).

[27] Exec Order No 13, 693, Federal Leadership on Climate Change and Environmental Sustainability, 80 Fed Reg 15871 (19 March 2015); Exec Order No 13690, Establishing a Federal Flood Risk Management Standard and a Process for Further Soliciting and Considering Stakeholder Input, 80 Fed Reg 6425 (30 January 2015); Exec Order No 13677, Climate-Resilient International Development, 79 Fed Reg 58229 (26 September 2014); Exec Order No 13653, Preparing the United States for the Impacts of Climate Change, 78 Fed Reg 66817 (6 November 2013); Exec Order No 13514, Federal Leadership in Environmental, Energy, and Economic Performance, 74 Fed Reg 52117 (8 October 2009).

Some State laws address climate change more directly and comprehensively than do federal laws. California has been a longtime leader in this regard, first enacting a suite of legislative measures in 2006.[28] Other States, including but not limited to the nine members of the Regional Greenhouse Gas Initiative,[29] have adopted climate policy measures that constrain the emissions intensity of their corners of the electric grid.[30] However, given the inherently inter-State nature of the energy and transportation sectors,[31] these efforts must navigate the constraints of the US Constitution's (dormant) Commerce Clause and Supremacy Clause.[32]

B. Laws Addressing CCS/U Activities and Facilities

This sub-section describes two categories of laws: the first (and more complex) is regulatory; the second relates to support for RD&D of CCS/U technologies. As the following short summaries reflect, with the notable exception of EPA's regulation of new or modified coal-fired power plants, existing federal and State laws that regulate carbon capture, transport and sequestration are geared toward EOR activities.[33] Carbon utilisation is not the focus of any federal or State laws or regulations.

i. Regulations and Carbon Capture

The EPA's new source performance standard (NSPS) for new or modified coal-fired power plants sets GHG emissions limits at 1,400 pounds of CO_2 per megawatt-hour, and thereby requires plants either to co-fire with natural gas or to employ at least partial capture technology.[34] This NSPS sets the floor below which States' decisions

---

[28] Global Warming Solutions Act of 2006 ('AB 32'), 2006 Cal Stat c 488, codified at Cal Health & Safety Code §§ 38530–99. See also California Air Resources Board, 'First Update to the Climate Change Scoping Plan' (May 2014).

[29] The statutes and regulations authorising RGGI participation are as follows: Conn Gen Stat § 22a-200c (Connecticut); 7 Del Code § 6043 (Delaware); 38 Me Stat ch 3–B (Maine); Md Code Ann §§ 1-101, 1-404, 2-103, and 2-1002(g) (Maryland); MGL c 21A, § 22 (Massachusetts); NH Stat §§ 125-O20-29p (New Hampshire); 21 NYCRR pt 507 (New York); RI Gen Laws § 42-17.1-2(19), § 23-23 and § 23-82 (as amended) (Rhode Island); 30 VSA § 255 (Vermont).

[30] Wash Admin Code c 173-442 (15 September 2016) (imposing cap on GHG emissions from large emitters and requiring average annual reductions of 1.7% by 2020 from the 2011–16 baseline period).

[31] Hawaii and Alaska are geographic exceptions to this general characterisation; Texas, which is home to ERCOT, an exclusively intra-State electricity transmission grid and wholesale marketplace, is an institutional exception with respect to electricity.

[32] See, eg, *North Dakota v Heydinger*, No 14–2156, 2016 WL 3343639 (8th Cir, 15 June 2016) (explaining affirmation of lower court's decision to strike down Minnesota's 2007 Next Generation Energy Act on three grounds: violation of dormant Commerce Clause, pre-emption by Federal Power Act and pre-emption by Clean Air Act). See also S Ferrey, 'Carbon Outlasts the Law: States Walk the Constitutional Line' (2014) 41 *Boston College Environmental Affairs Law Review* 309 (summarising Commerce Clause in context at 313–19, and pre-emption by the Federal Power Act at 336–41).

[33] See PM Marston and PA Moore, 'From EOR to CCS: the Evolving Legal and Regulatory Framework for Carbon Capture and Storage' (2008) 29 *Energy Law Journal* 421.

[34] EPA, Final Carbon Pollution Standards for New, Modified and Reconstructed Power Plants, 80 Fed Reg 64510, 64529–43 (23 October 2015), codified at 40 CFR pts 60, 70, 71. See also EPA, Reconsideration of Standards of Performance for Greenhouse Gas Emissions From New, Modified, and Reconstructed Stationary Sources: Electric Utility Generating Units, 81 Fed Reg 27442 (6 May 2016) (denying five requests for reconsideration of the NSPS). This regulation has been challenged in ongoing litigation. *North Dakota v EPA*, Case No 15–1381 (DC Circuit, 13 October 2016).

about air pollution control technologies cannot go.[35] (Although carbon capture has been considered multiple times as a pollution control technology to potentially install in a new or modified power plant, it has never yet been adopted as a means of complying with EPA regulations.[36])

This requirement is especially significant because power plant developers typically recoup their costs from electricity ratepayers only after a public utility commission authorises it, and a commission only authorises recoupment of 'just and reasonable' costs that developers 'prudently' incur to provide ratepayers with safe and reliable electricity services.[37] Can it be just, reasonable and prudent to incur the costs of adding carbon capture to a facility at present, given the state of the technology? To date, even though the EPA has characterised the technology as 'adequately demonstrated',[38] State authorities have said no. Specifically, Mississippi's Supreme Court and public service commissions in Virginia and West Virginia have rejected proposals that ratepayers should cover the costs of developing various carbon capture technologies. The Mississippi Court did so on the grounds that the Mississippi Public Service Commission had provided insufficient evidence to support prudent authorisation of cost recovery from shareholders for 'construction of a new power generation facility that would employ a new technology not in operation anywhere else in the United States'.[39] Similarly, the Virginia and West Virginia Commissions objected to ratepayers paying for research, development and demonstration of a new technology.[40] The Virginia Commission also specifically rejected the argument that the project would be a prudent means of complying with *future* emissions regulations: 'The legal necessity of, and the capability of, cost-effective [CCS] in in this particular IGCC Plant, at this time, has not been sufficiently established to render APCo's Application reasonable or prudent.'[41] Notably, however, West

---

[35] Clean Air Act §§ 111(a)(1) (defining 'standard of performance'), (b)(1) (directing EPA to promulgate such standards for new or modified stationary sources).

[36] Those instances of considering whether to incorporate carbon capture technology have all occurred in the context of determining the best available control technology (BACT) for a power plant—a requirement of the Clean Air Act's New Source Review program, which governs new or modified sources of GHG emissions in areas currently in compliance with national ambient air quality standards (NAAQSs). BACT determinations arrive at prescribed technologies on a case-by-case basis. See WB Jacobs, 'Carbon Capture and Sequestration' in M Gerrard and J Freeman (eds), *Global Climate Change and US Law* 2nd edn (Chicago, IL, American Bar Association, 2014) 581, 586–87.

[37] See S Hempling, *Regulating Public Utility Performance* (Chicago, IL, American Bar Association, 2013), 219–34 (describing how 'just and reasonable' requirement is applied), 235–42 (describing prudence principles).

[38] 80 Fed Reg 64529–43.

[39] *Sierra Club v Mississippi Pub Serv Comm'n*, 82 So 3d 618, 618 (Miss 2012).

[40] W Va Pub Serv Comm'n, Case No 10-0699-E-42T Appalachian Power Co, 46 (30 March 2011) (deciding, 'given the "pilot project" nature of the CCS project to date', to 'exclude amounts booked in Account 103, "Experimental Electric Plant" from rate base', and explaining that '[w]e consider the project as a continuing preliminary investigation. In the future, we may consider it as used and useful plant in service and include it in rate base'); Va State Corp Comm'n, Case No PUE-2009-00030, Appalachian Power Co, 20–21 (15 July 2010) (final order) (rejecting proposal that ratepayers rather than shareholders should pay for a 'validation' project intended to 'test' a new technology); Va State Corp Comm'n, Case No PUE-2007-00068, Appalachian Power Co, 2–3 (14 April 2008).

[41] Va State Corp Comm'n, Case No PUE-2009-00030, 16.

Virginia's Commission, guided by a State law that encourages development of CCS, bucked this trend, granting conditional approval of a proposal for the Mountaineer IGCC Project in 2008 (the condition was that the American Electric Power 'pursue all reasonable and prudent tax credits and other incentives available to reduce the impact of the project costs to APCo's customers').[42] The Project never launched, however, because its financing also required approval from the Virginia State Corporation Commission, which rejected it.[43] Thus, at present, plans for new coal-fired power plants are caught between the EPA's NSPS requiring use of capture technology for new plants and State public service commissions' obligation to be sceptical on behalf of ratepayers of carbon capture's legal necessity and commercial viability. The significance of this impasse is reduced, however, by the fact that almost no new coal-fired power plants are planned in the US, due largely to the low cost of natural gas.

The other important category of regulations pertaining to carbon capture processes are those that govern the use and disposal of hazardous materials involved in separating the CO_2 from other flue gases, such as amines.[44] This aspect of capture's governance is much the same as a host of other industrial processes involving hazardous chemicals.

ii. Carbon Transport Regulations

The Federal Energy Regulatory Commission, the Surface Transportation Board and the Office of Pipeline Safety in the Department of Transportation's Pipeline and Hazardous Materials Safety Administration (PHSMA) regulate the siting, economics and safety of various types of inter-State pipelines in the US,[45] but only PHSMA, operating pursuant to the Pipeline Safety Reauthorization Act of 1988,[46] exercises

---

[42] W Va Pub Serv Comm'n, Case No 06-0033-E-CN, Appalachian Power Co, 2, 65–66 (6 March 2008). The Commission explained that 'State legislative policy, as set forth in specific statutory provisions relating to the Commission, directs the Commission to "[e]ncourage the well-planned development of utility resources in a manner consistent with state needs and in ways consistent with the productive use of the State's energy resources, such as coal" (W Va Code 524-1-1) and encourages the Commission to "authorize rate-making allowances for electric utility investment in clean coal and clean air technology facilities," (W Va Code 524-2-1 g)'.

[43] Va State Corp Comm'n, Case No PUE-2009-00030, 20–21 ('APCo and its customers are being asked to shoulder the entire financial burden and risk associated with AEP's [CCS] research and development').

[44] See GT Rochelle, 'Amine scrubbing for CO_2 capture' (2009) 325 *Science* 1652 (describing history of use of amine scrubbers to separate CO_2 from other flue gases).

[45] See generally BJ Murrill, 'Pipeline Transportation of Natural Gas and Crude Oil: Federal and State Regulatory Authority' (Washington, DC, Congressional Research Service, 2016) (describing laws and regulations pertinent to pipeline siting, construction, operation and safety).

[46] Pub L No 100–561, 102 Stat 2805 (31 October 1988), codified at 49 USC § 60102(i). Other sources of PHSMA's authority include the Hazardous Liquid Pipeline Act of 1979 and Hazardous Materials Transportation Act of 1975. Hazardous Materials Transportation Act of 1975, 40 USC §§ 5101-27; 40 CFR pts 171–180; Hazardous Liquid Pipeline Act of 1979, as amended, 49 USC §§ 60101-301; PHSMA, Transportation of Carbon Dioxide by Pipeline; Final Rule, 56 Fed Reg 26922, 26923 (12 June 1991), codified at 49 CFR pt 195.

federal regulatory authority over those that carry CO_2.[47] Its regulations pertaining to hazardous materials classify CO_2 as a 'non-flammable, non-corrosive gas'.[48] States regulate intra-State pipeline safety.[49] Agencies in several States—all home to oil and gas operations that use EOR—have issued regulations addressing aspects of CO_2 pipeline siting, construction and operation as well.[50]

iii. Carbon Sequestration Regulations

The EPA has issued regulations pursuant to the Safe Drinking Water Act specifying safety standards for CO_2 injection and sequestration,[51] and has, pursuant to the Clean Air Act, issued GHG emissions reporting requirements for injection activities and sequestration sites.[52] The EPA has also excluded (conditionally) CO_2 injected for sequestration purposes from the Resource Conservation and Recovery Act.[53]

State law generally defines property rights and governs liability arising from property ownership. Thus it is State law that answers questions about acquisition, possession and use of the deep saline aquifers and pore space capable of storing CO_2, as well as about who owns and is liable for the effects of injected CO_2, and

---

[47] FERC and the Surface Transportation Board (which assumed the role of the Interstate Commerce Commission pursuant to the ICC Termination Act of 1995, Pub L No 104–88, 109 Stat 803 (1995)) have both disclaimed jurisdiction over rate-setting and construction for pipelines carrying CO_2. Cortez Pipeline Co, 7 FERC ¶ 61,024 (1979) (Natural Gas Act provides no authority over CO_2 pipelines); Cortez Pipeline Co, Petition for Declaratory Order: Commission Jurisdiction over Transportation of Carbon Dioxide by Pipeline, 45 Fed Reg 85177 (24 December 1980); Cortez Pipeline Co, Petition for Declaratory Order: Commission Jurisdiction over Transportation of Carbon Dioxide by Pipeline, 46 Fed Reg 18805 (26 March 1981). See also PW Parfomak and P Folger, 'Carbon Dioxide (CO_2) Pipelines for Carbon Sequestration: Emerging Policy Issues' (Washington, DC, Congressional Research Service, 2008) 6–10, 16–18. For a proposal to update these regulations, see RR Nordhaus and E Pitlick, 'Carbon Dioxide Pipeline Regulation' (2009) 30 *Energy Law Journal* 85.

[48] The PHSMA has explained its classification of CO_2 as a Class 2.2 material, and its appearance in the same table as various 'hazardous materials', 49 CFR § 172.101, as an effort to avoid 'an awkward title'. Notice of Proposed Rulemaking: Transportation of Carbon Dioxide by Pipeline, 54 Fed Reg 41912, 41914 (12 October 1989). The PHSMA does *not* include CO_2 in its list of 'hazardous liquids' (see 49 CFR § 195.2), and has made clear that this distinction sets CO_2 pipelines apart from those used to transport such liquids: 56 Fed Reg 26923.

[49] See PHSMA, 'State Pages' (US Department of Transportation), at primis.phmsa.dot.gov/comm/States.htm?nocache=8261 (collecting links to state regulatory authorities' websites and relevant regulations); J Pless, 'Making State Gas Pipelines Safe and Reliable: An Assessment of State Policy–Federal and State Responsibilities' (National Conference of State Legislatures, 2011) (tabulating state role in oversight of particular categories of inter- and intra-State pipeline).

[50] CCSReg.org, 'State CCS Policy' (Carnegie Mellon University, 2008), at www.ccsreg.org/bills.php (tabulating links to laws and regulations in Indiana, Kentucky, Louisiana, Montana, North Dakota, South Dakota, Tennessee and Texas).

[51] EPA, Federal Requirements Under the Underground Injection Control (UIC) Program for Carbon Dioxide (CO_2) Geologic Sequestration (GS) Wells Final Rule, 76 Fed Reg 56982 (10 December 2010), codified at 40 CFR pts 124, 144–147 (citing Safe Drinking Water Act of 1974, 42 USC §§ 300f-300j-26, 300h(b)(2)).

[52] 40 CFR pt 98 subparts PP (CO_2 suppliers), RR (CO_2 geologic sequestration), and UU (CO_2 injection).

[53] EPA, Hazardous Waste Management System: Conditional Exclusion for Carbon Dioxide (CO_2) 79 Fed Reg 350 (3 January 2014), codified at 40 CFR § 9, 260, 261.

for how long.[54] A handful of States have enacted legislation specifying the particular treatment of CO_2 injected for EOR and/or sequestration,[55] but no State has developed a comprehensive legal regime to govern sequestration,[56] leaving the US a patchwork of diverse and incomplete rules of ownership and liability.[57] Even Illinois' Clean Coal FutureGen Act of 2011, which addressed these issues as they relate to the FutureGen project, described that project as exploratory, and did not contemplate a generalised expansion of ownership and liability provisions relating to its operation.[58]

iv. CCS/U RD&D

The Energy Policy Act of 2005, the Energy Independence and Security Act of 2007, and the American Reinvestment and Recovery Act of 2009 all include provisions authorising funding for CCS/U RD&D. The cumulative total of appropriate funds is roughly $7 billion.[59] The Department of Energy, based on statutory directives and on recommendations of the Interagency Task Force on Carbon Capture and Storage,[60] has allocated those funds to efforts to develop capture technologies, characterise sequestration reservoirs, develop monitoring, verification and accounting

---

[54] JR Zadick, 'The Public Pore Space: Enabling Carbon Capture and Sequestration by Reconceptualizing Subsurface Property Rights' (2011) 36 *William and Mary Environmental Law and Policy Review* 257, 268–74 (discussing subsurface ownership); AB Klass and EJ Wilson, 'Climate Change, Carbon Sequestration, and Property Rights' (2010) *University of Illinois Law Review* 363, 391–93 (detailing ownership rights). See also JJ Monast, BR Pearson and LF Pratson, 'A Cooperative Federalism Framework for CCS Regulation' (2012) 7 *Environmental and Energy Law & Policy Journal* 1, 27–33 (describing existing law); Marston and Moore, n 33 above, 425–26.

[55] See, eg, Montana Code Ann 82-11-188 (2015) (authorising Montana Board of Oil and Gas Conservation to certify amount of CO_2 stored incidentally in EOR project); Wyoming Stat § 30-5-502 (2015) (similar). See also H Vidas et al, 'Analysis of the Costs and Benefits of CO_2 Sequestration on the US Outer Continental Shelf' (Herndon, VA, US Department of the Interior, Bureau of Ocean Energy Management, 2012) 47 (listing legislation addressing various aspects of CCS in the following States: Illinois, Kansas, Kentucky, Louisiana, Michigan, Montana, New Mexico, New York, North Dakota, Oklahoma, Pennsylvania, South Dakota, Texas, Utah, Washington, West Virginia and Wyoming).

[56] This in contrast to Alberta, Canada, which has developed an integrated regime for regulating CO_2 emissions, capture, transport, storage and liability for sequestration. See M Fernandez, C Leask and C Arnot, 'Liability for sequestered CO_2: the path forward for Alberta' (2013) 37 *Energy Procedia* 7709 (describing Carbon Capture and Storage Statutes Amendment Act of 2010, relevant provisions of the amended Oil and Gas Conservation Act, and the Carbon Sequestration Tenure Regulation).

[57] See M Faure, 'Liability and Compensation for Damage Resulting from CO_2 Storage Sites' (2016) 40 *William & Mary Environmental Law & Policy Review* 387, 419–32 (noting lack of legal guidance regarding liability and listing policy options for imposing liability).

[58] See Clean Coal FutureGen for Illinois Act of 2011, 20 ILCS 1108 (2011).

[59] P Folger, 'Carbon Capture: Research, Development, and Demonstration at the US Department of Energy' (Washington, DC, Congressional Research Service, 2014) 1. See also American Recovery and Reinvestment Act of 2009, Pub L No 111–5, § 1131, 123 Stat 115, 325 (17 February 2009); Energy Independence and Security Act of 2007 (EISA), Pub L No 110–140, § 712(b)(3)(C), 121 Stat 1492 (7 December 2007); Energy Policy Act of 2005, Pub L No 109–58, Title IX, Subtitle F, § 963, 119 Stat 594 (8 August 2005).

[60] Interagency Task Force on Carbon Capture and Storage, 'Report of the Interagency Task Force on Carbon Capture and Storage' (Washington, DC, US Department of Energy, 2010).

(MVA) tools and techniques, and seed research into utilisation technologies.[61] This support has yielded multiple demonstration projects and an increasingly thorough and detailed version of the CCS Atlas, which identifies potential sequestration reservoirs and notes their degree of characterisation.[62]

In addition to these direct grants for particular projects, the Emergency Economic Stabilization Act of 2008 also created a tax credit of $20 per ton of CO_2 captured and sequestered, and $10 per ton of CO_2 used for EOR, which will be available until 75 million tons have been injected for either purpose.[63] One estimate (not yet confirmed or revised by government data[64]) is that about half of this subsidy budget has been spent[65]—meaning that it has been spent on EOR projects, effectively making it a subsidy for fossil fuel production rather than sequestering CO_2.

One further statutory provision relating to RD&D bears mention, § 402(i) of the Energy Policy Act of 2005:

> No technology, or level of emission reduction, solely by reason of the use of the technology, or the achievement of the emission reduction, by 1 or more facilities receiving assistance under this act, shall be considered to be adequately demonstrated for purposes of [Section 111].[66]

This provision anticipates future reference by the EPA to a CCS/U demonstration facility in the context of an NSPS promulgated for new or modified coal-fired power plants pursuant to Clean Air Act section 111(b).[67] By prohibiting the EPA from relying on a facility subsidised pursuant to the Energy Policy Act of 2005 as a demonstration of a 'best system of emissions reduction', it seeks to prevent the EPA from integrating CCS/U into climate policy.[68]

---

[61] P Folger, n 59 above, 6–23.

[62] National Energy Technology Laboratory and US Department of Energy, 'Carbon Storage Atlas' (5th edn, US Department of Energy, 2015) (collecting surveys of sequestration reservoir characterizations).

[63] Emergency Economic Stabilization Act of 2008, Pub L No 110-343, div B, tit I, § 115(a), 122 Stat 3829 (3 October 2008), codified at IRC § 45q (2016).

[64] See Letter from Friends of the Earth and others to Rhonda O'Reilly, US Internal Revenue Service, regarding Freedom of Information Act request for 'records pertaining to tax credits disbursed for carbon capture and sequestration' (9 August 2016) bit.ly/2aQvQMQ.

[65] D Koplow, 'The Trouble with Q: Why the US should not be subsidizing carbon capture and sequestration' (EarthTrack, 8 August 2016) bit.ly/2cuOxHL.

[66] Energy Policy Act of 2005 § 402(i).

[67] See State of North Dakota's Opening Brief, *North Dakota v EPA*, Case No 15-1381, 11 (DC Circuit, 13 October 2016) (The Energy Policy Act of 2005 prohibits the EPA from considering projects subsidised by the US Department of Energy's Clean Coal Power Initiative to support a finding that a BSER is 'adequately demonstrated'). See also US EPA, 'Basis for Denial of Petitions to Reconsider the CAA Section 111(b) Standards of Performance for Greenhouse Gas Emissions from New, Modified, and Reconstructed Fossil Fuel-Fired Electric Utility Generating Units' (Washington, DC, EPA, 2016) (rejecting petitioners' claim that Canadian SaskPower Boundary Dam Unit 3 facility does not provide adequate demonstration of CCS technologies).

[68] But see 80 Fed Reg 64548 ('the EPA interprets these provisions as allowing consideration of EPAct05 facilities provided that such information is not the sole basis for the BSER determination, and particularly so in circumstances like those here, where the information is corroborative but the essential information justifying the determinations comes from facilities and other sources of information with no nexus with EPAct05 assistance').

C. Siting Sequestration Reservoirs: Politics atop Legal Requirements

Implementing the sequestration component of CCS/U would involve navigating a number of legal requirements, both substantive and procedural. Several authors have compiled lists of the federal and international laws that would pertain to onshore and offshore sequestration reservoir siting.[69] Their lists reflect the functional and legal overlaps among sequestration sites, injection facilities and pipeline-based CO_2 transportation infrastructure. The federal laws governing siting for onshore and offshore locations require a thorough characterisation of the site, and of the impacts of the installation and operation of the transport, injection and monitoring components involved.[70] State law addressing CO_2 sequestration facility siting and operation is, as noted in section III.B.iii, generally incomplete (even in cases where it addresses EOR) or wholly absent.

For both onshore and offshore locations, legal requirements can be expected to inform political aspects of the siting process. This is true not only in relation to the relatively straightforward tasks of transferring and specifying property rights, but also in relation to the more diffuse tasks of persuading communities to accept the risks of a siting decision. In this, siting of a CO_2 sequestration reservoir resembles that of a nuclear waste repository in certain respects (though perhaps not as likely to engender fervent State-level opposition). Comparing the legal and political underpinnings of two nuclear waste repositories—the Waste Isolation Pilot Plant (WIPP) of Carlsbad, New Mexico, which became operational in 1999, and the Yucca Mountain high-level waste repository, whose development was halted in 2009—provides an object lesson in why merely complying with legal requirements is not sufficient to ensure that even a well-planned, congressionally mandated and legally sound facility will become operational.[71] The WIPP's siting involved a thorough engagement with political leaders in New Mexico and Carlsbad, including appointment of the independent Environmental Evaluation Group pursuant to a memorandum of understanding signed by the Department of Energy and New Mexico's Governor.[72] Extensive negotiation between State and federal actors *preceded*

---

[69] Interagency Task Force on Carbon Capture and Storage, n 60 above, 61–67, 126, app G; Jacobs, n 36 above, 589–601; SM Carpenter, 'Preliminary Evaluation of Offshore Transport and Storage of CO_2,' (Southeast Regional Carbon Sequestration Partnership, 2011) 13–16.

[70] See, eg, US Department of Energy, 'FutureGen 2.0 Project Final Environmental Impact Statement' (DOE/EIS-0460) (Washington, DC, US Department of Energy, 2013); US Department of Energy, 'Record of Decision and Floodplain Statement of Findings for the FutureGen 2.0 Project' 79 Fed Reg 3577 (22 January 2014).

[71] RB Stewart and JB Stewart, *Fuel Cycle to Nowhere: US Law and Policy on Nuclear Waste* (Nashville, TN, Vanderbilt University Press, 2011) 162–85 (describing the legal and political history of WIPP), 186–230 (describing the history of Yucca). See also MB Gerrard, *Whose Backyard, Whose Risk: Fear and Fairness in Toxic and Nuclear Waste Siting* (Cambridge, MA, MIT Press, 1994).

[72] Stewart and Stewart, n 71 above, 162–75. This is not to say that the road to the WIPP's siting or development was smooth. Distrust and recrimination featured at several points in the process, which succeeded only after federal and State actors stipulated and memorialised various procedural and substantive conditions based in part on the double-checking by the independent Environmental Evaluation Group of technical conclusions proffered by the Department of Energy: ibid.

Congress's adoption of legislation cementing decisions about the site and its use.[73] Siting Yucca Mountain followed from an unrealistic time-table mandated by the federal Nuclear Waste Policy Act of 1982, and involved a series of manoeuvres in Congress that made the Yucca location a *fait accompli* for reasons at least somewhat unrelated to its technical suitability.[74] Subsequent efforts to reassure Nevadans of the facility's safety were drowned out by a series of well-publicised lawsuits and political campaigns that made opposition to Yucca Mountain a litmus test for statewide and congressional elections,[75] and the Department of Energy's decision to press ahead anyway ultimately ran aground on the political shoals of the 2008 presidential election.[76]

Whether a location for injection and sequestration is sited on private property, State lands, federal lands, in the state-managed coastal zone or in the US exclusive economic zone (EEZ), the siting process will necessarily involve installation of pipelines and injection facilities, as well as limitations on competing uses of the location. As the Department of Energy's experience with Yucca Mountain demonstrates, even if all facilities are located entirely on federal lands (Yucca Mountain is, but the train lines that would connect it to nuclear power plant locations are not), it may not suffice for federal or State agencies to conduct extensive and legally sufficient environmental reviews of planned facilities.[77] Siting will likely also require persuading a critical mass of the affected public about the utility and safety of carbon sequestration technology in general and about the characteristics of the selected location in particular.[78] This is not to say that Yucca Mountain's siting necessarily presages similar problems for siting and developing CO_2 sequestration facilities, only that it provides an important cautionary tale for federal and State entities tasked with siting.[79]

D. CCS/U Will Not Become Commercially Viable until Climate Policy Becomes Coherent and Stable

United States law does not impose a price on CO_2 emissions on a consistent basis, nor are the regulations by which it imputes a partial and inconsistent carbon

---

[73] See WIPP Land Withdrawal Act of 1992, Pub L No 102–579, 106 Stat 4777 (30 October 1992, as amended by the National Defense Authorization Act for Fiscal Year 1997, Pub L No 104–201, 110 Stat 2422 (23 September 1996).
[74] Stewart and Stewart, n 71 above, 201–09.
[75] ibid 209–17.
[76] ibid 226–30 (describing then-Senator Obama's political commitments to Senate Majority Leader, Harry Reid (D-NV) in the 2009 election).
[77] See *Nuclear Energy Institute v EPA*, 373 F3d 1251, 1289–97 (DC Circuit 2004) (rejecting Nevada's challenge to approval of Yucca facility by the EPA and Nuclear Regulatory Commission).
[78] See generally PW Parfomak, 'Community Acceptance of Carbon Capture and Sequestration Infrastructure: Siting Challenges' (Washington, DC, Congressional Research Service, 2008).
[79] See Vidas et al, n 55 above (noting that at least nine States have established commissions to locate and characterise potential carbon sequestration sites).

price stable. Carbon capture, sequestration and utilisation cannot achieve commercial viability in this context, because it cannot compete with the other options available to such major CO_2 emitters as gas-fired power plants, refineries and cement plants, namely, compliance with modest or non-existent CO_2 emissions restrictions and mandatory energy efficiency improvements. A 2016 MIT review of the status of integrated CCS demonstration projects highlights this point by explaining how a lack of reliable financing from sources other than federal RD&D subsidies has undermined several large projects, including FutureGen 2.0, Basin Electric, Hydrogen Energy, Mountaineer and Plant Berry.[80] As the report put it, for CCS/U to become viable, its '[a]ccess to markets has to move beyond EOR'.[81] And such access will only result from emissions regulations or charges that make CCS/U valuable to emitters by foreclosing the option of emitting CO_2 at low or no cost.[82]

Practically, bringing coherence and stability to climate policy by pricing the emissions responsible for climate change would probably mean either:

(a) Congress adopting a carbon tax or national cap and trade scheme that raises the price of carbon; or
(b) the EPA adopting a new nationwide emissions regulation pursuant to Clean Air Act section 115; or
(c) the Clean Power Plan surviving the judicial and political attacks on it *and* the EPA subsequently tightening its emissions requirements for gas-fired power plants enough to make CCS/U indispensable for compliance. Note that it would not suffice for the Clean Power Plan merely to survive. In that circumstance, one could reasonably expect the current pattern of GHG emissions reduction to persist: limited efforts beyond the electricity sector; no construction of new coal-fired power plants; replacement of aging coal- and nuclear-fired plants with gas-fired ones, renewables, energy efficiency and demand-side management; and construction of a fleet of new gas-fired power plants and industrial facilities without carbon capture compatibility or technology.[83] As a scenario analysis conducted by the National Renewable Energy Laboratory concluded: 'Without a carbon target enforced, natural gas generation ... grows over the long-term,

---

[80] H Herzog, *Lessons Learned from CCS Demonstration Projects and Large Pilot Projects* (Cambridge, MA, MIT, 2016) 10.
[81] ibid 38.
[82] ibid 9–11, 30, 38.
[83] See US Energy Information Administration, 'Annual Energy Outlook 2016 with Projections to 2040' (US Department of Energy, August 2016); US Energy Information Administration, 'Today in Energy: Coal made up more than 80% of retired electricity generating capacity in 2015' (US Department of Energy, March 2016). See also VR Clark and HJ Herzog, 'Assessment of the US EPA's Determination of the Role for CO_2 Capture and Storage in New Fossil Fuel-Fired Power Plants' (2014) 48 *Environmental Science & Technology* 7723. ('Requiring CCS on NGCC power plants would not only promote technological development of CCS but would also promote other low carbon generation options. By allowing what we call the "NGCC loophole", just about all capacity issues in the electric power sector will be solved using natural gas as a fuel (with the exception of renewables where they are mandated through portfolio standards and/or subsidized through tax credits). This will result in little to no incentive to invest in low carbon technologies like CCS, renewables, or nuclear power generation systems.' (ibid at 7727))

showing no indication of a natural gas bridge that eventually phases out over time'.[84]

The election of Donald Trump and a Republican-controlled Congress in November 2016 means, at best, continued incoherence and instability in US climate policy, and at worst a wholesale departure from any federal support for climate change mitigation efforts in the US or the rest of the world. Perhaps the most direct consequence of this turn of events for CCS/U is the likely cancellation of the only regulatory program that currently requires use of CCS/U technology: the NSPS for new coal-fired power plants that the EPA issued pursuant to Clean Air Act section 111(b) in October 2015.[85] The appointment of several high officials, including the Administrator of the EPA, who deny the existence of anthropogenic climate change will also reduce the impetus for developing technologies to reduce greenhouse gas emissions. The States that are most committed to action on climate change (such as California and New York) make little or no use of coal, and thus are unlikely to develop CCS/U on their own. Other consequences are difficult to predict with precision, but are unlikely to provide any part of the foundation needed to support commercially viable applications of CCS/U.

IV. THE FUTURE CLIMATE POLICY CONTEXT AND CCS/U

Climate stability requires humanity not to exceed its GHG emissions 'budget'. According to the Intergovernmental Panel on Climate Change, staying within this budget would require a 40–70 per cent reduction in emissions by 2050 from a 2010 baseline.[86] The Deep Decarbonization Pathways Project, having mapped out what this basic parameter would mean for key US sectors, concluded that no fossil-fuelled electricity generating facilities—new or existing, coal- or gas-fired—could forgo use of CCS/U by 2050.[87] Because the natural gas combined cycle (NGCC) plants

---

[84] W Cole et al, 'Considering the Role of Natural Gas in the Deep Decarbonization of the US Electricity Sector Natural Gas and the Evolving US Power Sector Monograph Series: Number 2' (Golden, CO, National Renewable Energy Laboratory, 2016) 28. Another analysis concludes that natural gas can only serve as a bridge to decarbonisation if it is consistently priced higher than $26.45/mmBTU by 2050. YF Mak, 'Conditions for Natural Gas to Become an Effective Bridge Fuel to a Low-Carbon Future' (Master's Thesis, MIT, 2016) 65. See also C Nicholsa and N Victor, 'Examining the relationship between shale gas production and carbon capture and storage under CO_2 taxes based on the social cost of carbon' (2015) 7 *Energy Strategy Reviews* 39, 50 (concluding that US cannot meet GHG reduction targets without mandating that gas- as well as coal-fired power plants use CCS/U).

[85] See US EPA, 'Standards of Performance for Greenhouse Gas Emissions From New, Modified, and Reconstructed Stationary Sources: Electric Utility Generating Units' 80 Fed Reg 64509 (23 October 2015).

[86] IPCC, 'Climate Change 2014: Synthesis Report, Summary for Policymakers. Contribution of Working Groups I, II and III to the Fifth Assessment Report of the Intergovernmental Panel on Climate Change' [Core Writing Team, RK Pachauri and LA Meyer (eds)] (IPCC, Geneva, Switzerland, 2014) 18. The US announced a comparable reduction—83% from a 2005 baseline—at the 2009 Copenhagen Conference of the Parties to the UNFCCC.

[87] JH Williams et al, 'Pathways to Deep Decarbonization in the United States' (Energy and Environmental Economics, Inc, Lawrence Berkeley National Laboratory, Pacific Northwest National Laboratory, revised November 2015) 19–20, table 7. The report also discusses industrial facilities, such as those that produce cement or glass, but this chapter focuses on the electricity sector for simplicity and due to space constraints.

currently being built can operate for 25 to 55 years,[88] keeping to this emissions trajectory would require at a minimum incorporating CCS/U into all gas-fired plants built after 2025, whether by making it a design feature (less expensive) or eventually retrofitting (more expensive). The US climate policy context circa 2030 could depart from that of today through adoption of robust GHG emissions pricing, or it could reflect only incremental tightening of what already exists. The role of CCS/U in both scenarios is considered here.

Imposition of a robust carbon price would make CCS/U the preferred option for natural gas-fired generation facilities that (i) could not afford to pay the price of their GHG emissions but (ii) could afford to incorporate carbon capture technologies into their operations without being priced out of wholesale electricity markets. Thus CCS/U would only be incorporated into a facility's operations in circumstances where (i) demand for reliable electricity capacity could not be met by renewables and nuclear (buttressed by storage and demand side management) alone *and* (ii) the marginal cost of CCS/U was less than the prevailing carbon price. The market segment that would satisfy this pair of conditions could potentially be substantial or very small.[89] If natural gas lives up to its promise as a 'bridge fuel' then this segment would be substantial at first and wane over time. But the key point for this chapter's purposes is this: merely pricing carbon might not be enough to ensure the commercial viability of CCS/U in a future policy context, particularly if renewables and storage continue to experience falling prices and rising capacity factors.[90] If the fate of gas resembles that of coal, mandatory use of CCS/U could simply put gas at the end of the wholesale electricity market's merit order (behind renewables, hydro, nuclear and demand response), where revenues are thin and flow infrequently.

A future scenario in which there is no carbon price but only an incremental ratcheting-down of electricity sector emissions limits would be even less promising for CCS/U. In such a scenario, given the currently rapid rate of development of natural gas-fired transmission and generation capacity,[91] not only would natural gas-fired plants potentially avoid substantial limits on emissions for a decade or more, but their ubiquity and sunk costs would make their continued operation valuable to an even larger constituency than the one currently pushing for their proliferation.[92] Such a constituency would be well positioned to resist a program of mandatory carbon capture retrofits, and would presumably argue instead for requiring CCS/U installation in new or modified plants—what one commentator calls a climate policy 'dead end' because it forces a choice between meeting climate goals or

---

[88] See J Logan et al, 'Natural gas scenarios in the US power sector' (2013) 40 *Energy Economics* 183, 194 (estimating NGCC plant lifespan).

[89] Notably, smallness would be even more problematic for CCS/U's commercial viability in so far as the cost of accessing CCS/U technologies responded strongly to network effects.

[90] C Stark et al, 'Renewable Electricity: Insights for the Coming Decade' (Golden, CO, National Renewable Energy Laboratory, 2015) 7, 17–18, 42.

[91] See US Energy Information Administration, 'Today in Energy: Natural gas expected to surpass coal in mix of fuel used for US power generation in 2016' (US Department of Energy, 2016).

[92] See TJ Foxon, 'Technological Lock-In' in *Encyclopedia of Energy, Natural Resource, and Environmental Economics* (London, Elsevier, 2013) 123–27.

stranding assets.[93] In this scenario, persistence in renewables' current trends of falling prices and rising capacity factors would not likely put pressure on gas-fired plants to adopt CCS/U. Indeed in the absence of a carbon price, greater price competition from renewables, buttressed by storage, would presumably *increase* gas-fired plant owners' aversion to the expense of incorporating CCS/U technologies.

V. CONCLUSION

Whereas other chapters in this volume have addressed technical, legal and regulatory particulars of CCS/U and its governance, this chapter has sought to consider how CCS/U fits into the context of US climate policy in its current state, as well as prospective future states. Based on an overview of CCS/U's key features and the existing body of regulations that address it, this chapter identifies various obstacles currently in the way of CCS/U deployment and highlights the crucial importance of a carbon price to CCS/U's prospects.

---

[93] MG Morgan, 'Climate policy needs more than muddling' (2016) 113 *Proceedings of the National Academy of Sciences* 2322, 2324.

7
Confronting the Bleak Economics of CCS in the United States

DAVID E ADELMAN

THIS CHAPTER WILL argue that carbon capture and sequestration (CCS) policies must be re-evaluated in light of the dramatic changes in electricity markets. Coal-fired power has progressed from being the cheapest to one of the most expensive sources of electricity in the United States (US), and while it will remain an important source of electricity for decades, it is projected to be in 'terminal decline' by 2020.[1] The Donald J Trump Administration may prolong the transition away from coal, but it will not reverse it because of the underlying economics. Three factors are driving this transformation: (i) dramatic declines in the cost of renewables; (ii) the projected long-term low price of natural gas; and (iii) strong signs that electricity storage will be widely cost-competitive by the mid-2020s. I have omitted environmental and climate change regulations because, though important, their status is highly uncertain in the near term given the current political climate in the US.

The clearest sign of this transition is that conventional coal plants, fully or partially amortised, have been retired or operated less frequently as the cost of electricity has declined from renewables and natural gas combined-cycle (NGCC) power plants. Of course, if conventional coal plants are uncompetitive, the economics of new or retrofitted coal plants with CCS are prohibitively worse—without new technologies or revenue streams. These changes have prompted a strategic shift within the coal industry, away from simply opposing climate policies to seeking tax breaks and other policies putatively to offset federal subsidies for renewables.[2] The coal

---

[1] Bloomberg New Energy Finance, 'New Energy Outlook 2017' (Bloomberg, 2017), at www.bloomberg.com/company/new-energy-outlook/#form.
[2] National Coal Council (NCC), 'Leveling the Playing Field: Policy Parity for Carbon Capture and Storage Technologies' (NCC, November 2015), at www.nationalcoalcouncil.org/studies/2015/Leveling-the-Playing-Field-for-Low-Carbon-Coal-Fall-2015.pdf. See also NCC, 'CO_2 Building Blocks: Assessing CO_2 Utilization Options' (2016), at www.nationalcoalcouncil.org/Documents/CO_2-Building-Blocks-2016.pdf; State CO_2-EOR Deployment Work Group, 'Putting the Puzzle Together: State & Federal Policy Drivers for Growing America's Carbon Capture & CO_2-EOR Industry' (2016), at www.betterenergy.org/EORpolicy.

industry now asserts that '[carbon capture, utilization, and storage] is not just about coal, nor is it just about fossil fuels generally. Rather, it is a *sine qua non* for achieving stabilization of greenhouse gas concentrations in the atmosphere'.[3] The scope of these policies anticipates technological change that industry proponents hope will make coal competitive again and, in the interim, coal-fired power plants retrofitted with CCS economically viable.

The changes in the electricity sector necessitate a re-evaluation of the strategy for deploying CCS that is built around coal-fired generation. If, as many energy experts believe, rising market competition is inexorably undercutting the viability of coal-fired generation, plans and policies for CCS must adapt to the new economic realities. The greatest barrier to deployment of CCS is the low price of natural gas, which is displacing coal-fired generation and foreclosing the construction of new plants—a factor also independent of the expected demise of President Obama's Clean Power Plan. At the same time, the costs of renewables and electricity storage are projected to continue their decline and to reach grid parity long before widespread commercialisation of CCS.[4] As a consequence, even under optimistic scenarios, coal plants with CCS will have to compete in a market increasingly dominated by technologies with more rapid innovation cycles, modularity and low barriers to deployment at both the utility-scale and as distributed generation.

This chapter will begin by reviewing the changes in electricity markets and the current state of CCS policies in the US. It will also examine the opportunities for generating revenue from the sale of CO_2 for use in enhanced oil recovery (EOR), a key element of pending legislation in Congress, and for deploying CCS in industrial sectors other than electric utilities. I shall argue that neither of these options will play more than a minor role in US carbon mitigation without advances in carbon capture technologies that dramatically improve the economics of CCS. In this light, US policies should be reoriented towards research and development (R&D) on CCS that has the potential to produce major technological advances.

I. THE ECONOMICS OF LOW-CARBON ELECTRICITY

Most commentary on CCS, while recognising the obvious importance of economics, has focused on regulatory barriers and public opposition to carbon sequestration. In the US, the regulatory issues are important, but they pale in comparison to the economic headwinds. Electricity markets have been transformed by the emergence of fracking technologies that have opened up enormous domestic gas reserves; NGCCs are now the cheapest source of electricity in most US markets, and the potential for natural gas price volatility has greatly diminished. In parallel, electricity generated from onshore wind farms has become competitive with NGCCs in regions with good wind resources, and advances in solar photovoltaics have reduced the levelised cost

---

[3] NCC, 'CO_2 Building Blocks', n 2 above, 1.
[4] Bloomberg, n 1 above (predicting that wind and solar will be the cheapest sources of electricity in OECD countries by 2027).

of electricity (LCOE) by more than 80 per cent since 2008, such that utility-scale solar is becoming cost competitive in some markets. Collectively, these advances are upending the economics of traditional base-load generation, including many coal-fired power plants that are now struggling to stay competitive. For CCS, these developments represent a critical (and rising) barrier to deployment in the utility sector.

The rate of technological change makes it difficult to stay current with shifts in electricity markets. The resulting lags are reflected in the variance of reported capital costs and LCOEs. Table 7.1 makes clear that recent comparisons of CCS with renewables do not reflect the latest US trends in the cost of renewables.[5] The disparities are most evident in the LCOEs and costs of carbon abatement, but significant differences also exist in the reported capital costs of solar. Whereas the US Energy Information Administration (EIA), which is known for its conservatively high cost estimates, and the widely cited Lazard firm find that wind is cheaper or comparable to coal- and-gas-fired generation, the 2015 report issued by the Global CCS Institute (GCCSI) includes estimates that are substantially higher and finds that wind is not competitive with NGCCs. Much greater differences exist for the costs of utility-scale solar, which the EIA and Lazard estimate to be competitive or cheaper than coal and moderately more expensive than NGCCs. By contrast, the GCCSI report finds that solar is two to three times more expensive than coal-fired generation, and roughly three to five times more expensive than NGCCs. The disparities in carbon-abatement costs are similarly striking, with the EIA and Lazard calculating that electricity generated by wind and solar is substantially cheaper than electricity from a conventional coal-fired power plant (ie, CO_2 abatement costs are negative), whereas GCCSI reports that carbon abatement could cost up to \$19/tonne of CO_2 (t CO_2) for wind and \$101–\$223/t CO_2 for solar.

In the near to medium term, the price of natural gas will remain the single most important factor impacting the viability of coal-fired generation and CCS. Recent studies of CCS assume that prices for natural gas will be \$5 per million British Thermal Units (MMBtu) or higher.[6] This assumption is conservative given current prices of roughly \$3.25/MMBtu and projections that they will stay below \$5/MMBtu in the US through at least 2025.[7] However, even if these projections prove to be overly optimistic, the LCOE of new NGCC power plants is likely to remain substantially lower than that of new coal plants indefinitely. A 2015 report issued by the National Energy Technology Laboratory (NETL) finds that the price of natural gas would

---

[5] Global CCS Institute (GCCSI), L Irlam, 'The Costs of CCS and Other Low-Carbon Technologies in the United States: 2015 Update' (July 2015), at www.globalccsinstitute.com/publications/costs-ccs-and-other-low-carbon-technologies-2015-update, 8; M van den Broek, N Berghout and ES Rubin, 'The Potential of Renewables Versus Natural Gas with CO_2 Capture for Power Generation under CO_2 Constraints' (2015) 49 *Renewable and Sustainable Energy Reviews* 1296.

[6] See, eg, GSCCI, n 5 above, 11; van den Broek et al, 'The Potential of Renewables', n 5 above, 1312; NETL, 'Cost and Performance Baseline', n 8 above, 17 (similar to the other studies, NETL used a relatively high price for natural gas of \$6.13/MMBtu in its calculation and fuel cost accounted for 53–71% of total costs).

[7] EIA, 'Annual Energy Outlook 2016 MT-23' (Department of Energy, August 2016), at www.eia.gov/outlooks/aeo/pdf/0383(2016).pdf (the price of natural gas in reference case for Figure MT-23 stays below \$5/MMBtu through 2025).

Table 7.1: Comparison of Costs Between Coal, Natural Gas and Renewable Generation

	Pulverized Coal		NGCC		Onshore Wind	Solar PV
	w/o CCS	w/ CCS	w/o CCS	w/ CCS		
Capital Costs ($/kW)						
Rubin (2015)[8]	2313–2990	4091–5252	808–1378	1422–2626		2250–3000
GCCSI (2015)[9]	2950	3517–6749	1050	1918–2142	1250–2264	2707–4263
NETL (2015)[10]	2429–2507	4267–4333	901	1945		
EIA (2016)[11]	3636	5084	978		1877	2671
Lazard (2016)[12]	3000–8400		1000–1300		1250–1700	1300–1450
LCOE ($/MWh)	w/o CCS	w/ CCS	w/o CCS	w/ CCS		
Rubin (2015)	61–79 (70)	95–150 (113)	42–83 (64)	63–122 (92)		
GCCSI (2015)	79	115–160	55	82–93	66–94	162–264
NETL (2015)	82	143	58	87		
EIA (2016)[13]		140	48	85	52	71
Lazard (2016)	60–143		48–78		32–62	46–61

(continued)

[8] ES Rubin, JE Davison and JH Herzog, 'The Cost of CO$_2$ Capture and Storage' (2015) 40 *International Journal of Greenhouse Gas Control* 378, 382.
[9] GCCSI, 'The Costs of CCS and Other Low-Carbon Technologies', n 5 above, 8.
[10] National Energy Technology Laboratory (NETL), 'Cost and Performance Baseline from Fossil Energy Plants Volume 1a: Bituminous Coal (PC) and Natural Gas to Electricity' (US Department of Energy, Rev 3, July 2015), available at www.netl.doe.gov/File%20Library/Research/Energy%20Analysis/Publications/Rev3Vol1aPC_NGCC_final.pdf, 17.
[11] US Energy Information Administration (EIA), 'Capital Cost Estimates for Utility Scale Electricity Generating Plants' (EIA, November 2016), available at www.eia.gov/analysis/studies/powerplants/capitalcost/pdf/capcost_assumption.pdf, 2–11.
[12] Lazard, 'Lazard's Levelized Cost of Energy Analysis—Version 10.0' (December 2016), available at www.lazard.com/media/438038/levelized-cost-of-energy-v100.pdf.
[13] EIA, 'Levelized Cost and Levelized Avoided Cost of New Generation Resources in the Annual Energy Outlook 2016' (August 2016), available at www.eia.gov/forecasts/aeo/pdf/electricity_generation.pdf, 12.

Table 7.1: (Continued)

	Pulverized Coal		NGCC		Onshore Wind	Solar PV
CO_2 Avoided (\$/t CO_2)[14]	CCS	CCS & EOR	CCS	CCS & EOR		
Rubin (2015)[15]	45–70 (63)	–5 to 58	58–121 (87)	10–112		
GCCSI (2015)	48–109		74–114		–16–19	101–225
NETL (2015)	89–91		94			
DO						
EIA (2016)					–34	–10
Lazard (2016)					–31	–13

[14] The cost of CO_2 emissions avoided is based on emissions reductions relative to that emitted by a conventional coal-fired power plant with a CO_2 emissions rate of 0.79 t CO_2/MWh. The estimates include the costs of transportation and storage.
[15] Note that Rubin et al used a relatively high range, \$15–40/t CO_2, for the price of CO_2 sold for use in EOR: Rubin et al, n 6 above, 388, 390. In 2014, CO_2 prices for use in EOR were \$17–27/t CO_2 for crude oil prices ranging from \$30–70 per barrel, which suggests the likelihood of net negative costs for CCS is low unless oil prices rise substantially from current levels. See IHS Energy, 'CO_2 EOR Potential in North Dakota' (June 2016), at www.legis.nd.gov/files/committees/64-2014%20appendices/IHS%20Energy%20-%20Final%20Report.pdf, 7.

have to exceed $10/MMBtu before coal generation is cheaper than an NGCC.[16] Moreover, for natural gas prices below $5/MMBtu, the study finds that the LCOE of an NGCC with CCS would be lower than that of a conventional coal plant.[17] These projections highlight the large competitive deficit of new coal-fired generation and the extent to which NGCCs with CCS are economically favoured over coal plants in US electricity markets.

The economics are less problematic for retrofitting existing coal plants with CCS than for building CCS into new ones, but the characteristics of existing coal plants (ie, age, efficiency, capacity factor) will limit deployment. A 2011 NETL report assessed the feasibility of CCS retrofits on US coal plants, in total 738 generating units with a collective capacity of 282 gigawatts (GW).[18] The report estimated that about 70 per cent of existing coal-fired plants could be retrofitted at $50/t CO_2 or less. However, only about 20 per cent of the generating units (56 GW) could be retrofitted at an added cost for electricity of $55/MWh or less, and the percentage of units fell to less than 5 per cent if coal plants operated on average less than 65 per cent of the time (increasingly an optimistic assumption).[19]

A 2015 study using more up-to-date data has analysed the viability of CCS retrofits under the Clean Power Plan. It found that CCS would be uneconomic for most coal-fired power plants, as CCS retrofits with just a 30 per cent CO_2 capture rate would increase LCOEs by 31–43 per cent and result in an average increase in electricity costs of $43/MWh.[20] Similar to the 2011 NETL study,[21] about 50 GW of coal-fired generation, 98 generating units located across 22 states, had relatively favourable economics.[22] Within this select group, the average LCOE was $38/MWh for CCS with a 30 per cent CO_2 capture rate and $61/MWh for CCS with a 90 per cent CO_2 capture rate.[23] A 2016 study of CCS retrofits on coal plants in Texas generated comparable estimates, with 85 per cent CO_2 capture rates achievable at LCOEs of $60–71/MWh.[24] These studies indicate that LCOEs for retrofitted coal plants

---

[16] NETL, n 8 above, 19. See also H Zhai and ES Rubin, 'Comparative Performance and Cost Assessments of Coal- and Natural-Gas-Fired Power Plants under a CO_2 Emissions Performance Standard Regulation' (2013) 27 *Energy & Fuels* 4290, 4297 (estimating that coal-fired power plants become competitive with new NGCC at gas prices above $9/MMBtu).

[17] NETL, n 8 above, 19.

[18] NETL, 'Coal-Fired Power Plants in the United States: Examination of the Costs of Retrofitting with CO_2 Capture Technology,Revision 3' (4 January 2011), at www.netl.doe.gov/File%20Library/Research/Energy%20Analysis/Publications/GIS_CCS_retrofit.pdf, 13, 33 (the key factors were plant efficiency, existing emissions controls, water availability, space; strictly limited by >100 MW, heat rate <12,500 Btu/KWh, w/in 25 miles of CO_2 repository).

[19] ibid 35. See also Zhai and Rubin, n 16 above, 4290 (estimating that a 66% reduction in CO_2 from coal plants would add $38.9/MWh to the cost of electricity generated).

[20] H Zhai, Y Ou and ES Rubin, 'Opportunities for Decarbonizing Existing US Coal-Fired Power Plants via CO_2 Capture, Utilization and Storage' (2015) 49 *Environmental Science and Technology* 7571, 7574.

[21] NETL, n 18 above.

[22] ibid 7574–75 (the coal plants determined to be 'feasible' were required to have an LCOE with the CCS retrofit that was comparable to that of a fully amortised NGCC, which was $37.2/MW; other feasibility factors included plant age, net summer capacity, capacity factor, heat rate and net unit efficiency).

[23] ibid 7576.

[24] S Talati, H Zhai and MG Morgan, 'Viability of Carbon Capture and Sequestration Retrofits for Existing Coal-Fired Power Plants under an Emission Trading Scheme' (2016) 50 *Environmental Science and Technology* 12567, 12568, 12571 (the CCS retrofits added $48–50/MWh to pre-retrofit LCOEs of $12–22/MWh; however, the estimates did not include all of the added costs associated with the capture technology).

will often be higher than the LCOEs for wind and solar power today. The option to sell the captured CO_2 for use in EOR has the potential offset this competitive disadvantage, and may be critical if the costs of wind and solar decline as projected.[25] Anticipating this issue, the 2015 study estimated that the increase in LCOE from CCS retrofits on coal plant could be fully offset by CO_2 prices of $20–30/t CO_2 at a 90 per cent CO_2 capture rate.[26] While promising, this added revenue would not materially alter the article's estimate that CCS retrofits are viable on only about 20 per cent of the coal-fired generation in the US.

The prevailing focus of applying CCS to coal-fired generation often obscures the option of retrofitting existing or constructing new NGCCs with CCS. Yet if one factors in a price on CO_2, new NGCCs would be a cheaper source of electricity than new coal plants for gas prices below $10/MMBtu and CO_2 prices below $51/t CO_2. Further, even at carbon price of $100/t CO_2, electricity generated by a new NGCC with CCS would be cheaper than electricity from a new coal plant with CCS if the price of gas is below $6/MMBtu.[27] The number of US electricity markets in which NGCCs are dominant could also increase if significant investments are made in new infrastructure (transmission lines, gas pipelines), which may be a priority of the Trump Administration.

Shifting the focus from coal to natural gas generation would not necessarily provide a significant pathway for CCS. The lower CO_2 emissions rate from NGCCs complicates the economics, because while the added cost of capturing CO_2 is lower than that for a coal plant, resulting in an LCOE of roughly $92/MWh versus $113/MWh,[28] respectively, the quantity of CO_2 emissions captured per unit of electricity produced is much lower. This is evident in the CO_2 abatement costs, which are estimated to be $-5 to $58/t CO_2 for coal-fired units and $10–110/t CO_2 for NGCCs.[29] Thus, whether in the form of emissions credits or the direct sale of CO_2, the potential economic value of emissions reductions is much lower for an NGCC. Low gas prices therefore exacerbate the weak economics of CCS on coal plants without necessarily providing an alternative pathway for CCS on an expanding fleet of NGCCs.

II. CURRENT AND FUTURE US POLICIES FOR PROMOTING CCS

A great deal of excellent commentary has centered on the regulation of CCS and public opposition to geologic sequestration of CO_2. This work has informed policies in the US and elsewhere through development of model laws and frameworks for evaluating regulatory options, compilations of CCS policies and international cooperation involving governments, non-governmental organisations and industry.

---

[25] Bloomberg, n 1 above.
[26] Zhai et al, n 20 above, 7576; Talati et al, n 24 above, 12572–73 (finding that a price of $10/t CO_2 for use in EOR reduced the LCOE to $40/MWh for 85% CO_2 capture).
[27] NETL, n 8 above, 20 (finding that a new NGCC with CCS is cheaper than a new coal plant with CCS at gas prices below roughly $13/MMBtu).
[28] Rubin et al, n 6 above, 382.
[29] ibid 390.

Although the specific standards and forms of CCS regulations vary across jurisdictions, several technical and legal issues have risen to the surface. Among the technical issues, the characterisation and monitoring of carbon sequestration sites have received extensive consideration, and continue to evolve as research and implementation progress. Among the legal issues, short- and long-term liability for harmful releases of CO_2, along with subsurface ownership rights, have stimulated considerable debate. These issues are unlikely to be fully resolved in the near term, but a common set of principles and legal frameworks now exist that are sufficient to guide policies as CCS is deployed and sequestration practices mature.

In the US, federal and State policies are in place, though still evolving. A key development was the Environmental Protection Agency's (EPA's) issuance of regulations and supporting guidance on geologic sequestration of CO_2 pursuant to the Underground Injection Control (UIC) program of the federal Safe Drinking Water Act.[30] The new 'Class VI' well program establishes a comprehensive program for regulating geologic sequestration of CO_2, including site characterisation requirements, injection testing protocols, site closure and monitoring plans, and proof of adequate financial resources. Importantly, sites that use captured CO_2 for EOR are subject to much more limited regulations under the UIC's 'Class II' well program, and need only obtain a Class VI permit if a site transitions to injecting CO_2 predominantly for geologic sequestration. Several US States have issued their own complementary sets of regulations for CO_2 sequestration, which vary in scope and relative stringency.[31] The principal elements of State regulations have centered on property rights, supplemental permitting rules and requirements for long-term stewardship of sequestration sites. Most of the State laws have been passed to facilitate deployment of CCS, and enable carbon sequestration by resolving uncertainties around property rights and legal liability. Thus, while policies will undoubtedly change as CCS deployment progresses, the essential regulatory framework is in place, and legal barriers are no longer a rate-limiting obstacle to deployment of CCS in the US.

Texas is among a handful of States with the most promising conditions for deploying CCS, and thus is a valuable illustrative case study. It is one of four that account for 40 per cent of the coal-fired generation capacity nationally for which CCS retrofitting is projected to be economic,[32] and it has the largest market in the country for CO_2 used in EOR.[33] These technical advantages are complemented by favourable regulations and generous State incentives. Consistent with EPA regulations,

---

[30] US EPA, Federal Requirements Under the Underground Injection Control (UIC) Program for Carbon Dioxide (CO_2) Geologic Sequestration (GS) Wells, 75 Fed Reg 77229 (10 December 2010); EPA, 'Class VI Guidance Documents', at www.epa.gov/uic/final-class-vi-guidance-documents.

[31] Interstate Oil & Gas Compact Commission (IOGCC), 'A Review of State and Provincial Action to Create a Legal and Regulatory Infrastructure for Storage of Carbon Dioxide in Geologic Structures' (September 2010), at www.groundwork.iogcc.ok.gov/topics-index/carbon-sequestration/iogcc-white-papers/a-review-of-state-and-provincial-action-to-crea.

[32] Zhai et al, n 20 above, 7575.

[33] G Cooney et al, 'Evaluating the Climate Benefits of CO_2-Enhanced Oil Recovery Using Life Cycle Analysis' (2015) 49 *Environmental Science and Technology* 7491, 7491; NETL, 'Near Term Projections of CO_2 Utilization for Enhanced Oil Recovery (DOE and NETL, 2014), at www.netl.doe.gov/research/energy-analysis/search-publications/vuedetails?id=632, 16–17.

EOR operations in Texas are not subject to regulations beyond those required for conventional oil and gas production, and offshore geologic storage of CO_2 is being facilitated by a 2009 law that requires State agencies to establish regulations for and to assume ultimate ownership and long-term liability over a major offshore geologic CO_2 repository.[34] In terms of incentives, Texas provides a sales tax exemption for all equipment used to separate, capture, transport and geologically inject CO_2; substantial property tax abatements for CCS operations and sequestration sites; and a 75 per cent reduction in the State severance tax on oil production for EOR that utilises anthropogenic CO_2.[35] Relative to other States, the principal countervailing factor is the low price of electricity in Texas, which makes the economics of CCS less attractive due to the lower revenue from base-load electricity generation.

Despite this unique mix of natural advantages and favourable policies, deployment of CCS in Texas has been mixed. The Air Products & Chemicals CCS project, which recently surpassed capturing 3 million tonnes of CO_2 from a methane purification process, is the leading example of CCS in the State.[36] The much larger Petra Nova coal-fired power plant went online in January 2017 capturing about 1.3 million tonnes of CO_2 annually, which will be used in an EOR project partially owned by the parent company NRG.[37] Nevertheless, failed CCS projects still outnumber the successes, with the future of the Texas Clean Energy Project uncertain and three other CCS projects either on hold or cancelled in 2016.[38] At the same time, the viability of conventional coal-fired power in Texas is itself in jeopardy. Several recent reports project large losses of coal-fired capacity, including a 2016 report from the Electric Reliability Council of Texas (ERCOT), the local grid regulator, that projects 50 to 90 per cent of coal-fired generation could be retired by 2031 with no new coal plants in the pipeline.[39] These projections underscore the dramatic changes in US electricity markets and the obstacles they present to deploying CCS. As the

---

[34] An Act Relating to the Development of Carbon Dioxide Capture and Sequestration in this State HB NO 1796. See IOGCC, n 31 above, 10–11.

[35] Texas currently accounts for about two-thirds of all EOR operations, and is projected to produce roughly half of all EOR-extracted oil in the longer term. See ibid.

[36] GCCSI, 'Air Products Steam Methane Reformer EOR Project' (26 September 2016), at www.globalccsinstitute.com/projects/air-products-steam-methane-reformer-eor-project.

[37] J Schwartz, 'Can Carbon Capture Technology Prosper Under Trump?' New York Times (2 January 2017), at www.nytimes.com/2017/01/02/science/donald-trump-carbon-capture-clean-coal.html?_r=0.

[38] T Overton, 'DOE Poised to Pull Out of Texas Clean Energy Project' Power Magazine (17 May 2016); MIT, 'Carbon Capture & Sequestration Technologies, Cancelled and Inactive Projects', at sequestration.mit.edu/tools/projects/index_cancelled.html (listing Trailblazer and ZENG Worsham-Steed projects as cancelled and the Sweeney Gasification project as on hold as of 30 September 2016).

[39] Electric Reliability Council of Texas (ERCOT), '2016 Long-Term System Assessment for the ERCOT Region' (26 December 2016), at www.ercot.com/content/wcm/lists/89476/2016_Long_Term_System_Assessment_for_the_ERCOT_Region.pdf, 10–11 (projecting coal plant retirements of from roughly 9.5 to 16 GW or about 50 to 90 per cent of total coal generation capacity); I Shavel et al, 'Exploring Natural Gas and Renewables in ERCOT, Part IV' (The Brattle Group, 17 May 2016), at www.brattle.com/system/news/pdfs/000/001/066/original/Exploring_Natural_Gas_and_Renewables_in_ERCOT__Part_IV_-_The_Future_of_Clean_Energy_in_ERCOT.pdf?1464037646; D Schlissel, Institute for Energy Economics and Financial Analysis, 'The Beginning of the End: Fundamental Changes in Energy Markets are Undermining the Financial Viability of Coal-Fired Power Plants in Texas' (September 2016), at www.ieefa.org/wp-content/uploads/2016/09/The-Beginning-of-the-End_September-2016.pdf.

experience in Texas exemplifies, market economics, far more than regulatory gaps or public opposition, are the principal barrier to deployment of CCS.

With conventional coal plants losing ground to other generation sources, technological innovation and secondary revenue streams are the only options for overcoming what is becoming an existential threat to the coal industry. Climate change policies, when they eventually do arrive, will accelerate this process if CCS is not close to being economically competitive. In these circumstances, the critical policy objective ought to be transformative technological innovation, with deployment of CCS that propels incremental cost reductions from 'learning by doing' remaining a secondary goal until new technologies advance beyond the pilot project phase.

Electricity market trends and economics in the US make it essential that government resources and policies be used to promote development of new technologies with dramatically superior economics. First, the strongest case for relying on existing, relatively proven technologies (ie, carbon capture based on amines) is that the economics of retrofitting *existing* power plants with CCS are relatively close to being competitive with other low-carbon technologies. While plausible, this argument overlooks the sensitivity of CCS retrofits to plant characteristics and projections that the economics are likely to be favourable for less than a fifth of the existing fleet of coal plants, and given their shorter lifetime of roughly 25 years, the economics of retrofitting existing NGCCs is unlikely to be better. These constraints severely limit the potential impact of incremental changes in CCS technologies and make it hard to justify significant government investments on the basis of existing fleets alone.

Secondly, the economics of *new* coal-fired power plants, with or without CCS, are not competitive with low-carbon technologies under all but the most pessimistic assumptions about NGCCs and renewables. The poor economics of coal generation are the principal reason that almost no new coal plants are projected to be built in the US. Conventional coal-fired power is on the order of 40 per cent more expensive than NGCCs and wind, and at least 15 per cent more costly than utility-scale solar in markets such as Texas; with CCS, the LCOE of coal-fired power is more than double the LCOEs of wind and solar.[40] Similarly, while the LCOE of an NGCC with current CCS technologies is 25 per cent lower than coal-based CCS, it is still more than 50 per cent higher than the LCOEs for wind and solar. Only fundamental technological advances have the potential to make CCS economically competitive, and while a path forward likely exists for NGCCs with CCS, the prospects for coal-fired generation are far more challenging.

Policymakers should also be realistic about the impact of EOR on the economics of CCS. Given the relatively low costs of CCS retrofits, one could imagine EOR substantially enhancing CCS deployment if CO_2 prices for EOR were at least \$20–30/t CO_2; however, the universe of CCS retrofits, as we have seen, is still likely to be quite limited. Enhanced oil recovery is far less likely to bridge the gulf between the high costs of new coal plants and renewable generation; the high CO_2 prices necessary, more than \$50/t CO_2, are unlikely to occur in the EOR market, particularly if the low price of oil persists, or in the form of federal tax credits. Concerns

---

[40] See Table 7.1.

about federal budgets and the declining costs of renewables and storage are likely to be powerful countervailing forces against large subsidies. Moreover, given the large volumes of CO_2 emitted by coal plants, it is not difficult to foresee significant deployments of CCS, resulting in a market awash in CO_2 supplies and the price of CO_2 for use in EOR collapsing.

The preceding analysis cannot be squared with the leading policies under consideration in Congress. Pending bills focus foremost on deployment of CCS technologies through policies that reduce the cost of capital financing and fixed minimum prices on CO_2 used in EOR (\$30–35/t CO_2) or geologically sequestered in deep saline formations (\$30–50/t CO_2).[41] To begin with, it is perverse for government policies to establish minimum prices for the sale of CO_2, as opposed to imposing a price on its release, to incentivise CO_2 abatement. As a general rule, market failures associated with innovation or deployment of technologies should not be conflated with environmental externalities, particularly through such an inverted pricing mechanism.

More to the point, these policies create only indirect incentives, through 'market pull' mechanisms, for investments in fundamental R&D, which, as I have argued, is far more important than deployment of CCS technologies that have little prospect of ever being economically competitive. My overriding concern is that the pending legislation may be sufficient to stimulate limited deployment of CCS at existing power plants, as well as some industrial facilities, but that it will do so by stimulating over-investment in dead-end technologies with only marginal impacts on CO_2 emissions. In so far as generous tax credits reduce government support for fundamental CCS R&D, they also risk slowing progress on new CCS technologies. Further, if the impacts on CO_2 emissions are marginal, these policies are likely to reinforce scepticism in the US about CCS. In essence, current policies risk throwing good money after bad to provide a short-term, largely symbolic political response to structural changes in electricity markets that will not meaningfully revive the coal industry or serve the interests of deploying CCS.

Proponents of CCS should be wary of policies that are politically expedient but economically untenable: CCS has little prospect of playing more than a niche role in the US without dramatic improvements in its economics. A 2016 analysis by the Department of Energy (DOE) based on several scenarios that incorporated technological advances and federal policies supports this view.[42] Under the most optimistic scenario, in which CO_2 capture costs declined to \$30/t CO_2 and federal tax credits were \$35/t CO_2 for EOR and \$50/t CO_2 for geologic sequestration, the study projected that by 2040 there would be CCS retrofits on 34 GW of coal-fired generation (roughly 10 per cent of the current fleet), less than 1 GW of new coal-fired generation with CCS, and 14 GW of new NGCCs with CCS.[43] Most of the CCS retrofits

---

[41] C Marshall, 'Carbon Capture: Heitkamp, Whitehouse Bill Would Boost Incentives' (13 July 2016), at www.eenews.net/greenwire/stories/1060040224/; US Department of Energy (DOE), 'Carbon Capture, Utilization, and Storage: Climate Change, Economic Competitiveness, and Energy Security' (August 2016), at https://energy.gov/sites/prod/files/2016/09/f33/DOE%20-%20Carbon%20Capture%20Utilization%20and%20Storage_2016-09-07.pdf, 7.
[42] DOE, n 41 above.
[43] ibid 8–9.

on coal plants (roughly 29 GW) occurred by 2030, whereas almost all of the new NGCCs with CCS were built after 2030.[44] This analysis provides further evidence that deployment of CCS on coal plants is likely to be low in the US, and it offers only modestly more hope for deployment of CCS on NGCCs longer term. All of the existing studies reinforce the conclusion that the future of coal-fired power rests on major advances in both CCS and combustion technologies. The potential of NGCCs with CCS is more difficult to predict, but the DOE study suggests at minimum that carbon capture costs must drop below $30/t CO_2 for it to be widely deployed.

The specific mix of policies is less important than recognising that despite decades of work, fundamental technological advances are still needed for CCS to play more than a minor role in the US. Potential policies could include funding of basic research, grants for demonstration projects, loan guarantees and prizes for significant advances based on cost or performance metrics. In addition, federal policies should be directed more systematically towards industrial sources of CO_2 for which the economics of CCS are promising but significant practical or technical barriers exist. Currently CCS is the only option for mitigating CO_2 emissions from many industrial sources, and they have the virtue of not being subject to the brutal competitive environment characteristic of electricity markets. Carbon capture and sequestration policies should also be prioritised and calibrated according to the volume of CO_2 emissions in the industry and the prevailing economics. In sectors where the costs are relatively low and the existing technologies adequate, such as natural gas processing plants, policies should be directed at deployment; whereas in sectors for which technologies are less developed or costly, basic R&D along with demonstration projects should be the principal focus.

III. CONCLUSION

This chapter has focused somewhat artificially on developments in the US without considering the potential global implications, which are likely to be substantial because climate change is global in scope and because technology transfer transcends borders. The US is idiosyncratic, however, in at least two critical respects: opportunities for CCS retrofits on coal plants are limited by the old age of the US fleet, and the weak economics of CCS are greatly exacerbated by the persistently low price of natural gas. Neither of these conditions exists in China or India, which together account for about 60 per cent of the coal consumed globally. Their fleets are relatively young and projected to expand, and the price of natural gas in each country is high due to limited domestic supplies.[45] The potential universe of CCS retrofits is therefore much greater outside the US among the other leading coal-consuming countries. This market provides a plausible rationale, albeit an extraterritorial one,

---

[44] ibid.
[45] M Finkenrath, J Smith and D Volk, 'CCS Retrofit: Analysis of The Globally Installed Coal-Fired Power Plant Fleet' (International Energy Agency, 2012), at www.iea.org/publications/freepublications/publication/information-paper---ccs-retrofit-analysis-of-the-global-installed-power-plant-fleet.html, 34.

for the prevailing focus of US policy on CCS deployment. A less parochial view thus complicates the case for US policies to focus on groundbreaking CCS technologies, although it is unclear whether the potential gains from US deployment of CCS would be meaningful at the global level. The global context should not be lightly dismissed, but two factors make me sceptical about whether such external factors should be given controlling weight—the exceptional capacity for technological innovation in the US and the modest scale of CCS deployment projected even under very favourable assumptions. In short, forgone US R&D is more likely to be irreplaceable, whereas a US focus on deployment of CCS is more likely to fail to reach critical mass. Whatever balance is ultimately struck, this chapter has sought to highlight the critical importance to the success of CCS policies of current and projected competitive dynamics in US electricity markets.

8

Gaining Economic Credit for CCS in the United States

ROBERT F VAN VOORHEES[*]

I. INTRODUCTION

ONCE THE ATTEMPT to establish a mandatory national cap and trade program for greenhouse gas (GHG) mitigation fell short in 2009 without enactment by Congress of the Waxman-Markey bill,[1] which had been passed by the House of Representatives,[2] the effort to put a national price on carbon in the United States (US) effectively stalled. Since then, the focus has shifted to other sources of funding and support for the development of carbon dioxide (CO_2) capture and storage (CCS) (often called 'sequestration' in the US). These other sources at the national level have included tax credits for the storage of CO_2 in subsurface geologic formations and investment tax credits for CO_2 capture projects, in addition to the very extensive funding through grants, loan guarantees and other means provided by the US Department of Energy (DOE) through its network of seven Regional Carbon Sequestration Partnerships (RCSPs) and its other research, development and demonstration efforts.[3] At the State and regional levels, this has included several other types of tax credits, as well as cap-and-trade programs.

II. NATIONAL LEVEL CREDIT

A. Credit for Carbon Dioxide Sequestration under Section 45Q

One economic credit available at the national level for CCS in the US comes in the form of a tax credit for CO_2 sequestration under section 45Q of the Internal

---

[*] The author acknowledges with appreciation the assistance of John Kindschuh, Associate, Bryan Cave LLP, in the preparation of this chapter.
[1] The American Clean Energy and Security Act of 2009, HR 2454, 111th Cong (2009).
[2] Les Lo Baugh referenced the Waxman-Markey bill and Robert Nordhaus described its provisions in the first edition of this book: L Lo Baugh, 'Legal and Regulatory Challenges of Geological Carbon Capture and Sequestration: US Hurdles to Reducing CO_2 Emissions', and RR Nordhaus, 'Treatment of CCS under GHG Regulatory Programmes' in I Havercroft, R Macrory and RB Stewart (eds), *Carbon Capture and Storage: Emerging Legal and Regulatory Issues* (Oxford, Hart Publishing, 2011).
[3] See US Department of Energy (DOE), Office of Fossil Energy, 'Carbon Capture Research' (2016), at energy.gov/fe/science-innovation/carbon-capture-and-storage-research.

Revenue Code (IRC).[4] Enacted in 2008 and amended the following year, the provision allows a credit of $20, adjusted for inflation, per metric ton of CO_2 stored in geologic formations through CCS operations not associated with oil and gas production, and $10, adjusted for inflation, per metric ton of qualified CO_2 that is stored in association with enhanced oil recovery (EOR).[5] In each case, the CO_2 must be captured by the taxpayer at 'a qualified facility' and disposed of in 'secure geologic storage'.[6] A qualified facility is a facility owned by the taxpayer where carbon capture equipment is placed in service and at least 500,000 metric tons of CO_2 are captured during the taxable year. In order to qualify, the CO_2 must be both captured and stored in the US. The CO_2 itself must be 'captured from an industrial source' where it 'would otherwise be released into the atmosphere as industrial emission of greenhouse gas', and it must be 'measured at the source of capture and verified at the point of disposal or injection'. The statute expressly precludes credit for CO_2 'that is re-captured, recycled, and reinjected' for EOR to avoid double counting.

i. Secure Geologic Storage—IPCC Guidelines

Specification of what constitutes 'secure geologic storage' was assigned to the Secretary of the Treasury—'in consultation with the Administrator of the Environmental Protection Agency [EPA], the Secretary of Energy, and the Secretary of the Interior'—to 'establish regulations for determining adequate security measures for the geological storage of carbon dioxide'. Rather than promulgate regulations, the Internal Revenue Service (IRS), acting for the Secretary, published in 2009 a Notice[7] providing interim guidance ('pending the issuance of regulations') on 'determining eligibility for the credit and the amount of the credit, as well as rules regarding adequate security measures for secure geological storage of CO_2'. The IRS 2009 Notice adopted the approach of basing secure storage on guidance developed for national GHG inventories instead of a scheme directly applicable to CCS storage operations. Specifically, the IRS adopted 'procedures outlined in the 2006 Intergovernmental Panel on Climate Change Guidelines for National Greenhouse Gas Inventories (IPCC Guidelines)'.[8]

---

[4] 26 USC § 45Q (2015). Section 45Q was enacted by § 115 of the Energy Improvement and Extension Act of 2008, Pub L No 110-343, 122 Stat 3829 (3 October 2008), as amended by § 1131 of the American Recovery and Reinvestment Tax Act of 2009, Division B of Pub L 111-5, 123 Stat 115 (17 February 2009), at www.gpo.gov/fdsys/pkg/USCODE-2015-title26/html/USCODE-2015-title26-subtitleA-chap1-subchapA-partIV-subpartD-sec45Q. The credit is essentially applicable against any tax imposed on a business under Chapter 1 of the IRC, subject to the limitations, carryback and carryforward provisions of §§ 38 and 39: 26 USC §§ 38 and 39 (2015).

[5] Generally, this means that the $20 credit would apply to CO_2 injected through wells regulated under the Class VI provisions of the underground injection control (UIC) program, while the $10 credit would apply to CO_2 injected through wells regulated under the Class II provisions.

[6] As originally enacted, the requirement for 'secure geologic storage' did not apply to EOR: Pub L No 110343, 122 Stat 3829 (2008). That provision was expanded to include EOR in 2009: Pub L No 1115, 123 Stat 325.

[7] IRS, 'Credit for Carbon Dioxide Sequestration Under Section 45Q', Notice 2009–83, 44 Internal Revenue Bulletin 588 (2 November 2009).

[8] Intergovernmental Panel on Climate Change 2006, National Greenhouse Gas Inventories Programme. HS Eggleton et al (eds), *2006 IPCC Guidelines for National Greenhouse Gas Inventories*, 2: *Energy* (Hayama, Japan, Institute for Global Environmental Strategies, 2006), ch 5. 'Carbon Dioxide Transport, Injection and Geological Storage'.

The IRS noted, however, that the EPA had proposed rules for geologic sequestration of CO_2, and stated:

> The requirements in the final [underground injection control (UIC)] program rules (or any successor rules) will apply in lieu of the requirements of the IPCC Guidelines ... However, any taxpayer that is not covered by the final UIC program rules must continue to follow the procedures outlined in the IPCC Guidelines ...

The IRS also noted that the EPA had announced 'plans to propose new rules to require reporting of the amount of CO_2 that is geologically sequestered', and stated 'When the proposed geologic sequestration rules are finalized, such rules (or any successor rules) will apply in addition to the final UIC program rules (to the extent applicable), and the requirements of the IPCC Guidelines ... will no longer apply.'

ii. Secure Geologic Storage—Subpart RR

The EPA finalised mandatory GHG reporting rules for the underground injection of CO_2 on 1 December 2010.[9] In the preamble to the final rule, the EPA states that 'taxpayers claiming section 45Q tax credit must follow the [monitoring, reporting and verification (MRV)] procedures that are being finalized under 40 CFR part 98, subpart RR in this final rule'.[10] In the aftermath of the EPA's action, the IRS did not promulgate the mandated regulations or even revise the published 2009 Notice. Instead, in 2013 the IRS added a section to the Internal Revenue Manual (IRM), with instructions to IRS examiners on how to handle credits claimed under section 45Q.[11] The 2013 IRM text instructs IRS examiners that subpart RR applies to taxpayers claiming the section 45Q credit after 2010. The IRM references the subpart RR Preamble, saying:

> EPA's final rule states in plain language that, under the final rule, operators of facilities that are sequestering CO_2 in geologic storage must comply with Subpart RR regardless of whether the CO_2 is currently used as a tertiary injectant in an EOR project.

It further instructs examiners that 'credits claimed by the taxpayer in years after 2010 should be reconciled with annual volumes reported by the operator of the facility to the EPA under its subpart RR rules'. The IRM further instructs that if a taxpayer has claimed the tax credit for years beginning after 2010 but the injection operator did not submit an MRV, 'the examiner should contact local IRS Counsel and Petroleum Subject Matter Experts regarding the treatment of those previously or currently claimed credits'.

Where this leaves the qualification for 'secure geologic storage' under section 45Q is not as clear as it could be, because the IRS has not issued the regulations called for by the statute or revised the 2009 Notice, choosing instead to bury its response to the EPA's rules in the less authoritative IRM. What does seem clear is that a taxpayer who wants to claim a credit for CO_2 that is injected for secure geologic

---

[9] Mandatory Reporting of Greenhouse Gases: Injection and Geologic Sequestration of Carbon Dioxide, 75 Fed Reg 75,060 (1 December 2010).
[10] ibid 75,064.
[11] Internal Revenue Manual (IRM), § 4.41.1.3.5 (3 December 2013).

storage without being used for EOR must obtain a Class VI UIC permit to inject the CO_2 and comply with the GHG reporting requirements under 40 CFR part 98 subpart RR (CO_2 received, injected, produced and emitted), which are mandatory for Class VI geologic sequestration projects. It is less clear whether the same subpart RR reporting requirements are mandatory for taxpayers claiming the lower credit for CO_2 used for EOR. Those operations inject through wells having Class II UIC permits, are not covered by the final UIC program rules for 'geologic sequestration' and therefore, arguably, 'must continue to follow the procedures outlined in the IPCC Guidelines' under the terms of the as yet unaltered IRS interim guidance statements in the IRM to the contrary notwithstanding.[12]

Any project that is injecting CO_2 as part of a qualified EOR project will use Class II injection wells and be required to report GHG emissions under subpart W, which applies to all petroleum and natural gas production operations and requires the reporting of CO_2, CH_4, and N_2O emissions. In addition, anyone injecting CO_2 for EOR (or any other purpose) must also report under subpart UU 'the annual mass of CO_2 received'. The GHG reporting program is expressly designed to allow anyone who 'injects the CO_2 stream for long-term containment in subsurface geologic formations' to choose to report under subpart RR rather than subpart UU by obtaining EPA approval of a 'monitoring, reporting, and verification (MRV) plan'. The EPA announced that '[o]il and gas operations that use CO_2-EOR are only required to report under subpart UU, unless they opt into subpart RR to establish that CO_2 is being geologically sequestered'.[13] Although the IRM instruction is that EOR operators must comply with the requirements of subpart RR in order to obtain 45Q credit for CO_2 used for EOR, uncertainties remain because of the loose ends left by the language of the 2009 Notice and the IRS's failure to issue regulations, which presumably would have more binding effect on taxpayers than the 2009 Notice and 2013 IRM instructions to examiners. It does seem clear, however, that anyone claiming 45Q credit for CO_2 injected without complying with subpart RR is swimming against the current.

iii. Questions about Subpart RR

The intent that subpart RR reporting be used whenever someone is seeking credit of some type for storing CO_2 in geologic formations—at least on the part of the EPA, if not the IRS—is shown by the EPA's actions in promulgating regulations for the control of GHG emissions from fossil fuel-fired electric generating units (EGUs).[14]

---

[12] Curiously, the instructions on IRS Form 8933, used to claim the 45Q credit, say nothing about subpart RR. For 'secure geologic storage' the instructions say '[t]his includes storage at deep saline formations, oil and gas reservoirs, and unminable coal seams under such conditions as the IRS may determine under regulations. See Notice 2009-83, 2009-44 I.R.B. 588, for more information on secure geological storage.' The form only references the non-existent regulations and the unrevised 2009 Notice.

[13] Mandatory Reporting of Greenhouse Gases: Injection and Geologic Sequestration of Carbon Dioxide, 75 Fed Reg 75,060, 75,077.

[14] EPA, Standards of Performance for Greenhouse Gas Emissions from New, Modified, and Reconstructed Stationary Sources: Electric Utility Generating Units; Final Rule, 80 Fed Reg 64510 (23 October 2015). EPA, Carbon Pollution Emission Guidelines for Existing Stationary Sources: Electric Utility Generating Units, 80 Fed Reg 64,662 (23 October 2015).

Where CCS is used to achieve compliance with those rules, the EGU capturing the CO_2 is required to send the CO_2 to an operation that reports under subpart RR, regardless of whether it is a geologic sequestration project without hydrocarbon recovery or an EOR project. The EPA's actions prompted expressions of concern and both administrative and judicial challenges to these regulatory requirements on the grounds that the requirements of subpart RR would interfere with normal EOR operations to the point of being 'fundamentally incompatible' with the use of any EGU-captured CO_2 for EOR and on administrative procedure grounds.[15]

The fundamental problem expressed with subpart RR was that compliance would involve more than a reporting obligation. The claim is that subpart RR imposes operational constraints and uncertainties through the requirement to operate under an approved MRV plan that imposes obligations extending beyond the EOR operator's ability to continue its field operations under the existing oil and gas legal framework, including leases and contracts. Specific cited problems include the administrative process for approval of an MRV, which includes potential delays for administrative and judicial appeals and for frequent revisions with further administrative proceedings; the inherent defect of being designed for a 'waste disposal operation' (a notion also reflected in the section 45Q use of 'disposed' in secure geologic storage); and the implicit requirement to continue monitoring and other operations at an EOR project for an extended period after oil and gas production has ceased. As explained, the underlying mineral leases for EOR operations are granted for the purpose of hydrocarbon recovery and do not authorise the lessee to convert the owners' property into a storage site. The leases are held by production of the oil or gas. Hence, following completion of oil or gas operations, the leases will come to an end and the property will revert to the owner. Some EOR operators explained that it is fundamentally inconsistent with the nature of these underlying property rights to convert a hydrocarbon recovery operation into a 'waste disposal' operation. Yet that appears to be what is contemplated by subpart RR. The overriding assertion was that the imposition of subpart RR requirements would have the effect of unduly penalising the use of anthropogenic CO_2 captured from EGUs.

The alternative recommendation is for the EPA to allow EGU operators to direct captured CO_2 streams to EOR operators who comply with subpart W and subpart UU reporting, which is already required, has been successfully implemented by the Agency and the reporting community for a number of years, and imposes no new mandatory requirement on the EOR operators. The assertion is that the EPA's Class II permitting program for CO_2 injection wells is already designed to fully protect underground sources of drinking water from endangerment and is the regulatory framework for tens of thousands of existing active Class II wells, CO_2 supplies to which are regularly reported under subpart UU. Under this proposed alternative, emissions reported under subpart W would be subtracted proportionately from total CO_2 received from the EGU source, which must report the total CO_2 sent under subpart PP.

---

[15] Petition of Denbury Onshore, LLC for Reconsideration of 40 CFR § 60.5860(F)(2) and Expedited Stay Pending Reconsideration—Before EPA (21 December 2015); *Denbury Onshore, LLC v EPA*, Case No 15-1475 (DC Cir, filed 21 December 2015), consolidated with *State of West Virginia v EPA*, Case No 15-1363 (DC Cir, filed 23 October 2015).

iv. Subpart RR Reporting

From 2010 until 2015, no one reported under subpart RR because all of the non-EOR Geological Sequestration (GS) projects injecting CO_2 into geologic formations had qualified for research exemptions,[16] and no EOR operations had opted to report under subpart RR rather than under subparts W and UU. On 22 December 2015, the EPA ushered in the first ever use of subpart RR reporting for a CO_2-EOR operation by approving a MRV plan submitted by Occidental Petroleum for the Denver Unit in the Permian Basin of West Texas.[17] The EPA's approval provided insight into how some concerns and uncertainties surrounding the use of subpart RR reporting for storage associated with CO_2-EOR could be addressed, and the decision indicates significant flexibility to adapt parts of subpart RR requirements to a context substantially different from non-EOR geologic storage.[18] These include questions about whether subpart RR reporting can be discontinued before EOR operations are terminated, and whether a MRV plan must be revised every time any type of new well is installed.

Some significant concerns over the application of subpart RR to CO_2-EOR operations were alleviated by the EPA's approval, which also provided reason for optimism that other concerns could potentially be resolved through give and take with the EPA during the MRV plan development and approval process. Because there were no appeals of the EPA's approval, any potentially disruptive administrative proceedings were avoided. Moreover, the MRV plan was for an existing EOR operation and not for a CO_2 capture operation dependent on approval for regulatory compliance. Thus, other questions remain unanswered and could limit the usefulness of 45Q credits.

As of 26 September 2016, the aggregate amount of qualified CO_2 taken into account for purposes of section 45Q was 44,590,130 metric tons.[19] This is very significant, because section 45Q was enacted as a temporary incentive to encourage the development and use of CCS technologies. The credit expires after the 'end of the calendar year in which … 75,000,000 metric tons of qualified carbon dioxide have been taken into account' for the credit.[20] Because this type of tax information is confidential, it is not possible to identify exactly who has used the credits, or to be sure how long the credits or how many credits will be available. These latter uncertainties loom large for projects seeking financing in reliance on 45Q credits. Nor does the fact that the credits have been claimed indicate that they have been audited and accepted by the IRS. If all of the section 45Q claims made so far are allowed,

---

[16] See US Environmental Protection Agency (EPA), 'Greenhouse Gas Reporting Program (GHGRP): Subpart RR—Geologic Sequestration of Carbon Dioxide' (2016), at www.epa.gov/ghgreporting/subpart-rr-geologic-sequestration-carbon-dioxide.

[17] EPA, 'Technical Review of Subpart RR MRV Plan for the Denver Unit' (December 2015), at www.epa.gov/ghgreporting/denver-unit.

[18] RF Van Voorhees, 'Crediting carbon dioxide storage associated with enhanced oil recovery' (13th International Conference on Greenhouse Gas Control Technologies, GHGT-13, Lausanne, Switzerland, 14–18 November 2016) (2017) 114 *Energy Procedia* 7659.

[19] IRS, Internal Revenue Notice 2016-53, Internal Bulletin 2016-39 (26 September 2016).

[20] 26 USC § 45Q(e) (2015).

the entire 75,000,000 metric tons will be consumed, and the credit will expire, at the end of calendar year 2018 if claims continue at the currently trending rate.

Those uncertainties prompted the National Enhanced Oil Recovery Initiative (NEORI) to call upon Congress to eliminate the expiration provision and amend the section 45Q program to:

— Designate the owner of the CO_2 capture facility as the primary taxpayer;
— Establish a registration, credit allocation, and certification process;
— Change the recapture provision to ensure that any regulations issued after the disposal or use of CO_2 shall not enable the federal government to recapture credits that were awarded according to regulations that existed at that time; and
— Authorize limited transferability of the credit within the CO_2 chain of custody, from the primary taxpayer to the entity responsible for disposing of the CO_2.[21]

The NEORI recommendations were incorporated in proposed legislation in 2012[22] and have been introduced in every session of Congress since then.[23] Similar proposals were reflected in President Obama's FY 2016 budget, which also included provisions for 'new separate investment and production tax credits available for up to 10 and 20 years, respectively'.[24] In July 2016 legislation was introduced[25] that would extend and expand the tax credits under section 45Q by eliminating the 75 million ton cap, creating credits aimed at industrial capture of CO_2 (with a lower eligibility threshold) in addition to capture at EGUs, significantly increasing the value of the credits (from $20 to $50 per ton for non-EOR storage and from $10 to $35 per ton for EOR), and adding flexibility to allow others involved in capture and storage projects to take advantage of the credit. Other legislative proposals introduced in 2016 would amend section 45Q to authorise reporting under subpart UU as the basis for 'secure geological storage' for CO_2 stored in association with EOR.[26]

B. Investment Tax Credits under Sections 48A and 48B

In 2005, Congress enacted two investment tax credits that have helped to support the development of projects with CO_2 capture technologies: the section 48A advanced

---

[21] National Enhanced Oil Recovery Initiative (NEORI), Recommended Modifications to the 45Q Tax Credit for Carbon Dioxide Sequestration (February 2012), at www.neori.org/publications/neori-45q/, 1.
[22] S. 3581—A bill to amend the Internal Revenue Code of 1986 to modify the credit for carbon dioxide sequestration, 112th Congress (2011–2012).
[23] NEORI, 'Legislation', at www.neori.org/legislation; Center for Climate and Energy Solutions, 'National Enhanced Oil Recovery Initiative', at www.c2es.org/initiatives/eor.
[24] NEORI, 'NEORI Welcomes Proposed CCUs Tax Credits in President's Budget' (12 February 2015), at www.neori.org/neori-welcomes-proposed-ccus-tax-credits-in-presidents-budget.
[25] S. 3179—A bill to amend the Internal Revenue Code of 1986 to improve and extend the credit for carbon dioxide sequestration,114th Congress (2016). The bill would also extend credit to other forms of CO_2 utilization, including production of biomass, biofuels and plastic.
[26] S. 3459, A bill to amend the Internal Revenue Code of 1986 to enhance the requirements for secure geological storage of carbon dioxide for purposes of the carbon dioxide sequestration credit, 114th Congress (2015–2016); HR.6295—CO_2 Regulatory Certainty Act, 114th Congress (2015–2016).

coal project credit, and the section 48B gasification project credit.[27] Section 48A(a) provided an investment tax credit of 20 per cent for any qualifying advanced coal project using integrated gasification combined cycle (IGCC) technology, and 15 per cent for any other qualifying advanced coal project. The total credits were limited to $1.3 billion, with $800 million allocated to IGCC projects and $500 million allocated to other advanced coal projects (2006 allocation figures).[28] Section 48B(a) provided an investment tax for any qualifying gasification project up to a total amount available for award of $350 million (2006 allocation figure). 'Gasification Technology' is

> any process that converts a solid or liquid product from coal, petroleum residue, biomass, or other materials that are recovered for their energy or feedstock value into a synthesis gas composed primarily of carbon monoxide and hydrogen for direct use or subsequent chemical or physical conversion.[29]

Taxpayer claims for these section 48A and section 48B credits are subject to a competitive application and allocation process: 'Taxpayers are awarded an amount of credit based upon their qualified project application and a Department of Energy project feasibility certification and ranking of the application.' To qualify for these credits, a project must obtain a DOE certification of feasibility and consistency with energy policy goals.[30] A number of other criteria were established relating to types of coal used, heat rates, efficiency, capacity and percentage of CO_2 captured. The types of projects and amounts of credits were separated into pools. A number of projects received credit awards under this program, but not all of them were ultimately constructed.[31]

C. Advanced Fossil Energy Project Loan Guarantees

Advanced Fossil Energy Project loans are authorised by section 1703 Title XVII of the Energy Policy Act of 2005.[32] Under this program, the DOE made available

---

[27] 26 USC § 46 (2015) provides that the amount of investment credit for purposes of § 38 for any taxable year is the sum of the credits listed in § 46. Section 1307(a) of the Energy Tax Incentives Act of 2005, Pub L 109-58, 119 Stat 594 (8 August 2005) (more commonly referred to as the Energy Policy Act of 2005 or EPA 2005) amended § 46 to add these two new credits to that list.

[28] IRS, 'Audit Technique Guide for Sections 48A and 48B—Advanced Coal and Gasification Project Credits', LMSB-4-0209-005 (updated 19 January 2016), at www.irs.gov/businesses/audit-technique-guide-for-sections-48a-and-48b-advanced-coal-and-gasification-project-credits.

[29] 16 USC § 48B(c)(2).

[30] IRS, Internal Revenue Notice 2006-24, 'Qualifying Advanced Coal Project Program', Internal Revenue Bulletin: 2006-11 (13 March 2006).

[31] See, eg, IRS, 'Announcement of the Results of 2009–10 Allocation Round of the Qualifying Advanced Coal Project Program and the Qualifying Gasification Project Program', Announcement 2010-56, Internal Revenue Bulletin: 2010-39 (27 September 2010); IRS, 'Announcement of the Results of the 2010–2011 Allocation Round of the Qualifying Advanced Coal Project Program', Announcement 2011-62, Internal Revenue Bulletin: 2011-40 (13 October 2011); IRS, 'Reallocation of section 48A credits under the qualifying advanced coal project program', Internal Revenue Notice 2012-51, Internal Revenue Bulletin 2012-33 (13 August 2012); IRS, 'Announcement of the Results of the 2011–2012 Allocation Round of the Qualifying Advanced Coal Project Program', Announcement 2013-2, Internal Revenue Bulletin: 2013-2 (7 January 2013).

[32] Pub L No 109-58.

up to $8 billion in loan guarantees to support 'innovative, advanced fossil energy projects in the US that reduce, avoid, or sequester greenhouse gases'. Carbon capture projects were specifically covered, including 'CO_2 capture from synthesis gases in fuel reforming or gasification processes; CO_2 capture from flue gases in traditional coal or natural gas electricity generation; and CO_2 capture from effluent streams of industrial processing facilities'.[33] On 21 December 2016, the DOE offered 'a conditional commitment to guarantee loans of up to $2 billion to Lake Charles Methanol, LLC to construct the world's first methanol production facility to employ carbon capture technology'. This loan guarantee would be the first of any kind made under the Advanced Fossil Energy Projects loan guarantee program. The project would produce methanol from petroleum coke (petcoke), and the captured CO_2 would be sent to Texas for storage in association with EOR.

III. STATE AND REGIONAL CREDITS

A. California Cap-and-Trade Program

Assembly Bill 32 (AB 32), the California Global Warming Solutions Act of 2006,[34] charged the California Air Resources Board (ARB) with 'monitoring and regulating sources of emissions of greenhouse gases that cause global warming in order to reduce emissions of greenhouse gases'.[35] The ARB prepared a 'scoping plan' that identified a cap-and-trade program as one of the strategies to reduce the GHG emissions. In October 2011, the ARB approved the California Cap on Greenhouse Gas Emissions and Market-Based Compliance Mechanisms Regulation (Cap-and-Trade Regulation). The Regulation provides for the establishment, administration and enforcement of the California Greenhouse Gas Cap-and-Trade Program by applying a statewide GHG emissions cap on covered entities and providing a mechanism for trading instruments used to comply with the cap.

California is working with British Columbia, Ontario, Québec and Manitoba through the Western Climate Initiative to develop harmonised cap and trade programs that will allow greater flexibility for compliance and credit trading across their respective programs. On 1 January 2014, the California Cap-and-Trade Program and Québec Cap-and-Trade System linked and agreed to mutual acceptance of compliance instruments. The ARB and Québec's Ministry of Sustainable Development, Environment and the Fight against Climate Change (MDDELCC) now hold joint auctions of GHG allowances.

The Cap-and-Trade Program provides flexibility for compliance. One alternative allows covered entities to use a limited number of offset credits to satisfy a portion of their compliance obligation. An offset credit comes from a GHG reduction

---

[33] DOE, 'Advanced Fossil Energy Projects Loan Guarantee Solicitation' (2013), at www.energy.gov/sites/prod/files/2014/04/f14/Advanced-Fossil-Fact-Sheet-FINAL.pdf.
[34] AB 32, Cal Statutes of 2006, Chapter 488.
[35] Cal Health & Safety Code § 38510.

or removal activity that can be measured, quantified and verified. Credits from individual offset projects can be sold and used by a covered entity for compliance under the Cap-and-Trade Regulation.[36] The Cap-and-Trade Regulation allows offset projects to be located in the US, US Territories, Canada or Mexico.[37] Individual Compliance Offset Protocols (COPs) may specify a more limited geographic applicability area.

An offset credit is equivalent to a GHG reduction or GHG removal enhancement of 1 metric ton of CO_2e. The GHG reduction or GHG removal enhancement must be real, additional, quantifiable, permanent, verifiable and enforceable, and may only be issued to offset projects using approved COPs. At present there is no approved COP for carbon capture and geologic sequestration, but ARB is currently developing a quantification methodology for CCS. The Regulation recognised the potential for using CCS by defining the category of 'Carbon Dioxide Supplier' to be facilities that

> capture a CO_2 stream for purposes of supplying CO_2 for commercial applications or that capture the CO_2 stream in order to utilize it for geologic sequestration where capture refers to the initial separation and removal of CO_2 from a manufacturing process or any other process.[38]

In establishing the compliance obligation for Carbon Dioxide Suppliers, the Regulation provides that the emissions exclude 'CO_2 verified to be geologically sequestered through use of a Board-approved carbon capture and geologic sequestration quantification methodology that ensures that the emissions reductions are real, permanent, quantifiable, verifiable, and enforceable'.[39] In addition, any offset credits that are 'invalidated' must be replaced by the holder of the credit or the Offset Project Operator.[40]

B. Regional Greenhouse Gas Initiative

Another public 'cap-and-trade' program is the Regional Greenhouse Gas Initiative (RGGI, pronounced 'Reggie'), the first US mandatory, market-based program to reduce GHG emissions.[41] It was created in 2005 as a regional cooperative among nine States, including Connecticut, Delaware, Maine, Maryland, Massachusetts, New Hampshire, New York, Rhode Island and Vermont, to reduce carbon emissions from the power sector.[42] The Initiative is composed of individual CO_2 Budget Trading Programs in each participating State. Through independent regulations, based on the RGGI Model Rule (2013) and the Summary of RGGI Model Rule Changes,

---

[36] California Air Resources Board, Cap-and-Trade Regulation Instructional Guidance, ch 6.2. See at www.arb.ca.gov/cc/capandtrade/guidance/guidance.htm.
[37] Cal Code of Regulations (CCR) tit 17 §§ 95972(c) and 95973(a)(3).
[38] CCR tit 17, § 95802(a)(58).
[39] CCR tit 17, § 95852(g).
[40] CCR tit 17 § 95985 (covering invalidation provisions and requirements for replacement of credits).
[41] Regional Greenhouse Gas Initiative (RGGI), 'Welcome' (2017), at www.rggi.org.
[42] RGGI, 'Program Design', at www.rggi.org/design. New Jersey withdrew from RGGI in 2011.

each State's CO_2 Budget Trading Program limits emissions of CO_2 from electric power plants, issues CO_2 allowances and establishes participation in regional CO_2 allowance auctions.

In 2014, RGGI States implemented a cap of 91 million short tons of CO_2.[43] The cap is projected to decline 2.5 per cent yearly from 2015 to 2020.[44] Fossil fuel plants having a capacity of over 25 megawatts (about 163 facilities) are required by RGGI to obtain an allowance annually for each ton of CO_2 emitted.[45] States in RGGI sell their emission allowances through quarterly regional auctions. As an alternative to purchasing CO_2 allowances, CO_2 offset allowances may be used to satisfy a limited portion of a regulated power plant's compliance obligation. Carbon dioxide offset allowances may be used to satisfy up to 3.3 per cent of a regulated source's compliance obligation during each Interim Control Period. At this time, the RGGI States limit the award of offset allowances to five project categories (not including CCS), each of which is designed to reduce or sequester emissions of CO_2, methane (CH_4) or sulphur hexafluoride (SF_6) within the nine-State region:

— landfill methane capture and destruction;
— reduction in emissions of sulphur hexafluoride (SF_6) in the electric power sector;
— sequestration of carbon due to US forest projects (reforestation, improved forest management, avoided conversion) or afforestation (for Connecticut and New York only);
— reduction or avoidance of CO_2 emissions from natural gas, oil, or propane end-use combustion due to end-use energy efficiency in the building sector; and
— avoided methane emissions from agricultural manure management operations.

One problem with RGGI is 'emissions leakage', because RGGI does not regulate emissions from electricity generated outside the region (ie, other States) and then used within the region (eg, 'imported electricity'), but this issue is, it is hoped, addressed by caps on the individual States.[46]

C. State Severance Tax Reductions

Some States have created tax incentives for carbon capture utilisation and storage (CCUS). The Texas Legislature enacted House Bill (HB) 3732 in 2007[47] to provide a reduction in the tax rate on oil produced from enhanced recovery projects using anthropogenic CO_2.[48] The bill authorised the Texas Railroad Commission (RRC)

---

[43] ibid.
[44] ibid.
[45] RGGI, 'Program Overview', at www.rggi.org/design/overview.
[46] RGGI, 'Potential Emissions Leakage and the Regional Greenhouse Gas Initiative (RGGI): Evaluating Market Dynamics, Monitoring Options, and Possible Mitigation Mechanisms' (14 March 2007), at www.rggi.org/docs/il_report_final_3_14_07.pdf.
[47] HB 3732, 84th Leg (Tex. 2015) (HB 3732).
[48] HB 3732 also established an 'Advanced Clean Energy Project Grant and Loan Program', which does not appear to have been used to date. See, eg, Texas Comptroller of Public Accounts, 'A Report of the Texas Economic Development Act' (7 January 2013).

(which regulates oil and gas operations) to issue a certification for a severance tax rate reduction on oil produced using anthropogenic CO_2 in an EOR project, if that CO_2 is to be sequestered in a reservoir productive of oil or natural gas, and the Commission finds that there is a reasonable expectation that the operator's planned sequestration program will ensure that at least 99 per cent of the CO_2 sequestered will remain sequestered for at least 1,000 years. The bill also requires that the operator employ appropriately designed monitoring and verification measures for a period sufficient to demonstrate whether the sequestration program is performing as expected.

An EOR operator producing oil that qualifies for the reduced recovered oil tax rate already applicable to such projects is entitled to an additional 50 per cent reduction if:

> the EOR project uses carbon dioxide that:
>
> (1) is captured from an anthropogenic source in Texas;
> (2) would otherwise be released into the atmosphere as industrial emissions;
> (3) is measurable at the source of capture; and
> (4) is sequestered in one or more geological formations in this state following the EOR process.[49]

The tax reduction is 'proportional to the percentage of anthropogenic carbon dioxide that satisfies these criteria'.

i. Certification of Sequestration

To qualify for the tax rate reduction, the operator must obtain a certification. The RRC provides the certification if the CO_2 is used in an EOR project and sequestered in a reservoir that is productive of natural gas or oil. The Texas Commission on Environmental Quality (TCEQ) issues the certification if anthropogenic CO_2 is used in an EOR project and then is sequestered in a formation that is not productive of natural gas or oil. If the CO_2 used in the EOR project will be sequestered in an oil or gas reservoir and also in a geological formation that is not an oil or gas reservoir, the operator must obtain certifications from both agencies. The certifications are then submitted to the Texas Comptroller with an application for the tax reduction.

ii. Monitoring and Verification

The agencies may issue a certification only if they find, based on substantial evidence, that the project will meet the criteria and include sufficient monitoring and verification measures to demonstrate whether the sequestration program is performing as expected. House Bill 3732 requires approval of an application if the operator submits the requisite certification and the oil satisfies the pre-existing

---

[49] 33 Tex Reg 114 (4 January 2008).

EOR requirements. The tax rate reduction is set to expire seven years after the first approved reduction for a Texas project or the EPA adopts a final rule regulating CO_2 as a pollutant, whichever comes later.

iii. Railroad Commission Certification Rule

The RRC certification rule[50] requires the operator of the CO_2 project to implement a monitoring, sampling and testing (MST) plan that starts with analysis of chemical and physical characteristics of the CO_2 stream. It also requires continuous monitoring of injection pressure, rate of injected CO_2 and volume of injected CO_2. Annual monitoring of the injection zone pressure in the productive reservoir is required, supplemented by a pressure fall-off test at least once every five years. The plan also must use 'indirect, geophysical techniques to determine the position of the CO_2 fluid front'.

As an alternative to preparing a new MST plan for the RRC, the operator may comply with the RRC rule by submitting a copy of the information submitted to the EPA to comply with the GHG Mandatory Reporting Program. The rule expressly reaffirms that EOR injection wells will be regulated as Class II wells, and provides that certification 'does not preclude the operator of an enhanced recovery project from opting into a regulatory program that provides carbon credit for the geologic storage of anthropogenic CO_2 incidental to enhanced recovery'—for example, the EPA subpart RR program.

In all cases, the operator will be required to develop an accounting scheme and demonstrate that it that will track the anthropogenic CO_2 on a proportional basis that avoids overstating the quantities of anthropogenic CO_2 stored. To allow 'an operator to make a determination by mass balancing or actual system modelling of the quantities of anthropogenic CO_2 permanently stored', the plan must 'ensure that the injected anthropogenic CO_2 is confined to the productive reservoir' and account for the CO_2 injected, separated from produced oil, entrained in produced oil, recycled and injected, emitted and received for injection.

iv. Other States

Other US States have begun to enact legislation that would create tax credits and authorise their oil and gas regulators to certify the quantities of anthropogenic CO_2 that are incidentally stored in association with CO_2-EOR operations.[51] The RRC certification regulations also served as a starting point for the development of an International Standards Organization (ISO) standard for the recognition and quantification of anthropogenic CO_2 incidentally stored in association with CO_2-EOR.

---

[50] 16 Texas Admin Code §§ 5.301–5.308.
[51] See, eg, Wyo Stat § 30-5-502 (2015).

IV. VOLUNTARY CARBON CREDIT MARKET

In April 2015, the American Carbon Registry (ACR)[52] approved a final methodology that outlines the requirements and process for CCS Project Proponents that store CO_2 in oil and gas reservoirs to qualify their projects for carbon credits under the ACR program. The methodology is based on the accounting framework developed by the Center for Climate and Energy Solutions.[53] The methodology specifies how credits are to be quantified, and requires the replacement of lost credits through insurance, the establishment of a reserve account with ACR or other means of mitigation. Projects are eligible that capture, transport and inject anthropogenic CO_2 during EOR operations into an oil and gas reservoir located in the US or Canada. Projects are required to have clear and uncontested ownership of the pore space and all necessary land surface use rights to conduct post-injection monitoring activities and, if necessary, remediation. The current methodology does not apply to non-EOR CO_2 geologic storage.

Based on its accounting protocols, the ACR oversees the registration and verification of carbon offset projects and issues offsets through its registry system. These offset credits can be used by California entities to help meet their emissions reductions obligations. In the voluntary market, the ACR issues verified emissions reduction credits as Emission Reduction Tonnes (ERTs), and one ERT represents the reduction or removal from the atmosphere equivalent to 1 metric tonne of CO_2. For the California Cap-and-Trade Program, the ACR is an approved registry and works with the ARB to oversee the listing and verification of carbon offset projects developed using the ARB's approved protocols.

V. CONCLUSION

In the absence of national legislation that would give rise to market forces or create more direct incentives for advancing the development of CCS technologies, progress has come primarily from direct DOE support for pilot and demonstration projects. Programs and provisions described in this chapter are in place at the national, regional and State levels that could provide some level of economic assistance. There is no clear evidence, however, that any of these means of support has yet contributed substantially to fostering the development of CCS technologies. This could change as programs are modified and implemented more fully.

For the section 45Q tax credits, inherent limitations imposed by the minimum 500,000 tons per year CO_2 capture threshold and the 75 million ton cap on available credits have limited availability to larger projects requiring longer planning times owing to the lack of certainty on availability of the support, where greater

---

[52] The ACR was founded in 1996 as the first private voluntary GHG registry in the US.
[53] M McCormick, Center for Climate and Energy Solutions, 'Greenhouse Gas Accounting Framework for Carbon Capture and Storage Projects' (February 2012), at www.c2es.org/publications/greenhouse-gas-accounting-framework-carbon-capture-and-storage-projects.

certainty could be used to garner additional financing. Although information on who has used these credits to date is not publicly available, there is little evidence to suggest the program has provided significant incentives or benefits for new CCS projects. Nor has the IRS provided sufficient certainty about what must be done to demonstrate 'secure geologic storage'. After publishing interim guidance in its 2009 Notice 'pending the issuance of regulations', the IRS has not after seven years either established the regulations as directed by the statute or provided legally enforceable revisions that would tie up loose ends dangling from the initial Notice. With more than half of the available credits already apparently claimed, more definitive action by the IRS seems overdue. Congressional adoption—either individually or in some combination—of the legislative proposals described above could allow section 45Q to provide more reliable and beneficial long-term support to advance CCS technologies. All have support from members of the Republican majority in Congress, and some have Democrats as co-sponsors.

Investment tax credits have been claimed but have not been sufficient, as many of the supported projects have failed to advance to full operation. Because the loan guarantee program has taken years to reach the stage of initial commitments, its potential contribution to fostering further development remains to be shown. The first step to support a CO_2 capture project shows promise.

The regional and State cap and trade programs operated by RGGI and California could offer some potential for support. California is expanding its program to include CCS as an available offset program, but RGGI has not taken steps to include CCS. Although some State severance tax reductions are currently available, and others are being developed, it remains to be shown that these can prove sufficient to support desired significant increases in use of anthropogenic CO_2 for EOR.

Notwithstanding these limitations, the US support for CCS development through DOE research, coordination and funding, along with supplemental support from States and strong contributions from companies willing to host and support specific projects, has placed the US at the forefront of advancing CCS technologies. Although the US has announced its withdrawal from the 2015 UNFCCC Paris Agreement,[54] continuing US use and marketing fossil fuels internationally (both of which the new administration supports) will require a resolute and expanding commitment to CCS, especially in light of the commitments that 197 nations and other parties made to GHG reductions in the Paris Agreement.

---

[54] UN Framework Convention on Climate Change (UNFCCC), Decision 1/CP.21, 'Adoption of the Paris Agreement' (29 January 2016) UN Doc FCCC/CP/ 2015/10/Add.1, Annex, at www.unfccc.int/paris_agreement/items/9485.php.

9

The Legal Framework for Carbon Capture and Storage in Canada

HENRY J KRUPA

CARBON CAPTURE AND storage (CCS) maintains strong political support, as much because of the fiscal benefits it offers to Canada's economy as because it offers a means of reducing Canada's greenhouse gas (GHG) emissions. Canada has a number of the essentials necessary to make the use of carbon capture technologies a practical alternative for addressing GHG emissions: large final emitters of GHGs; suitable geology; and a wealth of transferable experience with the technologies used in CCS through the enhanced oil recovery (EOR), enhanced coal-bed methane recovery and acid-gas disposal activities of its oil and gas sectors. Canada has also implemented market-based programs to ensure that the costs for emitting carbon are elevated, and has enacted legislation and regulations to control GHG emissions, which are frequently seen as necessary for the long-term viability of CCS.

This chapter considers the status of the legal framework applicable to current and potential CCS activities by examining property rights and the regulatory and liability frameworks across Canada, and incentives supporting the use of CCS techniques.

I. AUTHORITY—CANADA'S CONSTITUTIONAL STRUCTURE

Canada is a federation of 10 provinces. Canada's Constitution[1] creates two orders of government: a central Federal authority and the provinces as self-governing authorities with the powers assigned by the Constitution. The Federal Government and provincial governments are effectively co-equal orders of government, because the Constitution assigns primacy over specific subject-matter to each order of government.[2] Canada also has three territories that are creatures of the Federal

---

[1] The Constitution Act 1867 (30 & 31 Vict, c 3) (UK) (The Constitution Act) as amended.
[2] From east to west: Newfoundland and Labrador, Nova Scotia, Prince Edward Island, New Brunswick, Québec, Ontario, Manitoba, Saskatchewan, Alberta and British Columbia.

Government, created under its constitutional authority.[3] Substantial self-governing authority has been granted to the territories, although they remain under Federal jurisdiction.

The doctrine of pre-emption does not apply in Canada in the sense known to proponents of CCS technologies in the United States (US).[4] Pre-emption refers to the displacement of State law by federal law. In Canada there is a presumption of jurisdictional limits. In enacting a law, it is assumed that the Federal Government and the provincial governments are aware of, and intend to conform to, the limits of their constitutional authority. Canadian constitutional law has further recognised that spheres of jurisdiction can be occupied by different levels of government, a concept that is known as the dual-aspect doctrine.[5] Consequently, if the principal purpose of a law—its pith and substance—affects matters within the competence of the enacting order of government, the law will be upheld even though it may impact on matters within the legislative competence of the other jurisdiction, unless it is shown to impair an essential and vital element of the other jurisdiction's power as opposed to merely affecting it.[6] Accordingly, jurisdiction for the environment is shared between the Federal Government and provincial governments.

Among the constitutional responsibilities assigned to the provinces are local works and undertakings, property and civil rights, and non-renewable natural resources.[7] Resource exploitation activities, therefore, fall predominantly under provincial jurisdiction, as do the groundwater resources. These are the constitutional subject-matters under which the provinces have traditionally sheltered their control of CCS activities. For that reason, the provinces have a substantial amount of constitutional authority to govern CCS activities within their borders. Advances in the development of local laws that govern CCS activities reflect the provinces' political autonomy and responses to such factors as the local geology, previous experiences with natural resources or the industrial sectors involved, needs and demographics, and the current provincial government's priorities, which have generally included the more active control of GHG emissions. Not surprisingly, policy or legislative road blocks to the growth of CCS projects stem from similar factors. Another dynamic relates to the development of the province's legal framework regarding subsurface ownership rights (something fundamental to CCS). The nature of these rights can depend on the date that the province joined the federation. Constitutional authority alone, therefore, is not enough to stir a province to develop its CCS capacity. Consequently, the inconsistent development of the CCS legal framework across Canada can be attributed to provincial dominance of the subject-matters most closely associated with CCS.

---

[3] From east to west: Nunavut, Northwest Territories and the Yukon.
[4] United States Constitution, Art VI: 'This Constitution, and the Laws of the United States ... *shall be the supreme Law of the Land*' (emphasis added).
[5] *Multiple Access Ltd v McCutcheon* [1982] 2 SCR 161.
[6] *R v Latouche* [2010] AJ No 631 (J Shriar Prov Ct J). An Application was brought for an order that a City by-law and its enabling provincial statute were ultra vires the jurisdiction of City and province and therefore unconstitutional. Shrair J dismissed the Application, holding that the scope of the statute or by-law did not impair the essential elements and core purposes of Federal jurisdiction over navigation and shipping.
[7] The Constitution Act, n 1 above, ss 92 and 92A.

The Government of Canada's authority over CCS activities has to be found under one of the heads of power assigned to it under the Constitution, or from a conceptual power derived from one of the functional heads of power granted to it under section 91 of The Constitution Act 1867.[8] In either case, these powers may be exercised independently by the Federal Government, such as with its authority over the management of sea beds, national borders, international relations[9] or on matters of national concern.[10] The Federal Government's powers may also be exercised in collaboration with a province acting under the provincial government's constitutional authority. International and inter-provincial pipelines, for example, fall under the exclusive jurisdiction of the Federal Government, while pipelines wholly situated within a province fall under exclusive provincial jurisdiction. However, where a pipeline connects with an international and inter-provincial pipeline, the Federal Government becomes involved, and cooperation between governments is required. Inter-government cooperation can extend to resource development that has an international component. For example, the Government of Canada and the government of Saskatchewan agreed with the US to commit new funding for the International Energy Agency GHG Weyburn-Midale CO_2 Monitoring and Storage Project in Weyburn, Saskatchewan. This project was a public- and private-sector initiative to create the world's first monitoring site for the geological storage of carbon dioxide (CO_2) in two depleted oilfields in southern Saskatchewan. The CO_2 was transported by pipeline from a coal gasification operation in North Dakota. This project ran from 2000 to 2012.[11]

There are further examples of cooperation between the Federal Government and provincial governments. In 2008, a collaborative Federal, provincial and territorial initiative to address key CCS issues of common interest across Canada was launched under the direction of the Canadian Council of Energy Ministers.[12] The Federal Government is also working in partnership with Alberta and Saskatchewan to fund CCS initiatives that may require both federal and provincial regulatory approvals.[13]

---

[8] The Constitution Act, n 1 above.
[9] Due to Canada's constitutional division of responsibilities, the powers to give effect to Canada's treaty obligations often fall within provincial authority.
[10] Again, under Canada's constitutional division of responsibilities, the Government of Canada's jurisdiction may require the provinces to exercise their powers to give effect to federal legislation of national scope. An example is the Canada Health Act, which details the conditions that provincial and territorial health insurance programs must meet in order to receive transfer payments of Federal Government funding.
[11] Petroleum Technology Research Centre, 'The IEAGHG Weyburn-Midale CO_2 Monitoring and Storage Project' (July 2017), at www.ptrc.ca/projects/weyburn-midale.
[12] The Canadian Carbon Capture and Storage Network. See Canada's CO_2 Capture and Storage Information Source (July 2017), at ccs101.ca/about_us.
[13] Some of the factors that could trigger a federal assessment of the project under the Canadian Environmental Assessment Act 2012, SC 2012, c 19 are if there are any direct or incidental effects on the environment that are linked to a federal decision, if federal funding is provided, if the project has cross-provincial or international boundary effects or if there are impacts on Aboriginal people. In cases where the Federal Minister of the Environment is satisfied that the substantive requirements of the federal environmental assessment process can be met by the provincial process, and if the province requests it, the provincial environmental assessment process can be substituted for the federal process.

For instance, the Government of Canada invested CAN$150 million from its Clean Energy Fund for two large-scale CCS demonstration projects, which included the construction in partnership with Alberta of one of the world's first fully-integrated CCS projects;[14] and CAN$240 million for the world's first commercial-scale CCS coal-fired power plant at Saskatchewan's Boundary Dam.[15] A further CAN$12.6 million from Canada's ecoENERGY Innovation Initiative is being directed to research and development projects to advance the technologies involved in CCS.[16]

II. THE REGULATION OF GHG EMISSIONS

A. Canada and International: Climate Change Law

The global drive to reduce GHG emissions underlies the development of CCS resources. This campaign is founded on the United Nations Framework Convention on Climate Change (UNFCCC) and the subsequent treaties made under the UNFCCC that record the international consensus for the principles of the UNFCCC and for the prevailing specific objectives of each of the treaties in which the objectives are recorded.[17] Canada has committed to the UNFCCC and to each of the ensuing treaties to reduce GHG emissions: the Kyoto Protocol,[18] the subsequent Copenhagen Accord[19] and, most recently, the Paris Agreement.[20] The Kyoto Protocol committed Canada to the specific emissions reduction target of reducing its GHG emissions by 6 per cent below 1990 levels by 2012. Canada's acceptance of the Protocol's compliance mechanisms was followed a few years later by the enactment of the Kyoto Protocol Implementation Act.[21] However, timely and effective national and sub-national (the provinces and territories) schemes to reduce GHG emissions did not follow. This resulted in Canada's GHG emissions rising to 17 per cent above

---

[14] Natural Resources Canada, 'Large Scale CCS Demonstration Projects' (February 2016), at www.nrcan.gc.ca/energy/funding/current-funding-programs/4951.

[15] Natural Resources Canada, 'Boundary Dam Integrated Carbon Capture and Storage Demonstration Project' (January 2016), at www.nrcan.gc.ca/energy/publications/16235.

[16] Natural Resources Canada, 'ecoENERGY Innovation Initiative Research and Development (R&D) Projects' (July 2016), at www.nrcan.gc.ca/energy/funding/current-funding-programs/eii/4987.

[17] 1771 UNTS 107; S Treaty Doc No 102–38; UN Doc A/AC 237/18 (Part II)/Add 1; (1992) 31 ILM 849.

[18] UN Doc FCCC/CP/1997/7/Add 1, 10 December 1997; (1998) 37 ILM 22; UN Framework Convention on Climate Change, 'United Nations Framework Convention on Climate Change' (Kyoto 1998); on 29 April 1998 Canada was one of the first countries to sign the Kyoto Protocol, while formal ratification came more than four years later on 17 December 2002.

[19] FCCC/CP/2009/L 7, 18 December 2009; United Nations Framework Convention on Climate Change's 15th session of the Conference of the Parties (Copenhagen 2009). The Copenhagen Accord established a climate change agreement for the period following the expiration of the commitment period under the Kyoto Protocol in 2012. Canada inscribed its 2020 economy-wide target of a 17% reduction in GHGs from 2005 levels in the Copenhagen Accord on 29 January 2010.

[20] FCCC/CP/2015/L.9; UN Framework Convention on Climate Change, 'Adoption of the Paris Agreement: 21st Conference of the Parties' (Paris 2015). The Paris Agreement is a non-binding accord to keep global warming below 2°C this century. The Agreement came into force on 4 November 2016.

[21] SC 2007, c 30.

1990 levels by 2010.[22] Faced with purchasing costly international credits to fulfill its Protocol obligations and with having to deal with the potential disadvantages arising from its biggest economic trading partner, the US (which is responsible for nearly 20 per cent of global GHG emissions), not being covered by the Protocol,[23] Canada withdrew from the Protocol in December 2011 and subsequently rescinded the Kyoto Protocol Implementation Act.[24]

In 2009 Canada followed by committing to the emissions limitations under the Copenhagen Accord. Canada has not had markedly better results meeting its Accord target than it did with meeting its Protocol target. Despite the allowance provided by the decline in Canada's GHG emissions resulting from the 2007–08 recession, an internal government report shows that Canada will fall substantially short of its 2020 Copenhagen Accord target.[25]

Next, Canada was one of countries that made a non-binding commitment to the 2015 Paris Agreement's common goal to keep global warming below 2°C this century. The non-binding nature of the Paris Agreement meant that signatory nations were not faced with the threat of binding enforcement mechanisms to measure and control CO_2 emissions if this goal were not met. The Paris Agreement's enforcement mechanisms are essentially peer pressure and apprehension about the consequences of global warming flowing from the transparent reporting of GHG emissions. The Agreement requires best efforts through nationally determined contributions (NDCs), which are to be updated and reported every five years.[26] To assess the collective progress made in achieving the goals of the Agreement, a 'global stocktake' is to occur in 2023, and every five years thereafter. Canada ratified the Paris Agreement on 5 October 2016. Significantly, the possibility has already been raised of the need to purchase carbon offsets to meet Canada's Paris Agreement commitment in the event that global resource prices rebound and oil sands production increases to the levels anticipated by the recent pipeline expansion approvals.[27]

Canada's international commitments to reduce GHG emissions have provided evolving structured goals but do not direct the actions that Canada will need to take to achieve the desired outcome. The Paris Agreement accommodated the development of each signatory nation's goals by allowing those nations the opportunity to

---

[22] UN Framework Convention on Climate Change, 'Report of the individual review of the annual submission of Canada submitted in 2010'(UN Framework Convention on Climate Change, 2011); The Conference Board of Canada, 'Greenhouse Gas (GHG) Emissions' (July 2017), at www.conferenceboard.ca/hcp/details/environment/greenhouse-gas-emissions.aspx.
[23] Environment and Climate Change Canada, 'A Climate Change Plan for the Purposes of the Kyoto Protocol Implementation Act 2012' (June 2013), at www.ec.gc.ca/Publications/default.asp?lang=En&n=EE4F06AE-1&xml=EE4F06AE-13EF-453B-B633-FCB3BAECEB4F&offset=3&toc=hide.
[24] Repealed 2012, c 19, s 699.
[25] Environment Canada, *Canada's Emissions Trends 2013* (Environment Canada, 2013).
[26] The NDC Registry can be found at www4.unfccc.int/ndcregistry/Pages/Home.aspx.
[27] D Sawyer, 'After Paris, here's how Canada can achieve a low-carbon future', *The Globe and Mail* (15 December 2015), at www.theglobeandmail.com/opinion/after-paris-heres-how-canada-can-achieve-a-low-carbon-future/article27762660; see also J Wilt, 'The Carbon Offset Question: Will Canada Buy its Way to the Climate Finish Line?' *Desmog Canada* (13 December 2016), at www.desmog.ca/2016/12/13/carbon-offset-question-will-canada-buy-its-way-climate-finish-line.

weigh their national priorities, capabilities and circumstances to prepare a declaration of their NDC, which should balance those factors to produce an achievable commitment. Underlying factors, such as political support and the motivation of the electorate, will invariably influence the assessment of those factors. In theory the process of coming up with Canada's Paris Agreement NDC should have paralleled how the decision was reached for the country to commit to its previous international GHG-related commitments. However, the structure of Canada's federal state means that the relative influence of each of these factors will be impacted by a variety of national and sub-national conditions, which makes the measuring of the factors less than precise. In this regard, Canada's mixed record in meeting its national commitments since signing on to the Kyoto Protocol can in part be attributed to the Federal Government's not being held politically accountable for its failure to take meaningful action. This process resulted in Canada's 2010 GHG emissions being 17 per cent above the 1990 base-year levels of the Kyoto Protocol.[28]

Canada's federal and provincial leaders periodically participate in meetings to consider matters of national importance. These meetings are the modern expressions of the constitution conventions that took place in the early years of the Canadian federation in the nineteenth century.[29] In its current form, it is the Prime Minister of Canada who has the discretion to call a meeting of the First Ministers of the Confederation. Typically the provincial leaders meet immediately before the First Ministers' meeting for the purpose considering the concerns of all of the provinces, and possibly to put together a united provincial position before the full meeting of the First Ministers.[30] By their very nature, First Ministers' meetings serve to document the political priorities of the Canadian federation. For example, although the First Ministers have met 81 times since 1906, with 19 of these meetings having occurred since 1990, stand-alone environmental or climate change subjects have been on the agenda at only the three most recent First Minister meetings, which have all occurred since November 2015.[31] The March 2016 First Ministers' meeting saw the beginning of a coordinated national approach to carbon risk mitigation, with the release of the 'Vancouver Declaration on Clean Growth and Climate Change'. The Vancouver Declaration reiterated Canada's Paris Agreement NDC pronouncement

---

[28] NDC Registry, n 26 above.

[29] There have also been a few federal, provincial and territorial Ministerial and Deputy Minister meetings held to discuss environmental issues. Ministers are typically serving politicians, while a Deputy Minister is the civil service head of a ministry serving at the pleasure of the elected government.

[30] Since the territorial governments are constitutional creatures of the Federal Government, they are typically invited to First Ministers' meetings only when the agenda contains an issue relevant to the territories.

[31] A First Ministers' Conference is a meeting of the provincial and territorial premiers and the Prime Minister of Canada. The 79th First Ministers' meeting held on 23 November 2015, the 80th First Ministers' meeting held on 3 March 2016 and the 81st First Ministers' Meeting held on 9 December 2016 are the only First Ministers' Conferences at which climate change was on the agenda that were released to the public. On the other hand, a partial list of agenda items at First Ministers' meetings since 1990 finds that the economy was on the agenda for six First Ministers' meetings, health care and social programs were on the agenda for seven First Ministers' meetings and the Constitution was on the agenda for three First Ministers' meetings. There have also been a very few federal, provincial and territorial Ministerial and Deputy Minister meetings held to discuss environmental issues.

The Legal Framework for CCS in Canada 155

by promising 'GHG mitigation policies in support of meeting or exceeding Canada's 2030 target of a 30% reduction below 2005 levels of emissions'.[32] The first opportunity the First Ministers had to fulfil this pledge as a group came about with the First Ministers' meeting in December 2016. At that time, by a divided consensus, the First Ministers adopted the Pan-Canadian Framework on Clean Growth and Climate Change.[33] Although it is still very much a plan to make a plan, the Pan-Canadian Framework did catalogue purposed mitigation policies, which could encourage the development of industrial CCS resources. The mitigation policies include phasing out the use of coal, 'protecting and enhancing carbon stored in forested lands, wetlands and agricultural lands', pricing carbon emissions and 'reducing methane emissions from the oil and gas sector'.

The Federal Government had a limited risk in persuading the provinces to accept a national carbon policy (NCP) scheme under the December 2016 Pan-Canadian Framework. First, Canada had sent a very large delegation to the 2015 Paris Climate Conference. The delegation included representatives from the provinces and territories.[34] The options available to achieve the Paris Agreement's goals were well known to the attendees, although any consensus regarding the preferred means to do so tended to discount practical economic and political considerations. Secondly, by December 2016, Ontario, Québec, Alberta and British Columbia, Canada's four biggest provinces, representing 86 per cent of Canada's population, either had a carbon pricing scheme in place or had announced that a carbon pricing scheme would be introduced in 2017.[35] Therefore, the implications of a carbon pricing scheme would have been well known to Canada's sub-national jurisdictions. Thirdly, the Federal Government's interest in an NCP scheme should not have been a surprise to the provinces or the country as a whole: the Federal Government's intention to introduce an NCP scheme had already been made public in October 2016, weeks before the Pan-Canadian Framework was announced.[36] Nevertheless, not all of the provinces initially bought into the Pan-Canadian Framework. The Communiqué of Canada's First Ministers that was released following the December 2016 meeting tried to mask the reluctance of Manitoba, Saskatchewan and British Columbia

---

[32] Canadian Intergovernmental Conference Secretariat, 'Vancouver Declaration on clean growth and climate change' (March 2016), at www.itk.ca/wp-content/uploads/2016/04/Vancouver_Declaration_clean_Growth_Climate_Change.pdf. Canada's NDC can be found at www4.unfccc.int/ndcregistry/PublishedDocuments/Canada%20First/INDC%20-%20Canada%20-%20English.pdf.

[33] Communiqué of Canada's First Ministers (9 December 2016), at pm.gc.ca/eng/news/2016/12/09/communique-canadas-first-ministers.

[34] E Thompson, 'Trudeau's delegation to Paris conference costs more than $1m', *iPolitics* (12 March 2016), at ipolitics.ca/2016/03/12/trudeaus-delegation-to-paris-conference-cost-more-than-1-million/.

[35] In November 2016, Nova Scotia announced that it will implement a cap-and-trade system by 2018. Nova Scotia released a discussion paper of the proposed cap-and-trade program for public comment, which can be found at climatechange.novascotia.ca/sites/default/files/Cap-and-Trade-Document.pdf. Aside from an emissions tax on the use of petroleum coke in industrial facilities, Manitoba currently does not have plans for carbon taxation or pricing. New Brunswick, Prince Edward Island, Newfoundland and Labrador do not have plans for carbon taxation or pricing. Canada's three territories have indicated that they will implement carbon taxation or pricing, but have yet to do so.

[36] Hansard, Number 086, 42nd Parliament, 1st Session, 3 October 2016, 1205.

to sign on to it.[37] British Columbia's concerns were about fairness: it wanted to be sure that regulated parties in British Columbia would not be paying a higher carbon price than in other provinces when the costs of the national scheme were added to the costs of British Columbia's home-grown carbon tax (in the other provinces that have implemented carbon pricing, this has taken the form of cap-and-trade or a blended carbon tax and cap-and-trade program). Saskatchewan based its opposition to any sort of carbon pricing on the declarations of then US President-Elect Donald Trump regarding scrapping many of the green-friendly regulations that were implemented by President Barack Obama. Saskatchewan felt that an NCP scheme would have an uncertain effect on reducing GHG emissions but could impair the growth of Saskatchewan's economy, and, as purposed, fell outside of the Federal Government's constitutional authority.[38] Manitoba's reluctance, on the other hand, can be characterised as a more customary theme of First Ministers' meetings: the desire to increase federal transfer payments to the provinces. Manitoba's view was that healthcare funding from the Federal Government should be the number one priority. The Federal Government responded by announcing that it would impose a national carbon price scheme despite the objections of any province. In the end, only Saskatchewan did not adopted the Pan-Canadian Framework.[39]

The Pan-Canadian Framework remains consistent with Canada's Paris Agreement NDC by adopting the Vancouver Declaration's GHG-related reduction target date of 2030. The Pan-Canadian Framework also proposed GHG reduction measures that are, for the most part, of indifferent benefit to the development of CCS projects. Without doubt, adding to the costs of carbon emissions and proposing to reduce methane emissions from the oil and gas sector are incentives for CCS projects. However, the Pan-Canadian Framework shifts the focus away from large final GHG emission sources to the more wide-ranging issue of GHGs in the atmosphere and to GHG management schemes that involve the use of natural carbon sinks. Unfortunately, no information has been provided regarding whether the preparations leading up to the Pan-Canadian Framework included weighing the relative merits of the GHG management options, to explain why the Pan-Canadian Framework ignores the potential of employing engineered carbon capture schemes to address known and potential future large final emission sources. The Pan-Canadian Framework's remedy for existing large final emission sources like coal-fired electricity generation facilities is to ban the use of coal rather than to support the employment of electrostatic precipitators (scrubbers) and end-of-pipe solutions like CCS, although since the actual amendment of legislation is beyond the capacity of the Pan-Canadian Framework, the statutory option of an equivalency agreement under the Canadian Environmental Protection Act 1999, which would recognise the provinces' use of an alternative CO_2

---

[37] JP Tasker, 'Trudeau announces "pan-Canadian framework" on climate—but Sask., Manitoba hold off', *CBC News* (9 December 2016), at www.cbc.ca/news/politics/trudeau-premiers-climate-deal-1.3888244.
[38] J Warick, 'Sask. Alone in threatening carbon tax suit: Brad Wall', *CBC News* (1 December 2016), at www.cbc.ca/news/canada/saskatoon/wall-threatens-legal-action-carbon-tax-1.3876489.
[39] Environment and Climate Change Canada, n 23 above.

emissions reduction strategy, was not removed.[40] The Pan-Canadian Framework's ban on the use of coal was conceived in the context of a number of earlier federal and provincial prohibitions relating to the use of coal. Undoubtedly the ban is helpful to deal with small GHG, nitrogen oxide, sulfur oxide and PM 2.5 and PM 10 emission sources. However, some provinces have already addressed small sources of these emissions, such as space heaters. In any event, the Pan-Canadian Framework appears to disregard the history of successful engineered carbon capture schemes in Canada, such as the Boundary Dam coal-fired electricity CCS project and Weyburn-Midale coal gasification CCS projects.[41]

A number of federal election cycles have taken place since the UNFCCC was created in the early 1990s. Some of these have resulted in ideological swings in the Federal Government's political leadership.[42] Although there were concerns that a swing of the federal governing party from Liberal to Conservative would influence the Federal Government's support for international climate change initiative and support for the UNFCCC, every federal governing party since the Kyoto Protocol was negotiated has treated Canada's climate change-related commitments as politically binding, albeit with different levels of adherence. This has brought about the peculiar situation whereby the federal leadership that replaced the one that brought Canada into the Kyoto Protocol proposed to implement arguably more constructive Kyoto Protocol-related initiatives than did its predecessor, the latter having been criticised for doing little to help Canada meet the Kyoto commitment to which it bound Canada.[43]

Historically Canada has tried to moderate its climate-change-related plans with practical economic and political considerations. For Canada the dilemma has always been one of balancing the potentially competing objectives of addressing climate-change factors and obtaining real environmental rewards, while achieving real economic benefits for all Canadians. To fully appreciate the predicament facing Canadian policy makers, it is important to bear in mind the context in which the planning of these efforts has taken place. Canada is a large, typically very cold country with a relatively small population, with long distances between population and economic centres, and with an economy that has a significant

---

[40] SC 1999, c 33, s 10 Agreements Respecting Equivalent Provisions.
[41] Canada's CO_2 Capture and Storage Information Source, n 12 above; Natural Resources Canada, n 15 above.
[42] 1997—Liberal majority; 2000—Liberal majority; 2004—Liberal minority; 2006—Conservative minority; 2008—Conservative minority; 2011—Conservative majority; 2015—Liberal majority.
[43] Eg, in 2005 the Conservative Government proposed the 'Climate Change Plan for Canada', which would have implemented a Large Final Emitters System, an Offset System and the Climate Fund. The Large Final Emitters System was a mandatory market-based program, which aimed to reduce GHG emissions in the mining, manufacturing, oil, gas and thermal electricity sectors, which at the time accounted for roughly half of Canada's national GHG emissions. The 'Climate Fund' (officially the Canada Emission Reduction Incentives Agency) was to be capitalised for the purpose of reducing or removing GHGs through the purchase of GHG emission reduction and removal credits on behalf of the Federal Government. The 'Climate Change Plan for Canada' strategy was to be implemented by 2009, but this had not been done by the time that Canada withdrew from the Kyoto Protocol at the end of 2011. The timing to implement the 'Climate Change Plan for Canada' strategy had to be weighed against the impossibility of Canada's meeting its Kyoto target and the failure of the US to accept the Kyoto Protocol.

resource-based component. The result of this is that for the period between 1990 and 2014, the period during which the Kyoto Protocol and Copenhagen Accord were negotiated, a significant part of the increase in Canada's GHG emissions can be attributed to 'a 79% ... increase in emissions in the oil and gas sector and a 32% ... increase in the transportation sector'.[44] In 2014, the oil and gas sector was the largest GHG emitter in Canada, accounting for 26 per cent of Canada's total GHG emissions.[45] However, in that same year, the oil and gas sector was also reported to be 'the single largest private sector investor in the country', and provided a significant amount of government revenues by way of royalty payments, land payments, and corporate and municipal taxes.[46]

There is some justification for the paradox of Canada's policy makers striving to expand the foreign markets for Canada's fossil fuels at the same time that Canada is supporting global action on climate change. This apparent inconsistency has not gone unnoticed. For instance, Canada's actions attracted criticism at the COP 22 meeting held in Marrakech, Morocco, in November 2016.[47] Nonetheless, this did not prevent the Federal Government from announcing that federal approvals had been granted for two major export pipelines from the oil sands in Alberta not long after the First Ministers' meeting in December 2016, which introduced the Pan-Canadian Framework to combat climate change. One of the approved pipelines, the Line 3 Pipeline Replacement Project, will run from eastern Alberta to the Canadian–US border in south-west Manitoba near Superior, Wisconsin, at the head of the Great Lakes. The Line 3 Pipeline Replacement Project will nearly double the existing daily pipeline capacity of Line 3.[48] The second approval was for the Trans Mountain Expansion Project.[49] When completed, this Project will nearly triple the daily capacity of the existing pipeline running from Edmonton, Alberta, to the west coast near Vancouver. Both projects satisfied a regulatory review that included confirmation that the direct and upstream GHG emissions linked to the projects would not be significant. In addition, both projects are required to operate within the Alberta government's proposed oil sand emissions cap of 100 megatonnes of CO_2 per year.[50] The Canadian Prime Minister's announcement regarding the federal approval of these two projects included the assertion that '[t]here isn't a country in the world that would find billions of barrels of oil and leave it in the ground

---

[44] Environment and Climate Change Canada, 'Canadian Environmental Sustainability Indicators: Greenhouse Gas Emissions' (Environment and Climate Change Canada, 2016) 9, at www.ec.gc.ca/indicateurs-indicators/FBF8455E-66C1-4691-9333-5D304E66918D/GHGemissions_EN.pdf.

[45] Environment and Climate Change Canada, *Canada's Emission Trends 2014* (June 2017), at www.ec.gc.ca/ges-ghg/default.asp?lang=En&n=E0533893-1.

[46] Canadian Association of Petroleum Producers, *Canadian Economic Contribution* (July 2017), at www.capp.ca/canadian-oil-and-natural-gas/canadian-economic-contribution.

[47] B Cheadle, 'Canada criticized over fossil fuel expansion at Morocco climate summit', *The Globe and Mail* (Ottawa, 16 November 2016), at www.theglobeandmail.com/news/national/canada-criticizied-over-fossil-fuel-expansion-at-morocco-climate-summit/article32874253/.

[48] Natural Resources Canada, 'Line 3 Replacement Project' (May 2017), at www.nrcan.gc.ca/energy/resources/19188.

[49] Natural Resources Canada, 'Trans Mountain Expansion Project' (May 2017), at www.nrcan.gc.ca/energy/resources/19142.

[50] Oil Sands Emissions Limit Act SA 2016, c O-7.5, s 2(1).

while there's still a market for it'.[51] Yet not long after making this assertion, Prime Minister Trudeau advised a town-hall meeting in Ontario that while 'Canada can't shut down the oil sands immediately [it] would need to eventually'.[52] The former statement put Prime Minister Trudeau at odds with environmental activists, who are recognised as being an important constituency of the Prime Minister, as well as a sizable number of Albertans, notwithstanding that few would argue that while Alberta's (and Saskatchewan's) oil resources are large, these resources are not limitless.[53] The shutting down of the oil sands may be a predictable eventuality but it is one that reasonably will not have to happen for many years. The Prime Minister's views appear to be more than merely off-the-cuff comments playing to an audience, because Prime Minister Trudeau repeated the essential elements of these statements to a conference of oil executives in Texas in March 2017. This suggests that these statements were more likely an indication of the inclination of the Trudeau Government.[54]

Oddly enough, Prime Minister Trudeau's view regarding the end of oil sands production is in line with the opinion of his immediate predecessor, of whose government's environmental policies Prime Minister Trudeau was critical when the Prime Minister sat in the opposition gallery. At a 2015 meeting of the G7 meeting, then Prime Minister Steven Harper stated that the world needs to stop burning fossil fuels by the end of the century.[55] This suggests that the choice between the long-established options of either addressing climate change factors or achieving real economic benefits, which has typically been framed as choosing to realise either one goal or the other, will over time devolve into a reasonably balanced approach, striving to achieve environmental benefits while factoring in the potential economic consequences.

Moderating Canada's climate change commitments with practical economic and political considerations has included harmonising climate and energy policies with those of Canada's biggest economic trading partner, the US. In 2011, Canada had reasoned that the potential economic disadvantages to Canada arising from the failure of the US to sign on to the Kyoto Protocol justified withdrawing from the Protocol. However, the US subsequently committed to the GHG reduction targets

---

[51] Prime Minister Justin Trudeau; see G Morgan, 'Ottawa approves two pipelines, rejects one while imposing tanker ban on northern BC coast', *Financial Post* (29 November 2016), at business.financialpost.com/news/energy/ottawa-approves-two-pipelines-rejects-one-while-imposing-tanker-ban-on-northern-b-c-coast?__lsa=a0ec-5e6c.

[52] Wall Street Journal, 'Canada Needs to Phase Out Oil Sands, Prime Minister Says', *Wall Street Journal* (13 January 2017), at www.wsj.com/articles/canada-needs-to-phase-out-oil-sands-prime-minister-says-1484368920.

[53] B Jean, 'Statement on Trudeau's vow to phase out the oil sands' (January 2017), at www.wildrose.ca/jean_statement_on_trudeau_s_vow_to_phase_out_the_oil_sands; Brian Jean, the leader of Alberta's conservative Wildrose Party, stated that 'If Mr Trudeau wants to shut down Alberta's oil sands, ... let him be warned: He'll have to go through me and four million Albertans first'.

[54] A full transcript of Prime Minister Trudeau's keynote address at the CERAweek Global Energy and Environment Leadership Award Dinner in Houston, Texas, on 9 March 2017 is available at www.macleans.ca/economy/justin-trudeaus-speech-in-houston-read-a-full-transcript/.

[55] S McCarthy and K Cryderman, 'Trudeau's oil sands "phase-out" comments spark anger in Alberta', *The Globe and Mail* (Ottawa and Calgary, 13 January 2017), at www.theglobeandmail.com/news/alberta/trudeaus-oil-sands-phase-out-comments-spark-anger-in-alberta/article33622908/.

under the Copenhagen Accord. Therefore, to improve its trade relations with its largest trading partner, Canada harmonised its 2020 economy-wide target GHG reduction commitments with those of the US under the Copenhagen Accord. Doubts about the future of harmonisation arose from the uncertainty about the future actions of the US raised during the 2016 US Presidential race.[56] These doubts became certainties when President Trump's Executive Order 13783, 'Promoting Energy Independence and Economic Growth', was issued in March 2017,[57] which was followed not long after by the President's announcing that the US would be withdrawing from the Paris Accord.[58] Canada will have to weigh the economic risks that could follow should Canada's harmonisation of its 2020 GHG reduction commitments becoming inconsistent with the US GHG reduction plans. The potential of policy discord with the US did not delay the Federal Government's announcement of its intention to implement an NCP scheme, nor did this deter a number of Canada's sub-national jurisdictions from proceeding with their own carbon pricing schemes and policies that are reflected in the Pan-Canadian Framework, even though these may make those sub-national jurisdictions uncompetitive. Similarly, Canada and its sub-national jurisdictions continued to phase out electrical power generation options that involve large final emitters of GHGs, while the future of the US Clean Power Plan, which dealt with US power plants, remained judicially undecided.[59] In any event, the Trump Presidency's Executive Order directing US federal agencies to take regulatory action to review Obama-era climate policies could result in the complete elimination of the Clean Power Plan and similar regulation, which means that there will be less chance of achieving harmony between Canadian and US regulations and GHG reduction commitments.[60] However, at this time there is no indication that the Canadian national and sub-national initiatives will be revised to accommodate changes in the US.

In 1991, before the Kyoto Protocol, the Copenhagen Accord and Paris Agreement, Canada and the US arranged to address 'air-related issues of a global nature, such as climate change' by an agreement directed at trans-boundary air pollution.[61] Coal-fired power plants were recognised as being significant sources of GHGs. Both countries (and independently many of Canada's sub-national jurisdictions)

---

[56] R Cho, 'Trump vs Clinton: What the Election Could Mean for Climate Policy' (*Earth Institute*, 2016).

[57] Office of the Federal Register, Executive Order 13783, 'Promoting Energy Independence and Economic Growth', issued on 28 March 2017, available at www.federalregister.gov/documents/2017/03/31/2017-06576/promoting-energy-independence-and-eco.

[58] MD Shear, 'Trump Will Withdraw US From Paris Climate Agreement', *New York Times* (1 June 2017), at www.nytimes.com/2017/06/01/climate/trump-paris-climate-agreement.html.

[59] 40 CFR pt 60, Carbon Pollution Emission Guidelines for Existing Stationary Sources: Electric Utility Generating Units. On 9 February 2016 the US Supreme Court stayed the implementation of the 'Clean Power Plan' pending judicial review. This did not impact the work of individual States that undertook to cut GHG emissions from power plants.

[60] Executive Order 13783, n 57 above.

[61] 'Agreement Between the Government of the United States of America and the Government of Canada on Air Quality', available at www.epa.gov/sites/production/files/2015-07/documents/agreement_between_the_government_of_the_united_states_of_america_and_the_government_of_canada_on_air_quality.pdf.

implemented regulations and pressed for the use of technologies that focused on regulating and controlling the discharge of particulate matter and gases such as CO_2, carbon monoxide, nitrogen oxide, sulfur dioxide and various hydrocarbons from coal-fired power plants. For example, effective 1 July 2015, the federal Reduction of Carbon Dioxide Emissions from Coal-fired Generation of Electricity Regulations came into force.[62] In addition, where a large final emitter like a coal-fired power plant has access to favourable geology, CCS has been employed to limit the discharge of GHGs. The example of the Boundary Dam coal-fired power plant project in Saskatchewan has previously been noted.

In 2014, the electricity sector was Canada's fourth largest source of GHG emissions, accounting for 11 per cent of total national emissions, even after a decrease of 17 per cent of GHG emissions from combustion-based electricity generation since 1990. This decline in GHG emissions is attributed to '[t]he growing share of electricity generated from non-GHG-emitting sources (such as hydro, nuclear and other renewables) and from fuels less GHG-intensive than coal'.[63] Carbon capture and storage did not contribute to this decrease, because the Saskatchewan-based Boundary Dam coal-fired power project, which is the first large-scale coal-fired power plant fitted with CCS technology, did not come on line until October 2014.

In Canada, Nova Scotia, New Brunswick, Ontario, Manitoba, Saskatchewan and Alberta have had coal-fired electricity generation plants. Going back to the period before significant reductions in coal-fired generation capacity, in 2006 Ontario and Alberta, in that order, were the provinces with the largest coal-fired generation capacity.[64] However, Canada has moved away from the continuing use of coal-fired electricity generation plants seen in the US. The human health and environmental risks associated with air emissions from coal-fired electricity generation plants were viewed as being significant enough to warrant taking on the economic risk linked with replacing the mid-range capital costs and mid-range fuel and operating costs for the generation capacity provided by coal-fired electricity generation plants with higher-cost alternative generation sources like renewables.

In 2014, Ontario became the first jurisdiction in North America to fully eliminate coal as a fuel source for electricity generation. This process was started in 2007, with Ontario enacting a regulation to force the closure of all coal-fired generating stations in the province.[65] This was reinforced by banning the use of coal to generate electricity.[66] The Ontario government stated that its decision to do so was based

---

[62] SOR/2012-167.

[63] Environment and Climate Change Canada, n 44 above, 11.

[64] National Energy Board, 'Coal-Fired Power Generation: A Perspective' (National Energy Board (NEB), 2008); Ontario 6,329 MW and Alberta 6,217 MW. In 2006, coal-fired electricity generation provided the following percentages of total electricity generation capacity: Nova Scotia—52.3%, New Brunswick—11.9%, Ontario—19.5%, Manitoba—1.7%, Saskatchewan—46.4%, Alberta—52.9%. The 2015 'End of Coal: Ontario's Coal Phase Out' Report by The International Institute for Sustainable Development (IISD) states that coal-fired generation provided 25% of Ontario's electricity in 2007. The NEB was reporting capacity, while the IISD is reporting the electricity that was provided.

[65] Ontario Regulation 496/07 Cessation of Coal Use—Atikkoan, Lambton, Nanticoke and Thunder Bay Generating Stations.

[66] Ending Coal for Cleaner Air Act 2015, SO 2015, c 2, which amended the Environmental Protection Act RSO 1990, c E19, by adding pt VI.1, 'Cessation of Coal Use at Generating Facilities'.

on a 'cost–benefit analysis that assumed about CAN$3 billion in annual savings to the health care system would come from the reduction of smog-related air contaminants'.[67] However, the province's rationale did not connect the elimination of GHG emissions with the elimination of smog-forming emissions. At any rate, the utility of phasing out the use of coal for air quality and public health reasons has been questioned. A recent study concluded that

> the coal phase-out yielded small improvements in air quality in some locations ... which were comparable in size to projected air quality improvements that could have been achieved through the installation of new pollution control systems rather than closing the plants.[68]

This study serves as a caveat for the other Canadian jurisdictions planning to phase out the use of coal for ambient air-quality purposes.

In any event, Ontario's actions to eliminate coal-fired electricity generation from the province were heralded as the single largest GHG emissions reduction initiative in North America.[69] The phase out of coal-fired electricity generation was taken to be the only option available to Ontario. While the subsurface geology of Ontario is not uniformly favourable for the use of CCS technology, the fundamental barrier to the development of CCS was one of mind-set: prior to the shut-down of the coal-fired electricity generation plants, the Ontario government (which at that time owned Ontario's principal electricity generator) did not consider CCS technology as a suitable response to deal with the air emissions from coal-fired electricity generation plants. Ontario instead focused on replacing coal-fired generation with natural gas and renewable generation sources. Although Ontario has eliminated coal as a GHG emission source from its electric power generation system, it is still home to industries that are large GHG emission sources. To deal with this, Ontario proposes to develop programs that will maximise GHG emission reductions from sectors outside of the electricity sector.[70] Regrettably this scheme appears to carry forward the Ontario government's view that CCS technology is not a suitable response to deal with the GHG emissions, so CCS technology is not on the Ontario government's list of potential technologies to be considered. This does not, however, prevent the private sector's taking advantage of CCS technology in the right circumstances.

By 2016 the Federal Government and the province of Alberta had followed Ontario's example by announcing their own intentions to phase out coal-fired electricity generation by 2030. At the time the Federal Government did not release the details of its plan. However, as an example of climate change commitments being moderated by practical economic and political considerations, the Federal Government has shown that it is open to tempering its plans to eliminate coal-fired generation by 2030. Nova Scotia was granted 'an exemption to continue its

---

[67] R McKitrick and E Aliakbari, *Did the Coal Phase-out Reduce Ontario Air Pollution?* (Vancouver, The Fraser Institute, 2017) iii.
[68] ibid iii–iv.
[69] Ministry of the Environment and Climate Change, Press Release, 25 November 2013.
[70] O Reg 46/17, Ontario Climate Change Solutions Deployment Corporation.

use (of coal-fired generation) beyond that deadline'.[71] This exemption relied on the equivalency agreement provisions of the Canadian Environmental Protection Act 1999.[72] This action followed Nova Scotia's 2014 exclusion from the federal Reduction of Carbon Dioxide Emissions from Coal-fired Generation of Electricity Regulations.[73]

The Alberta government released a Climate Leadership Plan in late 2015.[74] This Plan outlines Alberta's aim to replace all coal-fired electricity generation facilities with renewable sources and natural gas sources by 2030.[75] The way the current Alberta government has overlooked CCS-based opportunities to address GHG emissions from coal-fired electrical generation facilities can perhaps be explained by the fact that coal-fired electricity generation is not a process that had much support within the current Alberta government before it was elected. It would not have been expected to become an acceptable electricity generation process to this government simply on election—notwithstanding the availability of appropriate subsurface geology, the examples of functioning CCS technology within the province that are provided by the Shell Canada Energy Quest Project[76] and the Alberta Carbon Trunk Line integrated carbon capture and storage project,[77] and decades of experience with EOR projects.[78]

Canada has the second largest established crude oil reserves in the world, outranked only by Saudi Arabia. Although up to 80 per cent of the GHG emissions from a barrel of oil come from consumption, such as from internal combustion engine exhaust emissions, about 20 per cent are created during oil production. While the fall in the price of a barrel of oil has resulted in a decrease in the production of oil, the oil and gas sector's production phase remains a significant contributor to GHG emissions. Post-production GHG emissions are being addressed. Internal combustion engine exhaust emissions are open to regulation across Canada in a way that helps to mitigate the economic impact of these regulations, but these emissions are not a source of product for CCS schemes. Based on the volume of GHG emissions

---

[71] 22 November 2016; see K Harris, 'Liberals present plan to phase out coal-powered electricity by 2030', *CBC News* (21 November 2016), at www.cbc.ca/news/politics/canada-coal-electricity-phase-out-1.3860131.

[72] See n 40 above.

[73] Order Declaring that the Reduction of Carbon Dioxide Emissions from Coal-fired Generation of Electricity Regulations Do Not Apply in Nova Scotia, SOR/2014-265. This Order came into force on 1 July 2015.

[74] Alberta Government, 'Climate Leadership Plan' (July 2017), at www.alberta.ca/climate-leadership-plan.aspx (Climate Leadership Plan).

[75] Alberta Government, 'Climate Leadership Plan: Carbon Levy and Rebates' (July 2017), at www.alberta.ca/climate-leadership-plan.aspx#toc-1.

[76] Natural Resources Canada, 'Shell Canada Energy Quest Project' (September 2016), at www.nrcan.gc.ca/energy/funding/current-funding-programs/18168.

[77] Natural Resources Canada, 'Enhance Energy—Alberta Carbon Trunk Line Carbon Capture and Storage Project' (February 2016), at www.nrcan.gc.ca/energy/funding/current-funding-programs/18170.

[78] The election of the current Alberta government represented a striking ideological shift in governing for Albertans. The current New Democratic Party, which forms the Alberta government, has a strong left-wing history and base. Its election in 2015 ended an unbroken 36-year period of Alberta's being led by the same right-of-centre Progressive Conservative government. This was also the first time that the New Democratic Party had formed the government in Alberta.

from either pre- or post-production sources that are potentially available for CCS schemes, it is the major oil-producing regions of Canada—principally Alberta, Saskatchewan and, to a lesser degree, the Maritime Provinces on the east coast—that are at greatest risk of becoming uncompetitive, and so which are exceedingly aware of the need to reduce GHG emissions.[79] Oil sands and fossil fuel production in general are the principal sources of concern for Alberta, Saskatchewan and British Columbia. However, these concerns also arise because of the use of fossil fuels to generate electricity, which, at least as regards coal, are scheduled to be phased out across Canada by 2030, with limited exceptions. The Maritime Provinces are also concerned about maintaining the viability of their oil and gas sectors. The coal-mining sector is an important component of the local economy of the Maritime Provinces, which offers a rationale for Nova Scotia's being excluded from the federal ban on coal-fired electricity generation. These requirements, along with and, in some cases, because of the recognised need to address public perception and attitudes, are no less important to other natural resource or energy sectors, such as mining and forestry, and to coal-fired electricity generation, which despite actions to eliminate coal-fired electricity generation still represents a sizeable share of the electricity production in many provinces. Taken together, these sectors are the source of a significant amount of Canada's GHG emissions, and make significant contributions to Canada's economic activity.

The provinces have taken four approaches to addressing GHG emissions: (i) the general regulation of air emissions; (ii) the specific regulation of GHGs; (iii) the use of market-based programs as incentives to reduce GHG emissions,; and (iv) the direct support and regulation of CCS. Each of these will now be examined in further detail.

B. General Regulation of Air Emissions

All of the provinces regulate the emission of contaminants into the natural environment. As a result, all of the provinces also regulate the equipment or processes that do or *may* emit a contaminant into the natural environment. Carbon capture technologies are characterised as either pre-combustion or modified combustion technologies, such as coal gasification or an oxy-fuel process, or post-combustion technologies involving ammonia, amines or porous membranes. Depending on the specific wording of the provincial regulations, employing a technology from any of these groupings may require a permit or approval from the environmental regulator, or at least proof that the technology that is being employed will not result in the discharge of a contaminant, or that any discharges will not exceed the local emissions thresholds that have attracted the permitting requirement.[80]

---

[79] 'Action on Climate Change & Responsible Energy Development: Enabling Carbon Capture and Storage', presentation of Alberta Premier E Stelmach and Saskatchewan Premier B Wall to the Council of the Federation, Québec City, PQ (July 2008).

[80] Ontario's Environmental Protection Act RSO 1990, c E9, s 9, is typical of the requirements. An Environmental Compliance Approval or an amendment to a Environmental Compliance Approval is

C. Specific Regulation of GHGs

Regulating GHGs typically starts with monitoring and reporting GHG emissions, followed by the regulation of the GHG emissions. It is important to keep in mind that although the two paradigms are related, there is a fundamental difference between regulating GHGs for reporting or accounting purposes and regulating GHGs for the purpose of reducing GHG emissions. Further, a GHG reporting obligation may serve two purposes: to implement market-based GHG reduction programs, and as essential groundwork for the regulation of GHG emissions. For example, in 2016 the Province of Newfoundland and Labrador enacted legislation that provides for two years of monitoring at industrial facilities before the province forms its emission reduction targets.[81] Similarly, other provinces required the reporting of GHG emissions before reduction targets were set. Manitoba enacted legislation that permits the making of regulations that require GHG reporting and the setting of GHG reduction targets.[82] Alberta has regulated industrial GHG emissions in general by setting intensity-based limits, which will require the monitoring and reporting of GHG emissions.[83] Alberta has also set limits on total oil sands emissions, which again will require the monitoring and reporting of GHG emissions.[84]

British Columbia,[85] Ontario,[86] Québec[87] and Nova Scotia[88] require industrial facilities that emit GHGs above a prescribed threshold to report their GHG emissions. Fortifying this requirement in Ontario and Québec and with emitters under the federal jurisdictions, are the measures taken by those jurisdictions to have CO_2 declared to be a contaminant. The discharge of CO_2 in those jurisdictions would have to be reported as discharge of a contaminant into the natural environment. Notionally this will require minor CO_2 emission sources to report their discharges to the environmental regulator. However, from a practical perspective there will still be a number of low-emission sources of GHGs that are not counted, notwithstanding this regulatory obligation.

To fully account for GHG emissions, those gases that have a higher global warming potential than CO_2, such as methane, nitrous oxide and hydrofluorocarbons, are accounted for in Canada's National GHG Inventory either under their own designations or as carbon dioxide equivalents (CO_2e). There gases are

---

required for the construction, altering, extension or replacement of 'any plant, structure, equipment, apparatus, mechanism or thing that may discharge or from which may be discharged a contaminant into any part of the natural environment'.

[81] Management of Greenhouse Gas Act SNL 2016, c M-1.001.
[82] Climate Change and Emissions Reductions Act, CCSM, c C135.
[83] Climate Change and Emissions Management Act SA 2003, c C-16.7; Specified Gas Emitters Regulation, Alta Reg 139/2007, s 4.
[84] Oil Sands Emissions Limit Act SA 2016, c 0-7.5.
[85] Greenhouse Gas Emission Reporting Regulation, BC Reg 249/2015, s 8.
[86] Quantification, Reporting and Verification of Greenhouse Gas Emissions, O Reg 143/16, s 5, as amended by O Reg 474/16.
[87] Regulation Respecting Mandatory Reporting of Certain Emissions of Contaminants into the Atmosphere, RQ c Q-2, r 3.3, s 4.
[88] Greenhouse Gas Emissions Regulations, NS Reg 260/2009, as amended NS Reg 305/2013.

also regulated.[89] For example, at the North American leaders' summit in June 2016, Canada, the US and Mexico agreed to emission reductions for methane.[90] Fifteen per cent of Canada GHG emissions were from methane in 2013, and the oil and gas sectors are recognised as major sources of methane gas emissions.[91] British Columbia, Alberta and Saskatchewan, the jurisdictions in which the majority of onshore oil and gas activities take place, already regulate methane to some degree. However, the Province of Alberta intends to have a Methane Reduction Regulation in place by the end of 2017.[92] The Federal Government proposes to fulfil its commitment under the Pan Canadian Framework for a 45 per cent reduction in methane emissions by 2025, by bringing into force a methane regulation that will have both general requirements and specific requirements that will apply to facilities which produce and receive at least 60,000m^3 of methane in a year.[93]

The GHG emission targets found in international climate-change agreements to which Canada is a signatory have served to validate federal and provincial declarations of a hard economy-wide and sector-based GHG emissions target having standing ahead of the emission thresholds that are commonly found in environmental protection regulations. British Columbia, Alberta, Ontario and Québec have set GHG emission caps, while Nova Scotia plans to do so by 2018. British Columbia was the first province to set a hard cap for CO_2 emissions and has set reduction targets. Québec and Ontario have also set CO_2 emission caps, while Nova Scotia is planning to do so for 2018.

The federal Greenhouse Gas Emissions Program under the Canadian Environmental Protection Act 1999 imposes a GHG reporting requirement on facilities that emit the equivalent of 50 kilotonnes or more of CO_2e.[94] Furthermore, the prohibiting of the use of coal for electricity generation has taken the Federal Government significantly beyond the emission-intensity limit of 420 tonnes of CO_2 for each gigawatt-hour of electricity produced from coal per year at each power plant, as provided by the Reduction of Carbon Dioxide Emissions from Coal-fired Generation of

---

[89] United Nations Climate Change Secretariat, 'October Climate Change Session: Experts Say Paris Can Help Cut Non-CO_2 Gases' (July 2017), at newsroom.unfccc.int/unfccc-newsroom/bonn-meeting-identifies-ways-to-curb-non-c02-gases/. The Intergovernmental Panel on Climate Change Fourth Assessment Report reports that the global warming potential of methane is 72 times higher than CO_2 20 years after release—see Intergovernmental Panel on Climate Change, 'Climate Change 2007: Working Group I: The Physical Science Basis' (July 2017), at www.ipcc.ch/publications_and_data/ar4/wg1/en/ch2s2-10-2.html.

[90] S McCarthy, 'Trudeau, Obama and Pena Nieto agree to emission-reduction goals at summit', *The Globe and Mail* (Ottawa, 29 June 2016), at www.theglobeandmail.com/report-on-business/industry-news/energy-and-resources/three-amigos-agree-to-clean-energy-partnership/article30674952/. At that same summit the North American leaders also agreed develop projects to demonstrate 'the capture of carbon for ... sequestration underground'.

[91] The Intergovernmental Panel on Climate Change Fourth Assessment Report reports that the global warming potential of methane is 72 times higher than CO_2 at the 20-year mark; see n 89 above.

[92] Alberta Government, 'Reducing methane emissions' (July 2017), at www.alberta.ca/climate-methane-emissions.aspx#toc-0.

[93] Regulations Respecting Reductions in the Release of Methane and Certain Volatile Organic Compounds (Upstream Oil and Gas).

[94] Above n 40, s 49.

Electricity Regulations.[95] From a CCS perspective, though, the Federal Government's efforts at eliminating coal as a source of CO_2e emissions in electricity generation is a two-edged sword. Although there are obvious benefits from this requirement, it also undercuts the provisions of the Reduction of Carbon Dioxide Emissions from Coal-fired Generation of Electricity Regulations that permit the use of CCS technology to meet the prescribed emission-intensity limit.[96]

D. Market-based Approaches to Reduce GHG Emissions

Provincial market-based carbon pricing programs have been introduced as an economic incentive to reduce GHG emissions. The Federal Government has announced the NCP to bolster the provincial programs. While many of the provinces were taking action before the federal NCP was announced, there is no doubt that the implementation of provincial market-based programs has been spurred by the terms of the federal NCP policy. Characteristically, market-based programs add a cost to something that previously was essentially free—discharging CO_2e into the natural environment. The cap-and-trade approach, the carbon tax approach or a combination of both are the market-based approaches that are used to add costs to this previously no-cost activity. What are the merits of the market-based carbon-pricing systems' being used or being developed by the provinces and territories? Undoubtedly, by establishing a limit or cap on GHG emissions, the cap-and-trade alternative creates a certainty that there will be a reduction in GHG emissions. However, permitting GHG allowances or offset credits to be purchased creates a level of uncertainty regarding the impact that a cap-and-trade system would have on reducing GHG emissions in that jurisdiction. Presumably at some stage the costs of allowances or offset credits will rise to the point that reducing GHG emissions through improved operational practices or equipment, or deciding to close a particular emission operation, becomes a viable option. In any event, in theory the level of the cap can be managed down to meet a desired target level. Uncertainty arises, however, because the price of carbon is determined by the market and the availability of credits. In contrast, a carbon tax or levy uses market pressures to provide a cost-effective means to reduce GHG emissions, while providing certainty regarding the price of carbon.[97] Canada's sub-national jurisdictions are currently employing both of these systems. Subject to specific restrictions, CCS proposals may be acceptable under either of these carbon-pricing systems either to create carbon emission offsets, or to directly reduce carbon emissions into the atmosphere. From the regulator's perspective, GHG emissions into the atmosphere should be effectively reduced, while from the perspective of a CCS proponent, its operations are likely to receive an overall economic benefit under either carbon-pricing system.

---

[95] Reduction of Carbon Dioxide Emissions from Coal-fired Generation of Electricity Regulations, n 62 above, s 3(1).
[96] ibid, s 9.
[97] Environmental Economics; see T Haab and J Whitehead, 'ECON 101: Carbon Tax vs Cap-and-Trade', *The Cromulent Economics Blog* (11 July 2017), at www.env-econ.net/carbon_tax_vs_capandtrade.html.

The Federal Government's plan to introduce an NCP scheme is contrary to the direction chosen by the US. However, a number of Canada's sub-national jurisdictions have already taken steps to implement carbon-pricing schemes that would also puts these jurisdictions at variance with the US. This pattern, of Canada's sub-national jurisdictions either taking the lead in reducing GHG emissions or playing an essential albeit integral part in the regulation of GHG emissions, is founded on the constitutional separation of powers between the provincial governments and the Federal Government. Canada's constitutional separation of powers effectively places primary (but not exclusive) responsibility for the environment under the jurisdiction of the provinces. Given the provinces' constitutional responsibility over local works and undertakings, their responsibility for the local economy—essentially operational matters—as well as their environmental responsibilities, it is understandable that any real environmental and economic benefits flowing from the alternatives available to address GHG emissions and the impacts of poor environmental and economic governance would be more directly and immediately felt at the local or provincial level.[98] Further, the separation of powers anticipates that some international commitments made by the Government of Canada, such as those found under the Paris Agreement, will depend on the provinces for their implementation because of their constitutional powers. Therefore, the provinces have a legitimate interest in the options available to address climate change, including any actions taken to regulate GHG directly. To this end, carbon-pricing schemes were already in place or were being planned by Québec, Ontario, Manitoba, Alberta and British Columbia at the time the Federal Government announced its intention to introduce an NCP scheme in October 2016.[99] Almost 90 per cent of Canada's population resides in these five provinces.

Québec, Ontario and Manitoba have negotiated a Memorandum of Understanding[100] to operate a cap-and-trade system under the Western Climate Initiative.[101] A subsequent change in government in Manitoba acted on the doubts that were raised about the worth of cap-and-trade systems. Manitoba is now reviewing its options. However, the election platform of the current elected government pledged '"to develop a made-in-Manitoba climate action plan" involving carbon pricing'.[102] This will bring Manitoba into line with the carbon tax schemes of Alberta and British Columbia.

---

[98] The Constitution Act, n 1 above, s 92(10).
[99] Hansard, n 36 above; Government of Canada, 'Government of Canada Announces Pan-Canadian Pricing on Carbon Pollution' (October 2016), at www.canada.ca/en/environment-climate-change/news/2016/10/government-canada-announces-canadian-pricing-carbon-pollution.html.
[100] Memorandum of Understanding Between the Government of Ontario, the Government of Quebec and the Government of Manitoba Concerning Concerted Climate Change Actions and Market-Based Mechanisms, 7 December 2015; see at news.ontario.ca/opo/en/2015/12/memorandum-of-understanding-between-the-government-of-ontario-the-government-of-quebec-and-the-gover.html.
[101] Western Climate Initiative Inc (July 2017), at www.wci-inc.org/.
[102] S Reklev and M Szabo, 'Ontario, Manitoba cap-and-trade schemes facing new threats' *Carbon Pulse* (27 April 2016), at carbon-pulse.com/18590/.

The Federal Government released a technical paper on its purposed NCP scheme in May 2017.[103] The NCP scheme is intended to ensure that a floor or backstop price for carbon emissions, to be 'applied in jurisdictions that do not have carbon pricing systems that align with the benchmark' set by the Federal Government, will be in place across Canada by 2018.[104] The essential components of the NCP scheme are as follows. First, Canada's provinces and territories are allowed to choose how they will implement their own carbon-pricing systems. Secondly, the price that Canada's sub-national jurisdictions charge for carbon emissions under their authority must 'meet or exceed the federal benchmark'.[105] Thirdly, the Federal Government has indicated that either 'a direct price on carbon pollution' system or 'a cap-and-trade system' are acceptable options for the sub-national carbon-pricing systems. Fourthly, the price-based backstop price has to be a minimum of CAN$10 per tonne in 2018, rising to CAN$50 per tonne by 2022, and will be composed of two elements: a carbon tax or levy applied to fossil fuels, or a hybrid 'composed of a carbon levy and an output-based pricing system for industrial facilities that emit above a certain threshold'.[106] Fifthly, if a cap-and-trade system is chosen, it will be required to have annual cap adjustments that correspond to the emissions reductions achieved through the price-based system.[107] Lastly, '[t]he output-based pricing system will apply to all industrial facilities that emit 50 kilotonnes (kt) or more of CO_2e per year'.[108] The effectiveness of the NCP scheme in meeting Canada's GHG emissions target will be reviewed in 2022.[109]

Québec's Regulation Respecting a Cap-and-Trade System for Greenhouse Gas Emission Allowances[110] is central to the province's 2013–2020 Climate Change Action Plan.[111] The Action Plan describes this Regulation as having 'established an ambitious GHG emission cap-and-trade system within the framework of the Western Climate Initiative'.[112] Québec's cap-and-trade scheme is directed at companies in the industrial and electricity sectors that emit 25,000 metric tonnes or more of CO_2 equivalent (CO_2e) annually.[113] This Regulation assigns responsibility to fossil fuel distributors for the GHG emissions associated with all products they distribute in

---

[103] Government of Canada, 'Technical Paper on the Federal Carbon Pricing Backstop, Environment and Climate Change Canada' (Government of Canada, 2017), at www.canada.ca/en/services/environment/weather/climatechange/technical-paper-federal-carbon-pricing-backstop.html.

[104] ibid, 5.

[105] Hansard, n 36 above.

[106] Above n 103, 4.

[107] ibid 6.

[108] ibid 17.

[109] Hansard, n 36 above.

[110] Ch Q-2, r 46.1.

[111] Québec Government, *Québec in Action: Greener by 2020*, Climate Change Action Plan 20132020 (Quebec Government, 2012), at www.mddelcc.gouv.qc.ca/changements/plan_action/pacc2020-en.pdf.

[112] ibid 3.1. The Western Climate Initiative promotes North American market-based programs to reduce GHG, such as cap-and-trade, including recognising GHG emission offsets. Membership has varied, but currently the members are British Columbia, Manitoba, Ontario, Québec and the US State of California.

[113] The Organisation for Economic Cooperation and Development (OECD) defines carbon dioxide equivalent as a measure used to compare the emissions from various GHGs based upon their global warming potential.

Québec (gasoline, diesel fuels, propane, natural gas and heating oil).[114] It permits emitters to offset their emissions by purchasing offsets to decrease the compliance costs borne by the emitter.[115] The use of offset credits as a means of regulatory compliance is limited to 8 per cent in order to maximise emission reductions by entities and sources covered by the system. Offset credits can be granted for sequestering GHG emissions in sectors of activity or sources other than those that are subject to the compliance obligations of the Regulation.

In 2017, Ontario implemented a cap-and-trade program to address carbon emissions.[116] Similar to Québec's system, Ontario's cap-and-trade system is directed at the electricity, industrial and large commercial, institutional, fuel transportation and natural gas distribution sectors. Significantly, Ontario's system requires that extra-jurisdictional carbon emissions that benefit the province be considered: the sources of imported electricity for consumption in Ontario are included in the definition of the electricity sector. Under the Climate Change Mitigation and Low-carbon Economy Act 2016, emitters can apply to register an offset initiative.[117] However, as with Québec, the use of offset credits is limited to meet up to 8 per cent of the emitters' cap-and-trade compliance obligations. Ontario will consider offset initiatives undertaken anywhere in Canada. Offset credits are assessed in a discussion paper published by Ontario, 'Compliance Offset Credits Regulatory Proposal'. The discussion paper does not include any actual offset protocols, which are the government-approved methodologies for eligible offset initiatives, but it does leave open the possibility of using sequestration and non-sequestration offset methodologies. However, bearing in mind that Ontario, together with Québec, is investigating offset protocols that expressly relate to the capture and *destruction* of certain methane and ozone-depleting substances and projects that involve the agricultural and forestry sectors, and bearing in mind the less than ideal subsurface geology for CCS that is typical in many areas of the province, along with the historical indifference to CCS technology, carbon capture with subsurface storage methodology is not likely to be given precedence as a government-sponsored initiative.[118]

Manitoba's immediate goal is to reduce GHG emissions by one-third of its 2005 levels by 2030. Manitoba's long-range target is to be carbon neutral by 2080.[119] The Premier of Manitoba has ruled out using a cap-and-trade system, but has not yet made a decision on supporting a carbon tax because of the possible effects of such a tax on the agriculture industry in Manitoba.[120] Manitoba has a Climate

---

[114] Chapter Q-2, r 46.1.
[115] ibid, regs 19 et seq.
[116] The Cap and Trade Program, Ontario Regulation 144/16.
[117] SO 2016, c 7, s 34(2). This Act came into effect on 1 January 2017.
[118] Ministry of the Environment and Climate Change (Ontario), 'Compliance Offset Credits Regulatory Proposal' (Ministry of the Environment and Climate Change, 2016), at www.downloads.ene.gov.on.ca/envision/env_reg/er/documents/2016/012-9078.pdf.
[119] Government of Manitoba, 'Manitoba's Climate Change and Green Economy Action Plan' (Government of Manitoba, 2015) 11, at www.gov.mb.ca/conservation/climate/pdf/mb-climate-change-green-economy-action-plan.pdf.
[120] R Laychuk, 'Carbon pricing could take money from Manitoba Farmers, industry group says', *CBC News* (Manitoba, 4 October 2016), at www.cbc.ca/news/canada/manitoba/carbon-pricing-manitoba-agriculture-1.3791170.

Change and Emissions Reductions Act, although it is currently limited in scope and does not have any significant regulations.[121] Manitoba also has an Emissions Tax on Coal and Petroleum Coke Act, which imposes an emissions tax on taxable fuels. The fuels listed under this statute are limited to petroleum coke, bituminous and sub-bituminous coal, lignite and anthracite, 'and any other grade of coal'.[122] To date there have not been any regulations made under this Act.

Saskatchewan has not been an enthusiastic supporter of the Federal Government's initiatives to reduce GHG emissions, such as the Pan-Canadian Framework, which the province did not sign, or the NCP, which Saskatchewan Premier Brad Wall opposes, calling the federal white paper on this carbon tax a 'ransom note'.[123] Premier Wall has also said that the province is considering commencing a constitutional challenge of the NCP. Under Saskatchewan's Management and Reduction of Greenhouse Gases Act, facilities that emit more than 50,000 tonnes of GHG will be required to reduce their annual emissions to a provincially established target.[124] This Act was assented to in 2010 but has yet to be proclaimed in force. There are no plans to implement a provincial carbon-pricing scheme, which presumably would give an added incentive to reduce GHG emissions. Nevertheless, the province has not been unmindful of climate change-related challenges. Saskatchewan has been a world leader in the implementation of CCS projects, for example the Weyburn-Midale CO_2 Monitoring and Storage Project, which was the world's first monitoring site for the geological storage of CO_2, and the world's first commercial-scale CCS coal-fired power plant at Saskatchewan's Boundary Dam.[125] The success of the Boundary Dam CCS project is also important for the equivalency agreement between Saskatchewan and the Federal Government, to allow coal-fired power generation to continue in the province.[126]

Alberta has been actively regulating GHG emissions since the Climate Change and Emissions Management Act (CCEMA) became law in 2003.[127] Alberta is now purposing to implement a carbon tax across all sectors by 2018. In 2004, the Specified Gas Reporting Regulation (SGRR) came into force under the CCEMA. The SGRR introduced reporting requirements for large industrial and other emitters with over 100,000 tonnes of CO_2e emissions annually.[128] In 2007, the Specified

---

[121] The Climate Change and Emissions Reductions Act, CCSM, c C135.
[122] The Emissions Tax on Coal and Petroleum Coke Act, CCSM, c E90, s 3. The emissions taxes range from $31.90 for petroleum coke to $14.27 for lignite.
[123] D Baxter, 'Sask. Premier describes federal carbon tax plan as a "ransom note"', *Global News* (18 May 2017), at globalnews.ca/news/3462367/sask-premier-describes-federal-carbon-tax-plan-as-a-ransom-note/.
[124] SS 2010 Chap M-2.01 ch 2010.
[125] Canada's CO_2 Capture and Storage Information Source, n 12 above; and Natural Resources Canada, n 16 above.
[126] S McCarthy, 'Saskatchewan, Ottawa strike accord on coal-fire power generation', *The Globe and Mail* (Ottawa, 28 November 2016), at www.theglobeandmail.com/report-on-business/industry-news/energy-and-resources/saskatchewan-reaches-deal-with-ottawa-on-future-of-coal-fired-power-plants/article33068106/.
[127] SA 2003, c C-16.7.
[128] Alta Reg 251/2004.

Gas Emitters Regulation (SGER) under the same Act set emission intensity limits for those facilities, as well as the requirement that the facilities annually reduce GHG emissions in comparison to their historical baseline emissions.[129] The SGER combined elements of a carbon tax and a cap-and-trade system, and also established emission offsets and credits for emission reductions of specified gases, the geological sequestration of specified gases or a capture of specified gases that are geologically sequestered.

In 2005, Alberta considered a policy that would use '[s]ector-specific, output-based allocations of emissions rights' to 'mitigate competitiveness and employment impacts in trade-exposed sectors and to protect electricity consumers from significant and unnecessary rate increases'.[130] This objective is one element of Alberta's Climate Leadership Plan.[131] Another element is the Carbon Competitiveness Regulation (CCR), which the Alberta government purposes to be law in 2018. Large industrial emitters will continue to be subject to the SGER framework until the end of 2017, when the implementation of the CCR will transition the province to product- and sector-based performance standards. The result of this shift will see a facility's specific emission intensity reductions no longer being based on the facility's specific GHG baseline emissions. Instead, under the CCR, the facility's GHG emissions will be compared to the GHG emissions from other similar facilities. In effect, all facilities in the same sector will be subject to the same emissions reduction obligations, regardless of their historical baseline emissions. The other elements of Alberta's Climate Leadership Plan are replacing all coal-fired electricity facilities with renewable sources and natural gas sources by 2030, and oil sands emission limits, methane emissions reduction and a carbon price on GHG emissions.[132]

Another step for Alberta was to impose 'a carbon levy on consumers of fuel to be effected through a series of payment and remittance obligations that apply ... throughout the fuel supply chains', through the 2016 Alberta Climate Leadership Act.[133] The Climate Leadership Regulation under this Act was also promulgated in 2016.[134] This Regulation provided details of the kinds of activities caught by that Act, the stages of the fuel supply chain at which the carbon levy is payable and the exemptions from the carbon levy. The exemptions are significant. Fuel used in the operation of a facility to which the SGER applies are exempt from the carbon levy if the emissions from the fuel are direct emissions and are marked as such. Therefore a consumer identified as a large industrial emitter, which could be a power plant or large oil sands facility, will not have to pay the levy on marked gasoline or diesel. A consumer is also exempt from paying the carbon levy on fuel that is used in a production process before 2023, if the fuel is not flared or vented.

British Columbia set targets for reducing GHG emissions in 2008 under the Greenhouse Gas Reduction Targets Act.[135] British Columbia's Carbon Tax Act also

[129] Alta Reg 129/2007.
[130] Alberta Government, Climate Leadership: Report to the Minister' (Alberta Government, 2015). The report can be found at www.alberta.ca/documents/climate/climate-leadership-report-to-minister.pdf.
[131] Climate Leadership Plan, n 74 above.
[132] ibid.
[133] SA 2016, c C-16.9, s 3(1).
[134] Alta Reg 175/2016.
[135] Greenhouse Gas Reduction Targets Act, SBC 2007, c 42.

became the law in 2008.[136] The province stresses that its carbon tax is not just another gas tax and that it is revenue neutral.[137] Carbon tax revenues by law must be returned as personal and business tax reductions.[138] The Carbon Tax Act applies a tax on CO_2e emissions generated from the burning of fuels in the province, based on the emission factor for the fuel that has been established by a federal agency, Environment Canada. Since the amount of CO_2e generated can differ with the type of fuel that is burnt, a distinct tax may be applied to gasoline, diesel, natural gas, fuel oil, propane and coal. The Carbon Tax Act allows regulations to be made for exemptions from the payment of the carbon tax for fuel that does not emit GHGs as a result of the GHGs' being captured and stored.[139] While the Carbon Tax Act applies to any party that purchases or uses fuels within the province, which the province estimates accounts for 70 per cent of its total GHG emissions, the large final emitters that could benefit from the use of CCS technology will also be regulated by the Greenhouse Gas Industrial Reporting and Control Act (GGIRCA).[140] Undoubtedly there will be some overlap in the application of the GGIRCA and the Carbon Tax Act, because the GGIRCA requires '[a]ll greenhouse gas amounts to be measured ... documented and reported in tonnes of' CO_2e. However, the GGIRCA allows for the calculation of a facility's CO_2e emissions to take into account credits for emission offset projects.[141] Emission offset projects may include a 'storage project', defined in the regulation as a project providing for the storage in non-biological reservoirs of GHG or components of GHG, which have been 'captured before [being] emitted into the atmosphere, or removed from the atmosphere by an industrial process'.[142]

E. Direct Support and Regulation of CCS

The last approach covers active preparation for the employment of carbon capture and utilisation processes, which could include CCS. These efforts could involve preparing the regulatory framework for carbon capture and utilisation processes, and in some case direct support of these initiatives. The provinces that are involved are Nova Scotia, Québec, Manitoba, Saskatchewan, Alberta and British Columbia. The Federal Government has also implemented initiatives to advance CCS.

Capture and utilisation processes are being promoted in more provinces than those listed above. Of the provinces listed, all except Manitoba are currently actively pursuing both active and planned CCS activities, commercial-scale analogues to the geological storage of CO_2, or, along with Manitoba, capturing and utilising captured

---

[136] SBC 2008, c 40.
[137] British Columbia Ministry of Finance, *Myths and Facts About the Carbon Tax* (July 2017), at www.fin.gov.bc.ca/tbs/tp/climate/A6.htm.
[138] Above n 136, s 3(2).
[139] Above n 136, s 84(3)(o).
[140] SBC 2014, c 29.
[141] ibid, s 12(1).
[142] Greenhouse Gas Emission Control Regulation BC Reg 250/2015, s 11(1).

CO_2 for other non-emission purposes. Québec is actively supporting an enzyme-enabled carbon capture project and carbon capture for greenhouse development. The business behind these initiatives in Québec has promoted carbon capture and utilisation processes in Ontario and Alberta. Constitutionally, provinces have the lead for setting the regulatory context for the development of carbon capture and utilisation processes, but the Federal Government has financially supported a number of these initiatives.

British Columbia amended its Petroleum and Natural Gas Act[143] and the Oil and Gas Activities Act[144] in 2015 to facilitate CCS activities.[145] The province built on its exiting regulatory regime for underground natural gas storage and acid-gas disposal to allow CCS to be utilised as a permanent solution to disposing of CO_2. The Petroleum and Natural Gas Act definition of a storage reservoir as 'a naturally occurring underground reservoir that is capable of being used for the introduction, disposal, storage or recovery of ... waste or any other prescribed substance' provides the basis for a CCS-related use, while the exploration and permit requirements under the Oil and Gas Activities Act expand that definition to allow the disposal of 'prescribed substances', such as CO_2, when appropriate. The Petroleum and Natural Gas Act addresses the designation and ownership of the storage reservoir, which directs that title vests in the government subject to certain limitations.[146] British Columbia employed its oil and gas regulations to regulate the capture, transport, storage, ownership and liability issues arising from CCS activities because of the subject-matter and due to the natural gas sector's being a major source of large CO_2 emissions. In addition British Columbia led the other provinces in initiating a market-based approach to reducing GHG emissions by taxing carbon emissions and offering the opportunity to use CCS as a means to lessen the overall costs of the operation emitting CO_2. These provisions were first introduced in 2008. For industrial facilities in 2016, these were replaced by the Greenhouse Gas Industrial Reporting and Control Act and regulations that set GHG emissions benchmarks for liquefied natural gas facilities and coal-based electricity generation operations, and for other industrial facilities or sectors.[147] This Act provides authority for the Greenhouse Gas Emission Control Regulation, which continues to outline the requirements for a CCS proposal to create emission offset units, to be used to meet that Province's GHG reduction targets.[148] The requirements are straightforward: a risk-mitigation and contingency plan, and the reasonable likelihood that the plan will achieve its purpose. The Regulation also establishes the BC Carbon Registry to enable the issuance, transfer and retirement of offsets and credits on an electronic platform.

Alberta's support and regulation of CCS is built into its regulation of the exploitation of fossil fuels. This province has a considerable history of utilising and regulating CCS-type techniques, such as EOR and acid-gas injection, and more recently

---

[143] RSBS 1996, c 361.
[144] SBC 2008, c 36.
[145] Natural Gas Development Statutes Amendment Act 2015, Bill 40 2015.
[146] Oil and Gas Activities Act, n 144 above, s 126.
[147] SBC 2014, c 29.
[148] BC Reg 250/2015.

genuine CCS. Indeed, CCS was a prominent element of Alberta's 2008 Climate Change Strategy.[149] The potential offered by CCS technology increased in importance following the November 2015 release of Alberta's Climate Leadership Plan and the coming into force of the Climate Leadership Act, which put elements of the Climate Leadership Plan into effect.[150] The Plan's strategy is for a regulatory transition from the historical facility-specific emissions reduction approach under the Specified Gas Emitters Regulation, to a product-specific or output-based sector-wide emissions allocation and reduction approach, which will be put into place under a carbon competitiveness regulation in 2018. Large industrial facilities producing more than 100,000 tonnes of CO_2 per year will pay a carbon tax as they emit CO_2, with emission allocations and reductions being determined on a sector-wide basis. Regardless of the availability of emissions allocations, subsidies and offsets, this should provide industrial facilities with an incentive to find technologies to decrease CO_2 emissions to the atmosphere.

Alberta's experience with CCS technology has resulted in a comprehensive regulatory regime centred around the Mines and Minerals Act.[151] To adapt its regulatory regime to deal with the issues arising from CCS activities, the province passed the Carbon Capture and Storage Statutes Amendment Act 2010[152] to amend the Mines and Minerals Act and Energy Resources Conservation Act,[153] to address the questions of long-term liability for CO_2 stored underground, pore space access and ownership, and the funding of maintenance and remediation following closure.

The Mines and Minerals Act takes a 'cradle to grave' approach to CCS. The Act regulates the sequestration of captured CO_2 by prohibiting the injection of 'any substance into a subsurface reservoir ... unless ... authorized to do so under the Act or by agreement'. The Act requires the province to enter into a carbon sequestration lease, and the lessee is required to prepare and comply with an approved monitoring, measurement and verification plan (MMV) and an approved closure plan. Long-term liability for a storage site is assumed by the province once the site has been properly closed down and long-term monitoring has provided evidence that the stored CO_2 is stable. The Act establishes the Post-Closure Stewardship Fund for the purpose of monitoring captured CO_2, fulfilling the obligations assumed by the Crown (the state), and paying suspension, abandonment or reclamation costs, which is funded by fees paid by the storage site operator.[154] The Act makes clear that the province is the owner of the pore space, while not changing the ownership of the mine or mineral resources. A number of regulations have been enacted to support this Act. The Carbon Sequestration Tenure Regulation[155] deals with tenure or lease

---

[149] Alberta Government, 'Alberta's Climate Change Strategy' (Alberta Government, 2008), at aep.alberta.ca/forms-maps-services/publications/documents/AlbertaClimateChangeStrategy-2008.pdf.
[150] SA, 2016, C C-16.9.
[151] RSA 2000, C M-17.
[152] SA 2010, c 14.
[153] RSA 2000, c E-10.
[154] Carbon Capture and Storage Statutes Amendment Act, n 152 above, 122.
[155] AR 68/2011.

rights and MMVs for pore space for CCS activities, while the Mines and Minerals Administration Regulation[156] regulates rental fees for a carbon sequestration lease. The Metallic and Industrial Minerals Tenure Regulation deals specifically with sub-surface reservoir leases.[157]

Also in 2010, Alberta enacted the Carbon Capture and Storage Funding Act to provide funding for the construction and operation of CCS projects in the province, up to a maximum aggregate amount of CAN$2 billion.[158] The Carbon Capture and Storage Funding Act (Extension of Expiry Date) Amendment Regulation extended the expiry date of this Act to 30 April 2020.[159]

A number of CCS-related projects have been advanced in Alberta. Penn West's Joffre Viking sands project and the Glencoe Resources Chigwell Viking sands project are two CO_2-EOR projects that are currently operating in Alberta.[160] The Joffre Viking sands project has been operating for three decades and is Canada's oldest CO_2-EOR operation. The Glencoe Resources' Chigwell Viking sands project started in 2007. Supporting CO_2-EOR activities is the Alberta Carbon Trunk Line (ACTL).[161] Characterised as a large-scale CCS demonstration project, the ACTL is a 240 km pipeline, which transports captured CO_2 from Alberta's Industrial Heartland north-east of Edmonton to the Clive Nisku and Leduc mature oil reservoirs in central Alberta for use in CO_2-EOR projects. There is supposed to be capacity to store additional CO_2 after the EOR operations have been completed.[162] The Shell Canada Energy Quest Project is a dedicated CCS project that captures CO_2 at the Scotford oil sands upgrading facility near Edmonton, and then compresses and transports the captured CO_2 to a storage site about 64 km to the north, where the CO_2 is injected into deep saline formations about 2km underground.[163] The Quest project started operating in late 2015 and has the capacity to sequester about 1 million tonnes of CO_2 per year. Total project cost is CAN $1.35 billion, with the Province of Alberta providing funding of CAN $745 million and the Federal Government providing funding of CAN$120 million.[164] The Quest project also has a two-for-one carbon credit arrangement with Alberta for each tonne of CO_2 sequestered.

Saskatchewan has been relying on its existing oil, gas and environmental laws to regulate the use of CCS technology in the province. Although Alberta's fossil fuel regulatory framework appears to be more comprehensive than Saskatchewan's for

---

[156] AR 262/1997.
[157] AR 145/2005.
[158] SA 2009, C C-2.5.
[159] AR 64/2010.
[160] Enhance Energy Inc, 'Enhanced Oil Recovery Projects in Canada' (Enhance Energy Inc), at www.enhanceenergy.com/pdf/News/releases/Handout_EOR_in_CA_web.pdf.
[161] Natural Resources Canada, 'Alberta Carbon Trunk Line (ACTL)' (January 2016), at www.nrcan.gc.ca/energy/publications/16233.
[162] Enhance Energy Inc, 'The Alberta Carbon Trunk Line' (Enhance Energy Inc), at www.enhanceenergy.com/pdf/News/releases/ACTLBrochure2017_web.pdf.
[163] Global CCS Institute, 'Quest' (June 2017), at www.globalccsinstitute.com/projects/quest.
[164] Natural Resources Canada, 'Shell Canada Energy Quest Project' (September 2016), at www.nrcan.gc.ca/energy/funding/current-funding-programs/18168.

this purpose, there is no doubt that Saskatchewan has been able to regulate and support a very successful and—by all accounts—environmentally safe CCS-related sector (CCS and CCS-EOR) by using its existing oil and gas and environmental legal framework.

Saskatchewan's experience with a CCS-type activity such as EOR dates back to 1984, and includes a CCS technology demonstration project starting in 2000 and an actual CCS activity starting in 2005.[165] This experience has continued into more recent times, with details of the world's first commercial-scale CCS project at SaskPower's Boundary Dam facility being made public in late 2014.[166] Saskatchewan's confidence in CCS technology is reflected by its use of CCS technology in the province: the International Energy Agency estimated that in 2009, 46 per cent of the annual amount of CO_2 being stored worldwide was stored at the Weyburn and Midale fields in Saskatchewan, which began as CO_2-EOR projects.[167] Even since 2009, during which time the worldwide acceptance of CCS has increased and additional CCS projects have been developed, in 2012 the Province of Saskatchewan was estimated to be responsible for sequestering about 15 per cent of the total subsurface stored CO_2 in the entire world.[168] The province's experience with CCS-type activities and the fact that this largely rural province has the highest per capita GHG emissions in Canada and is responsible for 10 per cent of Canada's GHG emissions explains, at least in part, why Saskatchewan actively encourages the local use of CCS technology to reduce the province's contribution to global GHG emissions, as well as GHG emissions from US sources south of the international boarder.[169] The province produces around 10 million tonnes of coal per year, with about 44 per cent of Saskatchewan's electricity generation coming from coal in 2014.[170] Carbon capture and storage is so highly favoured by the province that CCS technology was put forward as the basis for an Equivalency Agreement with the Federal Government as a response to the federal ban on coal-fired electricity generation, in order to allow the province to continue the use of coal-fired generation facilities.

The application of CCS technology in Saskatchewan is governed by the Oil and Gas Conservation Act,[171] which regulates the storage of oil-and-gas substances and non-oil-and-gas substances, as well as by the Environmental Management and

---

[165] Natural Resources Canada, 'Carbon Capture and Storage: Canada's Technology Demonstration Leadership' (Natural Resources Canada, 2013), at www.nrcan.gc.ca/sites/www.nrcan.gc.ca/files/energy/files/pdf/11-1416_eng_acc.pdf.

[166] SaskPower, 'Capturing Carbon and the World's Attention' (July 2017), at www.saskpower.com/our-power-future/carbon-capture-and-storage/capturing-carbon-and-the-worlds-attention/.

[167] Canada's CO_2 Capture and Storage Information Source, n 12 above.

[168] Global CCS Institute, 'Global Status of CCS: 2012' (Global CCS Institute, 2012), at www.globalccsinstitute.com/publications/global-status-ccs-2012.

[169] E Flanagan et al, 'Race to the Front: Tracking pan-Canadian climate progress and where we go from here' (Pembina Institute, 2016) 8, at www.pembina.org/pub/race-to-front.

[170] A Marsh and J Berenyi, 'An Overview of Coals in Saskatchewan' (Saskatchewan Ministry of Energy and Resources, 2008), at publications.gov.sk.ca/documents/310/95116-OH2008_TS4_Marsh.pdf.

[171] The Revised Statutes of Saskatchewan, 1978, C O-2, as amended by the Statutes of Saskatchewan, 1982–83, c 1; 1983, c 54; 1988–89, c 31; 1989–90, c 54; 1990–91, c 39; 1993, c 35; 1998, c 30; 2000, c 50; 2001, c 26; 2003, c 29; 2007, c7; 2010, c E-9.22; 2011, c 11; 2014, c E-13.1 and c 21; and 2015, c 21.

Protection Act[172] and the Saskatchewan Environmental Code.[173] A project may also be required to complete an assessment under the Environmental Assessment Act.[174]

It has previously been noted that Saskatchewan's Management and Reduction of Greenhouse Gases Act was passed in 2010 but has not yet come into force.[175] It has also been noted that when this Act does come into force, facilities that emit more than 50,000 tonnes of GHGs will be further motivated to reduce their annual emissions to provincially established targets.[176] However, for the purpose of promoting CCS technology, the Act will also set up the Saskatchewan Technology Fund Corp. This Fund will have the legislative the power, inter alia, to 'provide financial assistance by way of a loan, grant, guarantee, investment or any other means ... to assist in activities related to ... carbon capture and storage'.[177] As noted, despite being passed in 2010, this Act has yet to be proclaimed in force and the emission limits have not yet been set by regulation. Undoubtedly the endorsement of an Equivalency Agreement by Saskatchewan and the Federal Government will force the province to take action on those two outstanding matters.

In addition, to promote CCS-type activities within the province, the government of Saskatchewan had previously introduced a number of initiatives: the Saskatchewan Petroleum Research Incentive; the Saskatchewan Carbon Dioxide Enhanced Oil Recovery and Storage Initiative; and the Saskatchewan Oil and Gas Industry Upstream Emission Reduction Initiative.[178] The province also supports the International Test Centre for Carbon Dioxide Capture[179] and the International Performance Assessment Centre for the Geological Storage of Carbon Dioxide at the University of Regina. BHP Billiton is joining SaskPower, a Crown utility, contributing to a research centre located next to the university for the purpose of supporting CCS technology and commercial viability research.[180]

Saskatchewan is also using its experience with CCS technology to advance a collaborative effort with Québec 'to accelerate the development and deployment of technologies related to carbon capture and storage (CCS)'.[181] However, Québec's interest appears to be not directed at CCS, that is the capture, transport and permanent sequestration of the carbon, but at the capture and short-term storage

---

[172] SS 2010, c E-10.21.
[173] Government of Saskatchewan, 'Saskatchewan Environmental Code: Moving Forward in Partnership' (Government of Saskatchewan, 2014), at publications.gov.sk.ca/documents/66/89764-Consolidated%20SK%20Environmental%20Code%20November%202014.pdf.
[174] SS 1979–80, c E-10.1.
[175] Management and Reduction of Greenhouse Gases Act, n 124 above.
[176] SS 2010, c E-10.22.
[177] Management and Reduction of Greenhouse Gases Act, n 124 above, s 24.
[178] Saskatchewan Upstream Petroleum Industry Associated Gas Conservation Directive Directive S-10, November 2015.
[179] International Test Centre for CO_2 Capture (ITC). See at www.co$_2$-research.ca.
[180] CBC News, 'BHP Billiton pledges $20m toward carbon capture research in Regina', *CBC News* (5 February 2016), at www.cbc.ca/news/canada/saskatchewan/bhp-billiton-will-contribute-20-million-dollars-to-carbon-capture-research-in-regina-1.3436112.
[181] Cision, 'Quebec Government to Invest $15m to Enhance Carbon Capture Technology Developed by CO_2 Solutions', *Cision* (18 March 2016), at www.newswire.ca/news-releases/quebec-government-to-invest-15-m-to-enhance-carbon-capture-technology-developed-by-co$_2$-solutions-572533751.html.

of carbon for a productive use. For example, Québec is financially supporting 'a consortium to promote adoption of ... (an) enzyme-enabled technology'.[182] Québec's interest in CCS technology is founded on supporting its cap-and-trade regulations by promoting the 'reuse (of) carbon dioxide in applications that are crucial to Québec's economy—the conversion of biofuels, the production of reinforced concrete and enhanced hydrocarbon recovery'. Undoubtedly this is a worthwhile purpose, which benefits from experience with 'technologies *related* to carbon capture and storage (CCS)' (emphasis added), but this is not a characteristic CCS technology venture. In any event, this proposal will be regulated by the Québec Environmental Quality Act[183] and, if the promoter intends to use an underground storage reservoir to store the collected carbon, also by the Mining Act[184] and the regulation respecting petroleum, natural gas and underground reservoirs.[185]

Nova Scotia is investigating the potential for CCS technology within the province. In 2008, the Province of Nova Scotia, Nova Scotia Power Inc and Dalhousie University incorporated a joint venture called the Carbon Capture and Storage Research Consortium of Nova Scotia (CCSNS).[186] A multi-phase development program was planned, involving research into the technical and preliminary economic feasibility of utilising CCS in Nova Scotia, which took place between 2009–15; followed by the Pilot Plant and Injection Phase that will be based on the findings of the Phase 1 research, which is planned to take place between 2015–18; and finally a third phase—a commercial-scale operation based on the Phase 2 findings—which is planned for between 2018–25. The Federal Government provided financial support for the injection site characterisation.[187] Unfortunately, the characterisation of the potential injection site did not confirm the presence of a suitable reservoir. Although the conclusion was that 'the geological storage of carbon dioxide will not be possible within Nova Scotia', finding a satisfactory potential reservoir is still stated as a focus of the project.[188]

Manitoba's efforts have been modest and focused on the use of CCS-type technologies to perform what has been characterised as a value-added CCS option.[189] In this regard Manitoba's efforts have been directed at commercial-scale CO_2-EOR projects rather than at dedicated sole-purpose CCS projects. This focus

---

[182] Canadian Underwriter, 'Quebec and Saskatchewan join forces for carbon capture and storage technologies', *Canadian Underwriter* (17 June 2016), at www.canadianunderwriter.ca/technology/quebec-saskatchewan-join-forces-carbon-capture-storage-technologies-1004094700/.

[183] RSQ, c Q-2.

[184] RSQ, c M-13.

[185] CQLR c M-13.1, r 1.

[186] A Henry, 'Geological Storage of Carbon Dioxide in Nova Scotia' (NS Energy R&D Forum, 2008). Available at www.oera.ca/wp-content/uploads/2013/05/Andrew-Henry-Geological-Storage-Assessment-Project.pdf.

[187] Natural Resources Canada, 'Carbon Storage Onshore Nova Scotia–Injection Site Characterization' (May 2016), at www.nrcan.gc.ca/energy/funding/current-funding-programs/eii/16057.

[188] CCS Nova Scotia, 'CCS Nova Scotia: Executive Summary' (CCS Nova Scotia, 2015), at www.nspower.ca/site/media/Parent/CCSNS%20Geological%20Research%20-Executive%20Summary%20-April%202015.pdf.

[189] Government of Canada, 'Canada's CO_2 Capture & Storage Technology Roadmap' (Government of Canada, 2006) 53, at www.nrcan.gc.ca/energy/coal/carbon-capture-storage/4327.

has been aided by the Manitoba Drilling Incentive Program. One of the objectives of this Program is to encourage technologies to maximise the recovery from Manitoba's oil pools.[190] Captured carbon and waterflooding are substances that are used and regulated to fulfil this goal. It appears that other uses have been made of potential injection wells and storage reservoirs. Manitoba indicates that at a time when about 6,500 wells had been drilled in the province, '[a]pproximately 400 wells are used for purposes other than production, such as disposal of produced water'[191] (a more recent announcement states that more than 8,500 wells have been advanced[192]). Current oil production is located in southwest Manitoba on a sedimentary basin, called the Williston Basin, that also occupies portions of southern Saskatchewan, North Dakota, South Dakota and Montana.[193] Outwardly, then, with the province's potential hydrocarbon-bearing formations occurring to depths of up to 2,300 metres (7,500 feet) and the geological trapping of hydrocarbons for millions of years, even without detailed pore space characterisation data, Manitoba would seem to offer similar CCS opportunities as its neighbour to the west, Saskatchewan, which by any measure has excelled at exploiting CCS technology. However, aside from the CO_2 used for EOR, a dedicated CCS project has not been planned. Manitoba relies on Oil and Gas Act[194] and the Drilling and Production Regulation[195] to regulate EOR operations using either captured carbon or waterflooding, and subsurface storage reservoirs, which could include CCS-type storage projects.

III. GEOPHYSICAL SURVEY AND GHG EMISSIONS SOURCES

Canada is the world's second largest country by total area.[196] However, Canada's geology is not uniformly appropriate for the geological storage of CO_2, which is recognised as being best achieved in tectonically stable sedimentary basins.[197] Large parts of Canada, which include provinces in which major CO_2 emitters are located, are underlain by less suitable Canadian Precambrian Shield, which is an area of mostly igneous or metamorphic rocks formed more than 1 billion years ago. This presents a challenge to matching large source emitters with the appropriate geology and the motivation and will power to take action.

The Maritime Provinces—Newfoundland and Labrador, Nova Scotia, Prince Edward Island and New Brunswick—accounted for only about 6 per cent of

---

[190] 'Manitoba Mineral Resources Division: Petroleum Branch' (Williston Basin Petroleum Conference, Saskatchewan, 1 May 2013).
[191] Government of Manitoba, 'Manitoba Oil Facts' (Government of Manitoba). Available at www.gov.mb.ca/iem/petroleum/pubcat/oilfacts.pdf.
[192] Government of Manitoba, 'Manitoba Oil Facts' (Government of Manitoba). Available at www.manitoba.ca/iem/petroleum/oilfacts/oilfacts.pdf.
[193] Above n 190.
[194] CCSM c O34, ss 160–161, 166.
[195] Regulation 111/94.
[196] Central Intelligence Agency, 'The World Factbook' (July 2017).
[197] S Solomon, 'Fact sheet: CO_2 Storage' (The Bellona Foundation, 2007) 1, at network.bellona.org/content/uploads/sites/3/Fact_sheet_CO_2_storage.pdf.

Canada's total GHG emissions in 2015.[198] Promising full-scale sequestration opportunities are offered by the basalt formations of the Atlantic Basin off the coast of Nova Scotia and Newfoundland, the coal basins underling the northern part of Nova Scotia and Prince Edward Island, and by the deep salt caverns in Nova Scotia. However, there are relatively few large final emitters to take advantage of these opportunities. Nova Scotia has an important coal-mining sector and an economy that is based on fossil fuels, notwithstanding that it must deal with a substantial seasonal employment component. Its economy is sustained by a significant, local coal-fired electricity generation capacity. This has provided the province with sufficient motivation to investigate the feasibility of using the geological storage of CO_2 to control its GHG emissions, which the province has done through its partnership in CCS Nova Scotia.

Moving west from the Maritime Provinces to central Canada we find Québec, Ontario and Manitoba. Québec and Ontario account for about 37 per cent of Canada's GHG emissions. Since almost two-thirds of Canada's population lives in Québec and Ontario, a good portion of the GHG emissions are from small, diverse emission sources.[199] However, large parts of Québec and Ontario are heavily industrialised, and so are also home to a number of large GHG emission sources.

Québec has strong mining, smelting and refining, forestry and pulp and paper and manufacturing sectors, but its electricity generation facilities consist mainly of hydroelectric power plants, which account for 94 per cent of the available power. Thermal plants, which burn petroleum products, and a nuclear power plant generate the remaining power.[200]

Québec has six sedimentary basins: the St Lawrence Lowlands, the Lower St Lawrence, Gaspesia, the St Lawrence Estuary, the St Lawrence Gulf and North Québec. Important natural gas deposits have been found in three locations. Public hearings regarding the development of the shale gas resources of the St Lawrence Lowlands began in 2010, with a report of the inquiry and hearings published by the Bureau d'audiences publiques sur l'environnement in 2011.[201] However, shale gas is associated with high concentrations of CO_2, which has raised concerns amongst Québec-based environmentalists about the venting of CO_2 to the atmosphere as the gas is processed to market standards. Capturing and disposing of the CO_2 in a sedimentary basin is an option.

Large portions of Québec and the large central section of Ontario, as well as most of Labrador and a large part of Manitoba and northern Saskatchewan stretching to the Arctic Ocean—a broad area surrounding Hudson's Bay in central Canada— are underlain with Canadian Precambrian Shield. This offers limited opportunities

---

[198] All data regarding GHG emissions in Canada have been obtained from Environment and Climate Change Canada, 'National Inventory Report 1990–2015: Greenhouse Gas Sources and Sinks in Canada'. The data are also available at Environment and Climate Change Canada, 'Canadian Environmental Sustainability Indicators: Greenhouse Gas Emissions' (2017), at www.ec.gc.ca/indicateurs-indicators/default.asp?lang=En&n=FBF8455E-1.

[199] Statistics Canada, '2006 Census of Population' (Statistics Canada, 2006).

[200] Government of Québec, Ministère de l'Énergie et des Resources naturelles, 'Abundant and Accessible Energy'. See at mern.gouv.qc.ca/english/energy/index.jsp.

[201] Bureau d'audiences publiques sur l'environnement (2011) Sustainable Development of the Shale Gas Industry in Québec Inquiry and Hearing Report February 2011, Report, 273 (excerpts translated, original in French).

for sequestration activities due to the low porosity and permeability of the rock. More promising are the limited areas of younger sedimentary rocks in Ontario, to the south and the extreme north of the vast central area covered by Canadian Precambrian Shield. The southern area is the Michigan Basin, centred on the Lower Peninsula of the US State of Michigan. This feature is a nearly circular pattern of geologic sedimentary strata, which runs under southwest Ontario and Lake Erie. Located in this region are active and depleted oil and gas reservoirs, saline aquifers and salt caverns. There is uncertainty about using depleted oil and gas reservoirs for CCS purposes because of the risks posed by the many shallow-depth reservoirs, the large number of undocumented and unplugged well-bores (out of the more than 50,000 well-bores constructed for oil and gas development) and the limited pore volumes available.[202] Nevertheless, the costs of completing a captured CO_2 disposal project have been studied, although the CCS concept has never been favoured by an Ontario government.[203] The availability of large final emitters located close to this area, however, kept the possibility of CO_2 sequestration alive for many years.[204]

Candidate reservoirs also exist relatively close to some large emissions sources in that part of the Michigan Basin that is centred in the Lower Peninsula of Michigan. However, Ontario's use of Michigan as the disposal site for Ontario's CO_2 would have to overcome political hurdles, notwithstanding the precedent set by international CO_2 transfer agreement governing the transport of captured CO_2 from the source in North Dakota to the Weyburn-Midale Project sequestration sites in Saskatchewan. The success of the Weyburn-Midale Project demonstrates that the potential political obstacles are not insurmountable. Historically Michigan had been the repository for a large amount of Southern Ontario's non-hazardous wastes, while hazardous waste is often transported in the opposite direction. Non-hazardous waste shipments from Ontario to Michigan became an issue in the US at both the State and Federal levels, and with Ontarians from a variety of backgrounds. In fact the 2002 gubernatorial race saw the question of stopping Ontario's waste at the border become an election issue. It would be a stretch to imagine that there would now be no political roadblocks to Michigan's agreeing to be the disposal site for Ontario's captured industrial GHG emissions. At the same time, Ontario's government was actively carrying forward its promise from before it was elected in the 2003, to close down the province's remaining coal-fired generating plants. Additionally, since 2003 consecutive Ontario governments having been actively pursuing green, renewable energy sources. There was, therefore, little motivation to pursue the option of CO_2

---

[202] A Shafeen et al, 'CO_2 sequestration in Ontario, Canada. Part I: Storage Evaluation of Potential Reservoirs' (2004) 4 *Energy Conversion and Management* 2645.

[203] A Shafeen et al, 'CO_2 sequestration in Ontario, Canada. Part II: Cost Estimation' (2004) 4 *Energy Conversion and Management* 3207. This investigation focused on the capital and operating cost for CO_2 sequestration in southwestern Ontario from a 500 MW coal-fired power plant. Although many uncertainties associated with the cost estimation were identified, the study's authors estimated the cost of sequestration of 14,000 ton per day of CO_2 at approximately 110 bar in southwestern Ontario to be at between US$7.5 and 14 per ton (2003 dollars) of CO_2 stored.

[204] See, eg, T Carter et al, *Geological Sequestration of Carbon Dioxide: A Technology Review and Analysis of Opportunities in Ontario* (Peterborough, Ont, Ontario Ministry of Natural Resources, 2007).

sequestration, which could have provided Ontario's coal-fired electricity generation facilities with an extended life as well as attending to industrial large final emitters. Instead, since 2003 Ontario has had to adjust to less reliable and considerably more expensive renewable energy sources.

It is on the Western Canadian Sedimentary Basins that large final emitters and very promising geological formations come together. These Basins cover the southern part of Manitoba and Saskatchewan, most of Alberta and parts of British Columbia. Historically, these formations have hosted commercial-scale analogues to the geological storage of captured CO_2, such as EOR, enhanced coal-bed methane recovery and acid-gas disposal operations.

Beyond the volumes potentially available from utilising EOR and enhanced coal bed methane recovery production methods, the options for the geological storage of CO_2 in Western Canada also include depleted gas reservoirs, which will become more abundant in Saskatchewan, Alberta and British Columbia over time. There are many advantages offered by these pools. First, there is proof of containment, since these pools have held hydrocarbons for millions of years. Secondly, the volumes available for CO_2 storage are well understood, since the hydrocarbons that were removed were measured. A third advantage is that the historical production rates of these pools provide a good understanding of the potential for future CO_2 insertion into the geological strata. Lastly, these sites typically have existing infrastructure in place, such as wellbores and pipelines.

Unfortunately, the storage space in depleted gas pools cannot be fully realised until production operations cease, which is estimated to be decades away. There is also the risk of commercial conflict with adjoining oil or gas pools that have not yet been drained, and the risk of leakage from existing well-bores if the CO_2 plume migration dynamics are not well understood. Also, the distance to some of the pools from the source emitters can increase the costs of transporting the captured product.

Saskatchewan, Alberta and British Columbia also have CO_2 sequestration potential in deep saline formations. In areas such as northern British Columbia, it is also possible to utilise coal seams and deep saline formations to bridge the timing gap for short- to intermediate-term requirements.[205] Notwithstanding the risk of leakage that was noted above, the general risk to human health and the environment at all these sites is viewed as low.

IV. SUBSURFACE PROPERTY RIGHTS[206]

A fundamental component of a CCS legal framework is property rights. Surface rights, pore space ownership and subsurface rights, and property assembly rights

---

[205] B Ryan and D Richardson, 'The Potential for CO_2 Sequestration in British Columbia Coal Seams' (Resource Development and Geosciences Branch, British Columbia Ministry of Energy, Mines and Petroleum Resources, 2004); A Hartling,' Carbon Capture and Storage in British Columbia' (British Columbia Ministry of Energy, Mines and Petroleum Resources, 2008).

[206] For a more detailed review of this subject, the reader should consult ch 10 of this volume, by Nigel Bankes, entitled 'Pore Space Ownership in Western Canada'.

can influence site selection and characterisation. Indeterminate or fragmented ownership of surface or subsurface rights can hinder the assembly of suitable subsurface disposal space, or prevent locating injection sites in a favourable place for activities related to both the transport and injection of captured CO_2.

Two propositions are fundamental to understanding Canadian property rights: first, the mineral interest may be severed from the surface interest; and, secondly, the owner of the mineral interest continues to have ownership over the geological formation even after all the minerals have been removed.[207] It follows that the ownership of pore space and the subsurface storage or disposal rights likely accrues to the owner of the mineral rights, who may be different from the surface right owner.[208] Consequently, the legal maxim *cujos est solum, ejus est usque ad coelum et ad inferos* ('for whoever owns the soil, it is theirs up to Heaven and down to Hell') has limited relevance to the subsurface property rights framework across Canada.[209]

A peculiarity of the regulatory and property right frameworks across Canada is that subsurface hydrocarbon storage has commonly been anticipated, while subsurface storage or disposal rights for non-hydrocarbons have developed inconsistently and belatedly.

Some jurisdictions either presume the subsurface rights to be vested in the Crown (the state), or take this for granted. Nova Scotia's petroleum and mineral legislation, for example, appears to assume that these rights are vested in the Crown.[210] Nova Scotia also addresses only hydrocarbon storage, not subsurface disposal or non-hydrocarbon storage rights. In a similar fashion Nova Scotia allows surface rights access with compensation to the surface rights holder, but only for the purpose of storage operations.

New Brunswick and Québec clearly vest pore space and subsurface storage rights in the Crown (the state).[211] However, these rights are again limited to storage uses; neither jurisdiction extends pore space ownership rights to disposal uses. Pore space ownership rights in Québec are further limited by not being extended to the storage (or disposal) of non-hydrocarbons. In New Brunswick, surface right access with compensation to the surface right holder is allowed, but again for storage operations only.

Ontario,[212] Manitoba[213] and Saskatchewan[214] assume that subsurface storage rights follow mineral rights. As a result, these rights may be vested either in the

---

[207] JL Lyndon, 'The Legal Aspects of Underground Storage of Natural Gas-Should Legislation be Considered before the Problem Arises?' (1961) 1 *Alberta Law Review* 543, 545.

[208] For a contrasting legal position concerning ownership in the US, see I Havercroft, R Macrory and RB Stewart (eds), *Carbon Capture and Storage—Emerging Legal and Regulatory Issues*, 1st edn (Oxford, Hart Publishing, 2011) ch 4.

[209] W Blackstone, *Commentaries on the Laws of England* (Oxford, Clarendon Press, 1769); *Star Energy Weald Basin Ltd v Bocardo SA* [2010] UKSC 35.

[210] Mineral Resources Act, SNS 1990, c 37, s 4; Petroleum Resources Act, RSNS 1989, c 342; Underground Hydrocarbons Storage Act, SNS 2001, c 37.

[211] Underground Storage Act, SNB 1978, c U-1.1; Mining Act, RSQ, c M-13.1, s 3.

[212] Mining Act, RSO 1990, c M-14; Exploration Licences, Production and Storage Leases for Oil and Gas in Ontario, O Reg 263/02.

[213] Oil and Gas Act, CCSM, c O-34.

[214] The Crown Minerals Act, SS, 1984-85-86, c 50.2, as amended. The Crown Minerals Act applies to Crown minerals and Crown mineral lands, but not to privately-owned minerals.

Crown (the province or federal authority, as the case may be) or in a private owner, depending on mineral ownership. In regard to the assembly of subsurface rights, Ontario allows compulsory acquisition with compensation from a private owner for natural gas storage, but does not address compulsory acquisition for disposal uses.[215] Similarly, neither Manitoba nor Saskatchewan has specific legislation to deal with compulsory acquisition. Lastly, while these jurisdictions do not deal with the pore space rights for subsurface disposal purposes, practice suggests that in Saskatchewan, pore space ownership for disposal purposes appears to follow the mineral ownership rights, while pore space ownership for disposal purposes is uncertain in Ontario and Manitoba. Pore space ownership for EOR activities would follow the mineral ownership rights.

Saskatchewan and Alberta have a long history of exploiting their mineral resources. In Alberta, the Crown (the state) owns the pore space and therefore the storage rights below the surface of all land in the province, regardless of who is the owner of the title to the petroleum and natural gas mineral estate in an underground formation.[216] The Crown can enter into an agreement for 'the use of the subsurface reservoirs'.[217] Since the Alberta Mines and Minerals Act defines storage rights as meaning 'the right to inject fluid mineral substances into a subsurface reservoir for the purpose of storage', and distinguishes this activity from permanent disposal or sequestration, it is clear that these provisions relate to oil and gas production and related activities, and not to the disposal of 'substances'.[218] This framework has been sufficient for the development of CCS undertakings, and indeed has been used to accommodate both CO_2 and acid-gas disposal, the latter being characterised as a commercial-scale analogue to CO_2 geological storage.

Alberta has vested all rights associated with surface or subsurface water in the provincial Crown (the state).[219] This will include saline aquifers. Consequently, rights to dispose of CO_2 in saline formations can be granted by the Crown. In addition, the owners of the freehold disposal rights are able to grant those disposal rights to others by way of contract. Lastly, Alberta allows surface access to the holder of the mineral estate and requires compensation be provided to the surface rights owner.

Subsurface rights in British Columbia have not been included in most land grants from the late nineteenth century, and continue to be reserved to the Crown.[220] Therefore, to a substantial degree, the subsurface rights for petroleum, natural gas and coal are held by the provincial Crown, as is the case in Alberta. However, in areas of early settlement, such as the Fraser Valley, mainly private, individual owners hold the subsurface rights. Notwithstanding the apparent clarity of ownership rights, British Columbia has approved a relatively clear legislative framework for the development of storage projects, which takes into consideration the possibility that the ownership of pore space rights for natural gas storage may vest in either the surface

---

[215] Ontario Energy Board Act, 1998, SO 1998, c 15, s 38(1).
[216] Carbon Capture and Storage Statutes Amendment Act, n 152 above, s 15(1).
[217] ibid, s 102(1).
[218] Carbon Capture and Storage Statutes Amendment Act, n 152 above, s 1(1)(z) and s 1(1) (y.1).
[219] Water Act, RSA 2000, c W-3, s 3(2).
[220] Land Act, RSBC 996, c 245, s 50(1)(b): [no right, title or interest is conveyed to] (i) geothermal resources as defined in the Geothermal Resources Act, (ii) minerals and placer minerals as defined in the Mineral Tenure Act, (iii) coal, (iv) petroleum as defined in the Petroleum and Natural Gas Act, or (v) gas.

or mineral rights holder.[221] Differing from Alberta's approach, British Columbia includes the function of disposal as one of the functions for which a storage reservoir may be used.[222] The British Columbia framework deals with storage reservoirs on a case-by-case basis. The Crown can designate an area as a storage area with these rights vesting in the Crown by law, subject to the payment of compensation where the holder of the subsurface rights can show that it has been divested of its ownership rights.[223] This provides some certainty regarding the assembly of rights for storage projects, albeit not on the level that would be afforded by vesting storage rights in one category of owner. However, this is a small qualification in light of the Crown's predominance over the ownership of subsurface rights in the province. A provincial policy discussion paper on CCS recognises that suitable geological storage sites will include the 'deep saline formations and depleted oil and gas reservoirs' located in northeast British Columbia.[224] This policy discussion paper also appears to distinguish CO_2 'produced through the production of petroleum and natural gas' and CO_2 from other sources. It suggests that the geological storage sites could accept CO_2 from a variety of sources if these captured gases were a prescribed substance. The province is also considering the options for clarifying the tenure requirements for CCS. Tenure agreements give rights to specific areas or certain geological formations, and may include rights to all depths. Current agreements typically run for three to 10 years, with renewal options.[225] The province recognises that this timeframe accommodates only the pre-abandonment phase of a CCS undertaking, as it is also examining long-term liability issues.

V. THE REGULATORY FRAMEWORK

In common with other undertakings that create a potential risk to human health and the environment, the approval of a CCS project should be contingent upon the regulator's being satisfied of a number of factors.

First, the regulator will have to assess the selected site. A detailed characterisation and assessment of the underlying geology and land features is essential to inform a longer-term risk profile, and may involve stakeholder engagement to help weigh the key elements of the site characterisation and the range of potential impacts and liabilities.

Secondly, the approval and permitting of the proposal will require the regulator to consider how the venture will operate, including the following elements: the capture of the carbon; pressurisation, transport and injection site equipment that will be used; injection-well construction; mitigation measures; and a proposed

---

[221] Oil and Gas Activities Act, n 144 above, pt 14; Petroleum and Natural Storage Reservoir Regulation, BC Reg 350/97.
[222] Oil and Gas Activities Act, n 144 above, pt 4, s 1.
[223] ibid, pt 14, ss 127–129.
[224] British Columbia Ministry of Natural Gas Development, 'Carbon Capture and Storage Regulatory Policy: Discussion and Comment Paper' (British Columbia Ministry of Natural Gas Development, 2014) 1.
[225] British Columbia Ministry of Energy and Mines Titles Division, Victoria, BC.

decommissioning plan that considers longer-term risks and remediation actions, as well as any conditions that should be imposed on the project as a requirement of the project's approval in order to mitigate potential human and environmental risks. Stakeholder engagement will be desirable.

Thirdly, during the life of the project, the regulator will have to consider operational matters relating to the intended purpose of the project, as well as engineering and scientific design, calculations and assurances. This will involve comparing the actual operations against the criteria tendered during the site selection and during the approval and permitting phase, and monitoring the storage reservoir and injected CO_2.

Fourthly, the regulator should be prepared to observe and regulate the decommissioning of the project, ensuring that monitoring continues and that the project conditions are assessed against identified performance criteria, such as pressure levels, the percentage of CO_2 dissolved into subsurface formations or groundwater, and that the CO_2 that remains is contained.

Lastly, for the post-closure phase to officially commence, the regulator will have to be satisfied that the decommissioning plan and all of the conditions of approval have been met or completed.

Economic regulation has historically played a central role in the development of subsurface storage operations, albeit in the context of hydrocarbon storage. The review of the subsurface property right issues in section IV illustrates that hydrocarbon storage, not non-hydrocarbon storage or disposal rights, has been the principal focus of the law in most of the provinces. In provinces such as Alberta and British Columbia, where the regulatory framework can accommodate or has developed to deal directly with subsurface disposal of captured CO_2 or processing by-products such as acid gas, the management of hydrocarbon resources (including the full utilisation of these resources) and subsurface hydrocarbon storage provides the historical basis for the regulation of CCS activities. Traditionally, an economic regulator, in the form of the provincial utility, energy board or commission, is often the primary approval mechanism. However, the principal focus of the economic regulator has been consumer protection and the rational development of hydrocarbon storage capacity. Nova Scotia, Québec, Ontario, Manitoba and Alberta all have provincial regulators and regulatory schemes that contemplate the regulation of subsurface storage capacity, whether site selection, or rates or both. Nonetheless, at least in the context of economic regulation, the trend has been towards deregulation and a move towards a competitive market with market-based rates for new storage, rather than regulated rates based upon the cost of service. Though subsurface hydrocarbon storage and CCS projects share a number of features, these two types of undertakings differ in their fundamental objectives. Therefore, neither the limited role of an economic regulator occasioned by deregulation nor the more traditional role of the economic regulator fits squarely with the needs of a comprehensive CCS legal regime.

All Canadian jurisdictions regulate the safety and environmental and resource conservation aspects of each of the component elements, ie carbon capture, compressing, transport, subsurface injection and storage, of both publicly- and privately-owned storage projects, using the regulatory mechanism of issuing either a licence or a permit for each component that requires compliance with standard terms provided in a regulation, or an approval that may have conditions attached. The requirements for a licence or permit, however, differ between the provinces. The process of capturing, compressing and transporting CO_2 would nevertheless have undoubtedly required a provincial environmental approval, or an amendment to an approval that has been issued, because this would involve the operation, construction or alteration of a plant, equipment or mechanism that may discharge, or from which may discharge, a contaminant into the natural environment.[226]

In addition, each of the component elements of a CCS undertaking may require a federal and/or provincial environmental assessment to evaluate the possible environmental, social, economic and cultural impacts, as well as, if the environmental assessment foresees the possibility of potential impacts, to assess mitigation or risk management measures to deal with those impacts. A component of a CCS undertaking may be designated an activity subject to a mandatory environmental assessment. For example, the federal Clean Energy Fund's[227] funding of the Shell Quest CCS Project triggered an environmental assessment under the Canadian Environmental Assessment Act 1999, which was the law in force at the time.[228] However, provincial environment regulations typically also allow for a discretionary assessment to be ordered, again, for all or part of the CCS undertaking. For example, although not required under provincial regulations, Alberta directed an environmental impact assessment of the carbon storage component of the Shell Quest CCS Project to be prepared and submitted to the Energy Resources Conservation Board (ERCB), which was at that time the energy regulator, at the same time as Shell's application to the ERCB for the licensing of that component.[229]

The conditions that would trigger an environmental assessment are not the same for all of the provinces. For example, Nova Scotia requires an environmental assessment for hydrocarbon storage projects,[230] while it is not clear whether an environmental assessment for a subsurface storage or disposal project will be required in New Brunswick or Québec. In Ontario, the requirement to complete an environmental assessment depends on whether the project is characterised as a major commercial or business enterprise, but even then a Ministerial Order may exempt the project, or an otherwise excluded project could be 'bumped up' to requiring an environmental assessment.[231] Saskatchewan leaves open the possibility of having an environmental assessment, but does not require one in all circumstances. The threshold question is whether the project is likely to have significant environmental implications, in which case the proponent is required to receive the approval

---

[226] See, eg, the Ontario Environmental Protection Act, RSO 1990, c E.19, s 9(1).

[227] Natural Resources Canada, 'Clean Energy Fund Program' (July 2016), at www.nrcan.gc.ca/energy/funding/current-funding-programs/cef/4949.

[228] SC 1992, c 37, s 5(1)(b); repealed, 2012, c 19, s 66.

[229] Shell Canada Ltd, 'Proposed Terms of Reference Environmental Assessment Report for the Proposed Quest Carbon Capture and Storage Project' (Shell Canada Ltd, 2010).

[230] Environmental Assessment Regulations under the Environment Act, SNS 1994–95, c 1 OIC 95-220 (21 March 1995), NS Reg 26/95, as amended up to NS Reg 2009-386 (15 September 2009), NS Reg 277/2009.

[231] Environmental Assessment Act, RSO 1990, c E18, s 3.

of the Provincial Minister of Environment under the Environmental Assessment Act before proceeding with the development.[232] Significantly, the landmark Weyburn-Midale project did complete an environmental assessment. However, the fact that this project is part of an approved active and depleted oil and gas field may have influenced this decision.

Where the statutory power of decision rests determines both the route for getting all of the necessary approvals for the project and the options available to question the decision to grant or not to grant an approval, as well as any conditions that may be prescribed. Ontario and Saskatchewan provide examples of possible ministerial or government executive, or executive committee, involvement in regulatory decision making, the latter exemplified by an issue's being brought to Cabinet. This is in contrast to public service staff decision making and quasi-judicial decision making, or judgments of boards, commissions or tribunals. Public service staff decision-makers are part of the government. Boards, commissions and tribunals, on the other hand, usually stand at arm's-length to the government. However, appointments to a board, commission and tribunal remain with the prerogative of the executive, and financial responsibility for the operation of the board, commission or tribunal often, if not usually, falls to the government. Public service staff decision-makers and boards, commissions and tribunals are all subject to the tenets of administrative law.

There are two important differences between ministerial or executive decision making and the decisions or judgments of public service staff decision-makers and boards, commissions and tribunals. First, as a rule, ministerial or executive decisions are shown a great deal of deference by the courts. As a result, the grounds available to appeal a ministerial or executive decision are limited. Appeals are typically by way of judicial review founded on one or more grounds from a very limited number of available grounds of appeal, such as bias. However, a judicial review may also be founded on there being no other reasonable and effective manner for the issue to be resolved. Ministerial or executive decisions in Canada are ultimately controlled by elections. If the voting population is not happy with the ministerial or executive decision, the theory goes, then at the next election the ministerial or executive decision-makers can be replaced (admittedly this may be of limited utility to the people who have to live with the offensive decision in the interim). On the other hand, the decision or judgments of public service staff decision-makers and boards, commissions and tribunals are subject to judicial review or appeal on both the law and the facts, and there is a range of avenues of appeal. Secondly, the decisions or judgments of public service staff or boards, commissions and tribunals are required to be based on existing and available policy, the law and scientific or engineering certainty applied to the context of the case. However, certainty is not aided by the application of the general principle of environmental protection to an innocent party.[233] In contrast,

---

[232] Environmental Assessment Act, SS 1979–80, c E-10.1, s 8.
[233] In *The Corporation of the City of Kawartha Lakes v Director, Ministry of the Environment* 2012 ONSC 2708, the Divisional Court affirmed the reasoning of the Environmental Review Tribunal (ERT) that innocent parties who are not responsible for discharging pollution into the environment may nonetheless be ordered by the environmental regulator and the ERT to remediate the contamination that has impacted properties through no fault of their own.

the courts have accepted that ministerial or executive decision-makers can weigh a number of factors that would be considered of limited or no relevance to public service staff or boards, commissions or tribunals. Underlying ministerial or executive decision making is the belief that these decision-makers are in a position to soften the sometimes harsh application of government policy or of the law in order to accommodate broader public concerns. To date, only the Shell Quest CCS Project has untaken a provincial environmental impact assessment of the storage component of the undertaking, and that was voluntary. However, due to federal funding, a federal environmental assessment was completed.

On the west coast, CO_2 disposal projects are exempted from environmental assessments in British Columbia. However, because a permit is required for any oil and gas activity, which includes the operation or use of a storage reservoir, public consultation is mandatory. 'Storage reservoir', as previously noted, is defined in such a way as to include a reservoir for the permanent sequestration of CO_2. The demands of ratepayer groups can be substantial, and can force the information required to support an application and the accompanying public consultation to contain substantial details of the proposal. This will still not be as extensive as the information that is required for an environmental assessment, unless the ratepayers make further demands, and even then it is unlikely to be as comprehensive.[234] This view is supported by the mandate of the provincial regulator, the Oil and Gas Commission, which is required to make decisions regarding oil and gas activities that balance broad environmental, economic and social outcomes.[235] However, if the province views a CCS proposal as a matter of provincial interest, it has the statutory option of designating land as a storage area. This designation starts the time running for the right, title and interest in any underlying storage reservoir to vest in the province. The landowner may apply to the Surface Rights Board for compensation.[236]

Historically, projects that were on or that crossed federal lands, or that required federal approval or received federal funding, or that crossed provincial or international borders, were required to complete a federal environmental assessment. The approach of the former Canadian Environmental Assessment Act 1999 was to require an environmental assessment if the project required the Federal Government to exercise a listed power, or required the Federal Government to perform one of the duties or functions listed in that Act. The approach of the current Canadian Environmental Assessment Act 2012 is to require an environmental assessment for projects or activities that have been designated by regulation.[237] However, currently, CCS projects and the project components of CCS undertakings are not listed as designated activities. Although the new Act has a potentially broader application than

---

[234] Presumably, the tendency will be to follow the example of an environmental assessment proceeding by way of screening. However comprehensive and detailed the information that is provided to the ratepayers, this does not address the issue of the ratepayers' being able to afford to retain a qualified person or persons to assess the information and to advise the ratepayers.
[235] Oil and Gas Activities Act, n 144 above, s 1.
[236] ibid, ss 127–129.
[237] Canadian Environmental Assessment Act 2012, SC 2012, c 19, s 52; Regulations Designating Physical Activities, SOR/2012-147.

the former Act, it is reasonable to anticipate that the question of designating fresh projects under the new Act and regulation will fall back on the same triggers as under the former Act. It is possible, therefore, that all or part of a proposed CCS undertaking may draw in both federal and provincial environmental assessment regulations, thereby placing the project at risk of requiring an environmental assessment to be accepted by both orders of government, and perhaps by more than one province. This difficulty has been dealt with in two ways. First, on a case-by case basis, where the environmental assessment requirements of the two jurisdictions are comparable, one or both of the jurisdictions may vary or dispense with the environmental assessment requirements imposed under its legislation.[238] The second method is to enter into an omnibus agreement to address potential duplicate environmental assessments.[239] In either case, the intention is to have 'one project–one review'.[240]

A government that is functioning as both the regulator and the regulated party can create an issue. The Federal Government or a provincial government may hold the rights to the pore space. This is the situation in Alberta. In that case, the Crown's role as both the regulator and the owner of the pore space has to be questioned, if for no other reason than that this creates the potential for a conflict of interest. It is axiomatic that the regulator should not regulate itself. Therefore, where storage or disposal rights are vested in the Crown, the prudent course of action is to ensure that the Crown does not regulate these privileges. Unfortunately, this is not practised across the board. Nova Scotia, Ontario and Alberta, for example, have delegated the regulatory responsibilities to arm's-length boards or commissions, while provincial storage rights are managed by a separate government organisation. British Columbia and Québec are anomalies. The British Columbia Oil and Gas Commission is an exception, because section 3 of its founding legislation, the Oil and Gas Activities Act, declares the Commission to be an agent of the government. Yet that Act also provides the province with the statutory authority to gain the right, title and interest in storage reservoirs, which are regulated by the Oil and Gas Commission. Similarly, Québec has shown an interest in commercial-scale analogues and alternatives to the geological storage or disposal of captured CO_2, but does not clearly separate its regulator and regulated community functions.

VI. THE LIABILITY FRAMEWORK

Canada and the provinces are making efforts to develop a comprehensive legal and regulatory framework to address the liability challenges that are distinctive to

---

[238] Ie Environmental Assessment Act, RSO 1990, c E.18, s 3.1, 'Harmonization'.

[239] Ie Government of Canada, 'Canada-Saskatchewan Agreement on Environmental Assessment Cooperation' (Government of Canada, 1999), renewed 2005. Available at www.canada.ca/en/environmental-assessment-agency/corporate/acts-regulations/legislation-regulations/canada-saskatchewan-agreement-environmental-assessment-cooperation/canada-saskatchewan-agreement-environmental-assessment-cooperation-2005.html.

[240] Government of Canada, 'Basics of Environment Assessment', at www.canada.ca/en/environmental-assessment-agency/services/environmental-assessments/basics-environmental-assessment.html.

CCS undertakings.[241] Short-term or operational liabilities arise in relation to the environmental, health and safety risks associated with capturing, transporting and injecting CO_2. The technology and risks associated with these component activities of a CCS project are similar to those that have already been dealt with by the oil and gas industries in the regulation of comparable activities in that sector, and have been employed with success for many years in commercial-scale analogues to the geological storage of captured CO_2. The inclination, therefore, has been to use the existing fossil fuel and mining regulatory framework whenever possible, to deal with these liabilities from the exploration stage through to capture and transport to decommissioning.

Regulatory gaps in the liability framework derived from the oil and gas and mining sectors emerge once a CCS project enters its post-closure phase. This issue goes beyond the standard for the appropriate decommissioning of a CCS project. The potential inadequacies of the liability framework are known and, from a liability perspective, are much more controversial then specific operational risks.[242] These shortcomings increase the risk that liability will arise in circumstances that may preclude accountability and responsibility. Storing captured CO_2 in geological formations that may have latent faults resulting in uncertain integrity, for extended periods—perhaps hundreds or thousands of years—means that risks and liability may manifest long after the typical liability time-frames found under existing federal and provincial environmental liability regimes have passed. Therefore, a properly planned long-term liability regime for CCS would address the following: Who is responsible for the geological storage of the captured CO_2 and for how long? Will the initial operator be liable in perpetuity, or will liability transfer to an entity with a longer life span, such as the Crown (the state)? What will happen to the source emitter's past statutory reporting records and any claimed carbon credits (of both the source emitter and the CCS undertaking) in the event of a discharge of the captured CO_2 into the atmosphere? Unfortunately, Canadian jurisdictions have not yet addressed these issues in full.

One of the issues noted above touches a potential administrative issue that falls under both operational and long-term liability considerations. Greenhouse gas reporting is required by the Federal Government and by a number of the provinces, including Alberta, Saskatchewan and British Columbia. The release of CO_2 after capture anywhere along the supply and transport chain to the storage reservoir or after injection will have to be accounted for either in the original emitter's CO_2 emissions reporting account, or in the account of the captured CO_2 disposal project, and an appropriate adjustment will have to be made to any carbon credits.

It is not surprising that the jurisdictions with the greatest incentive to consider the adequacy of their existing liability frameworks are those making active use of CCS

---

[241] See, eg, International Energy Agency, *Carbon Capture and Storage: Progress and Next Steps* (Paris, International Energy Agency, 2010) 20.

[242] Eg, Alberta Carbon Capture and Storage Development Council, *Accelerating Carbon Capture and Storage in Alberta: Interim Report* (Edmonton, Alberta Carbon Capture and Storage Development Council, 2008) 16.

technologies, or are the jurisdictions that are making use of commercial-scale analogues to the geological storage of CO_2. The senior members of this group include Alberta, Saskatchewan and British Columbia. The junior members are Nova Scotia, which is in the planning stages of its first CCS pilot project, and Manitoba, which has a relatively small EOR project.

Altogether, three broad approaches to address the liability issues associated with CCS can be distinguished: civil remedies; adapting existing liability frameworks; and creating new liability frameworks. These approaches are not mutually exclusive. A new liability framework can arise by adapting the existing liability framework to meet an emerging liability issue, or by directly addressing the limitations of the civil liability framework.

The civil remedy approach relies on the private law remedies of tortious liability and contractual liability to address the problematic consequences of CO_2 capture, transport, and injection, disposal and storage operations. Tort liability is a well-recognised means to compensate an injured party for any legally cognisable costs.[243]

Canadian courts have applied established common law tort-based principles such as negligence or nuisance. The tort of negligence is founded on an act or omission by the defendant that constitutes a breach of the defendant's required duty of care to the plaintiff. Nuisance requires an unreasonable and substantial interference with the use and enjoyment of land.[244] A likely application of this tort would be to plead nuisance where migrating CO_2 has entered local aquifers and water wells and impacted the potable water supply,[245] or has damaged crops on reaching the surface. It is not a defence to plead that best available technology or all reasonable skill and care were used, or that the damage is only to a particularly sensitive crop.

Also available to the plaintiff is the strict liability tort of trespass. Trespass is more readily understood in the context of the migration of stored gas to a reservoir to which the operator does not have any rights. Inadvertently over-pressurising a reservoir stratum may result in the reservoir seal either fracturing or pushing the captured CO_2 to the nearest porous stratum. Trespass is a tort that is actionable per se, and so it requires no special proof of actual harm.[246] An injunction may also be available to prevent the defendant from causing an injury or from trespassing on to a neighbouring property, even harmlessly.

Strict liability principles are also useful to a plaintiff that cannot maintain a negligence or nuisance action. When the defendant carries on a potentially hazardous activity or makes a 'non-natural' use of the land involving a dangerous substance, the rule in *Rylands v Fletcher*[247] can be used to impose strict liability on the defendant for any and all damage that results from the hazardous activity or that was caused by the escape of the substance. Taking all reasonable, precautionary steps to avoid the injury is no defence.[248]

---

[243] G Thompson, ML McConnell and LB Huestis, *Environmental Law and Business in Canada* (Aurora, Ontario, Canada Law Book Inc, 1993) 109.
[244] *Tock v St John's Metropolitan Area Board* [1989] 2 SCR 1181.
[245] *Interprovincial Coop Ltd v Manitoba* [1976] 1 SCR 477, 53 DLR (3d) 321.
[246] *Mann v Saulnier* [1959] NBJ No 12, 19 DLR (2d) 130 (NBCA).
[247] *Rylands v Fletcher* (1868) LR 3 HL 330.
[248] *Bisson v Brunette Holdings Ltd* [1993] OJ No 3378, 15 CELR (NS) 201 (Ont CJ GD).

The typical standard of originality displayed by civil litigation counsel means that tortious liability claims may be adapted to a wide variety of factual situations. However, tortious liability claims require a plaintiff with both the motivation and the wherewithal to pursue the claim. Notwithstanding the prevalence of contingency fees (a fairly recent development in a number of Canadian jurisdictions but still not universally accepted), the cost of retaining expert witnesses may fall directly on the plaintiff. There is also always the risk that if the plaintiff is not successful, it will be required to pay the defendant's legal costs. The plaintiff will also need to weigh a number of practical matters before commencing an action. The plaintiff must consider its ability to prove causation, a duty of care owed by the defendant to the plaintiff, and that the defendant did not exercise the requisite standard of care and as a result caused the plaintiff's injury. Notwithstanding the availability of joint and several liability based on directives commonly found in provincial legislation,[249] the plaintiff should also be able to identify the defendant, which, in the circumstance of the geological storage of CO_2, may not be certain. Sharing pore space or migrating captured CO_2 over a considerable distance from the injection point could make this difficult, albeit not fatal so long as one defendant is identified. Lastly, there is the need to have a defendant at hand, and a defendant that is solvent and has the resources to pay a damages award. In light of the expected time-frames over which CCS undertakings will operate, the injury may become apparent long after a private sector operator has left the scene. In conclusion, the issue of long-term responsibility for the geological storage of captured CO_2 could present a very real limitation to recovery on a tortuous liability claim.

In spite of this, to address the risk of an absent or impecunious private sector operator, an injured party may be assisted by bringing a claim of regulatory negligence against the provincial (or federal) ministry or agency responsible for enforcing the regulations governing that part of the undertaking from which the damages arise. The Federal Parliament's House of Commons' Standing Committee on Environment and Sustainable Development warned:

> There is a growing body of case law that holds that if there is a regulated standard in place and the public has a reasonable expectation of a given standard of performance, the Crown could be held at least partially liable for any damage caused by its failure to live up to that standard ... [therefore] it is not inconceivable that such an action might be brought in future, given the [Crown's] limited resources and selective enforcement practices.[250]

A private law duty of care must be found, since the law is rarely intended to protect the private interests of specific individuals. However, if the facts support the allegation that the responsible ministry (or agency) had been negligent in the conduct of its regulatory duties, and as a result damage was suffered, a regulatory negligence claim could effectively substitute a public sector defendant for an absent private sector defendant and avoid the risk of an impecunious defendant.[251]

---

[249] Ie Negligence Act, RSO 1990, c N l, s 1.
[250] *Enforcing Canada's Pollution Laws: The Public Interest Must Come First!* (Standing Committee on Environment and Sustainable Development, Ottawa, 1998) 59.
[251] *Just v British Columbia* [1989] 2 SCR 1228.

The common law, therefore, may provide the answer to who will be taking long-term responsibility for the CCS undertaking, and that would appear to be, one way or another, the responsible government or governments.

Contracts are used to manage liability. Transferring the ownership of the captured CO_2 to a party down the supply chain is a fundamental method of limiting exposure to civil liability; although this may not be effective in limiting regulatory liability, since control of the contaminant immediately before its release can be determinative, and past charge, management or control of the contaminant can attract liability to those farther down the supply chain. Contracts allow for as much innovation as can be agreed upon (and paid for) by the parties. For example, captured CO_2 could be supplied to a CCS undertaking under a contract with an agreed standard of performance, such as an acceptable rate of loss or leakage.[252] Contract provisions could also anticipate future breaches of the contract's terms, as well as the possibility that the contracting party might cease to exist or become insolvent. For instance, carbon credits could be placed in escrow to compensate the source emitter in the event of leakage, or a portion of the funds paid for the service could be held in escrow or trust until containment is verified and assured. The source emitter, therefore, could be protected well into the post-closure phase. Lastly, contractual indemnity can be applied to every stage along the supply chain, from capture and compression, through transport, to injection and storage, and to closure. Again, established common law contract principles that are well recognised by Canadian courts provide some certainty in determining contractual liability. However, contractual liability will not have an effect on regulatory liability for the release of a contaminant into the natural environment.

The second approach to addressing the liability issues associated with CCS relies on adapting the existing regulatory framework to address liabilities arising from a CCS undertaking. In Canada there is a wide body of existing laws that govern the full spectrum of CCS-type activities, with the liability issues that are peculiar to CCS drawing on the laws that deal with well development, subsurface mineral exploration and storage.

Regulatory liability during the active, closure and immediate post-abandonment phase of a CCS project is usually not an issue. The provinces and, on federal lands, the Federal Government regulate the development of wells, whether for extraction or injection purposes, mineral production, disposal site abandonment and discharges into the natural environment, which may include the migration of substances from a property. Generally, environmental regulations apply to an event if an adverse effect occurs or is threatened as the result of a release of a contaminant into the natural environment. In that case, the party that had charge or management of, or control over the contaminant immediately before its release is mandated by law to take remedial action, failing which it may be ordered to do so by the appropriate regulatory authority. The atmospheric release of captured CO_2 is not likely to cause an adverse effect unless the release is catastrophic and complete, and even then the

---

[252] MA de Figueiredo et al, *Regulating Carbon Dioxide Capture and Storage* (Cambridge, MA, Center for Environmental Policy and Research, 2007) 10.

effect will likely quickly dissipate. This draws into question the reasonableness of any remedial action. However, because CO_2 has been designated a 'contaminant' by a number of jurisdictions in Canada, the discharge of captured CO_2 will likely attract regulatory liability, if only as a reporting requirement.

The Federal Government,[253] Alberta[254] and Saskatchewan[255] regulate operational monitoring and the early loss detection of CO_2 through legislation directed at oil and gas sector activities that can be applied to CCS-related undertakings in the transport and injection phases. British Columbia's regulation of transport and injection-type activities of its oil and gas sector imposes an obligation to take measures to contain leakage.[256] Consequently, any release or leakage of CO_2 into the atmosphere, at least during the early parts of the CCS supply chain, is more likely to be discovered, with regulatory liability more certain to follow independently of establishing that there has been an actual adverse impact on the natural environment.

Alberta's[257] and Saskatchewan's[258] oil and gas legislation also holds the owner or licensee of a well, which would include a captured CO_2, injection well, responsible for the well, even after it has been abandoned. However, this provision only applies to the well, wellhead or injection site or facility. It does not appear to cover captured CO_2 that leaks from a geological formation along natural faults or fractures in the rock, though Saskatchewan explicitly includes liability for the area immediately adjacent to the site.[259]

In Alberta, for the province to assume long-term liability for a storage site the operator must demonstrate that the stored CO_2 is stable. Alberta also has a Post-Closure Stewardship Fund for the purpose of monitoring captured CO_2 and fulfilling the obligations assumed by the province.[260] However, there is no explicit statutory requirement regarding length of time that the stored fluids have to be monitored to determine if the captured CO_2 is leaking from distant faults or fractures. All that is required is for the operator to demonstrate that the stored CO_2 is stable. However, these requirements could be added as conditions of approval by the Alberta Energy Board[261] in Alberta, or in Saskatchewan by the Minister responsible for the administration of the Act,[262] with or without the recommendation of the Provincial Oil and Gas Conservation Board following a hearing.[263] Nonetheless, environmental

---

[253] Canada Oil and Gas Operations Act, RSC 1985, c 0-7.

[254] Pipeline Act, RSA 2000, c P-15; Oil and Gas Conservation Act, RSA 2000, c O-6; Energy and Utilities Board Directive 020; Abandonment Guide and Directive 055; Storage Requirements for the Upstream Petroleum Industry.

[255] Oil and Gas Conservation Act, RSS 1978, c O-2 as amended; Oil and Gas Conservation Regulations 2012, O-2, reg 6; The Pipelines Act 1998, SS, c P-12.1.

[256] Pipeline Act, RSBC 1996, c 364, ss 38–39; Oil and Gas Activities Act, SBC 2008, c 36, s 37.

[257] Oil and Gas Conservation Act, RSA 2000, c O-6, s 29.

[258] Oil and Gas Conservation Regulations, n 255 above.

[259] Oil and Gas Conservation Act, n 255 above.

[260] Carbon Capture and Storage Statutes Amendment Act, n 152 above, s 122.

[261] The Alberta Energy Board is an independent, quasi-judicial agency of the government of Alberta that has jurisdiction over oil and gas production, and deep-well injection and disposal. Alberta's Department of Environment is responsible for groundwater protection.

[262] Oil and Gas Conservation Act, n 255 above.

[263] ibid, s 7.11; The Minister has authority to issue licences for 'drilling for, and the resources, occurrence, production, transportation, distribution, disposition and processing of, oil or gas' (s 6), but may refer 'any matter or thing in relation to' these matters to the Oil and Gas Conservation Board for an investigation, hearing or inquiry.

legislation in both Alberta[264] and Saskatchewan[265] could require that the responsible party take remedial action if there is a distant leak that causes an adverse effect.

If more than one CCS undertaking has used the pore space for captured CO_2 disposal, it may be difficult to identify who would be responsible for post-abandonment leaks along faults or fractures. Typically, the Crown takes no fewer rights than a private litigant pursuing a civil claim, so liability will likely be joint and several between all pore space users. In Alberta, the Crown must be compensated for any damage caused by an injection well into a geological formation owned by the Crown. However, an individual that seeks compensation for damage caused by a leak may have to take the Crown to court.

In British Columbia, the obligations of the permit-holder of an 'eligible disposal well' do not cease on abandonment.[266] Comparable to Alberta and Saskatchewan, the well must be completed or abandoned, or operations suspended, in accordance with the regulations and any directions given by the province's regulator, which in British Columbia's case is the Oil and Gas Commission.[267] As previously noted, British Columbia's amendments to the Oil and Gas Activities Act expanded the existing definition of a storage reservoir to include prescribed substances such as captured CO_2.[268] This Act also makes clear that the permit-holder or former permit-holder has continuing liability to complete work required under the permit or any directions of the Oil and Gas Commission, or for any liability imposed under specified enactments such as the province's Environmental Management Act.[269]

The third approach to addressing the liability issues associated with CCS is to create a new liability framework. In some ways it is inappropriate to consider this as a distinct approach, because before a new liability framework is created, the shortcomings of the existing framework must be recognised and any emerging liability issues identified. Once those factors have been acknowledged, as a practical matter the simplest way of moving forward is to adapt the tools that are already available. Following the example of Alberta, this can be done with long-term liability concerns.

As a rule, across Canada the private sector operator has primary accountability and responsibility for monitoring and remedial action in the advancement, injection and intermediate post-abandonment phases of a well or mining or waste disposal undertaking, and nearly all other industrial undertakings. This is certainly the case where financial assurance or security is held by the government to ensure the proper decommissioning of the undertaking so that the risk that the private operator will no longer be able meet its financial, operational or monitoring commitments is minimised. In Alberta, the Oil and Gas Conservation Act provides for the continuing liability of the licensee, approval holder or a working interest participant for doing work in relation to the abandonment of the well or facility.[270] However, the Alberta Energy Regulator can require this work to be done by a party other than the licensee

---

[264] Environmental Protection and Enhancement Act, RSA 2000, c E-12, ss 108–109.
[265] Environmental Management and Protection Act, 2002, SS 2002, c E-10.21, ss 4 and 7.
[266] Petroleum and Natural Gas Act, n 143 above, s 61.1.
[267] ibid, s 8.
[268] Oil and Gas Activities Act, n 144 above.
[269] SBC 2003, c 53, as amended.
[270] RSA 2000, c O-6, s 29.

or approval holder.[271] In the event that any of the suspension, abandonment or related reclamation costs are not recovered from the defaulting licensee or approval holder, the costs may be recovered from the Province's 'Orphan Fund'.[272] Alberta, Saskatchewan[273] and British Columbia[274] currently use dedicated Orphan Funds to mitigate the impact of an orphan site in the oil and gas sector. However, these funds do not compensate for losses or damages suffered by third parties; the funds are directed at the actual orphan site.

The Orphan Funds offer the provinces functional examples of one alternative to address many of the long-term liabilities associated with CCS activities and practical experience of how this would be done. Bearing in mind the risk of underfunding current potential liabilities by simply expanding the application of the current Orphan Funds to CCS undertakings, the Orphan Fund principle could be adapted to address the wider spectrum of long-term liability issues and costs associated with CCS undertakings even in situations where the rights, tile and interest in the storage reservoir have vested with the province. The alternative is a dedicated fund such as Alberta's Post-Closure Stewardship Fund, which is funded by mandatory contributions from CCS operators.

Those with experience of government will immediately appreciate the benefits of a dedicated fund compared to relying on general or consolidated government revenues. A dedicated fund allows payments from the industry to be earmarked for the purposes of the fund, and not to be comingled with revenue from other sources in the jurisdiction's consolidated revenue fund. Taking funds from the consolidated revenue fund requires that the funds be clearly appropriated both as to amount and purpose by the parliament or legislature of the day. Since the legislative body cannot be compelled to vote in a particular way, even by the highest court of the land, funds appropriated from the consolidated revenue fund can never be assured and are subject to budgetary demands, while a dedicated fund provides a reserve limited by its founding purpose and balance. In addition, no matter how restricted the purposes of an Orphan Fund, there is still the potential of a wider group that can draw on the fund when compared to those having to deal with post-closure CCS issues, and likely nowhere near the certainty of the quality of the undertaking—after all it is an 'orphan' fund—that is required before the Province of Alberta assumes the long-term liability.

The Alberta Energy Regulator also oversees a Licensee Liability Rating Program. The purpose of this program is to prevent the costs of suspending, abandoning, remediating and reclaiming a well or facility in the License Liability Rating Program from being borne by the public, should a licensee become defunct. Another purpose is to reduce the risk to Alberta's Orphan Fund posed by the unfunded liability of licensees in the program.[275]

---

[271] ibid, s 28.
[272] ibid, ss 68–77.
[273] Canada Oil and Gas Operations Act, n 255 above, ss 20.91–20.98.
[274] Oil and Gas Activities Act, n 144 above, ss 44–47.
[275] Directive 006, Licensee Liability Rating Program and Licence Transfer Process, Energy Resources Conservation Board, revised 15 September 2009, s 1.

Alberta is one of the provinces that also has dedicated environmental remediation funds that could be used to deal with actual environmental events.[276] Unfortunately, due to the structure of environment remediation funds (which may receive some start-up funding from the government but typically rely on continued financial support from the payment into the fund of fines and penalties or, occasionally, permit fees), there is a risk of having unfunded liabilities. Simply, at some point there may be a shortfall between what is owed to cover the liabilities and what is available in the environment remediation fund to pay for those liabilities. Topping-up is usually not an issue, because the government, as the remediator of last resort, would know that a deficient account would have been rendered to the government in any event, and recorded in the province's books for distribution across the entire tax base.

There are at least three important limitations to keep in mind when considering environmental remediation funds, whether general environmental remediation, Orphan Funds or a Post-Closure Stewardship Fund along the Alberta model. First, like the Orphan Funds, environmental remediation funds may not compensate for all losses or damage to third parties. It is reasonable to anticipate that third parties would be properly insured, but in any event, this issue should be considered and suitably addressed if the environmental remediation funds (or for that matter, the Orphan Funds) are the vehicle chosen by the government to fully deal with the short- and long-term liabilities associated with the geological storage of CO_2. Secondly, there is the risk that the contribution base for the Post-Closure Stewardship Fund and the environmental remediation funds is too small to adequately fund all of the potential liabilities arising from the widespread injection of CO_2 into the geological substrata. Thirdly, the conceptual model underlying environmental remediation funds is not as appropriate for CCS activities as the conceptual model that underlies the current Orphan Funds and the Alberta Post-Closure Stewardship Fund. The Orphan Funds and the Alberta Post-Closure Stewardship Fund depend on contributions by operators that are actually in the industry, that make a profit from the activity and that benefit from the overall regulation of the industry. In theory, this is a relatively predictable funding source. Funding for the environmental remediation funds comes from compliance and enforcement activities, which, by their very nature—a favourable result for the Crown (the state) at trial being one uncertainty—offer an unpredictable funding source. Consequently, the better the compliance record of the target sector, the less funding that will be available. The contributions from a sector with an excellent safety and compliance record, therefore, may be inadequate to address the costs of remediating and fully compensating for a future catastrophic event. This could mean that the Crown, through the provincial tax base, would have to fund the remedial activities. The best solution could be some combination of these two types of funds or, following Alberta's example, starting a Post-Closure Stewardship Fund to cover the costs of ongoing monitoring and any required maintenance. However, the Orphan Fund concept also offers a good model, and valuable experience, to address many of the potential long-term liabilities associated with the geological storage of captured CO_2 for jurisdictions.

---

[276] Saskatchewan's environmental remediation fund became the province's Orphan Fund.

Regardless of whether the Orphan Fund model is fully adapted to CCS activities and remains focused on the private sector, or the long-term ownership of the stored CO_2 reverts to the Crown, the Crown is effectively the remediator of last resort in any event. Therefore, given enough time, the liability for the stored CO_2 will ultimately transfer to the Crown. The Orphan Fund model and Post-Closure Stewardship Fund at least offer a scheme for avoiding the situation where the full costs of long-term liability are borne solely by the Crown, and therefore burden the tax base in general.

Lastly, carrying out the policy work to support proposed or amended legislation is a constant theme with both the Federal Government and the provincial governments. A basic requirement of such work is that the people in charge of creating these policies understand any inadequacies of the existing regulatory arrangement to meet changing or new situations. In the past few years British Columbia has amended its oil and gas framework to accommodate placing CO_2 in geological storage reservoirs, and is working in consultation with industry to clarify issues regarding policy, regulation and long-term liability associated with CCS.[277] In Alberta, the 2008 announcement of a CAN$2 billion CCS-related program, along with pressures on the oil and gas sectors to limit their GHG emissions, highlighted the need to update the province's legal framework for CCS, which was done with the Carbon Capture and Storage Statutes Amendment Act 2010. Questions still remain, however, involving the transformation of CO_2-EOR projects to dedicated CCS projects. Nova Scotia has committed to investigating the viability of a commercial-scale CCS undertaking, although its regulatory framework is adequate if rudimentary.

VII. CONCLUSIONS

There are few inherent or fundamental inadequacies with any of the existing legal frameworks in Canada—subsurface property rights, regulatory and liability issues—that will hinder the utilisation of CCS technologies. This is because the existing regulatory frameworks can be and have been adapted to meet almost any exigency arising from a CCS development. This is demonstrated by the fact that Canada has considerable experience with commercial-scale analogues to the geological storage of CO_2 and with actual dedicated CCS undertakings. This is not to suggest that improvements to the existing legal frameworks are not warranted, or that these improvements should not be made expeditiously.

There are two apparent weaknesses within the existing legal frameworks across Canada. One is the failure to statutorily address the geological disposal or storage of CO_2. The other is the need to sort out how to deal with the long-term liabilities associated with CCS. Alberta and British Columbia have addressed the former, but the other provinces are using legislation directed at hydrocarbon storage and

---

[277] BC Ministry of Energy, Mines and Petroleum Resources Oil and Gas Division, *British Columbia Natural Gas and Petroleum Yours to Explore 2010* (BC Ministry of Energy, Mines and Petroleum Resources Oil and Gas Division, 2010).

have failed to deal with disposal rights in general. The Saskatchewan, Alberta and British Columbia Orphan Fund model and the Alberta Post-Closure Stewardship Fund offer a basis for funding long-term monitoring, abandonment, closure and remediation activities.

The provinces have different rating on their success in dealing with subsurface property rights and regulatory and liability frameworks, in part because demands made of the provinces have not been uniform across the country. This is a factor of both differing needs and the inconsistent promise of the available geology across Canada.

Alberta and British Columbia are strong in the realm of subsurface property rights legal frameworks, and Saskatchewan is adequate in managing subsurface property rights issues. Nova Scotia and Québec both need to move their subsurface property rights legal frameworks beyond hydrocarbon storage issues into explicitly addressing non-hydrocarbon storage and disposal matters. The remaining provinces are also focusing on hydrocarbon storage and ignoring non-hydrocarbon storage and disposal. Nova Scotia's subsurface property rights framework would benefit from a clear articulation of its subsurface ownership rights, rather than the proxy of logical inference. In this respect, Ontario, Manitoba and Saskatchewan find themselves in only a slightly better situation.

While the regulatory frameworks of all of the provinces are adequate to meet the needs of CCS, British Columbia's, Alberta's and Saskatchewan's long experience with the oil and gas sector gives these provinces the advantage in regulating CCS undertakings. Finally, the key national shortcoming of addressing long-term liability issues has been addressed to a great degree by Alberta, and again the extensive involvement by Alberta, British Columbia and Saskatchewan with the oil and gas sector has given these provinces an edge in addressing the long-term liability issues associated with CCS undertakings.

10

Pore Space Ownership in Western Canada

NIGEL BANKES

THE PROVINCES OF western Canada are global leaders in implementing carbon capture and storage (CCS) projects on a commercial scale. The two main projects are SaskPower's Boundary Dam Project in Saskatchewan[1] and Shell's Quest Project in Alberta.[2] In addition there is the Weyburn/Midale Enhanced Oil Recovery (EOR) Project (Saskatchewan),[3] as well as numerous acid gas disposal (AGD) projects in both Alberta and British Columbia.[4] These AGD projects have provided valuable learning for implementing CCS projects.[5] Lastly, there is the Alberta Carbon Trunk Line Project, which is a carbon dioxide (CO_2) pipeline infrastructure project designed to supply a number of CO_2/EOR projects in central Alberta.[6]

This chapter examines how each of the three provinces of British Columbia, Alberta and Saskatchewan has dealt with the problem of pore space ownership for

---

[1] For a synopsis of the Boundary Dam project, see Global CCS Institute, 'Boundary Dam Carbon Capture and Storage Project' (26 September 2016), at www.globalccsinstitute.com/projects/boundary-dam-carbon-capture-and-storage-project. Following capture at a coal-fired plant, most of the CO_2 will be used for EOR operations at Weyburn (see n 3 below), but some portions of the CO_2 will be injected into the Winnipeg and Deadwood formations of the Williston Basin. This part of the project is known as the Aquistore Project.

[2] For a synopsis of Shell's Quest Project, see Global CCS Institute, 'Quest' (26 September 2016), at www.globalccsinstitute.com/projects/quest. CO_2 is captured at the Scotford upgrader and then injected into a deep saline formation in the basal Cambrian sands. By August 2016 the project had captured and injected 1 million tonnes of CO_2.

[3] The Weyburn/Midale Project was launched in 2000 as a CO_2/EOR project. The project has served as an international study and monitoring site. For project details, see Petroleum Technology Research Centre, 'Weyburn-Midale', at www.ptrc.ca/projects/weyburn-midale.

[4] S Bachu and W Gunter, 'Overview of Acid-Gas Injection Operations in Western Canada' in ES Rubin, DW Keith, and CF Gilboy (eds), *Proceedings of the 7th International Conference on Greenhouse Gas Control Technologies*, vol 1 (London, Elsevier, 2005).

[5] ibid.

[6] The project involves capture at two different facilities, the Sturgeon Upgrader and an ammonia products and fertiliser plant. For project details, see Global CCS Institute, 'Alberta Carbon Trunk Line ('ACTL') with North West Sturgeon Refinery CO_2 Stream' (15 September 2016), at www.globalccsinstitute.com/projects/alberta-carbon-trunk-line-actl-north-west-sturgeon-refinery-co₂-stream, and Global CCS Institute, 'Alberta Carbon Trunk Line ('ACTL') with Agrium CO_2 Stream' (15 September 2016), at www.globalccsinstitute.com/projects/alberta-carbon-trunk-line-actl-agrium-co₂-stream.

all three project types (where relevant to that jurisdiction). Since all three jurisdictions share the same common law heritage, the chapter begins with some general comments on the common law of pore space ownership before examining how these jurisdictions might have changed these rules.[7] The chapter does not discuss the regulatory and liability frameworks of these jurisdictions. Those issues are dealt with elsewhere in this volume.[8]

I. THE COMMON LAW RULES

The common law ownership issue is frequently framed in terms of who owns the geological pore space into which CO_2 will be injected. This issue arises where there has been a severance of the mineral estate from the surface estate such that there are two or more owners, one (B) owning the surface estate and another (C) owning the mineral estate. Where there is a single owner (S) of the surface and mineral estate (ie, no severance) the position is clear; the pore space must be owned by that person (S). A party seeking to operate a CCS project or any other project involving use of the subsurface will require permission from S.

Severance of the surface and mineral estates is most likely to occur when the Crown (the state) creates the first title in favour of a private party, 'reserving thereout all mines and minerals'. In such a case the Crown retains ownership of the mineral estate and settler B acquires ownership of the surface estate. But equally, a party (S) that acquires all rights (ie, the surface and the mineral estate) from the Crown might subsequently sever the two estates as part of a later transaction.[9] Who owns the pore space in either of these situations?

Barry Barton has written the definitive contribution on this issue and concludes that the answer in the common law is clear.[10] All that the mineral owner obtains through a reservation or grant of the minerals is rights in relation to the minerals. All other rights in relation to the subsurface remain with the owner.[11] For present purposes that would mean that injection operations not associated with a mineral tenure operation (eg, a natural gas storage operation, disposal of CO_2 into a saline formation, or

---

[7] Some of the material in the following section draws on N Bankes and E Brennan, 'Enhanced oil recovery and the geological sequestration of carbon dioxide: Regulation and carbon crediting' (Report prepared for Natural Resources Canada, March 2013), at www.law.ucalgary.ca/files/law/final_june7_enhanced-oil-recovery-and-the-geological-sequestration-of-carbon-dioxide.pdf.

[8] See in particular chs 9 and 15 in this volume by Henry Krupa and Ian Havercroft respectively.

[9] N Bankes, 'Disputes Between the Owners of Different Subsurface Resources' in DN Zillman et al (eds), *The Law of Energy Underground: Understanding New Developments in Subsurface Production, Transmission, and Storage* (Oxford, Oxford University Press, 2014).

[10] B Barton, 'The Common Law of Subsurface Activity: General Principle and Current Problems' in Zillman et al (eds), n 9 above. For a broader survey of different approaches, see J Morgan, 'Digging Deep: Property Rights in Subterranean Space and the Challenge of Carbon Capture and Storage' (2013) 62 *ICLQ* 813.

[11] See in particular *Bocardo SA v Star Energy UK Onshore Ltd* [2011] 1 AC 380 (SC(E)) (*Star Energy*). Star Weald was held liable for trespass in a case of directional drilling under Bocardo's land. Star Weald had acquired rights to petroleum from the Crown, but that alone did not give it a defence to the claim in trespass. The Court rejected the proposition that a surface owner's rights under the maxim *cuius est solum eius est usque ad coelum ad inferos* only extended so far as to permit full use and enjoyment of the surface.

disposal of a waste stream into a depleted and abandoned oil and gas reservoir) would have to be authorised, as a matter of property law,[12] by the surface owner. The same would apply to AGD into a subsurface formation. By contrast, the injection of CO_2 as part of EOR operation would only require the authorisation of the mineral owner.

While there is significant public ownership of surface lands in western Canada, public ownership of the mineral estate is even more dominant,[13] with the consequence that while in many areas there will be a single owner of the mineral rights (the Crown), in other areas a Crown mineral estate will coincide with private surface ownership with potentially many different owners. Given the geographical scale of CCS operations,[14] a fragmented surface ownership scenario may significantly increase the challenges of obtaining the necessary consents where, as a result of the common law rule, pore space rights are held by surface owners.

With this as the background, we can turn to examine how these three western provinces have changed the background rules of the common law to accommodate the three types of activities of interest in this volume.

II. ALBERTA

Of the three westernmost provinces, Alberta has made the most significant changes to the common law rules in order to accommodate pure saline CCS operations. It achieved this through an amendment to its Mines and Minerals Act[15] (MMA) in 2010,[16] to declare that:

(a) no grant from the Crown of any land in Alberta, or mines or minerals in any land in Alberta, has operated or will operate as a conveyance of the title to the pore space contained in, occupied by or formerly occupied by minerals or water below the surface of that land,

(b) the pore space below the surface of all land in Alberta is vested in and is the property of the Crown in right of Alberta and remains the property of the Crown in right of Alberta whether or not

 (i) this Act, or an agreement issued under this Act, grants rights in respect of the subsurface reservoir or in respect of minerals occupying the subsurface reservoir, or

 (ii) minerals or water is produced, recovered or extracted from the subsurface reservoir, and

(c) the exception of pore space under this section is deemed to be an exception contained in the original grant from the Crown for the purposes of ... the Land Titles Act.

---

[12] The operator would also require regulatory approvals, but, as noted, this chapter is only concerned with the property issues.

[13] For example, in Alberta only about 9% of mineral rights are privately owned; approximately 40% of surface titles are held by private owners.

[14] See JT Birkholzer, CM Oldenberg and Q Zhou, 'CO_2 migration and pressure evolution in deep saline aquifers' (2015) 40 *International Journal of Greenhouse Gas Control* 203, 204, noting that a 1000 MW power plant will provide enough CO_2 over the life of the plant to create a subsurface CO_2 plume with linear dimensions of 10 km with a pressure plume extending over 100 km.

[15] Mines and Minerals Act RSA 2000, c M-17.

[16] SA 2010 c 14. The amendment was enacted by a conservative government. It did attract some criticism for interfering with property rights, but there is no constitutional protection of property rights in Canada and it is clear that a provincial legislature has the jurisdiction to make such a law under s 92 of the Constitution Act, 1867. See *Reference re Upper Churchill Water Rights Reversion Act* [1984] 1 SCR 297.

The section goes on to make it clear that no person has a claim to compensation as a result of this enactment. Based on this definitive resolution of the ownership issue, the amendment then went on to add a new Part 9 to the MMA, which provides a disposition system for the acquisition of sequestration rights for captured CO_2.[17] The disposition scheme involves evaluation permits and carbon sequestration leases.[18] Shell's Quest Project followed this route to acquire storage leases for its operation.[19]

In sum, the legislation dealt with the property issues in relation to CCS in two steps: first, a declaratory provision vesting ownership of pore space in the Crown (the state); and, secondly, a leasing scheme designed to allow proponents to acquire exploratory permits and storage leases for their operations.[20]

Acid gas disposal operations were first permitted in Alberta in 1990, well before CCS operations and well before the adoption of the declaratory provision referred to. These operations were therefore authorised under (and continue to be authorised under) a different provision of the MMA,[21] which simply requires an applicant to acquire a licence from the Crown in addition to any regulatory approvals required from the Alberta Energy Regulator under the terms of the Oil and Gas Conservation Act.[22]

The property aspects of EOR projects turn on the terms of private or freehold leases (where the mineral rights are privately held) and Crown leases, and on the provisions of the MMA and the Petroleum and Natural Gas Tenure Regulations[23] (where the mineral rights are owned by the Crown). A private petroleum and natural gas lease will typically authorise injection activities for EOR operations for so long as there is continuing production. Once production ceases, the lease terminates. Thus, while a private lease provides an adequate base for CO_2/EOR operations for so long as there is production, a private petroleum and natural gas lease will not support a pure storage project in a depleted reservoir. At that point the operator must acquire new rights from the relevant owner, and that owner, as a result of

---

[17] See also the Crown Sequestration Tenure Regulation, Alta Reg 68/2011.

[18] A carbon sequestration lease is granted for a renewable 15-year term.

[19] Shell has six sequestration leases (copies on file with the author) covering some 263,000 hectares that represent the 'area of interest' for the Project. See N Bankes, 'Quest. The Energy Resources Conservation Board Approves the First Commercial Scale Carbon Capture and Storage Project in Alberta' (*ABlawg*, 3 August 2012), at www.ablawg.ca/2012/08/03/quest-the-energy-resources-conservation-board-approves-the-first-commercial-scale-carbon-capture-and-storage-project-in-alberta/, commenting on a decision of Alberta's Energy Resources Conservation Board, *Shell Canada Limited, Application for the Quest Carbon Capture and Storage Project, Radway Field*, July 10, 2012, 2012 AERCB 008, at www.aer.ca/documents/decisions/2012/2012-ABERCB-008.pdf.

[20] Alberta conducted a very thorough expert assessment of the adequacy of its legislative framework for dealing with CCS projects. See Alberta Energy, *Carbon Capture and Storage: Summary Report of the Regulatory Framework Assessment* (Alberta, Alberta Energy, 2013), at www.energy.alberta.ca/CCS/pdfs/CCSrfaNoAppD.pdf. Most of the report deals with regulatory issues, but it addresses the tenure regime at 54–76.

[21] Mines and Minerals Act RSA 2000, c M-17, s 56. For discussion of this procedure, see N Bankes, J Poschwatta and M Shier, 'The Legal Framework for Carbon Capture and Storage in Alberta' (2008) 44 *Alberta Law Review* 585. The licence is not so much a regulatory licence but a licence in the classical property law sense, in that the operator would be a trespasser but for the licence.

[22] Oil and Gas Conservation Act RSA 2000, c O-6, s 39.

[23] Petroleum and Natural Gas Tenure Regulations Alta Reg 363/976.

the declaratory amendment to the MMA quoted above, will be the Crown. In this situation a party that wishes to continue injecting needs to acquire a Crown sequestration lease under Part 9 of the MMA, referred to above.

Essentially the same conclusion follows for Crown petroleum and natural gas leases, with the clarification that there is no automatic termination for lack of production or operations on the leased lands. Instead, the regulations contemplate that the Minister may give a party a notice of non-productivity with respect to the lease. If the lessee fails to re-establish production, the lease may be terminated.[24] The operator of any continuing sequestration operations would now need a new authorisation under Part 9, as above.

III. BRITISH COLUMBIA

There are no CCS saline disposal projects in British Columbia, but there are AGD projects, EOR projects and a natural gas storage project.[25] In a January 2014 Discussion Paper released for consultation, the province indicated that it was considering authorising CCS saline projects under Part 14 of its Petroleum and Natural Gas Act[26] (PNGA). This Part of the Act deals generically with 'underground storage' in a 'storage reservoir'.[27] These provisions are deliberately agnostic with respect to pore space ownership rights in such storage reservoirs. They contemplate that the executive may designate an area as a storage area,[28] following which any private rights in the designated area vest automatically in the government.[29] The Act goes on to provide that any person affected by this automatic vesting may apply for compensation from the Surface Rights Board (SRB) established under Part 17 of the Act.[30]

---

[24] ibid, s 18.
[25] I would like to thank Jenny Biem, Senior Policy Analyst, Policy and Royalty Branch, Upstream Development Division, Ministry of Natural Gas Development, Government of British Columbia for her comments on this part of the chapter.
[26] Petroleum and Natural Gas Act RSBC 1996 c 361 (PNGA).
[27] PNGA, pt 14; and see British Columbia Ministry of Gas Development, 'Carbon Capture and Storage Regulatory Policy, Discussion and Comment Paper' (January 2014), at www2.gov.bc.ca/assets/gov/farming-natural-resources-and-industry/natural-gas-oil/uploads/ccs_rpf_discussion_paper_final_2014.pdf (hereafter CCS Regulatory Policy Paper). A summary report of consultation on the Discussion Paper was released in October 2014. See British Columbia Ministry of Gas Development 'Carbon Capture and Storage Regulatory Policy, Consultation Summary Report' (October 2014), at www2.gov.bc.ca/assets/gov/farming-natural-resources-and-industry/natural-gas-oil/ccs/ccs_consultation_summary_report.pdf. The province has not yet indicated whether or the extent to which some of the recommendations in the Paper may be implemented or modified based on that consultation. Other recommendations, such as the requirement to obtain a storage lease to conduct a CCS project, were implemented through the Natural Gas Development Statutes Amendment Act, 2015.
[28] PNGA, s 127.
[29] PNGA, s 128. For further discussion of this provision, see N Bankes and J Gaunce, 'Natural Gas Storage Regimes in Canada: A Survey' (University of Calgary, Institute for Sustainable Energy, Environment and Economy, Research Paper, 2009), at www.law.ucalgary.ca/files/law/bankes_and_gaunce_natural_gas_storage_regimes_in_canada-1.pdf, 21–33.
[30] PNGA, s 129. The principal job of the Surface Rights Board (SRB) is to provide entry orders for surface operations (eg, a well site) and to fix appropriate compensation to be paid to the owner of the surface. Section 154 provides guidance as to the factors that the SRB should take into account; they are evidently more directed at surface rights disturbance issues than they are at the situation of compensating for the loss of storage/disposal rights.

In sum, the Act does not express a view as to who owns the storage rights; but it does provides a mechanism for vesting such rights in the government (to the extent that they are not already so vested), as well as a mechanism for a person who believes that his or her rights were divested by the designation to seek compensation. The onus will be on such a party to demonstrate that he or she owned disposal/storage rights before the automatic vesting occurred.

Storage rights in a 'storage reservoir owned by the government' may be acquired by way of a lease of a storage reservoir by a person who holds a petroleum and natural gas authorisation (permit, licence or lease) for the area, or by a person who holds a licence to explore for a storage reservoir.[31] While the current scheme indicates that a storage reservoir licence or lease may be issued 'on application', the province's 2014 Discussion Paper indicated that it may amend the legislation to provide for competitive bidding for storage rights.[32] The Discussion Paper also suggested three categories of storage reservoir lease: developmental, operational and post-closure. A developmental lease issued for up to seven years might be converted to an operational lease if the lessee has been able to demonstrate the suitability of the site for storage and containment purposes in accordance with international best practices. An operational lease is expected to have a 30-year initial term, renewable for further 10-year periods. Unused areas of the lease area might be subject to reversion.

Acid gas disposal projects in British Columbia have never been authorised through the storage provisions of the PNGA. Instead, these projects have been authorised under a 'special projects' provision in the legislation, which is currently found in section 75 of the Oil and Gas Activities Act (OGAA).[33] This is likely justified on the basis that AGD projects are designed to handle the acid gases (especially CO_2 and H_2S) produced with some gas streams, and thus an inherent part of production activities and proper conservation practices.[34] The property basis of the government's entitlement to authorise AGD activities has yet to be questioned, and this may be because the disposal wells are being drilled into formations included in the applicant's lease. However, the 2014 Discussion Paper suggested that in the future, the province may require petroleum and natural gas lessees to acquire a storage tenure for these activities so as 'to ensure effective management of the zones where substances are being disposed'.[35]

The property aspects of EOR operations in British Columbia, much as in Alberta, will turn on the terms of the leases, which could be expected to authorise, explicitly or implicitly, the injection of CO_2 as part of EOR operations. While such leases

---

[31] PNGA, s 130 and see Petroleum and Natural Gas Storage Reservoir Regulation, BC Reg 350/971.
[32] CCS Regulatory Policy Paper, n 27 above, 5.
[33] Oil and Gas Activities Act SBC 2008, c 36 (OGAA). The predecessor provision used to authorise these activities was s 100 of the PNGA (which was repealed in 2008, also dealing with the approval of experimental schemes).
[34] OGAA, s 75 contemplates that the Commission may make a special project order in the following four circumstances: (a) to enhance recovery, (b) the application of innovative technology as defined by regulation, (c) 'an innovative method of carrying out oil and gas activities and related activities' or (d) any other prescribed activity. Notably, there is no express mention of disposal activities. It is hard to characterise AGD activities as 'innovative' in 2018, since this method of handling an acid gas stream is now business as usual.
[35] CCS Regulatory Policy Paper, n 27 above, 6.

(whether freehold or Crown) would ordinarily come to an end when production ceases, section 61.1 of the PNGA provides that where there is an 'eligible disposal well' on the lease lands (which included a well used to dispose of CO_2 or other waste fluids), the relevant official may continue the lease—but only for another year.[36]

IV. SASKATCHEWAN

Unlike Alberta, Saskatchewan has not enacted declaratory legislation vesting pore space ownership for geological sequestration purposes in the Crown. Neither has the province enacted legislation, such as that in British Columbia, to allow storage/disposal rights to be clarified by a procedure for vesting rights in the government. As a result, the matter should be governed by the common law and storage/disposal rights vested in the surface owner. Not all commentators share this view. Zukowsky, for example, concludes that 'there is no role contemplated for surface owners' in relation to pore space ownership in Saskatchewan law, but offers no authority to support this conclusion.[37] The government of Saskatchewan also shares that view and takes the position that pore space is owned by the owner of the mineral rights. According to this view, where the mineral rights are owned by the Crown, the Crown is able to dispose of pore space rights by way of 'a lease of spaces' under section 27.2 of the Crown Minerals Act.[38] This section provides as follows:

(1) In this section, 'spaces' means the spaces occupied or formerly occupied by a Crown mineral.
(2) Notwithstanding the terms or conditions of any Crown lease, all spaces are the property of the Crown and remain the property of the Crown whether or not a Crown lease is issued for the Crown mineral within the space and whether or not the Crown mineral is produced, recovered or extracted from the space.
(3) The minister may enter into agreements to lease spaces.
(4) An agreement entered into pursuant to subsection (3) may be for any period and contain any terms and conditions that the minister considers appropriate.
(5) All agreements to lease spaces that were made by the minister before, on or after the coming into force of this section are ratified and confirmed.

Thus the Aquistore Project operates on the basis of a 'lease of spaces agreement' issued under this section of the Act. However, in that particular case SaskPower, the operator and provincial Crown corporation, owns the surface while the Crown owns the mineral rights.[39] There is therefore little risk that anybody will challenge

---

[36] PNGA, s 61.1.
[37] R Zukowsky, 'The Regulatory Framework Governing Injection and Storage of Carbon Dioxide at the Cenovus Weyburn and Apache Midale Enhanced Oil Recovery Operations in Saskatchewan' (IEA GHG Weyburn-Midale CO_2 Monitoring and Storage Project, 22 March 2010), at ccs101.ca/assets/Documents/The%20Regulatory%20Framework%20Governing%20Injection%20and%20Storage%20of%20Carbon%20Dioxide%20%20in%20SaskatchewanApril%206%202010.pdf, 45–46.
[38] Crown Minerals Act, SS 1984-85-86, c C-50.2, s 27.2.
[39] Email from Floyd Wist, Executive Director, Energy Policy, Ministry of the Economy, Government of Saskatchewan, to author (3 May 2013).

the property basis of this arrangement. The agreement is for a term of 20 years, renewable for a second 20-year term.[40] It grants the lessee (SaskPower) 'all rights and interests in the spaces, which may be found to exist within the Winnipeg Formation and Deadwood Formation in the lands described [as] Lsd [legal subdivision] 5 of Sec. 6-2-8W2M in the Province of Saskatchewan, containing an area of 16.11 hectares more or less', and authorises the lessee to 'use the said spaces for the purpose of injecting commingled CO_2 and brine and for no other purposes'. It is not clear why the agreement covers such a small area, since the CO_2 plume is likely to extend well beyond the immediate injection site.[41]

In sum, while the decision of the Supreme Court of the United Kingdom in *Star Energy*[42] suggests that the Crown's mineral title alone does not provide a secure basis for storage operations, the government has proceeded on the basis that it does; that view has yet to be challenged.

While there are no AGD operations in Saskatchewan, there are significant EOR operations in the province, including the much-studied Weyburn/Midale EOR project, most of which operates on the basis of freehold leases and a unitisation agreement. The property analysis of this arrangement is much the same as in Alberta and British Columbia for so long as there is production. Thus, the petroleum and natural gas leases held by the operator authorise the injection activities for so long as there continues to be production from the unitised zone. Should the operator propose to convert the project to a pure storage project, the leases would likely no longer provide adequate title for the operation. In that situation the operator would need to consider who can provide the additional property authorisation: *Star Energy* would suggest that the relevant surface owners would need to provide the authorisation; the government's position suggests that it is the mineral owner (but note that in this project, most of the mineral rights are held by private parties, not the Crown).

V. CONCLUSIONS

Commentators have been suggesting for years that in order to encourage commercial-scale adoption of CCS, it is necessary to clarify the different elements of the legal regime within which CCS will operate. These elements include property rules, regulatory rules, liability and CO_2 accounting rules. This chapter has examined the applicable property rules in three neighbouring jurisdictions in western Canada.

---

[40] Lease of Spaces Agreement between Her Majesty the Queen in right of the Province of Saskatchewan, as represented by the Minister of Energy and Resources, and Saskatchewan Power Corporation, 26 June 2012; copy provided to the author by Paul Mahnic, Executive Director, Lands and Mineral Tenure, Ministry of the Economy, Government of Saskatchewan. A legal subdivision is 40 acres or 16.1874 hectares. Contrast this with the series of six sequestration leases issued to Shell for the Quest Project (n 19 above).

[41] Paul Mahnic, n 40 above, suggests (telephone conversation with author (8 November 2016)) that the province uses 'lease of space agreements' to provide the property authorisation for a variety of disposal activities as well as salt cavern storage activities. The agreement serves 'to flag' the existence of the operation so that the other leasing activities of the Department are placed on notice. Given this purpose, the geographical size of the space may not be based on a scientific assessment of plume size.

[42] See n 11 above. See also Barton, n 10 above.

The results are perhaps surprising since, notwithstanding a common legal heritage, they show a surprising degree of diversity, as well as some lack of clarity as to the relevant rules in relation to one of those jurisdictions (Saskatchewan).

Of the three provinces it is Alberta that has grasped the nettle most firmly by enacting declaratory legislation to vest pore space in the Crown. In addition, it has enacted a clear set of rules by which a private party can acquire storage permits and leases. British Columbia has a workable regime for vesting pore space in the Crown on a case-by-case basis and for clarifying any potential claims to compensation, but continues to study the design of an appropriate form of tenure for CCS projects. Saskatchewan proceeds on the questionable premise that in the case of severed surface and mineral titles, it is the owner of the mineral title that owns the pore space. It has not yet chosen to confirm that premise through legislation, or otherwise to vest pore space in the Crown. Saskatchewan also follows the questionable practice of granting storage rights for actual site of the injection well—not for the more extensive CO_2 footprint. While this does not seem to have caused a problem for the Boundary Dam and Aquistore Project, this may be due to the identity of the main actor (a Crown corporation) and the ownership configuration of the injection site (Crown surface and mineral ownership). If other CCS projects come forward in Saskatchewan, it may be necessary for the government to re-examine its position in relation to both of these issues.

11
The Regulation of Underground Storage of Greenhouse Gases in Australia[*]

MEREDITH GIBBS

I. INTRODUCTION

AUSTRALIA HAS ONE of the most comprehensive legal and regulatory regimes for the underground storage of greenhouse gases (GHGs).[1] It has detailed regimes covering underground storage in its offshore waters under Australian Federal and Victorian jurisdictions, together with onshore regimes in Victoria, Queensland and South Australia. In addition, Western Australia has project-specific legislation for the Gorgon LNG Project sequestration of carbon dioxide (CO_2).[2] Despite having no carbon capture and storage (CCS) regulatory frameworks in other States and Territories, Australia's regimes were rated as the 'most comprehensive models' of regulation across the CCS project lifecycle, ranking number one globally in the Global CCS Institute's recent global assessment of legal and regulatory regimes for CCS.[3]

Much of this regulatory framework was developed in the mid- to late 2000s. At that time, government funding was provided to a number of CCS projects and, notably, the Australian Federal Government established the Global CCS Institute. Commentators have observed that '[t]he scope, complexity and geographical coverage observed in the various regulatory models, complement the bold policy positions and strong support that were originally adopted by the Federal Government and many of the state governments in Australia'.[4] However, this early momentum

---

[*] The views in this chapter are those of the author and do not necessarily represent those of HWL Ebsworth. This chapter is a general overview and is not intended to be legal advice.
    [1] T Dixon, S McCoy and I Havercroft, 'Legal and Regulatory Developments on CCS' (2015) 40 *International Journal of Greenhouse Gas Control* 431.
    [2] *Barrow Island Act 2003* (WA).
    [3] Global CCS Institute, *Global CCS Institute Legal and Regulatory Indicator: A global assessment of national legal and regulatory regimes for carbon capture and storage* (Global CCS Institute, 2015), at hub.globalccsinstitute.com/sites/default/files/publications/196443/global-ccs-institute-ccs-legal-regulatory-indicator.pdf, 5.
    [4] Dixon et al, n 1 above, 440.

waned, and since the late 2000s there has not been a sufficient level of policy certainty or support in Australia for further development of a CCS industry.[5]

This chapter examines the underground storage legislation enacted by Australian governments, paying particular attention to how the different regimes in Australia have dealt with long-term liability for stored GHGs. In section II, the chapter addresses the following topics:

(1) the differing approaches to regulation taken by Australian Federal and State Governments;
(2) GHG storage tenures;
(3) regulation of the environmental, health and safety aspects of GHG activities;
(4) how the different regimes manage competing interests; and
(5) enforcement of the regimes, including the powers for dealing with serious situations such as leaks and unexpected migration of stored GHG.

In section III, this chapter explores the differences between the approaches to long-term liability and discusses some of the reasons for these differences.

II. OVERVIEW OF AUSTRALIA'S GHG STORAGE LEGISLATION

In the context of regulating the geological storage of GHGs, under Australia's federal system the various State and Territory governments have jurisdiction in respect of GHG storage activities both onshore and offshore out to three nautical miles. From this point, the Australian Federal Government has jurisdiction in offshore waters. These arrangements mean that Australia has three categories of GHG storage legislation: (i) State or Territory onshore legislation; (ii) State or Territory offshore legislation; and (iii) Federal offshore legislation.

Generally, the Australian Acts define eligible GHGs to include CO_2 (in gaseous or liquid state), prescribed substances or mixtures of the same.[6]

A. Approaches to Regulation

As of October 2016, the legislation shown in Figure 11.1 was in place in Australia regulating geological storage of GHGs.

Unfortunately, the approach taken across the jurisdictions has not been consistent.[7] One approach has been to amend existing petroleum regimes to include

---

[5] M Gibbs, 'Wither Carbon Capture and Storage: What do recent developments in Australia suggest about its future?' (2016) 31 *Australian Environment Review* 8.
[6] For example, *Offshore Petroleum and Greenhouse Gas Storage Act 2006* (Cth), s 7.
[7] M Gibbs and P McCormack, 'No Consistent Approach to CCS Legislation', *Greenhouse Update* (Melbourne, Blake Dawson, 10 October 2008); Western Australian Parliament Standing Committee on Uniform Legislation and Statutes Review, *Report 47: Petroleum and Energy Legalisation Amendment Bill 2009 April 2010* (Perth, Parliament of Western Australia, 2010), at www.parliament.wa.gov.au/Parliament/commit.nsf/(Report+Lookup+by+Com+ID)/C69CCC218613CDB348257831003E9848/$file/us.pel.100422.rpf.047.xx.doc.pdf; S Singleton and R Gawrych, 'Overlapping Land Interest

Australian Federal
Offshore: *Offshore Petroleum and Greenhouse Gas Storage Act 2006*

Western Australia
Barrow Island Act 2003

Queensland
Onshore: *Greenhouse Gas Storage Act 2009*

South Australia
Onshore: *Petroleum Act 2000*

Victoria
Onshore: Greenhouse Gas Geological Storage Act 2008

Offshore: *Offshore Petroleum and Greenhouse Gas Storage Act 2010*

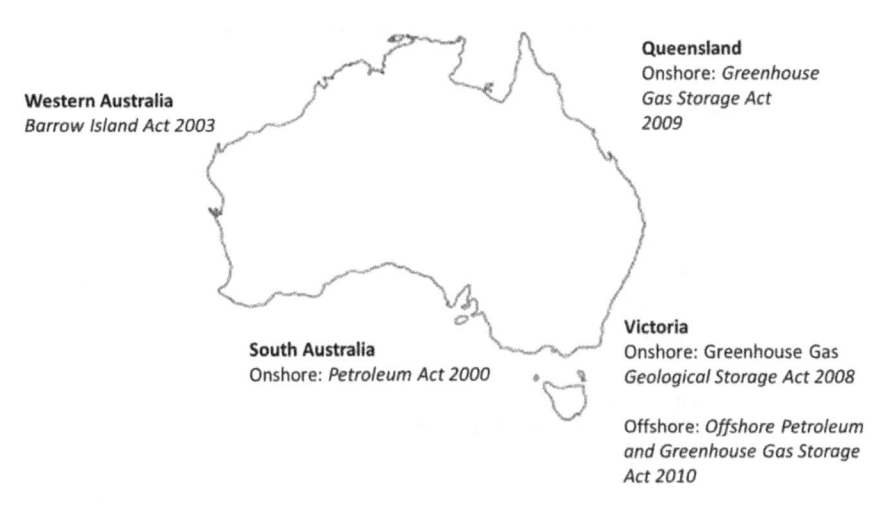

Figure 11.1: Australian GHG Storage Legislation

provisions regulating GHG storage. This approach is reflected in the *Offshore Petroleum and Greenhouse Gas Storage Act 2006* (Cth) ('Federal offshore Act'), the *Offshore Petroleum and Greenhouse Gas Storage Act 2010* (Vic) ('Victorian offshore Act') and the *Petroleum Act 2000* (SA) ('South Australia's onshore Act'). The second approach has been to enact stand-alone legislation, as illustrated by the *Greenhouse Gas Geological Storage Act 2008* (Vic) ('Victorian onshore Act') and the *Greenhouse Gas Storage Act 2009* (Qld) ('Queensland onshore Act'). Although the approach is different in many key respects, for example the tenure process and the application of environmental and safety regulations, the stand-alone legislation closely follows existing petroleum legislation. A third approach has been to enact project-specific legislation, such as Western Australia's *Barrow Island Act 2003* (WA), which applies to project-specific storage under Barrow Island as part of the Gorgon LNG Project.

Leaving aside project-specific legislation, this chapter examines Australia's broad-scale GHG storage legislation and concentrates on the Australian Federal and

---

Issues for Greenhouse Gas Grants and Activities' [2009] *AMPLA Yearbook* 283; G Campbell, 'Carbon Capture and Storage: Legislative Approaches to Liability—Managing Long-Term Obligations and Liabilities' [2009] *AMPLA Yearbook* 324; Dixon et al, n 1 above. See also J McLaren and J Fahey, 'Key Legal and Regulatory Considerations for the Geosequestration of Carbon Dioxide in Australia' (2005) 24 *Australian Resources & Energy Law Journal* 46; A Warburton et al, 'Geosequestration Law in Australia' in T Bodyhady and P Christoff (eds), *Climate Law in Australia* (The Federation Press, 2007); G Dwyer, 'Emerging Legislative Regimes for Regulating Carbon Capture and Storage Activities in Australia: To what extent do they facilitate access to procedural justice?' (2015) 32 *Environmental & Planning Law Journal* 3.

Victorian offshore Acts and the Victorian and Queensland onshore Acts (collectively referred to as 'the Acts') as the two key approaches to regulation of GHG storage in Australia.

B. GHG Storage Tenure

Each of the Acts implements a system of GHG tenures similar to that used for petroleum. Greenhouse gas tenure is required, first, to explore for suitable geological storage formations and undertake injection testing in set areas released by the relevant government, and, secondly, to inject and store GHGs in a specified storage formation. Environmental, and sometimes planning and development, approvals will also be required, often as a condition precedent to obtaining the relevant GHG authority. Tenure is also available to 'hold' an area that has been the subject of an exploration authority until a source of GHGs is ready to be injected. Each of the various Acts creates slightly different processes, with different time frames and information requirements. Periods of tenure vary slightly also.

Importantly, under each Act, it is an offence to explore for geological storage formations or to inject and store GHGs without holding the relevant GHG authority.[8]

Reflecting the risk management approach of the Australian regulatory framework, GHG tenures are granted subject to statutory and discretionary (project-specific) conditions. Additional approvals may be required to undertake certain GHG storage activities under the relevant tenure. For example, under the Federal offshore Act, each GHG exploration authority is subject to a condition that the authority holder must not carry on a 'key GHG operation' unless an additional approval is obtained from the relevant Federal Minister.[9] Detailed work plans, generally in the form of risk management plans, are also required.[10] The Victorian onshore Act has similar risk management provisions requiring the prior approval of an injection testing plan, for example. The relevant Victorian Minister is required to be satisfied that the proposed injection testing will not present a risk to public health or the environment, and will not present a significant risk of contaminating or sterilising other resources in the permit area, before granting approval.[11] Similar provisions are required before ongoing, operational injection may take place.[12]

Each Act provides for a process to surrender an injection and storage authority once injection of GHGs has ceased. Again reflecting a risk management approach, approval of an application to surrender an injection and storage authority will depend on the risk profile of the site and include consideration of whether: (i) the

---

[8] Victorian onshore Act, s 18; Queensland onshore Act, s 386 (although note that injection for enhanced oil recovery is an exception to this under the Queensland legislation—see Queensland onshore Act, s 386(2)); Federal offshore Act, ss 289 and 356.
[9] Federal offshore Act, s 291(3).
[10] ibid, s 292.
[11] Victorian onshore Act, s 40. See also the *Greenhouse Gas Geological Sequestration Regulations 2009* (Vic).
[12] Victorian onshore Act, s 96.

authority holder has complied with all laws and conditions of the authority; (ii) all wells have been plugged or closed off; (iii) the sequestered GHG is behaving, and will continue to behave, as predicted; (iv) the authority holder has reduced all risks to as low a level as is reasonably practicable; and (v) the stored GHG will not present a risk to public health or the environment.[13]

After site closure, the relevant State government or Federal Government becomes responsible for monitoring and verification of stored GHGs, at the storage proponent's cost.[14] As will be discussed in detail in section III, this signals the end of the period for which the GHG authority holder is 'on risk' in respect of statutory liabilities. Long-term common law liabilities vary under the Acts and are discussed further in section III.B. There is no obligation for the relevant Minister to approve an application to surrender an injection and storage authority, although the decision-maker must not act unreasonably, and normal rules of administrative law apply.[15] Nor is there any set time frame in which this decision must be made under the Victorian and Queensland Acts. There is, however, a right in some jurisdictions to appeal against a decision not to approve a surrender application.[16] This leaves the possibility that the authority holder will remain liable for an indefinite period of time if, for example, the GHGs are not behaving as predicted, or there is a risk to human health or the environment. Under the Federal offshore Act, the surrender decision must be made within five years.[17] As a result, the GHG authority surrender process is a key risk for storage proponents.

Other risk exposures for GHG storage proponents exist. In particular, it has been argued that the high levels of Ministerial discretion and the significant protections afforded to petroleum titleholders provided for in the Federal offshore Act diminish the security and certainty of GHG tenures.[18] These discretions include the ability to impose conditions on GHG authorities, significant powers to issue directions to GHG authority holders where failure to comply with such is a ground for cancellation of the relevant GHG authority, powers to suspend or cancel GHG authorities in certain circumstances, and, as already noted, with respect to the issuing of a Site Closure Certificate.[19] The Federal Minister can also impose additional conditions at any time by notice in writing.[20] Further, if regulations are enacted that establish a regime for third-party access to identified GHG storage formation(s) or GHG infrastructure, an injection licensee must comply with that regime.[21] The Federal offshore

---

[13] ibid, ss 168–178; Queensland onshore Act, ss 176–179; Federal offshore Act, ss 338, 442; Victorian offshore Act, ss 420–422, 474.
[14] Victorian onshore Act, s 174; Queensland onshore Act, s 177; Federal offshore Act, s 391.
[15] Victorian onshore Act, s 168(3); Federal offshore Act, s 442(4); Victorian offshore Act, s 474(4).
[16] Queensland onshore Act, s 395(1).
[17] Federal offshore Act, s 383(8).
[18] M Gibbs, 'Greenhouse Gas Storage in Offshore Waters: Balancing Competing Interests' (2009) 28 *Australian Resources and Energy Law Journal* 52; Australian Parliament Senate Standing Committee on Economics, *Report on the Offshore Petroleum Amendment (Greenhouse Gas Storage) Bill 2008* (Canberra, Parliament of the Commonwealth of Australia, 2008) 22.
[19] Federal offshore Act, ss 291, 316, 317, 320, 351, 352, 358, 376, 378, 383, 385 and 446.
[20] ibid, s 358(12).
[21] ibid, s 358(10) and (11).

Act also allows the Minister to suspend, for a specified period or indefinitely, a GHG assessment permit or holding lease if satisfied that it is necessary to do so in the 'national interest'.[22] The Act provides no guidance as to the definition of 'national interest'. These measures all create uncertainty with respect to GHG authorities and may act as a barrier to CCS projects.

C. Environmental, Health and Safety

Onshore in Victoria and Queensland, existing environmental and health and safety legislation will apply to GHG storage activities. Under the Queensland onshore Act, a GHG storage proponent is required to obtain all necessary approvals prior to the grant of the relevant GHG authority.[23] This ensures that all environmental and public health impacts are considered before any decision is made with respect to the GHG tenure itself. The Victorian onshore Act takes a different approach. With the exception of certain planning approvals,[24] existing environmental requirements remain unaffected by the Victorian onshore Act. In addition, environmental assessments are included in the GHG decision-making process by requiring that, for the purposes of determining whether the relevant GHG activity will present a risk to the environment, the matter must be referred to the Minister administering the *Environment and Protection Act 1970* (Vic), the Minister administering the *Water Act 1989* (Vic) and the Victorian Environment Protection Authority before key decisions are made with respect to the grant of various GHG tenures and other approvals.[25] Each has a right of veto if it considers that the activity under consideration will present a risk to the environment, or that the relevant risk management plan in relation to the environment is inadequate.

Under the Federal offshore Act, the existing frameworks applicable to petroleum activities for the management of environmental impacts also apply to GHG injection and storage activities.[26] In addition, major offshore projects, which will include most GHG injection and storage operations, require assessment under existing Federal laws such as the *Environment Protection and Biodiversity Conservation Act 1999* (Cth) and the *Environment Protection (Sea Dumping) Act 1981* (Cth). Similar to the situation onshore, under the Victorian offshore Act all relevant environmental legislation must be complied with.[27]

This position is consistent with the approach to environmental impact assessment in respect to other resource-based activities in Australia. Generally, environmental

---

[22] ibid, s 438.
[23] Queensland onshore Act, s 40.
[24] Victorian onshore Act, ss 189 and 190.
[25] ibid, ss 41, 97 and 136.
[26] *Offshore Petroleum and Greenhouse Gas Storage (Environment) Regulations 2009* (Cth) and *Offshore Petroleum (Safety) Regulations 2009* (Cth).
[27] Including *Environment Protection Act 1970* (Vic); *Dangerous Goods Act 1985* (Vic); *Aboriginal Heritage Act 2006* (Vic); *Coastal Management Act 1995* (Vic); *Flora and Fauna Guarantee Act 1998* (Vic); *Water Act 1989* (Vic); and *National Parks Act 1975* (Vic).

and public health concerns, together with appropriate public consultation and submission rights, are dealt with under relevant environmental and planning legislation rather than in the resource allocation framework. This approach ensures a consistency of environmental regulation across different resources within each jurisdiction.

D. Managing Competing Interests

Greenhouse gas storage operations may impact on other activities being undertaken in the same, or adjacent, geographical and spatial areas. These competing interests are sometimes referred to as 'overlapping titles' or 'overlapping interests'. In offshore areas, many of the geological formations suitable for the storage of GHGs occur in close or overlapping proximity to petroleum operations.[28] Any leaks or unexpected migration of stored GHGs could cause adverse impacts to adjacent petroleum interests, such as the spoiling of petroleum reserves, changes in reservoir pressure and effects on the structural integrity of the subsurface.[29] In addition, where a spent oil or gas well is used for GHG storage, there are potential risks depending on the adequacy of the plugging and abandoning of wells.[30] Onshore, a range of potentially competing interests exist, including mining interests, groundwater uses and geothermal energy sites. In addition, surface land-owner rights may be affected.

The issue of competing interests generated a high degree of stakeholder concern, and the Acts have very detailed provisions in this respect.[31] The Acts take differing approaches concerning *when* in the tenure process competing interests will be considered, as well as the *extent* of protections given to existing rights as compared to GHG storage interests. Significantly, the offshore Acts give existing petroleum titleholders a right of veto over the establishment of new GHG operations in certain circumstances. This level of protection is not replicated in the onshore Acts. Where competing interests cannot co-exist, all of the Acts provide mechanisms for the relevant decision-maker to decide which interest will be given priority, using a 'public interest' test, and override any relevant commercial arrangements between competing stakeholders.

---

[28] International Energy Agency, *Geological Storage of Carbon Dioxide*, at www.ccsassociation.org/docs/2008/IEA%20GHG%20geological%20storage%20of%20CO$_2$%20February%2008.pdf. See also International Panel on Climate Change (IPCC), Working Group III of the IPCC, B Metz, O Davidson, H de Coninck, M Loos and L Meyer (eds), *IPCC Special Report on Carbon Dioxide Capture and Storage* (Cambridge, Cambridge University Press, 2005).

[29] McLaren and Fahey, n7 above, 52–53; IPCC, n 28 above; Australian Government Department of Resources Energy and Tourism, *Discussion Paper—Greenhouse Gas Injection and Storage Legislation Overview of Regulations and Guidelines*, Attachment 3, 'Greenhouse Gas Injection and Storage Legislation, Significant Risk of a Significant Adverse Impact Test, Public Interest Test' (Canberra, Australian Government, nd).

[30] For a discussion of issues arising from abandoned oil and gas fields and CCS, see IPCC, n 28 above, 215, 221–24, and 227–28 in relation to integrity of plugging.

[31] Gibbs, n 18 above.

i. Federal and Victorian Offshore Acts

The Federal and Victorian offshore Acts contain almost identical, comprehensive provisions requiring the relevant Minister to assess the impact of GHG storage operations on overlapping interests.[32] These Acts utilise a 'significant risk of a significant adverse impact' (SROSAI) test. The Acts set out a detailed methodology for this determination, requiring the decision-maker to consider the probability of the adverse impact's occurring, its economic consequences and the economic consequences of the adverse impact relative to the potential economic value of the affected petroleum activities.[33] Further, an adverse impact will be found to exist only where the relevant GHG operations will result in an increase in the capital or operating costs of the affected petroleum exploration or recovery operations, or a reduction in the rate or quantity of recovery of petroleum.[34] The adverse impact will be treated as significant only if it exceeds the amount of the probability-weighted impact cost thresholds set by regulation.[35]

Where the Minister forms the view that a SROSAI exists, the protection afforded the adversely affected petroleum interest depends on its timing and nature. The two Acts provide greater protections for pre-existing petroleum interests—those in existence prior to passage of the relevant GHG provisions under each Act—giving these petroleum titleholders a right of veto over the establishment of new GHG storage operations.[36] This same protection is also afforded to any petroleum title that is in production at the time the SROSAI test is satisfied, regardless of when the title came into existence. In other cases, the Acts establish a 'level playing field' for interests, generally giving the prior tenure in time priority, but subject to Ministerial discretion exercised in the 'public interest'.[37] In the latter case, depending on where the public interest lies, the Minister can approve a GHG operation or a petroleum activity that has an adverse impact on the other, even where that adversely affected stakeholder does not consent. The Acts allow for affected parties to enter into commercial agreements, but these are not definitive and can be overridden in the public interest.

ii. Victorian and Queensland Onshore Acts

In contrast, the State regulatory regimes give a greater role to commercial agreements.[38] For example, under the Queensland onshore Act there is a heavy

---

[32] ibid; and Singleton and Gawrych, n 7 above.
[33] Federal offshore Act, ss 25–29; Victorian offshore Act, ss 27–31.
[34] Federal offshore Act, ss 25–29; Victorian offshore Act, ss 27–31.
[35] Federal offshore Act, ss 25–29; Victorian offshore Act, ss 27–31. See *Offshore Petroleum and Greenhouse Gas Storage (Greenhouse Gas Injection and Storage) Regulations 2011* (Cth); Australian Government Department of Resources Energy and Tourism, n 29 above. See also *Offshore Petroleum and Greenhouse Gas Storage Regulations 2011* (Vic).
[36] Gibbs, n 18 above.
[37] ibid.
[38] J Hedge, 'Geothermal Regulation Heating Up' [2006] *AMPLA Yearbook* 564, 576. For a discussion of coordination agreements see D McGann, 'Coordination Agreement for Coal Seam Gas' [2005] *AMPLA Yearbook* 380; and L Hill, 'Mineral Sharing Contracts and Coordination Agreements' [2005] *AMPLA Yearbook* 389.

reliance on private arrangements, called 'coordination agreements',[39] but Ministerial discretion, exercised primarily at the point of the decision to grant GHG tenure, also plays a role. Ministerial discretion can only be exercised subject to specified criteria, which include likely impacts on the relevant competing interest, the extent to which the competing and GHG interests might co-exist, safety issues and the public interest.[40]

Where an application for a GHG injection and monitoring authority is made and there is an overlapping authority in place, the Queensland Minister may only grant priority to the overlapping interest where he or she is satisfied that a coordination agreement is unlikely or not commercially or technically feasible, and that the public interest would be best served by not granting the GHG authority.[41] In the case of exploration activity, if an overlapping authority holder objects to GHG exploration activities, the Minister must resolve the dispute after taking into account the submissions of the relevant parties.[42] In addition, where a non-GHG authority holder has already begun authorised activities, the GHG exploration permit holder cannot undertake activities that will adversely affect the non-GHG authority holder's activities.[43]

Even where a coordination agreement has been reached, the Queensland Minister retains considerable discretion, including to cancel a coordination agreement.[44] The Minister's approval is required for the agreement to be effective.[45]

Under the Victorian onshore Act, the balancing of competing interests comes not at the stage of approval of the relevant GHG tenure but instead when various work plans are required, after tenure has been obtained. This means that GHG storage proponents may have invested substantial resources in obtaining tenure only to find that the Minister does not allow the operations to go ahead 'in the public interest'. This is another risk that storage proponents must manage. For example, in relation to an injection and monitoring authority, an injection and monitoring plan is required prior to any injection of GHGs, and this must contain an assessment of the effect any leakage of a GHG might have on public health, the environment and other resources.[46] The Victorian Minister must not approve an injection and monitoring plan if there is either: (i) a significant risk of contaminating or sterilising other resources; or (ii) a risk to public health or the environment.[47] If there is a significant risk of contamination or sterilisation, but no risk to public health or the environment, approval may be given if the other resource authority holder has consented, or if approval is in the public interest.[48] The authority holder must enter into a compensation agreement with the other resource authority holder, or have a

---

[39] Queensland onshore Act, ss 186–194.
[40] ibid, ss 196, 197, 202, 212.
[41] ibid, s 203.
[42] ibid, s 221.
[43] ibid, s 220.
[44] ibid, s 193.
[45] ibid, ss 187(3), 189.
[46] Victorian onshore Act, ss 94–95.
[47] ibid, s 96.
[48] ibid, s 98.

special administrative tribunal[49] determine the amount of compensation to be paid in respect of access prior to commencement of injection activities.[50]

E. Enforcement

The Acts have comprehensive enforcement regimes, with extensive enforcement powers and a variety of enforcement tools that allow relevant regulators to take a risk-based approach to enforcement of the Acts.[51] These powers and tools are backed up by detailed monitoring and verification requirements, together with reporting obligations, that span the lifecycle of a CCS project: prior to commencement of GHG activities to establish a 'baseline' for further monitoring, during GHG the injection phase and then after site closure.[52]

In particular, the Acts have extensive powers for the Minister to intervene in a 'serious situation'.[53] For example, under the Federal offshore Act, the Minister has wide-ranging powers to deal with a leak or unintended release of GHGs from a storage site, where the GHG plume is behaving other than as predicted, or where there are significant risks to the geotechnical integrity of the storage formation.[54] The direction can cover matters relating to GHG operations both inside and outside the permit area, and require various actions to avoid, remedy or mitigate the 'serious situation'. The Minister can also require the GHG storage operator to cease injecting GHGs, either temporarily or permanently. Further, the Minister has general powers to issue directions in respect of GHG storage activities and to make remedial directions to operators in respect of removal of property, plugging or closing wells, conservation and protection of natural resources, and making good any damage to the seabed or subsoil.[55] Similar provisions are found in the other Australian regimes.

When exercising these Ministerial discretions, regulators must rely on relevant data that evidence that the specific tests under the legislation have been met.[56] This is particularly important given the seriousness of the potential enforcement consequences.

One area that has come under criticism is the failure of the Australian regimes to define what constitutes a 'leak' of GHGs from a storage site, or to place any

---

[49] The Victorian Civil and Administrative Tribunal.
[50] Victorian onshore Act, ss 48–49.
[51] M Gibbs, *Effective Enforcement of Underground Storage of Carbon Dioxide* (Melbourne, HWL Ebsworth Lawyers, 2016), at www.globalccsinstitute.com/publications/effective-enforcement-underground-storage-carbon-dioxide.
[52] ibid.
[53] Federal onshore Act, s 379; Victorian onshore Act, s 6; Queensland onshore Act, s 363 (definition of 'serious situation').
[54] Federal onshore Act, s 380.
[55] ibid, s 591.
[56] Gibbs, *Effective Enforcement of Underground Storage of Carbon Dioxide*, n 51 above, 21; I Havercroft and R Macrory, *Legal Liability and Carbon Capture and Storage: A Comparative Perspective* (Global Carbon Capture and Storage Institute, 2014), at www.globalccsinstitute.com/publications/legal-liability-and-carbon-capture-and-storage-comparative-perspective.

requirement that the 'leak' be significant or have an impact on a relevant receptor before Ministerial powers can be used.[57] This is in contrast to the International Energy Agency's *Carbon Capture and Storage Model Regulatory Framework*, which requires that there be a '*significant* leakage, unintended migration or other irregularity' for the exercise of enforcement powers.[58] It is also out of step with much environmental legislation, which provides that the concentration of the relevant substance must be above the concentration normally present at that location *and* that the presence of the substance at that level presents a risk of harm to human health or any other aspect of the environment before it will be considered 'pollution' or 'contamination' and trigger enforcement powers.[59] This issue, and the potentially high compliance obligation that it places on storage operators, is seen by the CCS industry as a barrier to further development of the CCS industry, and therefore is an area that warrants further consideration by Australian policy-makers.[60]

III. LONG-TERM LIABILITY

The issue of long-term liability for stored GHGs is a crucial one both for governments and for the CCS industry. It is also one that has attracted much public attention. When the Federal offshore Act was before Parliament, this was the issue that raised the most stakeholder concern, from the perspective of GHG storage proponents, those likely to be adversely affected by such activities, environmental groups and the public alike.

A. What is Long-term Liability?

Long-term liability in the context of CCS refers to liability that might arise in the post-operational phase. The key risks include:

— Leakage: the leakage of stored GHGs to the surface of land and into the atmosphere; and
— Migration: the (unexpected) migration of stored GHGs to contiguous underground areas.[61]

These situations could arise for a range of reasons, including seismic or volcanic activity, reservoir failures, equipment failures, decommissioning activities and interference by third parties (for example, drilling in the vicinity).

The types of harm that may occur include:

— Leakage: harm to human health and safety, the environment and property; impacts on climate change through increased emissions; and

---

[57] Gibbs, n 51 above, 37–40.
[58] International Energy Agency (IEA), *Carbon Capture and Storage Model Regulatory Framework: Information Paper* (OECD/IEA, 2010), Model text 6.8.2 (emphasis added).
[59] Gibbs, n 51 above, 38.
[60] ibid.
[61] For a discussion of these risks under the Australian regimes, see ibid, 35–47.

— Migration: harm to the environment and property; sterilisation, pollution or other adverse impacts on other resources (for example, oil and gas, groundwater).

If a leakage or migration event occurs, liability could be owed to the general public, surface or overlying land owners, competing interest stakeholders and, more generally, under both statute and the common law (for example, negligence, nuisance, trespass and the common law action of breach of statutory duty).[62] Liabilities may also arise under contract.

B. How do the Acts Deal with Long-term Liability?[63]

The Federal offshore Act is unique in that it contains specific provisions under which the Federal Government assumes liability for sequestered GHGs in the long term.[64] The Victorian (onshore and offshore) and Queensland Acts do not contain any such government indemnity, leaving the authority holder responsible for ongoing liabilities, primarily common law liabilities, indefinitely.[65]

i. Federal Offshore Act

Once injection ends, an authority holder must apply to surrender the injection and storage authority under the Federal offshore Act. This is a two-step process. First, as soon as injection ceases, the authority holder must apply for a 'Site Closure Certificate'. Secondly, if this certificate is granted (a decision must be made within five years) then, after at least 15 years, the authority holder may apply for a declaration stating that the 'Closure Assurance Period' has come to an end. During this Closure Assurance Period, the authority holder is responsible for monitoring and verification of the site, and remains fully liable for stored GHGs. The Closure Assurance Period will be declared to be at an end when the sequestered GHGs do not pose any significant risks, the gas is behaving as expected and no further injection has taken place. Significantly, this declaration triggers the end of the period where the authority holder is on risk and the point when the Federal Government takes over liability for the site and the sequestered GHGs. The Closure Assurance Period, together with the five-year period from the time of ceasing injection to the issue of

---

[62] See Havercroft and Macrory, n 56 above; N Swayne and A Phillips, 'Legal Liability for Carbon Capture and Storage in Australia: Where should the losses fall?' (2012) 29 *Environment & Planning Law Journal* 189. For a discussion of how long-term liabilities might be managed under contract, see Campbell, n 7 above, and S Golding, 'Some Considerations in Drafting Carbon Capture and Storage Contracts' (2009) *Australian Resources & Energy Law Journal* 418.

[63] See generally Swayne and Phillips, n 62 above. For a discussion of the Victorian onshore Act, see Havercroft and Macrory, n 56 above.

[64] Warburton et al, n 7 above, 52–53; IPCC, n 28 above, 61–65; R Campbell, 'Long-Term Liability for Offshore Geosequestration' [2006] *AMPLA Yearbook* 515.

[65] Campbell, n 7 above.

the Site Closure Certificate, means that the authority holder will remain 'on risk' for at least 20 years after injection ceases.[66]

At the end of the Closure Assurance Period, long-term liability passes to the Federal Government by operation of law. The Federal offshore Act specifically provides that the Federal Government will indemnify the former authority holder for any liability of that party:

(a) in damages;
(b) attributable to any act done or omitted to be done in carrying out operations authorised by the relevant authority; and
(c) incurred after the end of the Closure Assurance Period.[67]

The Federal Government also takes on liability in circumstances where the authority holder ceases to exist.[68] This statutory indemnity includes liabilities arising under the common law.

No other Australian GHG storage legislation provides for the relevant government to indemnify the former authority holder after surrender of the injection and storage authority, including the Victorian offshore Act, which, in all other principal respects, mirrors the Federal offshore Act.[69] The Victorian offshore Act does not contain the more complex 'Closure Assurance Period' provisions of the Federal Act, and does not contain the indemnity and liability provisions of the Federal offshore Act. Instead, it follows the liability model of the Victorian onshore Act, which was enacted some 15 months prior and which is now discussed.

ii. Victorian Onshore, Victorian Offshore and Queensland Onshore Acts

The Victorian onshore, Victorian offshore and Queensland onshore Acts do not provide any indemnity for long-term liabilities. However, these Acts specify that all GHG storage formations are owned by the State and, on surrender of the relevant GHG injection and storage authority, the GHGs stored in the formation become the property of the State.[70] As noted in section II.B, the relevant State government will also take over responsibility for monitoring and verification of the storage site.

The issue of ownership of storage formations and stored GHGs impacts on liability. At common law, where a GHG is stored in a subterranean formation and becomes part of that land, for example by process of chemical or mineral trapping, ownership of the gas will pass to the owner of the land. If, however, the gas remains separate from the land, capable of extraction at a later time, for example, then ownership of the gas will not pass to the owner of the geological formation but stays

---

[66] Federal offshore Act, ss 386–398. See also M Gibbs and P McCormack, 'New greenhouse gas storage legislation commences', *Greenhouse Update*, 5 December 2008 (Melbourne, Blake Dawson, 2008).
[67] Federal offshore Act, s 400.
[68] ibid, s 401.
[69] See M Gibbs, 'Victoria Enacts Greenhouse Gas Storage Legislation for its Offshore Waters', *Greenhouse Update*, 27 May 2010 (Melbourne, Blake Dawson, 2010).
[70] Victorian onshore Act, ss 14, 16; Queensland onshore Act, ss 27, 181; Victorian offshore Act, ss 65, 67.

with the owner of the gas. In some geological formations, both situations may occur contemporaneously. In addition, onshore in Australia, there are some situations where the ownership of the subsurface will be in private hands rather than with the Crown, which is otherwise the norm. For example, in Victoria, the Crown owns all land 50 feet (15.24 metres) or more below the surface, except in the case of freehold land alienated before 1892.[71] In order to resolve these uncertainties, the Victorian onshore and offshore Acts specifically provide for Crown ownership of both stored GHGs, post-closure, and storage formations at all times. Queensland followed suit when enacting its onshore legislation.

This means that onshore and offshore in Victorian waters, in the post-closure period, the primary risk and liability for the storage formation and its stored GHGs is with the State government. However, the former authority holder will remain liable for any harm arising as a result of its actions, even where the harm arises after surrender of the relevant GHG authority. This exposure to long-term liability is a key risk for storage proponents. In the case of a leak or migration event occurring long after surrender, it is likely that a person suffering damage or injury would take action in the courts, listing as many causes of action as possible, including negligence, nuisance, trespass and breach of statutory duty as relevant.[72] Under the Victorian onshore Act, the authority holder is deemed, for the purposes of occupier's liability, to be the occupier of any premises on which any operation is being carried out under the authority.[73] Given that the relevant State government owns both the storage formation and the stored GHGs in the post-surrender period, it is likely that the initial action would be directed against the State government. Having said this, the plaintiff or the State would likely join the former authority holder as a co-defendant in any such action. In some instances, such as in trespass cases, the ownership of the storage formation and the stored GHGs in the post-surrender period will create a presumption of State government liability.

Without canvassing the intricacies of the common law, a crucial element in all these causes of action is likely to be causation.[74] As has been the case in US litigation,[75] evidentiary issues around causation are likely to be difficult to resolve. Highly technical expert evidence will be required to establish that a particular act or omission of the defendant, such as the storage operator, actually caused the harm concerned. There may be added difficulties where more than one source of GHGs is involved. Further, some of the common law causes of action have not yet been tested in the GHG storage context and do not neatly fit with the CCS context, largely due to the fact that the common law has developed to deal with different kinds of situations. However, if GHG storage becomes common, courts may seek to adapt the common

---

[71] *Land Act 1958* (Vic), s 399A(1). See also Victorian Government Department of Primary Industries, *A Regulatory Framework for the Long-Term Underground Storage of Carbon Dioxide in Victoria: Discussion Paper* (Melbourne, Victorian Government, 2008) 23–26.
[72] Havercroft and Macrory, n 56 above.
[73] Victorian onshore Act, s 187.
[74] Havercroft and Macrory, n 56 above, 24.
[75] For example, *Chance v BP Chemicals, Inc*, 670 NE 2d 985 (Ohio 1996); *Mongrue v Monsanto Co*, 249 F 3d 422 (5th Cir 2001).

law to respond to the kinds of scenarios that arise due to leaks and migration events. For example, in the context of negligence, a court may be willing to find that a storage operator owes a duty of care to an adjoining landowner or the overlying surface landowner. This could include a duty of care in relation to site selection, operation of reservoirs, including injection of GHGs for testing or permanent storage, and, later, for decommissioning the storage site and monitoring of stored GHGs.

C. Why the Difference in Liability Regimes?

The Federal offshore Bill, the first of Australia's broad-scale GHG storage Acts, attracted considerable attention, and the issue of long-term liability was hotly debated as the Bill went through Parliament. Long-term liability was identified as a crucial issue, and stakeholders knew that the then Labor Federal Government needed the support of either the Conservative Opposition or the Greens in the Upper House (the Senate) to pass the Bill.

As a general proposition, the Labor Government had originally intended that any liability post-closure should 'lie where it falls'. Consistent with the Victorian and Queensland policy positions, the Federal offshore Bill provided that after site closure, storage proponents would remain liable indefinitely under common law in respect of post-closure leakage or migration. It was acknowledged by the Federal Government that under this approach the long-term risk would, 'in a sense', pass to the community over time:

> For example if greenhouse gas operations were to result in personal injury or loss to individuals, at a time when there were no project participants still available to be sued, or where damages were for some other reason irrecoverable, the cost would in practice be borne by the community. This would however, be the consequence of the passage of time, not of any assumption of liability on the part of government.[76]

The Government argued it could see 'no reason' to favour CCS over other technologies for reducing GHG emissions, and therefore opposed calls to actively take over long-term liability right up until the Bill was before the Senate.[77]

In the Senate, Labor had to choose between amendments put forward by the Opposition and those of the Greens. The Greens were proposing a raft of amendments, some of which required extensive changes to the Bill. The Greens supported making CCS project participants fully liable for any future leakage or migration, and

---

[76] Australian Government, *Regulation Impact Statement: Amendments to Offshore Petroleum Legislation to provide for Greenhouse Gas Transport, Injection and Storage in Commonwealth Waters* (Canberra, Australian Government, 2008) 27. See also Australian Parliament Senate Standing Committee on Economics, n 18 above, 24.

[77] Australian Government House of Representatives Standing Committee on Primary Industries and Resources, *Down Under: Greenhouse Gas Storage, Review of the draft Offshore Petroleum Amendment (Greenhouse Gas Storage) Bill* (Canberra, Parliament of the Commonwealth of Australia, 2008). See also the Australian Government's response: Australian Government, *Response to the House of Representatives Standing Committee on Primary Industries and Resources Recommendations* (Canberra, Australian Government, 2008) 8.

proposed that the Bill be amended to 'explicitly set out an independent process for determination of an adequate bond to be paid by companies to cover the full liability into future'.[78] The Opposition's required amendments were few in comparison. The Opposition argued that the liability for a GHG storage site should pass to government 20 years after site closure, and expressed concern that without such a provision in the legislation, it would be near impossible for company directors to sign off on CCS projects due to the indefinite liabilities involved.

At the last minute, the Labor Government accepted the Opposition's amendments and the long-term liability provisions discussed in section III.B were included in the Act, passing liability to the Federal Government a minimum of 15 years after the issue of the Site Closure Certificate. A further amendment in the Opposition's package required the decision to issue the Site Closure Certificate to be made within five years of site closure, thus creating an approximate 20-year period during which the project proponent remains on risk for all liabilities.[79]

The Victorian and Queensland State governments, both at the time Labor and both having the necessary majorities in their respective Parliaments, did not have to compromise their policy position on long-term liability. When the Victorian offshore Act was debated in Parliament, the issue of the differing Federal and Victorian offshore liability provisions was raised.[80] The Victorian government argued that the Victorian regime of leaving common law liabilities with GHG storage participants 'provides the greatest incentive for companies injecting to ensure the permanence of their injection activities'.[81] However, the Victorian government also said:

> If the long-term liability affects the take-up of tenements, this can be dealt with on a case-by-case basis by agreement with the State. In the meantime, it is preferred not to set up a regime that embeds unlimited liability being assumed by the [Victorian government].[82]

This suggests that early-mover and demonstration projects may be able to obtain Victorian government indemnities similar to those provided in the Federal offshore Act.

These two different policy positions are likely to have some challenging practical consequences, and may impact on the take up of GHG tenure in Victorian offshore waters—out to three nautical miles—as compared to in Federal offshore waters, where long-term liability passes to the Federal Government. More significantly, it will create crucial uncertainties for GHG storage proponents where storage reservoirs cross from the Victorian to Federal jurisdiction.[83] This is highly possible, as many potential reservoir systems offshore from the Victorian coast have physical

---

[78] Australian Parliament Senate Standing Committee on Economics, n 18 above, 24.
[79] Parliament of the Commonwealth of Australia, The Senate, *Offshore Petroleum Amendment (Greenhouse Gas Storage) 2008, Schedule of the amendments made by the Senate* (Canberra, Parliament of Commonwealth of Australia, 2008).
[80] *Victorian Parliamentary Debates*, Legislative Assembly, 23 February 2010, 361. See also Gibbs, n 69 above.
[81] *Victorian Parliamentary Debates*, Legislative Assembly, 25 February 2010, 579. See also Havercroft and Macrory, n 56 above, 43.
[82] *Victorian Parliamentary Debates*, Legislative Assembly, 25 February 2010, 579.
[83] Gibbs, n 5 above.

characteristics that mean that gases injected offshore will tend to migrate towards the shore from the Federal-governed areas to Victorian (offshore and, possibly, onshore) jurisdictions.

This situation is unsatisfactory. In any court action, the exact cause of the leak or migration, and its precise location, will need to be proved. Did GHGs leak or migrate from a storage reservoir governed under the Victorian Act or the Federal Act? What if a storage proponent holds authorities under each jurisdiction and it is impossible to know in which part of a reservoir the leak originated? What if more than one source of GHGs is involved? Answers to such factual questions will be crucial in determining the party liable for any losses suffered, and will be particularly important where the storage company is impecunious or no longer exists. As noted, the Victorian government has indicated that it may take on long-term liability for particular offshore projects on a case-by-case basis, which may overcome some of these issues in certain cases or in early projects. However, there would still be a debate concerning whether the State government or Federal Government is liable.

D. 'De-risking' Early Mover Projects

In this early stage of the CCS industry's growth, the willingness of governments to 'de-risk' CCS projects and take over long-term liabilities appears to be crucial in CCS projects moving to implementation stage. This has been the experience internationally,[84] and the indemnities given by the Australian Federal Government and the Western Australian government to the proponents of Gorgon LNG Project at Barrow Island, Western Australia, provide a precedent for this to occur.[85]

Under the *Barrow Island Act 2003* (WA), the State of Western Australian will indemnify the Gorgon Project proponents for any 'common law liability' to third parties arising after the 'liability assumption date', being at least 15 years from the time that injection ceased, in respect of loss or damage caused by the injection of CO_2 from the project. The loss or damage must be attributable to an act done, or omitted to be done, in the carrying out of injection operations under the authority of the relevant statutory approval.[86] Under an agreement between the two governments, the Australian Federal Government in turn indemnifies the West Australian government for 80 per cent of liability.[87] These government indemnities reduce the long-term liability of the Gorgon Project proponents significantly, resulting in a similar liability position for the proponents as if injection had occurred under the Federal onshore Act.[88]

---

[84] ibid.
[85] ibid; M Gibbs et al, 'Carbon Capture and Storage Moves Forward', *Greenhouse Update*, 23 November 2009, 5.
[86] *Barrow Island Act 2003* (WA), s 14D.
[87] *Barrow Island Amendment Bill 2015* (WA) *Explanatory Memorandum*, at www.austlii.edu.au/au/legis/wa/bill_em/biab2015235/.
[88] Gibbs, n 5 above.

IV. CONCLUSION

Australia has one of the most well-developed, comprehensive regulatory frameworks permitting GHG storage activities. All of the Acts discussed in this chapter—the Federal and Victorian offshore Acts and the Victorian and Queensland onshore Acts—establish GHG storage tenure that reflects existing petroleum tenure systems. The Acts take a risk-minimisation approach to environmental and safety issues, consistent with Australia's well-developed environmental laws.

However, the Australian GHG storage framework contains considerable Ministerial discretions, which arguably result in uncertainties that may be a barrier to the rapid deployment of CCS projects and, in the longer term, the establishment of a viable GHG storage industry in Australia. Perhaps even more concerning are the different long-term liability regimes and the different processes for managing, and levels of protection for, competing interests under the various Acts. These differences create further uncertainties and complexities for GHG storage proponents and their financiers. This is particularly the case with respect to long-term liability, where the different liability regimes under the Federal offshore Act and the other Acts will create crucial difficulties for storage proponents and investors as they attempt to assess the risk profile of projects. Greenhouse gases will migrate across jurisdictional boundaries, most likely in the Victorian coastal region where some of the first large-scale projects are likely to be established, but also in other areas. This will raise questions concerning who will be liable for any future damage or losses arising as a result of leakage or unexpected migration of those GHGs. In order to provide the necessary degree of certainty and to reduce long-term risk exposures, it is likely that early-mover and demonstration projects will seek government indemnities where they are not provided in legislation.

This chapter has presented some possible explanations for the different policy positions taken under the various Acts. While the differing positions may have explanations, be they rational or merely political, it is regrettable that a more consistent approach across the Australian jurisdictions has not eventuated. In order to encourage investment in CCS, the statutory framework should not add to the already considerable risk exposures of GHG storage proponents, particularly in the context of a commodity that has no economic value in and of itself; its only economic value being in an avoided cost imposed by other legislation for climate change mitigation purposes. Given these economics and the longevity of the risks involved in CCS, it may be that we see changes to the Australian liability regimes in the future. Accordingly, whilst Australia has a highly developed regulatory framework for the storage of GHGs, there is some way to go before it offers complete certainty to GHG storage proponents.

12
Tenure, Title and Property in Geological Storage of Greenhouse Gas in Australia

MICHAEL CROMMELIN

I. INTRODUCTION

THE DISPOSAL OF greenhouse gas (GHG) by underground storage in geological formations provokes several questions of legal entitlement: to the land in which the formations occur; to the formations that accommodate the stored gas; to the stored gas; to locate these formations; to store gas therein; to deal with these exploration and storage rights; and to protect them. This chapter examines how those questions arise and are resolved, onshore and offshore, in Australia.

II. LAND TENURE

Legal entitlement to land within Australia and offshore is derived from a number of distinct sources: Aboriginal customary law and practice, English land law, Australian statutes and international law.[1]

In 1992, the High Court of Australia acknowledged that the indigenous inhabitants of Australia were entitled, in accordance with their traditional laws and customs, to their traditional lands at the time of the establishment of the Australian colonies in the eighteenth and nineteenth centuries. The acquisition of sovereignty over the Australian continent by the United Kingdom (UK) gave it radical title to all land in the colonies. Unlike beneficial title, however, radical title was merely residual in nature; it did not extinguish native title, although it provided the UK with the authority to do so.[2]

The content of native title is not fixed. Rather, it is determined in each case by the traditional laws and customs of the relevant Aboriginal group.[3] Usually native title

---
[1] See M Crommelin, 'Australian Responses to Subsurface Conflicts: Greenhouse Gas Storage v Petroleum' in DN Zillman et al (eds), *The Law of Energy Underground* (Oxford, Oxford University Press, 2014) 419–423.
[2] *Mabo v Queensland (No 2)* (1992) 175 CLR 1, [1992] HCA 23.
[3] *Native Title Act 1993* (Cth), s 223. See also *Western Australia v Ward* (2002) 213 CLR 1, 65–66; [2002] HCA 28.

confers surface rights of access, occupation and utilisation, rather than entitlement to underground geological formations or any pore space therein.[4]

The colonisation of Australia led to the adoption of English law,[5] including English land law with its array of estates and interests harking back to feudal times and, notably, the presumption that *cujus est solum, ejus est usque ad coelum et ad inferos*.[6] The estate in fee simple, or freehold tenure, usually confers rights of exclusive possession not only to the surface, but also to the subsurface and to the airspace above the surface of land. Accordingly, freehold tenure may include rights to underground geological formations and any storage space therein.[7] Moreover, the grant of freehold tenure extinguishes native title to the land.[8]

During the early years of the Australian colonial era, the UK made land grants to settlers in the form of freehold tenure, sometimes (but not always) subject to the reservation of title to gold, silver and coal. However, the extensive use of freehold tenure was short lived.

New South Wales and Victoria acquired self-government in 1855, Tasmania and South Australia in 1856, Queensland in 1859 and Western Australia in 1890.[9] Self-government brought control of unallocated land: the 'entire Management and Control of the Waste Lands belonging to the Crown' were vested in each colonial legislature.[10] The Australian colonies seized this opportunity to make radical changes to land tenures, ensuring that they, rather than private landholders, were entitled to subsurface resources.

The most significant change was the shift away from reliance upon freehold land tenure in favour of statutory land tenures, frequently called 'leases' or 'licences'[11] but usually very different in legal character from their English namesakes. The rights conferred and obligations imposed by these newly devised tenures are specified in their relevant statutes, giving rise to 'a bewildering multiplicity of tenures'[12] similar to one another only in their legislative origin and in the existence of a legal relationship between the granting polity and the holder of each particular title.[13]

---

[4] *Native Title Act 1993* and *Western Australia v Ward*, n 3 above.

[5] Australian Courts Act 1828 (UK), s 24.

[6] 'Whoever owns the surface of land also owns up to the heavens and down to hell'; ie, the concept of entitlement to land is three-dimensional rather than two-dimensional. The presumption is subject to exceptions such as the royal metals, gold and silver. See *Cadia Holdings Pty Ltd v New South Wales* (2010) 242 CLR 195, [2010] HCA 27.

[7] B Barton, 'The Common Law of Subsurface Activity: General Principle and Current Problems' in Zillman et al (eds), n 1 above, 21.

[8] *Mabo v Queensland (No 2)* (1992) 175 CLR 1, 63–71; [1992] HCA 23.

[9] RD Lumb, *The Constitutions of the Australian States*, 5th edn (Brisbane, University of Queensland Press, 1991) chs 1, 2.

[10] Eg, New South Wales Constitution Act 1855 (UK), s 2. The term 'Waste Lands' encompassed all lands not already subject to freehold tenure. See also *Cudgen Rutile (No 2) Pty Ltd v Chalk* [1975] AC 520.

[11] Eg, 'Crown lease', 'pastoral lease', 'perpetual lease', 'grazing licence', 'timber licence'.

[12] TP Fry, 'Land Tenures in Australian Law' (1946–47) 3 *Res Judicatae* 158, quoting AC Millard and GW Millard, *The Law of Real Property in New South Wales*, 4th edn (BA Helmore ed, Sydney, Law Book Co of Australasia, 1930) 474.

[13] Crommelin, n 1 above, 421.

Notwithstanding their diversity, these statutory tenures are readily distinguishable from freehold tenure.[14] They confer limited rights of possession, occupation or utilisation of the land, typically confined to narrowly specified activities, with no entitlement to geological formations or the storage spaces therein. The *cujus est solum* presumption does not apply to them.

Only 20 per cent of Australian land is now held under freehold tenure, compared with more than 40 per cent held under statutory tenures. The rest is made up of reserves for public purposes (about 23 per cent) and special tenures, distinct from native title, conferred on Aboriginal organisations by Commonwealth, South Australian and Queensland legislation (about 14 per cent).[15] The proportion of land subject to freehold tenure ranges from a high of 68 per cent in Victoria to a low of 8 per cent in Western Australia.

The Australian colonies also curtailed the application of the *cujus est solum* presumption by a series of measures limiting the rights of holders of freehold tenure to exploit specified subsurface resources. Despite its extensive grants of freehold tenure, Victoria retained entitlement to most subsurface resources by imposing a depth limitation on all grants of freehold tenure on and after 1 March 1892.[16] Moreover, during the second half of the nineteenth century, all colonies adopted the practice of reservation of minerals and petroleum from subsequent grants of freehold tenure.[17] Many years later, the Northern Territory,[18] South Australia,[19] New South Wales[20] and Victoria[21] took the further step of compulsory acquisition of privately owned mineral rights in freehold land that had been granted prior to their adoption of this reservation practice. All States and the Northern Territory now assert property in all petroleum, without exception, located naturally within their territorial boundaries.[22] Some also declare property in geothermal energy resources.[23]

Offshore, pursuant to the Offshore Constitutional Settlement reached between the Commonwealth, the States and the Northern Territory in 1979,[24] the States and

---

[14] *Wik Peoples v Queensland* (1996) 187 CLR 1, [1996] HCA 40.
[15] Geoscience Australia, 'Australian Land Tenure 1993' (App C), at ecat.ga.gov.au/geonetwork/srv/eng/search#!a05f7892-b78d-7506-e044-00144fdd4fa6.
[16] The limitation is 15.24 metres (50 feet).
[17] M Crommelin, 'Resources Law and Public Policy' (1983) 15 *University of Western Australia Law Review* 1.
[18] *Mineral (Acquisition) Ordinance 1953* (Cth).
[19] *Mining Act 1971* (SA).
[20] *Coal Acquisition Act 1981* (NSW). See *Durham Holdings Pty Limited v New South Wales* (2001) 205 CLR 399, [2001] HCA 7.
[21] *Mines (Amendment) Act 1983* (Vic).
[22] Eg, *Petroleum Act 1990* (Vic), s 13: 'The Crown owns all petroleum on or below the surface of any land in Victoria that came to be on or below that surface without human assistance.'
[23] *Petroleum and Geothermal Energy Resources Act 1967* (WA), s 9: '[A]ll petroleum, geothermal energy resources and geothermal energy on or below the surface of all land within this State, whether alienated in fee simple or not so alienated from the Crown, are and shall be deemed always to have been the property of the Crown.' See also *Geothermal Energy Act 2010* (Qld), s 28; *Geothermal Energy Resources Act 2005* (Vic), s 12; *Petroleum and Geothermal Energy Act 2000* (SA), ss 4, 5; and *Geothermal Energy Act* (NT), s 9.
[24] *Offshore Petroleum and Greenhouse Gas Storage Act 2006* (Cth), s 5. See also M Crommelin, 'Offshore Mining and Petroleum: Constitutional Issues' (1981) 3 *Australian Mining and Petroleum Law Journal* 191.

the Northern Territory have jurisdiction over their coastal waters that extend offshore from the seaward boundaries of their land territory to a distance of three nautical miles from the international baselines used to define the limits of Australia's territorial sea.[25] They also hold statutory title to the seabed beneath those coastal waters.[26]

Beyond coastal waters, the Commonwealth has sovereignty in respect of the remainder of Australia's territorial sea, rights and jurisdiction in Australia's exclusive economic zone, and sovereign rights in Australia's continental shelf for the purpose of exploring it and exploiting its natural resources.[27] However, the Commonwealth Parliament has not sought to exercise Australia's sovereignty and sovereign rights in these areas by assertion of statutory title to the seabed.

III. TITLE

Legal entitlement to underground resources in Australia is thus public rather than private, apart from minor exceptions. Nevertheless, usually the Commonwealth, the States and the Northern Territory do not themselves undertake exploration for and exploitation of underground resources. Instead, they engage private enterprise to do so, pursuant to legislative regimes relating to specific resources within each jurisdiction[28] or agreements between government and private enterprise relating to specific projects.[29] These legislative regimes and government agreements, while numerous and highly variable in content, have some common features. First, they typically confirm the public proprietorship of the relevant underground resources in their natural state, prior to recovery. Secondly, they create statutory titles that authorise exploration for and production of the resources by the holders thereof on detailed terms and conditions. Thirdly, they prohibit the exploration for and production of the resources otherwise than in accordance with the provisions of these regimes and agreements.

In recent years, the Commonwealth and several States have established distinct legislative regimes, and Western Australia has entered into a project agreement, relating to geological storage of GHG, offshore and onshore.

A. Offshore Areas

The Commonwealth regime for GHG storage applies in offshore areas within Australian jurisdiction beyond coastal waters. The regime is incorporated in the *Offshore Petroleum and Greenhouse Gas Storage Act 2006* (Cth), presumably on

---

[25] *Coastal Waters (State Powers) Act 1980* (Cth); *Coastal Waters (Northern Territory) Powers Act 1980* (Cth).
[26] *Coastal Waters (State Title) Act 1980* (Cth); *Coastal Waters (Northern Territory) Title) Act 1980* (Cth).
[27] *Seas and Submerged Lands Act 1973* (Cth), ss 6, 10A, 11.
[28] M Crommelin, 'Mining and Petroleum Titles' (1988) 62 *Australian Law Journal* 863.
[29] M Crommelin, 'State Agreements: Australian Trends and Experience' [1996] *AMPLA Yearbook* 328.

the basis that depleted petroleum reservoirs offer the best prospects for offshore GHG storage.

The Act regulates various activities in offshore areas, including exploration for petroleum, recovery of petroleum, exploration for potential GHG storage formations, and injection and storage of GHG substances,[30] which are defined to include carbon dioxide (CO_2) and prescribed GHGs.[31] Atypically, the Act does not assert property in the seabed of Australia's territorial sea and continental shelf, as previously noted,[32] or in petroleum, GHG storage formations or GHG substances therein. Instead, it prohibits specified activities unless they are authorised by the Act, pursuant to a statutory title or otherwise. These activities are exploration for petroleum,[33] recovery of petroleum,[34] construction or operation of an infrastructure facility[35] or pipeline,[36] exploration for a potential GHG storage formation or a potential GHG injection site,[37] and injection and storage of GHG substances.[38]

The regime for GHG storage includes three statutory titles that authorise the principal activities relating to injection and storage of GHG substances.[39] The GHG assessment permit allows the holder to explore in the permit area for potential GHG storage formations and potential GHG injection sites, and to conduct limited injection and storage operations in a geological formation on an appraisal basis.[40] Upon identification of a GHG storage formation in a permit area,[41] the holder of a permit may apply for a GHG injection licence[42] that authorises the holder to conduct injection and storage operations for GHG substances in the licence area.[43] Alternatively, the holder of a permit who has identified a storage formation, is not yet in a position to inject and store a GHG substance but is likely to be able to do so within 15 years, may apply for a GHG holding lease[44] that authorises further exploration in the lease area and injection and storage operations on an appraisal basis,[45] before making an application for a GHG storage licence.[46]

B. Coastal Waters

The States and the Northern Territory do have statutory title to the seabed beneath their coastal waters, as already noted.[47] In accordance with the Offshore

---

[30] *Offshore Petroleum and Greenhouse Gas Storage Act 2006* (Cth), s 4.
[31] ibid, s 7.
[32] Section II.
[33] *Offshore Petroleum and Greenhouse Gas Storage Act 2006* (Cth), s 97.
[34] ibid, s 160.
[35] ibid, s 193.
[36] ibid, s 210.
[37] ibid, s 289.
[38] ibid, s 356.
[39] ibid, s 287.
[40] ibid, s 290.
[41] ibid, s 312.
[42] ibid, s 361.
[43] ibid, s 357.
[44] ibid, ss 324–325.
[45] ibid, s 319.
[46] ibid, s 361.
[47] Section II.

Constitutional Settlement, Victoria has established a legislative regime, modelled closely upon the Commonwealth offshore regime, for the exploration and recovery of petroleum and for the injection and storage of GHG substances in its coastal waters. The *Offshore Petroleum and Greenhouse Gas Storage Act 2010* (Vic) also declares that the State owns all underground geological storage formations within the seabed beneath its coastal waters,[48] and becomes the owner of any GHG substance that has been injected into a formation pursuant to a statutory licence upon cancellation or surrender of that licence.[49]

C. Onshore

In South Australia, the *Petroleum and Geothermal Energy Act 2000* declares that property in petroleum and other regulated resources is vested in the State.[50] Regulated resources are naturally occurring underground accumulations of regulated substances (petroleum, hydrogen sulphide, nitrogen, helium, CO_2, any other substance that occurs naturally in association with petroleum, and any other declared substance), sources of geothermal energy, and natural reservoirs (geological structures in which petroleum or some other regulated substance has accumulated, or which are suitable for storage thereof).[51] The Act also prohibits engagement in a regulated activity unless that activity is authorised under the Act.[52] Regulated activities include exploration for and production of regulated resources, utilisation of a natural reservoir for storage of regulated substances, and production of geothermal energy.[53]

The Act establishes a licensing regime applicable to regulated resources based upon three principal titles—exploration, retention and production licences; each of these titles has three categories, petroleum, geothermal and gas storage.[54] The gas storage exploration licence authorises the holder to carry out exploratory operations in the licence area for a natural reservoir.[55] The gas storage retention licence authorises the holder to carry out operations in the licence area to establish the nature and extent of utilisation of a natural reservoir to store a regulated substance such as CO_2.[56] The gas storage licence authorises operations for the use of a natural reservoir for the storage of a regulated substance such as CO_2.[57]

In Victoria, the *Greenhouse Gas Geological Sequestration Act 2008* declares that the State owns all underground geological storage formations below the surface of

---

[48] *Offshore Petroleum and Greenhouse Gas Storage Act 2010* (Vic), s 65. See also s 66.
[49] ibid, s 67.
[50] *Petroleum and Geothermal Energy Act 2000* (SA), s 5.
[51] ibid, s 4.
[52] ibid, s 11.
[53] ibid, s 10.
[54] ibid, pts 4–6.
[55] ibid, s 21.
[56] ibid, ss 10, 29.
[57] ibid s 34.

any land in Victoria, despite any prior alienation of Crown land,[58] and any GHG substance that has been injected into a formation under a statutory licence upon cancellation or surrender of the licence.[59] It also prohibits exploration for a potential underground geological storage formation and injection of a GHG substance into a formation for permanent storage except in accordance with the Act.[60]

The Act establishes a regime for storage of GHG substances, comprising three statutory titles. The exploration permit authorises the holder to carry out GHG sequestration exploration in the permit area.[61] The retention lease enables the holder of an exploration permit to retain the right to an underground geological storage formation identified as likely to be geologically suitable for the injection and permanent storage of a GHG substance that is not yet commercially viable to develop under an injection and monitoring licence, but which might become viable to develop within 15 years.[62] The retention lease authorises the holder to carry out GHG formation exploration, with a right to apply for an injection and monitoring licence.[63] The GHG substance injection and monitoring licence authorises the holder to carry out GHG substance injection and monitoring in the licence area.[64]

In Queensland, the *Greenhouse Gas Storage Act 2009* declares that all GHG storage reservoirs in land in the State are and are taken always to have been the property of the State, regardless of whether a person creates or discovers the reservoir and whether or not the land is freehold or other land,[65] and that any GHG injected into a GHG storage reservoir pursuant to a statutory lease becomes the property of the State upon surrender of the lease.[66] Further, each grant under another Act of a right relating to land is taken to contain a reservation to the State of all GHG storage reservoirs in the land, and the exclusive right to enter and carry out any GHG storage activity.[67]

The Act provides two main authorities for GHG storage activities. The GHG exploration permit allows the holder, within the permit area, to explore for GHG storage sites and to conduct feasibility studies relating to storage of CO_2 therein.[68] The GHG injection and storage lease allows the holder, within the lease area, to inject CO_2 into a storage reservoir for storage purposes, and to monitor and verify its behaviour in the reservoir.[69]

---

[58] *Greenhouse Gas Geological Sequestration Act 2008* (Vic), s 14. The declaration does not apply to any land (other than Crown land) where the underground geological storage formation is within 15.24 metres of the surface of the land. This proviso accords with the statutory requirement that grants of freehold tenure made on and after 1 March 1982 extend only to a depth of 15.24 metres from the surface of the land. See also s 15 (Crown land).
[59] ibid, s 16.
[60] ibid, ss 17, 18. See also ss 3–5.
[61] ibid, s 19.
[62] ibid, s 58.
[63] ibid, s 59.
[64] ibid, s 71.
[65] *Greenhouse Gas Storage Act 2009* (Qld), s 27.
[66] ibid, s 181.
[67] ibid, s 28. See also s 23 for the definition of 'greenhouse gas storage activity'.
[68] ibid, s 30. See also ss 14, 15.
[69] ibid, s 110. See also s 14.

In Western Australia, the *Barrow Island Act 2003* ratifies and authorises the implementation of the Gorgon Gas Processing and Infrastructure Agreement between the State and four private entities, the Joint Venturers.[70] The terms of the Agreement are set out in a schedule to the Act. The long title of the Act states that the Agreement relates 'to a proposal to undertake offshore production of natural gas and other petroleum and a gas processing project on Barrow Island', and provides for 'underground disposal of carbon dioxide recovered during gas processing on Barrow Island'.[71]

The provisions for underground disposal of CO_2 are meagre indeed. Section 13 of the Act merely prohibits the injection of CO_2 into an underground reservoir or other subsurface formation for disposal purposes without the approval of the responsible Minister. An application for approval must provide particulars of the proposed disposal project. The Minister must consult other specified State Ministers and consider their advice. The Minister may then grant approval, 'subject to any condition or restriction'.

IV. PROPERTY

The legislative regimes that authorise the injection of GHG into underground reservoirs that are usually publicly owned,[72] and the storage of GHG in these reservoirs, present difficult questions of legal characterisation of the statutory titles they provide for injection and storage. One significant question is whether a statutory title is property; if so, there may be a further question of whether the title is an interest in land or personal property.

Occasionally, a statute declares that titles are not property either for a particular purpose or of a particular kind. The *Offshore Petroleum and Greenhouse Gas Storage Act 2006* (Cth) states that none of its statutory titles that authorise activities relating to injection and storage of GHG substances is personal property for the purposes of the *Personal Property Securities Act 2009* (Cth),[73] which establishes a national regulatory regime for dealings with personal property as defined therein. Each of the *Petroleum and Geothermal Energy Act 2000* (SA),[74] *Greenhouse Gas Geological Sequestration Act 2008* (Vic)[75] and *Greenhouse Gas Storage Act 2009* (Qld)[76] has a provision to the same effect. Furthermore, the *Greenhouse Gas Storage Act 2009* (Qld) declares that the granting of a GHG authority does not create an interest in any land.[77]

---

[70] *Barrow Island Act 2003* (WA), s 5.
[71] Barrow Island is part of the State of Western Australia.
[72] Or otherwise publicly controlled.
[73] *Offshore Petroleum and Greenhouse Gas Storage Act 2006* (Cth), s 780H.
[74] *Petroleum and Geothermal Energy Act 2000* (SA), s 13A.
[75] *Greenhouse Gas Geological Sequestration Act 2008* (Vic), s 187A.
[76] *Greenhouse Gas Storage Act 2009* (Qld), s 8A.
[77] ibid, 369.

The legal character of statutory titles is necessarily determined by statutory interpretation. The legislative regimes seldom state explicitly whether or not their statutory titles are property. The legal character of each title must therefore be inferred from the relevant provisions of its statute, having regard to the purposes of the regime and the particular rights conferred and obligations imposed by the title. That character is not immutable. It may differ according to the context in which the question of characterisation arises.[78]

A. Dealings and Registration

The legal character of statutory titles is especially significant in relation to the nature, extent and enforcement of commercial dealings with those titles and interests therein by the holders of the titles. The legislative regimes regulating injection and storage of GHG clearly contemplate such dealings, although they usually fail to authorise them expressly or to specify the legal basis for conducting them. Instead, they impose restraints of two kinds upon dealings. One is a requirement for government approval of proposed dealings, while the other is a requirement for registration of appropriate instruments that effect those dealings. For example, the *Offshore Petroleum and Greenhouse Gas Storage Act 2006* (Cth) provides that a transfer of a title is 'of no force' until it is approved by the Titles Administrator and an instrument of transfer is registered in accordance with the Act.[79] Any dealing with a specified interest in a title is similarly constrained.[80] The other statutory regimes contain comparable provisions.[81] These constraints themselves support the premise underlying the legislative regimes that their statutory titles are proprietary in character, at least to the extent required to allow their holders to deal with them and proprietary interests therein.

B. Security of Title

Statutory titles are inherently vulnerable to legislative amendment. Their legal character may, however, limit that vulnerability somewhat. The Australian Constitution confers power on the Commonwealth Parliament to make laws with respect to the 'acquisition of property on just terms from any State or person for any purpose in respect of which the Parliament has power to make laws'.[82] The High Court of

---

[78] *TEC Desert Pty ltd v Commissioner of State Revenue (Western Australia)* (2010) 241 CLR 576, [2010] HCA 49.
[79] *Offshore Petroleum and Greenhouse Gas Storage Act 2006* (Cth), s 524.
[80] ibid, 538.
[81] *Offshore Petroleum and Greenhouse Gas Storage Act 2010* (Vic), ss 566, 580; *Petroleum and Geothermal Energy Act 2000* (SA), s 112; *Greenhouse Gas Geological Sequestration Act 2008* (Vic), ss 164–167, 281–282; *Greenhouse Gas Storage Act 2009* (Qld), s 8AA; and *Mineral and Energy Resources (Common Provisions) Act 2014* (Qld), ss 6, 16, 17.
[82] Constitution, s 51(xxxi).

Australia has long held that this provision implicitly denies Parliament the power to enact legislation that effects an acquisition of property otherwise than on just terms, thereby providing a small measure of constitutional protection against compulsory acquisition of property. The Court has frequently endorsed the following encapsulation of the doctrine:

> [Section] 51(xxxi) is not to be confined pedantically to the taking of title by the Commonwealth to some specific estate or interest in land recognised at law or in equity and to some specific form of property in a chattel or chose in action similarly recognised, but ... extends to innominate and anomalous interests and includes the assumption and indefinite continuance of exclusive possession and control for the purposes of the Commonwealth of any subject of property. Section 51(xxxi) serves a double purpose. It provides the Commonwealth Parliament with a legislative power of acquiring property; at the same time as a condition upon the exercise of the power it provides the individual, or the State, affected with a protection against governmental interferences with his property rights without just recompense. In both aspects consistency with the principles upon which constitutional provisions are interpreted and applied demands that the paragraph should be given as full and flexible an operation as will cover the objects it was designed to effect.[83]

According to this doctrine, statutory titles for GHG injection and storage may well be characterised as property within the scope of section 51(xxxi) of the Constitution. However, characterisation of statutory titles as property is not enough for them to obtain constitutional protection against variation or extinguishment by statutory amendment. Section 51(xxxi) requires an acquisition of property. Deprivation of property does not always amount to acquisition of property. The legislative abrogation of a statutory title must, in addition to depriving the former holder of the title, confer property on the Commonwealth, a person or some other entity, in order to attract the constitutional requirement of just terms.[84]

Whether a legislative abrogation of statutory rights amounts to an acquisition of property within the scope of section 51(xxxi) of the Constitution depends upon the interpretation of the statute that creates the rights and the statute that amends it. The High Court has recently confirmed that any provisions of the primary statute providing for alteration or extinguishment of its titles will mitigate against an acquisition of property in the event of its subsequent amendment.[85] In the words of Gageler J:

> Where Parliament exercises a legislative power to create a statutory right in the nature of property, attention to the particular statutory characteristics of that statutory right is needed in order to determine whether a subsequent legislative alteration of the right meets the threshold condition of a law with respect to the acquisition of property ...
>
> One potential characteristic of a statutory right of property created in the exercise of another grant of legislative power is that the right may be created on terms that make that right susceptible to administrative or legislative alteration or extinguishment without acquisition.[86]

---

[83] *Bank of NSW v The Commonwealth* (1948) 76 CLR 1, 349–50; [1948] HCA 7; *ICM Agriculture Pty Ltd v The Commonwealth* (2009) 240 CLR 140, 197; [2009] HCA 51; *Cunningham v Commonwealth of Australia* [2016] HCA 39 [62].

[84] *Newcrest Mining (WA) Ltd v The Commonwealth* (1997) 190 CLR 513, [1990] HCA 38.

[85] *Cunningham v Commonwealth of Australia* [2016] HCA 39.

[86] ibid, [65], [66]. See also at [46] (French CJ, Kiefel and Bell JJ), [234]–[238] (Nettle J) and [328]–[329] (Gordon J).

The object of the *Offshore Petroleum and Greenhouse Gas Storage Act* (Cth) is to provide an effective regulatory framework for two sets of activities in Australia's offshore areas: (i) petroleum exploration and production, and (ii) the injection and storage of GHG substances.[87] Those activities are undertaken by private enterprise pursuant to statutory titles provided by the Act. The titles confer valuable rights and impose substantial obligations on their holders. The Act provides for commercial dealings with the titles and interests therein. The Act is replete with discretionary powers conferred upon government officers and agencies. Nevertheless, the effectiveness of the regulatory framework depends upon the legal security of its statutory titles. Legislative abrogation of any of these statutory titles could therefore amount to an acquisition of property, requiring just terms for its constitutional validity.

However, this conclusion may be difficult to reconcile with that of the High Court in *The Commonwealth v WMC Resources Limited*,[88] that legislative cancellation (in part) of an offshore petroleum exploration permit granted in 1977 pursuant to the *Petroleum (Submerged Lands) Act 1967* (Cth)[89] was not an acquisition of property within section 51(xxxi) of the Constitution. The decision in that case was not unanimous, and various reasons were given for it. One was that the permit was granted over an area of contested jurisdiction, suggesting that it was vulnerable from the outset.[90] Another was that crucial provisions of the *Petroleum (Submerged Lands) Act 1967* indicated that the exploration permit was inherently susceptible to legislative abrogation.[91] A third was that in the absence of any assertion of property in the seabed of Australia's continental shelf, the cancellation of the exploration permit conferred no benefit on the Commonwealth and thus amounted merely to a deprivation rather than an acquisition of property.[92] A fourth was that all rights that owe their existence to statute may be extinguished by statutory amendment without providing just terms.[93] None of these reasons gained the support of a majority of Justices, and all of them received trenchant criticism from dissenting Justices.[94]

The High Court referred to the *WMC Resources* case in its most recent decision on section 51(xxxi) of the Constitution without analysis of its diverse reasons.[95] Most members of the Court merely cited the case as an illustration of the accepted proposition that the particular language of legislation creating a statutory right may render that right inherently susceptible to abrogation without acquisition of property.[96]

---

[87] *Offshore Petroleum and Greenhouse Gas Storage Act 2006* (Cth), s 3.
[88] *The Commonwealth v WMC Resources Ltd* (1998) 194 CLR 1, [1998] HCA 8.
[89] This Act was the predecessor of the *Offshore Petroleum and Greenhouse Gas Storage Act 2006* (Cth).
[90] *The Commonwealth v WMC Resources Ltd* (1998) 194 CLR 1, 10 (Brennan CJ), 62–63 (Gummow J); [1998] HCA 8.
[91] ibid, 36–38 (Gaudron J), 56–58 (McHugh J) and 69–75 (Gummow J). The relevant language of the *Offshore Petroleum and Greenhouse Gas Storage Act 2006* (Cth) differs from that of the *Petroleum (Submerged Lands) Act 1967* (Cth).
[92] *The Commonwealth v WMC Resources Ltd* (1998) 194 CLR 1, 18–20 (Brennan CJ) and 37–38 (Gaudron J).
[93] ibid, 51–56 (McHugh J).
[94] ibid, 26–31 (Toohey J) and 86–102 (Kirby J).
[95] *Cunningham v Commonwealth of Australia* [2016] HCA 39.
[96] ibid [39], [44]–[45] (French CJ, Kiefel and Bell JJ), [153], [167], [189] (Keane J), [223], [229]–[230] (Nettle J) and [253], [329], [352]–[353], [358] (Gordon J).

However, Gageler J drew attention to the peculiar facts of the case in describing the *Petroleum (Submerged Lands) Act 1967* (Cth) as 'legislation creating and extending exclusive rights to explore for petroleum in an area of the continental shelf which at the time of creation and extension of those rights was subject to competing claims of sovereign rights in international law'.[97]

Significantly, the *Offshore Petroleum and Greenhouse Gas Storage Act 2006* (Cth) recognises the possibility that the exercise of broad discretionary powers that it confers on government officers and agencies could result in an acquisition of property from a person. In that event the Act makes the Commonwealth liable to pay a reasonable amount of compensation to that person,[98] to protect the Act from constitutional challenge.

The Constitutions of the Australian States do not impose any comparable limitation upon the powers of their legislatures to acquire property without just terms. Nevertheless, Australian courts do require State legislatures to employ clear and unequivocal language in acquiring property without any or adequate compensation. This requirement is an aspect of a long-established presumption of interpretation, derived from the principle of legality,[99] that statutes 'do not amend the common law to derogate from important rights enjoyed under that law, except by provisions expressed in clear language'.[100] Nevertheless, as previously noted, instances abound of acquisition of natural resources by State legislation without any or adequate compensation of previous proprietors of those resources.[101]

V. CONCLUSION

The Australian approach to disposal of GHG by underground storage in geological formations is derived from the principles and practices that have evolved since the nineteenth century for the management of public lands and natural resources such as minerals and petroleum therein. This approach treats geological formations and their storage space as underground natural resources.

The first principle is that the authority and responsibility for management and control of land and natural resources are vested in the States and the Northern Territory. This principle spawns various practices designed to retain public proprietorship of natural resources, including reservation of title to natural resources from grants of freehold tenure to land, expropriation of private title to natural resources, imposition of a depth limitation on grants of freehold tenure and, ultimately, reliance upon statutory titles granted for specified purposes rather than freehold tenure to land.

---

[97] ibid [68].
[98] *Offshore Petroleum and Greenhouse Gas Storage Act 2006* (Cth), s 780.
[99] B Chen, 'The Principle of Legality: Issues of Rationale and Application' (2015) 41 *Monash University Law Review* 329.
[100] *Durham Holdings Pty Limited v New South Wales* (2001) 205 CLR 399, 414; [2001] HCA 7. See also *The Commonwealth v Hazeldell Ltd* (1918) 25 CLR 552, 563; [1918] HCA 75.
[101] Section II.

The second principle is that, despite public proprietorship of land and natural resources, private enterprise usually undertakes exploration and exploitation pursuant to legislative regimes or government agreements ratified by legislation. This principle underlies the establishment of an ever-growing number of distinct legal regimes designed for particular resources such as minerals, petroleum, geothermal energy and storage reservoirs, or for specified projects in the case of government agreements, within a State or Territory.

The third principle is that these legislative regimes and government agreements provide for the grant of statutory titles, conferring substantial rights and imposing substantial obligations, prescribing the legal relationship between the State or Territory and the holders of the titles. The practice gives rein to the ingenuity of the framers of these regimes and agreements in the design of a plethora of particular illustrations of that relationship, but it offers little consistency in or clarification of its nature.

This approach to disposal of GHG by underground storage in geological formations rests precariously on the uncharted divide between public and private law. Questions of land tenure, title to underground resources and property arise together with matters of constitutional doctrine and statutory interpretation. None can be resolved in isolation.

13

Transportation of Carbon Dioxide in the European Union: Some Legal Issues

MARTHA M ROGGENKAMP[*]

I. INTRODUCTION

CARBON CAPTURE AND STORAGE (CCS) is a relatively new technology, aimed at combating climate change while continuing to use fossil fuels. As part of its climate policy, the European Union (EU) aims to reduce carbon dioxide (CO_2) emissions by 2020 by at least 20 per cent based on 1990 levels.[1] In this process, CCS is considered as a transitional instrument, as it limits the emission of CO_2 but not the use of fossil fuels. It may be used until other reliable means of clean energy can be applied on a larger scale.

A regulatory framework for CCS came into place in the EU following the entry into force of Council Directive 2009/31/EC (the CCS Directive) in June 2009.[2] The CCS Directive governs the geological storage of CO_2. As a result, each Member State may individually decide whether it wishes to regulate permanent storage of captured CO_2 in subsoil reservoirs. In practice, a Member State's decision will depend on the availability of suitable sites like depleted oil and/or gas fields and aquifers. Since some Member States may not have sufficient suitable sites within their territory, the CCS Directive also provides for cross-border CCS, in which an emitter in one Member State should have the opportunity to inject and store CO_2 in another Member State. Obviously, the concept of cross-border CCS is in line with the general principles of free movement of goods, services and capital in EU law.

---

[*] This chapter is a slightly amended and updated version of the chapter 'CO_2 Transportation in the European Union: Can the Regulation of CO_2 Pipelines Benefit from the Experiences of the Energy Sector?' by Martha M Roggenkamp and Avelien Haan-Kamminga in the 1st edn of this volume.

[1] The EU Council agreed to these targets in a Council Meeting of 8–9 March 2007, Presidency Conclusions presented on 2 May 2007, 7224/1/07 REV 1.

[2] Council Directive 2009/31/EC of 23 April 2009 on the geological storage of CO_2, [2009] OJ L140/114 (CCS Directive). See M Doppelhammer, 'The CCS Directive, its Implementation and the Co-financing of CCS and RES Demonstration Projects Under the Emissions Trading System (NER 300 Process)' in I Havercroft, R Macrory and RB Stewart (eds), *Carbon Capture and Storage: Emerging Legal and Regulatory Issues* (Oxford, Hart Publishing, 2011) ch 6, for a detailed discussion of the Directive.

Given that most emitters are located in industrial areas, and suitable storage locations are often situated in remote areas, both onshore and offshore, the process of CCS will require the transportation of the captured CO_2 to an underground storage facility. It will thus usually involve the following three stages: capture, transport and storage. In practice, several means of transportation can be applied. Although not explicitly stated, the focus of the CCS Directive seems to be transportation through subsoil pipelines. Sometimes it may be possible to use existing pipelines to transport CO_2, but it is equally likely that new pipelines will need to be constructed as part of a specific CCS project. In general, this mode of transportation is considered to be relatively safe and well suited to transporting large quantities of CO_2. However, due to the steadily increasing public opposition towards onshore storage of CO_2, there seems to be a general trend to consider CO_2 storage offshore, and subsequently attention is now also on the possibility to transport CO_2 by ship.[3]

This chapter will examine both means of transportation. When doing so, one should keep in mind that capturing and transporting CO_2 is not a new phenomenon. The soft drinks and agricultural sector, for example, already utilise CO_2, which is transported by lorry and subsoil pipelines.[4] By contrast, so far the development of CCS in the EU has been rather slow, and therefore the analysis presented below is still theoretical in scope. After discussing CO_2 transport via pipelines, the focus will turn to CO_2 transport by ship and how the regime governing Trans-European Networks may promote the development of CO_2 transport infrastructure in the EU.

II. TRANSPORTING CO_2 VIA PIPELINES

A. Qualifying CO_2 Pipelines

The CCS Directive contains few provisions on the role of (piped) transportation. The relevant provisions in the Directive focus on the composition of the CO_2 stream, the pipeline access regime, and the application of Directive 85/337/EEC (as amended) (the EIA Directive)[5] to transport and storage.[6] Due to the lack of regulatory guidance at the EU level, Member States are free to govern (i) the construction and siting of pipelines, (ii) the safety of pipelines and (iii) the use of pipelines, and this may lead to a variety of different national solutions.

Given the fact that CO_2 is a gaseous substance and can be transported via pipelines, it seems obvious to compare piped transportation of CO_2 with that of natural

---

[3] Pipelines are the cheapest option for large volumes, greater distances and a longer time-frame, whilst ships are the cheapest alternative for long distance, small volumes and short-term projects. Therefore, transport by ship might be feasible for smaller demonstration projects.

[4] Cf the Shell refinery in Rotterdam, where CO_2 is captured and transported by road to a range of industrial consumers, including the soft drinks industry.

[5] Council Directive 85/337/EEC of 27 June 1985 on the assessment of the effects of certain public and private projects on the environment [1985] OJ L175/40, as amended by Directive 97/11/EC of 3 March 1997 [1997] OJ L73/5 and Directive 2003/35/EC of 26 May 2003 [2003] OJ L156/17.

[6] Arts 12, 21 and 31 of the CCS Directive, n 3 above.

gas, specifically because both pipelines will be made of steel and that in order to avoid pipeline corrosion the captured CO_2 also needs to be dried before it is injected into the pipeline. It must also be compressed in order to reduce the volume that needs to be transported, and to facilitate its movement in the pipeline.[7] The gas sector, however, usually distinguishes between several types of pipelines: upstream, transportation and distribution. The qualification depends on the position of the pipeline in the energy chain and on the pressure under which the commodity is transported. The energy chain includes all activities ranging from the production of energy to the supply of energy to final consumers. In the case of natural gas, the energy chain begins with a reservoir from which natural gas is produced and transported through a so-called 'upstream' pipeline.[8] The upstream pipeline is connected to a 'transmission' pipeline, which in turn is connected to several 'distribution' pipelines. Apart from this, there may be dedicated pipelines, also known as 'direct' pipelines, connecting a limited number of producers with a limited number of consumers.[9] Each category of these pipelines may be subject to a different set of rules applying to their construction and/or use. These rules focus in particular on the need to create independent network operators (via unbundling procedures) and rules on third-party access to existing networks.

In the case of CCS, a CO_2 pipeline will connect a producer of CO_2 (an emitter) with a consumer/receiver of CO_2 (a subsoil storage facility). These storage facilities are often depleted oil and/or gas fields. In the case of storage in a depleted field, it is possible that abandoned pipelines are still present, and the existing infrastructure can be used.[10] However, if CO_2 is injected in a producing field, or if pipelines have been removed, it will be necessary to construct new pipelines. Considering that a pipeline is directly linked to the reservoir, it may be argued that CO_2 pipelines should be considered as some sort of 'reversed' upstream pipeline system. Instead of the reservoir being the starting point of the chain, ie the 'producer', it is now the terminus point of the chain, ie the 'consumer' or 'receiver'.

Although the terminus point of the pipeline—the reservoir—is known, it is less clear where the pipeline begins. It may be that the pipeline is directly connected to the emitter. In that case, the pipeline can also be considered as some sort of direct or dedicated (pipe)line. It may also be that several emitters are connected to the same pipeline. Does the assumption that a CO_2 pipeline should be considered a 'reversed'

---

[7] The CO_2 will then be pressured above 74 bar and transported at temperatures higher than 31°C. At that stage, it will become a substance somewhere between a gas and a liquid (supercritical phase). When stored, however, CO_2 will take the form of a high-pressured liquid (dense phase).

[8] Art 2(2) of Council Directive 2009/72/EC of 13 July 2009 concerning common rules for the internal market in natural gas and repealing Directive 2003/55/EC [2009] OJ L211/94, 101, defines an upstream pipeline network as 'any pipeline or network of pipelines operated and/or constructed as part of an oil or gas production project, or used to convey natural gas from one or more such projects to a processing plant or terminal or final coastal landing terminal'.

[9] Examples of direct lines can also be found in the oil and petrochemical industry, as well as the electricity sector.

[10] See also C Cronenberg et al, *Potential for CO_2 storage in depleted gas fields at the Dutch Continental Shelf, Phase 2: Costs of transport and storage* (Netherlands Oil and Gas Exploration and Production Association, 2009).

upstream pipeline change if several 'emitters', or 'consumers/fields', are connected to the pipeline? Not necessarily. In the upstream petroleum sector, it is common practice that several producers/fields are connected to one (sometimes very long) upstream pipeline. Although the injection of CO_2 is the opposite of the extraction of gas, they share the characteristic of being only one activity, or one-way traffic. This might indicate, again, that CO_2 pipelines can be considered as reversed upstream pipelines.

It follows from the above that there are sufficient arguments and reasons to treat CO_2 pipelines within the framework of CCS as some sort of reversed upstream pipeline. Consequently, these CO_2 pipelines could be governed by national petroleum or mining law, which also may govern the underground storage of CO_2.[11] This has certain advantages. First and foremost, it would provide that the oil and gas upstream regulatory and safety regime also applies to CO_2 pipelines. This is a regime which has proven itself effective, and already has competent regulatory authorities in place. Apart from this, it would also mean that the regulatory regimes applying to the use of the upstream pipelines could be applied. These consequences will be discussed in section II.B.

B. Health, Safety and the Environment

i. Health and Safety Regulation

The public acceptance of CCS is closely linked to the safe and environmentally friendly operations for both the transportation and storage of CO_2. Unsafe transportation can result in damaged pipelines, leading to leakages that harm the environment, health and safety, and the climate in general. Member States intending to apply CCS thus need to take into account the need to guarantee, as far as possible, that the activities are carried out in a safe manner. As the CCS Directive does not provide any clear instructions, each Member State may choose the relevant health and safety measures. National legal choices may differ between the application of national safety laws and/or pipelines laws (if any) to the construction and use of CO_2 pipelines. It may also be that no specific law applies, and consideration must be given to a large number of different, more general laws and regulations. Consideration would be based on which permit may be required, such as a building/construction permit or a spatial planning/zoning permit. These permits may again contain a variety of safety requirements.

---

[11] In The Netherlands, the Mining Code of 2003 provides for a special subsoil storage regime, which also applies to CO_2 storage. See MM Roggenkamp, 'Regulating Underground Storage of CO_2' in MM Roggenkamp and E Woerdman, *Legal Design of Carbon Capture and Storage—Developments in the Netherlands from an International and EU Perspective* (Antwerp, Intersentia, 2009). Several other EU Member States (eg, France, Denmark and Italy) also have a licensing regime under the national Mining, Petroleum or Subsoil Law. See, for these storage regimes, MM Roggenkamp et al, *Energy Law in Europe: National, EU and International Regulation*, 2nd edn (Oxford, Oxford University Press, 2007).

When classifying CO_2 pipelines as upstream pipelines, a comprehensive safety regime could be in place through the application of the existing upstream health and safety regimes, although it can be expected that certain amendments need to be made to facilitate CO_2 transportation. Hence, the operators of these pipelines could be made subject to health and safety regulations under the national (onshore and/or offshore) petroleum or mining laws. The safety guidelines and procedures would include requirements regarding the design, maintenance and integrity of the pipeline, the construction and operation of the pipeline, arrangements for incidents and emergencies, prevention of damage to pipelines and many other considerations.[12] Moreover, the construction and operation of CO_2 pipelines would also be subject to supervision by the national health and safety authority.[13] The same competent authority would then be charged with monitoring the subsoil storage reservoir and the subsoil pipeline.

In conclusion, when classifying CO_2 pipelines as upstream pipelines, CO_2 storage and transportation could be subject to a single health and safety regime and supervised by the same health and safety authority. The application of one health and safety regime will result in more transparency and, thus, fewer risks of unsafe operations.

ii. Protecting the Environment

The CCS Directive provides slightly more guidance concerning the need to protect the environment, as it requires operators to apply for an environmental impact assessment (EIA) covering the construction and operation of CO_2 pipelines.[14] The EIA shall identify, describe and assess the direct and indirect effects of a project on human beings, fauna and flora; soil, water, air, climate and the landscape; material assets and cultural heritage; and the interaction between these factors. This requirement, based on the EIA Directive, will be implemented in national legislation and procedures. These national requirements may go beyond the provisions in the EIA Directive.[15] Onshore pipeline development will usually entail a variety of licensing requirements, building permits, land use agreements, and, in general, provisions regarding ownership rights and pipeline registration.[16]

It also means that the public will be involved in the process of granting permits for the construction of pipelines. The EIA Directive requires that members of the public affected by, or having an interest in, the construction and use of the pipelines are

---

[12] See, eg, the UK Pipelines Safety Regulations 1996 (SI 1996/825) and the Dutch Mining Decree and Mining Regulations of 2003.
[13] In the UK, the Health and Safety Executive is charged with the supervision of upstream health and safety. In The Netherlands, it is the State Supervision of Mines.
[14] CCS Directive, n 3 above, recital 17, Art 31.
[15] The EIA Directive, n 5 above.
[16] National law may, eg, provide for the establishment of a pipeline register so as to avoid any construction activities taking place near the registered pipeline and so that the pipeline is protected from damage as a result of these activities. See also DA Lubach, 'Pipelines Transporting CO_2 from a Public and Private Law Perspective' in Roggenkamp and Woerdman, n 11 above, 198.

informed and able to participate in the decision-making process. This might mean that when the public are opposed to the construction of a pipeline, their means of having access to justice (ie appeal procedures) may slow down the permitting process, as illustrated by the Dutch 'Barendrecht' case, where a storage permit has not been awarded due to strong opposition from the public and local authorities.[17] Although there is little experience with constructing and operating CO_2 pipelines, it is striking that the experience so far has not resulted in any dangerous situations or appeals. The conversion of an abandoned 85 km long oil pipeline owned by NPM to a CO_2 pipeline early in 2000 by a company called OCAP Trading BV (OCAP),[18] and the additional construction of some 130 km of pipelines to supply greenhouse growers with pure CO_2, have not led to any public debate or opposition. Given that this pipeline is located in the same area, the difference in response to both projects is noticeable.

The CCS Directive clearly recognises the need to protect the environment from damage resulting from CCS. It provides for an amendment of the Environmental Liability Directive (ELD)[19] to ensure that adequate provisions are made regarding liability for damage to the environment (ie to protected species and natural habitats, water and land) resulting from any failure of permanent containment of CO_2. Does this amendment to the ELD also affect the transportation of CO_2? In principle, only the *storage* of CO_2 is covered by the ELD under the CCS Directive, thereby guaranteeing compensation by the operator for environmental damage on the basis of a regime of strict liability.[20] However, this strict liability applies only to subsoil storage of CO_2. Transport is not included in Annex III of the ELD.[21] Hence, a fault-based system of liability applies to damage resulting from CO_2 transportation, as a result of which only damage to protected species and natural habitats will be compensated. Since the ELD restricts the types of damage to be compensated, (pipeline) operators are liable only if the damage was caused by fault on the side of the operator.

Apart from applicable EU law, account needs to be taken of national law governing civil law claims for harm to persons and property resulting from damage to CO_2 pipelines. The national compensation or remediation obligations that result

---

[17] The 'Barendrecht' case concerns the storage of CO_2 captured at a Shell refinery in depleted gas-fields operated by Shell and located under (part of) the city of Barendrecht. The Government may limit the number of possible appeals by using the regulating of the coordination of large projects (*Rijkscoördinatieregeling*) based on para 3.6.3 of the Spatial Planning Act. See also CFJ Feenstra et al, *What happened in Barendrecht? Case study on the planned onshore carbon dioxide storage in Barendrecht, the Netherlands* (Energy Research Centre of the Netherlands and Global Carbon Capture Storage Institute, 2010) at www.globalccsinstitute.com/publications/what-happened-barendrecht.

[18] OCAP is an abbreviation of Organic Carbon Dioxide for Assimilation of Plants. OCAP Trading BV is a joint venture between the gas supplier Linde Gas Benelux BV and the contractor Volker Wessels.

[19] Council Directive 2004/35/EC of 21 April 2004 on environmental liability with regard to the prevention and remedying of environmental damage [2004] OJ L143/56.

[20] Art 34 of the CCS Directive amending Directive 2004/35. If there is a significant adverse effect in the environment, or if there are measurable adverse effects for humans, the Directive provides for the strict liability of the operator. Re environmental liability, see also JH Jans and HB Vedder, *European Environmental Law* (Groningen, Europa Law Publishing, 2007) 341.

[21] Only in the unlikely situation that the CO_2 stream is contaminated with substances that can be qualified as dangerous, toxic or waste, may transport fall under the strict liability regime.

from such claims may include costs such as reinstatement of habitats and species, compensation payments for victims of bodily injury or losses in property values, and business interruption claims where economic activity has been disrupted.

iii. Leakages and Impact on Climate Change

As the purpose of the CCS Directive is to avoid CO_2 emissions through permanent storage, any leakage of CO_2 should be avoided. This also applies to leakages from pipelines transporting the captured CO_2 to the storage sites. This is achieved first and foremost by safeguarding the external and internal safety of the pipeline. In addition to this, and due to the close link with the EU climate policy, any leakages need to be compensated by submitting sufficient emissions allowances.[22] The CCS Directive therefore amends the EU Emissions Trading System Directive (EU ETS) to state that stored CO_2 is not considered to have been 'emitted', and also introduces a regime of corrective measures in case of leakages. In addition, the CCS Directive brings the transport of CO_2 under the EU ETS as of 2013. Under the amended EU ETS, operators of CO_2 pipelines need to apply for an emissions permit.[23]

Article 4 of the EU ETS requires Member States to ensure that all installations listed in Annex I (including transport facilities) have a permit authorising them to emit greenhouse gases (GHGs). As a result, the same regime applies to pipeline operators, storage operators and the CO_2 emitters. Each of them needs an emission permit stating which activities are to be undertaken, the materials used, and a methodology for the monitoring and reporting of emissions. Member States are required to verify the annual emissions reports submitted by the facility, in accordance with the criteria contained in Annex V of the Directive.[24] The emissions report is to be submitted to the national regulatory (emissions) authority by 31 March each year, and the holder of the permit then surrenders sufficient allowances to meet its verified emissions before 30 April.

Obviously, neither the pipeline operator nor the storage operator aims to emit large quantities of CO_2. Emissions during the transportation of CO_2 are either fugitive emissions—emissions from venting—or the result of potential leakages from the pipeline. Since fugitive emissions are usually low, and leakages can easily be detected and repaired, a system of input and output measurement seems sensible, although measurement along the length of the pipeline does create more accuracy.[25]

---

[22] KJ De Graaf and JH Jans, 'Environmental Law and CCS in the EU and the Impact on the Netherlands' in Roggenkamp and Woerdman, n 11 above, 157–81.

[23] The amount of transported CO_2 determines whether or not an operator of a pipeline might be excluded from the ETS system. Based on Art 27 of the ETS Directive, small emitters do not have to apply for a permit. Considering the amount of CO_2 that is transported and the fugitive emissions rate estimated at 1.5%, an average pipeline will emit more than 25 kT CO_2 and will have to apply for the ETS permit. See, in the previous edition of this volume (Havercroft, Macrory and Stewart (eds), n 2 above), ch 8 (Bugge) for an analysis of state responsibility for leakages under public international law, and ch 5 (Nordhaus) for a discussion of various models for accounting for leakage being considered in the US.

[24] Such verification is to be carried out by an accredited verification body.

[25] S Wartmann, H Groenenberg and S Brockett, 'Monitoring and reporting of GHG emissions from CCS operations under the EU ETS' (2009) 1 *Energy Procedia* 4459.

The idea is that the amount of CO_2 is measured at the beginning and at the end of the pipeline. If these amounts are not equal, leakage has occurred, and the operator is obliged to buy emissions allowances which meet the level of CO_2 emissions.[26]

C. The Use of CO_2 Pipelines

i. Pipeline Owners and Users

The CCS Directive does not refer to the ownership of CO_2 pipelines. It is for Member States to decide whether these pipelines will be constructed and operated by the state, a state-owned company, private parties or a public-private partnership. In practice, we may see a variety of solutions, which may depend on previous experiences in Member States. In other words, the extent to which the current energy infrastructure is owned and operated by the state may also be decisive for choosing an ownership structure for CO_2 pipelines. Lower levels of government may also own and operate the energy infrastructure, as is the case regarding the transmission and/or distribution systems in, for example, The Netherlands or Denmark; alternatively, private parties may also own/operate the infrastructure, as is the case in Germany, or public-private parties, as in most offshore (upstream) pipelines.

In practice, the choice will also depend on (i) whether use will/can be made of existing infrastructure, (ii) the wish of the original owners (if any) to keep their shares in the pipeline, (iii) the guarantee of any profits on the transportation, and (iv) the risks concerning any liability for damages. In the case of new infrastructure, the costs of constructing and operating a CO_2 pipeline will be crucial, if not decisive. It is therefore possible that the national government will be involved in one way or another, either as a financial participant/shareholder in a new or existing pipeline, or as the party (exclusively) entitled to construct and operate CO_2 pipelines. It may also be that the above scenarios exist next to each other, depending on the location of the pipeline.

The CCS Directive leaves all options open. However, the choices made by national legislators will influence the way in which the pipeline is used. The case in which several CO_2 emitters have a share in a storage facility and a CO_2 pipeline differs from the situation where the state or another party exploits the pipeline. In the first situation, the emitters/shareholders will aim to use their share in the pipeline for their own needs. In the latter situation, the pipeline will be organised as a public facility, to be used by anyone who requests access. Although the CCS Directive does not contain any explicit provision on ownership and pipeline exploitation, it does recognise that pipelines and storage facilities may hold a monopoly position, and therefore some sort of access regime should be applied.

---

[26] Commission Decision of 8 June 2010 amending Decision 2007/589/EC as regards the inclusion of monitoring and reporting guidelines for greenhouse gas emissions from the capture, transport and geological storage of carbon dioxide [2010] OJ L155/34.

ii. Third-party Access Regime

Article 21 of the CCS Directive obliges pipeline operators/owners to negotiate access with any interested party on the basis of rules governing transparent and non-discriminatory access. A refusal of access may be based on:

— the lack of available capacity;
— incompatibility of technical specifications;
— duly substantiated reasonable needs of the owner; or
— CO_2 reduction obligations to be met through CCS.

This provision shows a striking resemblance with the regime under the EU Gas Directive governing third-party access to upstream pipelines[27] and the US Courts' Essential Facility Doctrine as applied by the European Commission and the European Court of Justice in cases of arbitrary or discriminatory refusal of access to infrastructures. It entails that if a party depends on the use of a specific facility and a parallel infrastructure is not economically viable (as in the case of a natural monopoly), Member States shall take the necessary measures to ensure that said party can obtain access to the facility (ie, an upstream pipeline).[28] The owner/operator of the facility/pipeline and the third party seeking access are thus required to negotiate access to the infrastructure, and a refusal of access is limited to:

— a lack of available capacity;
— incompatibility of technical specifications;
— the duly substantiated reasonable needs of the owner; and
— payment of adequate compensation to the owners/operator.

The objective of the regime is to identify whether the facility (infrastructure) is essential to the activities of the potential competitor, and whether a denial of such access constitutes an abuse of a dominant position. If so, general EU competition law applies.

Although the essential facility doctrine is of little relevance to the downstream transmission and distribution systems, as these systems are subject to a regime of regulated third-party access, the EU legislator apparently assumed it to be relevant in relation to access to upstream gas pipelines and CO_2 pipelines.[29] It is nonetheless for Member States to decide whether they wish to follow the requirements of the CCS Directive (minimum harmonisation) or go beyond these provisions and include stricter access provisions, ie apply a regime of regulated Third Party Access (rTPA), and thus the appointment of an ex ante regulator (national regulatory authority) who is charged with setting or approving the conditions and tariffs so that any

---

[27] The provision was introduced in the first Gas Directive of 1998 and has remained unchanged in the recent Council Directive 2009/73/EC of 13 July 2009 concerning common rules for the internal market in natural gas and repealing Directive 2003/55/EC [2009] OJ L211/94.
[28] J Faull and A Nikpay, *The EC Law of Competition* (Oxford, Oxford University Press, 2007) 353 ff; 1457 ff.
[29] See also MM Roggenkamp, 'The concept of third-party access applied to CCS' in Roggenkamp and Woerdman, n 11 above, 273.

interested third party knows beforehand the financial and technical conditions under which the commodity can be transported through the grid.

A reason for opting for such a regime could be the wish to avoid long periods of negotiations on tariffs and conditions. In a situation of many interested parties seeking pipeline access, it could be beneficial to introduce a system of ex ante access regulation, as this would minimise transaction costs and provide certainty. However, in contrast to the natural gas sector, with CCS there is less need to speed up negotiations because there is no supply security involved. Moreover, there will be relatively few parties interested in negotiating access to CO_2 infrastructure—both pipelines and storage facilities—because the parties interested in CCS usually involve some major industries qualifying as point emitters. In The Netherlands, for example, there are some 30 point emitters.[30] Introducing a system of regulated access would lead to high administrative costs, which is not in the interests of the few parties that may be interested in CCS and transporting CO_2. Furthermore, CCS is used as a temporary solution to reduce emissions until the dependency on, and use of, fossil fuels has decreased. Thus, creating a competitive market is not the main objective of regulating access to the CO_2 pipelines.

It can thus be concluded that there are no solid arguments to introduce a system of regulated access to CO_2 pipelines. There is limited need for such a regime, as there is no supply security at the end of the pipe as in the case of natural gas. In addition, any agreement on access will be part of a broader investment decision on CCS, which will nevertheless be time-consuming. Moreover, opting for a regime of negotiated access does not limit the possibility for Member States to further regulate the procedures and timing for such negotiations.[31]

iii. National Developments

When considering the overall situation in the EU, the picture is diverse. Whereas some Member States have decided not to allow CO_2 storage on their territory,[32] others have introduced restrictions such as restraints as regards the type of projects (demonstration projects only), the volumes to be stored or the location of the project (offshore only).[33] Other Member States (Belgium and Germany) expect that CO_2 will be exported and stored elsewhere.[34] The Netherlands, the UK and Norway

---

[30] These 30 point emitters involve 12 industrial installations such as refineries (73% of all industrial CO_2) and 20 installations in the electricity-generating sector (81% of all emissions in this sector). See *Advies van de Werkgroep Schoon Fossiel*, 'Platform Nieuw Gas (Platform New Gas)' (*Advies van de Werkgroep Schoon Fossiel*, 2007) 19.

[31] See, eg, the UK Infrastructure Code of Practice.

[32] These include Austria, Brussels Capital Region of Belgium, Estonia, Finland Ireland, Latvia, Luxembourg and Slovenia.

[33] The Czech Republic prohibits CCS activities until 2020. Germany sets the maximum volume of stored CO_2 per storage site at 1.3 million tonnes per year, and the total amount for Germany at 4 million tonnes of CO_2 per year. Poland only allows CCS in the framework of 'demonstration projects'.

[34] Information on national developments can be found in MM Roggenkamp et al, *Energy Law in Europe: National, EU and International Regulation*, 3rd edn (Oxford, Oxford University Press, 2016) and Milieu Law and Policy Consulting, 'Identification of future CO_2 infrastructure networks' (final report, 2015) at publications.europa.eu/en/publication-detail/-/publication/ddafc491-f70c-11e5-b618-01aa75ed71a1/language-en.

primarily focus on offshore storage, which can be the result either of an absence of onshore storage potential (Norway) or of public opposition (The Netherlands). Denmark has decided to postpone CCS until the experience from CCS projects in other Member States is available, unless the aim is to improve enhanced oil recovery (EOR) from Danish oilfields. Experience can be found in France, as Total has been running a CCS pilot project since January 2010, 'the Lacq Pilot', which entails that CO_2 is transported from the Lacq plant to the Rousse fields via a 27 km long pipeline formerly used to carry gas extracted from the Rousse fields to the Lacq plant. This pipeline can be considered as a reversed upstream pipeline, but it is limited to one user and no third parties make use of this dedicated pipeline.

The extent to which Member States allow for CO_2 storage has obviously a direct impact on the development and use of CO_2 transport networks. In general, Member States (and Norway) have implemented similar access provisions as provided for by the CCS Directive. This means that use is made of a rudimentary regime of negotiated third-party access. In order to facilitate access negotiations, several Member States require pipeline operators to make publicly available information about conditions and technical modalities for access,[35] or establish further requirements as regards the negotiations procedure.[36] If the parties do not manage to reach an agreement, several Member States provide that the competent authority may take a decision on its own merits. In France, an access agreement is also subject to an authorisation by the Minister of Environment, which is deemed to be granted if the administration has not responded within two months. In Norway, all agreements for CO_2 transport must be submitted for approval to the Ministry, which also is entitled to set transport tariffs and conditions.[37] In case of a refusal to provide access, Greek and Spanish laws require operators to inform the competent authority about the reasons for refusal. In such situation, the competent authority in Slovakia and Norway may still take a decision to grant third-party access.

D. Other CO_2 Pipelines

In the preceding sections the focus has been on carbon transport's being part of the CCS chain. In practice CO_2 can also be captured and used for different purposes and in different contexts, such as the soft drinks and horticulture industries. For example, in The Netherlands, the company OCAP[38] has operated, since 2005, an

---

[35] In Estonia such information has to be published on the operators' websites, and in Belgium such information must be published in the *Official Journal*. Other states have different requirements (eg, France and Denmark), although generally information must be updated regularly.

[36] In Belgium interested parties must submit a request with all relevant data to the operator, via registered mail. Similarly, in Denmark the operator has to notify the applicant of the receipt of the request for access and about whether or not the request can be accommodated. Negotiations must be completed within four months, unless another time period is agreed upon between the parties.

[37] The Ministry may alter the conditions that have been approved or determined, in order to ensure that CO_2 transport and storage is carried out with due consideration for the resources and that the owner of the facility will receive a reasonable profit, balancing investments and risk.

[38] See n 18 above.

extensive pipeline system through which it supplies approximately 160,000 kg of pure CO_2 per hour to 550 greenhouse growers in the area between Rotterdam and Amsterdam.[39] OCAP purchases the CO_2 from Shell Per+ at the refinery gate.[40] What kind of regulatory regime applies to this pipeline system, and how is it operated in comparison to those pipelines that are part of a CCS project?

A difference between the OCAP pipeline and pipelines needed for large-scale CCS is, inter alia, that the pressure used for transporting CO_2 to horticulturalists is considerably lower than the pressure needed for CCS. However, this is only a matter of economics, ie the amount of energy it takes to compress the CO_2 in combination with the size of the pipeline needed for transport—the more compressed it is, the more energy is needed, but it results in a cheaper pipeline construction. More importantly, however, is that these pipelines have a different position in the energy chain, as there are consumers of CO_2 at the terminus point of the pipeline. When end consumers, like greenhouse growers, are connected to the terminus point of the pipeline, it is more problematic to qualify these pipelines as an upstream pipeline. These pipelines may therefore be considered as direct lines instead. This qualification may also apply to CO_2 pipelines like OCAP.

A complicating factor is that the EU ETS regime does not apply to other CO_2 pipelines, such as pipelines not used within the framework of CCS. Carbon dioxide transported for purposes other than permanent storage does not count as a prevented emission under the EU ETS.[41] Sometimes pipelines may transport CO_2 to end consumers as well as to subsoil storage facilities, as was envisaged in the Barendrecht case (see section II.B) and the potential Rotterdam Nucleus Project (see section V.B). What kind of regime applies to such a dual-purpose pipeline? The OCAP pipeline system could serve several CO_2 suppliers, as well as several storage sites and CO_2 consumers. But only part of the CO_2 stream in the OCAP pipeline system would be subject to the EU ETS, and in cases of permanent storage counts as 'not emitted'. An emission permit will at least be required for the part of the pipeline connected to the subsoil storage facility. However, once the EU ETS applies to the transportation network, a complicated situation occurs when other CO_2 (non-EU ETS) is also transported through that pipeline, as it will be difficult to measure the input and output of CO_2 relevant for EU ETS separately. In case of such a dual-purpose pipeline, it may be difficult to provide the level of accuracy demanded by the EU ETS monitoring and reporting guidelines, while simultaneously meeting the business expectations of the other (non-EU ETS) users of the pipeline.

---

[39] The pipeline system consists of two parts: (i) an existing 85 km long pipeline running from the Rotterdam industrial area to the port of Amsterdam and passing a number of major greenhouse horticultural areas; and (ii) a new distribution network of 130 km, which has been connected to this main transportation pipeline. In addition, 500 delivery/metering stations (ie, horticulturists) are connected to this grid.

[40] The CO_2 is released during the production of hydrogen at the Shell PER+ refinery in the Botlek area and supplied to horticulturists, who save about 95 million cubic metres of natural gas per year (and increase the horticulturists' competitive position) and reduce some 170,000 tonnes of CO_2 emissions per year. The supply agreements are based on an all-in regime, ie no distinction between the supply and transportation of CO_2.

[41] De Graaf and Jans, n 22 above, 163.

III. TRANSPORT OF CO$_2$ BY SHIP

A. Qualifying CO$_2$ Transport by Ship

The current focus on offshore carbon storage has also led to a gradual shift towards another type of transportation than pipelines. The transport of CO$_2$ to the storage facility (underground reservoir or aquifer) can also be done by ship, in particular as this means of transportation may be economically more attractive if CO$_2$ has to be moved over large distances. An example is the Green Hydrogen Project, which would involve CO$_2$ capture by Air Liquide and the transportation of the captured CO$_2$ from the Maasvlakte by ship to the Danish Continental Shelf for permanent storage in some mature oilfields operated by MaerskOil, in combination with EOR. So far, the project has not been able to attract sufficient funding.[42]

In order to transport large volumes of CO$_2$ by ship the gas needs to be compressed, ie liquefied to 7 bar (–50°C). The entire process is similar to transporting LPG (liquefied petroleum gas) or LNG (liquefied natural gas) by ship. As in the case of shipping LPG and LNG, the pressure in the tank will rise during transport due to heat transfer from the environment through the wall of the cargo tank. Although it is not dangerous to discharge CO$_2$ boil-off gas together with the exhaust gas from the ship's engines, it is of course not in line with the objectives of CCS. Zero CO$_2$ emissions can nevertheless be achieved by using a refrigeration unit to capture and liquefy boil-off and exhaust CO$_2$; this will, however, entail additional construction costs. Given the similarities between the transport by ship of LPG, LNG and CO$_2$, this section will briefly examine the rules applying to the transport of LNG and LPG, as these rules most likely will also apply to shipped transportation of CO$_2$. The focus will be on the rules that are relevant for safety, cross-border transport and offshore liability.

B. Offshore Safety and the Environment

i. Safety Regulation

The safety of ships and their cargo can be endangered as a result of collision, wrecking, stranding and fire. Some of these failures can be avoided by careful navigation along prescribed routes, and by prescribing severe standards of construction and operation. Collision risks (ruptured tanks) can be minimised by making certain that the high standards of construction and operation applied to LPG and LNG are also applied to ships transporting CO$_2$.

The most important treaty governing the safety of merchant ships is the International Convention for the Safety of Life at Sea (SOLAS Convention). The current

---

[42] See Zero Emission Resource Organisation, 'Air Liquide Green Hydrogen Project', at www.zeroco$_2$.no/projects/air-liquide-green-hydrogen-project.

version of the treaty dates from 1974, but it has been amended several times since.[43] The SOLAS Convention requires signatories to ensure that ships sailing under their jurisdiction (flag-state jurisdiction) comply with minimum safety standards as regards their construction, equipment and operation, including the transport of dangerous goods. Consequently, contracting states are required to apply the International Maritime Dangerous Goods (IMDG) Code developed by the International Maritime Organisation (IMO).[44] Moreover, the construction and equipment of ships carrying liquefied gases in bulk and gas carriers need to comply with the requirements of the International Gas Carrier Code (IGC Code), which was adopted in 1983 and most recently amended in 2016.[45] The IGC Code applies to ships, regardless of their size, engaged in the carriage of liquefied gases having a vapor pressure exceeding 2.8 bar and a temperature of 37.8°C, as well as other products specified in the Code. In 2006 the Maritime Safety Committee added CO_2 to the list of specified products,[46] and the construction and operation of ships transporting CO_2 will thus need to be subject to these rules.[47]

The aim of the Code is to provide an international standard for the safe carriage by sea in bulk of liquefied gases by prescribing the design and construction standards of ships involved in such carriage, and the equipment they should carry so as to minimise the risk to the ship, to its crew and to the environment, having regard to the nature of the products involved. In order to demonstrate compliance with the requirements of the IGC Code, ships must have been awarded the International Certificate of Fitness for the Carriage of Liquefied Gases in Bulk.[48] For this purpose the ship will be regularly examined. Before being taken into service, gas tank ships will be subject to an extensive inspection process, including a full inspection of the construction, equipment, installations, facilities and materials of the ship, in so far as they are covered by the Code. To maintain the certificate, all gas tank ships are subject to a small annual inspection and to a more elaborate inspection every five years. If an inspector concludes that the ship or its equipment does not meet the requirements of the certificate, or that the ship is not seaworthy, the ship owner needs to take all necessary measures to meet the requirements set. If not, the certificate is revoked and the local authorities informed.[49]

---

[43] International Convention for the Safety of Life at Sea, 1974 (with annex and final act of the International Conference on Safety of Life at Sea, 1974) (concluded at London on 1 November 1974) 1184 UNTS 18961. The Solas Convention was adopted on 1 November 1974 and entered into force on 25 May 1980. In March 2016, SOLAS 1974 had 162 contracting states, which flag about 99% of merchant ships around the world in terms of gross tonnage.

[44] Solas Convention, n 43 above, ch VII.

[45] International Maritime Organisation, 'IGC Code' (2016), at www.imo.org/en/ourwork/safety/cargoes/cargoesinbulk/pages/igc-code.aspx.

[46] International Maritime Organisation, 'Adoption of Amendments to the International Code for the Construction and Equipment of Ships carrying Liquified Gases in Bulk', Resolution MSC.220(82)(2006), Annex, para 11.

[47] The 2016 IGC Code will in principle also apply to floating storage regasification units. Less clear, however, is the status of floating production storage and offloading units.

[48] IGC Code, Art 1.5.1.1–1.5.4.1.

[49] See also HD Boekholt, 'Scheepstransport van CO_2 voor permanente opslag offshore: Veiligheid van schepen en aansprakelijkheid voor schade door uitstroom van gevaarlijke stoffen' (2013) 4 *Nederlands Tijdschrift voor Energierecht* 182.

ii. Leakages and Climate Protection Offshore

Carbon dioxide releases from the ship may be the result of discharge of CO_2 boil-off gas, or from collisions or other incidents offshore. It is assumed that such releases will not to have long-term environmental impacts and would be different from LNG spills, because liquid CO_2 in a tanker is not as cold as LNG but much denser. Its interactions with the sea would be complex as hydrates and ice might form, and temperature differences could induce strong currents. Some of the gas would dissolve in the sea, but some would be released to the atmosphere. If there were little wind and a temperature inversion, clouds of CO_2 might lead to asphyxiation and might stop the ship's engines. These risks can be minimised by careful planning of routes and by high standards of training and management.

As already discussed, the CCS Directive aims at capturing and permanently storing CO_2, and consequently introduces a regime of corrective measures in the event of leakages. The CCS Directive therefore brings the transport of CO_2 via pipelines under the EU ETS. Given the specific reference to piped transportation, the obligation in the EU ETS for a emissions permit does not apply to transport of CO_2 by ship. In the case of a leakage of CO_2 transported by ship during its passage to the permanent storage location, there is no legal obligation in place such that the emitted quantities need to be compensated via the purchase of an equal amount of emissions allowances. The transport of CO_2 by ship is thus treated differently from transport via pipelines and this is not in the spirit of the CCS Directive. Given the possibility that more CO_2 will be transported by ship, there is an apparent need to amend current legislation. The question, however, will be who will be the subject of such legislation, as ships do not necessarily sail under the flag of an EU jurisdiction. So far this has been one of the reasons why shipping in general is not included in the EU ETS.[50]

iii. Liability Offshore

As discussed in section II.B.ii, the CCS Directive provides for an amendment of the ELD in order to ensure that adequate provisions are made regarding liability for damage to the environment (ie, to protected species and natural habitats, water and land) resulting from any failure of permanent containment of CO_2.[51] Apart from the fact that transport is not listed in Annex III of the latter Directive, the ELD applies neither to environmental damage nor to any imminent threat of such damage arising from an incident in respect of which liability or compensation falls within the scope of any of the international conventions listed in its Annex IV. This includes the International Convention on Liability and Compensation for Damage in Connection

---

[50] See Annex I of Council Directive 2009/29/EC of 23 April 2009 amending Directive 2003/87/EC so as to improve and extend the greenhouse gas emission allowance trading scheme of the community [2009] OJ L140/63, which lists all categories of activities to which the Directive applies (and excludes ships). See also E Woerdman and MM Roggenkamp, *Essential EU Climate Law* (Cheltenham, Edward Elgar, 2015) 55.
[51] Council Directive 2004/35/EC of 21 April 2004 on environmental liability with regard to the prevention and remedying of environmental damage [2004] OJ L143/56.

with the Carriage of Hazardous and Noxious Substances by Sea (HNS Convention) of 3 May 1996 and the 2010 HNS Protocol.[52]

The HNS Convention aims at compensating for damage (loss of life or personal injury, loss of or damage to property outside the ship, loss or damage caused by contamination of the environment and costs of preventive measures) caused by spillage of hazardous and noxious substances during maritime transportation. Whether a substance is hazardous or noxious is determined by the IMO. Substances listed under International Maritime Dangerous Goods Code (and thus CO_2) are, for example, considered HNS. The HNS Convention establishes a two-tier system for compensation in the event of accidents at sea involving hazardous and noxious substances. Tier one will be covered by the ship owner's compulsory insurance. Depending on the gross tonnage, the ship owner will be able to limit his financial liability.[53] In cases where the insurance is insufficient, a second tier of compensation (with a maximum of 250 million SDR) will be paid from a special HNS fund. Companies that import hazardous and noxious substances in states party to the Convention will be required to contribute to this fund. Contributions are based on the amount of substances companies receive each year.

Until the HNS Convention enters into force, the owners of ships transporting CO_2 will be able to limit liability under the Convention on limitation of liability for maritime claims (the LLMC Convention).[54] This Convention is to a large extent similar to the HNS Convention as it (i) limits liability to a certain maximum amount per incident, depending on the tonnage of the ship (Article 3) and (ii) provides for a fund to be established through the deposit of a sum of money or a financial guarantee (Article 5). The compensation limits, however, are significantly lower than provided for by the HNS Convention.[55] Moreover, although the LLMC Convention provides for the establishment of a fund, this fund is not intended as a safety net but is used for direct payment if liability has been established. Ship owners have, as in the case of the HNS Convention, no right to limit their liability if there is evidence that they have caused the damage themselves intentionally or as a result of recklessness.

At the EU level, Council Directive 2009/20/EC on insurance of ship owners for maritime claims applies. The objective of this Directive is to fill a legal vacuum, as there is no obligation to have insurance under international law, and to avoid substandard shipping in EU waters. Some level of harmonisation is achieved by 'endorsing' LLMC standards. The Directive applies to ships over 300gt, but excludes, for example, state-owned ships used for non-commercial purposes.[56] The latter could potential apply to transport of CO_2.

[52] In 2009 the Convention had still not entered into force since it had not been ratified by a sufficient number of countries. A protocol to the Convention was consequently adopted in 2010 (2010 HNS Protocol) to overcome the initial ratification problems.

[53] The Convention applies the International Monetary Fund's currency, ie special drawing rights or SDR. Liability is capped at 10 million and 100 million SDR for ships under 2,000 tonnes. If damage is caused by packaged HNS, the maximum liability for the ship owner is 115 million SDR.

[54] The Convention on Limitation of Liability for Maritime Claims, concluded at London on 19 November 1976, as amended by Protocol of May 1996. The protocol entered into force on 13 May 2004.

[55] Total liability limits for a ship with a gross tonnage of 50,000 tonnes under the LLMC Convention is 54.6 million SDR, while under the HNS Convention it will be 72 million SDR.

[56] Council Directive 2009/20/EC on the insurance of shipowners for maritime claims [2009] OJ L131/128, Art 2.

C. Transport

The ships transporting CO_2 will probably have to be specifically designed and constructed for this purpose, but can be owned and operated by a wide range of parties, including entities involved in a CO_2 emissions activity, a storage operator or an independent shipping company. Given the focus of the CCS Directive on transportation via pipelines, the transport of CO_2 by ship to an offshore storage location falls outside the scope of the CCS Directive and is thus governed by general principles of maritime law. In general, maritime transport is governed by two basic contracts: FOB or CIF. Whereas a FOB or 'Free on Board' contract entails that the seller delivers at the railing of the ship and the buyer takes all the risk, a CIF or 'Cost, Insurance Freight' contract means that the seller has responsibility for transport, insurance and freight charges to a destination chosen by the buyer. In the case of CCS, it can be assumed that the seller has to take all the risks until the CO_2 is injected in the geological formation, and use will be made of a CIF contract, the owner of the ship thus not taking any risk.

Given the special design and investments needed, there will probably be few ships available. This may result in a situation where the ship owners have a monopoly situation and may thus be in a position to favour certain cargoes above others. In that case the person affected by a refusal to transport certain quantities of CO_2 may have to rely on general competition law and the earlier-mentioned essential facility doctrine (see section II.C.ii).

IV. CROSS-BORDER TRANSPORTATION OF CO_2 OFFSHORE

Cross-border transportation of CO_2 is potentially hampered due to the need to safeguard the offshore environment. Two treaties are of special importance as regards the protection of the marine environment: the Convention on the Prevention of Marine Pollution by Dumping of Wastes and Other Matter (London Convention) of 1972; and the Convention for the Protection of the Marine Environment of the North-East Atlantic (OSPAR Convention) of 1998. Both Conventions have as their primary goal to 'protect the maritime area against the adverse effects of human activities'. However, whereas the London Convention did not refer to CO_2 at all, the OSPAR Convention originally abolished any CCS activities. In 2007, the OSPAR Convention was amended in order to remove all legal barriers to CCS. Similarly, attempts have been made to enable CCS under the London Convention. In 2006 the London Protocol of 1996 entered into force, replacing the London Convention.[57] One of the amendments concerns Article 6 of the Protocol, which prohibits the export of waste for dumping, and thereby poses a legal hurdle to the transboundary transport of CO_2.[58] It provides that CO_2 may be exported as long as the states concerned have

---

[57] For the number of ratifications as of 4 September 2012, see Overheid, '1996 Protocol to the Convention on the Prevention of Marin Pollution by Dumping of Wastes and Other Matter', at www.minbuza.nl/producten-en-diensten/verdragen/zoek-in-de-verdragenbank/1996/11/007463.html.

[58] C Armeni, 'Legal Developments for Carbon Capture and Storage under International and Regional Marine Legislation' in Havercroft et al (eds), n 3 above, 151.

agreed to do so.[59] This amendment was adopted in 2009 but has not yet entered into force, as it has so far not reached the required number of ratifications.[60] This means that states may permanently store CO_2 within their national boundaries, but storage outside their territory, and thus transboundary transport of CO_2, is still prohibited. The same applies to cross-border transport for enhanced hydrocarbons recovery (see section III.A).

V. TRANS-EUROPEAN NETWORKS

The preceding sections have shown that the CCS Directive provides little guidance and support for developing CO_2 transport infrastructure. The need for such support is becoming more apparent, as transport distances seem to increase given the trend to develop carbon storage offshore. At the EU level the regime governing the development of Trans-European Networks (TENs) has applied since 2013 to CO_2 infrastructure as well.

A. EU Legal Framework

The concept of TENs was introduced in 1992 (Treaty of Maastricht) and is now included in Title XVI (Articles 170 to 172) of the Treaty on the Functioning of the European Union (TFEU). It provides that the EU shall contribute to the establishment and development of TENs in the areas of transport, telecommunications and energy infrastructures in order to help achieve the objectives of an internal market, to strengthen economic and social cohesion, and to enable those concerned to derive the full benefit from the setting-up of an area without internal frontiers. This policy can be achieved by the increased interconnection and interoperability of national networks, as well as access to such networks, whilst particularly taking into account the need to link islands, landlocked and peripheral regions with the central regions of the Union.[61] These objectives can be achieved by removing two main obstacles, that is, lengthy permitting procedures and insufficient finances for developing TENs. The TENs policy thus aims at (i) streamlining administrative and permitting procedures in order to avoid delays when developing cross-border infrastructure projects and (ii) financially supporting TENs via, for example, feasibility studies, loan guarantees, interest rate subsidies or through the Cohesion Fund.[62]

---

[59] 'Report of the 31st Consultative Meeting and the 4th Consultative Meeting of Contracting Parties' IMO Doc LC 31/15 (2009), Annex 5: Resolution LP 3(4) on the amendment of Art 6 of the London Protocol (as described by Armeni, n 58 above).

[60] Art 21(3) of the London Protocol provides that an amendment cannot enter into force before two thirds of the Contracting Parties have deposited an instrument of acceptance of the amendment.

[61] Treaty on the Functioning of the European Union (TFEU), Art 170. Art 171(3) TFEU explicitly provides that for the purpose of TENs, the EU may also cooperate with third countries to promote projects of mutual interest and to ensure the operability of networks.

[62] Art 171(1) TFEU. If necessary the Union may also take specific measures in the field of technical standardisation.

These policy goals only apply to networks identified as projects of common interest (PCIs).[63] For this purpose the EU needs to establish for each sector a set of guidelines, which provide rules and procedures for the identification, selection and treatment of PCIs. Since the first guidelines for the energy sector (TEN-E) from 1996, the rules governing the identification of PCIs have gradually been intensified, and currently PCIs need to be part of 'priority corridors and areas of trans-European energy infrastructure'. The most recent guidelines are included in Regulation 347/2013 (the Regulation)[64] and aim at identifying PCIs that are necessary to implement priority corridors and areas falling under the energy infrastructure categories such as electricity, gas and oil, as well as CO_2.[65] This means that CO_2 networks are considered as an energy infrastructure category even if there is no direct link with the energy sector, as would be the case if CO_2 emissions from a cement producer were to be captured and injected into an aquifer. However, categorising all CO_2 networks under one TEN category is probably the most pragmatic solution to identifying and promoting the development of these networks.

B. Carbon Dioxide Networks

According to Regulation 347/2013, a project can be considered as a PCI if the infrastructure is part of a specific category.[66] The first category refers to dedicated pipelines, other than an upstream pipeline network, used to transport CO_2 from more than one source (ie, industrial installations that produce CO_2 gas from combustion or other chemical reactions involving fossil or non-fossil carbon-containing compounds) for the purpose of permanent geological storage of CO_2 pursuant to the CCS Directive. This category of networks consists of pipelines specifically developed to transport CO_2 as part of the CCS chain. Moreover, these pipelines should be able to transport CO_2 from several sources, and would thus exclude a pipeline connecting one CO_2 source and one storage facility. Although 'upstream pipeline networks' are specifically excluded from this category, the Regulation does not provide for a definition of 'upstream pipeline networks', and it is thus not clear what kind of pipelines the Regulation is actually excluding. Is it referring to the concept of upstream pipeline networks used in the Gas Directive, ie 'any pipeline or network of pipelines operated or constructed as part of an oil/gas production project, or used to convey natural gas from one or more such projects to as processing plant or terminal or final coastal landing terminal'? If so, it is not clear why this category is excluded, as a re-use of such pipelines could play a significant role in carbon storage. If the idea

---

[63] Art 172 TFEU provides the legislative procedure for establishing such guidelines.
[64] Regulation 347/2013/EU of 17 April 2013 on guidelines for trans-European energy infrastructure and repealing Decision No 1364/2006/EC and amending Regulations (EC) No 713/2009, (EC) No 714/2009 and (EC) No 715/2009 OJ L15/39 (Regulation). The Regulation is directly binding upon Member States as of 1 June 2013.
[65] Regulation, Art 1.
[66] Regulation, Annex II, s 4.

would be that existing pipelines should be excluded as these require fewer investments then a similar exemption should also apply to transport and distribution pipelines.[67]

The second category includes facilities for liquefaction and buffer storage of CO_2 in view of its further transportation (excluding infrastructure within a geological formation used for the permanent geological storage of CO_2 pursuant to the CCS Directive), and is thus of special relevance for transport by ship, but only as far as it concerns liquefaction and unloading facilities. A similar approach can again be found with regard to LNG infrastructure.

In order to qualify as a PCI, the project should be necessary for developing at least one energy infrastructure priority corridor or area, and involve at least two Member States either by directly crossing the border of two or more Member States (including a country from the European Economic Area) or by having a significant cross-border impact.[68] Unlike the electricity and gas sectors, there is no EU master plan for developing CO_2 networks. In the absence of such a plan, it seems that it would be sufficient that a plan is presented by at least two Member States, as long as it fulfils the requirements of the Regulation, ie that in addition to the project's having to cross two borders or have a significant cross-border impact, it states that the potential benefits of the project should outweigh it costs. In order to assess the latter it will be necessary to develop a common methodology for a cost–benefit analysis (CBA). Similarly, it is not yet clear what is understood by 'significant' cross-border impact. For this purpose a capacity or throughput capacity threshold could be applied.[69] Whichever threshold is being used, it must be carefully designed in order to avoid any unnecessary obstacles to developing CO_2 networks.

In addition, the project has to meet some general criteria, as it has to contribute to (i) the avoidance of CO_2 emissions whilst maintaining security of energy supply, (ii) increasing the resilience and security of CO_2 transport, and (iii) the efficient use of resources, by enabling the connection of multiple CO_2 sources and storage sites via common infrastructure and minimising the environmental burden and risks. The first criterion seems to be relevant to the energy sector only, and to focus more on the emissions/capture part of the CCS chain than the part involving the transport of CO_2. The need included in the second criterion, to increase the resilience and security of CO_2 transport, is relevant. As already discussed, so far no clear European legal framework applies, and given the potential different treatment of pipelines transporting CO_2 for storage purposes and other pipelines, a project promotor will need to present some clear views on this matter. The Regulation also seems to favour larger networks to be used by several users. This brings with it a clear financial aspect, as it may require the need to develop some larger/oversized infrastructure

---

[67] See also Milieu Law and Policy Consulting, 'Identification of future CO_2 infrastructure networks' (Final report, Milieu Law and Policy Consulting, 2015). The Report can be found at publications.europa.eu/en/publication-detail/-/publication/ddafc491-f70c-11e5-b618-01aa75ed71a1/language-en.
[68] Regulation, Annex III, s 2, para 6.
[69] See Milieu Law and Policy Consulting, n 67 above.

and thus anticipatory investments. Such projects could benefit from EU funding if they are classified as a PCI.

Last but not least, the Regulation provides that the identification and selection of PCIs for inclusion in the list of supported projects is made by regional or thematic groups consisting of the Commission, relevant Member States and project promoters. The groups identifying and selecting CO_2 networks are established on an ad hoc basis. A thematic group for a cross-border CO_2 network in the North Sea has been created, and on the basis of the criteria for project selection included in the Regulation, a template will be issued so that project promoters can identify possible candidate projects for PCI status in the next call of early 2017. A possible project could be the Rotterdam Nucleus PCI, which involves Belgium (emitters near/at the port of Antwerp), The Netherlands (emitters near/at the port of Rotterdam, the existing OCAP project as well as an offshore storage site P15/P18 operated by Taqa) and the UK (offshore storage site/UK Fizzy field), as well as possible future extensions to Germany and France. The project would involve transportation by ship (from Antwerp to P18) and via pipelines (The Netherlands to P18). If awarded the status of a PCI, the project could apply for a subsidy under the Connecting Europe Facility for a feasibility study.[70] From 22 May 2017 to 15 August 2017 the European Commission organised a consultation on the third list of PCIs, which included a list of four potential carbon dioxide pipelines in the North Sea area, including the one mentioned above. The objective of this consultation is to receive views on the need for cross-border carbon dioxide pipelines from an EU energy policy perspective.

VI. CONCLUSION

The process of carbon capture and permanent storage of CO_2 implies that the captured CO_2 has to be transported to a storage facility. The CCS Directive seems to focus on piped transportation, given the many similarities between the transport of natural gas and CO_2, and has made use of schemes also applying to the (upstream) gas sector. Several Member States have, however, also decided not to select storage sites, or to limit storage to certain phases (pilots) or areas (offshore). The North Sea is thus becoming the main area for CO_2 storage, and as a result of this the focus is gradually shifting to transportation of CO_2 by ship instead of submarine pipelines. Shipped transportation is, however, subject to a completely different set of regulations. Irrespective of the means of transportation, the development of CO_2 transport and storage in the North Sea is restricted to the individual coastal states, as the London Convention is currently still hampering cross-border transport of CO_2.

Despite a large number of CCS project plans, only one CCS project has been realised, the Lacq pilot project in France. Lack of funding at the EU level (for example

---

[70] If such a feasibility study could take place in 2018 it would be possible to have a start-up in 2025. See also K Aursland, 'One Step Closer to European CCS Deployment: GATEWAY Pilot Case Chosen' (September 2016), at blog.sintefenergy.com/ccs/gateway-pilot-case-chosen/.

NER 300) and by national governments (for example co-funding) and low carbon prices are the main reasons for this slow development of CCS projects. As of 2013 an additional type of funding has been identified for CO_2 pipelines, and that involves some partial funding on the basis of the regime governing TENs. This regime may facilitate the development of cross-border CCS projects in the North Sea area, but it has had little impact so far.

Moreover, the CCS Directive is only focusing on pipelines connecting major point emitters and subsoil storage facilities, and does not take into account other transportation networks. As a result, pipelines transporting CO_2 for different purposes will be treated in different ways, especially within the framework of the EU ETS. This is surprising, as safety and environmental concerns are largely the same. It shows, once again, that the transportation of CO_2 needs to be considered from a broader perspective than CCS alone.

It follows from the above that, so far, little experience has been gained with CCS and thus with CO_2 transportation, but that in practice it will not be limited to piped transportation. The trend is towards developing several offshore hubs around the North Sea, and this would require a more integrated approach towards cross-border transport via pipelines as well as ships, and the integration of pipelines used for non-CCS transport (OCAP). When carbon prices increase and CCS becomes more attractive, it could be useful to apply a more holistic approach towards CO_2 transportation.

14
Regulation of Carbon Dioxide Pipelines: The US Experience and a View to the Future

PHILIP M MARSTON[*]

I. INTRODUCTION: A WORD OF CONTEXT

M Jourdain	What? When I say 'Nicole, bring me my slippers and give me my night cap', that is prose?
Philosophy Tutor	Yes, sir.
M Jourdain	Good heavens. For over forty years I've been speaking prose without even knowing it.

(Molière, *Le Bourgeois Gentilhomme*, Act IV, sc 4)[1]

SEVERAL CENTURIES AGO, Molière's famous fictional 'bourgeois gentilhomme' was astonished—but delighted—to discover that he had been speaking prose for over 40 years without even knowing it. In his mind, the discovery transformed his banal request for his slippers and night cap into something special—something learned and deserving of respect.

So it is with CO_2-based enhanced oil recovery (CO_2-EOR) and the associated (or 'incidental') geologic storage of the injected CO_2 that occurs as an inherent aspect of the hydrocarbon recovery operation—as well as with the pipeline infrastructure that supports that industry. For well over 40 years, CO_2-EOR operations were viewed as just one particular technique for oil recovery that could be used in certain hydrocarbon recovery operations. As explained in section II.A, the injection of CO_2

---

[*] The author's views are his own. He may be reached at pmarston@marstonlaw.com.
[1] Molière, *Le Bourgeois Gentilhomme*, Act II, sc 4 (English translation by author):

Monsieur Jourdain	Quoi, quand je dis 'Nicole, apportez-moi mes pantoufles, et me donnez mon bonnet de nuit', c'est de la prose?
Maître de Philosophie	Oui, Monsieur.
Monsieur Jourdain	Par ma foi, il y a plus de quarante ans que je dis de la prose, sans que j'en susse rien.

in certain reservoirs can significantly increase the percentage of the original oil in place (OOIP) that can be recovered, incidentally leaving the injected CO_2 in the geologic formation stored in place of the pre-existing reservoir fluids as an inherent aspect of the CO_2-EOR operation.

This 'incidental' or 'associated' storage of CO_2 has taken on new interest for policymakers in recent years in the context of efforts to reduce atmospheric emissions of CO_2. Hence, like the fictional character of M. Jourdain, the CO_2-EOR industry has in recent years sought to master the new terminology of 'carbon capture and storage' (CCS) in order to explain to policymakers unfamiliar with the industry how CO_2-EOR operations fit within the CCS linguistic paradigm and how these operations can advance the policymakers' goals of greenhouse gas (GHG) emissions reduction. This chapter is intended to further that basic educational objective, with particular focus on the regulation of the CO_2 pipeline component of the CO_2-EOR industry.

A regulatory scheme is necessarily overlaid on an underlying network of private property rights, commercial contracts and economic operational practices. It is the author's considered judgement that a successful regulatory framework must recognise these underlying considerations and take them into account. Accordingly, this chapter does not speak of 'sources' and 'sinks' of captured CO_2, but rather of 'suppliers' and 'customers' of the commercial CO_2 commodity. In the commercial world, the terms of trade in CO_2 are not governed by emission trading systems or cap and trade schemes, but rather by the Uniform Commercial Code (in the US), by privately-negotiated offtake agreements, and the more general law of contracts that applies in jurisdictions around the world. Similarly, the chapter does not speak of measuring the 'capacity' of a storage field, but discusses rather some of the legal and regulatory principles that are needed to allow commercial parties to match the 'output contract' that might be sought by a CO_2 industrial supplier with the 'requirements contract' needed by a buyer—and the role of the CO_2 pipeline in between the two, together with the potential regulatory implications of different ways of bridging this fundamental tension between two co-dependent commercial operations on either end of the pipeline.

The existing CO_2 pipeline infrastructure has been designed and built almost exclusively to meet the needs of CO_2-EOR operations.[2] The regulatory framework for this 'midstream' component of the industry reflects the integrated nature of the infrastructure and the respective requirements of the CO_2 suppliers and the customers they serve. A basic understanding of CO_2-EOR is therefore essential to understanding the design and operational requirements for CO_2 pipelines and the applicable regulatory framework, and will help explain some of the significant differences in the regulation framework for CO_2 pipelines as compared to pipelines carrying natural gas or petroleum.

---

[2] A few of the pipelines incidentally deliver some CO_2 volumes to customers for food and beverage or industrial gas use, accounting for perhaps 10% of overall CO_2 demand.

Since the CO_2-EOR operations are generally unfamiliar to the broader public, this chapter begins with an overview of the CO_2-EOR business before addressing the regulatory framework for the intermediary pipelines.[3]

II. CO_2-BASED ENHANCED OIL RECOVERY AND THE ROLE OF CO_2 PIPELINES

A. The CO_2-EOR Process

The process known as CO_2-EOR is one of a variety of 'enhanced oil recovery', or 'EOR', techniques that may include the injection of steam, polymers or other gases (eg nitrogen). The term 'EOR' refers to all of these 'tertiary' recovery techniques, so-called because they are generally used after primary and secondary (eg waterflooding) operations.[4] While 'EOR' refers to *all* these tertiary techniques, the term 'CO_2-EOR' refers only to the subset of EOR that involves injection and incidental storage of CO_2.

Primary production typically extracts approximately 10 to 20 per cent of the OOIP; waterflooding and other secondary techniques may then recover a roughly similar, or typically somewhat smaller percentage, still leaving well over half of the original oil remaining in the formation.[5] As a tertiary operation, CO_2-EOR may recover in the range of 5 to 15 per cent of the OOIP, with some operators experiencing even higher recovery factors.[6]

At standard temperature and pressure, CO_2 is a gas. Like many other substances, at the requisite combination of temperature and pressure, CO_2 can also exist as a

---

[3] For more detailed treatment of the underlying industry see, eg, P Marston, P Moore and G Schnacke, *Carbon Dioxide Infrastructure: Pipeline Transport Issues and Regulatory Concerns—Past, Present and Future* (2015) 52 *Rocky Mountain Mineral Law Foundation Journal* 275, on which the shortened summary in this chapter is partially based. See also Department of Energy, *Quadrennial Energy Review: Energy Transmission, Storage and Distribution Infrastructure* (April 2015) ch 7 (hereinafter 'DOE 2015 Quadrennial Energy Review'); B Hill, S Hovorka and S Melzer, 'Geologic carbon storage through enhanced oil recovery' (2013) 37 *Energy Procedia* 6808; and US Department of Energy, National Energy Technology Laboratory, *Carbon Dioxide Enhanced Oil Recovery: Untapped Domestic Energy Supply and Long Term Carbon Storage Solution*, at www.netl.doe.gov/File%20Library/Research/Oil-Gas/enhanced%20oil%20recovery/co_2%20eor/NETL_CO_2-EOR-Primer.pdf) (hereinafter 'DOE/NETL *Primer on CO_2-EOR*').

[4] For a good summary of primary, secondary and tertiary production, including CO_2-EOR, see E Tzimas et al, *Enhanced Oil Recovery using Carbon Dioxide in the European Energy System* (Institute for Energy, Petten, The Netherlands) (December 2005) 20–29.

[5] DOE/NETL *Primer on CO_2-EOR*, n 3 above, at 6. A study prepared for the US Department of Energy estimated that primary and secondary recovery techniques nationwide recover only about 32% of the OOIP. See 'Onshore Conventional Oil Including EOR', Paper #1-5, Working Document prepared by the Onshore Oil & EOR Subgroup of the Resource & Supply Task Group of the National Petroleum Council's North American Resource Development Study (made available 15 September 2011) at 16 (Table B-4) (referencing Advanced International Resources, Inc, *Storing CO_2 with Next Generation CO_2-EOR Technology*, prepared for the National Energy Technology laboratory of the US Department of Energy, DOE/NETL-2009/1350 (9 January 2009), Table 3, p 12, at www.npc.org/Prudent_Development-Topic_Papers/1-5_Onshore_Conventional_Oil_Incl_EOR_Paper.pdf.

[6] DOE/NETL *Primer on CO_2-EOR*, n 3 above, at 9.

solid (commonly called 'dry ice') or as a liquid.[7] Of relevance here, however, CO_2 is among a relatively small number of substances that—at particular combinations of temperature and pressure—may also exist as what is termed a 'dense-phase gas' (also termed a 'dense vapour' or a 'supercritical fluid').[8] While such CO_2 is sometimes referred to loosely as a 'liquid',[9] it is not: once the temperature and pressure pass a defined phase-change boundary (the 'critical point'), the CO_2 assumes a physical state that is indeterminate: it is neither a solid nor a liquid nor a gas. Rather it exhibits simultaneously certain physical characteristics of *both* a gas and a liquid. It is highly compressible, for example, like a gas and is sometimes termed 'spongy'. This compressibility allows for a given volume of CO_2 in this state to be much denser than gaseous CO_2, and it is more economical for long-distance transport by pipeline. Maintaining CO_2 in this dense phase generally requires pipeline pressures that range from 1,200 to 2,700 psi,[10] pressures that are higher than those typically used for long-line natural gas pipelines.[11] At the same time, however, supercritical CO_2 retains the ability of a gas to diffuse through a solid, such as a hydrocarbon-bearing rock formation.

In CO_2-EOR operations, the CO_2 is injected in a formerly-productive (or marginally-productive) oilfield by a pattern of injection wells that are drilled around each production well. In a common 'five-spot' pattern, there are four injection wells placed relatively evenly around each production well, while in a 'seven spot' pattern, there are six injectors around each producer, etc. The operation of these injection/production patterns creates a subsurface pressure gradient between the injectors and the producers, with the injected CO_2 generally moving from the higher pressure at the points of injection to the lower pressure created by the removal of reservoir fluids at the production wells. This process allows the operator to actively manage the subsurface pressure in the project.[12]

---

[7] A graph depicting the combinations of temperature and pressure at which these changes occur is termed a 'phase change diagram'.

[8] In the CO_2 industry, the terms 'dense phase' CO_2 and 'supercritical CO_2' are sometimes used interchangeably. More technically, however, a CO_2 stream may be quite dense, but yet not pass the supercritical boundary.

[9] For example, the American Society of Mechanical Engineers (ASME) standard that applies to CO_2 pipelines uses the term 'liquid' to refer to CO_2 that is compressed above its critical pressure. ASME, 'Pipeline Transportation Systems for Liquids and Slurries: ASME Code for Pressure Piping, B31' (ASME B31.4-2012), Revision and Consolidation of ASME B31.4-2009 and B31.11-2002 (R2008), Clause B400.2 (defining CO_2 for purposes of the Code as 'fluid consisting predominantly of carbon dioxide compressed above its critical pressure and for the purpose of this Code, shall be considered to be a liquid').

[10] Interstate Oil and Gas Compact Commission and Southern States Energy Board, Pipeline Transport Task Force, *A Policy, Legal, and Regulatory Evaluation of the Feasibility of a National Pipeline Infrastructure for the Transport and Storage of Carbon Dioxide* (December 2010) 14 (hereinafter 'IOGCC/SSEB CO_2 Pipeline Report').

[11] ibid. The operating pressures used in most natural gas pipelines typically range from 200 to 1,500 psi.

[12] The pressure equilibrium is maintained by balancing the fluids injected into the reservoir (CO_2) with fluids removed from the reservoir (petroleum, brine, and recycled CO_2). This dynamic equilibrium means that CO_2-EOR operations generally exhibit an essentially flat pressure profile over the life of producing operations (following an initial period of restoring the pressure to roughly pre-production levels). This is quite different from the pressure profile exhibited in a CO_2 storage operation where the injected CO_2 is *incremental* to the existing reservoir fluids (unless offsetting pressure relief wells are drilled, effectively making the storage operation resemble a CO_2-EOR operation, but without any economic value attached

During primary production from a hydrocarbon-bearing reservoir, significant quantities of the reservoir fluids are extracted (principally brine, in addition to the hydrocarbons). These fluid extractions reduce the subsurface pressure of the reservoir below the original, pre-preproduction levels.

In order to raise the subsurface pressure back to, or somewhat above, the original pre-production level, the operator may, at the beginning of an EOR operation, inject CO_2 for months, or even a year or more, with no offsetting fluid production.[13] Then, during the production phase, the operator generally seeks to maintain a stable pressure in the producing formation by balancing the total quantity of CO_2 injected with the quantity of oil, brine and CO_2 that is produced: in short, balancing *total fluids injected with total fluids withdrawn*.[14]

This 'balance' between 'fluids-in' and 'fluids-out' during production operations means that only a minimum pressure change occurs in the reservoir, reducing the risk of potential induced seismic events, as compared, for example, to CO_2 injections for non-EOR associated geologic storage in a saline or non-producing hydrocarbon-bearing reservoir, as explained by a report approved by the Governing Board of the US National Research Council of the National Academy of Science:[15]

> One reason for the apparent lack of induced seismicity with EOR may be that EOR operations routinely attempt to maintain the pore pressure within a field at levels near preproduction pore pressures. This 'balance' of the pore pressure means only a minimum pressure change occurs in the reservoir, reducing the possibility of induced seismic events;

to the brine production operation). As compared to non-EOR storage operations, this differing pressure profile for CO_2-EOR implies a lower risk of fracturing the overlying rock formation, lower risk of subsurface leakage, more efficient use of the available pore space, a smaller areal extent required to contain a given quantity of CO_2, a correspondingly reduced Area of Review, and a geographically smaller environmental monitoring area on the surface. See generally, P Marston, 'Pressure Profiles for CO_2-EOR and CCS: Implications for Regulatory Frameworks' (2013) 3(3) *Greenhouse Gases Science and Technology* 165, available at onlinelibrary.wiley.com/doi/10.1002/ghg.1348/full. See also Hill, Hovorka and Melzer, n 3 above.

[13] For more detail and for a schematic showing how the typical pressure pattern dips during primary production and is raised prior to tertiary operations and then held steady over the life of the CO_2-EOR production operation, see P Marston, n 12 above. The potentially lengthy initial period of CO_2 injections prior to beginning oil production must be taken into account in estimating the quantity of CO_2 that is injected (and incidentally stored in association with the oil production operation) in order to produce a barrel of oil. The initial barrel of oil production required a very large quantity of CO_2 injections; the second barrel, just half that, etc. In short, the unit amount of CO_2 injected per barrel of oil produced in a given field follows a descending asymptotic curve over time such that *net utilisation* can be calculated over the life of the particular operation. See N Azzolina et al, 'CO_2 storage associated with CO_2 enhanced oil recovery: A statistical analysis of historical operations' (2015) 37 *International Journal of Greenhouse Gas Control* 384, available at www.sciencedirect.com/science/article/pii/S1750583615001413; and S Bachu, 'Identification of oil reservoirs suitable for CO_2-EOR and CO_2storage(CCUS) using reserves databases, with application to Alberta, Canada' (2016) 44 *International Journal of Greenhouse Gas Control* 152, 159, available at doi.org/10.1016/j.ijggc.2015.11.013. It is this *net* utilisation over the life of the operation that best represents the relationship between CO_2 injections and barrels of oil produced.

[14] National Research Council of the National Academies (Committee on Induced Seismicity Potential in Energy Technologies; Committee on Earth Resources; Committee on Geological and Geotechnical Engineering; Committee on Seismology and Geodynamics; Board on Earth and Sciences and Resources; Division on Earth and Life Studies), *Induced Seismicity Potential in Energy Technologies* (Washington, DC, NRCNA 2013) 83.

[15] ibid.

this maintenance of pore pressure is achieved broadly by maintaining balance between the amount of fluid being injected and the amount being withdrawn. EOR using CO_2 injection is also considered one form of CCS, a technology under broader development in several other geological settings as part of the effort to reduce greenhouse gas emissions.

As the injected CO_2 diffuses through the hydrocarbon-bearing formation, it contacts the trapped oil droplets that remain in the pores of the rock. If conditions are right, the dense-phase CO_2 becomes *miscible* with the oil, which means that the two substances may flow together as if they were a single fluid.[16] The oil droplets swell and the surface tension that held the oil droplets attached to the pore surfaces is reduced, allowing the oil to become mobile and be carried to the production well.[17] The subsurface fluids (oil, CO_2 and the native brine) move along the subsurface pressure gradient to a producing well where they are brought to the surface. As the production stream rises to the surface, the pressure falls and the produced CO_2 exits the dense phase and reassumes a gaseous form. The produced CO_2 is separated from the oil and the brine and is usually dehydrated, pressurised and then recycled back into the formation to continue the process.[18] At the end of an EOR operation, 'effectively all' of the injected CO_2 is ultimately retained in this closed-loop EOR system;[19] it is 'inherently stored'[20] in the oilfield as an 'intrinsic part'[21] of the CO_2-EOR process.

---

[16] MA Raines et al, *A Review of the Pennsylvanian SAC ROC Unit*, West Texas Geological Society, Fall Symposium (2001) 70.

[17] ibid. A small percentage of CO_2-EOR operations are 'immiscible' operations, meaning that the CO_2 does not enter into a single fluid with the oil. In immiscible CO_2-EOR operations, the injected CO_2 serves to increase the formation pressure and helps push the oil towards the producing wells, but does not function as efficiently as in miscible operations. Fewer than 10% of US CO_2-EOR projects are currently identified as involving immiscible operations: Oil and Gas Journal, *Survey: Miscible CO_2 Continues to Eclipse Steam in US EOR Production*, Table C (7 April 2014) (hereinafter Oil and Gas Journal Survey) (as corrected in 5 May 2014 issue, at 100–103) (identifying 8,525 CO_2 injection wells active at the time of the 2014 survey). This survey was conducted biennially from the 1980s, but was discontinued after 2014. The 2014 survey is thus the end of this particular data series. See also Tzimas et al, n 4 above, 31 (and fig 3.8 showing the virtual disappearance of immiscible flooding projects in the US after 1986).

[18] Recycling of the produced CO_2 is the general practice in the United States (US), undertaken for economic reasons to minimise the amount of CO_2 that must be purchased for the operation. Such recycling is not technically required, however, and some EOR operations contemplated in other parts of the world may emit the produced CO_2 until such time as surface separation and recycle facilities are installed.

[19] S Whittaker and E Perkins, *Technical Aspects of CO_2-Enhanced Oil Recovery and Associated Carbon Storage* (Melbourne, Global CCS Institute) (October 2013) 12 ('[r]etention of the injected carbon dioxide within the reservoir is an intrinsic part of the CO_2 EOR process, and effectively all CO_2 purchased for injection will ultimately remain stored within the oil field at the end of EOR operations'). The Global CCS Institute was founded in 2009 with initial funding from the Australian Government and has a diverse membership of national governments, global corporations, small companies, research bodies and non-governmental organisations (see at www.globalccsinstitute.com/institute). See also LS Melzer, *Carbon Dioxide Enhanced Oil Recovery (CO_2 EOR): Factors Involved in Adding Carbon Capture, Utilization and Storage (CCUS) to Enhanced Oil Recovery* (February 2012) 4 (report prepared for the National Enhanced Oil Recovery Initiative, Center for Climate and Energy Solutions).

[20] Carbon Sequestration Leadership Forum, *Final Report by the CSLF Task Force on Technical Challenges in the Conversion of CO_2-EOR Projects to CO_2 Storage Projects* (September 2013) 58 (CO_2 'is inherently stored in CO_2-EOR operations, with a retention rate of the purchased (new) CO_2 greater than 90–95%' and 'almost all of the purchased CO_2 is retained (stored) in the reservoir'). The Carbon Sequestration Leadership Forum (CSLF) is a government to government, Ministerial-level international climate change initiative comprised of the EU and some 25 member nations, including the US. The CSLF members represent approximately 60% of the world's population. See at www.cslforum.org/cslf/About-CSLF.

[21] Whittaker and Perkins, n 19 above, 12.

While the initial transportation of CO_2 by pipeline dates from over 80 years ago (for use in dry-ice and beverage production),[22] use of CO_2 for EOR operations only began a quarter century later,[23] and large-scale commercial operation began in 1972, at the SACROC project in the Permian Basin, and continues there to date.[24] Today, there are over 100 CO_2-EOR projects in the US, with over 8,000 active CO_2 injection wells, with projects located in multiple States, including Colorado, Louisiana, Michigan, Mississippi, Montana, New Mexico, Texas (accounting for the single largest number of projects), Oklahoma, Utah and Wyoming.[25] By 2013, cumulative injections of CO_2 in US CO_2-EOR operations (net of recycle) had exceeded 1 billion metric tonnes,[26] and were increasing by over 60 million metric tonnes per year.[27]

To date, CO_2-EOR has been very largely a North American industry, particularly as regards miscible CO_2 operations. One major reason for the absence of CO_2-EOR in other areas has been the unavailability of large supplies of relatively low-cost CO_2, as recognised in an extensive study of CO_2-EOR potential in Europe:[28]

> The major barrier has been the availability of low cost CO_2 at the injection site. Given the absence of significant natural CO_2 resources in the proximity of the European oil-rich regions, large combustion plants, such as power stations, are potentially the only source.

There are exceptions, however, and CO_2-EOR operations are now being conducted in a number of non-North American locations. They have been applied in Hungary since the 1960s,[29] as well as in Turkey (at the Bati Raman field).[30] In Brazil,

---

[22] R Allis et al, *Natural CO_2 Reservoirs on the Colorado Plateau and Southern Rocky Mountains: Candidates for CO_2 Sequestration* (Proceedings of the First National Conference on Carbon Sequestration, Washington DC, May 2001), at www.files.geology.utah.gov/emp/co₂sequest/pdf/reservoirs.pdf).

[23] Field trials of CO_2 injections for EOR were conducted in Oklahoma at least as early as 1958 (injection of carbonated water). The first pure CO_2 pilot project commenced in 1964 (Mead Strawn Field in Texas). M Klins, 'CO_2-Heavy Oil Flooding-Economic Design' in E Okandan (ed), *Heavy Crude Oil Recovery* (The Hague, Springer, 1984) 264. See generally, US Office of Technology Assessment, *Enhanced Oil Recovery Potential in the United States* (January 1978) App B and sources cited therein.

[24] Operations at the SACROC project are described in detail by Raines et al, n 16 above; and WS Han et al, 'Evaluation of Trapping Mechanisms in Geologic CO_2 Sequestration: Case Study of SACROC Northern Platform, a 35-Year CO_2 Injection Site' (2010) 310 *American Journal of Science* 282-324.

[25] Oil and Gas Journal, Survey, n 17 above.

[26] Calculation of cumulative net injections by author based on analysis of CO_2-EOR production data from ibid, and prior year surveys back to 1984, and an estimated usage factor of about 9.5 Mcf of net CO_2 injected per barrel of oil produced (per Global CCS Institute, *The Global Status of CCS: 2012* (2013)). See also Hill, Hovorka and Melzer, n 3 above, at 6811 (estimating cumulative net injections by 2012 of about 850 million metric tonnes).

[27] L Bacanskas, 'CO_2-EOR and EPA's Greenhouse Gas Reporting Program', presentation at EPA workshop, *Workshop: Introduction to Carbon Dioxide Enhanced Oil Recovery (CO_2-EOR)* (11 June 2013), slide 6 (data from 65 million metric tonnes reported as 'supplied' under Subpart PP of the GHG reporting rules for 2011 reporting year). The Subpart PP reports are from 'suppliers' of CO_2, and may include some quantities that are not transported via pipeline. Since the vast majority of CO_2 is supplied to markets via pipeline, the Subpart PP data are used here as a surrogate for CO_2 pipeline throughput.

[28] Tzimas et al, n 4 above, 6. See also J Pearce et al, 'A review of natural CO_2 accumulations in Europe as analogues for geological sequestration', Geological Society, London, Special Publications, 2004, 233, 29–41 (doi:10.1144/GSL.SP.2004.233.01.04).

[29] G Nemeth, J Papay and A Szittar, 'Experience with CO_2 EOR Process in Hungary' (1988) 43(6) *Oil and Gas Science and Technology—Rev IFP*, at dx.doi.org/10.2516/ogst:1988048 (published online 1 November 2006).

[30] S Sahin, U Kalfa and D Celebioglu, *Bati Raman Field Immiscible CO_2 Application: Status Quo and Future Plans* (presented at Latin American & Caribbean Petroleum Engineering Conference, 15–18 April, Buenos Aires, Argentina) (see at dx.doi.org/10.2118/106575-MS) (2007).

Petrobras has been using CO_2 for EOR for more than 25 years in onshore fields, and is now developing an offshore project as well.[31] Several small-scale CO_2-EOR tests have been undertaken recently in China using CO_2 separated from natural gas production,[32] and other projects are under active development.[33] Industry experts also see a large potential for CO_2-EOR in various other parts of the world as well.[34]

B. CO_2 Supply and Demand

i. CO_2 Supply: Large, 'Bulky' Increments of Both 'N-CO_2' and 'A-CO_2'

As of the mid-2010s, about three-quarters of the CO_2 used in North American EOR operations came from a handful of large, high-purity, naturally-occurring sources of CO_2 that require relatively minimal processing and from which CO_2 is extracted via production wells similar to the production of natural gas (ie CH_4).[35] These natural CO_2 resources have been geologically trapped, like oil or gas resources, for millions of years. In the case of the Jackson Dome in Mississippi, for example, the CO_2 is produced from the site where it is estimated to have been naturally trapped in the formation for around 65 million years.[36] Carbon dioxide produced from such

---

[31] See EF de Souza, 'Understanding CO_2-EOR and its application in Brazil' *Carbon Capture Journal* (22, November 2012), at www.carboncapturejournal.com/news/understanding-co$_2$-eor-and-its-application-in-brazil/2832.aspx?Category=all).

[32] See, eg, Global CCS Institute, *Sinopec Zhongyuan Carbon Capture Utilization and Storage Pilot Project*, at www.globalccsinstitute.com/projects/sinopec-zhongyuan-carbon-capture-utilization-and-storage-pilot-project; and *Sinopec Shengli Oilfield Carbon Capture Utilization and Storage Pilot Project*, at www.globalccsinstitute.com/projects/sinopec-shengli-oilfield-carbon-capture-utilization-and-storage-pilot-project.

[33] L Lan-Cui et al, 'Developments towards environmental regulation of CCUS projects in China' (2014) 63 *Energy Procedia* 6903 (paper presented at GHGT-12, October 2014). Some studies have examined the use of CO_2 as a fracturing fluid. See, eg, R Middleton et al, 'Potential for commercial-scale shale gas production and CO_2 sequestration' (2014) 63 *Energy Procedia* 7780 (paper presented at GHGT-12 conference in Austin Texas, 2014). It should be stressed, however, that using CO_2 as a fracturing fluid for producing natural gas is a completely different process than injecting CO_2 in an EOR operation. In CO_2-EOR, it is important *not* to fracture the formation, as that would undermine the efficiency of the CO_2 sweep of the reservoir. The Global CCS Institute maintains a map-based worldwide database of CCS projects that can be filtered by proposed storage type (EOR or Dedicated Geologic Storage). Many of the projects anticipate injecting the captured CO_2 for EOR operations. See at www.globalccsinstitute.com/projects/large-scale-ccs-projects#map. See also Global CCS Institute, n 26 above, at 148 (noting potential for CO_2-EOR in Europe (offshore and onshore), the Middle East, China, Brazil, Mexico and Indonesia), and Global CCS Institute, *The Global Status of CCS: 2016* (Summary Report, at 23) (noting growing interest in EOR in China and parts of Central and Latin America and the Middle East).

[34] Global CCS Institute, n 26 above, at 148 (noting potential for CO_2-EOR in Europe (offshore and onshore), the Middle East, China, Brazil, Mexico and Indonesia). See also Global CCS Institute, *The Global Status of CCS: 2016* (Summary Report, at 23) (noting growing interest in EOR in China and parts of Central and Latin America and the Middle East).

[35] For a compilation of some of the principal CO_2 sources in the world, see M Stenhouse, *Natural and Industrial Analogues for Geological Storage of Carbon Dioxide* (Cheltenham, Greenhouse Gas R&D Programme, 2009) App 2: Compilation of Natural Occurrences of CO_2.

[36] US Environmental Protection Agency, *Federal Requirements Under the Underground Injection Control (UIC) Program for Carbon Dioxide (CO_2) Geologic Sequestration (GS) Wells: Proposed Rule*, 73 Fed Reg 43492, 43495 (25 July 2008).

naturally-occurring sources is sometimes referred to as 'N-CO$_2$'. There are other, anthropogenic supply sources as well, including:

— lower-purity geologic sources where the CO$_2$ must be separated and 'captured' from a raw production stream that is produced principally for its content of methane (CH$_4$) (commonly called 'natural gas');[37]
— industrial operations such as ammonia manufacture, a 1980s era coal-to-methane plant in North Dakota, steam methane reforming to produce hydrogen, and methanol production; and
— CO$_2$ captured from electric power generation facilities, including the Sask Power plant in Saskatchewan, Canada (beginning in 2014), and the 240 megawatt Petra Nova retrofit project at the WA Parish power plant in Texas (commenced operations in January 2017).[38] In June 2017, the developer suspended start-up operations on Mississippi Power's 582 megawatt generating station in Kemper County, Mississippi, pending review of potential future operations.[39]

All of these principal existing sources of CO$_2$ supply are individually large, whether 'N-CO$_2$' from naturally-occurring sources or 'A-CO$_2$' captured from industrial activities. In looking to a possible future in which CO$_2$ capture technology begins to be deployed more broadly, the practicalities and economics of the capture processes suggest strongly that future sources of A-CO$_2$ supply will continue to be individually large, complex and capital-intensive projects for many years to come. This is of considerable importance to the design and pattern of future CO$_2$ pipeline infrastructure, because it implies a relatively limited number of large supply sources that will only be developed if assured of market commitments—and of pipeline transportation capacity to reach those markets.

In short, CO$_2$ supply increments will likely continue to be 'bulky' increments, where each new supply tranche requires large amounts of capital and involves long-lived assets (measured in decades). This means that the supply side of the CO$_2$-EOR industry will continue for the foreseeable future to be characterised by

---

[37] See, eg, the Shute Creek facility of Exxon Inc, processing a raw production stream that is roughly one-third CH$_4$ and two-thirds CO$_2$. Note that in common parlance, the term 'natural gas' refers essentially to methane (ie CH$_4$) and that is the way the term is used here. The legal practitioner should be warned, however, that in fact the term 'natural gas' has differing meanings in the US under different legislative schemes. For example, the federal regulator under the Natural Gas Act of 1938 (as amended) has ruled on several occasions that the term 'natural gas' under that statute does *not* include a CO$_2$ stream, but the Bureau of Land Management (BLM), interpreting the federal Mineral Leasing Act of 1920, has reached the contrary result. See *Exxon Corp v Lujan*, 970 F 2d 757 (10th Cir 1992) (distinguishing the rulings under the Natural Gas Act and affirming the BLM determination under the Mineral Leasing Act that the term 'natural gas' as used there includes CO$_2$).

[38] Press Release, 'NRG Energy, JX Nippon Complete World's Largest Post-Combustion Carbon Capture Facility On-Budget and On-Schedule' (10 January 2017), at www.nrg.com/generation/projects/petra-nova.

[39] At 582 MW capacity, Kemper County is by far the largest coal-based electric generating facility in the world to be designed to capture associated CO$_2$ from coal (lignite). The plant commenced start-up operations in 2017 and began gasifying lignite and combusting the resulting syngas to generate electricity while separating and capturing CO$_2$. In June 2017, however, the operator suspended start-up operations pending further review of the potential future of the project, operating the generator instead with natural gas and without CO$_2$ capture.

a relatively small number of large supply points, a fact with considerable consequences for project planning, financing, pipeline siting and operations—and not least for regulatory rules and practices governing transportation access, which point is discussed in section II.B.ii.

ii. CO_2 Markets: Large, Long-lived 'Bulky' Demand Increments

Roughly 90 per cent of the CO_2 supply is dedicated to use in CO_2-EOR operations.[40] There are presently over 100 CO_2-EOR projects in operation in the US, ranging in size from projects comprising a few dozen to many hundreds of CO_2 injection wells. The non-EOR markets are comprised principally of food and beverage uses (accounting for approximately 5 per cent of total demand), while various other industrial uses account for the remainder, as illustrated in Figure 14.1.[41]

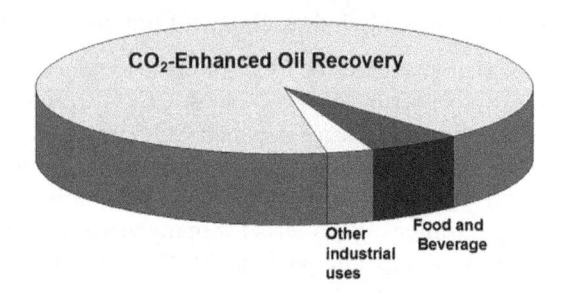

Figure 14.1: US markets for CO_2

While CO_2 supply mix may evolve in coming years to include a greater proportion of 'A-CO_2,' captured in significant part with an eye toward reductions in atmospheric emission, the bulk of the new supply is expected to continue to be used in EOR operations, as recognised, amongst others, by the International Energy Agency.[42] Because these new supply sources will be integrated into the supply portfolios of EOR operators, much (if not nearly all) of the new A-CO_2 supplies may be expected to be commingled at some point in its journey to market (and in varying proportions) in the existing pipeline transport infrastructure.

---

[40] Bacanskas, n 27 above, 6. Review of the Subpart PP reports for 2011 shows that of the 65 million tonnes reported, about 59 million tonnes went for EOR, 4 million tonnes for food and beverage operations, with the remainder to other uses.

[41] ibid. See also *IPCC Special Report on Carbon Dioxide Capture and Storage* (Intergovernmental Panel on Climate Change, Geneva, 2005) 332 (Section 7.3.2). See esp ibid, Table 7.2, 'Industrial applications of CO_2,' (and estimating yearly worldwide market by chemical product class or application).

[42] International Energy Agency, *Tracking Clean Energy Progress 2013: IEA Input to the Clean Energy Ministerial* (Paris, IEA, 2013) 59 (70% of the projects worldwide that are under construction or at an advanced stage of planning intend to use captured CO_2 for EOR). See also US Department of Energy, *Lake Charles Carbon Capture and Sequestration Project Draft Environmental Impact Statement* (April 2013) 1–6 (explaining that CO_2 from project would be transported to an existing pipeline that transports CO_2 obtained from anthropogenic and from natural sources, and used in EOR to supplement or replace other anthropogenic and naturally-occurring sources).

This commingling during pipeline transportation of A-CO_2 and N-CO_2 supply sources is not uncommon. For example, supplies of A-CO_2 captured from an industrial facility that had received nearly $250 million in federal financial assistance for CO_2 emission reduction purposes began delivering the captured CO_2 in 2012 into a pipeline already carrying supplies of naturally-occurring CO_2, and additional supply sources of A-CO_2 captured from an ammonia production facility were added to the supply portfolio in 2013.[43]

Depending on how the legal and regulatory rules evolve, such commingling of CO_2 supplies from anthropogenic and non-anthropogenic sources may carry legal or regulatory consequences that should be carefully reviewed by the practitioner. To the extent that some CO_2 supply sources carry regulatory characteristics or requirements that differ from other supplies, the commingling of these differing supply sources during pipeline transportation presents the risk that regulators may impose these regulatory requirements on all downstream CO_2 transportation and end-use customers who receive deliveries of the commingled stream.[44]

These CO_2-EOR projects tend to be long-lived, as is illustrated by the fact that the earliest commercial CO_2-EOR operation (SACROC in West Texas)—begun in 1972—is still operating some 45 years later. This means that in initial planning for a CO_2-EOR flood, the operator must plan for a CO_2 supply to be available for years or even decades into the future. This in turn implies large future financial commitments, since the cost of acquiring CO_2 is typically one of the largest (if not the largest) expenses for a CO_2-EOR project.

In sum, these projects are characterised by complexity, the necessity of ensuring reliable supplies of large quantities of CO_2 over a relatively long-term planning horizon and larges amounts of capital. As a result, increments of new EOR demand—like increments of new supply—tend to be 'bulky' and consist of individually large demand 'tranches'.

---

[43] See, eg, Department of Energy (DOE), Office of Fossil Energy, *Air Products & Chemicals, Inc: APCI Port Arthur ICCS Project*, at energy.gov/fe/air-products-chemicals-inc, describing the DOE-supported steam methane reforming facility in Port Arthur, Texas, constructed by Air Products and Chemicals, Inc.

[44] The risk is not theoretical. The federal regulator of interstate natural gas pipelines and electricity transmission adopted exactly this legal approach for both natural gas and for electricity. The regulator ignored the contractual allocations and imposed federal regulation *on the entire commingled stream*, an approach that was affirmed by the Supreme Court. See *California v Lo-Vaca Gathering Company*, 379 US 366 (1965) and *FPC v Florida Power & Light Co*, 404 US 453 (1972). In the intervening half-century, the 'commingling doctrine' has continued to generate legal disputes and complicated regulatory compliance. See, eg, Federal Energy Regulatory Commission (FERC), Order to Show Cause and Notice of Proposed Penalties Energy Transfer Partners, LP, 120 FERC ¶ 61,086 (2007) 174–77 (order directing pipeline to show cause why it should not be fined $82,000,000 and required to disgorge $69,866,966, plus interest in alleged unjust profits) and Order Approving Uncontested Settlement, Energy Transfer Partners LP, 128 FERC ¶ 61,269 (2009) (resolving proceeding through uncontested settlement imposing $5 million in civil penalties and establishing a $25 million compensation fund). In light of the long history involving natural gas pipelines and electric transmission facilities, the uncertainty and risk that may result from commingling CO_2 supplies that may be subject to different present or future regulatory obligations was identified in the literature as early as 2008, and has informed consideration of various regulatory matters since then. See PM Marston and PA Moore, 'From EOR to CCS: The Evolving Legal and Regulatory Framework for Carbon Capture and Storage' (2008) 29 *Energy Law Journal* 421, 455 and fn 154, available at www.felj.org/energy-law-journal/previous-issues/energy-law-journal-volume-29-no-2-2008.

C. CO$_2$ Pipelines: The 'Few-to-Few' Midstream Component of an Integrated Industry

As observed in section II.B, the CO$_2$ pipeline infrastructure has been developed to link supply sources to the markets. The 'midstream' CO$_2$ pipeline infrastructure is intimately interconnected with the 'upstream' CO$_2$ supply segment at one end and the 'downstream' CO$_2$-EOR oilfield operations and other markets at the other. Hence, regardless of how ownership of the various asset components may be held, the co-dependent nature of these assets and the attendant operations of the upstream and downstream components means that the upstream, midstream and downstream components must be planned, developed, constructed and operated as interdependent parts of a larger whole.

The CO$_2$ pipeline infrastructure necessary to support EOR operations has grown to serve the EOR markets. As of 2015, there were some 5,233 miles (8,373 km) of CO$_2$ pipelines in the US (including both interstate and intrastate pipelines), as reported to the US Department of Transportation and shown in Table 14.1.

Table 14.1: CO$_2$ pipeline reported mileage in United States[45]

Year	Mileage (as reported to PHMSA)	Kilometres (calculated at 1 mile = 1.6 km)
2004	3,221	5,154
2005	3,846	6,154
2006	3,827	6,123
2007	3,884	6,214
2008	4,203	6,725
2009	4,192	6,707
2010	4,560	7,296
2011	4,735	7,576
2012	4,840	7,744
2013	5,190	8,304
2014	5,276	8,442
2015	5,233	8,373

---

[45] US Department of Transportation, Pipeline and Hazardous Materials Safety Administration (PHMSA), *Annual Report Mileage for Hazardous Liquid or Carbon Dioxide Systems*. The current data are available only from the PHMSA's website. See, eg, at www.phmsa.dot.gov/pipeline/library/data-stats. The direct link for annual report mileage for CO$_2$ pipelines is currently located at phmsa.dot.gov/pipeline/library/data-stats/annual-report-mileage-for-hazardous-liquid-or-carbon-dioxide-systems. For a list of individual CO$_2$ pipelines in the US, see *Report of the Interagency Task Force on Carbon Capture and Storage* (August 2010), at B-2 (Table B-1) (report of Task Force co-chaired by the DOE and the Environmental Protection Agency (EPA)).

These pipelines facilities are found in three principal interstate groups, as illustrated on the map in Figure 14.2. The three largest networks are:

(a) the southern Rocky Mountain/Permian basin region, with natural CO_2 sources in Colorado, Utah and New Mexico supplemented by industrial CO_2 from the Permian Basin feeding CO_2-EOR projects in the Permian Basin;
(b) the Gulf Coast region, comprising primarily Mississippi, Louisiana, Texas, supplied by naturally-occurring CO_2 from Mississippi and CO_2 from various industrial or power-generating CO_2 capture projects in each of those States; and
(c) the upper Rocky Mountain area, carrying CO_2 captured from hydrocarbon processing and production operations to CO_2-EOR projects in Wyoming and Montana (with potential extension into North Dakota).

Smaller CO_2 pipeline systems serve CO_2-EOR operations in Kansas, Oklahoma and Michigan.

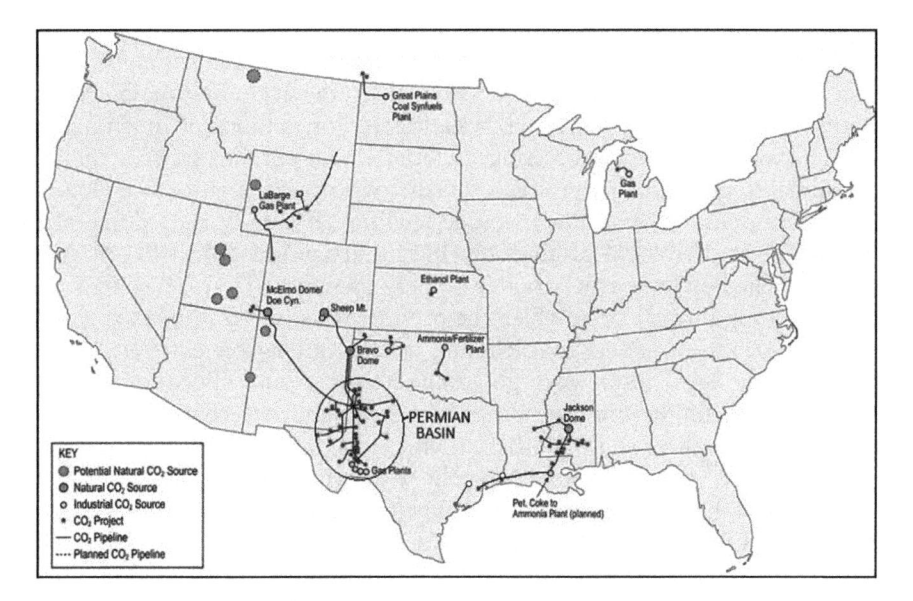

Figure 14.2: Active U.S. CO_2 Pipeline and Injection Site Infrastructure[46]

---

[46] Adapted from Melzer, n 19 above and reproduced with permission). A number of very useful, detailed maps of pipeline infrastructure feeding the Permian Basin projects may be found at Melzer Consulting's website at melzerconsulting.com/maps/.

A conceptual framework for future expansion has even been suggested to potentially link the existing pipeline networks into a so-called 'horseshoe pipeline' configuration that could conceivably provide the beginning of a national CO_2 pipeline network.[47]

The underlying pipeline infrastructure is similar in many respects to pipeline infrastructure for other valuable commodities, such as petroleum, refined products, anhydrous ammonia or natural gas (methane or CH_4). There are important differences as well. But, as already noted, both supply and demand increments of CO_2 are characterised by relatively small numbers of relatively large individual increments. This fact has important implications for the shape of the pipeline networks that link the two: CO_2 pipeline networks tend to be 'few-to-few' networks, where a relatively small number of large-quantity supply points are linked to a relatively small number of large-quantity delivery points. New supply sources and new markets tend to come in individually large 'chunks', and both require long-term future contractual commitments from both the commodity counterparty and any transporting pipeline involved.

This 'few-to-few' character of the network is fundamentally different from the existing US network of natural gas pipelines that effectively link many thousands of continuously-producing individual wells to tens of millions of individual retail consumers (with upstream processing facilities or oil-refining sources that range from minimal to huge and in between), together with vast amounts of geologic (and much smaller amounts of surface) storage facilities. It is also quite different from the petroleum or petroleum product pipelines that tend to link field area storage facilities (supplied by pipe, truck, rail or refinery operations) to market area storage facilities (eg 'tank farms') from which the product is delivered to further wholesale and retail distribution networks (including trucks, rail tanker cars, etc). Business practices and the legal framework governing access to and allocation of pipeline capacity for each of these commodities when demand exceeds pipeline capacity must be adapted to these sharply different underlying commercial realities.

Another point of comparison with pipelines carrying natural gas and petroleum should be noted here. Like the natural pipeline industry (and unlike petroleum product pipelines), CO_2 pipeline operations are essentially a *continuous process type business* in which new supplies are continually introduced into the pipeline, transported and delivered out of the pipeline in an uninterrupted flow. This differs from petroleum product pipelines, which have significant components of a *'batch' business* in which defined quantities of differing products may be flowing in a given pipe at the same time (either with or without a physical separation device

---

[47] See, eg, CM Ming and LS Melzer, *CO₂-EOR: A Model for Significant Carbon Reductions* (2010) 6, cited in MIT Energy Initiative, *Role of Enhanced Oil Recovery in Accelerating the Deployment of Carbon Capture and Sequestration*, Report of Symposium of MIT Energy Initiative and Bureau of Economic Geology at University of Texas Austin (23 July 2010) (Cambridge, MA, MIT Energy Initiative, 2010); MIT Energy Initiaitive, ibid at 21.

(ie a 'pig') between the products)[48] and with storage tanks or depots for the appropriate product located at both ends of the pipeline. The continuous process aspect of CO_2 pipelines means that the pipeline operator—working with its suppliers and customers—must be able to accommodate necessary operational variations in supply, demand and maintenance on essentially a real-time basis.

In the US, all of these distinctive aspects of CO_2 pipelines are generally accommodated by the current US regulatory framework. This has allowed for private investment in supply, transport and consumption infrastructure to go forward as EOR demand has increased over the decades. As noted in section IV, however, alternative regulatory frameworks for CO_2 pipelines are sometimes discussed in the literature that fail to recognise these commercial realities, and if adopted could impose significant new regulatory hurdles to the use of captured A-CO_2 in future CO_2-EOR operations.

III. THE CURRENT REGULATORY FRAMEWORK FOR CO_2 PIPELINES IN THE UNITED STATES

The legal and regulatory framework for CO_2 pipelines in the US has evolved in conjunction with the development of the industry itself. As will be seen, it is the various State governments, not the Federal Government, that play the principal regulatory role. Note also that many of the siting and permitting issues faced by CO_2 pipelines are common to many other large infrastructure projects and are intensely site specific. The discussion here is limited and intended only to highlight a few of the major aspects of generally applicable permitting and regulations. This is emphatically not a checklist for regulatory compliance, however, and counsel working with pipeline developers should carefully review the environmental, land use and permitting requirements that are applicable to each individual project.

A. Federal Regulation of Construction and Operation

The initial CO_2 pipelines to support EOR operations in the Permian Basin in West Texas in the early 1970s were relatively short and were located entirely within the State of Texas, which meant that questions of potential federal regulation of interstate CO_2 pipelines did not arise (except in the rather limited instances in Texas where the pipeline might cross federally-owned land). But after the CO_2-EOR process was successfully demonstrated in the initial commercial operations, the potential increased demand for CO_2 far exceeded the availability of CO_2 from the original gas-processing facilities located close to the target field, and industry looked to

---

[48] DC Cafaro and J Cerdá, 'Optimal scheduling of multiproduct pipeline systems using a non-discrete MILP formulation' (2004) 28 *Computers and Chemical Engineering* 2053. The article indicates that pigs are now seldom used. Where no pig is used, some intermixing between the adjoining batches occurs on either side of the product interface and must be accounted for by the operator.

develop larger sources of CO_2 to supply expanded EOR operations. The target CO_2 sources were very large, naturally-occurring reserves of high-purity CO_2 streams located hundreds of miles from the target fields, which would require longer, high-capacity pipelines to deliver the CO_2 to market. Such pipelines would be interstate in character, and so developers sought regulatory certainty of the potential regulatory status of interstate CO_2 pipelines under two federal statutes: the Natural Gas Act of 1938 ('Natural Gas Act' or NGA) and the Interstate Commerce Act (ICA). Developers petitioned the relevant administrative agency under each statute, seeking a determination whether pipelines carrying CO_2 came under the regulatory ambit. In each case, the agency ruled they did not. In addition, the Bureau of Land Management (BLM), which manages federally-owned lands (commonly found in the western US) resolved certain threshold questions with regard to permitting of CO_2 pipelines proposed to cross federal lands. These three proceedings are summarised in the following subsections.

i. Jurisdictional Status under the Natural Gas Act

The Natural Gas Act, as amended, applies to certain interstate wholesale transactions and to interstate transportation of 'natural gas'. Section 7(c) requires persons proposing to construct or operate a pipeline for the interstate transportation of 'natural gas' to obtain a certificate of public convenience and necessity from the Federal Energy Regulator Commission (FERC). The grant of such a Section 7(c) certificate grants the certificate holder a federal power to invoke eminent domain in a State proceeding to acquire the right of way approved by the FERC in granting the Section 7(c) certificate, thereby effectively making the FERC the 'siting agency' for jurisdictional natural gas pipelines.

The statute does not define the term 'natural gas', however. Accordingly, in the late 1970s, Cortez Pipeline Company sought a determination that the CO_2 stream to be transported in a pipeline that it planned to construct was not 'natural gas' within the meaning of the statute. In 1979, the FERC ruled that the proposed pipeline did not come within the agency's jurisdiction since the gas stream in question would be 98 per cent pure CO_2 with traces of methane in the remaining 2 per cent (which was not separated from the main production), and hence was not 'natural gas' under the statute.[49] The FERC thus declared that Cortez Pipeline Company would not become a 'natural-gas company' under the Natural Gas Act by constructing or operating the proposed CO_2 pipeline.[50] This declaratory ruling provided regulatory certainty under the Natural Gas Act and allowed development to proceed. Right of way acquisition proceeded either through privately negotiated transactions, or under relevant State law (discussed further in section IV.B). In 2006, the FERC applied the *Cortez* ruling

---

[49] *Cortez Pipeline Company*, 7 FERC ¶ 61,024 (1979), 1979 FERC LEXIS 1799.
[50] ibid at ¶ 61,042 (stating that jurisdictional result was reached 'by considering the source of the production, the use of the production, and the actual chemical composition of the production involved, in light of the goals of the NGA').

to a proposal to convert a natural gas pipeline to CO_2 transportation and found that, following conversion to CO_2 transportation, the pipeline transportation would no longer be subject to the Natural Gas Act or the FERC's jurisdiction.[51]

ii. Jurisdictional Status under the Interstate Commerce Act

Through the Hepburn Act in 1905, Congress expanded the pre-existing regulatory responsibilities of the Interstate Commerce Commission (ICC) under the 1887 Interstate Commerce Act (ICA) to include the regulation of oil pipelines.[52] The 1905 statute extended ICC regulation to include those engaged in 'the transportation of oil or other commodity, except water and except natural or artificial gas, by means of pipe lines'.[53] The effect of adding these new pipelines was treat oil pipelines as 'common carriers' under ICC regulation, treating them the same as railroads. At essentially the same time as the request for a jurisdictional ruling from the FERC under the NGA, developers of CO_2 pipelines sought comparable declarations from the ICC that CO_2 was not subject to the ICA. Following public comment on the issue, the ICC issued the requested ruling in 1981.[54]

The ICC was terminated by legislation adopted in 1995 (the ICC Termination Act of 1995) (ICC Termination Act), but Congress made no substantive change in the scope of federal jurisdiction over pipelines, simply assigning the pre-existing regulatory responsibilities of the ICC to the newly created Surface Transportation Board (STB).[55] The statutory jurisdiction of the new Board was unchanged in this regard and continued to extend to the interstate transportation by pipeline of a commodity 'other than water, gas or oil'.[56] Note that the savings provision of the ICC Termination Act specifically provided that all relevant orders and determinations issued by the ICC 'shall continue in effect according to their terms' until they are changed

---

[51] Order Approving Abandonment, *Southern Natural Gas Company*, 115 FERC ¶ 62,266 (2006) (at fn 26) (approving abandonment by sale of 142 miles of natural gas pipeline (principally 8 and 18 inches in diameter) for its conversion from transportation of natural gas to transportation of CO_2). For further discussion, see Marston and Moore, n 44 above, 454; and Nordhaus and Pitlick, 'The Regulation of CO_2 Pipelines' (2009) 30 *Energy Law Journal* 85, 88–90, available at www.felj.org/energy-law-journal/previous-issues/energy-law-journal-volume-30-no-1-2009.

[52] 34 Stat 584, 59th Cong, 1st Sess 1, ch 3591, enacted 29 June 1906.

[53] ibid.

[54] *Arco Oil and Gas Company, Petition for Declaratory Order—Jurisdiction Over Interstate Pipeline Transportation of Carbon Dioxide*, No 37529, 46 Fed Reg 18805 (26 March 1981) ('Final Declaratory Order'). The Final Declaratory Order affirmed the earlier, tentative rulings in *Cortez Pipeline Company, Petition for Declaratory Order—Commission Jurisdiction Over Transportation of Carbon Dioxide by Pipeline* and *Arco Oil and Gas Company, Petition for Declaratory Order—Jurisdiction Over Interstate Pipeline Transportation of Carbon Dioxide*, Nos 37427 and 37529, 45 Fed Reg 85177 (24 December 1980) ('Tentative Declaratory Order').

[55] ICC Termination Act of 1995, Pub L No 104-88, 109 Stat 803 (1995), at www.gpo.gov/fdsys/pkg/PLAW-104publ88/pdf/PLAW-104publ88.pdf.

[56] As amended by the ICC Termination Act, Interstate Commerce Act, 49 USC § 15301(a) provides in material part that the STB has jurisdiction over 'transportation by pipeline, or by pipeline and railroad or water, when transporting a commodity other than water, gas, or oil'.

in accordance with the law.[57] Hence, the prior jurisdictional determinations of the ICC from 1981 continue to apply.[58]

In sum, notwithstanding the changes in the statutory wording over the decades, the transfer of oil pipeline regulation to the FERC and of other regulatory responsibilities

---

[57] Section 204(a) of the ICC Termination Act. The saving provision was not included in the codification of the Termination Act, but may be found in the notes to the codification of 49 USC § 701 that established the STB (see at www.gpo.gov/fdsys/pkg/USCODE-2011-title49/pdf/USCODE-2011-title49-subtitleI-chap7-subchapI-sec701.pdf). The STB itself has recognised that the saving provision of the ICC Termination Act 'provides that ICC precedent applies to the Board': *GWI Switching Services, LP, et al*, (12 August 2001), mimeo at 4 (fn 12), available at www.stb.dot.gov/decisions/readingroom.nsf/UNID/9C C76279022BAB0085256A8E006BFB45/$file/30183.pdf; *accord*, 'Class Exemption For Motor Passenger Intra-Corporate Family Transactions', STB Finance Docket No 33685 (18 February 2000), available at (www.stb.dot.gov/decisions/readingroom.nsf/UNID/4B9598F2477DF0828525688900662DA5/$file/30325.pdf), *mimeo*, at 10 (under s 204(a) of ICC Termination Act, ICC precedent in effect on the date of enactment 'continues in effect until modified or revoked in accordance with law'). Some confusion as to the scope of STB jurisdiction under the ICA appears to have been created by a 1998 report from the General Accounting Office (now Government Accountability Office) that stated—without source or citation and without discussion of the contrary controlling precedent—that CO_2 pipelines were subject to STB regulation under the Interstate Commerce Act. See US General Accounting Office, *Surface Transportation: Issues Associated with Pipeline Regulation by the Surface Transportation Board* (April 1998) (GAO/RCED-98-99) 7 (including CO_2 among products carried by pipelines subject to the STB's jurisdiction). The error was corrected by a subsequent report of the Congressional Research Service that discussed the legal precedents and recognised that CO_2 pipelines are *not* in fact subject to regulation by the STB under the ICA. A Vann and P Parfomak, *Regulation of Carbon Dioxide (CO_2) Sequestration Pipelines: Jurisdictional Issues* (7 January 2008 and 15 April 2008) (Congressional Research Service, Order Code RL34307), at digital.library.unt.edu/ark:/67531/metadc94130/, at CRS-5 and CRS-6 (noting that 'ICC concluded that Congress intended to exclude all types of gas, including CO_2 from ICC regulation' and that, following public comment, the 'ICC confirmed its view that CO_2 pipelines were excluded from the ICC's jurisdiction'). Subsequent CRS reports on CO_2 pipelines have recognised the non-jurisdictional nature of CO_2 pipelines under current law and explored potential resulting policy implications for new CO_2 pipeline construction. P Partomak and P Folger, *Carbon Dioxide (CO_2) Pipelines for Carbon Sequestration: Emerging Policy Issues* (updated report of 17 January 2008 correcting prior version dated 19 April 2007) (Order Code RL33971), fn 92.

[58] Thus, it is incorrect to state that the STB is 'not bound' by the prior ruling of the ICC in the 1980 *Cortez* proceeding (*Cortez Pipeline Co*, 45 Fed Reg 85,178), as does one article that did not reference the savings provision of the ICC Termination Act and hence did not recognise its legal effect on the STB. See Nordhaus and Pitlick, n 51 above, 92. Similarly, some other authors have stated that the STB has not addressed the jurisdictional status of CO_2 pipelines, while ignoring the fact that the STB is bound by the savings clause by the prior rulings of the ICC declaring that CO_2 pipelines are not included. Rather, it is plain that the prior rulings of the ICC remain just as valid and binding on the STB following adoption of the ICC Termination Act as they were prior to that time. While an administrative agency—like a court—may depart from prior precedent in appropriate cases, such departures from existing precedent must be considered and supported by a reasoned analysis. Prior agency precedents may not be simply ignored. *Motor Vehicle Mfrs Ass'n v State Farm Mutual Auto Ins Co*, 463 US 29, 42, 103 S Ct 2856, 2866, 77 L Ed 2d 443 (1983) (an agency changing its course is obligated to supply 'a reasoned analysis for the change beyond that which may be required when an agency does not act in the first instance'). Moreover, the Supreme Court has cautioned that an agency interpretation of a statute or regulation that conflicts with a prior interpretation is entitled to 'considerably less deference' than a consistently held interpretation. See, eg, *Thomas Jefferson Univ v Shalala*, 512 US 504, 515, 114 S Ct 2381, 2388, 129 L Ed 2d 405 (1994) and *Cardoza-Fonseca*, 480 US at 446 n 30, 107 S Ct (1987) at 1221 n 30 (citations omitted) ('[a]n agency interpretation of a relevant provision which conflicts with the agency's earlier interpretation is "entitled to considerably less deference" than a consistently held agency view').

to the STB,[59] the jurisdictional scope of the 1905 Hepburn Act has not been altered and does not extend to CO_2 pipelines.[60]

iii. Jurisdictional Status under the Mineral Leasing Act of 1920 Administered by the Bureau of Land Management

The BLM is the agency of the Federal Government that manages federally-owned real estate. In particular, the BLM has permitting authority to allow for use of federal land for various purposes, including the constructing and operating of pipelines. In the 1980s, a unit of Exxon Inc applied to the BLM for a permit for a proposed CO_2 pipeline to cross certain federally-owned land, requesting authorisation under the Federal Land Policy and Management Act (FLPMA).[61] The BLM, however, determined CO_2 to be 'natural gas' within the meaning of a different statute the agency administered, the Mineral Leasing Act of 1920 (MLA),[62] and therefore processed the permit application under that statute instead, ultimately granting the requested permit for the CO_2 pipeline. This was significant in part because any right of way granted under the MLA (but not the FLPMA) for a pipeline to cross federal land requires that the pipeline must operate as a common carrier.

The applicant objected, but the federal district court found that the MLA statutory text was ambiguous and that BLM's interpretation that the term 'natural gas' included CO_2 was a reasonable interpretation. That ruling was affirmed on appeal.[63] Neither the district court nor the appellate court was troubled by the fact that the FERC had previously interpreted the term 'natural gas' as not including a CO_2 stream. Rather, the courts distinguished the FERC rulings on the ground that FERC had acted under a different statute and that its interpretation under that other statute had 'no bearing' on the BLM's interpretation of the statutes that it administered.[64]

Note that there are very great difference in the extent of federal ownership of land in the US. The percentages are generally quite low in the eastern States, but potentially very high in some western States. For example, the Federal Government owns only 1.7 per cent of the total acreage in Texas, but it owns over 34 per cent of neighbouring New Mexico, 36 per cent of Colorado and nearly 85 per cent of the land in Nevada.[65] Hence the practical significance of the *Lujan* case may vary greatly depending on the location of a particular CO_2 pipeline or pipeline proposal.

---

[59] The statutory wording was changed in 1977, as a result of the transfer of oil pipeline regulation under the ICA to the FERC, under the Department of Energy Organization Act (s 402(b) of the Department of Energy Organization Act, originally codified at 42 USC § 7172 (b), repealed by Pub L 103-272, 108 Stat 1379), and in 1978 as a result of the recodification of the US Code, which deleted the qualifiers 'natural or artificial' and left the exclusion of simply 'gas': 49 USC § 15301(a).

[60] 49 USC § 15301(a).

[61] 43 USC § 1761(a)(2) (1988).

[62] Mineral Leasing Act of 1920, as amended, 30 USC § 185.

[63] *Exxon Corp v Lujan*, 970 F 2d 757 (10th Cir 1992) (hereinafter *Lujan*), affirming *Exxon Corp v Lujan*, 730 F Supp 1535 (Wyo, 1990).

[64] *Lujan*, n 63 above, n 111, at 762.

[65] US Department of Interior, Bureau of Land Management, *Public Land Statistics 1999* (vol 184, BLM/BC/ST-00/001+1165) (March 2000), Table 1-3: US General Services Administration Table: Comparison of Federally Owned Land with Total Acreage of States (viewed 8 March 2017).

iv. Conclusion as to Federal Regulatory Jurisdiction over CO_2 Pipelines

The net effect of these various rulings on the status of CO_2 pipelines under federal permitting and licensing legislation over the last four decades has been summarised as follows:[66]

> [I]t seems fair to say that CO_2 pipelines are neither 'common carriers' under the Interstate Commerce Act nor 'natural gas companies' under the Natural Gas Act. They may however be 'common carriers' under the Mineral Leasing Act if (a) they cross Federal land that is subject to that act and (b) if the BLM issues right of way authorization under the MLA rather than the FLPMA. The operation of CO_2 pipelines remains subject of course to other generally applicable federal law.

B. State Regulation of Construction and Operation

The absence of federal jurisdiction under the NGA or the ICA does not mean that CO_2 pipelines are not regulated, but rather that it is State law that governs. Thus, it is the legislatures of the States where CO_2 pipeline development has actually occurred that have taken the lead, addressing issues as the need has arisen. State legislation has generally recognised CO_2 as a mineral resource in itself, or indeed recognised its role in helping to maximise the recovery of the State's hydrocarbon resources. This focus on the role of CO_2 pipelines in developing natural resources emphasises the interdependence of these CO_2 pipelines with the State's specific interest in conservation of oil and gas resources, their orderly and efficient development and safe operations. Recognising the role CO_2 pipelines play in allowing for the recovery of otherwise unrecoverable hydrocarbon resources, State legislation has also been promulgated to aid in the acquisition of the necessary rights of way for the CO_2 pipelines in order to make such oil and gas projects achievable.

The Texas experience illustrates this. The same impetus that prompted the need for the *Cortez* decisions from federal regulators fuelled legislative changes to facilitate transportation of out-of-State natural sources of CO_2 into EOR operations in west Texas. In 1981, the Texas legislature considered whether to grant condemnation authority (compulsory purchase) to common-carrier CO_2 pipelines. In the Texas Senate proceedings on the bill that would extend condemnation authority for CO_2 pipelines, it was made clear that the legislative purpose was to facilitate oil production, thereby generating additional revenues for the State.[67] Just as pipelines carrying

---

[66] IOGCC/SSEB CO_2 *Pipeline Report*, n 10 above, 26.

[67] For example, the analysis of the proposed law prepared for the legislators stated: 'The purpose of the bill was in connection with new developments in the field of secondary recovery to recover energy resources in West Texas through the use of CO_2.' Bill Analysis of Tex SB 829, Committee on Energy Resources (available at www.lrl.state.tx.us). Similarly, the author of the legislation explained: 'The purpose of [making CO_2 pipelines common carriers] is secondary recovery programs we anticipate in the oil fields. ... CO_2 is even more effective and efficient in recovering oil that we would otherwise not be able to get.' Act Relating to Regulation of Carbon Dioxide Pipelines as Common Carriers: Hearings on Tex SB 829, before Senate Committee on State Affairs, 67th Leg, RS (6 April 1981) (statement of Senator Farabee) (available at Texas State Library, Transcript and Audio Archived Files, Tape 2, Side 2).

oil had been granted the ability to exercise eminent domain because increased oil production was in the public interest, so pipelines that brought CO_2 required to produce such oil were also deemed in the public interest.

The same dynamic was at work in other States, though the precise conditions under which the State may extend eminent domain power varies by State and is not infrequently the subject of litigation.[68] In Mississippi, development of the Jackson Dome natural source of CO_2 for use in EOR operations prompted the legislature to recognise its value to the State. The 1984 Mississippi law acknowledged that pipelines that transport CO_2 for use in enhanced recovery operations in Mississippi could invoke eminent domain for the same reason—that it was in the public interest to make use of the State's natural mineral resources (which could not be produced without the CO_2 supplied by the pipeline).[69] In Louisiana, the pre-existing statutory provisions governing the condemnation of land (called 'expropriation', in Louisiana) for CO_2 pipelines serving EOR projects within the State was amended to apply to CO_2 pipelines carrying CO_2 to CO_2-EOR projects in 'other states or jurisdictions' as well, thereby underscoring the interdependence of such pipelines with an interstate undertaking.[70] Wyoming statutory law that recognises pipelines utilised in the movement of 'oil-related products' includes the construction of CO_2 pipelines under the authority of its condemnation laws.[71]

By allowing for increased oil production, CO_2 would help 'produce a large amount of revenue for the state': Act Relating to Regulation of Carbon Dioxide Pipelines as Common Carriers: Hearings on Tex SB 829, before Senate Committee on State Affairs, 67th Leg, RS (30 March 1981) (statement of Senator Farabee) (available at Texas State Library, Transcript and Audio Archived Files, Tape 2, Side 3).

[68] For example, the Texas courts have in a recent series of cases considered the minimum evidentiary showing required to support the extension of eminent domain power for pipelines carrying CO_2 as a common carrier under Texas law (and indeed other commodities). See *Denbury Green Pipeline-Texas, LLC v Texas Rice Land Partners, Ltd*, Supreme Court of Texas No 15-0225, Opinion delivered 6 January 2017, Opinion revised 7 April 2017, and cases cited therein. In *Denbury*, the Texas Supreme Court required a showing of a 'reasonable probability that, at some point after construction' the pipeline in question would serve the public by transporting CO_2 for one or more customers who will either retain ownership of their gas or sell it to parties other than the carrier.

[69] Miss Code Ann §11-27-1 (1972 amended) (1984) (provides the right of condemnation to oil, gas and EOR-related CO_2 pipelines in Mississippi). Note also that the production of CO_2 is regulated by the Mississippi Oil & Gas Board as a natural resource under Miss Code Ann (1972 amended) § 53-1-3.

[70] La Rev Stat Ann §19:2(10) (addressing expropriation rights for property in Louisiana) was added to provide eminent domain authority for entities engaged in 'the piping or marketing of carbon dioxide for use in connection with a secondary or tertiary recovery project for the enhanced recovery of liquid or gaseous hydrocarbons approved by the commissioner of conservation'. The statute was amended in 2007 to extend expropriation for the transportation of CO_2 for underground injection in connection with such projects located in Louisiana 'or in other states or jurisdictions'. Acts 2007, No 428, §1, eff 11 July 2007, codified at La Rev Stat Ann §19:2(10). In this case, the commissioner's approval consists of confirmation that the applicable regulatory authority of the State where the project is located has approved or authorised the CO_2 injection in association with such project.

[71] Wyo Stat §1-26-814 states: 'Whenever any utility or any petroleum or other pipeline company authorized to do business in this state, has not acquired ... land for construction, maintenance and operation of their facilities ... or which may be affected by any operation connected with the construction or maintenance of same, the utility or company has the right of eminent domain and may condemn the easement required by the utility or company.' The court process then becomes solely the determination regarding compensation prescribed by Wyo Stat § 1-26-701-713, as measured on date of evaluation determined under Wyo Stat §1-26-704.

Just as the operator's right under private leases to inject CO_2 into a subsurface oil and gas reservoir is permitted by the regulatory authority governing oil and gas production, the legislative authority granted to acquire the rights of way for a CO_2 pipeline stems from that same need to allow use of CO_2 to maximize the ultimate recovery of a state's mineral resources, thereby avoiding waste of resources. In sum, the CO_2 pipeline is simply an adjunct needed for the development of certain oilfields.

C. Safety Regulation

As detailed in section III.C.i, in 1988 Congress brought CO_2 pipelines explicitly under the pre-existing federal safety framework for pipelines.

i. The Federal Statutory Framework for Pipeline Safety Regulation

With the construction of long-line CO_2 pipelines in the 1980s, Congress brought CO_2 pipelines under the already-existing federal framework for pipeline safety regulation. At the time, federal safety regulation covered natural gas pipelines (since 1968)[72] and hazardous liquid pipelines (since 1979).[73] The term 'natural gas pipelines' was understood in those regulations to refer to pipelines carrying flammable methane (CH_4), and the term 'hazardous liquid' was essentially defined to include petroleum, petroleum products or anhydrous ammonia.[74] As stated by the Department of Transportation at the time, CO_2 as a gas 'is considered to be inert and does not easily react with other gases in the atmosphere'.[75] Hence, neither of these statutes applied to pipelines carrying CO_2, whether carrying gaseous or dense-phase CO_2.

In reporting out the bill that became the Pipeline Safety Reauthorization Act of 1988, the House Committee on Energy and Commerce noted that the Committee had 'for some time' recommended the adoption of safety regulation for CO_2 pipelines.[76] The Committee Report recognised the role CO_2 played in the already-expanding EOR industry and stressed that it '[did] not want to limit the future construction of CO_2 pipelines because of unnecessary safety regulations';

---

[72] Natural Gas Pipeline Safety Act of 1968 (NGPSA), Pub L 90-481, 12 August 1968, 82 Stat 720.

[73] Pipeline Safety Act of 1979, Pub L No 96-129, §§ 201–218, 93 Stat 989 (1979) (adding the Hazardous Liquid Pipeline Safety Act in Title II).

[74] See, eg, Department of Transportation, Office of Pipeline Safety, *Notice of Proposed Rulemaking: Transportation of Carbon Dioxide by Pipeline*, 54 Fed Reg 41912 (12 October 1989) (hereinafter '1989 CO_2 Pipeline NOPR') ('[h]azardous liquid is defined to include petroleum, petroleum products, or anhydrous ammonia' and '[t]herefore, part 195 does not currently apply to the transportation of carbon dioxide (CO_2) by pipeline'). In addition to including 'petroleum or any petroleum product', the definition of 'hazardous liquid' in the 1979 statute gave the Secretary authority over transportation of other materials 'in liquid state' (excluding liquefied natural gas) which 'which, as determined by the Secretary, 'may pose an unreasonable risk to life or property when transported by pipeline facilities'. Safety Act of 1979, 93 Stat. 1003. The Secretary had never made such a determination with respect to CO_2 pipelines carrying dense-phase CO_2.

[75] 1989 CO_2 Pipeline NOPR, n 74 above, 54 Fed Reg at 41912.

[76] Quoted ibid at 41913.

nonetheless, it concluded that CO_2 pipelines should have 'appropriate Federal safety regulations'.[77] Accordingly Section 211 of the Pipeline Safety Reauthorization Act of 1988 amended the Hazardous Liquid Pipeline Safety Act of 1979 by adding a new provision, Section 219, which placed CO_2 pipelines under the safety regulatory framework. That section provided that 'in addition to hazardous liquids', the Secretary shall regulate 'carbon dioxide which is transported by pipeline facilities'.[78] The statute did not distinguish between pipelines carrying gaseous CO_2 and those carrying dense-phase or supercritical CO_2. The new provision was made effective 18 months after the date of enactment.[79]

The effect of the 1988 legislation was to bring CO_2 pipelines under the pre-existing regulatory structure established for natural gas pipelines (in 1968) and for hazardous liquid pipelines in 1979. Several subsequent statutes have added to the basic framework, generally seeking to strengthen the safety regulation regime and the regulators' powers in implementing it.[80] In general, the regulatory approach that Congress had adopted in those statutes was a cooperative federal–State approach under which the federal safety regulator was directed to establish minimum federal standards that would apply to both interstate and intrastate facilities. Enforcement of the standards, however, was divided between federal and State regulators. The federal regulator was granted exclusive jurisdiction over *interstate* facilities, but was precluded from enforcing the federal standards on *intrastate* facilities in those States that met certain statutory conditions, which included a requirement for the State to certify annually that it had adopted the federal safety standards and was enforcing those standards by inspections conducted by qualified personnel.

Initially, implementation of the pipeline safety regime was assigned to the Office of Pipeline Safety (OPS), created as part of the original 1968 legislation and through the

---

[77] ibid.
[78] As originally enacted, the new section read as follows: '(a) GENERAL RULE.—In addition to hazardous liquids, the Secretary shall regulate under this title carbon dioxide which is transported by pipeline facilities. (b) REGULATIONS.—The Secretary, as necessary and appropriate, shall amend regulations issued with respect to hazardous liquids under this title and shall issue new regulations to ensure the safe transportation of carbon dioxide by pipeline facilities.' Pipeline Safety Reauthorization Act of 1988, Pub L No 100-561, § 102, 102 Stat 2805, 2806.
[79] 1988 Reauthorization Act, § 219(c).
[80] See, eg, the Pipeline Safety Act of 1992, Pub L No 102-508, 106 Stat 3289 (24 October 1992); the Accountable Pipeline Safety and Partnership Act of 1996, Pub L.104-304, 110 Stat 3793 (12 October 1996); the Pipeline Safety Improvement Act of 2002, Pub L No 107-355 (17 December 2002), 49 USC §§ 6103–6107 and 60104–60133); and the Pipeline Safety, Regulatory Certainty, and Job Creation Act of 2011, Pub L 112–90, 125 Stat 1904 (3 January 2012). This statutory evolution has been copiously addressed in the legal literature. The legislative and regulatory evolution of pipeline safety regulation during the earlier period is addressed in JT Scott and JE Graykowski, *The Federal Pipeline Safety Statutes: the Need for Increase Company Awareness* (Eastern Mineral Law Foundation) (White Paper, 1991) ch 20, available at www.emlf.org/clientuploads/directory/whitepaper/Scott_91_excerpt.pdf. For a discussion of the federal/State interplay (focused on natural gas pipelines), see Jim Behnke, 'Safety jurisdiction over natural gas pipelines' (1998) 19 *Energy Law Journal* 71. The 2002 pipeline safety legislation is addressed in SA Moore and TI Zolet, 'Pipeline Safety Improvement Act of 2002' (2003) 24 *Energy Law Journal* 107. Lastly, for a general overview of the statutory framework as it stood in 2013 (but focused on natural gas gathering), see M Diamond and J Curry, 'Pipeline Safety: An Overview of the Legal Framework, the Regulation of Gas Gathering, and How Current and Future Regulation May Affect Producers' (2013) 34 *Energy & Mineral Law Institute* 5 (see esp § 5.02 summarising the pipeline safety legal framework).

Research and Special Programs Administration (RSPA). In 2004, Congress created the Pipeline and Hazardous Materials Safety Administration (PHMSA) and assigned to it the duties and powers relating to pipeline and hazardous materials transportation and safety that were vested in the Secretary (that had previously been exercised by the RSPA).[81]

Under this federal statutory framework, State and local regulation of federally-regulated *interstate* pipeline facilities is generally pre-empted by the federal law.[82] With regard to *intrastate* pipeline facilities, however, the States were left free under certain conditions to adopt 'additional or more stringent safety standards' that were compatible with the federal standards, where the State authority has submitted a certification that it complies with certain provisions of the federal legislation.[83] The PHMSA Administrator has provided a good summary of the current federal/State framework:[84]

> Sections 60105 and 60106 of the Pipeline Safety Act continue to allow States to assume safety authority through PHMSA for the inspection and enforcement of intrastate pipelines. PHMSA sets the minimum Federal guidelines for pipeline safety, which the participating States then adopt into their State code and enforce. States are allowed, under Section 60104(c) of the Pipeline Safety Act, to adopt more stringent safety standards than the minimum standards PHMSA sets. This allows States to codify and enforce regulations that deal with specific, regional (or local) risks that might not be feasible or cost-beneficial to regulate on the Federal level. Many States have established safety regulations that are more stringent than the Federal regulations. [PHMSA] partner[s] with 52 State pipeline safety programs, containing approximately 300 full-time inspectors, through certification and agreements for the inspection of the Nation's intrastate gas and hazardous liquid pipelines. PHMSA also has interstate agent agreements with nine States to perform interstate pipeline inspections. With the exception of Alaska and Hawaii, which do not participate in the State pipeline safety program, State pipeline safety agencies are the first line of defence in protecting much of the American public from pipeline risks on lines that exist primarily where people live and work. State pipeline safety agencies have authority over approximately 80 percent of the total pipeline infrastructure under PHMSA's oversight and have always been a critical component of a sound pipeline oversight program.

---

[81] Norman Y Mineta Research and Special Programs Improvement Act, Pub L 108-426, 118 Stat 2423 (2004).

[82] 49 USC § 60104(c) provides in part that '[a] State authority may not adopt or continue in force safety standards for interstate pipeline facilities or interstate pipeline transportation' (except for certain one-call notification programs). See also *Olympic Pipe Line Co v City of Seattle*, 437 F 3d 872 (9th Cir, 2006) (city of Seattle's regulation of inter-State oil pipeline in addition to federal–State safety agreement was expressly pre-empted). See also Nordhaus and Pitlick, n 51 above, 95.

[83] 49 USC § 60104(c). See also *Shell Oil Co v City of Santa Monica*, 830 F 2d 1052, 1064 (9th Cir 1987). 'The legislative reports acknowledge broadly, and without qualification, that states may impose additional, compatible standards. ... [T]he HLPSA does not preempt Santa Monica from imposing all safety standards on intrastate pipelines.' (ibid at 1066) But see *ANR Pipeline Co v Iowa State Commerce Comm'n*, 828 F 2d 465, 469 (8th Civ 1987) ('Federal interest in intrastate safety issues remains strong' and state authority is subject to federal control).

[84] *A Review of the Pipeline Safety, Regulatory Certainty, and Job Creation Act of 2011: Hearing Before the Railroads, Pipelines, and Hazardous Materials Subcommittee of the House Committee on Transportation and Infrastructure*, 113th Cong 2d Sess (20 May 2014) (prepared statement of Cynthia L Quarterman, Administrator, PHMSA).

ii. Regulatory Implementation for CO_2 Pipelines in 1991

Following the 1988 legislation that brought CO_2 pipelines under the basic federal safety framework, the OPS commenced rulemaking proceedings to implement the change.[85] The governing statute provided that '[i]n addition to hazardous liquids, the Secretary shall regulate under this title carbon dioxide which is transported by pipeline facilities' and issue new regulations 'to ensure the safe transportation of carbon dioxide by pipeline facilities'.[86] Hence, CO_2 is not a hazardous liquid but is to be regulated 'in addition to hazardous liquids'. As stated by the proposed rule in 1991:[87]

> Hazardous liquid is defined to include petroleum, petroleum products, or anhydrous ammonia. Therefore, part 195 does not currently apply to the transportation of carbon dioxide (CO_2) by pipeline.

In petitioning for the new rule, the API had cautioned OPS against confusing CO_2 with hazardous liquids, 'to prevent the possibility of indiscriminate future application to CO_2 pipelines of regulations suited for hazardous liquid pipelines, and vice versa', a notion with which OPS explicitly agreed, 'especially since Congress distinguished the terms in the Reauthorization Act', and as a result the revised part 195 rules were applied to CO_2 pipelines 'without calling CO_2 a hazardous liquid'.[88] Nevertheless, the OPS chose to retain the pre-existing title of the part 195 regulations, that is, 'Transportation of Hazardous Liquids by Pipeline', believing that amending the title to include CO_2 'would result in an awkward title'.[89]

The final rules were adopted in 1991.[90] The term 'carbon dioxide' was defined to mean 'a fluid consisting of more than 90 percent carbon dioxide molecules compressed to a supercritical state'.[91] The Department of Transportation noted that it had the authority to regulate CO_2 transport in both a gaseous and a supercritical state, but limited its regulations to dense-phase (ie supercritical) CO_2:[92]

> At present, for economic reasons, CO_2 is transported by pipeline in a supercritical state, *ie* dense vapor state. In the future, if CO_2 is transported other than as a dense vapor where the part 195 regulations are inappropriate for such transportation, [the agency] will issue additional regulations for such transportation.

In 2012, however, federal legislation was adopted that directs the Secretary to prescribe minimum safety standards for gaseous CO_2 pipelines, and in so doing, to

---

[85] *1989 CO_2 Pipeline NOPR*, n 74 above. The agency action followed a petition filed by the American Petroleum Institute (API) to amend the pt 195 regulations to include the regulation of CO_2 pipelines. The API's petition was based on work of an industry task force that included representatives of nine companies that owned or operated CO_2 pipelines. ibid, 41,913.
[86] Pipeline Safety Reauthorization Act of 1988, n 78 above.
[87] *1989 CO_2 Pipeline NOPR*, n 74 above.
[88] ibid, 41914.
[89] ibid.
[90] *Final Rule: Transportation of Carbon Dioxide by Pipeline*, 56 Fed Reg 26922 (12 June 1991) (hereinafter 'CO_2 Pipeline Final Rule'). The time for compliance was subsequently extended for one year. *Final Rule: Transportation of Carbon Dioxide by Pipeline*, 56 Fed Reg 50665 (10 September 1991).
[91] Codified at 49 CFR § 195.2.
[92] *CO_2 Pipeline Final Rule*, at 26923.

consider whether applying the pre-existing minimum safety standards in the Code of Federal Regulations (CFR), title 49, part 195 for transportation of carbon dioxide in a liquid state would ensure safety.[93]

As codified, 49 CFR § 195(a) generally applies to both onshore and offshore pipelines,[94] while § 195(b) sets out various exceptions for certain production facilities, including, for example, onshore flow lines, refining and manufacturing facilities, or storage or in-plant piping systems associated with such facilities.[95] The final rule generally requires that all pipeline components, as well as any other commodity that may come into contact with the CO_2, must be 'chemically compatible' with the transported CO_2.[96]

The applicable rules have also incorporated certain portions of the consensus-based industry standards applicable for CO_2 pipelines that have been developed over the years. Thus, 49 CFR §§ 195.3 and 195.452(h)(4)(i) expressly incorporate certain provisions of the industry standards developed by the American Society of Mechanical Engineers (ASME), applicable, inter alia, to pipelines transporting CO_2.[97] The long-standing ASME standards based on US CO_2 pipeline industry experience provide a basis that may be used by countries that have not previously had a need to develop their own national standards for CO_2 pipelines.

iii. State Safety Regulation

Generally speaking, because of the pre-emptive effect of federal safety regulation by the PHMSA of all the major interstate CO_2 pipelines, the States have generally been precluded from entering this regulatory arena on their own, except through the adoption of rules the same as or stricter than those required under the PHMSA. Those States that have opted to exercise such regulatory authority, and in which there are located CO_2 pipelines, participate in the same manner as the PHMSA would otherwise in the construction, inspection and oversight on their intrastate CO_2 pipelines. In some States, such as Texas, there is a requirement to notify the State pipeline safety regulator prior to beginning construction of some intrastate lines.[98] In general, the federal requirement that any State program have consistent regulatory obligations does help achieve legal uniformity in the regulation of

---

[93] See § 15 of the Pipeline Safety, Regulatory Certainty, and Job Creation Act of 2011, n 80 above, amending 49 USC § 60102.

[94] 49 CFR § 195.1(a) (with certain exceptions applies to pipeline facilities and the transportation of hazardous liquids or CO_2 associated with those facilities in or affecting interstate or foreign commerce, including pipeline facilities on the Outer Continental Shelf).

[95] ibid § 195.1(b).

[96] ibid § 195.4.

[97] ibid § 195.3 and § 195.452(h)(4)(i) (expressly incorporating certain pipeline-integrity related provisions of ASME/ANSI B31.4–2006, 'Pipeline Transportation Systems for Liquid Hydrocarbons and Other Liquids' (20 October 2006)). Section 400(a) of the ASME B31.4 Standard (within ch 1 on 'Scope and Definitions') states explicitly that it applies, inter alia, to CO_2. See also fig 400.1.2: Diagram Showing Scope of ASME B31-4 for Carbon Dioxide Pipeline Systems.

[98] In Texas, for example, a pipeline operator or construction company must notify the Railroad Commission's Pipeline Safety Division before construction on a pipeline, when the construction involves an intrastate pipeline that is longer than one mile and is subject to safety regulation. See summary of Texas regulation in 39 Texas Reg 9969 (19 December 2014).

pipeline transportation safety, while recognising that the actual transport of CO_2 is a unique component that is interdependent with the source of the CO_2 and the end utilisation in the production of the State's natural resources.

iv. Safety Record of CO_2 Pipelines

Under the various federal statutes referenced in the preceding subsections, pipeline operators, including CO_2 pipeline operators, are required to report accidents to the Department of Transportation. The federal database allows the safety regulators at the PHMSA (and the public) to track and document the safety record of each type of pipeline operator. According to Congressional testimony from the PHMSA, the data demonstrate that CO_2 pipelines have had a 'particularly good' safety record since reporting began in the early 1990s.[99] Of a total of 3,695 serious accidents reported to the PHMSA on hazardous liquid and CO_2 pipelines between 1994 and 2008, only 36 involved CO_2 pipelines; and of those 36 incidents, only one involved an injury.[100] There have been no fatalities.[101]

IV. RELATED ISSUES: PIPELINE STANDARDS; CONTROL OF PRODUCT SPECIFICATIONS; AND CAPACITY ALLOCATION

A. CO_2 Pipeline Standards

i. ASME B31.4

As CO_2 pipelines expanded in the US during the 1980s and 1990s, the ASME included CO_2 pipelines within its design and safety standards for liquid pipeline transportation systems designated as 'B31.4'.[102] The AMSE B31.4 standard is intended to address

> safe design, construction, inspection, testing, operation, and maintenance of liquid pipeline systems for protection of the general public and operating company personnel, as well as

---

[99] Hearing on Regulatory Aspects of Carbon Capture, Transportation, and Sequestration before the Senate Committee on Energy and Natural Resources, 110th Cong 2d Sess (31 January 2008) at 19 (prepared statement of Krista L Edwards, Deputy Administrator of PHMSA), available at www.gpo.gov/fdsys/pkg/CHRG-110shrg41620/pdf/CHRG-110shrg41620.pdf.

[100] ibid. A review of the PHMSA database through 1 April 2015 shows that the industry's record of no fatalities has been continued to date. The accident reporting database is found on the PHMSA website at www.phmsa.dot.gov/portal/site/PHMSA/menuitem.6f23687cf7b00b0f22e4c6962d9c8789/?vgnextoid=fdd2dfa122a1d110VgnVCM1000009ed07898RCRD&vgnextchannel=3430fb649a2dc110VgnVCM1000009ed07898RCRD&vgnextfmt=print.

[101] Accident reporting database on the PHMSA website, n 100 above.

[102] Clause 400(a) of ASME B31.4 states that '[t]his Code applies to ... carbon dioxide'. See also fig 400.1.1-2: Diagram Showing Scope of ASME B31.4 for Carbon Dioxide Pipeline Systems. The B31.4 standards form one part of the ASME Code for Pressure Piping, ASME B31. It may be noted in this context that the online guidance provided by the UK's Health and Safety Executive (HSE) to the effect that ASME B31.4 'does not include CO_2 within the list of fluids to which the code is intended to apply' is directly at odds with the text of ASME B31.4, and thus appears to be erroneous. See UK HSE, *Pipeline design codes and standards for use in UK CO_2 Storage and Sequestration projects* (B31.4 'does not include CO_2 within the list of fluids to which the code is intended to apply').

for reasonable protection of the piping system against vandalism and accidental damage by others, and reasonable protection of the environment.[103]

Among other aspects of design, construction and operation, the ASME B31.4 standard addresses: pipeline design (including, inter alia, load classifications, combining loads, calculation of stresses; criteria for pipe wall thickness and allowances to prevent yield failure, buckling, fatigue, fracture), use of used pipeline; connections (flanges, valves, joints, etc); materials; construction, welding and assembly; restoration of right-of-way and clean-up; auxiliary CO_2 piping; inspection and testing (including qualification of inspectors, type and extent of examination required); repair of defects; record-keeping; operation and maintenance procedures affecting safety (including operation and maintenance plans and procedures; line markers and signs, right-of-way maintenance and patrolling); pipeline integrity assessments and repairs; leak detection; qualifying a piping system for a higher operating pressure; and corrosion control.[104] The 2012 revision of the standard added a new chapter, with certain requirements applicable exclusively to CO_2 pipelines.

Components of these consensus-developed industry standards have been given legal force in the US by incorporation by reference of various aspects of ASME B31.4 into federal regulations adopted by the PHMSA. These regulations are found in part 195 of title 49 of the Code of Federal Regulations.[105] Reflecting the incorporation of standards into federal law, Clause 400(g) of ASME B31.4 has, since at least 2002, specifically cautioned users that part 195 of the PHMSA regulations governs the transportation by pipeline in inter-State and foreign commerce of CO_2 in the US.

While the part 195 regulations apply to cross-border pipelines (known in the US as 'interstate' pipelines), similar requirements are applied by regulators in the applicable States to 'intrastate' CO_2 pipelines. The staff of the US EPA have prepared a helpful memorandum citing a number of instances where federal and State regulations incorporate the ASME B31 standards.[106]

ii. Other Standards and Recommended Practices for CO_2 Pipelines

In addition to the ASME standard applicable in the US (and as incorporated by reference in federal regulations), there are other standards or recommended practices for CO_2 pipelines elsewhere in the world. For example, Standard Z662, *Oil and Gas Pipeline Systems*, was developed by the Canadian Standards Association. That standard addresses many of the same matters as AMSE B31.4, but may have particular relevance to US operators where the CO_2 pipeline crosses the US-Canadian border. For this reason, in 2008, the PHMSA commissioned a study

---

[103] AMSE B31.4, section 400(c).
[104] See generally ASME B31.4 (2016).
[105] 49 CFR pt 195 (2016).
[106] Memorandum from Ross Elliott, US EPA in RCRA Docket No EPA-HQ-RCRA-2010-0695 (May 2013), 'Re: Examples Where ASME B31 Standards Are Incorporated by Reference by Federal and State Regulatory Agencies'.

comparing Z662 with the US ASME B31.4 standard, which resulted in a published detailed comparison (in Appendix B of the report) of the two standards.[107]

Other standards or recommended practices of potential interest include the International Organization for Standards (ISO) Standard 13623, *Petroleum and natural gas industries—Pipeline transportation systems*, and DNV-RP-J202, *Design and Operation of CO_2 Pipelines* (a recommended practice developed by the Norwegian-based consulting firm Det Norske Veritas (April 2010)). In addition, the ISO has developed a final draft standard, which was approved in 2016 and is expected to be published as an international standard during 2017. That ISO standard explicitly recognises various existing standards and addresses only certain matters not already covered by those existing standards, specifically including, inter alia, ASME B31.4 and the PHMSA's part 195 regulations as referenced in the standard's Bibliography.

B. Managing CO_2 Stream Quality Specifications

i. *A Word of Caution: 'One Size' CO_2 Stream Quality Specifications will not Fit All Projects*

Carbon dioxide is an extremely common element in the natural world. It is found in the subsurface in widely varying combinations with other elements, ranging from minor trace amounts to nearly pure concentrations (98 per cent or more). The specific chemical composition of a particular source defines the potential commercial uses for which that geologic resource may be developed. For example, in the US, natural gas pipeline tariffs typically allow CO_2 to be included in transported natural gas streams up to a level of either 2 or 3 per cent of total volume.[108] Natural gas production streams with higher CO_2 concentrations must be processed to remove the excess CO_2 to meet the allowed pipeline specification; the excess CO_2 is vented. Similarly, geologic resources that are produced principally for crude petroleum rather than methane also need to separate out the excess CO_2 content to meet oil pipeline quality specifications.

If the excess CO_2 content in a production stream is sufficiently high, however, the CO_2 itself may be converted to a commercially-valuable product. For example, one

---

[107] US Department of Transportation, Pipeline and Hazardous Materials Safety Administration, Office of Pipeline Safety, *Final Report: Comparison of US and Canadian Transmission Pipeline Consensus Standards* (submitted by Michael Baker Jr, Inc) (Delivery Order DTRS56-02-D-70036) (2008). For a summary and commentary on CSA Z662.03, see Canadian Standards Association, *Z662.1-03: Commentary on CSA Standard Z662-03, Oil and Gas Pipeline Systems* 2nd edn (Mississauga, Ontario, CSA, 2003).For a comprehensive review of various liquid pipeline integrity and safety considerations and how they are treated under various standards, including ASME B31.4, see *Oil and Gas Pipelines Integrity and Safety Handbook* (ed R Windston Revie) (Chichester. Wiley, 2015).

[108] One review of allowed CO_2 limits in natural gas pipeline tariffs noted that the tariffs generally allowed CO_2 to comprise up to either 2% or 3% of the product tendered for shipment. Submission of The Indicated Shippers in *Northern Natural Gas Company*, FERC Docket No RP07-425-000 (3 August 2007) (submittal # 20070803-5126), at elibrary.ferc.gov/idmws/common/opennat.asp?fileID=11414211. The average actual CO_2 content in US natural gas pipelines at that time was between 0.3% and 3.0% (ibid).

large natural gas project has commercialised a production stream containing 0.6 per cent helium (He), about 21 per cent methane (CH_4) and around 65 per cent CO_2.[109] The methane, helium and much of the CO_2 are each sold as separate commercial products, while the hydrogen sulfide (H_2S) content of about 5 per cent is disposed of.

But accumulations of nearly pure CO_2 (ie 98–99 per cent or higher) also exist in multiple locations around the world.[110] The map in Figure 14.3 illustrates the widespread nature of such natural accumulations of CO_2.

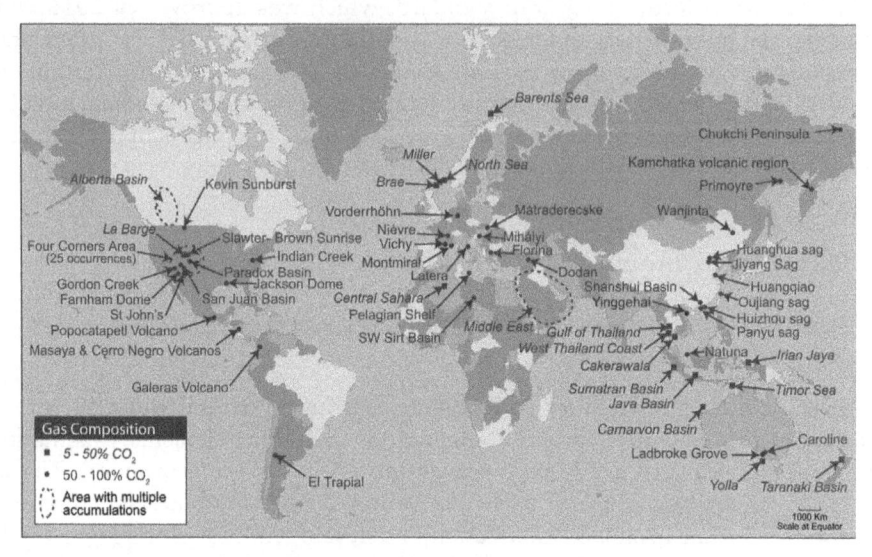

Figure 14.3: Illustrative Map of Natural CO_2 Accumulations[111]

The existence of such natural CO_2 resources has been known for over a century. The Bravo Dome reservoir in New Mexico was discovered in 1916.[112] Commercial production of naturally-occurring CO_2 began as early as 1931 in two separate locations: at Bravo Dome in New Mexico (produced for use in dry-ice and bottled liquids production) and at Farnham Dome in Utah (where the CO_2 was transported

---

[109] This is ExxonMobil Corporation's Labarge Field in Wyoming. See M Parker et al 'CO_2 Management at ExxonMobil's LaBarge Field, Wyoming, USA' (2011) 4 *Energy Procedia* 5455, 5456, available at dx.doi.org/10.1016/j.egypro.2011.02.531. This project is said to have the highest CO_2 content combined with the lowest BTU content for natural gas that is commercially produced in the world (ibid).

[110] For an overview of natural CO_2 reservoirs in the western US, see Allis et al, n 22 above. For CO_2 resources in Europe, see Pearce et al, n 28 above.

[111] Special Report from the Intergovernmental Panel on Climate Change (IPCC), IPCC 2005, Working Group III of the IPCC, B Metz et al (eds), *IPCC Special Report on Carbon Dioxide Capture and Storage* (Cambridge, Cambridge University Press, 2005) 210 (fig 5.11).

[112] Allis et al, n 22 above. In Germany, natural occurrences of CO_2 have been known for even longer, since the end of the 19th century. S Brune et al, *CO_2-deposits at Vorderrhön area (Thuringia)—gas migration from a deep reservoir to surface?* (proceedings of International Conference on Gas Geochemistry ICGG7 (2003)) 37–39.

by surface pipeline to a dry-ice plant).[113] The very large CO_2 reserves at the McElmo Dome CO_2 formation in Colorado were discovered in 1948.[114]

Each of these naturally-occurring mineral sources has its own unique chemical composition. Commonly occurring non-CO_2 components include methane (CH_4), hydrogen sulfide (H_2S), helium (He), nitrogen (N_2), oxygen (O_2) and water (H_2O). Similarly, the raw gas streams captured from the gasification or combustion of coal or during other industrial processes (eg methane stream reforming, methanol or ammonia manufacture) will each have its own unique composition profile.

In sum, managing the appropriate CO_2 content of hydrocarbon production streams in production and transportation piping as well as other facilities has been a routine aspect of oil and gas operations in the US for well over a century and, as noted, CO_2-specific production and CO_2 pipeline transportation began in 1931. Hence, planning and operational considerations of handling CO_2 are well understood by industry, and are addressed by private contracts among industry participants that are tailored to particular commercial projects as well as by government regulation.[115]

In the author's judgement, it would therefore be a significant error to conclude that new laws, regulations or construction or stream composition standards are required in order to accommodate the construction of CO_2 pipelines. The existing framework allowed for commercial CO_2 production, transport and use over the last 85 plus years and the contract models and standards developed in the US oil and gas industry have been adapted for use in many oil-producing areas of the world.

It should be noted, too, that much of the published literature discussing CO_2 stream composition in the context of CCS operations appears to focus principally on addressing acceptable composition of CO_2 streams *to be potentially captured* by emission sources. This analytic approach may be appropriate for future potential projects, where captured CO_2 is to be delivered for storage in non-EOR operations. In the context of EOR-related uses of captured CO_2, however, such an approach would appear to be largely 'upside-down', in the sense that it focuses on quality specifications from the standpoint of the CO_2 *supplier* rather than from the standpoint of the CO_2 *customer*. For a project that hopes to sell captured CO_2 for EOR or other economic uses, however, the commercial reality is likely to be quite the reverse: it is the *buyers or the end users* who will define the acceptable quality specifications of the product they are willing to purchase. The CO_2 supplier will need to ensure that its product meets *the buyer's quality specifications* at the delivery point. The extent of treatment or processing of the raw capture stream will thus be dictated by the technical and commercial requirements of the buyers.

The requirements of the buyers will be reflected in the composition standards applied by the various 'midstream' industry participants, such as the CO_2 pipeline operator. The pipeline operator provides the infrastructure used to deliver a valuable

---

[113] Allis et al, n 22 above.

[114] JA Cappa and DD Rice, *Carbon Dioxide in Mississippian Rocks of the Paradox Basin and Adjacent Areas, Colorado, Utah, New Mexico, and Arizona* (US Geological Survey Bulletin 2000-H) (Washington, DC, US Government Printing Office, 1995) H4.

[115] For example, as early as 1989, the US Government moved to include CO_2 pipelines within the federal pipeline safety framework. See CO_2 *Pipeline NOPR*, n 74 above.

commodity to paying shippers. In negotiations prior to entering into a contract to accept CO_2 from any supplier, the pipeline operator will work with the supplier to ensure that the product to be delivered to customers will meet the customers' commercial requirements. In short, the 'upstream' parties supplying a CO_2 stream will ultimately have to meet the quality requirements *of the downstream entities*—which is to say, whoever is willing to pay to purchase a commercial CO_2 product.

As a result, the product quality issues are analogous to those faced by pipelines for natural gas, petroleum or petroleum products. The delivered product on a given network will typically be a 'system average' composition (at least for any particular delivery point reflecting inputs that are upstream of that delivery point). This means that questions of equity may arise *among the suppliers* tendering product that varies from the 'system average' composition. Some may wish to tender 'above-average' quality product; others may tender 'off-spec' or 'below average' product. Pipelines receiving product from multiple supply sources typically have some capability to blend product streams to ensure that the delivered 'system average' product meets contracted delivery requirements. The technical and commercial parameters governing such blending can be highly fact-specific. In addition, a supplier tendering 'below average' product may be effectively subsidised by suppliers tendering average or above-average quality product, creating questions of *equity and cost allocation among shippers* on the pipeline system.

In order to provide equity among suppliers tendering product while ensuring delivery of 'in-spec' product to customers, industry participants have long developed pipeline- or project-specific solutions that are adapted to their particular circumstances, and which are embodied in private contracts, public tariffs and regulatory decisions. For example, crude petroleum pipelines may operate a 'gravity bank' or 'quality bank' to order, to treat equitably shippers who tender different quality product.[116] Similarly, the quality specifications of natural gas pipelines—including

---

[116] A good summary of one particular 'quality bank' on the Trans Alaska Pipeline Systems (TAPS) was provided in an Initial Decision in FERC, Docket No OR14-6-000, 147 FERC ¶ 63,008 (2014), *mimeo* at 2, *aff'd*, 149 FERC ¶ 61,149 (2014):

> Crude oil is a mixture of different hydrocarbon molecules, some of which are more valuable to refiners than others. In general, the types of molecules that refiners use to produce gasoline, diesel fuel and jet fuel are the most valuable. Each of the crude oil fields on the North Slope has its own unique mixture of hydrocarbon molecules. Because these crudes all have different qualities (that is, different proportions of the various types of hydrocarbon molecules), they all have different values to refiners.
>
> All of the North Slope crudes tendered at Pump Station No 1 are blended together and transported on TAPS as a single commingled common stream (that is, the ANS common stream). The quality of the ANS common stream is also affected by the operations of the refineries connected to TAPS. As a result of crude oil processing at those refineries, the qualities of the refinery return streams differ from the quality of the offtake streams at those locations, which, in turn, affects the quality of the ANS common stream delivered to the Valdez Terminal. At the Valdez Marine Terminal, all shippers receive delivery of the ANS common stream regardless of the quality of the crude oil that they tendered to TAPS.
>
> The TAPS Quality Bank was designed to compensate shippers for differences in the values of the crude oils which they tender to TAPS as compared to the value of the commingled ANS common stream. Shippers of crude oils that have a lower value than the ANS common stream are required to make payments into the Quality Bank, while shippers of crude oils with a value higher than the ANS common stream receive payments from the Quality Bank.

specifications for CO_2—are adapted to their particular circumstances and modified if and as conditions change, with varying impacts on different pipeline segments or supply or delivery points.[117]

In sum, pipeline quality specifications are specific to each pipeline and must take into account various design or operational requirements, including the commingling of available CO_2 supply sources and, of course, the customer requirements, whether for utilisation in CO_2-EOR or by the food and beverage industry. The applicable documents require careful drafting to reflect the actual operational and commercial requirements for the project in question. This need for flexibility and fit-for-performance drafting of pipeline quality specifications means that uniform CO_2 quality specifications or standards are neither appropriate nor desirable: 'one-size-fits-all' composition standards for 'pipeline quality' CO_2 are likely to prove ill-adapted to the technical and commercial requirements for many projects.[118] And of course, as is the case with pipelines carrying other materials (eg crude oil, refined petroleum products, natural gas, etc), each pipeline operator is required under US federal pipeline safety requirements to ensure that the CO_2 stream is compatible with the equipment and materials used for transportation.[119]

ii. Illustrative Pipeline Quality Specifications for CO_2 Pipeline Stream

Existing CO_2 pipeline quality specifications for CO_2 in the US are established by private contracts and are therefore not published, although in some instances these contracts have been included in published documents, such as filings with government agencies. The quality specifications provisions from two of these are reproduced in Figure 14.4.[120] They illustrate the wide range in acceptable CO_2 stream quality. In addition, those contracts show the kind of highly-detailed and individually-negotiated

---

[117] For an example of a dispute over proposed changes in quality specifications of a natural gas pipeline that included a proposed change in allowed CO_2 content (among other substances), see 'Order Following Technical Conference' issued in *Northern Natural Gas Company*, Docket No RP07-425-000, 121 FERC ¶ 61,122 (issued 31 October 2007). The case addressed in part the appropriate specifications for CO_2, as well as nitrogen (N_2), oxygen (O_2) and other substances. In particular, the record included considerable expert testimony and arguments concerning CO_2 interaction with water from the natural gas storage field, and illustrates some of the complex differences in positions that may arise among affected suppliers.

[118] The natural gas pipeline experience is informative. The natural gas pipeline industry in the US is well over 100 years old, and is many times the size of the CO_2 pipeline industry. Yet gas quality specifications are still individually established by the pipeline operators. For a detailed review of the evolution and present state of natural gas pipeline quality specifications, see M Foss, *Interstate Natural Gas— Quality Specifications and Interchangeability* (December 2004) (paper prepared by the Center for Energy Economics of the Bureau of Economic Geology, University of Texas). The paper includes a comparative table showing the then applicable quality specifications for a number of major natural gas pipelines, which vary considerably from each other. See Tables 1–4, 'Snapshot of Selected US/Canada Natural Gas Transmission Pipeline's General Terms and Conditions on Gas Quality and OFOs'.

[119] For example, the original Notice of Proposed Rulemaking to include CO_2 pipelines within the federal pipeline safety framework (*1989 CO_2 Pipeline NOPR*, n 74 above) specifically recognised the importance of ensuring the chemical compatibility of CO_2 with the pipeline.

[120] Contract Summary #1 is derived from Exhibit 10.12 to Securities Exchange Commission S-4 filing of 6 August 2009 by Resolute Energy Corporation. See also Exhibit 10.11 (additional contract). Contract Summary #2 is derived from Exhibit 10.31 to Securities Exchange Commission Form 10-K filing of 29, March 2011 by Chaparral Energy Inc.

provisions parties have developed to deal with variations in stream composition, for example by establishing two sets of product quality specifications. One provision sets minimum quality specifications, while another provision provides for 'typical' product specifications that are 'reasonably expected' but not contractually binding.

Contract Summary #1
9.1 Specifications. The Product * * * shall meet the following specifications, which herein are collectively called 'Quality Specifications':
(a) **Product.** Substance containing at least ninety-five mole percent (95%) of Carbon Dioxide.
(b) **Water.** ... no free water, and shall not contain more than thirty (30) pounds of water per MMcf in the vapor phase.
(c) **Hydrogen Sulfide.** ... not contain more than twenty (20) parts per million (two-hundred (200) parts per million if delivered from Canyon Reef Carriers Pipeline), by weight, of hydrogen sulfide.
(d) **Total Sulfur.** ... not contain more than thirty-five (35) parts per million (two-hundred (200) parts per million if delivered from Canyon Reef Carriers Pipeline), by weight, of total sulfur.
(e) **Temperature.** ... not exceed a temperature of one hundred twenty degrees Fahrenheit. (120°F).
(f) **Nitrogen.** ... not contain more than four mole percent (4%) of nitrogen.
(g) **Hydrocarbons.** ... not contain more than five mole percent (5%) of hydrocarbons and the dew point of Product (with respect to such hydrocarbons) shall not exceed minus twenty degrees Fahrenheit (-20°F).
(h) **Oxygen.** ... not contain more than ten (10) parts per million, by weight, of oxygen.
(i) **Other.** ... not contain more than 0.3 (three tenths) gallons of glycol per MMCF and at no time shall such glycol be present in a liquid state at the pressure and temperature conditions of the pipeline.

Contract Summary #2
5.01 Quality Specifications. The Contract Volume delivered by Coffeyville to Chaparral hereunder at the Title Transfer Point shall meet or exceed the following minimum specifications (the 'Quality Specifications'):
(a) CO_2: 96.0 mole % minimum;
(b) **Total Inerts:** 4.0 mole % maximum;
(c) **Water (H_2O):** Saturated at 80°F; and
(d) **Temperature:** 120°F

5.02 Typical Quality. The Contract Volume * * * is reasonably expected to be of the quality described below (the 'Typical Quality') * * *:
(a) CO_2: 99.60 mole %;
(b) **Water** (H_2O): <150 lbs per MMSCF;
(c) **Hydrocarbons:** 76 ppm vol.;
(d) **Sulfur:** 39 COS ppm vol.;
3 H2S ppm vol.;
(e) **Nitrogen:** 9.2 ppm vol.;
(f) **Oxygen:** 6.0 ppm vol.;
(g) **Temperature:** 60°F maximum; and
(h) **Carbon Monoxide:** 20 ppm vol

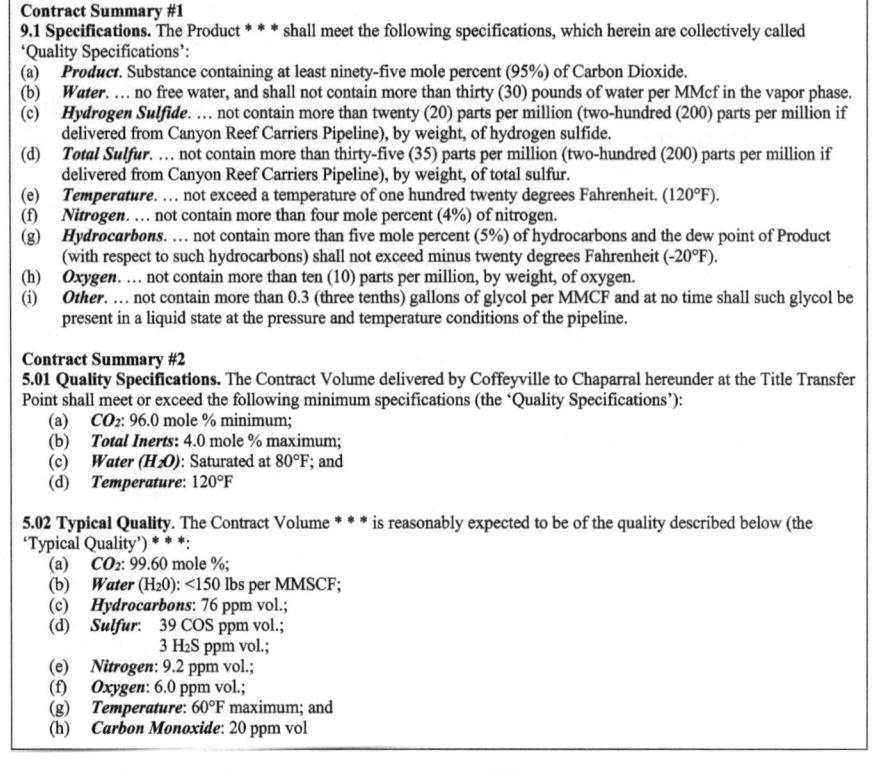

Figure 14.4: Illustrative CO_2 Quality Specifications[121]

C. Capacity Planning and Allocation: Ensuring Service While Avoiding Excessive Costs

As noted in section II.C, pipeline networks carrying CO_2 captured from power plant or other industrial sources to CO_2-EOR operations will tend to be 'few-to-few'

---

[121] 'MMcf' means 'million cubic feet'; 'MMSCF' means 'million standard cubic feet' (ie at standard pressure base of 14.65 pounds per square inch (psi) a dry and standard temperature base of 60°F). Air pressure of 14.65 psi is typically used in accounting for gas produced in States or regions that are significantly above sea level (eg New Mexico); gas is typically measured at 15.0125 psi in lower-lying Louisiana. A pressure base of 14.73 psi is also commonly used. In the US, CO_2 transactions are typically specified by a measure of *volume*, not weight, because in CO_2-EOR operations, the value of the CO_2 derives from its ability to contact the largest amount of residual oil in the target reservoir, which is a function of its volume, not its weight.

networks (at least for many years to come). They will likely link a limited number of large, capital-intensive supply projects requiring *long-term, firm take-away* service for all or defined portions of the expected CO_2 output, with a relatively limited number of similarly capital-intensive CO_2-EOR operations requiring similarly *long-term, firm CO_2 supply*. Both suppliers and customers will require firm commitments, but also provisions that accommodate various forms of operational or planning flexibility.[122]

The corollary of this fact is that increments of new pipeline capacity are likely to be tailored to particular projects, although they may include reasonably limited capacity to add incremental supply sources or incremental customer requirements in subsequent years. The necessary consequence is that there may not be transportation capacity available for CO_2 capture projects that were developed subsequent to the pipeline's construction or expansion, and that were not in a position to contract for a portion of the incremental pipeline capacity. Yet because of the various constraints on pipeline construction (including concerns over the environmental impact of pipeline construction and operation), it may be difficult to build new pipelines along the same routes to provide market access for the subsequently-developed projects.

Moreover, most scenarios for the deployment of CCS technology for CO_2 emission reduction anticipate that most initial CO_2 capture facilities will 'piggy back' on commercial CO_2-EOR operations and transportation infrastructure.[123] This is for three principal reasons: (i) revenues from sale of the captured CO_2 may help offset a portion of the cost of the capture facilities; (ii) existing CO_2 pipelines leading to CO_2-EOR target fields may be extended or expanded to attach new CO_2 sources; and (iii) the characteristics of target oil-bearing formations tend to be apt for the secure, long-term storage of CO_2 that occurs in association with EOR operations. Indeed, the US DOE has suggested that such industrially-sourced CO_2 supply may nearly exceed naturally-sourced CO_2 supplies by 2020.[124]

Reliance on CO_2-EOR operations to leverage construction of CO_2 pipelines means that the pipelines must meet the commercial requirements of the CO_2-EOR markets. One essential requirement will be the ability of parties to enter into contractual commitments that are adapted to their commercial needs. From the pipeline's standpoint that means the assurance that costs—including a return on investment—will be recovered; from the CO_2-EOR customers' standpoint, it includes assurance

---

[122] Agreements are likely to specifically define contract quantities and include provisions for variability (eg minimum monthly quantities, with provision for over- or under-deliveries; seasonal variability; downtime for maintenance or repairs, etc). For example, the contracts referenced in n 120 above include provision for a 'CO_2 Bank' that would allow netting out certain over- and under-deliveries. In addition, in some cases a party may have the ability to permanently release CO_2 from the contracts. Hence the terms 'output' and 'requirements' here are used as general terms and not as in Uniform Commercial Code Section 2-306, which addresses contracts that do not have specified quantity provisions but instead measure the quantity by the output of the seller or the requirements of the buyer.

[123] See, eg, Environmental Protection Agency, *Final Rule: Standards of Performance for Greenhouse Gas Emissions from New, Modified, and Reconstructed Stationary Sources: Electric Utility Generating Units*, 80 Fed Reg 64510, 64564 (23 October 2015).

[124] US DOE, *Quadrennial Energy Review: Energy Transmission, Storage, and Distribution Infrastructure* (2015) 7–24.

of contracted supply; and from the CO_2 suppliers' standpoint, it includes the assurance that their reliance on transport capacity will not be adversely affected by potential future CO_2 capture projects. That, in turn, means that the legal framework governing access to the pipeline must not allow demands for transportation from subsequently-constructed projects to jeopardise the investments of previously constructed facilities—the early movers.

The current legal framework allows for this requirement to be met by allowing pipeline operators to effectively dedicate portions of available capacity via private contracts, and to deny access to future customers in the event of inadequate unreserved capacity. A concern would arise, however, in the event regulatory rules were imposed that precluded a CO_2 pipeline's being able to honour capacity reservations or commitments. For example, the regulatory principles applied to oil pipelines regulated by the FERC generally allow for subsequent shippers to pre-empt a portion of pre-existing shipments on an oil pipeline by 'apportioning' available capacity among all requests for service, typically on some variation of a *pro rata* basis. This approach evolved in a world where oil pipelines serve many shippers of varying sizes in a given supply basin, typically with storage tankage available. In recent years, this approach has caused increasing concerns for pipelines serving new supply areas requiring major new investment and as the industry's structure evolved.[125] But such a 'pro rationing' approach to capacity for CO_2 pipelines would pose major difficulties for financing CCS capture projects, by injecting considerable uncertainty into the ability of the potential pipelines to ensure take-away capacity for the full contract quantity.[126] The interdependent nature of the CO_2 pipeline with the upstream CO_2 supply and the downstream CO_2 demand for EOR projects thus requires regulatory rules that allow the commercial parties to contractually accommodate the parties' individual needs, including those of the CO_2 source, the transporter and the EOR user.

In 2010, the Obama Administration's inter-agency task force to examine potential barriers to deployment of CCS for emissions reduction recognised this point:[127]

> Regulators may consider the impacts that common carrier laws will have on the future CCS industry. Power plants and other sources of CO_2 will likely need the flexibility to reserve capacity on the pipeline system. Power plants may need to cycle power production to meet demand, resulting in changes of emissions from the source, as well as bringing sources on and off line for maintenance. Under existing common carrier structures for natural gas transmission line, there exists the risk that another company could consume excess capacity

---

[125] The FERC has replied by modifying approach to capacity allocation in a number of cases. For an excellent analysis of how FERC's policy on oil pipeline capacity allocation had evolved as of 2011, see CJ Barr, 'Unfinished Business: FERC's Evolving Standard for Capacity Rights On Oil Pipelines' (2011) 32 *Energy Law Journal* 563.

[126] The approach the FERC applies to natural gas pipelines is quite different. The FERC allows for parties to dedicate capacity by contract (requiring open seasons for significant capacity expansion projects), effectively applying the 'first-come, first-served' principle it adopted in 1985 when it moved to adopt non-discriminatory third-party access. See *Associated Gas Distributors v FERC*, 824 F 2d 981 (DC Cir 1987) (discussing and ultimately dismissing as unripe challenges to adoption of the first-come, first served principle).

[127] *Report of the Interagency Carbon Capture and Storage Task Force* (August 2010) at M–5.

during a period of reduced emissions from an emissions source, essentially stranding the source from access to a storage site. Regulators ought to carefully consider allowing sources to reserve capacity on dedicated pipelines once a source is in operation, or consider the entire CCS system (capture, transport, and storage) as an integrated system which would not be subject to the typical common carriage requirements.

Similarly, the CO_2 Pipeline Transport Task Force of the Interstate Oil and Gas Compact Commission and the Southern States Energy Board noted that new capture sources 'will require pipeline off-take capacity that is specifically dedicated to receive the plant's CO_2 output' and that '[f]ailure to accommodate the requirement to ensure the availability of designated amounts of capacity for very lengthy periods could pose a significant regulatory barrier to wide-scale commercial deployment of CCS technologies'.[128] The Report cautioned against applying the oil pipeline 'apportionment' model:[129]

> Additionally, apportionment under the oil pipeline regulatory framework makes it incompatible with the dedicated business models contemplated above. Apportionment requires third party access that constrains the pipeline operator's ability to provide firm CO_2 transportation off-take capacity, a function assured under both the intrastate and interstate dedicated pipeline models. To meet possible future regulatory compliance obligations, new CO_2 capture sources will require pipeline off-take capacity that is specifically dedicated to receive the plant's CO_2 output. Absent the ability to structure transactions that ensure available firm transportation off-take capacity, generation facilities hoping to deploy CO_2 capture technologies will face challenges in financing and development. These underlying differences between the CO_2 pipeline network and the natural gas and oil pipeline models have major implications for potential legal and regulatory structures. An effective CO_2 pipeline regulatory framework will recognize and accommodate these differences in network purpose and design. The failure to accommodate the requirement to ensure the availability of designated amounts of capacity for very lengthy periods could pose a significant regulatory barrier to wide-scale commercial deployment of CCS technologies.

Some have advocated adoption of policy mechanisms to address this potential problem, and thereby hope to encourage the development of CO_2 pipelines that are sized to receive CO_2 from such potential subsequently developed CO_2 capture projects as may not materialise until an undefined number of years in the future—ie the construction of 'oversized' or 'supersized' CO_2 pipelines.[130] In effect, the suggestion

---

[128] IOGCC/SSEB, CO_2 Pipeline Report, n 10 above, 36.
[129] ibid, 53–54. For further discussion of potential CO_2 pipeline regulation, see PM Marston, *A regulatory framework for migrating from enhanced oil recovery to carbon capture and storage: the USA experience* (paper presented at 10th Greenhouse Gas Control Technologies Conference (GHGT–10)) (Amsterdam, 2010), available at ac.els-cdn.com/S1876610211008757/1-s2.0-S1876610211008757-main.pdf?_tid=582baa5e82d1568424f614484d966a9b&acdnat=1340118876_9ea8f2ebff4a991f4d5aa 99b7467f5cb (explaining how the practice of 'prorationing' or reducing service to pre-existing customers or shippers to make room for new customers, as typically done with federal 'common carriage' regulation of oil pipelines, is 'simply incompatible' with the underlying operational requirements because 'the unpredictability of service levels under this regulatory approach would fail to meet the fundamental requirement of customers for firm dedicated offtake service').
[130] See, eg, State CO_2-EOR Deployment Work Group, *21st Century Energy Infrastructure: Policy Recommendations for Development of American CO_2 Pipeline Networks* (February 2017); Global CCS Institute, *The Global Status of CCS* (2016) (Summary Report) 21 (discussing use of large-scale 'trunk

is to build pipeline infrastructure with capacity that is greater than what is justified by contractual commitments in order to ensure future take-away capacity for future CO_2 capture projects. In addition, the hope is to gain the benefit of lower unit costs when future capture projects are constructed and make increased utilisation of the pipeline. A larger pipeline than otherwise justified may allow for significantly lower *unit* transport costs if the total costs can be spread over the much larger number of units of transportation service that the larger pipeline can provide.[131] For example, increasing pipe diameter by 50 per cent, from 16 to 24 inches, might roughly triple the flow capacity, which—if the pipeline were fully utilised—could allow for significantly lower unit cost.[132]

While these suggestions may have superficial appeal for promoting CCS technology as a CO_2 emissions reduction tool, a note of caution should be sounded. Predicting the future is hard. The promised lower unit costs will only occur if the target levels of utilisation are actually achieved. This may never happen, or may be achieved only many years into the future. In the meantime, the commercial venture may have failed. In sum, a 'supersized' pipeline may become rather a supersized 'white elephant' with inflated losses—a result that has occurred in the past with pipeline or other large energy projects that were based more on government-supported policies or subsidies rather than on adequate contractual commitments from creditworthy partners.[133]

---

lines' for long-distance CO_2 transportation); JJ Dooley et al, 'Comparing Existing Pipeline Networks with the Potential Scale of Future U.S. CO_2 Pipeline Networks' (2009) 1 *Energy Procedia* 1595 (February 2009) (paper presented at GHGT-9); RS Middleton and JMA Bielicki, 'A comprehensive carbon capture and storage infrastructure model' (2009) 1 *Energy Procedia* 1111 (2009) (paper presented at GHGT-9); J Morbee et al, 'Optimal planning of CO_2 transmission infrastructure: The JRC InfraCCS tool' (2011) 4 *Energy Procedia* 2772 (paper presented at GHGT-10); E Mechleri et al, 'CO_2 capture and storage (CCS) cost reduction via infrastructure right-sizing', *Chemical Engineering Research and Design: Official journal of the European Federation of Chemical Engineering*, Part A, vol 119, 130–39 (March 2017), at dx.doi.org/10.1016/j.cherd.2017.01.016.

[131] A relatively small increase in pipe size allows proportionally much larger increase in transport capacity. As explained by I Png, *Managerial Economics*, 4th edn (Abingdon, Taylor and Francis, 2012) 131 (emphasis added): 'For example, the transport capacity of a gas pipeline depends on its cross-sectional area, which increases *with the square of the radius* of the cross section. By contrast, the amount of material required to build the pipeline depends on the circumference of the pipeline, which increases *with the radius* of the cross section. Hence, a 10% increase in the capacity of the pipeline requires less than 10% additional materials. In this case, the average variable cost falls with the scale of service.'

[132] See, eg, J Serpa, J Morbee and E Tzimas, *Technical and Economic Characteristics of a CO_2 Transmission Pipeline Infrastructure*, Report for the Joint Research Centre of the European Commission (JRC Scientific and Technical Report EUR 24731 EN—2011 (2011) 36 (fig 10)). Calculating the theoretical capacity of a proposed pipeline (and ultimately testing the actual capacity following construction) is in fact a much more complex undertaking and dependent on a variety of factors, including length, terrain, friction, etc.

[133] Examples are not difficult to find. One will suffice. The so-called 'pre-build' of the Alaska Natural Gas Transportation System resulting from the Alaska Natural Gas Transportation Act (ANGTA) in the 1970s was anticipated to allow early construction of pipeline infrastructure that would subsequently be used to deliver natural gas reserves from the north slope of Alaska—but 37 years later none of the Alaskan gas has been delivered. Around 1980, the American regulator had approved special tariffs that appeared—on paper—to ensure recovery of costs, in part by including a unit of throughput depreciation charge to regularly adjust rates to spread depreciation over actual throughput, decreasing rates if throughput rose, but increasing them if throughput declined. FERC, *Findings and Order Issuing Certificates Of Public Convenience and Necessity and Authorizing the Importation of Natural Gas*, issued in *Northwest*

Some authors have quite explicitly addressed the 'white elephant risk' in crafting governmental policies to support CO_2 'trunk' line systems, and have discussed the need for a robust *joint* regulatory and contractual framework to adapt to changes and avoid the risk.[134]

In the author's judgement, the contract-based approach that is presently used appears best suited to meeting the requirements for financing new pipeline construction and accommodating the planning and operational requirements of CO_2 suppliers and customers. It is decidedly difficult to determine the optimal size of any kind of major infrastructure. The long lead times required for planning and permitting and the long life cycles of the investment mean very large opportunities for market and policy changes that may result in stranded investments, even where initial capacity planning is backed by what appear to be carefully negotiated contracts. Deliberately planning to overbuild capacity is thus a decidedly chancy affair. Government policies have a tendency to change over cycles far shorter than the lifetimes of pipeline investment: the determined policy of President Carter and the Congress in 1977–80 to promote coal as a substitute for both natural gas and petroleum is distinctly different from current political preferences.[135] An investor in 1980 who expected those policies to ensure commercial success and political support rapid substitution of coal in place of both natural gas and petroleum would have been sorely disappointed. It is not clear why the current policy consensus on preferred energy sources should be any more permanent than the prior policy consensus.

Alaskan Pipeline, et al, (Docket Nos CP78-123, et al) (issued 28 April 1980) 17–18. The pipeline was completed in 1982, just in time for major changes in the US natural gas markets that led to its being 75% or more unused. Skyrocketing rates led to a required restructuring. Rather than ensuring recovery of capital costs, the unit-of-throughput feature quickly became a menace to remaining shippers: had the project financing not been restructured, the last Mcf of natural gas transported on the system would in theory have borne 100% of the depreciation for entire original construction of the pipeline—an absurd result.

[134] JP Banks, T Boersma and W Goldthorpe, *Challenges Related to Carbon Transportation and Storage—Showstoppers for CCS?*, Policy brief published by the Global CCS Institute (2017) 8, available at hub.globalccsinstitute.com/sites/default/files/publications/201363/Challenges%20related%20to%20 carbon%20transportation%20and%20storage.pdf ('Ensuring stability of income and returns on these assets therefore requires a sustained robust joint regulatory and contractual framework that can adapt to changes in circumstances and that addresses the following: ... Avoiding stranded asset (white elephant) risk by coordination of CO_2 supply and demand, from capture and storage respectively').

[135] The Carter Administration's National Energy Plan, adopted in 1977 (at the depth of the 1968–81 natural gas shortage) was based on the assumption that natural gas supplies were quickly running out and that it was essential to expand coal and nuclear electricity-generating capacity. P Marston and F Moring, 'Federal Restraints on Interstate Natural Gas Supply and Market Expansion' (1978) 54 *North Dakota Law Review* 377, 397–98. The Carter Administration's plan projected for coal to become the nation's principal energy source by 1985 (ibid). Indeed the Powerplant and Industrial Fuel Use Act of 1978 largely banned the use of natural gas in new electricity-generating facilities in order to encourage the use of coal in its place. By 1980 Congress had adopted the Energy Security Act of 1980, which created the Synthetic Fuels Corporation and authorised it to spend $88 billion to achieve the goal of producing at least 500,000 barrels of crude oil equivalent per day of synthetic fuels from domestic sources by 1987 and at least 2 million per day by 1992—essentially relying on coal to substitute for petroleum, as well replacing natural gas for electricity generation. The Corporation closed its doors in April 1986, however, after funding four projects, none of which survives today. HA Priddy, *United States Synthetic Fuels Corporation: Its Rise and Demise*, (PhD Dissertation) (2013). See also RL Bayrer, *The Saga of the US Synthetic Fuels Corporation: A Cautionary Tale* (Washington, DC, New Academia Publishing, 2011).

V. CONCLUSION

Knowledge is the beginning of wisdom—and wisdom is a window on tomorrow.
20th-century American proverb

Because they have developed to serve a specialised technique for oil recovery—and in addition are geographically concentrated in North America—CO_2 pipelines are broadly unfamiliar to the global public policy community that addressed atmospheric emissions of CO_2 and global climate issues. That the initial CO_2 pipeline was built at least as early as 1931, and that thousands of miles have been operating for decades subject to robust industry standards, governmental safety regulation and incident reporting, are facts that will come as a surprise to many. The intricate commercial interplay between CO_2 suppliers and CO_2 customers at opposite ends of the pipe, and the detailed contractual provisions addressing competing operational needs and economic parameters, are equally unfamiliar to nearly all but the limited universe of those directly involved in the transactions.

At best, that unfamiliarity may lead to misunderstandings and unnecessary policy disagreements. At worst it may produce self-defeating policies. Carbon dioxide pipelines and the EOR operations they serve may be able to play a discrete, but significant, role in providing a market for CO_2 that is captured by an industrial entity principally for emissions reduction purposes, and thereby defray a portion of the cost of the CO_2 capture facilities. In this way, CO_2 pipelines may facilitate initial deployment of CCS technology for GHG emissions abatement. But if policies or regulations fail to respect the legal, commercial and operational realities under which CO_2-EOR is conducted, the result will be but misbegotten alchemy, an odd craft in which valuable CO_2—a commodity that customers will willingly purchase and pipe in order to isolate it securely from the atmosphere by producing oil—transmutes into politically toxic waste that must be carefully excluded from commercial operations.

15
Long-Term Liability and CCS

IAN HAVERCROFT

I. THE CHALLENGE

THE ABILITY OF policymakers and regulators to regulate effectively and efficiently carbon capture and storage (CCS) processes remains a critical element of efforts to facilitate the technology's deployment. Central to this effort, and an ongoing focus for many regulators worldwide, has been the capacity of modern legal and regulatory frameworks to manage the risks associated with the particularly novel elements of the technology—their consideration and resolution within early policy and regulatory responses has proved critical.

A first example of these challenges may be found in the technical feasibility and novelty of the CCS process itself. While several individual aspects of the technical processes involved are well understood and have been practised for decades, their innovative application in sequence, across the full chain of the CCS process, has posed a number of challenges. The unique nature of aspects of these processes and applications has similarly created some uncertainty surrounding their future impacts. The risks and the management of the impact of CO_2 leakage from a storage site, upon the natural and human environment for example, was just one of the issues to be addressed in early legal and regulatory frameworks.

A further novel element, which is peculiar to CCS, are the temporal aspects to be addressed when contemplating geological storage. Unlike existing oil and gas operations, or analogous waste disposal activities, the climate mitigation objective of the technology ultimately requires the high threshold of the 'permanent' storage of the injected CO_2. The management and responsibility for the stored CO_2, beyond the traditional lifetime of a commercial entity, has therefore had to be addressed in many early legal models.

The need to address liability for CCS operations has been emphasised by policymakers, regulators and industry as one of the crucial elements for meeting these novel challenges. This requires defining the parameters and potential magnitude of liabilities during both the operational phase of a CCS project and following the cessation of injection activities, and has been viewed as critical for ensuring public, investor and operator confidence in the technology.

In the case of the wider public, liability regimes may offer confidence that a potential harm will be effectively addressed and that there are processes in place to manage the risks associated with many of the novel technical elements of the technology, or the impacts of a potential leakage. For operators and investors, liability regimes provide an opportunity to delineate responsibilities during the operational phases and, in some instances, afford an opportunity to limit exposure following the cessation of operations and the closure of a storage site.

This chapter considers the approach taken by regulators to date in the design of CCS-specific responses to liability, and the emergence of the dedicated regimes that attempt to address the technology's novel features. The author also considers the constraints and challenges of these new and varied approaches for those seeking to operate CCS projects, and the potentially wider consequences for the development and deployment of the technology as a whole.

II. EMERGENCE OF THE CCS-SPECIFIC REGIME

While many of the initial feasibility studies considered the technical, spatial and financial challenges of deploying the technology, early legal analysis largely focused upon the legality of deployment and the manner in which particular challenges were to be managed in national and supra-national regulatory regimes.[1] Broad consideration was given to the ability of existing environmental and energy law and regulation to address these technical processes, as well as whether current approaches to monitoring and verification would be capable of meeting the demands of permanent storage. Perhaps most challenging of all, however, were the temporal aspects and the significant time frames required by permanent geological storage.

The issue of liability and who should bear responsibility for both storage operations and the sequestered CO_2, during both the operational and post-closure phases, was a central consideration in many of these early studies.[2] The subject was discussed within both academic analysis and discussion papers and guidance that accompanied early drafts of legislation, and served to highlight the tensions at play between policymakers and regulators seeking to address all aspects of the technological process and those seeking to invest in and deploy the technology.

Despite these early challenges, the past decade has seen the emergence of a broad corpus of CCS-specific legal and regulatory models in many countries around the world. While this legislation ranges in its complexity and scope, a number of these individual examples contain well-characterised and detailed approaches to liability across the CCS project lifecycle.[3]

---

[1] These contrasting approaches are particularly evident in the 2005 Special Report from the Intergovernmental Panel on Climate Change (IPCC), IPCC 2005, Working Group III of the IPCC, B Metz et al (eds), *IPCC Special Report on Carbon Dioxide Capture and Storage* (Cambridge, Cambridge University Press, 2005).

[2] See, for example, the discussion in R Purdy and R Macrory, *Geological carbon sequestration: critical legal issues*, Tyndall Centre for Climate Change Research Working Paper Number 45 (2004); and C Hendriks, MJ Mace and R Coenraads, *Impacts of EU and International Law on the Implementation of Carbon Capture and Geological Storage in the European Union* (Brussels, European Commission, Directorate-General Environment, June 2005).

[3] An assessment of the status of legal and regulatory regimes for CCS across 55 countries was published by the Global CCS Institute: Global CCS Institute, *Global CCS Institute CCS Legal and Regulatory Indicator: A Global Assessment of National Legal and Regulatory Regimes for Carbon Capture and Storage* (Melbourne, Global CCS Institute, September 2015), at hub.globalccsinstitute.com/sites/default/files/publications/196443/global-ccs-institute-ccs-legal-regulatory-indicator.pdf.

A. The Nature of Liability

While only a few CCS-specific regimes specifically address the various types of liability to be borne throughout the project life cycle, it remains important in all instances to take into account the nature of these individual liabilities when considering the approach to be adopted and the extent of both operator and regulator responsibilities.

As described in an earlier work from 2014, there are conceivably three distinct strands of liability in the case of CCS operations: 'civil', 'administrative' liability and what is described as 'climate change liability'.[4] Civil liability encompasses those liabilities resulting from damage caused by CCS activities to the interests of a third party, and which are likely to be determined in legislation or through principles developed through decisions of the courts, depending on the nature of the jurisdiction in question. Despite limited experience with liability regimes for permanent storage to date, the application of these particular liabilities is likely to be broadly familiar to operators and regulators alike. A history of analogous industrial, oil and gas activities, in addition to a well-characterised body of case law, has resulted in a relatively well-understood civil liability regime in many jurisdictions. The specific regime may impose such liability on particular parties (such as the storage operator) but, as Lawrence describes in Chapter 16 of this volume, in practice commercial arrangements familiar to other industrial activities involving multiple parties are likely to be used to spread the potential liability risks.

The second category, 'administrative liability', may be borne by an operator and is in addition to the range of obligations required under a licence or permit for storage operations. These liabilities, traditionally observed within a jurisdiction's wider body of environmental and energy-related laws, result from the exercise of a competent authority's statutory powers and may compel an operator to undertake some form of action, be it to remediate or prevent a specific incident.

The peculiar nature of CCS is further highlighted by the fact that projects may have been incentivised (say, by gaining credits under an emissions trading scheme), and some liability accounting provisions must be made should leakage subsequently occur. This is also a form of administrative liability, but sufficiently distinctive that it has been characterised here as 'climate change liability', discussed in greater detail in section III.D.

B. Similarity in Approach

Closer examination of both the legal and regulatory frameworks and the policy positions adopted by several jurisdictions in recent years reveals a significant number of similarities in the approach adopted to managing liability. These similarities are particularly apparent when considering the legal and regulatory response to the storage

---

[4] I Havercroft and R Macrory, *Legal liability and carbon capture and storage: a comparative perspective* (Melbourne, Global CCS Institute, 2014).

aspect of the CCS process, which has posed a more significant challenge by virtue of the novelty of the time frames and technology involved.

Several early-mover jurisdictions, which have developed a comprehensive statutory response to CCS, have a permitting or licensing model at the core of their legal and regulatory frameworks.[5] It is in these permitting models, notably those found in the United States (US), Canada, Europe and Australia, where a number of parallels may be drawn in their treatment and management of liability.

In many instances the permitting models observed in these jurisdictions have sought to clearly allocate a wide range of potential liabilities between the operator and regulator, throughout the lifetime of a CCS project. In some instances this has been achieved through the design and implementation of new mechanisms; however, in other instances far broader obligations are likely to be borne by operators through the implicit application of a wider body of legislation and/or case law.[6]

Regulatory models that share similar methods to managing factors such as site selection, monitoring, measurement, verification and operator performance offer a further example of how many jurisdictions have approached the issue of liability. In several instances, law and regulation prioritise the identification and characterisation of the most suitable sites for storage, as well as ensuring that operator best practice is maintained. As a consequence, a strong emphasis is placed upon minimising and 'front-loading' risks in the early stages of the CCS project life cycle, and on ensuring that future liabilities (from leakage, etc) are minimised through initial good site selection and characterisation.

While there are noticeable differences in the approach adopted by many of the jurisdictions, it is clear that the opportunity for operators to 'transfer' some of their liabilities to the state at an agreed point it time has also proved to be a key element of these early regimes. To date, several of the CCS-specific models presently in operation include provisions that limit or envisage the transfer of an operator's responsibility for a storage site post-closure.[7]

A further feature of these early legal and regulatory frameworks, and one which is similarly allied to the management of risk throughout the project life cycle, is the inclusion of obligations concerning the provision of financial security or the use of broader 'financial mechanisms'. In addition to traditional insurance products, some

---

[5] A review of the development of these early regimes may be found in T Dixon, S McCoy and I Havercroft, 'Legal and Regulatory Developments on CCS' (2015) 40 *International Journal of Greenhouse Gas Control* 431.

[6] European Parliament and Council Directive 2009/31/EC of 23 April 2009 on geological storage of carbon dioxide and amending Council Directive 85/337/EEC, European Parliament and Council Directives 2000/60/EC, 2001/80/EC, 2004/35/EC, 2006/12/EC, 2008/1/EC and Regulation (EC) No 1013/2006 [2009] OJ L140/114 (CCS Directive), for example, applies the provisions of the EU's Environmental Liability Directive (European Parliament and Council Directive 2004/35/EC of 21 April 2004 on environmental liability with regard to the prevention and remedying of environmental damage [2004] OJ L143/56) and amends the EU Emissions Trading Scheme (European Parliament and Council Directive 2003/87/EC of 13 October 2003 establishing a scheme for greenhouse gas emission allowance trading within the Community and amending Council Directive 96/61/EC [2003] OJ L275/32) to address damage caused to the local environment and the climate resulting from any failure of permanent containment of CO_2.

[7] Examples of these transfer mechanisms are to be found in the CCS Directive, the Australian Commonwealth Government's *Offshore Petroleum and Greenhouse Gas Storage Act 2006* (Cth) and the Canadian province of Alberta's Mines and Minerals Act RSA 2000, c M-17.

regimes oblige operators to make up-front payments into funds or schemes, or specify forms of financial security products. These mechanisms are designed to ensure that the public purse is protected in the event of a serious incident, or to cover the costs of monitoring during the operational and post-closure phases.

C. Reliance upon Existing Liability Mechanisms

Early legal and regulatory models have often relied upon existing liability regimes to address discrete aspects, or indeed the entirety of the CCS process. In addition to the civil liability provisions observed in the decisions of the national courts, national regulators have also sought to include CCS activities within the scope of existing legislation.

An example of this approach may be found in the CCS Directive (2009/31/EC of 23 April 2009), which amends both the existing EU Emissions Trading Scheme (Directive 2003/87/EC) (EU ETS) and the Environmental Liability (ELD) CCS Directive (Directive 2004/35/EC) to explicitly include CCS activities. The implications for the EU ETS Directive are considered in greater detail in the climate liabilities section below, but the ELD Directive, which was designed to 'to establish a framework of environmental liability based on the "polluter-pays" principle, to prevent and remedy environmental damage',[8] and will ultimately apply to CCS storage operations, is discussed here.

Despite its title, the ELD is essentially confined to environmental restoration and the powers of regulators to impose obligations on operators (within the concept of 'administrative liability' as used here), rather than civil liability to third parties. Under the provisions of the ELD, CCS operations are included as an occupational activity within Annex III of the Directive, and are therefore subject to its strict liability provisions. An operator will be required to carry out preventive and remedial action as required under the ELD where damage, which is within the scope of the Directive, is threatened or has occurred. While not all forms of environmental damage are covered, the ELD does cover damage to protected species, water and damage to humans resulting from land contamination.[9]

An operator will remain liable under the provisions of the ELD throughout the operational and post-closure phases of a CCS project. These particular liabilities, however, may be transferred to the state in the event of a successful transfer of liability under the CCS Directive.

D. Transfer and Long-Term Stewardship

The significant geological time frames characterised by successful CCS operations, together with a desire to ensure the permanency of the storage of CO_2, have proved

---

[8] ELD, Art 1.
[9] ELD, Art 2(1). The limitations of the type of damage covered by the Directive are hardly logical, but represent political compromise during the legislative process and sensitivities as to the scope of EU competence in the field of liability.

to be a contentious issue during the design and development of legal and regulatory models. Regulators' ambition to achieve certainty around geologic storage and to ensure that the technology is comprehensively regulated has at times given rise to concern for those seeking to invest in the technology and develop projects. For potential operators, who would conceivably be liable for storage sites in perpetuity, the need for a distinctive approach to liability was a critical element of any proposed CCS regime.

To address these tensions, some regulatory frameworks contain provisions that allow for the transfer of liability from an operator to a state's 'competent authority', following the cessation of storage activities and the completion of several mandated requirements.[10] However, while these CCS-specific legal and regulatory models have largely adopted a similar perspective regarding the nature of liability across the project life cycle, there are a number of nuances in the operation and scope of these transfer provisions.

Where provision is made for a transfer, the focus of regulation has been the manner in which this is to be effected and the nature of the liabilities which are eventually to be transferred. Some of these regimes include explicit performance criteria that must be met by an operator prior to a transfer's being effected.[11] In some instances, this includes the completion of a post-closure time limit, during which an operator will remain fully accountable for the storage site and all associated obligations. The trigger conditions in some examples of law are expressed in strict language; others leave more discretion to the judgement of the Minister or relevant authority.

The nature of the liabilities to be transferred is also a critical consideration—more specifically, what forms of liability may be transferred to the state and, conversely, where no clear provision is made for their transfer, which liabilities will remain with an operator in perpetuity. Once again, the legal and regulatory models developed to date reveal a range of national and sub-national approaches.[12] For project proponents, the scope of the liability provisions offered, and any potential ambiguity in their application, remains a critical concern when considering their long-term risk exposure.

III. CONSTRAINTS AND CHALLENGES

The development and implementation of CCS-specific legal and regulatory frameworks in recent years have done much to clarify the nature and scope of liability for CCS operations. There are now several fully-defined models, which set out how policymakers and regulators intend to address the issue during both the operational and post-closure phases of a project.

Despite these developments, however, the topic of liability continues to be cited by a number of stakeholders as potentially challenging, and presents several issues that

---

[10] See n 7 above.
[11] The CCS Directive, Art 18, for example, requires that 'all available evidence indicates that the stored CO_2 will be completely and permanently contained'.
[12] For a comparison of the liabilities/responsibilities transferred in the UK, the Australian State of Victoria and the Canadian province of Alberta, see Havercroft and Macrory, n 4 above, 44.

will likely require further clarification.[13] It would appear that while policymakers and regulators have made considerable efforts to address the critical elements and provide comprehensive models, project proponents and investors have raised tangible examples of the challenges posed by these new and emerging models and how they represent ongoing barriers to investment.[14]

The need to address these particular issues in a timely manner will prove significant when considering their potential impact upon the taking of investment decisions and, ultimately, the deployment of CCS projects. Importantly for those jurisdictions contemplating and reviewing their own national regimes to regulate the technology, subsequent efforts to address these remaining issues will likely prove both persuasive and instructive.

A. The Scope and Practicality of Transfer Provisions

The design and implementation of mechanisms to transfer liabilities and broader responsibilities proved to be an intrinsic element of several of the early legal and regulatory models, and their development has proved a significant factor for improving operator and investor confidence in the regulatory framework. As such, their inclusion appears to have been driven by the need to balance a number of potentially competing interests. The establishment of time frames for effecting a transfer, and which have been clearly defined within law and regulations, is perhaps one example of where these interests have been reconciled.[15]

Two issues that remain critical to the effectiveness of these transfer mechanisms, however, are their scope and practicality. While some regulatory frameworks include clearly defined provisions, with the opportunity for the post-closure transfer of liabilities and obligations, others do not include these provisions, or remain silent as to the nature of the responsibilities and liabilities transferred. A further and perhaps more complex issue concerns the practicality of transfer provisions, and in particular the ability of operators to demonstrate their compliance with the thresholds defined within legislation.

In some jurisdictions, where the legal and regulatory model remains silent as to which liabilities are transferred to the relevant authority upon the surrender of a licence or authority, potential operators and investors face uncertainty as to their ongoing liabilities post-closure. One example may be found in the Australian State of

---

[13] See, for example, the various stakeholder perspectives included in the recent report prepared by consultants to support the European Commission's review and evaluation of the CCS Directive, as required by Art 38 of the Directive, and including consideration of the Directive under the new Regulatory Fitness and Performance programme (REFIT). European Commission, Directorate General for Climate Action, *Study to support the review and evaluation of Directive 2009/31/EC on the geological storage of carbon dioxide (CCS Directive)* (Luxembourg, Publications Office of the European Union, 2015), at www.publications.europa.eu/resource/cellar/3f0867e1-8e88-11e5-b8b7-01aa75ed71a1.0001.01/DOC_1.

[14] See, for example, the views concerning the Dutch ROAD project in T Jonker, The permitting process: Special report on getting a CCS project permitted (Melbourne, Global CCS Institute, 2013).

[15] The Australian Commonwealth Government's *Offshore Petroleum and Greenhouse Gas Storage Act 2006* (Cth), for example, requires the conclusion of a 15-year 'Closure Assurance Period' following the issue of a Site Closure Certificate, before an operator may apply to transfer liability to the Government. See further ch 11 of this volume.

Victoria's *Greenhouse Gas Geological Sequestration Act 2008* (Vic), where despite clear provision for the surrender of 'authorities', the legal framework is silent as to exactly which liabilities or responsibilities are transferred to the State. It may be presumed that all future administrative liabilities will be included within the surrender; however, it is unlikely that any civil liabilities will be transferred to the State. While this would appear to be in line with the Victorian government's policy position during the development of the legislation, the Victorian legislation stands at odds with the model developed under the Australian Commonwealth regime.[16] This misalignment was highlighted as an issue to be addressed by Victorian regulators in the recommendations of the State government's regulatory test toolkit exercise, undertaken in 2013.[17]

The State of Victoria's approach stands in contrast to that of the Canadian province of Alberta, where CCS-specific amendments to the existing regime will see the Crown assume future responsibilities under environmental legislation and a former licence holder may also be indemnified against damages in tort.[18] The policy decision by the Alberta government to indemnify lessees against liability for tort damages, which may arise in the post-closure period, has proved to be an important aspect of the province's regulatory response, and was highlighted in the province's Regulatory Framework Assessment.[19]

The ability of an operator to meet the standards and thresholds necessary to enable a transfer has been similarly highlighted as challenging, particularly where broad regulatory provisions prove ambiguous or offer very few (or no) technical parameters.[20] In this instance, it is likely that monitoring and verification (M&V) during the project's operational phase will become of critical importance to both the operator and regulator.

An example of this tension may be found in the CCS Directive's transfer provisions. Under the provisions of the Directive, a transfer may only take place once 'all available evidence' indicates that the CO_2 is completely and permanently contained.[21] A literal reading of these provisions imply a technical standard with which it will be challenging for an operator to comply. Indeed, it may be suggested that any opposing expert view may frustrate an operator's request.[22]

---

[16] N Swayne and A Phillips, 'Legal liability for carbon capture and storage in Australia: where should the losses fall?' (2012) 29 *Environmental and Planning Law Journal* 189.

[17] AECOM Pty Ltd, 'Carbon capture and storage regulatory test toolkit for Victoria, Australia: outcomes and recommendations' (Melbourne, Global CCS Institute and Victorian Department of Industry, 2013).

[18] Mines and Minerals Act RSA 2000, c M-17, s 121(2).

[19] Alberta Energy, *Carbon Capture and Storage—Summary Report of the Regulatory Framework Assessment* (Alberta, Alberta Energy, 2013), at www.energy.alberta.ca/CCS/pdfs/CCSrfaNoAppD.pdf.

[20] Jonker, n 14 above.

[21] CCS Directive, Art 18(1).

[22] The meeting report of the International Energy Agency's International CCS Regulatory Network, for example, highlighted that many regulators and operators found this term 'problematic to define', particularly given the natural variability of CO_2 levels in soil, air and oceans, and the technological limits of monitoring. International Energy Agency (IEA), '6th IEA International CCS Regulatory Network Meeting: Taking stock of progress and identifying next steps' (IEA/OECD, 2013).

The more demanding requirements of Article 18(1) of the CCS Directive are to some extent mitigated by the subsequent provisions of Article 18(2). Under this sub-section, an operator is obliged to submit a report demonstrating at least:

(a) the conformity of the actual behaviour of the injected CO_2 with the modelled behaviour;
(b) the absence of any detectable leakage;
(c) that the storage site is evolving towards a situation of long-term stability.[23]

The Directive's provisions in relation to transfer are further supported by Commission Guidance, aimed at 'providing an overall methodological approach to implementation of the key provisions of the CCS Directive'. Guidance Document 3, governing the transfer of responsibility to a competent authority, was adopted by the Commission in 2011 and provides further detail as to the manner in which Member States address the requirements of Article 18.[24] The Guidance confirms the reliance an operator will be required to place upon the M&V process and data gathering throughout the lifetime of a storage project, and its ultimate significance in the preparation of the transfer report. Reference is made throughout the document to the operator's ability to demonstrate conformity with predicted models, the absence of leakage and the site's evolution towards long-term stability.

It would appear, however, that the ultimate decision whether or not to transfer will rest with the regulator. The wording of Article 18 is such that only when the regulator is completely satisfied with an operator's compliance with the requirements, will a transfer be effected.

The more challenging provisions of the CCS Directive stand in contrast to those found in the Canadian province of Alberta's regulatory model. Under the province's Mines and Minerals Act, the Minister need only be satisfied that 'the captured carbon dioxide is behaving in a stable and predictable manner, with no significant risk of future leakage'.[25] The language avoids the more absolutist terminology of the CCS Directive, and explicitly rests responsibility on the judgement of the relevant Minister—a judgement that would be difficult to challenge in the courts unless there was evidence of irrationality.

B. Technical Cooperation

The need to engage technical expertise in the development and operation of legal and regulatory models similarly remains a critical consideration for addressing liability issues. In many instances regulators will be required to interpret profoundly technical information, when determining compliance with the requirements of the regulatory model. The role of regulators and project proponents, when seeking

---

[23] CCS Directive, art 18(2).
[24] European Commission, 'Implementation of Directive 2009/31/EC on the Geological Storage of Carbon Dioxide: Guidance Document 3 Criteria for Transfer of Responsibility to the Competent Authority' (European Commission, 2011).
[25] Mines and Minerals Act RSA 2000, c M-17, s 120(1).

to operationalise aspects of early regimes, is one area in particular where there is opportunity for far closer collaboration and engagement.

The interpretation of site-specific monitoring information, as well as efforts to determine a storage site's performance and impact upon the environment prior to a proposed transfer, are just two examples where a high degree of technical expertise and understanding will likely be necessary. Interpretation of these materials will require the operator to share their technical knowledge, or present data in a manner which is suitable for a regulator addressing a host of novel considerations.

For an operator faced with a regulatory model that contains many elements yet to be fully tested, it will be important to establish a flexible and practical relationship with the regulator. The effective operation of the many of the early CCS-specific regimes' regulatory mechanisms will likely depend upon the nature of this relationship and the ability for these parties to accommodate each other's requirements. Perhaps unsurprisingly, there are few examples of this type of cooperation to date. The novelty of the various legal and regulatory models, and the fact that early projects have yet to address the technical issues associated with long-term liability or transfer, means that this type of engagement remains hypothetical.

A 2016 Australian CCS workshop highlighted these issues, in particular the challenges faced by regulators and operators when determining the type and extent of M&V necessary to demonstrate compliance with regulatory requirements.[26] As suggested previously, M&V will undoubtedly play a significant role in determining whether CO_2 is behaving as predicted, whether leakage from a storage site has occurred or whether the regulatory criteria for enabling a transfer have been satisfied. Regulators and operators have suggested, therefore, that where M&V data are refined, updated and improved, perhaps as a part of an approved monitoring plan, it will be critical to maintain a dialogue and for industry to continue to educate regulators on the implications of the data.[27]

National regulators have, however, started to consider some of the technical elements associated with CCS operations in the permitting of early storage projects. The submission and approval of plans and programs for monitoring, corrective measures and financial security, all required as part of the permitting of projects, have required close cooperation between regulators and project proponents to identify thresholds and parameters for action.[28] A long history of oil and gas operations, including the operation of enhanced oil recovery projects, also provides an important analogy for both parties.

C. Liability Post-Transfer

For those regimes that do not include transfer provisions, it is clear that an operator will remain liable for a storage site in perpetuity. It will also be important

---

[26] Full details of the workshop may be found in MK Gibbs, *Effective enforcement of underground storage of carbon dioxide* (Melbourne, HWL Ebsworth Lawyers, 2016).
[27] ibid 42.
[28] Jonker, n 14 above.

to consider, however, whether an operator may also be held liable for operations following a formal transfer of its responsibilities to the state.

The CCS Directive includes a novel provision that allows the state to recover costs from an operator following a transfer. The 'claw back' provisions of Article 18 of the Directive allow recovery of costs where there has been fault on the part of the operator, notably in instances of 'deficient data, concealment of relevant information, negligence, wilful deceit or a failure to exercise due diligence'.[29]

In the UK, the transposed provisions of Article 18 enable the authority to recover any costs, to 'the extent that such costs arise due to fault on the part of the operator'.[30] The Storage of Carbon Dioxide (Termination of Licence) Regulations 2011, including the definition of fault, are drafted to apply to all liabilities to be transferred under the CCS Directive. Under the UK Regulations, however, other leakage liabilities are also included within their scope, including those arising out of tort. The information requirements prescribed by the UK Regulations also go further than those of the CCS Directive, and require an operator to provide a far wider range of materials following the issue of a termination notice.

While the claw-back provisions of Article 18 are broadly drafted and would appear to cover any activity where an operator is subsequently found to have been at fault, the UK Regulations go somewhat further. In both instances, these wide grounds mean that in the case of fault on the part of the operator, liabilities may be effectively 'reactivated' following their transfer.

For an operator, these requirements will place considerable emphasis upon the need to effectively monitor and accurately account for all activities throughout the lifetime of a project. In the case of operators in the UK, this will include exercising considerable diligence when preparing documentation at the point of transfer.

D. Climate Change Liabilities

A further and perhaps more complex sub-category of administrative liability may also be distinguished in the case of CCS operations. The technology's ultimate objective to mitigate the impacts of climate change, and the need therefore to ensure permanency of CO_2 storage, has required regulators to adopt a novel approach to liability in situations where there is a failure in storage operations. In these instances, a liability is borne because leakage of this nature would ultimately frustrate the environmental objective of the activity.

The need to address this form of 'climate change liability' is particularly significant where an operator has also secured a financial benefit for storing CO_2 as a part of a domestic emissions trading scheme. Consequently, the approach adopted by regulators to date will see an operator account for any leakages within a jurisdiction's national trading scheme through the surrender of an equivalent number of allowances.

---

[29] CCS Directive, Art 18(7).
[30] Storage of Carbon Dioxide (Termination of Licence) Regulations 2011 (SI 2011/1483), reg 16 (UK Regulations).

Liability of this nature, however, raises several unique challenges for operators and regulators alike. The ability of both parties to determine the exact amount of CO_2 that has leaked into the atmosphere from a storage reservoir, and the time frame within which such leakage occurred, are just two examples. Coupling climate change liabilities with any advanced financial security to be provided by storage operators, as required under the CCS Directive, adds further difficulties. Where liability is based on future unpredictable prices under emission trading schemes at the time of leakage, operators are faced with virtual unknowable and uninsurable risks. Placing caps on such liability (such as the financial benefits gains at the time of storage) may not be consistent with the pure economic logic of a trading scheme, but may be realistic from a practical perspective.

A further issue concerns the ability of an operator to transfer climate change liabilities in the post-closure period. To date, the early legal and regulatory models have adopted divergent approaches, the CCS Directive including these liabilities within the category to be transferred to a Member State's competent authority. A different approach has been adopted in the Canadian province of Alberta, where these liabilities have been formally excluded from those to be transferred to the Crown.[31]

IV. CONCLUSIONS AND THE WAY FORWARD

While liability throughout the project life cycle continues to be identified as problematic, it is important to assess the magnitude of the issue and consider how these liabilities may potentially be minimised for an operator.

A. Assessing Different Forms of Liability

Clarifying the 'type' of liability, in particular the exact nature of those liabilities applicable throughout the lifetime of a CCS project, is an important factor in determining the challenges posed to CCS operations. In many instances, it may be necessary for regulators and operators to approach each type differently.

In common law jurisdictions, the core principles governing civil liabilities, borne in instances where damage is caused to the interests of third parties, are largely determined through the courts' application of case law. The absence of any litigation to date means that suggestions as to the courts' application of these principles, particularly in instances of damage resulting from novel aspects of CCS operations, are at best hypothetical. The likelihood of some forms of damage caused by storage operations to remain undiscovered for many years, for example, would mean

---

[31] Note, however, that the final report of the Alberta Regulatory Framework Assessment (RFA) process included a recommendation that the Mines and Minerals Act be amended to include responsibilities under the province's Climate Change and Emissions Management Act SA 2003, c C-16.7. See Alberta Energy, *Summary Report*, n 19 above, recommendation 65.

that the application of limitation periods for bringing a civil claim will inevitably be brought into consideration. In some jurisdictions, therefore, it will be challenging to bring claims where legislation includes restrictive time limits, triggered from when the damages originally occurred.

It will likely prove difficult in many jurisdictions for regulators and policymakers to influence and/or determine the extent and application of third-party liabilities through legislation and in the absence of CCS-specific case examples. Notwithstanding these uncertainties, significant experience gained through analogous industrial, oil and gas activities, in addition to a substantial body of case law, may prove instructive and afford some clarity for potential investors and operators.[32]

Administrative liabilities, including the perhaps more complex sub-category of climate change liabilities, are likely to be viewed as more challenging for operators and regulators alike. These liabilities, which centre upon the powers afforded to public authorities to require an operator to take action in the event of actual or potential environmental damage, for example, will present several novel challenges for CCS operations. Contained within existing law and regulation, as well as more recent CCS-specific regimes, their provisions are broad enough to encompass incidents arising from storage operations. In many instances these liabilities are ambiguous in their scope, and contain limited rights to review or appeal a particular decision.

Climate change liabilities, notably those attaching to CCS activities where incorporated within a greenhouse gas trading scheme, will likely pose further challenges to both operators and regulators.[33] From an operator's perspective, these liabilities present a financial risk which it may prove difficult to forecast.

B. Positive Models of Law and Regulation

While there is no archetypal model of CCS-specific law and regulation, several early legal and regulatory frameworks contain particularly detailed approaches to addressing liability throughout the CCS project life cycle. Aspects of these regimes may serve as potential models, particularly for those jurisdictions still in the process of reviewing or developing legislation.

The approach taken to the transfer of liability, in instances where such a mechanism is contemplated, has proved a significant feature for regulators and project proponents globally. The clarity of these transfer provisions and the exact nature of the liabilities transferred are particularly critical to this approach. The UK's regulatory model, which envisages the transfer of liabilities relating to personal injury, damage to property and economic loss, may be highlighted as an example of a particularly

---

[32] D Adelman and I Duncan, 'The Limits of Liability in Promoting Safe Geologic Sequestration of CO_2,' (2011) 22 *Duke Environmental Law & Policy Forum* 1, 1.
[33] See, for example, the discussion on the management of climate-related leakage risk in the International Energy Agency Report, *IEA, 20 years of Carbon Capture and Storage: Accelerating future deployment* (Paris, IEA/OECD, 2016) 43.

comprehensive approach, and one which has the potential to offer operators and commercial proponents increased confidence. The conditions for enabling a transfer are also likely to be important, providing operators with clear thresholds and objectives. The inherent flexibility of the regulatory models found in the Canadian Province of Alberta and the Australian State of Victoria offer perhaps more practical models when contrasted with the more objective terms of models found in the UK and EU legislation.

The issue of financial security, and in particular the approach adopted by regulators when determining financial contributions to be made by the storage operator, is a further area where lessons may be drawn from early legal and regulatory frameworks. Aimed at reducing the state's exposure to an operator's insolvency, or inability to meet the demands of a regulatory framework, a number of schemes have been proposed by regulators worldwide. The example of the approach adopted by regulators in the Province of Alberta and the State of Victoria, which would see operators making financial contributions throughout a project's operational phase, rather than at the point of transferring responsibility to the State, may be viewed as a practical and realistic approach to addressing this particular issue.

C. Project-Specific Experience

Limited project-level experience of the operational elements of these new regulatory frameworks has meant that much of the commentary surrounding liability remains largely speculative. A small number of projects have, however, been permitted under these CCS-specific regimes, and their experiences to date reveal that some aspects of the liability frameworks are proving challenging.

Material published by projects participating in the former UK CCS Commercialisation Program reveal some of the challenges posed by liability regimes. The insurance strategy produced by the Peterhead CCS Project highlights a several issues with the UK's regime, noting in particular the absence of insurance solutions to address particular risks:

> Until the regulatory regime is defined, it is uncertain what the extent of liability for CO_2 release is. At present, no requirement for re-purchase of credits or financial penalties is expected in the case of accidental CO_2 release from the reservoir. Protection against repayment of carbon credits (European Union Allowances (EUAs)) is currently uninsurable.[34]

The Peterhead Project also noted that other liabilities, to be addressed throughout the construction and operational phases of the project, would have to be addressed by the venture in the absence of insurance solutions. Ongoing dialogue with the insurance and professional services sectors, as well as government and environment agencies, was similarly highlighted as critical to mitigating 'CO_2 risks exposures'.

---

[34] Shell UK Limited, *Peterhead CCS Project, Insurance Plan* (Shell UK Limited, 2014) 8. The plan is one of the 86 commercial, project management and lessons learned knowledge reports, gathered from the Peterhead and White Rose Carbon Capture and Storage Projects' Front End Engineering and Design (FEED) contracts.

A more collaborative approach between regulators and project proponents, in the design and implementation of these new regulatory regimes, is likely to be critical. The nature of this interaction will be particularly important where regulators are required to interpret profoundly technical information to establish an operator's compliance with the requirements of the regulatory model. Determining a storage site's effective retention of stored CO_2 and its associated impact upon the environment, prior to any proposed transfer of liability, is one example where a high degree of technical expertise will be needed to corroborate an operator's compliance.

16

Carbon Capture and Storage: Commercial Arrangements for Managing Liability Risks

DANIEL LAWRENCE

I. INTRODUCTION: THE COMPLEXITIES OF CCS
AND THE MANY LINKS IN THE CCS CHAIN

AN IMPORTANT ASPECT of emerging legislation on carbon capture and storage (CCS) has been concerned with apportioning civil and administrative liability for risks that may occur—particularly risks relating to the long-term storage of carbon dioxide (CO_2). For long-term storage often the model is to channel liability on the storage operator, but with some form of eventual transfer of liability to government, given the long time-scales over which CO_2 storage needs to be proved. Ian Havercroft, in Chapter 15 of this volume, explores various legislative models for liability apportionment that have been deployed or are envisaged in this regard. But whatever the apportionment of such liabilities under legislation, the reality is that commercial arrangements are likely to be made that further apportion liability as between the different parties involved in a full chain CCS project. This chapter explores the types of models that may be used by commercial parties for apportioning liabilities in practice, drawing on existing experience in the oil and gas industry but noting the particular challenges raised by CCS projects.

When considering the commercial arrangements for allocating liability risks, it needs to be borne in mind that each of the three basic elements of a full-chain CCS project—in particular the capture of CO_2 at the location where it is produced, the transportation of the captured CO_2 to the storage site, and ultimately its injection and storage there—involves distinct processes that require specialist technologies and related expertise. Also, it is not unusual for there to be arrangements in place to enable third parties to obtain access to CO_2 transport networks and storage sites on non-discriminatory terms, with a view to enabling the infrastructure to be used more efficiently.[1] The result is that a typical CCS scheme has the potential to involve a

---

[1] In the UK, for example, this is achieved by providing for the party seeking access to appeal to the Secretary of State in circumstances where the parties themselves are unable to reach agreement. See the Storage of Carbon Dioxide (Access to Infrastructure) Regulations 2011 (SI 2011/2305).

number of different actors. It also needs to be borne in mind that the respective operators of different parts of the CCS chain (power station operators, pipeline operators and operators involved with offshore platforms/infrastructure) come from very different backgrounds, in terms of the regulatory structures in place for the types of assets they operate and the rates of return they typically expect to receive on their investments. For example, investors in the offshore oil/gas sector are accustomed to risking considerable amounts of capital on exploratory work, on the prospect of discovering substantial hydrocarbon resources for which they would expect a high rate of return; whereas those investing in pipelines typically expect long-term certainty but at lower rates of return. The regulatory matrix and risk/return calculation for power station investors is again very different from that utilised by those investing in other elements in the CCS chain. There may also be other commercial tensions. For example, a CO_2 pipeline operator considering becoming involved in a CCS project may be concerned to ensure 'fairness of access', with a view to ensuring that various third-party producers of CO_2 will be able to access/utilise the pipeline for transporting the CO_2 they produce in future, whereas a single power station operator signing up to a CCS project is likely to be concerned foremost that potential access to the pipeline by other producers will not risk its own ability to throughput CO_2 to the storage site. The success of a full-chain CCS project will depend on the parties' collaborating in spite of these differences/tensions.

There are various ways in which those involved in the different stages of a CCS project might collaborate. For practical reasons, certain key participants may decide to organise themselves into a consortium arrangement, perhaps with a special purpose vehicle (SPV) acting as a single operator for the entire CCS chain but with personnel, expertise and other resources flowing from each of the respective members of the consortium, as well as from other contractors. For example, delivery of the proposed White Rose CCS Project[2] was to have been through an entity called Capture Power Limited, consisting of a consortium of General Electric, BOC and Drax, together with National Grid Carbon Limited, a wholly-owned subsidiary of National Grid. A consortium model is commonly used in the oil and gas industry for larger, more risky projects, as it enables the participants, through contractual arrangements, not only to apportion their respective entitlements (interests) in the project but also to allocate liabilities as between themselves. The need for funding or other support mechanisms may also influence the project structure, as where the project involves government funding and/or risk sharing.

As a concept, CCS is challenging because the full-scale capture and storage of large quantities of CO_2 is something of a novel activity, with the quantities of CO_2 to be handled being many orders of magnitude greater than has happened to date.

---

[2] Which would have comprised a new coal-fired ultra-supercritical oxy power plant (OPP) of up to 448 megawatts electrical (MWe) (gross) and a CO_2 transport and storage system (T&S System) that would transfer captured CO_2 from the OPP by pipeline for permanent storage under the southern North Sea. In November 2015, the UK Government announced that the £1 billion ring-fenced capital budget for the White Rose CCS Competition was no longer available, which meant that the CCS Competition could no longer proceed as planned.

For example, if equipped with CO_2 capture technology, a coal-fired power station consuming 8,000 tonnes a day of coal (in the region of 1 GW power generation) could produce up to 30,000 te/day of CO_2 to be captured and transported to long-term storage facilities.[3] Even though the technologies and infrastructure needed to realise a full-chain CCS project are well understood, the overall project costs can be high to the extent that the technologies/infrastructure necessary for a CCS project need to be put in place for the first time. Unlike many types of development for which the potential rewards of development are expected to outweigh the costs, there is little or no economic incentive for a CCS project that is intended solely for climate change mitigation purposes, in the absence of regulatory incentives/ imperatives (an exception is where CO_2 is injected for the purpose of enhanced hydrocarbon recovery). Where CCS involves the (proposed) re-use of existing offshore oil and gas platforms/infrastructure, there may also be challenges associated with how decommissioning liabilities will be dealt with, including (importantly) the timing for such liabilities being triggered, the extent to which they can effectively be assigned to the CCS injection/storage site operator and related tax considerations. In addition, full-chain CCS projects involve considerable 'project-on-project' risk (ie, the risk that an essential element of the chain could become uneconomic or otherwise fail in future). Uncertainty surrounding long-term gas, coal and carbon prices means that the gross margin for power generators is uncertain over time; moreover, the UK electricity generation mix is likely to evolve in future not only as a result of commodity prices, but also as a result of government policy (eg, more nuclear and renewables capacity could result in lower usage levels of CCS plants and therefore lower overall revenues). Notwithstanding that the capital costs of some elements of a CCS chain (such as pipeline systems) are better understood and are therefore more certain, where these form a large proportion of the total capital requirement, cost overruns can have a disproportionate impact on overall project returns. There is also uncertainty surrounding the thermal efficiency of power stations equipped with carbon capture technology, which can present significant risks of increased operational costs through fuel costs.[4] A further factor that complicates CCS technology's getting off the ground is that government support/encouragement for CCS demonstration schemes can wax and wane;[5] this is notwithstanding that many industry players regard at least some element of government funding/support to be necessary in order for CCS to be proved as a technology—particularly in the context of a large-scale demonstration project.

The novelty of the activity and the need for distinct elements of the project to remain viable/operational over long periods of time contribute to uncertainties as

---

[3] As discussed in P Harper, Health and Safety Executive, *Assessment of the major hazard potential of carbon dioxide (CO_2)*, advisers J Wilday and M Bilo (June 2011), at www.hse.gov.uk/carboncapture/assets/docs/major-hazard-potential-carbon-dioxide.pdf.

[4] See Scottish Centre for Carbon Storage, *Opportunities for CO_2 Storage around Scotland—an integrated strategic research study* (Edinburgh, Scottish Centre for Carbon Storage, Scottish Government, April 2009), at www.gov.scot/Resource/Doc/270737/0080597.pdf, ch 8.

[5] See K Stacey, 'High ambitions for carbon capture falter; CO_2 recovery', *Financial Times* (26 July 2016), at www.ft.com/content/bfcdcf44-2402-11e6-9d4d-c11776a5124d.

to how the technology will perform/operate in practice and the extent to which involvement in a CCS project may give rise to unexpected liabilities. It is against this backdrop that the issue of liability allocation for those participating in a CCS project needs to be considered.

II. KEY ROLES AND RISKS IN A CCS PROJECT

It is useful first to distinguish certain key roles that are likely to be involved in bringing a full-chain CCS project to fruition. The role of a 'developer' is to bring the project to a Final Investment Decision (FID), and this includes undertaking the necessary studies and characterisation work, as well as negotiating the overarching commercial arrangements. An 'owner' may provide all of the necessary project funding, or at least provide equity until project finance can be secured (indeed, there may be several 'owners' in the case of a consortium, as well as other investors and/or finance providers). The role of 'government' may also be critical in terms of offering funding/support. Various contractors and sub-contractors will be involved in the construction, and may also be involved in operating the project once completed. The 'operator' will be responsible for the operation of the facilities and other infrastructure that make up the CCS project; and there may be separate operators for different aspects of the CCS chain.

Various project structures are conceivable.[6] In the case of a CCS project that is funded in whole or part by government, it may well be important from government's perspective (as a party to the project development contract(s)) to be able to contract with a single entity (eg, an SPV) as 'developer', notwithstanding that other consortium members and subcontractors are involved in the project to provide particular elements of the CCS chain. Collaboration by the respective members of a CCS project is likely to be formalised thorough contractual arrangements that bind them to provide certain goods/technology/services for the project or parts of it.

Each of the parties involved in a 'full-chain' CCS scheme will be faced with certain potential liability risks, which will vary depending on the particular role(s) each party plays and the nature of potential liabilities associated with such role(s). Certain risks are more in the nature of commercial risks; however, a legal liability can also represent a commercial risk. As discussed in more detail in section IV, there are well-developed mechanisms for allocating and mitigating liabilities and other risks, and these are well understood by industry, who are typically involved in collaborating in relation to onshore and offshore industrial projects/activities. These mechanisms would also be relevant for a CCS project. Nevertheless, certain potential liability risks associated with a CCS project are peculiar to CCS, a key risk being an escape or leak of captured/stored CO_2. The mechanisms used to apportion liability risks may

---

[6] A number of different project structures and funding arrangements that might potentially be utilised for a CCS project are discussed in D Grosvenor et al, *A need unsatisfied: Blueprint for enabling investment in CO_2 storage* (Deloitte, February 2016), at www.thecrownestate.co.uk/media/502093/ei-a-need-unsatisfied-blueprint-for-enabling-investment-in-co$_2$-deloitte.pdf.

need to be more complex, such as where several operators are involved in the overall CCS chain or there is a common pipeline that is used by many. The principles and practice of liability allocation/apportionment can be applied for different project structures, technologies and CCS chain link configurations.

Before discussing in greater detail the mechanisms for allocating/apportioning liabilities in the context of a CCS project, it is useful to consider the different types of risks that may be relevant for those involved in a CCS project.

III. CATEGORIES OF RISKS/LIABILITIES ASSOCIATED WITH A CCS PROJECT, AND HOW LEGAL LIABILITY RISKS MAY ARISE IN PRACTICE

When considering the risks associated with a CCS project, it is useful to distinguish between 'usual course of business risks' and 'CCS-specific risks'. 'Usual course of business' in this context refers to risks that are commonly associated with many of the existing and familiar technologies and processes which would form part of the CCS chain—for example, risks associated with installing and operating pipelines and sub-sea drilling, both of which are well understood by the offshore oil and gas industry. Some types of risk cross both categories. For example, the risk of leakage from a sub-sea pipeline might be considered to be a 'usual course of business risk', in the sense that oil and gas pipeline operators must account for such risks in their business; however, to the extent that the transport of 'supercritical'[7] CO_2 through a sub-sea pipeline is a novel activity, the potential escape of CO_2 from such a pipeline presents a CCS-specific risk. Some of the CCS-specific risks will dissipate or diminish as the project progresses (eg, where it is proved over time that the design/construction of the transport pipeline is adequate to contain CO_2 whilst in transport), but some will remain throughout the project—and indeed certain risks may continue even after the storage site is closed, such as the long-term risks of CO_2 leakage.

Most of the risks associated with a CCS project are broadly similar to those that exist for many industrial projects, such as the development/construction of large-scale oil and gas and/or energy installations/pipelines, which typically involve collaboration by a number of different contractors. There are established industry practices and standard contractual provisions on liability apportionment, such as indemnities, warranties, claw-back provisions, insurance, etc, which are used to allocate risks associated with such projects. Examples of the sorts of risks involved include: poor design work or the inability to use standard components, meaning the project cannot be completed as originally designed; 'siting' risks associated with land where project infrastructure is to be sited, which may involve ownership and access issues; construction risks, such as those which give rise to project delays that impact on cost and schedule; 'change of law' risks, to the extent that changes in laws/regulations once the project commences can impact cost or the ability to

---

[7] A supercritical fluid exists above a substance's critical temperature and pressure (31.04°C and 73.82 bar for CO_2), above which supercritical CO_2 exhibits the density of a liquid and viscosity of a gas. See Harper, n 3 above.

operate the project; and technical, operational and decommissioning risks, such as where processes do not perform as expected, or costs otherwise turn out to be much higher than anticipated.

There are also the risks associated with obtaining and maintaining permits/consents for the project. These may relate to the construction, operation and/or decommissioning stages, and can either be general in nature (for example, requirements for planning consents for particular uses of land, and/or requirements to hold 'environmental permits' for certain activities) or CCS-specific (such as consents required in connection with CO_2 injection/storage activities). This category of risks includes delays in obtaining consents, refusal of consents, onerous conditions attached to consents and revocation/suspension of consents.

In addition, there is a category of risks that can be characterised as arising due to the imposition of some liability or other obligation by law or regulation, where crystallisation of the liability depends on the assertion/pursuit of a demand, claim, action or proceeding by a third party—including a governmental/regulatory authority. This is a complex category of risks because of the wide range of legal liabilities that might conceivably arise in connection with a CCS project. For example, this category includes legal liability risks associated with incidents that give rise to regulatory action asserting liabilities/obligations, and/or liability risks associated with claims by third parties who have suffered damage, injury or other losses arising from such incidents. It also includes liabilities that arise where there has been a breach of consents/permits or some other occurrence that results in regulatory enforcement action. Examples of incidents that might conceivably give rise to third-party claims include the sudden escape of supercritical CO_2 from a pipeline; the 'blowout' of CO_2 during injection (perhaps injuring employees/workers); and detrimental effects of CO_2 injection impacting surrounding oil/gas fields, etc.

Potential liabilities relating to escapes/leakage of CO_2 at or from a storage site are generally regarded as one of the most problematic of the categories of risk associated with CCS, simply because the activity of injecting industrial-scale quantities of supercritical CO_2 into strata/saline aquifers beneath the seabed is something of a novel activity, notwithstanding that there is some experience in certain jurisdictions.[8] Storage of CO_2 involves several phases: site selection, injection, closure and post-closure. Risks of CO_2 escape are perhaps at their highest during the injection phase, but with lingering risks of leakage during the post-injection phase. There are also certain technical metallurgical issues, associated with transporting supercritical CO_2 in high-pressure pipelines, which pose challenges in terms of unintended escapes of CO_2.[9] Incidents could potentially involve a sudden and catastrophic escape of

---

[8] Such as the Great Plains Synfuel Plant and Weyburn-Midale Project in Canada and the Snøhvit CO_2 Storage Project in Norway. See Global CCS Institute, *Great Plains Synfuel Plant and Weyburn-Midale Project* (15 September 2016), at www.globalccsinstitute.com/projects/great-plains-synfuel-plant-and-weyburn-midale-project. There are at the time of writing 19 active CCS operations, with a further 21 planned for the period 2017–25 according to Global CCS Institute, *Large-scale CCS facilities* (2016), at www.globalccsinstitute.com/projects/large-scale-ccs-projects#map.

[9] See P Shaladitya et al, *Material Selection for Supercritical CO_2 Transport* (Gateshead, The Welding Institute, The First International Forum on the transportation of CO_2, 2010), at www.twi-global.com/technical-knowledge/published-papers/material-selection-for-supercritical-co₂-transport/.

CO_2, such as might result from the failure of a pipeline,[10] or gradual leakage over time, as in the case of long-term seepage of CO_2 from an inadequately contained storage site.

Various categories of civil and administrative liabilities that potentially may arise in the context of unintended escapes/leakages of CO_2 are discussed in more detail by Ian Havercroft in Chapter 15 of this volume. The precise scope and formulation of these will depend on the particular jurisdiction where the relevant CCS activities take place. For example, under English law they may potentially include: various tortious liabilities, such as trespass,[11] private nuisance,[12] public nuisance[13] and negligence;[14] a range of administrative liabilities,[15] such as obligations to provide financial provision and/or to discharge remediation obligations; and (typically) potential criminal liabilities, such as where there is a breach of obligations/duties under permits or legislation. In general, liability is likely to fall on the operator, as the permit holder and/or person otherwise in control of the activity, although where the operator is a joint venture, it could potentially fall jointly and severally on the joint venture partners.

IV. MECHANISMS FOR APPORTIONING LIABILITY RISKS

What might be regarded as standard liability apportionment mechanisms used in many 'engineering procurement construction' (EPC)[16] contracts are likely to be appropriate for addressing many of the legal liability risks associated with a CCS project. The rationale for this is that project *construction* of onshore aspects of

---

[10] Whereas in existing CO_2-handling facilities, an inadvertent release of CO_2 may have created a small-scale hazard, potentially only affecting those in the local vicinity, a very large release of CO_2 from a CCS scale of operation has the potential to produce a harmful effect over a significantly greater area, and as such could affect a significant number of people. See Harper, n 3 above.

[11] Trespass occurs when there is an unjustified intrusion upon land in the possession of another. Trespass as a potential category of tortious liability is perhaps most likely to be relevant in an onshore context, as where CO_2 injected by a storage site operator into subsurface strata beneath an area of land leased to that operator had migrated (via the substrata) to affect neighbouring land owned by others.

[12] A private nuisance actionable in tort is caused by a person's doing something on his own land (which he may be lawfully entitled to do) that becomes a nuisance when the consequences of his act result in an unreasonable interference with a neighbouring landowner's enjoyment of his rights over his land.

[13] A public nuisance is actionable in tort but can also be a criminal offence. Public nuisance arises from an act that endangers the life, health, property, morals or comfort of the public, or obstructs the public in the exercise or enjoyment of rights common to all.

[14] Negligence essentially involves a failure by a person to exercise a standard of care which the law requires. Claimants must essentially prove: (1) that the defendant owed the claimant a duty of care, (2) the duty has been breached, (3) that breach resulted in loss or damage, and (4) the loss/damage was reasonably foreseeable.

[15] Various categories of administrative liabilities are discussed by Ian Havercroft in ch 15 of this volume. An example is liability for 'environmental damage' arising under European Parliament and Council Directive 2004/35/EC of 21 April 2004 on environmental liability with regard to the prevention and remedying of environmental damage [2011] OJ L143/56 (the Environmental Liability Directive), which is channelled to the operator.

[16] An EPC contract is one pursuant to which an engineering and construction contractor carries out the detailed engineering design of the project, procures all the equipment and materials necessary, and undertakes to construct and deliver a functioning facility to its client(s).

a full-chain CCS scheme carries no unusual risks, given that the onshore process facilities associated with onshore capture and transport of CO_2 are more or less the same as or similar to those that are already deployed all over the world in petrochemical, industrial and power plant installations. Similarly, the *construction* activities associated with the installation of pipelines, drilling platforms, injection equipment, etc offshore are the same as or similar to those already deployed by the oil and gas industry, and present no unusual risks beyond those which already exist for the industry. Notwithstanding this, as soon as the facilities go live, particular hazards may be presented, which are somewhat novel in view of the sheer quantities of CO_2 that are intended to be captured, transported and stored.

In the context of a full-chain CCS project that involves government funding, the government is likely to want to enter into the main project contract with an entity that has been designated as the prime contractor (or 'developer'), even though this may be/is often a joint venture or a special purpose company backed by a consortium. It is likely there would be a main project contract that would contain the principal contractual mechanisms for addressing risks that apply during the period before the CCS systems have completed commissioning. It would define the scope of the project and the services to be provided by the project developer. Typically, the developer would be obliged to design,[17] build, finance, commission, operate and maintain, and decommission the CO_2 capture facility and associated transportation, injection and offshore storage facilities. Where the 'developer' is a consortium, the project contract may require the developer to be owned (directly or indirectly through a holdco) by each of the consortium members, and for there to be a shareholders' agreement between the consortium members governing their inter-shareholder relationship and their obligations as shareholders in the developer. Certain other longer-term risks/obligations may also be addressed in the main project contract, such as post-injection site monitoring and long-term storage liabilities, even though such matters may be addressed at least in part by, and overlap with, obligations in the storage permit. In addition to the main project contract, there may also be key 'sub-contractor direct agreements' that will be entered into with the government authority responsible for promoting the project. Given the long-term nature of the obligations and liabilities associated with the storage of CO_2, the term of the project contract, in so far as it relates to the storage site, is likely to continue for several decades from the date it is executed, albeit subject to the possibility of early termination (eg, in circumstances where the operator fails to comply with storage permit or other requirements).

The various agreements that form part of the contractual arrangements discussed so far will likely contain a variety of mechanisms for allocating risks as between the respective parties. How the parties decide to allocate liabilities amongst themselves will depend on their respective responsibilities and obligations in relation to the CCS project, and the extent to which it is commercially reasonable for a particular party

---

[17] A 'front end engineering design' (FEED) contract may be required where a project proposal does not offer sufficient certainty of cost or risk to satisfy government that a full project contract should be offered. The FEED contract may, for example, be funded by government to cover the expected costs of performing engineering/design studies into particular elements of the CCS chain.

to be allocated a given liability risk as a matter of contract. The contractual mechanisms for allocating risks include not only the assignment of certain responsibilities/obligations to particular parties, but also warranties and representations given by such persons, which are usually addressed to a wide range of matters and typically include warranties/representations to the effect that the party giving them is in compliance with laws and has obtained and will maintain compliance with all requisite consents/permits.

A very common mechanism for allocating liabilities contractually is the indemnity. This defines the particular liability/or category of liabilities that is to be allocated, and provides that the party assuming the indemnity obligation undertakes to meet the indemnitee's losses to the extent they are within the scope of the indemnity. It is essentially a promise to be responsible for another person's loss. For example, the developer of a CCS project might agree to indemnify a governmental authority with which it contracts to provide a CCS scheme, from and against all liability for:

(a) death or personal injury;
(b) loss of or damage to property (including property belonging to the authority or for which it is responsible);
(c) breach of statutory duty; and
(d) actions, claims, demands, costs, charges and expenses (including legal expenses)

that may arise out of, or in consequence of, the design, construction, operation or maintenance of the CCS project, or the performance or non-performance by the developer of its obligations under the agreement.

Typically, such an indemnity would also expressly carve out particular circumstances in which the developer would not be liable under the indemnity, such as where the matters described in (a) to (d) arise as a direct result of the developer's acting on the instruction of the authority, or where any injury, loss, damage, cost and expense is caused by the negligence or wilful misconduct of the authority, its employees, agents or contractors, or by the breach by the authority of its obligations under the agreement.

The use of contractual mechanisms such as indemnities enables the parties to seek to allocate liabilities amongst themselves with a view to achieving a fair allocation of risk. For example, it might seem reasonable that the operator of a transport pipeline, as the person responsible for ensuring there are no unintended leakages from the pipeline infrastructure it controls, should bear any liabilities/losses that result from such leakages. However, this may not necessarily reflect the commercial reality where, say, the consortium members (or some of them) own the pipeline operator, as in such circumstances the shareholders may have agreed to indemnify the operator generally against liabilities/losses—other than where the liability/loss arises from the operator's gross negligence (the rationale being that the operator is run on a cash-lean basis, with its profits being mostly returned to its shareholders).

Similarly, a contractor with a minor (relatively low value) role in the project may aim to protect its position by seeking indemnities from other project members with whom it contracts, with a view to limiting its total liability to a certain amount by means of an indemnity in its favour to cover losses it may incur above such amount. Another common deployment of indemnity mechanisms is where a project involves a consortium, with each party to the consortium relying on indemnities from the other members aimed at ensuring that if one party suffers a loss, it will be able to recover it from the other members to the extent necessary to achieve a fair apportionment to reflect the respective percentage interests of the parties.

However, both warranties and indemnities share the common problem that they are only as good as the financial strength of the warrantor or indemnitor. This can be problematic in a full-chain CCS project that involves several actors with markedly different covenant strengths. If there are doubts about the warrantying/indemnifying party's creditworthiness, possible solutions may include taking out insurance (if the risk is commercially insurable), having a parent company guarantee, or having restrictions placed on intra-group reorganisations (although it is not possible to prohibit a company from entering into a liquidation process) or on any asset-stripping exercises.[18]

Another potential limiting factor when considering the use of an indemnity as a risk allocation tool is that, on ordinary principles, an indemnity will be construed against the person in whose favour it is given, and will not cover loss due to a person's own negligence or that of his servants unless adequate and clear words were used, or unless the indemnity could have no reasonable meaning unless so applied.[19] Where the loss in question arises concurrently from breach of statutory duty and negligence, the indemnity may be construed as not extending to the negligence.[20] These principles could potentially give rise to problems for an operator as 'indemnitee', in cases where it is alleged that the operator's negligent actions (or inaction) have caused or exacerbated a CO_2 release. Indeed, it may even be desirable from the perspective of members of the owning consortium for the liability to remain with the operating subsidiary (as an un-indemnified loss). On the other hand, it could be decided by the parties to the relevant agreements that the operating subsidiary should be indemnified even in cases where the operator is negligent, leaving it for the indemnifying parties to decide how to allocate the liabilities amongst themselves. That said, the legal doctrine of *ex turpi causa*[21] may become relevant in certain circumstances, as where an indemnitee (say, an operator) is seeking to recover fines or penalties, in as much as an agreement to indemnify a person against a criminal or civil penalty will not normally be upheld by the courts for public policy reasons; though for strict liability offences committed innocently or negligently, the position is less clear.[22] There is the potential for criminal liabilities to arise not only where there are breaches of permits/consents, but also where there are breaches of relevant legislation, such as (in the UK) the Health and Safety at Work etc Act 1974, which

---

[18] *Ricoh Europe Holdings BV & Ors v Spratt & Anor* [2013] EWCA Civ 92, [2013] 2 WLR 1398.
[19] *Canada Steam Ship Lines Ltd v The King* [1952] UKPC 1, [1952] AC 192; *Walters v Whessoe* [1968] 2 All ER 816n, 6 BLR 23.
[20] *EE Caledonia Ltd v Orbit Valve Company Europe* (QBD, 28 May 1993) [1993] 4 All ER 165; cf *Smith v UMB Chrysler (Scotland) Ltd* [1977] UKHL7, [1978] 1 WLR 165.
[21] The legal doctrine that a claimant is unable to pursue a legal remedy if the liability arises in connection with his own illegal act.
[22] *Safeway Stores Ltd & Ors v Twigger & Ors* [2010] EWCA Civ 1472, [2011] 2 All ER 841.

makes it an offence for employers to breach their statutory duties to ensure (as far as reasonably practicable) the health, safety and welfare of their employees and other persons who may be affected by their work.[23]

Insurance can also play an important role in mitigating certain liability risks, in as much as the effective allocation to insurers of certain categories of risks under insurance policies in which they agree to indemnify the insured, provides yet another mechanism for contractually allocating/mitigating risks (albeit subject to deductibles, exclusions and other limitations). However, some liabilities will remain uninsurable because of their nature (as discussed further below), and there can also be commercial challenges in obtaining insurance cover for certain risks. Ultimately, neither insurers nor storage operators are able to bear unlimited liabilities, so risk sharing with government is likely to be required if CCS is to be developed at scale in Europe.[24]

As discussed by Ian Havercroft in Chapter 15 of this volume, there can be particular challenges for a storage operator when it comes to achieving an effective transfer of liability risks associated with the CO_2 storage site to the state. For example, in the European Union, the CCS Directive[25] requires 'financial security' to be provided to meet not only CO_2 leakage risk, but also decommissioning cost risk and the risk that the storage permit may be prematurely withdrawn. Notwithstanding that the insurance industry has put forward for consideration some innovative potential insurance/risk solutions for transferring to insurers certain risks faced by storage operators (such as at least some of the risk associated with an operator's having to surrender emissions allowances under the EU ETS Directive[26] as a consequence of CO_2 leakage to atmosphere), insurance does not offer a comprehensive solution. Similarly, notwithstanding that certain structured financial products have been created to assist operators in managing the risks of incurring (premature) decommissioning liabilities if the operator's storage licence is temporarily or permanently withdrawn before the (planned) 'transfer of responsibility' to the competent authority (CA),[27] such products may not provide a complete solution. Not only is it difficult to quantify the amount of financial contributions that may be required by the CA in future, but there are also uncertainties associated with the regulatory mechanisms for transferring liability risk to the state once the storage site has been

---

[23] Health and Safety at Work etc Act 1974, s 2(1).

[24] See X Liang and A Voysey, *Managing Liabilities of European Carbon Capture and Storage: a ClimateWise Report on Developing Commercially Viable Insurance Solutions* (ClimateWise, 2012) at www.cisl.cam.ac.uk/publications/publication-pdfs/climatewise-ccs-report-nov-2012-full-report.pdf/view.

[25] European Parliament and Council Directive 2009/31/EC of 23 April 2009 on the geological storage of carbon dioxide and amending Council Directive 85/337/EEC, European Parliament and Council Directives 2000/60/EC, 2001/80/EC, 2004/35/EC, 2006/12/EC, 2008/1/EC and Regulation (EC) No 1013/2006 [2009] OJ L140/114 (as amended) (CCS Directive).

[26] European Parliament and Council Directive 2003/87/EC of 13 October 2003 establishing a scheme for greenhouse gas emission allowance trading within the Community and amending Council Directive 96/61/EC [2003] OJ L275/32 (as amended).

[27] This category of risk challenges the fundamental principles of insurability, as the risk is viewed as lacking sufficient fortuity to be insurable given that the timing of costs is the real risk.

closed, given the claw-back provisions, which typically allow the CA's post-transfer costs to be recovered from the operator in certain circumstances. Risks of this nature will continue to pose challenges to the extent that operators are unable to place reliance on insurance.

The extent to which a transfer to the state of liabilities associated with a storage site will include risks associated with existing or potential tort claims will depend on the law in the jurisdiction in question.[28]

V. INCENTIVISING CCS—LIABILITY CONSIDERATIONS

Apart from using CO_2 for enhanced hydrocarbon recovery, or where CO_2 storage is a co-benefit of injecting other materials for the purpose of disposal (eg, acid-gas injection with incidental CO_2 storage), the purpose of undertaking CCS is primarily climate change mitigation and should be regarded as a public good.[29] However, the technology is expensive and carries certain liability risks. Therefore, operators need to be incentivised if they are to engage in the deployment of CCS (even if the incentives involve principally mandatory regulatory requirements). The range of possible incentives includes mechanisms such as carbon taxes, cap-and-trade-based emission trading, feed-in tariffs and/or emissions performance standards, amongst others, but equally important are measures aimed at allocating, limiting or otherwise mitigating potential liabilities amongst those participating in CCS projects.

There is an important interplay between the incentives offered to CCS developers/operators and the extent of the liability risks they face, in as much as a developer or an operator is unlikely to undertake an activity for which the sum of potential (reasonably anticipated) liabilities outweighs the incentives—unless required to do so by regulatory imperatives. Also, the willingness of commercial entities to participate in a CCS project will be influenced by the extent to which potential liabilities can be allocated/shared effectively amongst the various CCS project participants (and/or their insurers), including the extent to which liabilities can be shared with/allocated to the state. In this sense, incentivising CCS optimally requires a combination of regulatory instruments that impose certain obligations/requirements on those involved in a CCS project and contractual devices for allocating responsibilities/obligations and liabilities amongst the various project participants. The choice of project structure will also influence how liabilities are allocated—particularly the extent to which the government itself is prepared give assurances to assume a share of the potential (contingent) liabilities or provide other support/funding for the project.

---

[28] For example: 'The [CCS] Directive does not deal with the transfer of any liabilities relating to civil actions (tort claims), nor does it deal with any administrative liabilities under national environmental laws, which are not encompassed under the [EU] Environmental Liability Directive. The extent to [which] these aspects of liability are transferred is left to each Member State.' See I Havercroft and R Macrory, *Legal Liability and Carbon Capture and Storage: A Comparative Perspective* (Canberra, Global CCS Institute, 2014).

[29] As discussed in International Energy Agency (IEA), *Carbon Capture and Storage: Model Regulatory Framework* (2010), at www.iea.org/publications/freepublications/publication/model_framework.pdf.

If it can be demonstrated over time that the large quantities of CO_2 involved can in fact be transported safely to and completely and permanently contained in a storage site, this is likely to increase confidence on the part of industry (including insurers) that the liability risks associated with CCS are commercially manageable. In the meantime, the potential owners/operators of CCS storage sites in jurisdictions where the relevant technologies/practices are as yet unproven, are likely to want binding assurances from government that certain liability risks associated with CO_2 storage/leakage will ultimately be shared/assumed by the state.

17

No Visible Means of Legal Support: China's CCS Regime

NAVRAJ SINGH GHALEIGH[*]

I. INTRODUCTION: WHITHER LAW?

IN THE SPACE of a few short years, the People's Republic of China (PRC) has transformed itself from villain to hero, the world's leading hope for avoiding anthropogenic climactic disaster. Notwithstanding its position as the world's leading emitter—its emissions being roughly double those of the second placed United States (US)[1]—China's embrace of the Paris Agreement, reaffirmed in the light of the Trump Presidency,[2] its pilot emissions trading schemes, and a vast renewables push have placed it in a position of great global moment. Against the backdrop of European Union (EU) peripherality and troubling signals from the post-Obama US, there is a great burden on China to demonstrate leadership in climate action.

Seen in this light, carbon capture and storage (CCS) serves as a particular instance of the general phenomenon of China as at the centre of climate change debates. China's energy system alone accounts for nearly half of the world's existing coal-fired power plants, and its first Nationally Determined Contribution (NDC) plans for its emissions to peak only around 2030, past the date by which 1.5°C warming is likely to have been reached. Notwithstanding this framing, the awe-inspiring numbers of China's climate challenge can be cast in an optimistic light. Retrofitting CCS to the Chinese coal power assets will contribute to the reversal of the '"lock-in" of emissions', as well as easing the domestic economic and social costs of premature closure of the fleet.[3] From a wider perspective, if China were to deploy CCS, even if slowly at first, such is its scale and networked system of governance that more rapid

---

[*] Sincere thanks are owed to the editors, and especially Ms Sonja Karikumpu for her superb research assistance.
[1] As of 2015, China's emissions (10,357Mt CO_2) were nearly double those of the US (5,414Mt CO_2), the second largest emitter in the world, and over one-quarter of the global total (36,262Mt CO_2). See TA Boden, G Marland and RJ Andres, *Global, Regional, and National Fossil-Fuel CO_2 Emissions* (Oakridge, TN, Carbon Dioxide Information Analysis Center, January 2017).
[2] P Clark, 'China Pledges to Uphold Paris Climate Commitments', *Financial Times* (29 March 2017).
[3] Organisation for Economic Cooperation and Development (OECD) and International Energy Agency (IEA), *20 Years of Carbon Capture and Storage: Accelerating Future Deployment* (Paris, International Energy Agency, 2016).

diffusion could push CCS past thresholds of cost, technology, social acceptance, governance, etc, with the effect that a tipping point might be reached.[4] Thus, the scale of China's climate change challenges contains within it the possibility to transform the demonstration and deployment of CCS globally.

What, though, is the role of law in this process? China's extant CCS regulatory regime is profoundly underdeveloped.[5] Consequently, this chapter places that regime, such as it is, in the context of domestic environmental law, but also in the light of larger debates about understanding the nature of law in legal systems that, unlike those in the West, do not give primacy to the professionalisation of law. It will be argued that notwithstanding major efforts of legal reform (ie consistency of law, rights-based normativity and restructuring of the legal system),[6] China's climate governance, legal norms and institutions only partially contribute to and safeguard the proper future of Chinese CCS. Moreover, such is the character of the Chinese legal system, any role it does play bears little resemblance to governance regimes in other jurisdictions.

From the first, it should be noted that China current lacks a comprehensive legal regime for climate action. Surveys undertaken by non-lawyers such as the GLOBE Climate Legislation Study make clear that there is no comprehensive climate change law in China.[7] This is despite the pledge made in 2010 for such a legal regime, and the optimistic thought that 'passage of the law is expected in 2015 or 2016'.[8] There is of course no denying that successive bureaucratic edicts from China's 11th Five-Year Plan (2006) onwards have promised economy-wide reductions in carbon intensity, which have been followed up by policies and measures to meet these targets. The powerful National Development and Reform Commission (NDRC) (dubbed the 'Little State Council'), which is the leading economic planning unit of central government, has developed a National Plan to Address Climate Change (2014–20), and carbon pricing schemes and measures for energy demand and supply abound.[9] All such policies, measures and schemes have been formalised into China's NDC under the Paris Agreement.[10] What many of these analyses fail to do, however, is to focus on the legal nature of the instruments in question. For example, the GLOBE study lists under 'China: legislative portfolio' genuine legal measures such as the

---

[4] See generally, G Heal and H Kunreuther, 'Tipping Climate Negotiations' in RW Hahn and A Ulph (eds), *Climate Change and Common Sense: Essays in Honour of Tom Schelling* (Oxford, Oxford University Press, 2012).

[5] X Zhaofeng et al, 'Guidelines for Safe and Effective Carbon Capture and Storage in China' (2011) 4 *Energy Procedia* 5966.

[6] C Thornhill, *A Sociology of Transnational Constitutions: Social Foundations of the Post-National Legal Structure* (Cambridge, Cambridge University Press, 2016) p 351–358.

[7] M Nachmany et al, 'Climate Change Legislation in China' in *The 2015 GLOBE Climate Legislation Study: A Review of Climate Change Legislation in 99 Countries* (GLOBE International and the Grantham Research Institute, London School of Economics, 2015) 2.

[8] ibid.

[9] For surveys of general climate change measures, see generally W Xi et al, 'Research and Scholarship on Climate Change Law in Developing Countries' in DA Farber and M Peeters (eds), *Encyclopedia of Environmental Law: Climate Change Law*, vol 1 (Cheltenham, Edward Elgar Publishing Ltd, 2016); AL Wang, 'Climate Change Policy and Law in China' in KR Gray, CP Carlarne and R Tarasofsky (eds), *The Oxford Handbook of International Climate Change Law* (Oxford, Oxford University Press, 2016).

[10] United Nations, 'NDC Registry' (May 2017), at www4.unfccc.int/ndcregistry/Pages/Home.aspx.

Renewable Energy Act (2006) and Energy Conservation Law (1997), along with the 12th Five-Year Plan for the Development of National Economy and Society (2011). But while China does indeed have a substantial body of environmental law properly so-called (discussed in section II), the regulation of climate action is dominated by 'Plans', 'Strategies' and other measures of questionable legal provenance.

This deficiency extends to the regulation of CCS. China lacks both a dedicated CCS regulatory regime (i.e. on the EU model) and the necessary array of CCS-orientated provisions bolted on to existing schemes for environmental protection, geological storage, etc, as seen in oil and gas legislation in Australia and Canada.[11] The consequences of the legal lacunae in which CCS finds itself in China are two-fold. First, the environmental regulation of CCS falls back on to the general environmental law governing environmental protection, Environmental Impact Assessments (EIAs), air pollution and so on. This is in itself hardly problematic. Other CCS regimes, including the EU's, make linkages to existing environmental laws such as environmental assessment and environmental liability.[12] After all, CCS is one type of industrial project that will fall within extant legal structures relating to environmental protection, hazardous substances, planning and permitting, and project approval, etc. In the case of China, however, it is questionable whether the general environmental law is capable of bearing this burden efficaciously. Secondly, and relatedly, as others have noted, 'CCS projects involve large investments and initially will most likely originate from the state-owned sector of the economy'.[13] The conflicts of interest that exist in the regulation of Chinese state-owned enterprises (SOEs) give reason to doubt the effectiveness of this mode of governance, not least when the limitations of enforcement and other governance considerations are taken into account.

II. ENVIRONMENTAL LAW IN CHINA

A. Basics of the Chinese Legal System

Although China's legal system falls into the family of 'socialist law' in David's classical taxonomy,[14] there are reasons to doubt that this is a helpful finding. As Mattei notes, this classification is both Euro-American-centric, and fails to account for the success of the Chinese political system and the influence of legal sinology.[15] A more compelling approach, he argues, is one that takes into account and seeks to unearth 'hidden law', that is, 'the hidden assumptions of different

---

[11] D Seligsohn et al, 'CCS in China: Toward an Environmental, Health, and Safety Regulatory Framework' (Issue Brief, World Resources Institute, 2010) 6–7. See further the chapters by Gibbs (ch 11) (Australia) and Krupa (ch 9) (Canada) in this volume.
[12] See further the chapter by Velkova on the CCS Directive (ch 2) in this volume.
[13] Seligsohn et al, n 11 above. Citing M Al-Juaied and A Witmore, *Realistic Costs for Carbon Capture* (Cambridge, MA, Belfer Center Harvard, 2009).
[14] R David, C Jauffret-Spinosi and M Gore, *Les Grands Systèmes de Droit Contemporains*, 12th edn (Paris, Dalloz, 2016).
[15] U Mattei, 'Three Patterns of Law: Taxonomy and Change in the World's Legal System' (1997) 45 *The American Journal of Comparative Law* 5, 10.

legal systems'.[16] In order to better arrive at this deeper view, Mattei proposes his own, now famous, classification of global legal systems. Rather than relying on formal categories (such as common law, civil law and socialist law), Mattei's categorisation revolves around 'three patterns of social incentives (or social constraints) which are at play in all legal systems simultaneously'.[17] These are the rule of professional law, the rule of political law, and the rule of traditional law. What varies among the legal systems of the world is the 'quantity, acceptability, and most importantly, hegemony' of these patterns of social incentives. The application of this approach has the advantage of being both non-western-centric and also dynamic, responding to developments as they occur. There will of course be circumstances in which the distinctions between approaches (ie the rule of political law and the rule of traditional law) will be difficult to parse, but this is no more than a proper recognition of the complexities of the task. In any event, Mattei's conclusion is that China's hegenomic legal approach is traditional, albeit with notable 'characteristics of the rule of political law'.[18] For context, this is to be contrasted with Japan, which although also classified as predominantly traditional, has professional law as its secondary pattern of social incentives.

It should be noted that Mattei's classification is not one that is routinely adopted by scholars working on China. A leading US textbook on Chinese law makes the wholly Eurocentric point that 'China's legal system is largely a civil law system'.[19] This is of course a recognition that, like Japan's, it is a system that has drawn very heavily on the German legal system, which has been grafted, far from unproblematically, on to Confucian systems of the state, authority and value.[20] Nonetheless, many of the abstract features identified by Mattei—of the interplay between tradition, politics, and professionalisation—are vividly present in the actual law-making processes of the PRC.

China's law-making processes are governed by the Constitution (1954) and the Legislation Law (2000).[21] Although law making must respect concepts such as 'the socialist road', democratic dictatorship by the people, Marxism, Leninism and thoughts of Mao Zedong among others, the Constitution vests all the political power in the national government.[22] The highest legislative organ of the PRC is the National People's Congress (NPC), and its Standing Committee adopts national environmental laws.

---

[16] ibid 13 (citing R Sacco).
[17] ibid 16.
[18] ibid 32.
[19] DCK Chow, *The Legal System of the People's Republic of China*, 3rd edn (Saint Paul, MN, West Academic Publishing, 2015).
[20] PR Luney, 'Traditions and Foreign Influences: Systems of Law in China and Japan' (1989) 52 *Law and Contemporary Problems* 129.
[21] C McElwee, *Environmental Law in China: Mitigating Risk and Ensuring Compliance* (Oxford, Oxford University Press, 2011) 44. See also The National People's Congress of the People's Republic of China, 'Constitution of the People's Republic of China' (May 2017), at www.npc.gov.cn/englishnpc/Constitution/node_2825.htm; and The National People's Congress of the People's Republic of China, 'Legislation Law of the People's Republic of China (Order of the President No 31)' (March 2000), at english1.english.gov.cn/laws/2005-08/20/content_29724.htm.
[22] Arts 9, 22 and 26 of the Constitution.

The State Council is China's highest 'executive' and 'state administration' body, and it oversees all the ministries and commissions.[23] Its functions include promulgating the regulations necessary to implement national laws passed by the NPC or its Standing Committee. The State Council is formally subordinate to the NPC, but in reality it operates relatively independently from it, which can create a bottleneck for laws waiting for implementing regulations.[24] Critically, it is constitutionally tasked with drawing up China's Five-Year Plans, which are drafted by the NDRC,[25] although its 'broad themes and goals ... are developed by the Communist Party of China (CPC) Central Committee'.[26] The role of the Five-Year Plans is essential to note. These are the pivotal policy documents in China, declaring and setting China's economy policies, objectives and long-term direction. Where it is deemed necessary and appropriate, the Plans are supplemented by NPC legislation and ministerial policy.[27]

As regards environmental law making specifically, the NPC has a number of special committees, one of which is the Environment and Natural Resources Protection Committee (ENRPC).[28] Similarly, the State Council has sub-units with cross-ministerial tasks, such as the Legislative Affairs Office that also has an Environmental Protection Department.[29] As environmental protection does not fall within the exclusive competence of either the NPC or its Standing Committee, it can be legislated by the NPC and the State Council and its ministries.[30]

For those who view 'law' strictly through the lens of western conceptions of the rule of law (a rough approximation of Mattei's rule of professional law), the Chinese approach bears only a slight resemblance to a system of generally applicable rules applied impartially, and enforceable via independent courts.[31] Essential to note is the role of the CPC. Although it formally derives no power from the Constitution, and has only a limited role in the law-making process,[32] it is the de facto highest power in the country. Its NPC is charged with formulating the basic orientation of the Party, and the Politburo of its Central Committee determines all key policy decisions and appointments.[33] Furthermore, the Third Plenum of the Central Committee usually introduces the new Party leadership's broad economic and political reforms.[34]

---

[23] McElwee, n 21 above, 41.
[24] ibid 78.
[25] The NDRC is 'China's most important economic planning body', and is also in charge of China's response to climate change. It is China's Designated National Authority under the Kyoto Protocol, and played a major role in drafting China's climate change 'white paper' released in 2008: ibid 92–94.
[26] ibid 72.
[27] Chow, n 19 above.
[28] McElwee, n 21 above, 35–36.
[29] ibid 42.
[30] ibid 45.
[31] See generally, J Waldron, 'The Rule of Law' in EN Zalta (ed), *The Stanford Encyclopedia of Philosophy* (Stanford, CA, Stanford University, 2016).
[32] RP Peerenboom, *China's Long March toward Rule of Law* (Cambridge, Cambridge University Press, 2002) 240.
[33] C Mackerras, DH McMillen and A Watson, *Dictionary of the Politics of the People's Republic of China* (Abingdon, Routledge, 1998) 66–68.
[34] Dezan Shira and Associates, 'Introduction to China's Plenary Sessions and the CPC Central Committee' (China Briefing, November 2013), at www.china-briefing.com/news/2013/11/11/introduction-to-chinas-plenary-sessions-and-the-cpc-central-committee.html.

A separate issue arises from the dispersal of legislative authority.[35] The 'lines of authority' are often unclear, within consequent uncertainties over whether given entities are acting within their powers.[36] Peerenboom describes the legislative processes as lacking in transparency, but also with a high degree of inconsistency between lower and superior legislation, as well as problems surrounding the publication and accessibility of laws.[37]

B. Environmental Law Making and Enforcement

In February 1978, the Chinese Constitution was amended to provide an explicit requirement for environmental protection—the current Article 26[38]—and shortly thereafter established an ideological basis for the state to fulfil its constitutional environmental obligations.[39] The development of modern Chinese environmental laws commenced in September 1979 with the introduction of the Environmental Protection Law of the PRC.[40] Legislative development has been rapid thereafter, and according to Wang, the Environmental Protection Law took precedence over other areas of law, such as economic construction.[41] This is partly due to the increasingly serious environmental problems that the nation had faced since the late 1950s, which were exacerbated during the Cultural Revolution.[42] In this formative period of the Republic, economic growth was prioritised over environmental protection, which was then marginalised.[43] An awareness on the part of the leadership of the public harm caused by industrialisation in the West and Japan was also a contributory factor in the formulation of the new regime.[44]

In the same period, the Leading Group of Environmental Protection in the State Council (LGEPSC) prepared policy instructions for cadres,[45] providing that the 'elimination of pollution and protection of the environment were a part of building socialism and realising the four modernisations enacted by Deng Xiaoping'.[46] As McElwee demonstrates, however, the effect of myriad mergers and administrative

---

[35] Peerenboom, n 32 above, 240.
[36] ibid 241.
[37] ibid 245.
[38] 'The state protects and improves the living environment and the ecological environment, and prevents and controls pollution and other public hazards. The state organizes and encourages afforestation and the protection of forests.' See generally, C Wang, 'The Rapid Development Of Environmental Protection Law' in D Cai and C Wang (eds), *China's Journey Toward the Rule of Law: Legal Reform, 1978–2008* (Leiden, Brill, 2010) 498. See also McElwee, n 21 above, 24.
[39] Wang, n 38 above, 499.
[40] The National People's Congress of the People's Republic of China, 'Environmental Protection Law of the People's Republic of China' (December 1989), at www.npc.gov.cn/englishnpc/Law/2007-12/12/content_1383917.htm (as amended). Formally implemented in 1989.
[41] Wang, n 38 above, 496.
[42] ibid.
[43] PB Potter, *China's Legal System* (Cambridge, Polity Press, 2013) 40–41, 155.
[44] Wang, n 38 above, 497–98.
[45] Roughly equivalent to a civil service. See AD Barnett, *Cadres, Bureaucracy, and Political Power in Communist China* (New York, Columbia University Press, 1967).
[46] McElwee, n 21 above, 25.

reforms of the LGEPSC, including its renaming as the Environmental Protection Bureau and subsequently the State Environmental Protection Administration (SEPA), served to weaken it, and proved to be a setback for environmental protection.[47] In 2008, however, SEPA was renamed the Ministry of Environmental Protection, and its Minister has gained membership of the State Council. As a corollary, its status has been elevated to the highest level of national administration[48]

The Environmental Protection Law serves as a framework law, providing principles, establishing an administrative system for protection and a legal basis for the development of various environmental protection institutions, and providing the system for implementation of environmental management.[49] The last of these includes the requirement that environmental protection efforts are to be implemented during the design, construction and operation of industrial facilities. Along with environmental impact assessment and emission fees, this serves as the basis of environmental management systems in China.[50] Under this framework, the NPC has promulgated nine environmental protection laws, and the State Council has enacted over 50 administrative regulations.[51] In addition, over 600 rules and regulations have been issued by the departments of the State Council and other subordinate congresses and governments, to implement the said laws and administrative regulations.[52]

In the cognate area of energy law, so critical for CCS, the Chinese Government has been regulating for broad environmental ends for decades. As early as 1980, the Government established multi-level bureaucratic roles, including within SOEs, specifically for the purpose of energy conservation. As noted by Wang, this was achieved not through positive law but rather through 'direct government intervention by means of administrative plan and order'.[53] Nor is this a historical anomaly. The Energy Conservation Law (2007)[54] is judged to be 'mostly a policy declaration and policy framework with weak operative nature [with] few punitive measures to deal with violations [and] governmental authorities having too much discretion in their functions of macro-regulatory and administrative supervision'.[55] Furthermore, as Wang patiently demonstrates, such 'defects and deficiencies' are endemic in fields beyond energy conservation law.[56] The Renewable Energy Law (2005) displays many such characteristics. After noting the widespread role of civil society

---

[47] ibid 25–28.
[48] ibid 29.
[49] Wang, n 38 above, 500–01.
[50] ibid.
[51] C Shi, 'Directors' Duties and Liabilities in China: Enforcement Difficulties in Protecting Investors and Other Corporate Stakeholders', *Political Determinants Of Corporate Governance in China* (Abingdon, Routledge, 2012) 182.
[52] ibid.
[53] Wang, n 38 above, 385.
[54] The National People's Congress of the People's Republic of China, 'Law of the People's Republic of China on Conserving Energy' (November 1997), at www.npc.gov.cn/englishnpc/Law/2007-12/11/content_1383579.htm.
[55] W Mingyuan, 'China's Plight in Moving Towards a Low-Carbon Future: Analysis from the Perspective of Energy Law' in DN Zillman et al (eds), *Beyond the carbon economy: energy law in transition* (Oxford, Oxford University Press, 2008) 385–86.
[56] Wang, n 38 above, 398.

organisations in formulating and enforcing environmental law, and of citizens' rights of information and participation, Wang observes that although Article 9 of the Renewable Energy Law requires that opinions be sought from, inter alia, the general public, 'the provision is not operational but a declaration of policy'.[57] Although others take a less critical stance on environmentally-related public engagement in China,[58] further examples of the shortcomings of Chinese environmental law abound.

A detailed analysis of the shortcomings of Chinese enforcement of environmental regulations, with a focus on the institutional framework by which regulations are enforced, comes from Andrews-Speed. His work on the closely related fields of energy policy and regulation (specifically, the regulation of township and village coalmines) identifies two basic institutional challenges: 'the ever-changing structure of government [and] the opaque, heterogeneous and ambiguous nature of government functions in China'.[59] There is, he observes, a hierarchically organised set of environmental agencies, bureaus and offices, ranging from central government to township, as well as a significant overlapping of responsibilities.[60] The consequent 'inadequate implementation and direct obstruction' are predictable, and are supplemented by 'the sheer number of vertical reporting lines [and] the overlap or duplication of roles amongst different agencies'.[61] The conclusion that the regulatory system has been 'largely ineffective [and] characterized by an ever-growing weight of laws and regulations and a highly complicated administrative structure' bodes ill for the broader character of energy and environmental regulation, as the 'higher levels of government are prevented from achieving their policy goals by policy modification, inadequate implementation and direct obstruction at intermediate and lower levels of government'.[62] In Andrews-Speed's estimation, not only are such outcomes typical of Chinese regulatory systems, but also 'in the energy and natural resources sectors the negative impact of such administration is particularly pronounced'.[63]

C. The Turn to the Climate

Although China ratified the United Nations Framework Convention on Climate Change (UNFCCC) from the first, and has been engaged in its negotiations ever since, domestic climate change action did not immediately follow. In the decade or so from 1992, China's primary policy goal was its development strategy and annual economic growth of 10 per cent. To the extent that environmental concerns were

---

[57] ibid 394.
[58] Q Zhao, 'China's Emerging Regulatory Framework for Safe and Effective CCS 2011–15' in I Havercroft, R Macrory and RB Stewart (eds), *Carbon Capture and Storage: Emerging Legal and Regulatory Issues* (Oxford, Hart Publishing, 2011) 229.
[59] CP Andrews-Speed, *Energy Policy and Regulation in the People's Republic of China* (The Hague, Kluwer Law International, 2004) 197.
[60] ibid 198.
[61] ibid 200.
[62] ibid 200–01.
[63] ibid 201.

articulated in major policy processes, they were manifested in the form of sustainable development planning. As early as 1994, China's 'Agenda 21: White Paper on China's Population, Environment and Development in the 21st Century' explicitly stated the wish to control greenhouse gas (GHG) emissions for purposes of climate change avoidance,[64] in terms that echo UNFCCC and post-Rio understandings of sustainable development. Similarly, the 10th Five-Year Plan (2001–05) placed great focus on sustainable development, including related objectives to, inter alia, increase forest cover, improve energy efficiency, and expand renewable energy. From reading Chinese scholars, however, it seems to be the case that the policy commitments in Agenda 21 and other policy documents of the era were not translated into law, much less complied with in spirit.[65]

However, from the 11th Five-Year Plan (2006–11) onwards, a new shift towards the environment and climate concerns became clear. Various explanations can be offered—the entry into force of the Kyoto Protocol and the economic opportunity offered by the Clean Development Mechanism, increasing international pressure for action as China's emissions matched those of the US, as well as the co-benefits for the climate associated with the domestic priority of action on air pollution in China's cities. The policy momentum that these Plans have given climate action in China has been considerable, ranging over fields as diverse as energy efficiency, adaptation, the built environment, forest management and tools from carbon tariffs to trading schemes.[66]

While the climate aspects of the Five-Year Plans are closely connected with the air pollution control policies[67] contained in the 11th Five-Year Plan (2006–10)[68] and the 12th Five-Year Plan (2011–15),[69] the Plans certainly have had broader environmental ambitions. As Sungin Na notes, the 11th Five-Year Plan was based on the 'Scientific Development Concept', promoted by then President Hu Jintao as the guiding socioeconomic ideology of the Communist Party of China.[70] At the core of concept was the goal of 'environmentally friendly and energy-efficient growth',[71] from which followed the Plan's policy of reducing unit GDP intensity by 20 per cent by 2010 compared with 2005, and a 10 per cent reduction in polluted substances. Notwithstanding these goals, such was the 'success' of China's energy-intensive

---

[64] State Council, 'Agenda 21' (1994), ch 18, 31–35, cited in J Xiaoyi, 'Climate Change and Energy Law' in Tianbao Qin (ed), *Research Handbook of Chinese Environmental Law* (Cheltenham, Edward Elgar Publishing, 2015).
[65] ibid. See also Mingyuan, n 55 above; Wang, n 9 above; and Sungin Na, 'Towards Sustainable Development in Developing Countries: Achievements and Problems of a Clean Development Mechanism' in H Niizawa and T Morotomi (eds), *Governing Low-carbon Development and the Economy* (Tokyo, United Nations University Press, 2014) amongst many others.
[66] W Weiguang and G Zheng (eds), *China's Climate Change Policies* (Abingdon, Routledge, 2012).
[67] See generally, CP Nielsen and MS Ho (eds), *Clearer Skies Over China: Reconciling Air Quality, Climate, and Economic Goals* (Cambridge, MA, MIT Press, 2013).
[68] 'The 11th Five-Year Plan' (December 2016), at www.gov.cn/english/special/115y_index.htm (focusing on sulphur control policies and a carbon tax).
[69] 'The 12th Five-Year Plan' (December 2016), at english.gov.cn/12thFiveYearPlan/ (advancing carbon pricing schemes and in particular the piloting of carbon trading schemes).
[70] Sungin Na, n 65 above, 73.
[71] ibid.

industries that coal consumption actually increased in this period.[72] The 13th Five-Year Plan is a yet more ambitious scheme, with increased carbon and energy intensity targets aimed at meeting China's Paris Agreement pledge to reduce carbon intensity by 60–65 per cent by 2030.[73]

It should also be noted that notwithstanding a historically uneasy relationship with international law,[74] China has engaged positively with the climate regime. This is especially true of the UNFCCC negotiations since the Copenhagen Conference of the Parties (2009), which marked a new era of BASIC leadership,[75] with China's then premier, Wen Jiabao, and other leading developing countries accepting the possibility of quantified emission reductions, in exchange for developed countries fulfilling their environmental commitments.[76] Arguably the Trump Presidency will deepen this process of engagement. Indeed, it has been argued that the 'America-first' approach of the Trump Administration means that 'China has an even greater stake in investing in international regimes, as well as more room for leadership. It is instructive that Beijing's immediate reaction to Trump's election was to call for reaffirmation of commitment to the Paris climate change deal'.[77]

As to the legal substance of China's current climate regime, a revealing account is provided by Wang.[78] It sets out the various targets for energy intensity, afforestation, pollution reduction, etc laid down in successive Five-Year Plans, the wide range of policies to adjust China's industrial structure, improve its energy efficiency and so on, as well as better-known initiatives such as the carbon trading pilot schemes. What is notable about this discussion, however, is the admission that 'the proliferation of discrete energy and climate-related plans, policies, and projects … has not relied on legislative authorization. A substantial program has emerged through the state planning process and related target and policy documents'.[79] Not merely is there no 'climate change law' on the model understood in many other jurisdictions, but the body of instruments understood as the Chinese climate regime exists without any visible means of legal support. Even more odd is Wang's insouciance: 'It is unclear what function legislation and their chosen allocations of authority would serve that is not already served by state planning.'[80] (discussed further in section III).

---

[72] ibid.
[73] 'The 13th Five-Year Plan' (March 2016), at en.ndrc.gov.cn/newsrelease/201612/P020161207645765233498.pdf.
[74] See generally, AE Kent, *Beyond Compliance: China, International Organizations, and Global Security* (Stanford, CA, Stanford University Press, 2007).
[75] Brazil, South Africa, India and China. See R Maguire and X Jiang, 'Emerging Powerful Southern Voices: Role of BASIC Nations in Shaping Climate Change Mitigation Commitments' in S Alam, S Atapattu, CG Gonzales and J Razzaque (eds), *International Environmental Law and the Global South* (Cambridge, CUP, 2015).
[76] L Rajamani, 'The Making and Unmaking of the Copenhagen Accord' (2010) 59 *International & Comparative Law Quarterly* 824.
[77] K Brown (ed), *The Critical Transition: China's Priorities for 2021* (London, Chatham House, 2017) 51. See also Clark, n 2 above.
[78] Wang, n 9 above.
[79] ibid 651.
[80] ibid.

III. CARBON CAPTURE AND STORAGE AND CHINA

A. Policy and Pilots

Given the scale and industrial profile of the Chinese economy, especially its reliance on coal-fired power generation, CCS in China is mutually supportive of Chinese decarbonisation, and global efforts at widespread CCS deployment. China's energy system alone accounts for nearly half of the world's 1,950 GW of existing coal-fired power plants,[81] and the role of CCS in contributing to China's suite of climate policies, and enabling them, has been publically recognised. In the Foreword to an important 2015 report by the Asian Development Bank, the Deputy Director General of the NDRC's Department of Climate Change discussed the urgent need 'to expand [CCS] deployment at a rapid scale to meet priority emission reduction targets in the short, medium and long-term'.[82] In China, as elsewhere, CCS deployment is a condition precedent to the lowest cost deployment of other climate change policies. For example, in the International Energy Agency's (IEA's) Roadmaps, the cost of meeting the 450 ppm target increases by around 40 per cent without CCS, owing to the absence of alternatives to fossil fuel power in industry sectors such as cement and chemicals, iron and steel, etc.[83]

In recognition of the imperative of widespread CCS deployment, China has invested considerable policy energy in the development of its CCS knowledge base. As Qin notes, China has for a number of years engaged in research projects, policy studies and roadmaps, pilots and demonstration projects on aspects of the CCS chain, including the world's largest capture project for coal-fired power plants.[84] However, detailed studies have found the CCS regulatory framework in China to be unfit for purpose, even when taking into account the scope for adaptation of existing laws.[85] Although some aspects of the regulation of the CCS chain hold out some hope (principally those related to industrial activities), others provide less scope for building upon (primarily those related to geological storage).[86]

B. The Adequacy of Amending Extant Regimes

Seligsohn et al survey the existing legal and institutional arrangements in a variety of CCS-relevant areas, such as environmental standards, geological storage, regulatory

---

[81] OECD and IEA, n 3 above.
[82] Asian Development Bank, *Roadmap for Carbon Capture and Storage Demonstration and Deployment in the People's Republic of China* (2015), at www.adb.org/sites/default/files/publication/175347/roadmap-ccs-prc.pdf.
[83] For the role of each of the other energy technologies necessary to achieve the 2050 target, see IEA, 'Technology Roadmaps' (May 2017), at www.iea.org/roadmaps.
[84] T Qin, 'Regulation of Carbon Capture and Storage in China: Lessons from the EU CCS Directive' in MZ Hou, H Xie and P Were (eds), *Clean Energy Systems in the Subsurface: Production, Storage and Conversion* (Berlin/Heidelberg, Springer, 2013), table 7 and accompanying text. See also Seligsohn et al, n 11 above, Box 2.
[85] Seligsohn et al, n 11 above.
[86] ibid 3, 6–9.

oversight, and health and safety. The purpose is to explore the scope for drawing upon these various bodies of law, and attaching CCS-specific provisions to them, in the absence of a dedicated CCS regime on the EU model. In many respects, this is a promising exercise, noting, for example, that 'China already has robust regulations for plant construction and air pollution that will impact all CS capture plants and form part of the CCS-specific regulations … under the current Law on Prevention and Control of Air Pollution'.[87] Other areas are considered in more neutral terms, however, and the generic limitations of Chinese environmental law are discussed. In addition to the shortcomings noted herein, a wide range of regulatory gaps are explored, the most pressing of which are capture, transportation and geological storage. To take the first of these, the water consumption aspects of capture are not addressed in the existing legislation. For a water-stressed society such as China, it is vital, therefore, that the impact of CCS plants on local water supplies is adequately approved and monitored. Whilst transportation regulation should be able to draw on cognate schemes for oil, gas and chemicals, new CO_2 purity standards will be required, as well as standards for pipeline materials.

Regarding geological storage, owing to the differences in storing CO_2 as compared with the existing storage regimes (for radioactive pollution, chemicals, hazardous materials, etc), a bespoke CCS storage regime would be required. There are, though, ample regimes for emulation in this respect. Gibbs has subjected this precise issue to exacting scrutiny, and developed criteria to examine the effective enforcement of underground storage of CO_2.[88] The four criteria are:

(1) comprehensive obligations addressing the risks;
(2) comprehensive monitoring and verification (M&V) requirements;
(3) enforcement mechanisms; and
(4) clear allocation of roles and responsibilities for enforcement.

Gibbs assesses the geological storage of CO_2 in five jurisdictions, including China's onshore regime. Each legal and regulatory regime is scored against each of the four criteria, and areas of potential improvement are recommended.[89]

Gibbs scores criterion (1) at 2/9 for China,[90] agreeing with Seligsohn et al that while current laws could be adapted for demonstration projects, larger-scale projects would need specific CCS laws, particularly in respect of the lack of technical and management standards, efficient policies for information disclosure and public engagement, and financial barriers and lack of efficient economic incentivising policies to cover the commerciality gap.[91] She identifies gaps in the application of the Chinese EIA process to CCS projects, and the fact that CO_2 is not a

---

[87] ibid 7.
[88] MK Gibbs, *Effective Enforcement of Underground Storage of Carbon Dioxide* (Melbourne, HWL Ebsworth Lawyers, 2016).
[89] ibid 7–8.
[90] ibid 30.
[91] ibid.

designated pollutant for licensing purposes.[92] Accordingly, while the Environmental Protection Law makes polluters liable for the failure to control pollution, not classifying CO_2 as a pollutant makes it unclear whether such rules could be enforced as regards CCS.[93]

By criterion (2), China similarly performs weakly. Gibbs scores China at 3/9, principally due to the absence of technical and management standards applicable to CCS.[94] In a similar fashion to Seligsohn et al, Gibbs notes that whilst other environmental regimes may potentially apply to closure and long-term monitoring, there are currently no requirements applicable to CCS.[95]

Criterion (3) also scores 3/9, with Gibbs noting the inadequacy of financial penalties for polluting, which leads to strategic non-compliance, as it is frequently cheaper to pollute and pay a fine than to abate. Furthermore, with patchy enforcement, pollution is often undertaken without cost, that is, without the payment of sanctions.[96] It is of course recognised that the Chinese legal system has a wide variety of administrative enforcement tools available for environmental matters, from the issuing of warnings and terminating licences, to fines, property seizures and mandatory shutdowns. Criminal sanctions are also available.[97] However, and as will be discussed at greater length in section III.C the effectiveness of environmental enforcement suffers from widespread local protectionism, not least since enforcement authorities are often major shareholders in polluting enterprises, which creates powerful conflicts of interest.[98] Lastly, environmental laws often lack clear obligations, having the character more of policy statements or ideals than binding norms.[99] Many of these shortcomings have been recognised by the state. Gibbs cites the 2016 acknowledgment by the Environmental Protection Minister of issues with local protectionism and interference.[100] One response to these problems that is noted with approval is the introduction of economic incentives, rewarding local government officials and enterprises who meet environmental targets, and fining and criticising those who fail to achieve their targets.[101]

Criterion (4)—the clear allocation of roles and responsibilities for enforcement—is scored 1/3 by Gibbs.[102] As is noted elsewhere, the wide range of possibly applicable laws is reflected in the fact that a variety of government bodies would be involved in the enforcement activities, with uncertainty as to their roles and responsibilities, a problem that has caused issues with the enforcement of environmental law

---

[92] ibid.
[93] ibid 31–32.
[94] ibid 31.
[95] ibid.
[96] ibid.
[97] ibid.
[98] ibid 32.
[99] ibid.
[100] ibid.
[101] ibid.
[102] ibid 33.

in the past.[103] In addition, problems of resources are not uncommon. The Ministry of Environmental Protection is reported to have limited resources, frequently leaving enforcement to local Environment Protection Bureaus. However, these bodies themselves are also understaffed, lack authority and are inevitably at risk of regulatory capture.[104] Again, these limitations have been acknowledged by the Minister for Environmental Protection.

In the light of the above, it is not surprising that China performs poorly in comparison with other Asia-Pacific nations.[105] Its score of 9 out of 27 indicates that significant reform of the regime is required for Chinese CCS enforcement to be effective. By comparison, the Australian Offshore Regime scored 25/27, and the Japanese and Malaysian Offshore Regimes scored 17/27 and 12/27, respectively.

C. State-Owned Enterprises

One further challenge for CCS in China, touched upon by Seligsohn et al but deserving of greater attention, is that posed by China's SOEs.[106] Given the need for large investments and familiarity with the operations of the power sector, it is a certainty that many of the leading industrial actors involved in CCS in China will be SOEs. The Chinese grid companies are owned by the state, and power generation is dominated by SOEs.[107] Indeed, several SOEs have considering large-scale demonstration projects,[108] and keys aspects of CCS infrastructure, such as the CO_2 pipeline network, could be organised as a full SOE.[109] Moreover, SOEs have the structural advantage of being 'better placed to manage risks than smaller, independent operators, and are therefore expected to be involved in a majority of the demonstration projects'.[110]

State-owned enterprises are but one of the contradictions within the Chinese state. Article 15 of the Constitution describes its mode of economic system as a 'socialist market economy'—a term that is undefined. One of the ways in which China manages the tension between these facts and norms is via SOEs, a means of protecting large parts of the industrial sector from competition, while simultaneously promoting market liberalisation.[111] Inevitably the relationship between the Chinese state

---

[103] ibid.
[104] ibid.
[105] ibid 2, 14–15, 30.
[106] For an early treatment of the issues, see R Macrory, 'Air Pollution and the Regulation of European State Enterprises: A Comparative Legal Model' in WE Butler (ed), *Yearbook on Socialist Legal Systems* (Dobbs Ferry, NY, Transnational Juris Publications Inc, 1989).
[107] MS Ho, Z Wang and Z Yu, *China's Power Generation Dispatch* (Washington, DC, Resources for the Future, 2017) 12–13.
[108] Asian Development Bank, n 82 above, 8.
[109] ibid 19.
[110] ibid 45.
[111] CA McNally (ed), *China's Emergent Political Economy: Capitalism in the Dragon's Lair*, 1st edn (Abingdon, Routledge, 2007) 3–17.

and SOEs is a complex one, mediated through the State-Owned Asset Supervision and Administration Commission (SASAC),[112] a commission of the State Council functioning as a supervisory authority and a holding company.[113] SASAC is the ultimate shareholder in 100–120 core companies and hundreds of downstream subsidiaries controlled through pyramid structures. State-owned enterprises managed by SASAC include PetroChina, Shenhua and the State Grid. Its control may be direct or indirect, and it is not unusual for SOEs to have close links to local governments.[114] SASAC is one of the entities needed to approve investment decisions for SOEs, including CCS projects.[115]

The Chinese state also has significant control over the executives of SOEs. The Communist Party and SASAC share an arrangement to appoint and rotate leading personnel in the spheres of business, government and the Party.[116] Such rotation is particularly common among the senior executives of different business groups in the same sector.[117] The state also has control in managerial incentives, such as compensation.[118] Moreover, success and promotion in business brings accompanying rewards in the area of politics, and vice versa.[119] For instance, a number of positions in elite government and Party bodies are reserved for leaders of SOEs.[120]

Of particular significance for present circumstances is that the Chinese state has less control over SOEs than may be supposed. Indeed, Milhaupt and Zheng conclude that Chinese state capitalism can be better explained by state capture rather than by ownership of enterprise. Large, successful firms exhibit a number of common characteristics: market dominance, receipt of state subsidies, proximity to state power and execution of the state's policy objectives.

Instances of SOE state capture abound, with the strictures of law routinely being eased where the exigencies of a situation so require. Lin and Milhaupt give the example of SASAC encouraging SOEs to collaborate in overseas projects so as to increase global competitiveness. Whilst such activities undoubtedly raised antitrust concerns under the Chinese Antitrust Law, 'SASAC-supervised enterprises have been virtually exempt from antitrust enforcement'.[121] Concerns of this nature inevitably raise the question of whether the intimate relations between SOEs and the state constitute a corruption problem—discussed in section III.D.

---

[112] The website of the State-Owned Asset Supervision and Administration Commission (SASAC) can be found at en.sasac.gov.cn/.
[113] CJ Milhaupt and W Zheng, 'Beyond Ownership: State Capitalism and the Chinese Firm' (2015) 103 *Georgetown Law Journal* 665; and LW Lin and CJ Milhaupt, 'We Are the (National) Champions: Understanding the Mechanisms of State Capitalism in China' (2013) 65 *Stanford Law Review* 697.
[114] Lin and Milhaupt, n 113 above, 725, 734.
[115] Seligsohn et al, n 11 above, 20.
[116] Milhaupt and Zheng, n 113 above, 677; Lin and Milhaupt, n 113 above, 707, 737, 741.
[117] Milhaupt and Zheng, n 113 above, 677; Lin and Milhaupt, n 113 above, 740.
[118] Milhaupt and Zheng, n 113 above, 680.
[119] Lin and Milhaupt, n 113 above, 707.
[120] ibid 726–27.
[121] ibid 723. See further the discussion regarding the position of SASAC under the Law on State-Owned Assets of Enterprises, ibid at 736.

IV. THE PROBLEM OF LAW AND THE ENVIRONMENT IN CHINA

A. Hostility to Legal Codes

The argument in section I that there is an absence of hard law in China regulating climate change, much less CCS, fits into a broad narrative about the role of law in Chinese society. At the highest level of generality, this sits well with the claims that there is a traditional Chinese hostility to legal codes and law. Dull wryly recounts the sixth-century BC story of Deng Xi, a man who sought to establish a system of lawful accountability for rulers, only to be executed for his troubles. Says Dull:

> [W]hen looking for the root causes of modern China's low opinion of lawyers, the story of Deng Xi should be examined for the source of a deep prejudice, not against laws, but *against public laws that could take on a life of their own and be used to challenge the authority of official policies and values*.[122]

Such approaches, emphasising a deep-seated hostility to law in China, are also to be found in the writings of contemporary human rights scholars, and those working in related fields such as criminal law and procedure. Recounting appalling litanies of human rights abuses—abduction, unauthorised detention, 'black jails', forced abortions and sterilisations, intimidation of activists and families of activists, interference with lawyers, 're-education through labour' and so on—the conclusion is that such violations of basic rights are suffered by millions of Chinese on an annual basis. As Cohen points out, all these are plain violations of the Chinese Constitution, but 'at present the government offers no effective means of enforcing constitutional protections'.[123] Nor is this merely a matter of administrative omission; the state is actively complicit in such violations: 'the police have mastered the range of lawless black arts, and the procuracy and the courts have too often proved accommodating'.[124] For western lawyers, the position of the courts is central. Writing in the context of Chinese criminal law, Cohen notes that 'the courts ... have often had difficulty fairly applying [the law]. Party interference, corruption, local protectionism and social networks have all led to distorted applications of the law.'[125] Indeed, at the time of writing, Zhou Qiang, President of the Supreme People's Court, denounced the idea of judicial independence (and presumably its corollary, the constitutional accountability of the executive), urging higher court officials to 'bare your swords towards false western ideals like judicial independence'.[126]

Mattei has stressed the dangers of slipping into stereotyped views of Chinese law, that 'traditional culture disparaged law, that Chinese law was devoid of concepts of rights, and that the domination of law by political considerations was and still is

---

[122] J Dull, 'The Deep Roots of Resistance to Law Codes and Lawyers in China' in K Turner-Gottschang, JV Feinerman and RK Guy (eds), *The limits of the rule of law in China* (University of Washington Press, 2000) 328–29 (emphasis added).

[123] JA Cohen, 'Foreword: Lawlessness in China' in X Youyu and H Ze (eds), *In the shadow of the rising dragon: stories of repression in the new China* (Basingstoke, Palgrave Macmillan, 2013) xii.

[124] ibid ix.

[125] ibid x.

[126] L Hornby, 'China's Top Judge Denounces Judicial Independence', *Financial Times* (17 January 2017).

viewed as legitimate in the Confucian tradition'.[127] Instead, the alternative approach is to seek to understand the 'different structural nature of law in [China]',[128] with a key hint being provided by which pattern of law comes out second in the competition. In the case of China, this is likely to be political law.

B. Administrative Measures and the Rule of Law

The preference for administrative fiat in place of ordinary law is evident in the case of Chinese climate law. This is not to criticise either its scope or its effectiveness. The argument can easily be made that Chinese climate action is at least as powerful, as extensive as other, more rule-based regimes. However, *pace* Wang, the issue is less one of brute effectiveness than normative. The key shortcoming of non-legislative rule making is routinely identified as one of epistemic accessibility. The rules governing a polity should be promulgated so that the demos can scrutinise, criticise, internalise and plan for it, and 'use it as a framework for their plans and expectations and for settling their disputes with others'.[129] Rules should be made in public and not in obscure bureaucratic contexts. Additionally, the institutions of state, including the courts, 'should be available to ordinary people to uphold their rights, settle their disputes, and protect them against abuses of public and private power'.[130] Rules should be clear and determinate, such that official interpretations do not leave citizens subject to official whims. At the heart of this latter point is the need for judicial independence, executive accountability, the absence of corruption, and so on.

Viewing Chinese environmental and climate regulation in the light of the rule of law, it is not surprising to conclude that it is an inadequate regime. At the highest level of abstraction, the difficulties of China to cohere with the strictures of this principle are well documented.[131] Indeed, when subjected to the various factors and criteria of the World Justice Project, China performs remarkably poorly for a jurisdiction of its wealth and sophistication. It ranked 80th out of 113 states surveyed overall, sandwiched between Burkina Faso and Zambia. Whilst performing well in fields such as order and security and civil justice, its constraints on government powers, regulatory enforcement and fundamental rights protection are negligible.[132] Such a system, in which the rule of politics dominates so decisively over that of law, is deeply inimical to the ideals of the rule of law. Scholars such as Tamanaha have termed this 'rule by law'.[133] Whereas the traditional, understood rule of law

---

[127] Mattei, n 15 above, 37.
[128] ibid.
[129] Waldron, n 31 above.
[130] ibid.
[131] For indicative surveys, see Cai and Wang (eds), n 38 above; K Turner-Gottschang, JV Feinerman and RK Guy (eds), *The Limits of the Rule of Law in China* (Seattle, WA, University of Washington Press, 2000).
[132] JC Botero, M Agrast and A Ponce, *World Justice Project: Rule of Law Index 2016* (Washington, DC, The World Justice Project, 2016).
[133] BZ Tamanaha, *On the Rule of Law: History, Politics, Theory* (Cambridge, Cambridge University Press, 2004) 3.

elevates law above politics, such that it stands in a position of equidistance from all people and institutions, rule by law deploys law as nothing more than a instrument of political will. Law in this sense is unidirectional, in that it is a tool by which the state can exercise dominion over its citizens without its citizens ever being able to exercise similar control over the state. The enforcement of environmental law generally, and in respect of the SOEs that will operate so decisively in the context of CCS, demonstrates precisely this.

C. Enforcement

The 'airpocalypses' of extreme air pollution events suffered by China are now annual events, making clear to global audiences that the environment of China has not been fundamentally improved by its corpus of environmental law and policy.[134] The causes of this ineffectiveness are numerous.[135] Competences to make and implement environmental policies are broadly dispersed among ministries and agencies, creating inconsistent approaches which hamper compliance.[136] Pivotal instruments such as the Environmental Protection Law have not been amended since 1989, meaning that many of its provisions are outdated and simplistic. The core task of affecting entities' behaviour will not be achieved, for example, when the benefits of non-compliance are greater than the cost of penalties.[137]

As discussed in section II.A, law has not always been the vehicle by which public behaviour has been modelled in China, and the concept of the rule of law has never been fully accepted by the Chinese state.[138] In the place of law, other considerations, often political or ideological, have mediated the application of law,[139] a particular instance of which is the informal *guanxi* networks.[140] In a style of law making straightforwardly antithetical to the rule of law, Chinese laws are often drafted at a high level of generality, which provides the interpretive space for corrupting practices.[141] In particular, local authorities have sufficient flexibility in the interpretation and implementation of legislation to undermine the certainty of law.[142] It is by the use of *guanxi* rather than transactional bribery that decision making is influenced, a system which weakens environmental law, legal authority and the prestige of the judiciary.[143]

---

[134] Wang, n 38 above, 350.
[135] ibid 352; McElwee, n 21 above, 3; Shi, n 51 above, 182.
[136] McElwee, n 21 above, 9.
[137] Shi, n 51 above, 183.
[138] Wang, n 38 above, 532–33; PB Potter, *The Chinese Legal System: Globalization and Local Legal Culture* (Abingdon, Routledge, 2001) 7.
[139] McElwee, n 21 above, 4–5.
[140] ibid 8; Potter, n 138 above, 7, 30.
[141] McElwee, n 21 above, 8; Peerenboom, n 32 above, 251.
[142] Peerenboom, n 32 above.
[143] Wang, n 38 above, 533; McElwee, n 21 above, 6.

Economic development is often considered to be of higher importance when it conflicts with environmental laws and regulations.[144] Both national and local governments have their own economic development goals and needs in mind, and routinely use pressure to obstruct enforcement.[145] When environmental obligations are to be enforced locally, authorities may be discouraged from enforcing them in the belief that the same may not be done in competing jurisdictions, thereby putting their local industries at a competitive disadvantage.[146] In this way, the geographic fragmentation of environmental responsibility, combined with economic considerations, can discourage authorities from enforcing the rules, defaulting instead to local protectionism.[147]

Institutionally, environmental enforcement agencies face difficulties in undertaking their duties due to their bureaucratic connections with environmental protection departments of local governments, whose staff and resources are controlled by the local seat of the People's Government.[148] Primary responsibility for environmental protection lies with the local authorities, and despite reporting obligations, there are opportunities to not follow the environmental laws.[149] The local People's Government may prioritise economic development over environmental protection, and in some cases the environmental protection departments may even become accomplices in illegal construction projects.[150] Refusing to follow the requests of the government and insisting on enforcing the law may lead to the dismissal of environmental officials.[151] More generally, routine problems of resourcing arise. Environmental protection departments have limited resources to enforce the law;[152] and they have difficulties in discovering polluters in their jurisdiction in a timely manner, and face challenges in collecting sufficient evidence to present in court due to the lack of appropriate equipment to monitor activities.[153] Where illegal construction projects are supported by government agencies and local governments behind the scenes, it is extremely difficult for environmental offices to enforce the law.[154]

As regards establishing liability, there are both substantive and procedural problems. Company law provides a not inconsiderable loophole, in that while polluting companies can face civil liability for harming the environment, there is no liability for directors.[155] As regards enforcement mechanisms, Gibbs notes that China's

---

[144] McElwee, n 21 above, 6; Potter, n 43 above, 159.
[145] Wang, n 38 above, 533.
[146] McElwee, n 21 above, 7.
[147] Shi, n 51 above, 184; McElwee, n 21 above, 7; Z Wang and K Tu, 'Chinese Constitutional Dynamics: A Decennial Review' in AHY Chen (ed), *Constitutionalism in Asia in the Early Twenty-First Century* (Cambridge, Cambridge University Press, 2014) 137.
[148] Wang, n 38 above, 533–34.
[149] McElwee, n 21 above, 5–6.
[150] Wang, n 38 above, 534.
[151] ibid.
[152] ibid; McElwee, n 21 above.
[153] Wang, n 38 above, 534.
[154] ibid 545.
[155] Shi, n 51 above, 182–83.

Tort Liability Law provides enforcement avenues for individuals.[156] If CCS causes damage or loss, these laws can provide remedies.[157] There is however a swathe of Chinese environmental law literature that runs in the opposite direction.

Environmental public interest litigation has struggled to make progress.[158] The reasons include the tradition of having citizens, legal persons or other groups who are direct stakeholders as plaintiffs, and this being resistant to change. Also, there is some concern that the system would appear to undermine the Government due to expanding democratic values.[159] The legislation on defending environmental rights is described as weak, lacking important procedural elements, such as rules on responsibility to provide evidence, determination of causation and on the scope of damages.[160] The laws have underdeveloped areas, which has caused many disputes to languish without a resolution, and some to end up in violent clashes over pollution.[161] Polluting industries are sometimes protected by local governments, meaning that impartial judgments are hard to obtain.[162] Often defence of environmental rights is also more challenging due to the quality of the judges in the judicial system, including their lack of education and systematic training in environmental law, and insufficient knowledge about how to handle pollution cases. The independence of judges is disrupted by central and local government involvement through personal relations, and appointment and funding powers.[163] In this way, environmental rights suffer from a negative impact caused by judges' reliance on civil cases where they lack specific knowledge on how to approach violations of environmental rights. Recently, local special environmental courts have been established to tackle the issues resulting from this lack of special knowledge, and the method has shown success.[164] That said, the lack of specialised knowledge on environmental law concerns not only judges but also bureaucrats.[165]

D. Corruption

Corruption as regards Chinese SOEs is 'widespread, and accompanied by institutionalised and pervasive cronyism'.[166] President Xi Jinping has run an anti-corruption campaign from 2012 onwards,[167] but corruption remains endemic, and there have

---

[156] Gibbs, n 88 above, 32.
[157] ibid.
[158] Wang, n 38 above, 537–38. For a more positive assessment, see J Thornton, 'Can we Catch-Up? How the UK is falling behind on Environmental Law' (UKELA Garner Lecture, 2015). Copy on file with the author.
[159] ibid.
[160] ibid 538–39.
[161] ibid.
[162] ibid 539–40.
[163] Shi, n 51 above, 171; Potter, n 138 above, 32; Wang, n 38 above, 541; Wang and Tu, n 147 above, 136–37.
[164] Wang, n 38 above, 541.
[165] McElwee, n 21 above, 5.
[166] Milhaupt and Zheng, n 113 above, 691 (citing the Heritage Foundation's *2013 Index of Economic Freedom*). See also W Cheng, 'An Empirical Study of Corruption within China's State-Owned Enterprises' (2004) 4 *China Review* 55.
[167] Milhaupt and Zheng, n 113 above, 682.

been struggles to carry out fundamental reforms.[168] The factors enabling corruption within SOEs include the

> complexity of the SOE operation, decentralisation of managerial power allowing direct control over distribution of resources, and the ability to make decisions generating corrupt benefits. Rampant corruption is further enabled by weak supervision systems and opportunities for corruption created both by the system and the use of legitimate managing power.[169]

All these features can be regarded as mechanisms to extract rents from governments, and as such risk undermining key aspects of CCS. Whilst SOEs may align with the interests, goals and priorities of the political leadership by developing CCS projects, they may be relatively indifferent to those aspects of project integrity to which the leadership are similarly indifferent. Poor site selection, monitoring, CO_2 purity or any number of other systemic defects may well go undetected, and may even be tacitly supported in an environment in which firms obtain special advantages through corrupt access to government, and where there is deep convergence of interests between managerial elites in the party-state and business.[170]

V. CONCLUSION

In the concluding chapter to this volume the editors observe that one of law's key functions is to provide the means to resolve conflicting interests, to articulate 'the framework for reconciling the complex issues and relationships involved [in GHG reductions]. This reinforces the importance of developing effective legal and regulatory structures.' If one agrees that law is a zone of institutionalised contestation between competing societal interests, the foregoing severely questions whether this is a universal truth, or one particular to certain legal systems. Certainly, the case cannot be easily made that Chinese law mediates effectively between the various stakeholders potentially implicated in a CCS project. That case is yet harder to sustain in relations between aggrieved individuals, and the state and its proxies.

One way to understand this would be to argue that there is in China simply an absence of law *tout court*. One might draw upon Gibbs and her finding that, having measured the Chinese CCS regime against her four criteria, there is a need for a permitting regime to be established, relevant standards to be developed, including monitoring and verification standards, for existing enforcement mechanisms to be adapted or new mechanisms developed for CCS, for the roles and responsibilities of the relevant authorities to be clarified, and for attitudes toward enforcement and compliance to be changed to ensure effective operation of CCS in China.[171] All this is undoubtedly correct, but 'mere' rulemaking would not address the problem in a legal system in which tradition and politics play as significant a part as they do in

---

[168] Heritage Foundation, *2017 Index of Economic Freedom: China* (Washington, DC, Heritage Foundation, 2017) 127.
[169] Cheng, n 166 above, 78–79.
[170] Milhaupt and Zheng, n 113 above, 688, 716.
[171] Gibbs, n 88 above, 33–34.

China. As Mattei notes, 'one should not confuse the rule of traditional law with the absence of law or even with the absence of formal legal institutions. In the rule of traditional law formal legal institutions do exist, but their working rule is different from what we are used to in Western societies'.[172] The deficit in this sense is then not the absence of law but the perceived shortcomings of the mode of law. In one sense, the story of China's climate regime, and its CCS regime, is one of the abundance of bureaucratic agreements, plans and schemes that have a degree of effectiveness more conventionally 'legal' regimes might envy. Such is the interlocking web of relations that the Chinese state, SOEs and local governments have between one another, that the 'absence' of law can be (and often in the literature is) eased out of sight. However, this is to do an injustice to the weight of the distinction between the rule of law and rule by law. The latter's elevation of politics above law serves to allow the state to exercise uncontested might over its citizens. For the purposes of enforcing environmental law in China, and in particular respect of the SOEs, which will operate so decisively in the context of CCS, there is little prospect of a CCS regime that both enables its widespread deployment *and* protects the broader interests of the environment and citizens.

---

[172] Mattei, n 15 above, 39.

Pulling the Threads Together

IAN HAVERCROFT AND RICHARD MACRORY

I. THE CONTEXT OF LEGAL DEVELOPMENT

THE FIRST EDITION of this book was published in 2011, when carbon capture and storage-specific (CCS-specific) legislation was at the early stages of development. The CCS Directive of the European Union (EU) had been agreed only a few years before, and was yet to be fully transposed into the national laws of Member States. Legislation had been agreed in Australia and Canada, but with little practical experience of the application of the law. The US experience was largely confined to the injection of carbon dioxide (CO_2) in the context of enhanced oil recovery operations, rather than for the purpose of climate change mitigation. Six years on there are 22 large-scale CCS projects in operation or under construction around the world, and several more in the pipeline.[1] While impressive, the scale-up and associated infrastructure necessary for CCS to make an effective contribution towards climate change mitigation are enormous. Consent procedures under new CCS laws have now been tested in practice. Yet is it clear that those seeking the widespread, commercial deployment of CCS face complex challenges. A host of competing interests, challenges and targets must be addressed and resolved simultaneously if the technology is to be effectively employed and contribute towards achieving the greenhouse gas (GHG) reductions needed to address global warming. While it is not the role of law to provide answers to the scientific, technological, economic and value questions that pervade the subject of CCS, law does have a key role in articulating the framework for reconciling the complex issues and relationships involved. This reinforces the importance of developing effective legal and regulatory structures.

The role of CCS and the extent to which it may mitigate the effects of climate change remain contentious issues, with environmental non-governmental organisations and sections of the public still sceptical about the claims made for the technology. Many in the scientific and climate-change communities have a different perspective. The 2005 Special Report prepared by the Intergovernmental Panel on Climate Change[2] demonstrated the considerable potential of CCS as part of a portfolio of mitigation options, a view which has been reiterated by successive reports from the International Energy Agency (IEA).[3] The 2015 Paris Agreement on Climate Change,

---

[1] See Global CCS Institute, *The Global Status of CCS: 2016 Summary Report* (GCCSI, 2016); and Global CCS Institute, *Large-scale CCS facilities* (May 2017), at www.globalccsinstitute.com/projects/large-scale-ccs-projects.

[2] B Metz et al (eds), *IPCC Special Report on Carbon Dioxide Capture and Storage* (Cambridge, Cambridge University Press, 2005).

[3] For the most recent review, see International Energy Agency, *20 Years of Carbon Capture and Storage* (Paris, International Energy Agency, 2016).

which entered in force on 4 November 2016,[4] also provides a potentially powerful framework for the greater deployment of CCS. Countries agreed to an ambitious temperature target of holding any increase in the global average temperature to 'well below 2°C' above pre-industrial levels, to pursue efforts towards 1.5°C and to balance emissions during the second half of the century. Carbon capture and storage is not mentioned explicitly in the Paris Agreement, but the goals of the Agreement will require extensive investment in deployment of in low-emissions technology, and CCS is likely to play a significant role, at least as a transitional technology. In the words of the IEA,[5] 'CCS is the potential "sleeping giant" that needs to be awakened to respond to the increased ambition of the Paris Agreement'.

In parallel to discussions surrounding the utility of the technology, a clearer consensus continues to emerge regarding the ability of the technology to meet these desired objectives. Many geologists worldwide are increasingly confident in their predictions of global storage potential and their skill in effectively characterising potential storage sites; whilst successful engineering developments have led to a number of industrial-scale projects at the planning and realisation phases. However, several risks associated with aspects of the CCS process remain unquantified, and greater investment and further research will be required if the technology is to be deployed globally and in a timely manner.

The roles and views of governments and industry remain vital for the development of the technology. Political commitments to the widespread deployment of CCS should be buoyed by the ever-increasing scientific certainty surrounding the causes and effects of climate change, as well as concerns for national energy security. Despite increased public and political opposition to their continued use, many developed and developing nations will inevitably continue to rely upon fossil fuels for energy generation in the short to mid-term. Carbon capture and storage remains an important element of the climate change mitigation response, and may continue to be viewed as a 'bridge' to the long-term ideals of de-carbonising the power sector and effecting the widespread deployment of renewable technologies.

The first edition of this text highlighted high-level intergovernmental commitments, as well as the anticipated mitigation contribution and ambitious projections for global deployment of the technology. In the intervening years, however, several of these forecasts have been re-adjusted in light of changing political and economic circumstances.

The IEA's 2016 Report[6] suggests that, despite a crystallisation of views regarding the technology's utility in mitigating the impacts of climate change, early deployment objectives have not been met with adequate political and financial support:

> More than USD 30 billion in public funding announcements were made and G8 leaders pledged to build 20 new large-scale CCS demonstration projects. However, this momentum

---

[4] The threshold for entry into force was reached in October 2016, when 129 parties to the Agreement had ratified it.

[5] International Energy Agency, n 3 above.

[6] Organisation for Economic Cooperation and Development and International Energy Agency, *20 Years of Carbon Capture and Storage: Accelerating Future Development* (Paris, International Energy Agency, 2016).

was not maintained as early CCS deployment proved to be more complex, expensive and politically challenging than anticipated. Of the USD 30 billion in public funding announcements, only around USD 2.8 billion was actually invested in large-scale CCS projects between 2007 and 2014.[7]

Despite these challenges, however, the outlook for CCS as a key component of global mitigation efforts has been buoyed by successive reports from climate change bodies. The Intergovernmental Panel on Climate Change's Fifth Assessment Report (IPCC AR5), published in 2014, highlighted the role CCS and CCS with bioenergy must play in future emissions reductions; while the UK's Committee on Climate Change has similarly emphasised the role CCS must play in meeting the UK's carbon targets at least cost.[8]

Although commercial interest in the technology has similarly fluctuated in recent years, there are now a number of operational facilities worldwide.[9] Storage projects are now capturing CO_2 from coal-fired generation, steel, natural gas processing, hydrogen and fertiliser production plants, demonstrating that the technology's application is far broader than just coal.

Law and regulation continue to play an important role in recognising and, to some extent, reconciling these challenges.

II. EMERGENCE OF CCS-SPECIFIC LEGISLATION

The history of legislation for this technology may be traced back to early analysis and reports[10] that predominantly considered the legality—or otherwise—of storing CO_2 in the subsurface and under the seabed, as well as its incorporation in the international climate change agreements. These studies sought clarification as to the prospect of undertaking CCS under international and regional law, and highlighted obstacles, examples of analogous regulation and issues requiring subsequent legislative amendment. This is not to say that such studies were unhelpful, and indeed their findings proved significant in the subsequent international treaty negotiations that marked the beginning of more focused legislation. One critical aspect of these studies, however, was their identification of issues that were distinctive to the technology, and which would prove pertinent in the design of subsequent regulation.

---

[7] ibid 10.
[8] IPCC, 'Summary for Policymakers' in O Edenhofer et al (eds), 'Climate Change 2014: Mitigation of Climate Change', Contribution of Working Group III to the *Fifth Assessment Report of the Intergovernmental Panel on Climate Change* (Cambridge and New York, Cambridge University Press, 2014). See also Committee on Climate Change, *Meeting Carbon Budgets—2016 Progress Report to Parliament* (London, Committee on Climate Change, 2016).
[9] A detailed review of large-scale CCS facilities is available on the Global CCS Institute's website at www.globalccsinstitute.com/projects/large-scale-ccs-projects and published in the Institute's annual Global Status of CCS report.
[10] See, eg, the legal and regulatory section of Metz et al (eds), n 2 above; and C Hendriks, MJ Mace and R Coenraads, *Impacts of EU and International Law on the Implementation of Carbon Capture and Geological Storage in the European Union* (ECOFYS and Foundation for International Environmental Law and Development, 2005) at pdf.wri.org/ccs_impact_of_eu_law_on.pdf.

The early amendments to both the London Protocol and the OSPAR Convention signified some of the first concerted efforts of the international community to regulate the technology. Strong support and policy drivers, particularly from European states and Australia, resulted in astonishingly swift revisions to the core treaty provisions likely to govern offshore storage activities, and provided much-needed models that addressed the features peculiar to CCS. For the first time, there was regulatory acknowledgement of the risks involved with sequestration and the long-term nature of the storage process, manifested in an iterative process for site characterisation, permitting and monitoring.

The challenges faced in reconciling both the over-arching concerns already discussed and many of the issues that are inherent to the technology have been addressed in the examples of CCS legislation which have now been developed in a number of jurisdictions, and discussed in earlier chapters of this book. In 2010, the IEA produced a valuable checklist of some 29 issues that required to be considered in the design of CCS-specific legislation.[11] Any national law, though, inevitably reflects political considerations and legislative practice distinctive to its jurisdiction, and five main models can been seen in the CCS legislation and regulatory frameworks that have emerged to date:

1. Stand-alone legislation of general application dealing with CCS as a technology requiring a distinctive regulatory regime, though in practice such legislation will almost inevitably contain some linkages with other existing laws to a greater or lesser extent. The 2009 EU CCS Directive,[12] for example, largely focused on storage provisions, and deliberately took the option of amending existing regulatory regimes to handle capture and transportation, as well as environmental assessment requirements, operational liabilities and public engagement. Other examples of stand-alone CCS legislation include the Australian State of Victoria's *Greenhouse Gas Geological Sequestration Act 2008*, which regulates onshore CCS activities. A similar approach was also adopted in Queensland, in the State's *Greenhouse Gas Storage Act 2009*.[13] A 2013 report to the New Zealand Government similarly advocated stand-alone legislation.[14]

2. Stand-alone legislation confined to specific projects, research or demonstration sites. Examples include Western Australia's *Barrow Island Act 2003*, which is applicable to a single site, and Germany's Gesetz zur Demonstration der dauerhaften Speicherung von Kohlendioxid, which transposes the requirements of the CCS Directive but restricts the scale of storage operations to demonstration projects.[15]

---

[11] Organisation for Economic Cooperation and Development and International Energy Agency, *Carbon Capture and Storage: Model Regulatory Framework* (Paris, International Energy Agency, 2010).

[12] Considered by Velkova in ch 2 in this volume.

[13] Discussed by Gibbs in ch 11 this volume.

[14] B Barton, K Jordan and G Severinsen, *Carbon Capture and Storage—Designing the Legal and Regulatory Framework for New Zealand* (Hamilton, University of Waikato, 2013). But for a counter-view that it is preferable to use existing well-established resource management regulatory regimes, see G Severinsen, 'Constructing a Legal Framework for Carbon Capture and Storage in New Zealand: Approaches to Legislative Design' (2014) 63 *Energy Procedia* 6629.

[15] See the analysis by Kramer in ch 4 of this volume.

3. Adaptation or amendment of existing and familiar petroleum and gas regimes to incorporate the storage of CCS, with examples including the Australian Offshore Petroleum and Greenhouse Gas Storage Act 2006 (offshore, non-territorial waters), South Australia Petroleum and Geothermal Energy Act 2000 (onshore).[16]
4. Mixed regimes involving effectively a stand-alone regime coupled with significant adaptation to the provisions found in existing legislation. An example would be Alberta's Mines and Minerals Act, amended in 2010 to include a new Part 9 dealing with CCS, focusing specifically upon tenure and transfer issues, which, together with amendments to the province's Oil and Gas Conservation Act, provides additional regulatory powers relating to CCS.[17]
5. Using adaptations of existing environmental laws as a medium for the development of comprehensive CCS regime. The US Environmental Protection Agency's development of a new class of wells, Class VI, under the authority of the Safe Drinking Water Act's Underground Injection Control (UIC) Program, is one example of this approach.

III. FUTURE PERSPECTIVES FOR REGULATION

The preceding chapters of this book have discussed and demonstrated the significant progress made in many jurisdictions globally, towards the adoption of legislation and regulation governing CCS. But they also highlight a wide variety of issues that have yet to be addressed or incorporated within a regulatory regime. Some of these issues have already been identified by regulators, policy-makers and stakeholders, whilst others have come to the fore as work begins upon the implementation of domestic and regional commitments to the technology. It will prove essential, in completing the regulatory sequence, to address these issues and ensure that all aspects of the processes involved are comprehensively and safely regulated.

Where gaps and obstacles have been identified, the focus has inevitably shifted back to aspects or features of the technology that remain peculiar or contentious; indeed, the novel aspects of the technology continue to pose particular issues for regulators and policy-makers. Although the early amendments and framework legislation have addressed some of the initial concerns, a range of issues still require further attention, particularly those relating to health and safety, property and tenure issues,[18] financing and long-term liability.

The last two issues have been considered at length in some of the earlier chapters to this book; however, they remain indicative of the type of unresolved concerns that remain in many jurisdictions. Financing, particularly with regard to the provision of incentives to secure both early investment and the continued operation of CCS activities, continues to be deliberated at length by the international community, as well as by regional and national governments. The EU incorporated the technology

---

[16] See Gibbs in ch 11 of this volume.
[17] See Krupa in ch 9 of this volume.
[18] In relation to Australia, see the discussion by Crommelin in ch 12 of this volume.

in the EU Emissions Trading Scheme (EU ETS), whilst many governments globally have committed considerable sums towards the financing of demonstration plants. Anxiety persists, however, given the uncertainty surrounding the mechanisms that are to ensure the continued commercial-scale deployment and operation of the technology worldwide. The EU decision to utilise the EU ETS to fund the long-term commercial deployment of the technology has similarly been met with scepticism, given the inability of the early phases of the scheme to secure a carbon price that would sustain commercial-scale CCS activities.

Focus is now shifting at the domestic level to other forms of regulatory incentives that would potentially drive the up-take of the technology. In light of the continuing constraints on public finance in many countries, however, these incentives are subject to political uncertainties and sudden changes of policy, as witnessed by the UK Government's sudden decision in 2015 to withdraw £1 billion capital funding support for its CCS demonstration competition.[19]

Liability for the long-term storage of captured CO_2 has also proved to be a challenging issue for many regulators, policy-makers and the public. The long-term nature of the storage phase, for time-frames well beyond the lifetime of conventional commercial organisations, has resulted in unfavourable comparisons being drawn between CO_2 storage and the disposal of nuclear waste. In view of this, many of the regulatory models developed to date include financial security mechanisms and provisions providing for the post-closure transfer of liability from the operator to the state. While the concept of post-closure transfer is common, the precise legal conditions that will trigger the provisions show marked differences in CCS legislation adopted across various jurisdictions.[20] Liability for localised environmental damage and risks to human health posed by the leakage or migration of CO_2 on a catastrophic scale has also been addressed in many of the early regulatory frameworks. There are, however, various inconsistencies and gaps in these frameworks, which would necessitate claims for damages being brought under a variety of traditional legal routes such as trespass and negligence. Until they are resolved in secondary legislation, or through the provision of more detailed guidance, these uncertainties may prove to be further barriers for those seeking to invest in the technology. In practice, CCS projects are also likely to involve a number of different commercial entities; and while legislation may focus liability on specific parties, such as the storage operator, commercial contractual arrangements, of the sort seen in other major industrial projects, will be employed to spread the risks.[21]

This chapter started with a discussion of a smaller set of wider over-arching concerns, which it would seem important to address in order to ensure the deployment of CCS. Reconciling these politically contentious aspects of the technology within legislation would therefore also appear challenging to regulators and policy-makers. The truly global deployment of the technology, on a scale required to meet the

---

[19] For a report on the competition process and the decision of the Government to cancel the competition, see National Audit Office, *Carbon Capture and Storage: the second competition for government support* (London, National Audit Office, 2017).
[20] See ch 15 by Havercroft in this volume.
[21] See the discussion by Lawrence in ch 16 of this volume.

climate change reduction objectives of the international community and the ambition of the IEA's emissions reduction models,[22] may prove difficult in the absence of sufficient political or financial incentives. However, the ambitious goals agreed in the Paris Agreement may see stronger commitments and a wider deployment of CCS. Similarly, the provision of adequate and quantifiable incentives at the national level may also promote greater confidence in the ability of the technology to deliver the anticipated emission reductions.

Public perception of the technology and, more significantly, the public's ability to engage in the decision-making processes surrounding CCS remain sensitive issues for the technology. Recent years have seen legal challenges and increased opposition to the development of 'clean coal' plants worldwide, as well as early opposition to the development of capture plants and storage sites in many jurisdictions. Despite the early development of EU-wide legislation on CCS, onshore CCS storage in Europe currently seems to be politically unlikely in the near future.[23] A significant volume of work has been now undertaken by social scientists to understand more fully the rationale for public concern, and the extent to which industry's ambitions and the public's opinions regarding the technology can be reconciled;[24] a study in 2014 identified 42 articles that had been published to date on public perception and CCS.[25] A greater analysis of the adequacy of legal mechanisms that enable public engagement and consultation is required in many jurisdictions. Here governments may see a conflict between a need to speed up decision-making processes for approving new infrastructure projects in the national interest and engaging in wide public consultation.[26] But short-cut measures, however tempting, could result in a failure to properly engage with public opinion, which may prove fatal to the widespread deployment of the technology. Here the law has an important role in prescribing decision-making frameworks.

The considerable number of political commitments to the technology also raises a temporal dimension to the regulation of the technology, which appears to have gone unnoticed by policy-makers thus far. In a number of jurisdictions, governments have committed to the deployment of CCS plants, or a standard for the technology by a given date; in several instances these pledges are linked to national obligations under international climate change agreements. The failure to identify or sufficiently address these regulatory roadblocks may result in the postponement of investment and of the ultimate deployment of commercial-scale CCS.[27]

From a regulatory perspective, it will continue to be important to identify gaps and obstacles within current and proposed legislation, and to then expedite the relevant

---

[22] Metz et al (eds), n 2 above.

[23] In relation to Germany, see the discussion by Kramer in ch 4 of this volume.

[24] See, eg, SJ Lock et al, 'Nuclear energy sounded wonderful 40 years ago: UK citizen views on CCS' (2014) 66 *Energy Policy* 428; P Ashworth et al, 'Public Preferences to CCS: How does it change across countries' (2013) 37 *Energy Procedia* 7410.

[25] SL Seigo, S Dohle and M Siegrist, 'Public Perception of Carbon Capture and Storage (CCS): A Review' (2014) 38 *Renewable and Sustainable Energy Reviews* 848.

[26] For a discussion of the recent changes in planning law for major infrastructure projects in the UK, see the discussion by Lewis and Westaway in ch 5 of this volume.

[27] For a recent study, see JP Banks, T Boersma and W Goldthorpe, *Challenges Relating to Transportation and Storage—Showstoppers for CCS?* (Melbourne, Global CCS Institute, 2017).

amendments. A greater consideration of the entire CCS chain will be essential when designing and implementing a regulatory framework for the technology; a more integrated approach will ensure that timescales inherent in particular regulatory processes are considered in advance.

The material contained within this book clearly demonstrates the significant developments made across many jurisdictions to regulate the various aspects of the CCS process. The pace at which legal amendments and regulatory frameworks have been drafted and agreed has been remarkable in many instances; however, a multitude of legal and regulatory issues remain and require further clarification.

For the technology to provide a bridge to a truly low-carbon future, of which many would argue it is capable, a global deployment of CCS is required. To achieve this ambition, commercial-scale deployment of the technology is required, as well as long-term funding mechanisms to provide all countries with the opportunity of including CCS within their mitigation efforts. As part of a portfolio of climate change mitigation options CCS offers considerable potential, but as a technology it encompasses a host of political difficulties and regulatory peculiarities. For regulators and policy-makers, the task of regulating the opportunities offered by the technology in a manner that reconciles environmental protection, human health, and public and investor confidence remains a challenge.

Carbon capture and storage has been hailed as a technology for the modern era, but in regulating its various components, much is to be garnered from pre-existing models of regulation. Analogous instances from the regulation of industrial activities can be found in existing environmental and energy law and regulation across many jurisdictions. Examination of these models will help to identify potential gaps and obstacles in proposed legislation, as well as provide an indication of the likely time-frames for decision making and consultation. An example may be found in the work undertaken by the IEA, under the auspices of its international CCS regulators' network,[28] which has proved invaluable in this field. Governments often meet to discuss and negotiate international energy and environmental agreements, and various networks of environmental regulators have been established to share information and experience of the implementation of existing environmental laws.[29] The international CCS regulators' network remains distinctive, in that it has allowed regulators to discuss CCS regulation at a very early stage in the design of CCS legislation. The network has provided a platform for regulators from around the world to discuss models of regulation, both in the developmental and post-settlement phases, and to work together to examine possible solutions to various regulatory obstacles. It is clear that greater collaboration of this kind is needed to enable the benefits provided by this form of knowledge transfer.

---

[28] This network was founded in conjunction with University College London's Carbon Capture Legal Programme, the Carbon Sequestration Leadership Forum and the IEA's Greenhouse Gas Programme. For more details see at www.iea.org.
[29] See, eg, within the EU, the European Network for the Implementation and Enforcement of Environmental Law (IMPEL), established in 1992.

Index

Australia:
  regulation of underground storage of GHGs, 3, 213–14
    conclusions, 230
    'de-risking' early mover projects, 229
    long-term liability, 223
      Acts dealing with, 224
        Federal Offshore Act, 224–25
        Queensland onshore Act, 225–27
        Victorian onshore and offshore Acts, 225–27
      difference in regimes, 227–29
      in context of CCS, 223–24
    overview of legislation, 214
      approaches to regulation, 214–16
      enforcement, 222–23
      environmental, health and safety, 218–19
      GHG storage tenure, 216–18
      managing competing interests, 219
        Federal and Victorian Offshore Acts, 220
        Victorian and Queensland Onshore Acts, 220–22
  tenure and ownership in geological storage of GHG, 3, 231
    conclusions, 242–43
    land tenure, 231–34
    property, 238–39
      dealings and registration, 239
      security of title, 239–42
    title, 234
      coastal waters, 235–36
      offshore area, 234–35
      onshore, 236–38

Canada:
  legal framework for CCS, 3, 149
    conclusions, 200–01
    constitutional authority, 149–52
    geophysical survey and GHG emissions sources, 180–83
    liability framework, 191–200
    regulation of GHG emissions:
      climate change law (Canada and international), 152–64
      direct support and regulation of CCS, 173–80
      general regulation of air emissions, 164
      market-based approaches to reducing GHG emissions, 167–73
      specific regulation of GHGs, 165–67
    regulatory framework, 186–91
    subsurface property rights, 183–86

pore space ownership, 3, 203–04
  Alberta, 205–07
  British Columbia, 207–09
  common law rules, 204–05
  conclusions, 210–11
  Saskatchewan, 209–10

carbon dioxide (CO_2) injection, *see* storage of CO_2 in deep subsurface

carbon dioxide (CO_2) storage:
  Australia, *see* Australia
  Canada, *see* Canada
  China's regime, *see* China
  context of legal development, 359–61
  deep subsurface, geological factors for legislation to enable and regulate, *see* storage of (CO_2) in deep subsurface
  Directive 2009/31/EC (CCS Directive), *see* CCS Directive
  emergence of CCS-specific legislation, 361–63
  future perspectives for regulation, 363–66
  liability:
    commercial arrangements for managing risks, 4
    categories of risks/liabilities associated with project, 327–29
    complexities of CCS and many links in chain, 323–26
    how legal liability risks arise in practice, 327–29
    incentivising CCS, liability considerations, 334–35
    key roles and risks in project, 326–27
    mechanisms for apportioning liability risks, 329–34
    framework, Canada, 191–200
    long-term, *see* long-term liability
    Member State as insurer for validation projects, 25–26
    progression, 27–28
    site specific monitoring required but total leakage small, 26–27
    UK, *see* United Kingdom
    US (sequestration), *see* United States

CCS Directive:
  Collingridge dilemma, 44–45, 49–50
  conclusions, 57–58
  Germany, and, *see* Germany
  implementation, *see* implementation of CCS Directive
  legislative history, 44–47
  public debate, 45, 47–49

risk management, 50
  underlying principles:
    conservatism, 52–57
    prevention, precaution, 50–52
    relationship between principles, 56
  stifling of technology in Europe, 43–58
  transfer provisions, 314–15
China, 4, 337–39
  carbon capture and storage:
    adequacy of amending extant regimes, 347–50
    policy and pilots, 347
    state-owned enterprises, 350–51
  conclusions, 357–58
  environmental law:
    basics of Chinese legal system, 339–42
    making and enforcement, 342–44
    shift towards environment and climate concerns, 344–46
  problem of law and the environment:
    administrative measures and rules of law, 353–54
    corruption, 356–57
    enforcement, 354–56
    hostility to legal codes, 352–53
commercial arrangements for managing liability risks, 4
  categories of risks/liabilities associated with project, 327–29
  complexities of CCS and many links in chain, 323–26
  conclusions, 357–58
  how legal liability risks arise in practice, 327–29
  incentivising CCS, liability considerations, 334–35
  key roles and risks in project, 326–27
  mechanisms for apportioning liability risks, 329–34
Copenhagen Accord:
  Canada, and, 152–53, 160

Directive on geological storage of carbon dioxide (2009/31/EC), see CCS Directive

environment and environmental issues, see health, safety and environment
European Union:
  CCS Directive, see CCS Directive
  transportation of CO_2, 3, 245–46
    conclusions, 265–66
    cross-border, 261–62
    trans-European networks, 262
      CO_2 networks, 263–65
      EU legal framework, 262–63
    transport by ship:
      offshore safety and the environment:
        leakages and climate protection offshore, 259
        liability offshore, 259–60
        safety regulation, 257–58
      qualifying, 257
      transport, 261
    via pipelines:
      health, safety and environment:
        health and safety regulation, 248–49
        leakages and impact on climate change, 251–52
        protecting the environment, 249–51
      other pipelines, 255–56
      qualifying pipelines, 246–48
      use of pipelines:
        national developments, 254–55
        owners and users, 252
        third-party access regime, 253–54

geothermal exploration and production, 8
Germany, 59
  actual situation and discussion of CCS, 67–68
  concluding remarks, 73–74
  elaboration of CO_2 Storage Act of 2012, 62–64
  KSpG (German Act) and land legislation, 64–67
  limitation to pilot projects, 61–62
  obligation to allow CO_2 storage, 59–61
  reasons for rejection of CCS technology:
    economic arguments, 71–72
    environmental arguments, 69–71
    policy considerations, 72–73
    public acceptance, 68–69
greenhouse gases (GHGs):
  Australia:
    regulation of underground storage of GHGs, 3, 213–14
    conclusions, 230
    long-term liability, 223
      Acts dealing with, 224
        Federal Offshore Act, 224–25
        Queensland onshore Act, 225–27
        Victorian onshore and offshore Acts, 225–27
      'de-risking' early mover projects, 229
      difference in liability regimes, 227–29
      in context of CCS, 223–24
    overview of legislation, 214
      approaches to regulation, 214–16
      enforcement, 222–23
      environmental, health and safety, 218–19
      GHG storage tenure, 216–18
      managing competing interests, 219
        Federal and Victorian Offshore Acts, 220
        Victorian and Queensland Onshore Acts, 220–22
    tenure and ownership in geological storage of GHG, 3, 231
      conclusions, 242–43
      land tenure, 231–34
      property, 238–39
        dealings and registration, 239
        security of title, 239–42
      title, 234
        coastal waters, 235–36
        offshore area, 234–35
        onshore, 236–38

Canada:
  legal framework for CCS, 3, 149
    conclusions, 200–01
    constitutional authority, 149–52
    geophysical survey and GHG emissions sources, 180–83
    liability framework, 191–200
    regulation of GHG emissions:
      climate change law (Canada and international), 152–64
      direct support and regulation of CCS, 173–80
      general regulation of air emissions, 164
      market-based approaches to reducing GHG emissions, 167–73
      specific regulation of GHGs, 165–67
    regulatory framework, 186–91
    subsurface property rights, 183–86

health, safety and environment:
  Australia, legislation, 218–19
  Germany, environmental reasons for rejection of CCS technology, 69–71
  China:
    environmental law:
      basics of Chinese legal system, 339–42
      making and enforcement, 342–44
      shift towards environment and climate concerns, 344–46
    problem of law and the environment:
      administrative measures and rules of law, 353–54
      corruption, 356–57
      enforcement, 354–56
      hostility to legal codes, 352–53
  EU, transportation of CO_2:
    transport by ship:
      offshore safety and the environment:
        leakages and climate protection offshore, 259
        liability offshore, 259–60
        safety regulation, 257–58
    via pipelines:
      health and safety regulation, 248–49
      leakages and impact on climate change, 251–52
      protecting the environment, 249–51
  UK, NSIPs and environmental assessment, 95–97
  US, regulation of CO_2 pipelines:
    safety regulation, 288
    pipeline, federal statutory framework, 288–90
    regulatory implementation for CO_2 pipelines in 1991, 291–92
    safety record of CO_2 pipelines, 293
    state, 292–93
hydrocarbon exploration and production, 7–8

implementation of CCS Directive, 33–34
  beyond legislation, 39
  conclusions, 41
  details of EU legislation, 34
    allowing storage or not, 34–35
    assessing storage capacity, 35–37
    permitting CO_2 storage sites, 37–38
    preparing for CCS retrofitting for new large-scale combustions plants, 38–39

Kyoto Protocol:
  Canada, and, 152–54, 157–58

leakage of CO_2, *see* storage of CO_2 in deep subsurface; transportation of CO_2
liability, 25
  commercial arrangements for managing risks, 4
  categories of risks/liabilities associated with project, 327–29
  complexities of CCS and many links in chain, 323–26
  how legal liability risks arise in practice, 327–29
  incentivising CCS, liability considerations, 334–35
  key roles and risks in project, 326–27
  mechanisms for apportioning liability risks, 329–34
  framework, Canada, 191–200
  long-term, *see* long-term liability
  Member State as insurer for validation projects, 25–26
  progression, 27–28
  site specific monitoring required but total leakage small, 26–27
long-term liability, 4, 307–08
  Australia, 223
    Acts dealing with, 224
      Federal Offshore Act, 224–25
      Queensland onshore Act, 225–27
      Victorian onshore and offshore Acts, 225–27
    difference in regimes, 227–29
    in context of CCS, 223–24
  conclusions and way forward, 318
    assessing different forms of liability, 318–19
    positive models of law and regulation, 319–20
    project-specific experience, 320–21
  constraints and challenges, 312–13
    climate change liabilities, 317–18
    liability post-transfer, 316–17
    scope and practicality of transfer provisions, 313–15
    technical cooperation, 315–16
  emergence of CCS-specific regime, 308
    nature of liability, 309
    reliance upon existing liability mechanisms, 311
    similarity in approach, 309–11
    transfer and long-term stewardship, 311–12

Paris Agreement on Climate Change 2015, 1, 7, 29, 147, 359–60
  Canada's non-binding commitment, 153–56
  China's endorsement, 4, 337
pipelines, *see* transportation of CO_2
planning and consent procedures in UK, *see* United Kingdom

risk management:
  CCS Directive, and, 50
    underlying principles:
      conservatism, 52–57
      prevention, precaution, 50–52
      relationship between principles, 56

safety, *see* health, safety and environment
storage liability, *see* liability
storage of CO_2 in deep subsurface, 1, 5–7, 9
  enhanced oil recovery, 23–25
  geothermal exploration and production, 8
  guidance on storage sites and monitoring zones, 12–13
    accommodating imperfect sites, 13
    leakage:
      natural processes of trapping, 13–14
      tracking and fingerprinting CO_2, 14
      pressure processes and extent around injection site, 14–15
  hydrocarbon exploration and production, 7–8
  injection and storage:
    accidents, 21–23
    concepts, 11–12
    consequences of injection, 17
    effects of injection, 16
    geometries of trap, 16
    incomplete containment, 17–18
    operational interventions, 18
      In Salah, Algeria, onshore, 18–20
      Snøhvit, Norway, offshore, 20–21
    passive depleted methane gas-fields or oilfields, 9
    roles of demonstrations and evolving regulation, 18
    types of trapping, 15–16
  Paris Climate Agreement of 2015, 29
  progression and outlook, 27–30
  shale gas production, 8–9
  'storage complex', 11
    concept, 12
    introduction, 11
    lateral extent, 11
    leakage, 13, 26
    subsurface containment, 30
  storage liability, 25
    Member State as insurer for validation projects, 25–26
    progression, 27–28
    site specific monitoring required but total leakage small, 26–27

subsurface zoning concepts, 9–11
summary, 30–31
shale gas production, 8–9

transportation of CO_2:
  European Union, 3, 245–46
    conclusions, 265–66
    cross-border, 261–62
    trans-European networks, 262
      CO_2 networks, 263–65
      EU legal framework, 262–63
    transport by ship:
      offshore safety and the environment:
        leakages and climate protection offshore, 259
        liability offshore, 259–60
        safety regulation, 257–58
      qualifying, 257
      transport, 261
    via pipelines:
      health, safety and environment:
        health and safety regulation, 248–49
        leakages and impact on climate change, 251–52
        protecting the environment, 249–51
      other pipelines, 255–56
      qualifying pipelines, 246–48
      use of pipelines:
        national developments, 254–55
        owners and users, 252
        third-party access regime, 253–54
  US, regulation of CO_2 pipelines, 3–4, 267–69
    capacity planning and allocation, 300–05
    conclusions, 306
    current regulatory framework, 281
      federal regulation of construction and operation, 281–82
        jurisdictional status:
          conclusion, 286
          Interstate Commerce Act, 283–85
          Mineral Leasing Act 1920 administered by Bureau of Land Management, 285
          Natural Gas Act, 282–83
      safety regulation, 288
        pipeline, federal statutory framework, 288–90
        regulatory implementation for CO_2 pipelines in 1991, 291–92
        safety record of CO_2 pipelines, 293
        state, 292–93
      state regulation of construction and operation, 286–88
    'enhanced oil recovery':
      CO_2-EOR process, 269–74
      CO_2 markets, large long-lived 'bulky' demand increments, 276–77
      CO_2 pipelines, 'few-to-few' midstream component of integrated industry, 278–81

CO_2 supply, large 'bulky' increments of 'N-CO_2 and 'A-CO_2', 274–76
managing CO_2 stream quality specifications, 295–300
pipeline standards:
ASME B31.4, 293–94
other standards and recommended practices, 294–95

United Kingdom, 75–76
CCS in planning regime:
Carrington decision, 80–81
CO_2 storage, 79–80
pipelines, 79
power plants:
Carbon Capture Readiness Regulations 2013, 78–79
former regime, 77
Planning Act 2008, 77–78
Yorkshire-Humber pipeline and White Rose CCS Project, 81–83
conclusions, 99–100
public participation:
application and project stages:
nationally significant infrastructure projects (NSIPs):
decision on an application, 97–98
environmental assessment, 95–97
examination of, 92–94
offshore pipelines and storage, 98–99
pre-application consultation, 90–92
national policy statements (NPSs), 83
dedicated, 88–89
energy NPSs, 83
Aarhus Convention, 86
consultation, 84–86
limitations of, and medications to, 89–90
strategic environment assessment (SEA), 87–88
United Nations Framework Convention on Climate Change (UNFCCC):
Canada, and, 152, 157
China, and, 344–46
United States:
climate change policy context, 101
CCS/U technologies, 101–04
current, and CCS/U, 104
commercial viability, 113–15
laws addressing activities and facilities, 106
carbon sequestration regulations, 109–10
carbon transport regulations, 108–09
funding for CCS/U RD&D, 110–11
regulations and carbon capture, 106–08
onshore/offshore sequestration reservoir sitings, 112–13
US climate policy, 105–06
future, and CCS/U, 115–17
nascent carbon capture, sequestration and utilisation (CCS/U), 101, 117

economic (tax) credits, 3, 133
conclusions, 146–47
national level:
Advanced Fossil Energy Projects loan guarantees, 140–41
credit for CO_2 sequestration under section 45Q of IRC, 133–34
National Enhanced Oil Recovery Initiative (NEORI), 139
secure geological storage:
Environmental Protection Agency (EPA) subpart RR rules, 135–39
Intergovernmental Panel on Climate Change (IPCC) Guidelines, 134–35
investment tax credits under sections 48A and 48B of IRC, 139–40
State and regional levels:
California Cap-and-Trade Program, 141–42
California Air Resources Board (ARB), 141–42
Regional Greenhouse Gas Initiative (RGGI), 142–43
State severance tax reductions, 143–44
certification of sequestration, 144
monitoring and verification, 144–45
other States, 145
Railroad Commission (RRC) certification rule, 145
voluntary carbon credit market, 146
American Carbon Registry (ACR), 146
regulation of CO_2 pipelines, 3–4, 267–69
capacity planning and allocation, 300–05
conclusions, 306
current regulatory framework, 281
federal regulation of construction and operation, 281–82
jurisdictional status:
conclusion, 286
Interstate Commerce Act, 283–85
Mineral Leasing Act 1920 administered by Bureau of Land Management, 285
Natural Gas Act, 282–83
safety regulation, 288
pipeline, federal statutory framework, 288–90
regulatory implementation for CO_2 pipelines in 1991, 291–92
safety record of CO_2 pipelines, 293
state, 292–93
state regulation of construction and operation, 286–88
'enhanced oil recovery':
CO_2-EOR process, 269–74
CO_2 markets, large long-lived 'bulky' demand increments, 276–77

CO$_2$ pipelines, 'few-to-few' midstream component of integrated industry, 278–81
CO$_2$ supply, large 'bulky' increments of 'N-CO$_2$ and 'A-CO$_2$', 274–76
managing CO$_2$ stream quality specifications, 295–300
pipeline standards:
  ASME B31.4, 293–94
  other standards and recommended practices, 294–95
understanding and re-evaluating potential of CCS, 2, 119–20
  conclusions, 130–31
  current and future CCS promotion policies, 125–30
  economics of low-carbon electricity, 120–25